THE PSYCHOLOGY OF WOMEN

THE PSYCHOLOGY OF WOMEN

Margaret W. Matlin

State University of New York at Geneseo

HOLT, RINEHART AND WINSTON, INC.

Fort Worth Chicago San Francisco Philadelphia
Montreal Toronto London Sydney Tokyo

Senior Acquisitions Editor: Susan Meyers
Senior Project Manager: Arlene Katz
Senior Production Manager: Nancy Myers
Art Director: Gloria Gentile
Text Design: Marilyn Marcus
Cover Photo: Colors of Nature

**Special thanks to Claudia Liepold Pretzer for her creative
and artistic chapter opener photos.**

Library of Congress Cataloging-in-Publication Data

Matlin, Margaret W.
   The psychology of women.

  Includes bibliographies and index.
   1. Women—Psychology. 2. Sex differences (Psychology)
3. Sex role. 4. Life cycle, Human. I. Title.
[DNLM: 1. Women—psychology—popular works.
HQ 1206 M433p]
HQ1206.M354   1987   155.6'33   86-3115

ISBN 0-03-063409-1

CREDITS

Chapter Opener, Chapter 1. Photo Credit: Claudia Liepold Pretzer.
Chapter Opener, Chapter 2. Photo Credit: Claudia Liepold Pretzer.
Figure 2.1. Money, J., et al. (1955). Hermaphroditism: Recommendations concerning assignment of
    sex, change of sex, and psychological management. *Bulletin of the Johns Hopkins Hospital, 97,*
    284–300.
Figure 2.2. Condry, J., & Condry, S. (1976). Sex differences: A study of the eye of the beholder. *Child*
    Development, 47, p. 817 (Table 3). Reprinted by permission.
Figure 2.3. Reproduced with permission from American Greetings Corporation, Card numbers 100G
    2788-E and 75G 2797-2E.

Figure 2.4. Sidorowicz, L. S., & Lunney, G. S. (1980). Baby X revisited. *Sex Roles, 6*, p. 71 (Table 1). Reprinted by permission.

Chapter Opener, Chapter 3. Photo Credit: Claudia Liepold Pretzer.

Figure 3.1. McArthur, L. Z., & Eisen, S. V. (1976). Achievements of male and female storybook characters as determinants of achievement behavior by boys and girls. *Journal of Personality and Social Psychology, 44*, p. 474 (Figure 1). Copyright 1976 by the American Psychological Association. Reprinted/Adapted by permission of the author.

Chapter Opener, Chapter 4. Photo Credit: Claudia Liepold Pretzer.

Figure 4.4. Reprinted by permission of Elsevier Science Publishing Co., Inc. from "College women's attitudes and expectations concerning menstrual-related changes," by J. Brooks, D. Ruble, and A. Clark. In *Psychosomatic Medicine*, Vol. 39, p. 293; by The American Psychosomatic Society, Inc.

Chapter Opener, Chapter 5. Photo Credit: Claudia Liepold Pretzer.

Figure 5.1. Gold, A. R., Brush, L. R., & Sprotzer, E. R. (1980). Developmental changes in self-perceptions of intelligence and self-confidence. *Psychology of Women Quarterly, 5*, p. 234 (Table 1). Reprinted by permission.

Figure 5.2. Deaux, K., & Emswiller, T. (1974). Explanations of successful performance on sex-linked tasks: What's skill for the male is luck for the female. *Journal of Personality and Social Psychology, 29*, p. 82 (Figure 1). Copyright 1976 by the American Psychological Association. Reprinted/Adapted by permission of the author.

Chapter Opener, Chapter 6. Photo Credit: Claudia Liepold Pretzer.

Chapter Opener, Chapter 7. Photo Credit: Claudia Liepold Pretzer.

Figure 7.3. Towson, S. M., & Zanna, M. P. (1982). Toward a situational analysis of gender differences in aggression. *Sex Roles, 8*, p. 909 (Table 1). Reprinted by permission.

Chapter Opener, Chapter 8. Photo Credit: Katherine Buck.

Figure 8.1. Moulton, J., Robinson, G. M., & Elias, C. (1978). Sex bias in language use: "Neutral" pronouns that aren't. *American Psychologist, 33*, p. 1035 (Figure 1). Copyright 1978 by the American Psychological Association. Reprinted/Adapted by permission of the author.

Figure 8.4. Zanna, M. P., & Pack, S. J. (1975). On the self-fulfilling nature of apparent sex differences in behavior. *Journal of Experimental Social Psychology, 11*, p. 588 (Table 1). Reprinted by permission.

Chapter Opener, Chapter 9. Photo Credit: Margaret W. Matlin.

Figure 9.3. Photo Credit: *Stanford Observer*, Stanford University.

Figure 9.4. Bernard, J. (1972). *The Future of Marriage*. New York: World Publishing, p. 33 (Figure 1). Produced with permission from Yale University Press.

Chapter Opener, Chapter 10. Photo Credit: Ron Pretzer.

Figure 10.2. Rathus, S. A. (1983). *Human Sexuality*. New York: Holt, Rinehart and Winston, pp. 190–191 (Figure 8.2). Reprinted by permission of the author.

Chapter Opener, Chapter 11. Photo Credit: Claudia Liepold Pretzer.

Poem, Chapter 11. "Breastfeeding" by Alice Mattison from *Animals*, published by Alice James Books, Cambridge, Massachusetts.

Chapter Opener, Chapter 12. Photo Credit: Claudia Liepold Pretzer.

Figure 12.1. Reprinted from *Social Forces, 58*, "Sex, marital status and psychiatric treatment" by W. R. Gove. Copyright © The University of North Carolina Press.

Chapter Opener, Chapter 13. Photo Credit: Claudia Liepold Pretzer.

Figure 13.1. Gutek, B. A., Nakamura, C. Y., Gahart, M., Handschumacher, I., & Russell, D. (1980). Sexuality and the workplace. *Basic and Applied Psychology, 1*, p. 259 (Table 1). Reprinted by permission.

Chapter Opener, Chapter 14. Photo Credit: Katherine Buck.

This book is dedicated to
the students in my Psychology of Women classes

PREFACE

Several years ago, I wandered among the textbooks on display at a psychology convention, in my annual quest for an ideal textbook for my course in Psychology of Women. I had taught this course since 1974 and had used four different textbooks and collections of readings. However, none of these books had met my needs or—more importantly—my students' needs. My search through the textbooks that year revealed nothing new. It was then that I approached Marie Schappert, Psychology Editor at Holt, Rinehart and Winston, who had provided invaluable guidance on my previous book, *Cognition*. She responded enthusiastically and encouraged me to develop my ideas into this textbook.

Psychology of Women has been highly praised for the completeness of its coverage. It includes many topics that are important in women's lives but are omitted or abbreviated in most other books. These topics include the development of sex-typing, women and work, love relationships, pregnancy and motherhood, and later adulthood. The reference section of this textbook includes 1253 books, chapters, and articles. These references represent only a portion of the literature I examined in writing this book. In fact, the amount of information now available on psychology of women is so overwhelming that I can now readily understand why writers have been reluctant to tackle a textbook in this area!

Just as important, *Psychology of Women* has been praised for being student-oriented. Here are some of the special features:

- The writing style is clear and interesting, with many examples and quotations reflecting women's experiences.
- True–false questions at the beginning of the chapters promote student interest and describe some of the issues covered in each chapter.
- Chapter outlines provide students with an overall structure prior to reading each chapter.
- Boldfaced print for new terms, accompanied by definitions, clarify new items to be mastered. A pronunciation guide is included for many unfamiliar words.

- Small-scale demonstrations are included to encourage involvement and to clarify experimental procedures.
- Three to four section summaries in each chapter allow frequent review prior to beginning new material.
- A "new terms" section at the end of chapters permits review of vocabulary.
- Chapter review questions at the end of chapters allow review and organization of concepts.
- Recommendations for additional reading provide extra resources for students who want more information on topics.

A final important feature of this textbook is its organization. Insofar as possible, I have adopted a lifespan developmental framework to provide structure for the book. The book begins with prenatal development and moves through infancy, childhood, adolescence, adulthood, and old age. For those instructors who prefer a different approach, however, each chapter is self-contained. A second organizational feature is the development of four general themes in psychology of women that can be traced through many aspects of women's lives. I hope that these features will provide a sense of continuity to an area that may otherwise seem overwhelming in its scope.

This book is intended for students from a variety of backgrounds. I have included enough learning aids that it will be readable for students who have taken only an introductory course in psychology. However, the coverage of topics is complete and the references are extensive, so *Psychology of Women* should also appeal to advanced-level undergraduates. This textbook is primarily designed for courses in psychology of women, psychology of gender, psychology of sex differences, and psychology of sex roles. Some instructors in courses focusing on gender or sex differences may wish to supplement the book with one of the textbooks now available on psychology of men.

A pleasurable part of writing a textbook is the opportunity to thank the many people who provide ideas, references, and help. Holt, Rinehart and Winston arranged for reviews from the following people: Mary Crawford, Gloria Cowan, Kay Deaux, Joan Fimbel DiGiovanni, Linda Lavine, Wendy Martyna, Michele A. Paludi, Letitia Anne Peplau, Rebecca Reviere, Barbara Sholley, Myra Okazaki Smith, Barbara Strudler Wallston, and Cecilia K. Yoder. Their suggestions, helpful criticisms, and support were extremely valuable. I am very grateful to them!

I would also like to thank friends and colleagues for suggesting important references: Christine Beard, Lawrence Casler, Jacques Chevalier, Johanna Connelly, George Rebok, and Mary Roth Walsh. Several other friends and colleagues also earn my gratitude for reading and reviewing first-draft chapters: Mary Clark, Karen Duffy, Meda Rebecca, Mary Roth Walsh, and Diony Young. Furthermore, I'd like to acknowledge the suggestions made by four students who read part or all of the book and provided useful feedback: Susan Flood, Zorayda Lopez, Kathleen Matkoski, and Marianne Rizzo. In addition, the students enrolled in my Psychology of Women and Issues in Feminism courses gave me numerous ideas and suggestions.

Many other people have helped in various phases of the preparation of this book. Mary Lou Perry and Constance Ellis provided numerous services that permitted me to devote more energy to writing. Four students, Victoria Beitz, Rachel Kelly, Stacy Rogers, and Shari Schultz, were especially helpful in locating references and helping with clerical tasks. I'd also like to thank Jean Amidon for typing the manuscript, and Nancy Smith and Pamela Wyant for typing the Bibliography and Name Index. Christine Finocchario and Thomas Crowley helped arrange for me to preview numerous films and videotapes for the media resources list in the Instructor's Manual for this book. Three members of the Milne Library staff at State University of New York, Geneseo, again demonstrated their professional expertise in tracking down elusive references and data; my thanks are due to Judith Bushnell, Paula Henry, and David Parish. Finally, Claudia Liepold Pretzer deserves special recognition for her creativity and persistence as textbook photographer!

Once again, I have appreciated the impressive skills of the people at Holt, Rinehart and Winston. My gratitude goes to Marie Schappert, for her support in initiating the project, and to Susan Meyers, for her expertise and enthusiasm in developing the book. David DeCampo, Editorial Assistant, has been invaluable in coordinating many phases of textbook preparation. Arlene Katz, Senior Project Manager, has been supremely supportive in expediting the editing of *Psychology of Women;* her carefulness, concern, and editorial talents deserve special acknowledgment. Others who merit my sincere thanks include Kathleen Nevils, Gloria Gentile, Catherine Buckner, and Charles Naylor.

Finally, I want to thank three important people for their help, love, and enthusiasm—my husband, Arnie, and my daughters, Beth and Sally. Their appreciation and pride in my work have been invaluable!

Margaret W. Matlin

CONTENTS

CHAPTER 3

Childhood and Adolescence   44

CHAPTER 4

Menstruation   88

CHAPTER 5 **Achievement Motivation and Achievement Attitudes 121**

CHAPTER 6 **Women and Work 148**

CHAPTER 11

Pregnancy, Childbirth, and Motherhood   358

CHAPTER 12

Women and Psychological Disorders   384

CHAPTER 13 **Violence against Women** 423

CHAPTER 14 **Later Adulthood** 462

THE
PSYCHOLOGY
OF
WOMEN

CHAPTER 1

INTRODUCTION

Women make up more than half of the population of our country. However, pick up a newspaper and determine whether even one woman is mentioned on the first page. It seems that women and their concerns are often neglected. Recently I received a form, sent to all the teaching faculty at my college, which requested information such as my birthday, my home address, and—what's this—my *wife's* birthday? The sender of the questionnaire had simply neglected the 20 percent of our faculty who are female.

Women and issues important to them are frequently neglected in psychology. In search of women-related topics in a popular introductory textbook, for example, I find no mention of pregnancy, but there is a reference to "praying mantis, disinhibition in." The topic of rape is similarly absent in that book, but under the letter "r" are multiple references to rapid eye movements, the reticular activating system, and—of course—rats. Even psychology authors who try to give women "equal time" may meet with resistance. In an earlier book, I wrote a sentence, "You know that the dependent variable should be reliable, valid, and sensitive (which sounds like a variation on the Girl Scout Law)" (Matlin, 1979, p. 25). One reviewer wondered why I didn't mention the *Boy* Scout Law instead, and also complained "Even the children to which she occasionally refers are daughters."

The purpose of psychology of women is to explore a wide variety of psychological issues that concern women. These issues may involve a comparison of females and males, when we consider questions such as the following: What forces in childhood encourage little girls and boys to behave differently? Are women and men substantially different? Are women and men *treated* substantially differently? Other issues that concern women are life events that occur exclusively for women, such as menstruation, pregnancy, childbirth, and menopause, or almost exclusively for women, such as rape, battering, and sexual harassment. The psychology of women may also focus on women's experiences in areas that are usually approached from the male point of view, such as achievement, work, sexuality, and retirement.

We need to introduce and define several terms that are central to the psychology of women. The first two terms—sex and gender—have produced considerable controversy (for example, Unger, 1979), and they are often used interchangeably. I will follow Deaux's (1985) distinction between these two similar terms. **Sex** refers to the biologically based categories of female and male. A study comparing females with males is therefore one that studies sex differences. **Gender** refers to the psychological features that are often associated with biological states, involving social categories, rather than biological categories. The term "gender stereotypes" refers to the psychological features that people believe to be associated with women and men.

However, the distinction between sex and gender is not always preserved (Henley, 1985). One journal that is frequently cited in this book is called *Sex Roles*, though—according to Deaux's definitions—it should be called "*Gender Roles.*" The term "sex-typing" has become standard in discussing the acquisition of gender roles, even though the term should really be "gender-typing."

We also need to discuss the term "feminist." A **feminist** is a person whose beliefs, values, and attitudes reflect a high regard for women as human beings (Hunter College Women's Studies Collective, 1983). A feminist therefore is someone who believes that women and men should be socially and economically equal.

Now that we've defined feminists we need to stress several additional points. First, reread that definition and notice that men can be feminists. In fact, think about some men you know who are stronger feminists than many of the women you know. Second, notice that many of your friends would probably qualify as feminists, even if they would be reluctant to label themselves as feminists. You probably have heard someone say, "I'm not a feminist, but I think that men and women should be treated the same." This person may mistakenly assume that a feminist must be a person who "hates men" or "wants only women to rule the world." The true definition stresses equality, not antagonism. Finally, the term "feminist" is preferable to other terms from the 1970s that now have a negative or trivial connotation, such as "women's libber."

A final relevant term is sexism. **Sexism** is sex-bias; it is prejudice against people on the basis of their sex. A person is sexist who believes that women couldn't be competent lawyers. A person is also sexist who believes that men couldn't be competent nursery-school teachers. Sexism can reveal itself in social behavior, in the representation of women and men by the media, and in discrimination. Sexism can be obvious, as when a chemistry professor tells a female premed student that women really belong in the home. It can also be relatively subtle, as in using the term "girl" to refer to a mature woman.

Now that we've covered these important terms, what other aspects of psychology of women need to be introduced? Let's start with a very brief history of psychology of women, and then discuss some of the problems that occur in research on this topic. The last section of the introduction describes this book, including a preview of the chapters, a discussion of several important themes, and a description of several special features.

☐ THE HISTORY OF PSYCHOLOGY OF WOMEN

The study of psychology began in the late 1800s, and psychological research on women began about the same time. The study of gender and sex differences is sufficiently intriguing to have attracted the attention of even the earliest researchers. In contrast to these early, often biased studies, the new discipline of psychology of women began in the late 1960s.

Early Studies of Sex Differences

Psychologists first paid attention to women in the study of sex differences. However, the majority of these early researchers were men, and their work was frequently guided by sexist biases. Stephanie Shields (1975) quotes an early evaluation of this research as "flagrant personal bias . . . unfounded assertions, and even sentimental rot and drivel . . ." (Woolley, 1910, p. 340).

One early "hot topic" involved the size of structures within male and female brains, a research area that was inspired by evolutionary theory (Shields, 1975). Early in this research, scientists believed that the highest mental capacities were located in the frontal lobes of the brain. The research at that time—not surprisingly—maintained that men had larger frontal lobes than women. Several years later, researchers decided that the highest mental capacities were *really* located in the parietal lobes of the brain, not the frontal lobes. Intriguingly, researchers hastily revised their statements about sex differences. Suddenly, women were found to have larger frontal lobes (neatly reversing the earlier findings). Women were also discovered to have stunted parietal lobes (Patrick, 1895). Research findings were revised in order to match whatever brain theory was currently fashionable.

A second facet of sex differences that intrigued early researchers was the suggestion that males might show more variability than females on a number of characteristics, such as intelligence (Shields, 1982). Men should be found in greater abundance at the upper and lower ends of the intelligence scale, whereas women should be clustered in closer to average. Researchers seemed to pay greater attention to the discrepancy at the upper end of the scale, ignoring the idea that there should be a larger number of incompetent men than women. However, a series of studies and articles by Leta Hollingworth in the early 1900s revealed no evidence on sex differences in variability either in the published literature or in her own additional studies.

The Emergence of Psychology of Women as a Discipline

There was little interest in either sex differences or in psychology of women from about 1920 until the late 1960s. By about 1970, however, a greater proportion of psychologists were female. Also, feminism began to be an issue on college campuses, and courses in women's studies were introduced. As Denmark (1977) notes, the rapidly growing interest in women had an impact on the field of psychology. By 1973, a new division of the American Psychological Association was established, bearing the name "Division of the Psychology of Women."

Many psychologists found themselves asking questions about gender that had never occurred to them before. I recall suddenly realizing in 1970 that I had completed my undergraduate degree in psychology at Stanford University and my Ph.D. in psychology at University of Michigan with only one female professor during my entire academic training! (Fortunately, that one female professor had been Eleanor Maccoby, whose classic book with Carol Jacklin helped to shape the discipline of psychology of women.) I wondered why there hadn't been more women, and why little of my training had focused on either women or gender.

During the mid-1970s, the field of psychology of women expanded dramatically, and nine new general books on the psychology of women were published between 1974 and 1976. Researchers were eager to explore topics such as achievement motivation, where women previously had been ignored. They also attacked issues that had been ignored because of commonly held assumptions. Macaulay (1985) lists a number of popular beliefs about aggression, such as the idea that women are innately nonaggressive. Another common assumption was that women have a "maternal instinct"; they automatically love and protect their babies. Previous researchers saw no point in examining topics such as these, but people interested in the psychology of women realized that unbiased, objective research was a better source of information than "common knowledge." Thus, the major efforts during the blossoming of psychology of women were to fill in the gaps in our information about women and to correct the misinformation.

During the late 1970s, people began to rediscover important women in psychology's history. We found out that many of the classic studies in psychology had actually been conducted by women! These courageous women provided us with models of achievement (O'Connell & Russo, 1980, 1983).

Looking back on the 1970s from the perspective of the 1980s, many people have remarked on the sense of excitement and discovery. However, there were two problems with some of the work done in the 1970s. First, we did not realize how complicated the issue of gender was; most of us optimistically thought that there were just a handful of factors that could explain questions such as: Why are there so few women in management positions? Now we realize that there are numerous factors, many of which haven't yet been identified.

A second problem was that women were sometimes blamed for their own fate. In trying to answer questions such as why women are scarce in management positions, two answers were commonly given. One was that women were not assertive enough, and the other was that they were afraid of success. The alternate idea—that the *situation* might be faulty—received little attention (Henley, 1985; Unger, 1983; Wallston, 1981). Some of the research (and most of the summaries of that research in the media) emphasized that the fault rested in women's personalities rather than in social structure, stereotypes, and institutions.

In the 1980s, there is an increasing realization that answers will be complex when we ask questions about psychology of women. Most theorists acknowledge the importance of external forces in society, which are responsible for who women are and what they can accomplish. Research on psychology of women continues at an amazing rate, perhaps even more than in the 1970s. At present, as Deaux (1985) states, "Sex and gender is an area of research whose time has come" (p. 74). The *amount* of research conducted in psychology of women is staggering. Examining just the work relevant to sex differences and gender roles, Deaux counted more than 18,000 articles published between 1967 and 1982 in the psychological literature. Furthermore, psychology of women is interdisciplinary in nature. In preparing this book, I consulted resources in areas such as biology, medicine, sociology, anthropology, history, media studies, economics, education, and linguistics. The number of articles and books that are potentially relevant to psychology of women, published in the last 15–20 years, comes close to 100,000.

Since the field of psychology of women is still young, many of the important elements of the big picture on gender are not yet visible (Mednick, 1978). At many points throughout this textbook, I will conclude something like, "We don't have enough information to draw conclusions." Furthermore, ideas change quickly. New research often makes us revise a previous generalization. It may be that sex differences in a particular behavior exist only when men and women are asked to describe themselves; in other situations, the sex differences may disappear. The field of psychology of women is challenging because women seem to be changing as we move toward the end of the 1900s. Other areas of psychology—say, the visual perception system—remain the same from year to year. However, women in the late 1980s are different from women in the 1950s. It is fascinating to contemplate what the psychology of women will be like in the twenty-first century!

At this point, we need to shift our attention to a different topic, though it is one that has been inevitable throughout the history of psychology of women. Specifically, what problems do researchers encounter when they examine the psychology of women?

☐ PROBLEMS IN RESEARCH ON PSYCHOLOGY OF WOMEN

The aim of research is to discover the truth. An unfortunate problem is that a variety of biases can interfere with this discovery. Biases are a problem in research on psychology of women, because this is a topic about which researchers are likely to have strong emotions and opinions. Strong emotions and opinions are less likely in most other areas of psychology; it's difficult to imagine researchers having strong emotional investments and preconceptions about the rat's nesting habits, for example. Biases can enter into research on psychology of women either in the area of sex differences or when doing research on women who do not conform to traditional stereotypes (for example, employed women, single women, and lesbian women).

There are many opportunities for these biases to influence the research process. As Table 1.1 shows, biases can interfere with the truth in formulating

TABLE 1.1   **Stages at Which Biases Can Influence the Research Process**

I. Formulating the hypothesis
   A. Using a biased theory
   B. Formulating a hypothesis on the basis of unrelated research
   C. Asking questions only from certain content areas

II. Designing the study
   A. Selecting the operational definition
   B. Choosing participants
   C. Choosing the experimenter

III. Performing the study
   A. Influencing the outcome through experimenter expectancy
   B. Influencing the outcome through participants' expectancies

IV. Interpreting the data
   A. Emphasizing statistical significance rather than practical significance
   B. Ignoring alternate explanations
   C. Supplying explanations for results not obtained in the study

V. Communicating the findings
   A. Leaving out analyses that show sex similarities
   B. Journal editors rejecting studies that show sex similarities
   C. Secondary sources emphasizing sex differences instead of sex similarities

the hypothesis, designing the study, performing the study, interpreting the data, and communicating the findings. Let's look at each of these phases in the research process.

Formulating the Hypothesis

Researchers are often strongly committed to a certain psychological theory. If this theory is biased against women, the researchers may be predisposed toward biased findings before they even begin to conduct their study. For example, the theory of Sigmund Freud, which we will mention throughout this book, is, in part, biased against women. For example, psychologists with a Freudian orientation are trained to believe that women are inferior to men in their moral standards. It may therefore be difficult for them to be entirely fair when conducting research on morality.

A second problem is that psychologists may formulate a hypothesis on the basis of previous research that is unrelated to the idea they want to study. Consider researchers several decades ago who wanted to determine whether children were harmed when their mothers worked outside the home. Their own biases against employed mothers led them to some studies in an area that was then called "maternal deprivation" but would more properly be called "parental deprivation." These studies showed that children raised in low-quality orphanages—without their parents—turned out poorly. Clearly, the situation of a child whose mother works outside the home is different from the situation of a child raised in an institution without mother or father. Yet these early researchers argued that the children of employed mothers should also turn out poorly!

The final way in which biases can influence the formulation of hypotheses concerns the kinds of questions that researchers ask. For example, researchers have ignored until recently the question of mothers' attitudes toward their newborn infants, perhaps partly because they had difficulty believing mothers could feel anything other than intense love toward their babies.

So far, we have seen that there are several ways in which biases can be influential in the early stage of hypothesis formulation. Biases can influence the theoretical orientation, the previous research that is considered relevant, and the content areas that are investigated.

Designing the Study

An important early step in designing a research study is the selection of operational definitions. **Operational definitions** tell us exactly how a variable in a study will be measured. Consider a study investigating sex differences in empathy, which involves feeling the same emotion that another person is feeling. For our operational definition, suppose that we decide to ask people a number of questions such as, "When your best friend is feeling sad, do you feel sad as well?" In other words, we will measure empathy in terms of self-report.

This operational definition for empathy may look perfectly innocent until we realize that there is a potential bias. Women and men may really be equal in their empathy, but men may be more hesitant to *report* that they feel empathic. Gender stereotypes stress that men are not supposed to be overly emotional or sensitive. Perhaps if we had used another measure (maybe watching people's facial expressions as they look at a sad movie), we might reach a different conclusion about sex differences in empathy. As Wallston and Grady (1985) stress, we can draw the best conclusions when a hypothesis is tested with several different methodologies. In summary, it is important to emphasize that researchers may unwittingly design a biased study when they select an operational definition. Details of the operational definition that seem trivial may really have important implications.

A second source of bias in research design is the choice of participants. Many investigations have shown that psychologists study men more often then women (Grady, 1981; Wallston & Grady, 1985). When researchers in the area of aggression were asked why they used only male participants, they responded that they did not want to use methods that would be physically harmful to female participants (Prescott, 1978). McKenna and Kessler (1977) confirmed this observation. They found that studies on aggression that used only male participants involved arousing strong feeling in people or exposing them to a hostile act. Studies on aggression that used only female participants (a much smaller number of studies) involved a less active kind of aggression, for example, reading a story about aggression. As a result of these biases, we don't have equivalent kinds of information about men and women.

Another source of bias in designing a study is the choice of the experimenter who will conduct the study. The sex of the experimenter may make a difference. For example, let's imagine that a researcher wants to determine whether there are sex differences in people's interest in babies. If the experimenter is male, female subjects may want to demonstrate a strong interest in babies, whereas male subjects may be embarrassed to do so; sex differences may be large. The same study done by a female experimenter could produce minimal sex differences.

Each of these problems in designing a study may lead us to draw inadequate or inappropriate conclusions. The underrepresentation of females in certain topics means that we don't know much about their behavior in certain areas. Furthermore, decisions about operational definitions and about the sex of the experimenter may influence the nature of the conclusions.

Performing the Study

Further complications enter when the study is actually performed. A source of bias at this point is called experimenter expectancy (Matlin, 1979; Rosenthal, 1976). **Experimenter expectancy** means that the biases that experimenters bring to the study can influence the outcome. (Some people prefer the term **researcher expectancy,** because biases influence surveys and case studies, as well as laboratory experiments. The effect is also called a **self-fulfilling prophecy.**) If experimenters expect males to perform better than females on a test of mathematical ability, they may somehow treat the two groups differently, thus fulfilling the prophecy they had made. It should also be noted that female researchers—not just male researchers—can produce experimenter-expectancy effects, as long as they have different expectations for males and females.

Other disciplines also encounter the problem of experimenter expectancy, but it can be reduced by designing the study so that the experimenter is unaware of which participant is in which condition. If experimenters in a study on memory don't know which people received a special training session and which did not, they won't have different expectations for the two groups. However, it's almost always impossible to make experimenters unaware of which participants are female and which are male! An experimenter who is told to rate female and male adolescents on their degree of independence couldn't help noticing the sex of the participant. The experimenter's ratings may therefore reflect his or her expectations and stereotypes about female and male behavior, rather than reflecting reality. As Maccoby and Jacklin (1974) observed, parents, teachers, and other observers may supply different ratings for males and females, when an objective frequency count of their actual behavior would reveal no sex differences.

Experimenters are not the only ones whose expectations and stereotypes influence the nature of the responses. The participants have grown up in the same culture as the experimenters and are likely to have absorbed expectations and stereotypes about their own behavior. For example, women have learned that they are supposed to be moody and irritable just before their menstrual periods. If they are told that they are participating in a study on how the menstrual cycle affects mood, they may supply more negative ratings during the premenstrual phase of the cycle. If they had been unaware of the purpose of the study, it is possible that their responses would be different. In summary, the expectations of both the experimenters and the participants may bias the results so that they are not an accurate reflection of reality.

Interpreting the Data

There are many ways in which data from experiments can be misinterpreted. One way concerns statistical versus practical significance. As we will discuss in Chapter 7, a difference between male and female performance on a math test may be *statistically* significant. **Statistical significance** means that the results are not likely to happen by chance alone. Statistical significance is calculated with mathematical formulas that give "extra credit" when the sample size is especially large. Returning to the example of the math test, the results may be statistically significant because the study tested 10,000 males and 10,000 females. Closer inspection might show that the males received an average score of 40.5, in contrast to females' average score of 40.0. This difference would be statistically significant because virtually *any* difference would be statistically significant with an enormous sample size. However, this difference has minimal *practical* significance. **Practical significance,** as the name implies, means that the results have some important implications for the real world. In the case of these hypothetical math scores, a half-point difference would have no imaginable implications for how males and females should be treated with respect to mathematics.

Unfortunately, researchers typically discuss only statistical significance. Instead, as Wallston and Grady (1985) point out, they should discuss whether a sex difference also has practical significance.

In interpreting the data, researchers may ignore alternate explanations. A researcher may claim that males' superior performance on a math test is due to their superior ability, ignoring the alternate explanation that males are likely to have had more math courses than females. Another researcher might conclude that there are significant differences between adult males and females in a study, when a careful examination of the participants might show that most of the males were employed and most of the females were not employed; differences should be attributed to employment status rather than sex of subjects (McHugh, et al., 1981). If females score higher on a test measuring anxiety, the difference might really be due to males' reluctance to *report* anxiety that they experience, rather than any sex differences in true anxiety (Jacklin, 1983). Unbiased research considers alternative ideas.

Researchers may sometimes supply explanations for the results, even when these explanations were never investigated in the study. For example—

on the subject of sex differences in math ability—some researchers have detected sex differences and concluded that these differences can be traced to biological sex differences. Yet biological components of mathematical ability were never examined in this particular study (Jacklin, 1983). In short, the interpretation phase of research offers several other opportunities for distortion of the truth.

Communicating the Findings

After conducting the research and performing the analyses, researchers usually want to publish their findings. Other sources of bias now enter. One important point to keep in mind is that sex similarities are not considered to be startling psychological news (Jacklin, 1983; Maccoby & Jacklin, 1974; Unger, 1979). Thus when a researcher is summarizing the results of a study, she or he may be likely to leave out a particular analysis showing that females and males had similar scores. However, any sex *difference* that was discovered is likely to be reported. This kind of selective reporting underrepresents the sex similarities that are found in research and overrepresents the sex differences.

Researchers then send their reports off to journal editors, who must decide whether the reports deserve publication. Journal editors, like the researchers themselves, are usually much more excited about sex differences than similarities. Studies that report sex similarities are likely to be rejected and sent back to gather dust in researchers' file drawers. Selective publication further underrepresents sex similarities and overrepresents sex differences.

Even further distortion occurs when the published journal articles are discussed by "secondary sources" such as the popular press, review articles, and textbooks. An introductory psychology textbook may discuss one study in which men are more assertive than women, but ignore several other studies in which there is no sex difference or in which women are more assertive than men. Sherif (1979) notes that research on the menstrual cycle has consistently shown that women's performance on various tasks did not vary substantially across the cycle. However, articles in popular magazines are likely to cite those articles that show mood changes during the menstrual cycle; you won't read about the *lack* of change in task performance.

In other words, researchers may have been unbiased in formulating their hypothesis, designing the study, performing the study, and interpreting the data. However, the communication process often introduces its own variety of bias so that readers may eventually receive a distorted version of the truth. This distorted version may represent sex differences as being larger than they really are, or it may misrepresent women's experiences. Ironically, this distorted version of the truth then often serves as the basis for future theories, and the cycle begins all over again. In addition, since researchers know that publishers and secondary sources favor studies demonstrating sex differences, they tend to examine areas where differences are likely and ignore areas where they expect to find sex similarities.

If the aim of research is really to discover the truth, we must identify and eliminate the sources of biases that can distort reality and underrepresent women. Only then can we have a clear understanding about women—an undistorted psychology of women.

☐ ABOUT THIS BOOK

Before you begin the following chapters, you need to know where you're going. Let's start with a preview of the chapters, and then move on to several important themes that occur throughout the book. We'll end this chapter with a description of the special features of this book and how they can help you in learning about the psychology of women.

Preview of the Chapters

In writing this book, a major issue was the order of topics. I decided to use a chronological approach, beginning with prenatal development and ending with later adulthood. However, there are some topics that are important for females throughout their entire lifespan. The issue of violence against women—sadly—can effect a baby girl as well as an elderly woman. Also, psychological disorders are as relevant for a teenage girl with eating disorders as for a middle-aged woman who is depressed. Therefore, the topics of violence against women and psychological disorders are each treated in a separate chapter. Otherwise, the book uses a chronological approach. This approach allows us to follow the development of a female, beginning with a fertilized egg, and continuing through infancy, childhood, adolescence, adulthood, and old age.

Throughout the early chapters, we will be trying to unravel a mystery: Adult women and adult men sometimes behave differently. Even more important, as people mature, they learn that women and men are "supposed to" be treated differently. What are the forces, beginning in infancy, that produce the differences in behavior and that teach people that men and women should be treated differently? To what extent are our answers still incomplete?

The middle chapters in this book examine aspects of adult women's lives in detail, sometimes focusing on topics that are unique to women and sometimes comparing women's and men's experiences. The last chapter examines older women, a group of individuals with admirable strength. Here is a brief description of each chapter.

Prenatal development and infancy (Chapter 2) begins with an overview of normal and abnormal development prior to birth. You'll then learn that sex differences in infancy are generally small; a baby girl and a baby boy behave similarly. However, adults make a big distinction between the two sexes, and they treat infant girls and boys differently.

Childhood and adolescence (Chapter 3) begins with four theories that attempt to explain the mystery of why females and males—two groups with similar beginnings—end up to be somewhat different and to be treated very differently. You will read about several important factors that may have a role in this mystery. Other topics include children's behavior and beliefs and a discussion of the female adolescent.

Menstruation (Chapter 4) is a chapter describing the first of a series of biological events that are unique to women. In this chapter, you will learn about the biological aspects of the menstrual cycle. However, the primary emphasis will be on the psychological aspects of menstruation, such as reactions to the beginning of menstruation, variations (and lack of variations) in mood and abilities across the menstrual cycle, and attitudes toward menstruation.

Achievement motivation and achievement attitudes (Chapter 5) describes an area that researchers once identified as an important factor in explaining why men have different kinds of occupations than women. During recent years, different groups of researchers argued that women were not interested in achieving, that they were afraid of success, that they lacked self-confidence in achievement situations, and that they were more likely than men to blame themselves for failure, yet take no credit for success. As you will see, more recent evidence shows that women and men are generally similar in these achievement-related areas. However, a woman's achievement is often *interpreted* differently from the same achievement when it is performed by a man.

Women and work (Chapter 6) begins with a section on women's preparation for work and continues with an examination of women in the workplace. A central theme is that women and men are steered into different occupations; women may experience discrimination in terms of entry into work, salary, and advancement. However, when men and women who work at the same jobs are compared, they are psychologically similar. You'll also learn about the effects of employment on personal life, including marriage, children, and personal adjustment.

Sex differences and similarities (Chapter 7) focuses on a comparison of women and men in adulthood. You'll find that sex differences in cognitive ability, personality, and social behavior are generally small and inconsistent, though men and women may show different communication styles in some areas.

Gender stereotypes (Chapter 8) provides a contrast with the previous chapter. Although men and women really are similar, they are perceived as being different. As you will learn in this chapter, men and women have been represented differently throughout history, in present-day language, and in the media. Furthermore, people's beliefs about men and women show an exaggeration and distortion of reality, a process that probably can be traced to our normal thought processes. This chapter also examines alternatives to these gender stereotypes.

Love relationships (Chapter 9) is the first of a series of three chapters that focus on adult women's interpersonal experiences. You will read about dating and cohabitation as well as three love-relationship options: marriage, lesbian or bisexual relationships, and being single. Surprisingly, much of the research about women in love (and out of love) seems to contradict society's stereotypes.

Sexuality (Chapter 10) is a topic that has important biological and psychological components. The chapter begins with an overview of the biological side of sexuality, and then it examines sexual behavior and attitudes. As you'll see, the so-called sexual revolution seems to have had both positive and negative implications for women's lives, and—despite the media's emphasis on sexual freedom for females—women aren't really free in sexual relationships. The last section in the chapter looks at birth control and abortion, two very controversial topics.

Pregnancy, childbirth, and motherhood (Chapter 11) are three aspects of a second biological event unique to women, but—unlike menstruation—women can make a choice about whether they will become mothers. As in the case of sexuality, there are biological and psychological reactions to pregnancy and childbirth. You will learn that there is a discrepancy between stereotypes about motherhood and the reality of motherhood.

Women and psychological disorders (Chapter 12) and the chapter on violence that follows both focus on tragic issues. Women are more likely than men to be the victims of both psychological disorders and violence. In both cases, the tragedies can be at least partially traced to our society's treatment of women. Their work is not respected, and their bodies are not respected. Psychological disorders and violence do not occur to the majority of women (though more women are affected than you might believe). Nonetheless, both areas provide extreme and poignant examples of what can happen when women, their accomplishments, and their bodies are not valued. Chapter 12 discusses three issues: why women are more likely than men to experience psychological disorders; the kinds of psychotherapy that can be used to help women with psychological disorders; and four specific psychological disorders.

Violence against women (Chapter 13) deals with three ways in which women can be victimized—by rape, battering, and sexual harassment. These three areas may initially seem different from each other, and there are some important distinctions. However, in all three cases, there is violence in some form. Furthermore, in these three areas men have more physical and psychological power than women and people tend to blame the victim for having provoked the violence.

Later adulthood (Chapter 14) begins with an overview of physical aspects of women's later adulthood, focusing on menopause, the last of the biological events unique to women. You'll also learn about women and retirement, a topic that has been largely ignored. The final section, on social aspects of later adulthood, emphasizes how negative attitudes toward women in general are even *more* negative in the case of older women. Older women have multiple responsibilities as mothers, daughters, and grandmothers, and the death of a spouse adds additional strain. However, older women are amazingly resilient; in general, they remain satisfied with their lives.

Themes in the Book

As I mentioned earlier, the subject of psychology of women is impressively complex, and the discipline is so recent that it is difficult to point to a large number of general principles that can summarize this diverse field. Nevertheless, there seem to be a small number of general themes that appear with some consistency throughout this book. We'll discuss these now to provide a framework for reading the book.

1. *Psychological sex differences are generally small and inconsistent.* In a previous section on problems in research on psychology of women, we mentioned that the research that is published probably represents the sex differences as being larger than they really are. However, even an examination of the published literature on men's and women's personalities and abilities shows that the sex similarities are generally more impressive than the sex differences. In terms of psychological characteristics, women and men simply aren't very different from each other. Furthermore, one study may demonstrate a sex difference, and yet a second study—apparently similar to the first—may demonstrate a sex similarity. As Unger (1981) remarks, sex differences often have a "now you see them, now you don't" quality. (Incidentally, you'll notice that I'm commenting on *psychological* sex differences, rather than *biological* or *anatomical* sex differences.)

   Often, too, sex differences may appear in some situations, but not in others. It seems that sex differences are most likely to occur (a) when people evaluate themselves, rather than when behavior is recorded objectively; (b) when people are observed in real-life situations, rather than in a laboratory setting; and (c) when people are aware that they are being evaluated by others. In these three kinds of situations, people drift toward stereotyped kinds of behavior. Women respond the way they think women are supposed to respond; men respond the way they think men are supposed to respond. In general, we can say that **sex as a subject variable**—a characteristic within a person that influences the way she or he acts (Parlee, 1981)—is not crucially important.

2. *People react differently to men and women.* We just pointed out that sex as a subject variable is not important. However, sex as a *stimulus variable* is important. When we refer to **sex as a stimulus variable,** we mean a characteristic of a person to which other people react (Parlee, 1981). For example, sex is an important stimulus variable when we are judging someone's accomplishments. As we will see in Chapter 5, people often treat the accomplishments of men and women differently, with males' accomplishments being rated more positively. In general, males are more valued than females. For example, people want a boy, rather than a girl, for their firstborn child; males are more valued in the workplace; and males are represented more positively in religion, mythology, and current language and media.

If people react differently to men and women, then this is an indication that people believe in sex differences. Unger (1979) calls this phenomenon "the illusion of sex differences." She stresses a point we will mention throughout this book: "Men and women are especially alike in their beliefs about their own differences" (p. 1086). Ironically, one sex similarity is that both women and men believe the sexes are different.

3. *Women are relatively invisible in many important areas.* As a partial extension of the second theme, we find that men are featured more prominently in areas that our culture considers to be important. As mentioned earlier in this chapter, a glance through the nearest newspaper will convince you that males and "masculine" topics receive more emphasis, and studies on all forms of media confirm that men are seen and heard more than women. Other examples include the relative invisibility of girls, in comparison with boys, in the classroom, and the invisiblity of women in our language, which uses terms such as "man" to include both women and men. Finally, psychologists have helped keep some topics invisible that are important to women. Three important biological events in women's lives—menstruation, pregnancy/childbirth, and menopause—have received too little attention from psychology researchers. Women *are* visible in many areas—in women's magazines, making costumes for the school play, and in the secretarial pool—but these are all areas that our culture does not consider important or prestigious.

   Minority women are particularly invisible (Simons, 1979). There are 8 million black women in this country, yet they are not represented in the psychological literature (Henley, 1985; Murray & Scott, 1982). As Murray and Scott note, "Our own research experiences reveal that black women remain invisible persons in American psychology...." (p. 259). Brown and her coauthors (1985) agree; they note that white, nonethnic middle-class women are deemed more worthy of scientific investigation than women who are black or members of ethnic minority groups. Chapter 8 will also point out how the media ignore minority women.

4. *Women show a wide range of variation from each other in their psychological characteristics, their life choices, and their responses to biological events.* In fact, there is so much variability among individual women that it is typically difficult to draw any conclusions about women in general. Think about the variability among women you know in the characteristic of aggressiveness or in sensitivity to the emotions of others. Women also vary widely in their life choices, in terms of careers, marital status, sexual preference, desire to have children, and so forth. Furthermore, women differ in their responses to biological events; some women have problems with menstruation, pregnancy, childbirth, and menopause, whereas others find the experiences neutral or even positive.

We have stressed that women show wide variation, and it is reasonable to believe that men show a similarly wide variation among themselves. These within-sex variabilities bring us full circle to the first theme of the book. Whenever variability *within* groups is large, the difference *between* those two groups is unlikely to be statistically significant. We will discuss this statistical issue in more detail in Chapter 7, but turn to Figure 7.2 for a preview. Suppose that this figure represents the scores of females and males on a test of verbal ability. On the average, females receive a score of 80, and males receive a score of 75, so the difference between those two groups is 5 points. However, the males' scores vary between 50 and 100, and the females' scores vary between 55 and 105, which means that there is a 50-point span for each sex. Compared to the 50-point variability *within* each group, the 5-point difference *between* the two groups will not be significant unless the sample size is large. The important point is that women (or men) show wide variability.

Another aspect of variability also needs to be stressed. Women's experiences are often likely to depend upon their race, ethnic group, and social class. However, as mentioned earlier, most research has been done on white, nonethnic, middle-class women. As Brown and her coauthors (1985) point out, it would be a mistake to conclude that findings on Euro-American middle-class women would apply to all women. Because researchers typically study such a narrow range of women, the true experiences of all women undoubtedly show more variability than is represented in the psychological literature.

How to Use This Book

This textbook was specially designed to provide you with a number of features that should be helpful in understanding and remembering the material. This last section of the chapter describes how you can use these features most effectively.

Each chapter begins with an outline. Before reading a new chapter, read over the outline to determine the scope of the chapter. Sometimes you can relate the topics in the outline to the themes we just discussed. For example, in Chapter 2 you'll notice that the major topics are: Prenatal Development; Sex Differences in Infancy; and How People Respond to Infant Girls and Boys. You might expect to find that actual sex differences are small, but that people respond differently to infant girls and boys.

A second feature is a set of ten true-false questions. I intentionally did not provide a list of answers elsewhere in the chapter, because it will be a better learning experience if you discover the answers for yourselves, in reading the chapter, rather than being tempted to peek at the answers.

The chapters themselves contain a number of demonstrations that you may try yourself or invite your friends to try. The purpose of these demonstrations is to make the material more concrete and personal. Research on memory has demonstrated that material is easier to remember if it is concrete and if it is related to personal experience (Matlin, 1983a; Rogers, Kuiper and Kirker, 1977).

In addition, every new term appears in boldface type (for example, **sex-typing**), and the definition appears in the same sentence. I have also included phonetic pronunciations in some cases, with the accented syllable appearing in italics. These pronunciation guides are not meant to insult your intelligence, but to help when the pronunciation might be ambiguous.

Many textbooks have summaries at the end of each chapter, but I prefer Section Summaries at the end of each of the major sections of the following chapters. Notice, for example, that Chapter 2 has three Section Summaries. This feature lets you review the material more frequently so that you feel confident about small, manageable portions of the material before you move on to new material. At the end of each section, you may wish to test yourself to see whether you can recall the important points. Then check the Section Summary to see whether you were accurate. Incidentally, students have reported that they learn the material more efficiently if they read only one section at a time, rather than an entire chapter.

There are three special features at the end of each chapter. First is a set of Chapter Review Questions, which sometimes test your specific recall and sometimes ask you to relate information from several parts of the chapter. A list of New Terms shows these items in their order of appearance in the chapter. Test yourself by seeing whether you can supply a definition for each term. Each of these terms also appears in the subject index at the end of the book, so that you can check on the more difficult terms. A final feature is a brief list of recommended readings of important articles, books, or special issues of journals that are particularly relevant to each chapter. These should be useful if you are writing a paper on one of the topics or if an area is personally interesting to you.

Chapter Review Questions

1. As this chapter mentioned, the terms "sex" and "gender" have somewhat different meanings, although they are sometimes used interchangeably. Define each term and decide which term would be used in connection with each of the following topics: (a) A theoretical paper about how boys learn "masculine" body postures and girls learn "feminine" body postures; (b) a study that contrasts self-confidence in adolescent males and females; (c) a survey that asks adults how the household tasks should be divided between a husband and a wife.
2. Often the popular usage of a word drifts considerably from its use in the professional literature. Define the terms "feminist" and "sexism" as used in this chapter and comment on how the popular usage differs in either connotation or detailed meaning from the definitions used here.

3. Describe two areas that were examined in the early studies of sex differences. In the later section on problems in research on psychology of women, there is a discussion about problems that arise in formulating a hypothesis. How might these problems be relevant in explaining this early research?
4. Briefly trace the development of psychology of women since 1920, mentioning as well the current state of the discipline.
5. At present, only a small portion of our senators and representatives are women. What kind of explanations might be given by those who support an approach that blames women for their fate? What kind of explanations might be given by those who support an approach that blames the situation?
6. Imagine that you would like to determine whether there are sex differences in leadership ability. Trace how a number of biases might influence your research at the five different stages of performing your research.
7. The description of problems in research on psychology of women can be applied to other areas of psychology as well. Select an area of research with which you are familiar (for example, from introductory psychology) and trace this topic through the five stages, noting the kinds of biases that might distort the truth.
8. Describe each of the four themes of this book. Do any of them contradict your previous ideas about women? If so, why?

☐ NEW TERMS

sex

gender

feminist

sexism

operational definitions

experimenter expectancy

researcher expectancy

self-fulfilling prophecy

statistical significance

practical significance

sex as a subject variable

sex as a stimulus variable

☐ RECOMMENDED READINGS

Deaux, K. (1985). Sex and gender. *Annual Review of Psychology, 36*, 49–81. ■ This valuable chapter provides an overview of the psychology of sex and gender, focusing on sex comparisons and gender belief systems.

Hunter College Women's Studies Collective. (1983). *Women's realities, women's choices.* New York: Oxford University Press. ■ Eight members of the women's studies program at Hunter College assembled this interdisciplinary introduction to women's studies, which will interest those who would like to pursue women's issues in areas beyond psychology.

O'Connell, A. N., & Russo, N. P. (1983). *Models of achievement: Reflections of eminent women in psychology.* New York: Columbia University Press. ■ This book contains autobiographies of 17 prominent women psychologists, providing interesting insights on the obstacles faced by women in the earlier days of psychology.

Psychology of Women Quarterly, (1981) Volume 5, Number 4. ■ Half of this journal issue is devoted to feminist research as an alternative to biased research about women; there are six articles on the topic.

Wallston, B. S., & Grady, K. E. (1985). Integrating the feminist critique and the crisis in social psychology: Another look at research methods. In V. E. O'Leary, R. K. Unger, & B. S. Wallston (Eds.), *Women, gender, and social psychology* (pp. 7–33). Hillsdale, N.J.: Erlbaum. ■ This chapter examines methodological biases, particularly with respect to their implications for social psychology.

PRENATAL DEVELOPMENT AND INFANCY

true or false?

- Every cell in your body has 46 chromosomes. *F*

- In the first weeks of prenatal development, females and *T ?*
males have identical sex glands and external genitals.

- If a person is genetically a male but is labeled a female *F*
because the external genitals look female, that person will
usually act masculine.

- Infant girls have greater perceptual sensitivity than infant *F*
boys; for example, their sense of smell is more acute.

- Infant boys are consistently more active than infant girls; for *F*
example, they kick and thrash more often.

- Infant girls are more dependent than infant boys; for *F*
example, they cry more when their mothers leave them.

- When people learn that a baby has just been born, they *F*
are more likely to ask if the baby or the mother is healthy
than to ask questions about the sex of the newborn.

- If people believe that an infant is a girl, they think "she" is *T*
softer and more fragile than if they believe that same infant
is a boy.

- If a baby is introduced as Johnny, people hand "him" a *T*
football, but if the baby is introduced as Jenny, people
hand "her" a doll.

- People touch their sons and daughters equally, and they *F*
are equally gentle in handling their children.

As we mentioned in Chapter 1, we have a mystery that needs unravelling. As adults, women and men are regarded as being different. They are treated differently and they hold different jobs. In some respects, they may behave differently. How did these differences emerge? What forces are responsible for shaping people in these two different directions? These questions all concern **sex-typing,** that is, how we acquire "sex-appropriate" preferences, skills, personality attributes, behaviors, and self-concepts (Bem, 1983). To begin to answer these questions, we must start before a baby is born, with a look at prenatal development. We will see that females and males may be genetically different at conception, but they are anatomically similar for the first few weeks of development in the uterus. A complicated series of biological events produces external genitals that are typically—but not always—consistent with the baby's genetic sex.

The obstetrician glances at a newborn's genitals and makes the pronouncement, "It's a boy!" or "It's a girl!" Once that label is assigned, parents, other relatives, and even strangers begin to shape the future of that infant. Look at the photograph of the infant at the beginning of this chapter and imagine that it is a girl. Think about the expectations people might have for this infant, knowing that she is female: "Sugar and spice and everything nice." Now try to erase that imagery and switch the infant's sex. If the task is difficult, notice what this tells us about the permanence of a label! However, try to convert this infant into a male, and contemplate the different set of expectations: "Snips and snails and puppy-dog tails." Even if you have no idea what a "snip" is, notice whether the baby now seems more solid, hearty, adventurous, and daring.

We have three topics in this chapter. We begin with a discussion of prenatal development, which includes an overview of genetics and a discussion of both normal and abnormal prenatal development. Next we consider whether there are any areas in which infant girls and boys differ. Finally, we will see how girls and boys are treated differently; in this last section we will look at infants, that is, children less than 18 months old. The treatment of older girls and boys will be a major topic in the next chapter.

☐ PRENATAL DEVELOPMENT

Let us begin this exploration of early development by looking at the prenatal period. We will discuss genetics and normal prenatal development. Our last topic is abnormal prenatal development, a topic that may have some interesting implications for gender-role development.

Genetics

If you are like most students, you learned about genetics in a biology course, but you would hesitate about delivering a spontaneous lecture on the genetic determinants of sex. A brief overview of the topic should be useful.

In normal humans, almost every cell in your body contains 23 pairs of chromosomes, or a total of 46 chromosomes. (The exceptions are the reproductive cells, that is, the egg cells and the sperm cells, which have only 23 *single* chromosomes when they are mature.)

The 23 pairs of chromosomes come in two varieties. Twenty-two of those pairs are called autosomes. The **autosomes** carry thousands of genes that have no influence on the sex of the embryo; instead, they determine body characteristics such as hair color, blood type, and the size of the big toe. The one remaining pair of chromosomes is called the **sex chromosomes;** these sex chromosomes determine whether the embryo will be female or male.

Females have a pair of sex chromosomes called X chromsomes, symbolized XX. Males have one sex chromosome called X and one called Y, symbolized XY. The Y chromosome is much smaller than the X chromosome.

Let us now see what happens at conception. We noted that the egg cell has 23 single chromosomes; this number includes one sex chromosome, an X chromosome. The sperm cell from the father that fertilizes the egg cell contains either an X chromosome or a Y chromosome. Therefore, the father determines the genetic sex of the offspring. Isn't it ironic that a human characteristic that is so important in our society—whether you are an XX person or an XY person—should be determined simply by whether an X-bearing sperm or a Y-bearing sperm is the first to penetrate the egg cell?

Normal Prenatal Development

The fertilized egg divides many times, forming an embryo that increases in size and complexity. However, the embryo shows no sexual differentiation until about six weeks after conception. In other words, males and females look the same in the early stages of development; they differ only in their chromosomes (Money & Ehrhardt, 1972). Let us trace the development of the gonads, the production of hormones, the internal reproductive system, and the external genitals.

Females and males even have identical **gonads,** or sex glands, during the first weeks of prenatal development. The primitive gonad has two parts, an outer portion and an inner portion. If the embryo is an XY embryo, the male testes begin to develop at six weeks of age. The development of the testes is influenced by messages that are contained in the genetic code of the XY pair of chromosomes. During development, the inner portion of the primitive gonad grows rapidly, and the outer portion shrinks until it almost disappears. The testes remain in the abdominal cavity until about seven months after conception. Then they migrate down into the scrotum, arriving there shortly before birth.

If the embryo is an XX embryo, a female ovary begins to develop somewhat later, at about 12 weeks of age. Messages in the genetic code of the XX chromosomes influence this development. In females, the outer portion of the gonad grows rapidly, whereas the inner portion essentially disappears (just the opposite of gonadal development in males). The ovaries remain permanently in the abdominal cavity.

We have discussed the gonads; now let us turn to the internal reproductive systems. At seven weeks after conception, each human fetus has two sets of primitive, internal reproductive systems. There is a female system, called **mullerian ducts,** which will eventually develop into a uterus, egg ducts, and part of the vagina in females. There is also a male system, called **wolffian ducts,** which will eventually develop into the appropriate internal reproductive system in males.

Obviously, as an adult, you no longer have two complete reproductive systems. How is this change accomplished? Secretions from the testes influence development in the male fetus. The testes secrete two substances. One of these is **androgen,** often called the male sex hormone. Androgen encourages the growth and development of the wolffian ducts. The other substance shrinks the mullerian ducts, and so it has been called, none too creatively, the **mullerian inhibiting substance.** At birth, then, a baby boy has only a male reproductive system.

If biology worked symmetrically, you might expect that the ovary would also secrete two substances. However, this is not the case. Instead, when the fetus lacks testes—which is the case with female fetuses—female development occurs spontaneously. That is, the mullerian ducts develop and the wolffian ducts shrink. At birth, a baby girl has only a female reproductive system. We know that the ovaries are *not* critical in early female development, because the rest of the female reproductive system develops normally even when both ovaries are absent (Money & Ehrhardt, 1972). Interestingly, therefore, the female pattern of development is the "standard" one, because something extra must be added to produce a male.

The last structures to develop prenatally are the external genitals. The early development of external genitals is identical for males and females, just as it was for the gonads and the internal reproductive systems. However, the external genitals develop into two different kinds of structures at about the same time that the internal reproductive systems are developing. Figure 2.1 shows details about how the same structure can develop in two different ways. Notice, for example, that the genital tubercle becomes the clitoris in females and the penis in males. Also, the labioscrotal swellings become the labia in females; these swellings fuse together to become the scrotum in males. Thus, the two kinds of external genitals that most people regard as being different from each other are structurally similar, and their origins are identical.

We have discussed the normal development of females and males prior to birth. The first event was conception, at which genetic sex is determined. Female and male embryos are anatomically identical for the first weeks of life until four further events occur to begin the differentiation of females and males. These four events are the development of the gonads, the production of hormones, the development of the internal reproductive systems, and the development of external genitals.

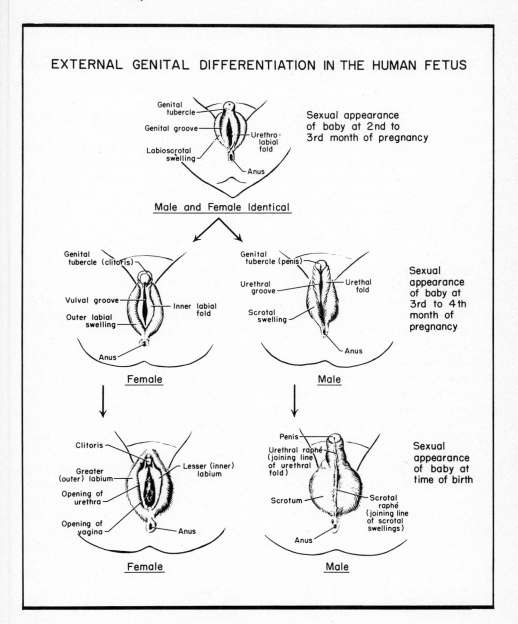

EXTERNAL GENITAL DIFFERENTIATION IN THE HUMAN FETUS

Genital tubercle
Genital groove
Labioscrotal swelling
Urethro-labial fold
Anus

Sexual appearance of baby at 2nd to 3rd month of pregnancy

Male and Female Identical

Genital tubercle (clitoris)
Vulval groove
Outer labial swelling
Inner labial fold
Anus

Female

Genital tubercle (penis)
Urethral groove
Scrotal swelling
Urethal fold
Anus

Male

Sexual appearance of baby at 3rd to 4th month of pregnancy

Clitoris
Greater (outer) labium
Opening of urethra
Opening of vagina
Lesser (inner) labium
Anus

Female

Penis
Urethral raphé (joining line of urethral fold)
Scrotum
Scrotal raphé (joining line of scrotal swellings)
Anus

Male

Sexual appearance of baby at time of birth

Abnormal Prenatal Development

The scenario we discussed is the typical one. However, mistakes occasionally occur during this elaborate developmental sequence, and a person's sex is ambiguous. In other words, some individuals receive biological influences that are female at some stages and male at other stages. An examination of these people may provide us with information about the importance of biological features in determining whether a person acts like a female or a male. Though there is some controversy (Hines, 1982; Huston, 1983), we will conclude that the more important factors are the label a child is given—female or male—and whether the child is treated like a girl or a boy.

The large majority of people have either an XX or an XY genetic pattern. However, a few people inherit either too many or too few sex chromosomes. **Turner's syndrome** is a condition in which people have an XO genetic pattern. That is, they have only one normal X chromosome; the other sex chromosome is missing, and so it is represented by a zero. A baby with Turner's syndrome has genitals that look like those of a normal girl, so she will be labeled a girl. She does not have normal ovaries, because she is missing an X chromosome. As a result, she will not menstruate at adolescence or develop breasts unless she is given hormonal treatment.

How do Turner's syndrome girls act? In one study, 15 girls with Turner's syndrome were compared with 15 normal girls (Ehrhardt, Greenberg & Money, 1970). In most respects, the Turner's syndrome girls and the normal girls behaved similarly in early adolescence. Both groups believed themselves to be girls and seemed to have no confusion or ambiguity about these beliefs. However, the Turner's syndrome girls had actually adopted the cultural stereotype of femininity to a greater extent than the normal girls, at least on three measures. They were more interested in jewelry, and they were less interested in athletic activities and childhood fights than the normal girls. We can conclude that neither beliefs about one's gender nor gender-stereotyped behavior seem to require a second X chromosome (Money & Ehrhardt, 1972).

There are several abnormalities that occur when the prenatal hormones do not function normally. One of them is **androgen-insensitivity syndrome,** a condition in which genetic males (XY) produce normal amounts of androgen, but a genetic defect makes their bodies insensitive to the androgen (Hines, 1982). As a result, they are born with female genitals, and they are usually labeled girls. They typically seem normal until puberty, when they do not begin to menstruate. A pelvic examination reveals that they have a shallow cavity rather than a complete vagina, and this cavity does not lead to a uterus.

An investigation of people with androgen-insensitivity syndrome who were raised as girls showed that they were strongly feminine. As Money and Ehrhardt (1972) conclude, the majority of these people "conformed to the idealized stereotype of what constitutes femininity in our culture" (p. 112).

It seems that their genetic background as males was largely irrelevant. For example, consider the case of a woman, married to a doctor, who went to a specialist to find out why she and her husband were unable to have children. She knew that something was wrong because she had been faking menstrual periods since adolescence. However, neither she nor her husband suspected that she was chromosomally a male, whose insensitivity to androgen had produced female genitals (Money & Tucker, 1975).

In another kind of abnormality, genetically normal fetuses have an excess of androgens during prenatal development. There are two reasons for this excess. One reason is an abnormality called **andrenogenital syndrome,** in which the adrenal gland produces excessive androgen, and the genitals look masculine. Another reason is that a drug was prescribed to some pregnant women in the 1950s to prevent miscarriage. In some cases, this drug produced genitals that looked masculine in children who were genetically female. (The use of this hormone was discontinued when the masculinizing effects were noticed.) In both of these cases—whether the extra androgen is from the baby's own body or from medication taken by the mother—the external genitals often look masculine. Genetic females may be labeled boys and raised as boys. Their ovaries and uteruses can be removed surgically, and androgen therapy can masculinize their bodies. In other words, despite their XX chromosomes, they can become men who do not look noticeably different from other men (Money & Tucker, 1975).

Table 2.1 summarizes these three kinds of abnormalities. Notice that the critical factor in determining the behavior of the individual seems to be the label given at birth, not the chromosome situation. Later in this chapter, we will see why this label is so important. First, however, we must see whether baby girls and baby boys differ from each other in the first months after birth.

TABLE 2.1   **Three Kinds of Abnormalities in Prenatal Development**

	Turner's Syndrome	Androgen-insensitivity Syndrome	Adrenogenital Syndrome
Genetic Pattern	XO	XY	XX
Disorder	XO genetic pattern	Body is insensitive to androgen	Too much androgen
Genital Appearance	female	female	male
Label	female	female	male
Behavior	"feminine"	"feminine"	"masculine"

☐ SECTION SUMMARY ▪ Prenatal Development

1. In humans, one of the 23 pairs of chromosomes is called the sex chromosomes, which are symbolized XX for females and XY for males.
2. For several weeks after conception, males and females are similar; then the primitive gonads develop into testes in males and ovaries in females.
3. All fetuses have two sets of reproductive systems; in females, the mullerian ducts develop and the wolffian ducts shrink, whereas the reverse is true in males. If the fetus is male, the testes secrete substances that promote the development of the male reproductive system; otherwise the female reproductive system develops automatically.
4. In early development, females and males have identical external genitals; the same structures grow into either female or male genitals during prenatal development.
5. In Turner's syndrome, an XO genetic pattern has external genitals that look female, and so the baby is labeled female; their later behavior is generally stereotypically feminine.
6. In androgen-insensitivity syndrome, XY babies are insensitive to androgen, their external genitals look female, and so the baby is labeled female; their later behavior is generally stereotypically feminine.
7. In adrenogenital syndrome, the fetus is exposed to too much androgen, and the external genitals of XX babies may look male; if they are labeled male, their later behavior is generally stereotypically masculine.

☐ SEX DIFFERENCES IN INFANCY

We will talk about sex differences in most of the chapters of this book. There is a reason, however, to focus upon sex differences in infancy. That is, research on infants may help clarify whether sex differences can be traced to biological explanations ("nature"), rather than explanations involving different experiences for females and males ("nurture"). Suppose that researchers find that at one day of age, female infants are much more responsive than male infants to human faces. We would be inclined to believe that there is an inborn, biological difference in this particular area. After all, it would be difficult to justify this sex difference by arguing that a baby girl and a baby boy had extremely different experiences from one another in those first 24 hours of life.

The areas we will investigate include the following: physical and perceptual development; activity level and temperament; and social behavior. We will see that sex differences in these areas are both small and inconsistent, congruent with the first theme of this book. These initial sex similarities argue for the importance of nurture rather than nature in the development of sex-typing.

Physical and Perceptual Development

There are several minor physical differences between infant boys and girls, other than the obvious difference in the genitals. When they are born, boys are slightly longer and heavier than girls. Infant girls are somewhat more advanced than infant boys in their bone development. For example, boys must reach the age of four to six weeks before their bones are as developed as those of newborn girls (Garai & Scheinfeld, 1968; Hutt, 1978). Boys also tend to be slower in their motor development; they sit, crawl, and walk later than girls do (Hutt, 1978).

Infant girls and boys are remarkably similar in their perceptual development. For example, Shepard and Peterson (1973) located 145 different comparisons of perceptual responsiveness in previous studies. In all, 13 comparisons showed that boys were more sensitive, and nine showed that girls were more sensitive. The clear majority of studies (123) concluded that boys and girls are similar in the way they see, hear, taste, smell, and respond to touch. Sex similarities are more common than sex differences in the area of perceptual development.

Activity Level and Temperament

Infant boys and girls are similar in their activity level and temperament. Consider motor activity in infancy. Although some studies have demonstrated that boys are somewhat more active on some measures (Block, 1976; Korner, 1969; Phillips, King & Dubois, 1978), other studies have concluded that there are no substantial differences (for example, Jacklin & Maccoby, 1983; Maccoby & Jacklin, 1974; Rothbart, 1983). A similar situation exists for sleeping patterns. That is, some research demonstrates that boys sleep less than girls (Moss, 1967; Phillips, et al., 1978), whereas other studies have found no sex differences (Moss & Robson, 1968). At present, we must conclude that any sex differences in motor activity or sleep patterns are small and inconsistent.

It is also difficult to draw conclusions about other aspects of infants' temperament. Moss (1967) found that baby boys cry more than baby girls at three weeks of age. However, Rothbart (1983) found no overall sex differences when she observed infants over a six-month period, beginning at three months. Observation of the babies, as well as parents' reports on questionnaires, showed that boys and girls were similar in their expression of fear, as well as the ease with which they could be soothed.

Some theorists believe that adult sex differences in areas such as aggression may be traced to early, inborn sex differences in activity level and temperament. However, sex differences in these areas during infancy are so small that the "early sex differences" explanation provides—at best—only a partial answer. The last part of this chapter and most of the next chapter attempt to uncover other explanations for the development of sex differences.

Social Behavior

Infant girls and boys are also similar in their social behavior. Baby girls and baby boys are equally likely to look at or to smile at faces (Maccoby & Jacklin, 1974).

Baby girls may be somewhat more sociable in other areas, however. For example, Brooks-Gunn and Matthews (1979) describe a study in which girls talked to, smiled at, and looked at their mothers more than boys did during the first two years of life. In other research, baby girls between the ages of six months and one year were more likely to begin social interactions with their mothers, in contrast with baby boys. Also, girls were more responsive than boys when their mothers spoke to them (Gunnar & Donahue, 1980). In Chapter 7, we will discuss some evidence that baby girls acquire language faster than baby boys, an advantage that might contribute to their social responsiveness. However, some researchers have found no sex differences in sociability (e.g., Rothbart, 1983).

There is a suggestion that baby girls may be more responsive to other babies, as well as to adults. For instance, Sagi and Hoffman (1976) found that one-day-old girls cried somewhat more than one-day-old boys in response to the cry of other infants. Eisenberg and Lennon (1983) summarize several other studies that confirm this tendency. However, they doubt that this kind of reflex-like crying is truly related to any kind of later social behavior. At present this finding is interesting, but we don't know whether it is important.

Do infant girls and boys differ in their dependency upon adults? The answer here seems to be a tentative "no." An early study discovered that 11-month-old baby girls cried more when a barrier separated them from their mothers (Goldberg & Lewis, 1969). Other research maintains that there are no substantial differences in dependency during infancy (Brooks-Gunn & Matthews, 1979; Jacklin, Maccoby, & Dick, 1973; Maccoby & Jacklin, 1974).

Once more, we see that sex differences in infancy are small and inconsistent. Furthermore, most of the studies that discover sex differences in social behavior involve older infants. Their sociability may well have been influenced by people's differential treatment of baby girls and boys. Let us turn now to that topic.

☐ SECTION SUMMARY ▪ Sex Differences in Infancy

1. Sex differences in infancy are theoretically interesting because they help clarify whether sex differences can be traced to "nature" or "nurture."
2. Infant girls are slightly shorter and lighter than infant boys, and their bone and motor development are somewhat more advanced.
3. Infant boys and girls are similar in their perceptual responses.

4. Although there are some studies that indicate sex differences in infant activity level and temperament, the differences are neither large nor consistent.
5. Although there are some studies that indicate sex differences in social behavior, the differences—once again—are neither large nor consistent.

☐ HOW PEOPLE RESPOND TO INFANT GIRLS AND BOYS

We consider a person's sex—the label "female" or "male"—to be very important. Remember that we discussed in the first section of this chapter that the label assigned at birth is even more important than a person's genetic or internal anatomical sex. Think about the most likely question to follow the announcement that a baby has been born: "Is it a boy or a girl?" One pair of researchers asked the parents of newborns to telephone friends and relatives to announce their baby's birth (Intons-Peterson & Reddel, 1984). In 80 percent of the cases, the first question concerned the baby's sex. Questions about the health of the mother or the baby were eventually asked, but only after establishing whether the baby was female or male! Sex is so important to some parents that they may be tragically disappointed if the baby doesn't meet their expectations. A friend of mine shared a room on a maternity ward in the late 1960s with a woman who was planning to give her baby girl up for adoption. She and her husband had wanted a boy.

Another index of the importance of a baby's sex is the enthusiasm with which some people seek a prediction for the sex of an unborn child. Brooks-Gunn and Matthews (1979) point out that a pregnant woman is like a mystery prize on a television game show, because everybody wonders about the surprise inside. Think about the prediction methods you have heard about. A fast heart rate indicates a boy; a slow rate, a girl. An active baby will certainly be a boy, according to legend—though the lack of clear-cut sex differences in activity levels for newborns should make you suspicious of this method. If the pregnant woman's belly is high, she should deliver a boy, whereas a low belly or spreading out to the sides signals a girl. My students have reported numerous other more exotic predictors, involving techniques such as swinging a ring above the mother's stomach and inspecting for varicose veins as a sure sign of a girl. Rumor has it that one entrepreneur charged $5.00 to predict the sex of unborn babies; the parents of newborns could reclaim the $5.00 if the prediction was wrong. Notice that this scam would assure a person, guessing the sex at random, a tidy income of about $2.50 on each pregnancy.

We know that people are intensely curious about the sex of an unborn baby. We also know that most parents hope that the baby will be a boy. In one study 90 percent of men and 92 percent of women wanted a boy as their firstborn (Peterson & Peterson, 1973). The birth of a daughter will be a disappointment—at least initially—to most people. Notice that the preference for male babies is an important example of the second theme of this book, that males and females are treated differently, with males being valued more than females.

Once the child is born, we find that people's reactions to baby girls are different from their reactions to baby boys. These reactions can be divided into three categories: judgments and expectations; toy choice; and parental behavior. Although not perfectly consistent, the research supports the important role of nurture in sex-typing. This section illustrates the second theme of this book, that people treat males and females differently. It is particularly important to stress that this differential treatment is evident in infancy.

Judgments and Expectations

Before you read further, try Demonstration 2.1, which is a modification of a study that demonstrated how we judge infants as a function of their sex. Did the friends who thought that the baby was a girl rate the baby as softer than the friends who thought that the baby was a boy? Were there other judgments that depended upon the sex that people believed the infant to be?

In their book, *He and She: How Children Develop Their Sex-Role Identity*, Brooks-Gunn and Matthews (1979) describe an infant daugher, Avery, who was dressed in a neutral outfit of overalls and a tee-shirt. People responded differently if they thought she was a girl, rather than a boy. Those who believed that she was a girl made remarks such as "O-o-oh, look at the tiny little teeth. Aren't they cute!" Notice how comments such as this one imply that teeth are purely ornamental. In contrast, a friendly supermarket manager, noticing these very same teeth but assuming that Avery was a boy, exclaimed, "H-ee-y there fella. Bet ya'll be biting into a big juicy steak this summer!" (p. 74).

We also have experimental evidence that people's judgments depend upon the infant's perceived sex—even when it is the same infant in both the "male" and "female" condition. Seavey, Katz, and Zalk (1975) introduced adults to a three-month-old infant, whose sex was not revealed. Later, these people were asked to guess the baby's sex and give reasons for their answers. Those who thought that the baby was a boy remarked about the strength of the baby's grasp or the lack of hair. Those who thought that the baby was a girl commented upon how round, soft, and fragile "she" was.

A baby's appearance, we have noticed, can look either feminine or masculine, depending upon our expectations. Similarly, our expectations determine whether the baby's *behavior* seems feminine or masculine. Condry and Condry (1976) prepared videotapes of an infant responding to a variety of stimuli. For example, the infant smiled, laughed, and reached out to a teddy bear and also stared and then cried in response to the opening of a jack-in-the-box. Adults were asked to watch the series of videotapes of the infant, who was labeled female half of the time and male half of the time.

Figure 2.2 shows how people rated the negative response that the infant gave to the jack-in-the-box. When people thought that the infant was a boy, they judged that "he" was showing anger; when they thought that the infant was a girl, they decided that "she" was showing fear. Remember that every-

Judgments about Infant Girls and Boys

Copy the rating scale at the bottom of this demonstration, making enough copies to pass out to people whom you can convince to participate in this exercise. Each person should be tested individually. Hand the participant the rating scale and explain that the picture at the beginning of the chapter is of an infant named Adam, and that Adam should be rated on each of the scales on the sheet. The next participant should receive the same instructions, except that the infant is named Emily. In all, half of the participants should rate "Adam" and half should rate "Emily."

X	X	X	X	X	X	X
Not at all soft						Very soft

X	X	X	X	X	X	X
Not at all alert						Very alert

X	X	X	X	X	X	X
Not at all timid						Very timid

X	X	X	X	X	X	X
Not at all strong						Very strong

X	X	X	X	X	X	X
Not at all cuddly						Very cuddly

X	X	X	X	X	X	X
Not at all intelligent						Very intelligent

one saw the same videotape of the same infant, yet the ambiguous negative reaction was given a more masculine label when the infant was perceived to be a boy. We are reluctant to believe that females can express such an active negative emotion as anger, and this reluctance also applies to older females. Recently, my 11-year-old daughter was wearing a negative expression and I remarked, "I'm sorry to see you're so sad, Sally." She corrected me, "I'm not sad, I'm *mad*."

The research we've discussed so far involves strangers' judgments about infants. However, the sex label attached to a child also influences parents' judgments. This finding is particularly important because infants spend so much more time with their parents than with supermarket managers or other friendly strangers. Rubin, Provenzano, and Luria (1974) met with parents during the first 24 hours after the birth of their first child. They interviewed 15 pairs of parents with sons and 15 with daughters, having made certain

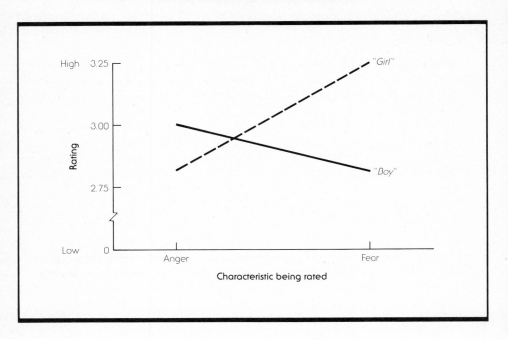

that the male and female infants were equivalent in critical factors such as birth weight, birth length, and overall health. In particular, they asked all parents to rate their infants on a number of scales such as the ones you tried in Demonstration 2.1.

Notice that this set-up cannot be as carefully controlled as those in which the same infant is sometimes presented as a female, sometimes as a male. However, the infants were physically similar, so that "unbiased" parents would rate daughters and sons equivalently. However, parents of sons rated their infants as being bigger, in contrast to the ratings supplied by the parents of daughters. Infant sons were also more likely to be seen as being large-featured, rather than fine-featured, and attentive, rather than inattentive.

Mothers and fathers were equally biased in judgment about these three characteristics—size, features, and attentiveness. However, on a number of other scales, fathers were more likely to be biased than mothers. Mothers rated their daughters and sons as being equally soft. Fathers, however, made a big distinction; fathers of daughters rated their infants as being very soft, in contrast to the ratings given by fathers of sons. In Chapter 3, we will mention that fathers continue their greater interest in sex typing throughout childhood.

Try noticing additional ways in which we judge baby girls differently from baby boys, even in the first few days after birth. Browse through greeting cards and notice the difference between cards to be sent to infant girls and those to be sent to infant boys. Figure 2.3 shows a typical contrast. The baby who receives these cards is only a few days old, and already we indicate our expectations.

Toy Choice

We have different impressions about baby girls and baby boys. However, these impressions may not shape the destinies of infants unless we somehow *behave* differently to girls and boys. For instance, do we give different toys to baby girls than we give to baby boys?

In one study, college students played with a young infant who was either introduced as Johnny or Jenny, or else no name was supplied (Sidorowicz & Lunney, 1980). In reality the baby in each condition was a boy on some occasions and a girl on other occasions. Just out of reach of the infant lay a small toy football (a stereotypically masculine toy), a doll (a stereotypically feminine toy), or a teething ring (a neutral toy).

The question of interest was whether people would hand different toys

FIGURE 2.3. **Representative cards to be sent to a baby girl and a baby boy (Note: In the original, the one for the girl is pink and the one for the boy is blue.)**

to infants as a function of their perceived sex. Figure 2.4 illustrates the results. As you can see, people were more likely to hand "Johnny" a football, rather than a doll. A child of unidentified sex received the doll slightly more often than the football. "Jenny" was handed the doll more than five times more often than the football. (The teething ring, incidentally, was not a popular choice for any infant.) Other studies have demonstrated a sex bias in toy choice for other groups of people, such as graduate students, secretaries, and people with both female and male children (Culp, Cook, & Housley, 1983; Seavey, Katz, & Zalk, 1975; Will, Self, & Datan, 1976).

These studies on biases on toy selection are important because other research, summarized by Sidorowicz and Lunney (1980), demonstrates that children who have been presented with "gender appropriate" toys tend to spend more time playing with them. Gradually, they develop competence in interacting with these toys. If Aunt Emma hands Jenny a doll—rather than

FIGURE 2.4. **Toys handed to infants perceived to be female or male or whose sex was not mentioned (based on Sidorowicz & Lunney, 1980)**

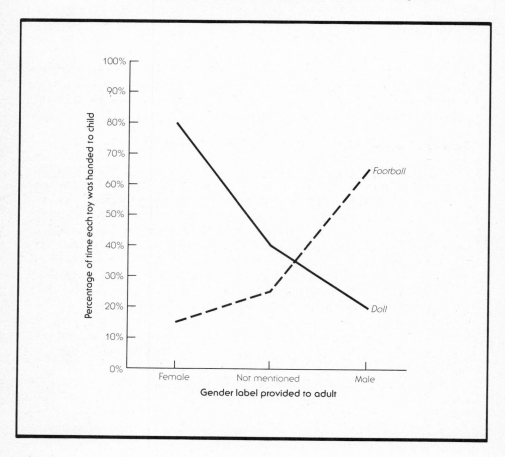

DEMONSTRATION 2.2

Choosing Toys for Infant Girls and Boys[1]

Find several acquaintances who did not participate in Demonstration 2.1. Ask them to imagine that they must buy a toy for an infant, whom you introduce either as a niece named Becky or a nephew named Robert. Show them, in either case, the picture at the beginning of the chapter. Ask them to list 4–5 toys that they would look for. Test half of the people in the "Becky" condition and half in the "Robert" condition.

If time permits, you can try a variant of this demonstration by visiting a toy store. Ask the clerk to help you choose either a toy or something to wear for a cousin who is one year old. Record whether the clerk asks about the sex of the child. (In all probability, this will be the very first question.) You might want to refuse to specify the sex of the child, noting the clerk's reaction. If you do (eventually) specify whether the child is a boy or a girl, does the clerk direct you to sex-typed gifts? What happens if you ask for an "inappropriate" item, such as a firetruck for a female child? Notice how gender-role conformity can be encouraged by people as seemingly innocent as department-store clerks!

[1] I would like to thank Dr. Mary Crawford for suggesting the second part of this demonstration, which was inspired by a study by Kutner and Levinson (1978).

---

a football—on one occasion, she will not be doomed to a life of unathletic nurturance, but repeated encouragement toward "feminine" toys could help shape her interests and areas of competence. Try Demonstration 2.2 to see whether people choose different toys for girls than for boys.

Parental Behavior

We saw earlier in the chapter that parents judge their sons and daughters differently. They also treat their baby girls differently from their baby boys in several respects. One obvious area is in the choice of clothing. Paul and Paula might both spend a large portion of their infancy in neutral sleepers, overalls, and tee-shirts, or—in hot weather—just a diaper. Still, for special occasions Paul is likely to be sporting a tailored blue outfit, while Paula wears a dress. Paula's parents can clothe her in a wide variety of colors, but her dress is likely to have flowers, smocking, bows, or frills. Parents are particularly likely to advertise their child's gender to the world on special occasions when infants make public appearances, perhaps because they want to save themselves and others the embarrassment of a mislabeled child. We mentioned earlier that the sex of an unborn child is important to us. Similarly, you have probably witnessed the obvious resentment that occurs when a bald, neutrally dressed infant is mistakenly called a boy.

Parents also treat girls differently from boys in their choice of bedroom decorations and contents. In one study, researchers visited the bedrooms of boys and girls between the ages of one month and six years (Rheingold & Cook, 1975). Boys' rooms were typically decorated with animal themes, whereas girls' were likely to have flowers, lace, fringes, and ruffles. Consistent with the previous section, the availability of toys also differed. Boys of all ages had a total of 375 vehicles, in contrast to 17 for girls. Boys were also more likely to have educational-art material, such as clay, and sports equipment. Girls, as might be expected, had more dolls. When boys' rooms did contain a doll, it was almost always a male doll, such as a toy soldier. As Rheingold and Cook conclude,

> Clear in the findings of this study was the extent to which the boys were provided objects that encouraged activities directed away from home—toward sports, cars, animals, and the military—and the girls, objects that encouraged activities directed toward the home—keeping house and caring for children. [p. 463]

We have other evidence, as well, that parents direct their daughters toward interpersonal interactions. Moss (1974) asked parents to encourage their seven-week-old infants to perform certain tasks. Both mothers and fathers spent more time urging their female infants to smile and to vocalize. It seems that we believe that girls must be social creatures, even if they are only seven weeks old. In Chapter 7, incidentally, we will see that adult women smile much more than adult men; we ensure this later sex difference by beginning the training early. Both parents were also more likely to apply terms of affection, such as "angel," "honey," and "precious," to baby girls than to baby boys.

In Chapter 7, we will also see that adult women have somewhat greater verbal ability than adult men. Could this difference be promoted by parents' early encouragement of verbal skills in their baby girls? There is some evidence for this suggestion, but it is not overwhelming. In one review of studies in the area, 19 comparisons showed that parents vocalized equally to boys and girls (Maccoby & Jacklin, 1974). Two other studies showed that boys received more vocalizations than girls, and ten studies showed that girls received more vocalizations than boys, though the differences occasionally applied only to a portion of the sample. It would be a mistake to conclude that parents *consistently* talk more to daughters than to sons, but it would also be a mistake to ignore those studies that demonstrated differential treatment. The truth is probably complicated, but parents' differential treatment of girls and boys may provide some extra encouragement to their daughters' verbal skills.

Parents interact with children physically, as well as vocally. Girls seem to be treated as if they were fragile, whereas boys can be handled more roughly (Maccoby & Jacklin, 1974). Parents are also more likely to play vigorously with their sons' arms and legs. These findings are reinforced by another investigation that showed that women were more likely to encourage large muscle activity in a child they believed to be a male, rather than a female (Smith & Lloyd, 1978).

We have looked at the rougher forms of physical contact with infants. How about the gentler kinds of touch? Here, parents' treatment of girls and boys seems to depend upon the age of the infant (Cherry & Lewis, 1976;

Goldberg & Lewis, 1969; Lewis, 1972). Boys seem to be touched and held more than girls for the first six months of life, but then a reversal occurs. For older infants, girls are touched and held more than boys. Brooks-Gunn and Matthews (1979) suggest that young boys may initially require more holding than young girls because of their somewhat greater irritability. Once boys have matured somewhat, however, independence training begins. When young boys reach the ripe old age of six months, we literally let go of them, although we keep cuddling young girls.

Another way in which we train boys—more than girls—to be independent is by encouraging them to venture forth. In the following observation of a one-year-old boy and his mother, notice the number of times that the mother encourages his exploration and independence. Would she have reacted similarly to a daughter?

> [The boy is] going toward mother. She is touching his head. He is touching her. . . . She throws the dog and cat far from her. He looks. He smiles and goes toward them. . . . Picks up the cat. Has mallet in right hand. Going toward the mother. Drops the cat. . . . Leans against mother. Looks up at her. Mallet in right hand. She vocalizes to him. She turns him around. He is facing away and smiling. Mallet in right hand. . . . Goes [away from mother]. Picks up the cat. Goes to mother again. Drops cat and goes to mother and leans against her. Looks up at her. Mallet in right hand. She turns him around. [Lewis, 1972, pp. 235–236]

This observation period lasted less than one minute; in this period, she encouraged him to leave her side three times. Boys are urged to go forth, even when they are barely able to walk.

The information on infancy does not provide us with a complete, satisfying resolution to the mystery of sex-typing. So far, we have seen that children can develop "feminine" behavior, even if their genetic makeup doesn't match that of a normal female. Thus, we must look beyond genetics for the clues. We have also seen that baby boys and baby girls may be somewhat different from each other in activity level and social behavior, but the differences are so small that they—by themselves—cannot explain sex-typing. There does seem to be at least a partial answer in the way people respond to infant girls and boys. People seem to think that infant boys are bigger and more attentive, and more capable of anger than fear. Adults also treat baby girls and boys differently with respect to toys, clothes, room decor, conversation, and cuddling. However, we will see that the differential treatment of boys and girls is still not a complete answer to the mystery of sex-typing. Instead, part of the answer seems to come from girls' and boys' own ideas about "femininity" and "masculinity."

☐ SECTION SUMMARY ▪ How People Respond to Infant Girls and Boys

1. We regard a baby's sex as important; the first question to a new parent concerns the baby's sex, and we also try to predict the sex.

2. A baby's appearance and behavior will be perceived as either feminine or masculine, depending upon the sex the baby is thought to be.
3. Parents judge sons as being bigger, larger featured, and more attentive than daughters, even when the infants are physically similar.
4. In general, people hand masculine toys to a child thought to be a boy and feminine toys to a child thought to be a girl.
5. Parents treat their daughters differently from their sons in clothing choices, name selection, and bedroom decoration.
6. Parents are somewhat more likely to encourage their daughters to smile and vocalize, in contrast to their sons, but the results are inconsistent.
7. Parents handle their sons more roughly than daughters; initially, they touch sons more than daughters, but in later infancy, they touch daughters more than sons, encouraging their sons to leave their sides.

Chapter Review Questions

1. Explain the genetic determinants of sex, using your own words.
2. List and briefly describe each of the three kinds of abnormal prenatal development we discussed in this chapter, and contrast each with normal prenatal development.
3. Early in prenatal development, infant boys and girls are identical. By the time they are born, they differ in their gonads, internal reproductive systems, and external genitals. Discuss how these three kinds of differences develop.
4. The evidence in this chapter provided more support for a "nurture" interpretation of sex-typing, rather than a "nature" interpretation. Discuss this statement, paying particular attention to the topics of abnormal prenatal development, differences in infancy, and the way people treat infant girls and boys.
5. The woman who lives next door is convinced that her newborn daughter behaves differently from the way her son behaved when he was a newborn. What information would you tell her about sex differences in infancy? How do you suppose her impressions were created? Now look back over the section in Chapter 1 about problems that can arise in research on sex differences and point out certain factors that might lead to exaggerated sex differences in her informal "study" based on her own children.
6. Suppose that a number of well-controlled research studies are conducted next year, using large samples of infants. They demonstrate that young infants do differ with respect to temperament and social behavior.

Explain how people's treatment of infant boys and girls might be influenced by these early sex differences.

7. In Chapter 1 we examined potential biases in the research process. Review the studies in the section on sex differences in infancy and point out how the findings could depend upon whether researchers had controlled for knowledge of infants' sex. Also, look at Table 1.1 and list the other ways in which biases could have influenced some of the conclusions about sex differences.

8. We pointed out that infants' sex is important to parents. Mention some of the ways in which this emphasis reveals itself and speculate about why we place such emphasis on whether a baby is a boy or a girl.

9. "Beauty is in the eyes of the beholder," according to the proverb. It also seems that newborns' masculinity and femininity is in the eyes of the beholder. Discuss this concept.

10. Chapter 3 discusses how parents encourage sex-typing in their children, beyond the infancy stage. In preparation for that discussion, summarize how parents perceive their infants and how they treat infant boys and girls differently.

☐ NEW TERMS

sex-typing
autosomes *Hair color etc*
sex chromosomes *Sex determinant*
gonads *Sex glands*
mullerian ducts *Female* > *Reproduction*
wolffian ducts *male*

androgen *Male sex hormone*
mullerian inhibiting substance *shrinks mullerian ducts*
Turner's syndrome *XO*
androgen-insensitivity syndrome *XY, but female external*
adrenogenital syndrome *XX but genitalia is male (Drug)*

☐ RECOMMENDED READINGS

Brooks-Gunn, J., & Matthews, W. S. (1979). *He & she: How children develop their sex-role identity.* Englewood Cliffs, N.J.: Spectrum. ■ This book would be an especially useful introduction to the area for nonprofessionals.

Huston, A. C. (1983). Sex-typing. In E. M. Hetherington (Ed.), *Handbook of child psychology*, Vol. IV (4th ed.). New York: Wiley. ■ This chapter provides a comprehensive overview of the literature on sex-typing, with coverage of the literature on infancy.

Jacklin, C. N., & Maccoby, E. E. (1983). Issues of gender differentiation. In M. D. Levine, W. B. Carey, A. C. Crocker, & R. T. Gross (Eds.), *Developmental-behavioral pediatrics* (pp. 175–184). Philadelphia: Saunders. ■ This chapter provides an overview of sex differences in infancy and of the treatment of female and male infants; it is an update on Maccoby and Jacklin's (1974) classic book, *The psychology of sex differences*.

CHILDHOOD AND ADOLESCENCE

- There is fairly strong evidence that girls have "penis envy" and feel that their own genitals are inferior.

- Girls imitate women and boys imitate men; in other words, children prefer to imitate same-sexed adults.

- Young children believe that a woman can become a man by cutting her hair very short.

- Parents are more likely to discourage a boy for his feminine behavior than a girl for her masculine behavior.

- Teachers give more attention to boys; boys are praised more, and they are also scolded more.

- When boys play together, they are more likely than girls to chase, hit, and wrestle.

- Children do not develop ideas about which personality characteristics are masculine and which are feminine until they are in kindergarten.

- Boys have more rigid stereotypes than girls about which careers are suitable for men and women.

- Adolescent women are more concerned than adolescent men about what other people think about them.

- Black adolescent females rate themselves higher than white adolescent females on characteristics such as warmth and responsibility.

Suppose that you have been reading a detective novel and have turned to the last page. Fancy New, brilliant young adolescent detective, has gathered all her chums around her to explain "who-dun-it." "It was the gardener," murmurs Fancy.

Detective novels are satisfying because by the time you reach the last page, there is only one guilty person responsible for the crime, and the evidence for that person's involvement in the crime is clear-cut. The mystery of gender development does not have such a satisfying resolution. You cannot look on the last page of this chapter (or even of this book) and find out "who-dun-it." We cannot point our finger at any single "criminal." Instead, there are many suspects, and the evidence for their involvement in the "crime" is often tentative and inconsistent. The reality is that, well before children reach adolescence, females have become "feminine" and males have become "masculine." Furthermore, both males and females know that men and women are supposed to be different kinds of creatures. The mystery about femininity and masculinity that we are trying to solve is often called sex-typing, and it has many components. **Sex-typing,** a term introduced in the last chapter, includes how we acquire "sex-appropriate" preferences, skills, personality attributes, behaviors, and self-concepts (Bem, 1983).

In an attempt to resolve the sex-typing mystery, dozens of psychiatrists, psychologists, and sociologists have proposed theories. The first section of this chapter examines four of these theories and comments briefly on how closely they fit the research evidence. The second section examines factors that shape sex-typing—people and forces who would be listed as the possible suspects in a detective novel. These include the family, peers, the school, and the media. The last two sections examine the "crime" itself. In the third section, we look at children's behavior—in particular whether girls and boys differ in their play activities—and children's beliefs about masculinity and femininity. In the fourth section, we discuss adolescent women, who are in transition between childhood and adulthood.

☐ THEORIES OF SEX-TYPING

In many areas of psychology, researchers have explored behavior in humans and in animals without the guidance of any developed theories. However, several important theories have been constructed that try to explain how children become sex-typed. The oldest of the theories we will examine, psychoanalytic theory, was developed out of a clinical, or case-study approach. Two other theories, social-learning theory and cognitive-developmental theory, were proposed in the 1960s. Both of these theories were derived from broad theories of learning and development, and both were based on results from a more experimental approach. Unfortunately, these two theories are far from perfect. During the last ten years, people interested in sex-typing have suggested a number of new theories, most of them borrowing from both social-learning theory and cognitive-developmental theory. We will look at one of these new theories, gender schema theory.

Psychoanalytic Theory

Psychoanalytic theory is a theory and method of treatment for psychological disorders; it emphasizes that people are not fully aware of their feelings. The theory was originally developed by Sigmund Freud, a Viennese psychiatrist who lived from 1856 to 1939. One of Freud's contributions was a theory of human development that had a tremendous influence on psychological theory, psychotherapy, and our culture in general. For many decades, Freudian theory formed the basis for "expert" opinion on women. As you'll see in Chapter 12 on Women and Psychological Disorders, therapists with a psychoanalytic orientation have a negative view of women that has undoubtedly had an enormous impact on women in therapy.

Freudian concepts are widespread throughout our culture. These concepts have invaded the health textbooks that our eighth graders read and the Sunday supplement of our local papers. Terms such as "super-ego," "repression," "Oedipus complex," and "castration anxiety" are now standard in our everyday conversations. Therefore, we need to discuss psychoanalytic theory because it has helped to *shape* the development of women, and not because it *explains* gender-role development accurately.

Freud proposed that sexuality is supremely important in explaining human behavior. As infants mature, the focus of their sexual energy shifts from one region of the body to another. Females and males develop similarly during the first two stages. In the first, or **oral stage,** babies focus upon the mouth region. In the second, or **anal stage,** children focus upon the anal region; the control of bowel movements is crucial. Both girls and boys are strongly attached to their mothers during these early years of life.

Girls and boys begin to differ from each other substantially at about the age of 4. During this third, or **phallic stage,** children focus upon their genitals. Boys in the phallic stage intensify their love for their mothers and suffer from a **castration complex,** fear that their genitals will be mutilated.

Freud suggested, though, that girls also suffer from a castration complex. A little girl presumably sees the male penis, notices the difference between those genitals and her own, and she feels inferior; she develops **penis envy.** As Freud (1933/1965) wrote, girls

> .... feel seriously wronged, often declare that they want to 'have something like it too', and fall a victim to 'envy for the penis', which will leave ineradicable traces on their development and the formation of their character and which will not be surmounted in even the most favourable cases without a severe expenditure of psychical energy. [p. 125]

Before we consider the consequences of this presumed penis envy, it would be wise to mention that there is little or no evidence for this concept.

In fact, most young girls do not express any major concern about genital differences. Some, indeed, are relieved that they are not similarly burdened. Tavris and Offir (1977) mention a little girl who took a bath with a young male cousin and observed the genital differences in silence. When her mother tucked her in bed that night, she said softly to her mother, " 'isn't it a blessing he doesn't have it on his face?' " (p. 155).

For Freud, though, penis envy was central to a girl's development during the phallic stage because it is this realization that makes her blame her mother for not supplying her with the proper equipment. She turns instead to her father, because she hopes that he will give her a penis as a gift. This desire for her very own penis is then transformed into an interest in dolls and a wish for a baby. (The students in my classes have trouble maintaining sober academic expressions at this point in the description of Freudian theory.) At this point, too, girls shift their interest from the "masculine" clitoris to the vagina. Girls never fully resolve the interest in their fathers. However, the problem is partly solved if they identify with their mothers, therefore symbolically achieving sexual relations with their fathers.

The fourth or **latency stage** is relatively boring, and psychosexual development does not move forward substantially. This stage lasts from approximately age six until puberty. At puberty, the **genital stage** begins, and both sexes are primarily concerned with intercourse, assuming that their development through other stages has been "normal."

This brief description of Freud's theory of female development provides you with an introduction to his complex ideas. The concept "anatomy is destiny" clearly dominates Freud's theory; a female's anatomy determines her further development. Notice that Freud's theory does not stress influence from outside forces. The specific characteristics of parents are generally unimportant. Other adults, peers, the school system, and additional important forces are not emphasized. Furthermore, there is no way in which development can be shaped by children's own ideas about what is "feminine" and what is "masculine." To examine these ideas, we must turn to more recent, more plausible-sounding theories.

Social-Learning Theory

Before you read further, try Demonstration 3.1. How did your friends respond? In all likelihood, "penis envy" did not figure prominently in the description. They probably also didn't mention complex thought processes, which are central in the two theories we will discuss later. Instead, your friends probably pointed out that children *learn* how to act "feminine" and "masculine." Their speculations are probably similar to social-learning theory.

According to **social-learning theory,** there are two major mechanisms that explain how girls learn about acting "feminine" and boys learn about acting "masculine": (1) they receive rewards and punishments for their own behavior, and (2) they watch and imitate the behavior of others. In fact, they learn sex-typing in the same way that they learn all other behaviors.

People's Informal Theories about Sex-Typing

Select several friends who have not had extensive backgrounds in psychology or sociology. Tell them that you are doing an informal survey and ask them how they think adult women and men come to be somewhat different. (Supply some examples, such as men being somewhat more aggressive than women, women being more likely than men to become nursery school teachers, and so forth.) If you question your friends in a group, responses should be written down to keep the answers independent.

Let us first see how rewards and punishments might operate. Jimmy, aged two, grabs a toy truck and, racing it back and forth between the dinner-guests' ankles, produces an admirable rumbling-motor sound. The doting parents smile and respond with praise; Jimmy's behavior is rewarded. His parents and their guests would probably not respond so positively if he donned his sister's pink tutu and waltzed among the dinner guests. His behavior would probably produce either a punishing silence or more active efforts to discourage him. Now imagine how Sarah, also two, might win smiles for the pink-tutu act and frowns for the roaring-truck performance. As Mischel (1966) describes social-learning theory, "Boys and girls discover that the consequences for performing such behaviors are affected by their sex, and therefore soon perform them with different frequency" (p. 60).

Social-learning theory points out, however, that children do not need to learn everything by trial-and-error. They often learn via a second method, by watching others and imitating them, a process called **modeling.** The extent to which they imitate a particular action depends upon the sex of the person performing the action, whether that person is rewarded or punished, and other situational factors. A little girl would be more likely to imitate her mother than her father, and more likely to imitate someone who has been praised for a behavior than someone who has been scorned.

According to social-learning theory, children might imitate actual people who have been observed, or they might imitate models whom they have read about or seen on television, called **symbolic models.** As we'll discuss later, the availability of gender-stereotyped models in the media helps explain why children reared in strongly feminist homes can produce some embarrassingly gender-stereotyped behavior. Recently, for example, two young daughters of friends of mine flounced seductively into the room and announced to their startled mother, "We're sexy ladies, Mommy." It seems likely that they learned about low-cut gowns and seductive body movements from television, rather than from their mother.

Unfortunately, social-learning theory has not been widely supported by research, in spite of the intuitive appeal of the theory. Maccoby and Jacklin (1974) considered whether parents reward or punish their sons and daughters for different kinds of behavior. They concluded that there is "a remarkable degree of uniformity in the socialization of the two sexes" (p. 348).

We will examine aspects of this process of reward and punishment in more detail in the next section. There is also little support for modeling, the second mechanism proposed by social-learning theory, as an explanation for gender-stereotyped behavior. Maccoby and Jacklin reviewed 23 studies and found no consistent tendency for young children to choose same-sex models. Instead, children copied indiscriminately from both female and male models. Notice how these findings are damaging to social-learning theory. Little Jenny is equally likely to copy her mother baking cookies and her father sawing a log; this lack of preference should not lead to gender-stereotyped behavior.

Let us look at typical research that examines modeling. Raskin and Israel (1981) asked third- and fourth-graders to watch female and male adults as they played with various toys. Then the children were observed to see which toys they would play with and how long it would take them to begin to play with the toys that the models had played with. Social-learning theory would predict that girls, for example, would more often select the toys that the female models had played with, and that they would also play with them sooner. The study was conducted twice, but only one measure in one study supported the predictions of social-learning theory. Girls who had been exposed to the female model played with the modeled toys sooner than girls who had been exposed to the male model. However, numerous other measures in both studies showed no tendency for children to imitate adults who were the same sex as themselves.

It is clear that social-learning theory cannot completely explain the acquisition of gender roles. It is equally clear that some parents, some of the time, encourage their children in "sex-appropriate" behavior. Block (1978) concluded from her review of the literature that fathers, more than mothers, were particularly likely to treat their sons and daughters differently. It seems that fathers are especially likely to expect their daughters to be "feminine" and their sons to be "masculine."

Cognitive-Developmental Theory

Social-learning theory proposes that adults shape children's acquisition of gender roles. **Cognitive-developmental theory,** in contrast, proposes that children are primarily responsible for shaping their own sex-typing. According to this theory, children's own thought processes are the real villain in the mystery of sex-typing.

You may be familiar with the Swiss psychologist Jean Piaget (pronounced "Pea-ah-*zhay*") and his theory of cognitive development. This complex theory proposes that children pass through a fixed series of stages as they mature into adulthood. The thinking of young children is qualitatively different from the thinking of older children. For example, young children believe that a row of M & M's has more candy if it is stretched out than if it is compact; they rely strongly on outward physical appearances when making judgments.

Lawrence Kohlberg (pronounced "*Kole*-berg") believed that the acquisition of gender roles could be explained within the broad framework of

Piaget's theory (Kohlberg, 1966; Kohlberg & Ullian, 1974). Children learn about gender-role concepts in the same way that they learn about other concepts, such as quantity and morality. Like Piaget, Kohlberg stresses that children actively work to figure out these concepts.

The major first step in sex-typing, according to Kohlberg, is **gender identity,** or a girl's realization that she is a girl and a boy's realization that he is a boy. Most children are quite accurate in labeling themselves by the time they are three.

Jenny may know that she is a girl, but correct self-labeling does not necessarily mean that she has a sophisticated appreciation for the classification system that divides the world into male and female. My daughter Sally carried on an extensive monologue when she was one and a half, "Sally good girl, Bethy [her sister] good girl, blanket good girl, hand good girl, light good girl, Daddy good girl, Mommy good girl, cup good girl." Children must learn how to classify people, just as they must learn numerous other classification systems during the course of cognitive development.

Once Jenny is four, she will probably be quite accurate in classifying people as female or male. However, correct classification does not mean that she understands gender constancy. **Gender constancy** means that a person's gender stays the same in spite of changes in outward physical appearance or behavior. (Recall that Piaget discovered that young children fail to appreciate that the number of objects in a row stays the same in spite of changes in the row's outward physical appearance.) Because young children do not appreciate gender constancy, they believe that a person can change genders very readily. A woman can become a man by cutting her hair very short, and a man can become a woman by holding a purse.

People can also change genders when they grow older, according to young children. Kohlberg (1966) recorded a conversation between Jimmy, almost four years old, and Johnny, who is four and a half:

Johnny: I'm going to be an airplane builder when I grow up.
Jimmy: When I grow up, I'll be a Mommy.
Johnny: No, you can't be a Mommy. You have to be a Daddy.
Jimmy: No, I'm going to be a Mommy.
Johnny: No, you're not a girl, you can't be a Mommy.
Jimmy: Yes, I can. [p. 95]

Once children have labeled themselves and have learned how to classify males and females, they begin to show systematic preferences. Specifically, they like things that are consistent with their own gender identity. A child who realizes that she is a girl, for example, likes objects and activities that are feminine. A woman in one of my classes provided a vivid example of these preference patterns. Her four-year-old daughter asked about the sex of every dog she met. If it was a "girl dog," she would run up and pat it lovingly. If it was a "boy dog," she would cast a scornful glance and walk in the opposite direction. Girls want to do stereotypically feminine activities because these activities are consistent with their female gender identity, and

TABLE 3.1   Causes and Effects in Social-Learning Theory and Cognitive-Developmental Theory

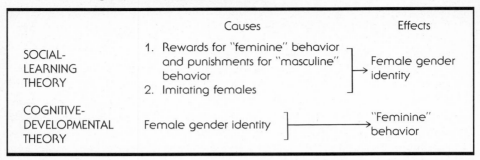

	Causes	Effects
SOCIAL-LEARNING THEORY	1. Rewards for "feminine" behavior and punishments for "masculine" behavior 2. Imitating females	Female gender identity
COGNITIVE-DEVELOPMENTAL THEORY	Female gender identity	"Feminine" behavior

not—as social-learning theory would suggest—in order to win rewards. Table 3.1 contrasts the two theories with respect to their explanations of why girls perform "feminine" activities.

Is there support for cognitive-developmental theory? Thompson (1975) tested children between the ages of two and three. He asked them a variety of questions about their own sex, the sex of people in various pictures, and their preferences for objects labeled as being either "for girls" or "for boys." Children who were two years old could accurately classify pictures of people as either "boys" and "daddies" or "girls" and "mommies." By two and a half, children correctly answered many questions about whether they most closely resembled a girl paper doll or a boy paper doll and questions about whether they would be daddies or mommies when they grew up. By three, children were likely to show preferences for objects consistent with their own gender identity; girls preferred "girl things" and boys preferred "boy things." (Notice that Thompson's ages are younger than those suggested by Kohlberg.)

As children grow older, they appreciate that the number of objects in a row does not change when the physical appearance of the row is changed. Emmerich and his colleagues discovered that children's appreciation of gender constancy shows a similar pattern of development (Emmerich, et al., 1977). They asked children questions such as, "If Janie puts on boys' clothes, what would she be?" Younger children thought that a person's gender depended upon physical appearance, but older children realized that gender would remain constant and stable, in spite of changes in physical appearance. They gave answers such as, "She would just look like a boy, but she wouldn't *be* a boy."

Cognitive-developmental theory has some compelling support, but there are also some difficulties. For example, cognitive-developmental theory predicts that a young girl must establish a firm gender-identity before she can show a preference for female activities. A girl must know she is a girl before she prefers dolls to trucks. Since gender identity is not acquired until about the age of three, children should not reveal gender-stereotyped behavior prior to that age. However, we have all seen girls acting stereotypically feminine and boys acting stereotypically masculine before that age.

Furthermore, as Bem (1983) observes, the theory does not explain why children focus upon sex as a critical factor in classifying people and activities. Why is sex so much more important than other possible categories, such as race or religion?

Many psychologists and sociologists have attempted to create new theories of how sex-typing develops. These theories often build upon some blend of social-learning theory and cognitive-developmental theory (Bem, 1983; Cahill, 1983; Markus, et al., 1982). Let us look at one of these theories, gender schema theory.

Gender Schema Theory

Gender schema theory, according to Sandra Bem (1981, 1983, 1985) proposes that children use gender as a cognitive organizing principle (or schema, pronounced "*skee*-mah") in order to structure and guide their perception of reality. That is, they are particularly likely to organize information about themselves and about the rest of the world according to the definitions of maleness and femaleness that are found in their society. Gender has a peculiar salience or prominence, so that we notice a person's sex and we mentally group people together who are the same sex. As we mentioned in Chapter 2, a person's sex is so important that our first question about a newborn is: Is it a boy or a girl?

Gender schema theory is based on both cognitive-developmental theory and social-learning theory. It resembles cognitive-developmental theory because it proposes that the child's own cognitive processing is responsible for sex-typing. However, like social-learning theory, gender schema theory specifies that sex-typing is a learned phenomenon. Children learn their society's definitions of what it means to be female and what it means to be male.

The theory proposes that sex-typing is the result of a child's readiness to blend his or her own self-concept into the gender schema. As children grow up, they learn about their own society's gender schema. They learn what attributes are important for them to possess. They learn that boys are supposed to be strong and girls are supposed to be weak. They learn that some attributes are highly relevant for one sex and largely irrelevant for the other sex. For example, the strong-weak attribute is very relevant for boys. Mike might learn that the way he throws a ball will be evaluated in terms of this dimension; adults will notice whether he is strong or weak. However, the strong-weak attribute is largely irrelevant for Mary; people will rarely comment upon either her strength or her weakness. On the other hand, nurturance is a dimension that is relevant for Mary but irrelevant for Mike.

Children learn to choose—out of all the possible dimensions that could be relevant for humans—only those attributes that are applicable to their own sex. As a result, their self-concepts become sex-typed. They learn that the two sexes are not only different in degree, but in kind; men are strong, for example, and women are nurturant.

Children also learn to evaluate their own adequacy as people in terms of the gender schema. The gender schema is a standard of comparison, and a child's self-esteem is greater if she or he compares favorably with the gender schema. Children regulate their behavior in order to conform to the cultural definitions of femaleness and maleness, as reflected in the gender schema. Mary realizes that she should be gentle and attentive to her baby brother in order to score well on the nurturance dimension, which adults will use to evaluate her.

Bem observes that a culture determines what kind of schema is most important. In American culture, gender is more important than other social categories. In our schools, boys and girls line up separately, and the teacher may tell the girls that they may line up first for recess. Children are not lined up separately according to race; the teacher does not tell black children to line up first. We try to deemphasize racial distinctions, but we continue to emphasize sexual distinctions.

You've probably noticed how readily children classify other children according to the gender schema. Recall those fifth-grade arguments about who was smarter, the boys or the girls, and remember the ritual of spraying for "cooties" when someone of the other sex had occupied your chair. Were there "boys' tables" and "girls' tables" at lunch? This preference for people of the same sex during childhood, as you may remember, is also a feature of Kohlberg's (1966) theory.

The three other theories proposed how sex-typing arose, but they did not provide a prescription for change. Bem (1983, 1985) outlines some strategies for child rearing. She stresses that parents must try to "inoculate" their children against gender-schematic processing, so that they can "build up their resistance" to the lessons they will receive from their culture. It should be mentioned that these suggestions have not yet been experimentally tested for their effects on sex-typing. Nevertheless, the suggestions are thought-provoking.

The first suggestion is that parents should eliminate gender stereotyping from their own behavior, so that activities are not rigidly divided into "female things" and "male things." Parents should share tasks such as bathing the children. Also, the children should receive both dolls and trucks, and they should be exposed to both women and men in nontraditional occupations.

Second, for young children, parents can select books and television programs that do not teach gender stereotypes, and they can alter some materials, for example by drawing long hair on a story book's male truck driver. Thus, parents should censor material for the early years.

Third, parents should emphasize that anatomy and reproduction are the essential characteristics that distinguish men from women. By focusing on these two areas, children will place less emphasis on cultural correlates of sex, such as traditional occupations, activities, clothing, and so forth.

Fourth, since parents should deemphasize gender-schematic processing, they should substitute other schemas for children to use in organizing their world. Children should be introduced to the "cultural relativism schema," which proposes that different people believe different things. This schema can help children who are old enough to be exposed to traditional books and television programs. Parents can discuss with school-aged children how a fairy tale was written long ago, when people thought that princesses were supposed to wait around in castles until they were rescued by princes. The "sexism schema" should be explained so that children will realize that "the view of women and men conveyed by fairy tales, by the mass media—and by the next-door neighbors—is not only different, but wrong" (Bem, 1983, p. 615). Children who are equipped with a sexism schema will actively oppose the constraints that people with a gender schema will inevitably try to enforce.

☐ SECTION SUMMARY ▪ Theories of Sex-Typing

1. Psychoanalytic theory, developed by Freud, proposes that sexuality explains human behavior.
2. According to psychoanalytic theory, boys and girls are similar in the oral and anal stages.
3. In psychoanalytic theory, during the phallic stage, girls develop penis envy, a concept for which there is minimal experimental support; girls turn to their fathers, but ultimately identify with their mothers.
4. In psychoanalytic theory, there is little psychosexual development during the latency stage; during the genital stage, both sexes are concerned with intercourse.
5. Psychoanalytic theory places less emphasis than the other three theories on the role of outside forces in the development of sextyping.
6. According to social-learning theory, children learn sex-typing by receiving rewards and punishments for their own behavior and by imitating the behavior of others.
7. Although social-learning theory may explain some aspects of sextyping, it has not been widely supported by research.
8. According to cognitive-developmental theory, children primarily shape their own sex-typing; gender-role acquisition can be explained within the broader framework of Piaget's developmental theory.
9. In cognitive-developmental theory, children first acquire gender identity, which is the ability to label themselves as a girl or a boy; later on, they can accurately label others.
10. In cognitive-developmental theory, young children do not appreciate gender constancy; they believe that gender changes when outward appearances change.

11. In cognitive-developmental theory, children prefer things that are consistent with their own gender identity.
12. Although cognitive-developmental theory has some support, it cannot explain why children are sex-typed before they have a firm gender-identity, and it does not explain why children focus upon sex as a method of classification.
13. According to gender schema theory, children use gender to organize the world.
14. In gender schema theory, children learn what attributes are important for them to possess, and they evaluate their own adequacy in terms of the gender schema.
15. Gender schema theory proposes that we can reduce the importance of gender schemas by eliminating gender stereotyping from adult behavior, censoring the media, focusing on the critical differences between men and women, and substituting other schemas.

☐ FACTORS THAT SHAPE SEX-TYPING

Social-learning theory, cognitive-developmental theory, and gender schema theory all describe how factors in the outside world shape the sex-typing of children. (Psychoanalytic theory, you'll recall, described a more spontaneous development of gender roles, which did not depend strongly on outside forces.)

According to social-learning theory, parents reward and punish children for their behavior and—together with characters in books and television programs—serve as models for their children's behavior. Cognitive-developmental theory states that parents and other people act as a source of data from which children draw information in their active pursuit of knowledge; a young girl learns what girls are *supposed* to enjoy doing. Gender schema theory describes how children learn from their parents and their broader culture that they are supposed to categorize people and activities as male-oriented and female-oriented.

We need to look at these influential shaping factors in more detail. Let us begin with the family, and then move on to peers, the school, and the media. As Katz (1979) points out, the relative importance of these factors shifts as children grow older. For preschool children, the family is the primary source of influence, with both parents and siblings contributing. During grade school, peers, school, and the media are dominant influences, so that the family's contribution decreases.

The Family

We know most about parents' role in sex-typing, so they will be our primary focus in this section. Consider, however, how important siblings were for you and your friends when you were growing up. An older brother might tease preschool-aged Joey about feeding Raggedy Ann with a baby bottle.

An eighth-grade girl may complain that her younger sister wears clothes that are too dirty, and more suitable for a boy. Younger children also frequently comment on their older siblings, sisters complain about brothers, and brothers complain about sisters. There are rich opportunities, in other words, for children to receive information from siblings about gender roles. Unfortunately, however, there has been little research on how siblings may influence sex-typing. As Huston (1983) concludes, the available information is tantalizing but inconclusive.

With respect to parents, you will remember that we discussed in the previous chapter how parents react somewhat differently to male and female infants. Jacklin and Maccoby (1983) point out that parents are particularly likely to react in a stereotyped fashion before they gain experience with their children. By the time their children are toddlers, parents are much better acquainted with the children's personalities and they are more likely to react to toddlers on the basis of personality characteristics than on the basis of sex. As a consequence, boys and girls are treated fairly similarly by their parents, from the time they are toddlers until they are adolescents, as we saw in the research on social-learning theory. We need to explore this idea in more detail and notice the areas in which parents encourage sex-typing and the areas in which sex-typing is not strong. We will discuss sex-typed activities, aggression, and independence.

Sex-typed activities.   Maccoby and Jacklin (1974) point out that parents may encourage their children to develop sex-typed interests by giving boys and girls different kinds of toys. This observation is consistent with the information on children's bedrooms that we already discussed in the last chapter. Maccoby and Jacklin argue that an even stronger force than encouragement is parents' *discouragement* of activities that they feel are inappropriate. Sons, rather than daughters, are particularly likely to be the targets of active protest about the wrong kind of activities.

Why is it worse for a boy to wear lipstick and put on high heels than it is for a girl to outline a moustache on her face and wear cowboy boots? To some extent, "sex-inappropriate" behavior may be more anxiety-arousing in boys than in girls because we tolerate a wider range of dress in adult women than in adult men. After all, adult women can wear cowboy boots, and jeans are the norm—rather than the exception—in many settings. A well-known designer has produced a line of underwear for women that mimic men's tee-shirts and jockey shorts. However, no one has seriously proposed a line of pink lace bikinis for men. Maccoby and Jacklin also speculate that parents, particularly fathers, are likely to interpret feminine behavior in a boy as a sign of possible homosexual tendencies. In contrast, masculine behavior in a girl is not as likely to suggest lesbian tendencies.

There is another likely explanation for why people are particularly worried about "sex-inappropriate" behavior in boys. Recall that one component of the second theme of this book is that males are more valued than females. A boy who doesn't show stereotypically masculine behavior is therefore failing to show the traits and behaviors that our culture values most highly.

In contrast, a girl who is a "tomboy" will not be seriously condemned for aspiring to show these highly valued characteristics (Crawford, 1984).

Let us look at some research that shows how parents encourage their children to develop sex-typed interests. In a study of toddlers, Fagot (1978) found that boys received more positive responses than girls for playing with blocks. Girls received more negative responses than boys for manipulating objects. In other words, boys receive more encouragement than girls for playing with spatial or mechanical toys. Furthermore, girls were more likely to be criticized for running, jumping, and climbing. Thus, girls are discouraged from large-motor activities. In addition, Fagot found that parents encouraged their daughters and discouraged their sons when they played with dolls.

Fagot found that fathers tended to be especially strong in their encouragement of sex-typed activities, an observation that was underscored in two other studies. Langlois and Downs (1980) discovered that fathers rewarded their children for playing with "sex-appropriate" toys and discouraged their children from playing with "sex-inappropriate" toys. Jacklin and her co-authors (1984) found that fathers were even more likely than mothers to encourage their daughters to play with stereotypically feminine items such as tea sets and baby dolls and to encourage their sons to play with stereotypically masculine items such as footballs and punching gloves.

In summary, parents do seem to promote some kinds of sex-typed activities in their children. Also, fathers are more eager than mothers to encourage sex-typing.

There are some intriguing questions in the area of sex-typed activities that have not yet been answered. Does ethnic group have an important influence on parents' behavior? Price-Bonham and Skeen (1982) studied upper middle-class black and white fathers, asking them to indicate whether various characteristics would be important for their sons and daughters. The black fathers were more likely than the white fathers to stress femininity in their daughters and masculinity in their sons. It would be interesting to see whether this finding is true for mothers as well as for people of lower-income brackets. Furthermore, would these beliefs translate into behavior? Are black fathers even more likely than white fathers to discourage "sex-inappropriate" behavior in their children?

Aggression. If you read popularized accounts about the development of gender roles, you may find a description of a scenario in which parents discourage aggression in their daughters and ignore—if not encourage—aggression in their sons. However intuitively appealing that description may seem, reality isn't that simple. In one review of the literature in this area, there are some studies that find no sex differences in parents' permissiveness when children are aggressive (Shepherd-Look, 1982). For example, when children had been attacked by someone else, boys and girls were equally discouraged from hitting back. Other studies completely contradict our intuitions, because they demonstrate that boys are scolded more frequently

Reactions to Aggression from Girls and Boys

Imagine that you are at home reading, with your four-year-old boy, Johnny, playing with a puzzle in the next room. Your one-year-old baby is in the same room with Johnny. You hear Johnny make the following remarks. After each remark, write what you think you would do or say.

1. Baby, you can't play with me. You're too little. _____
_____

2. Tell him he can't play with my puzzle—it's mine! _____
_____

3. Leave my puzzle alone or I'll hit you in the head! _____
_____

4. I don't like this game—I'm gonna break it! _____
_____

5. I don't like this game. It's a stupid game. You're stupid, Mommy. _____
_____

Now, repeat the exercise, imagining that you are in the same situation with your four-year-old girl, Susan. Check over your answers and see whether you would change any of them in this revised situation (adapted from Rothbart & Maccoby, 1966).

and more harshly than girls for their aggressive behavior (Shepherd-Look, 1982).

To complicate the picture even further, parents sometimes seem to be less tolerant of aggression in children who are the same sex as themselves. Try Demonstration 3.2, which is a modification of a study by Rothbart and Maccoby (1966).

In Rothbart and Maccoby's experiment, mothers and fathers listened to tape recordings of a child interacting with his or her parents. The child was sometimes introduced as Johnny, sometimes as Susan. In each case, the parents were asked to write down how they would respond to the situation, and their responses were rated according to the parent's tolerance of aggression.

We would have expected, according to social-learning theory, that parents would be more tolerant when "Johnny" was aggressive rather than "Susan." Rothbart and Maccoby did not find these results. Instead, they found that mothers allowed more aggression from their sons than from their daughters and fathers allowed more aggression from their daughters than from their sons. In other words, parents discourage aggression from same-sexed children. This finding puzzled the authors, and there doesn't seem to be a convincing explanation for the parents' reactions. However, keep in mind

Maccoby and Jacklin's (1974) observation that parents do not value aggression in either boys or girls.

As we have seen, parents are no more tolerant of aggression in their sons than in their daughters. The sex differences in aggression found in adults (which we will discuss in Chapter 7) cannot be explained by parents rewarding and punishing boys differently from girls. However, parents can provide information about power and aggression in other ways. Boys may learn to be aggressive by imitating their more aggressive fathers, as the second component of social-learning theory stresses. Furthermore, the structure of the family provides information for children's thoughts about proper "masculine" and "feminine" behavior, as stressed by cognitive-developmental theory. Children observe within their families that fathers make decisions, announce which television show will be watched, and may use physical intimidation to assert power. Children learn that aggression and power are "boy things" rather than "girl things."

Independence. According to the popularized accounts of the development of gender roles, parents not only show different responses to aggression in their sons and daughters, but they also show differential encouragement of independence. They encourage their sons to explore and do things on their own, but they encourage *dependency* in their daughters by restricting their activities, overprotecting, and over-helping them. Once again, the evidence is not as clearcut as we might expect. However, there are some hints that parents are more likely to encourage independence in their sons.

One way in which parents can encourage independence in their children is to allow them to go places by themselves, either inside or outside the home. We saw in the previous chapter that parents urge boys to leave their sides. Other studies have shown that boys are allowed to cross the street alone at an earlier age than girls are. They also can play away from home at an earlier age, and they are more likely to be left alone in a room as toddlers (Fagot, 1978; Hoffman, 1972). In other words, parents are more liberal about boys being by themselves and going places by themselves. Girls are more likely to be supervised and "chaperoned" (Block, 1983). However, some researchers have found no sex differences in this area (Newson & Newson, 1968).

Boys also may be allowed more independence in other kinds of activities, such as playing with potentially dangerous tools like scissors. However, it is not clear whether boys are encouraged to dress themselves and bathe themselves at an earlier age than girls are (Hoffman, 1972; Shepherd-Look, 1982).

Do parents help their daughters more than their sons? Hoffman (1972) provided an interesting suggestion that parents over-help their daughters, eagerly giving them assistance—even when it's not needed. The evidence suggests that there is some truth to that proposal, but only in certain situations.

Fagot (1978) studied toddlers and their parents in their own homes. When girls asked for help, they were likely to get it. When boys asked for help, they were likely to get a negative response. Rothbart and Rothbart (1976) watched mothers helping their children solve puzzles, and they found similar results. When help was requested, mothers were more likely to provide it to daughters than to sons. However, mothers were no more likely to *spontaneously* help their daughters than their sons. Also, parents give the same kinds of verbal directions to their sons and their daughters on a construction task (Bellinger & Gleason, 1982).

Notice that we do not have overwhelming, clear-cut support for the suggestion that parents push their sons to early independence, while leaping up to help their daughters at the slightest suggestion that they cannot do a task themselves. In some cases, at some ages, boys are more likely to be allowed to venture forth alone. They may be somewhat more likely to perform some other activities alone. However, the only way in which parents consistently help their sons and daughters differently is in responding to requests for help.

It is still possible that parents treat their sons and daughters differently in subtle ways that are difficult to measure. By their nonverbal cues, they may communicate anxiety to a daughter who is trying to be independent and they may communicate pride to a son performing the same activity. These nonverbal cues may be extremely important in shaping children's ideas about independence.

It also seems likely that some parents encourage their daughters to be independent, but other parents do not. Barnett (1981) offered support for this suggestion in her study on parents of preschool children. The parents were asked the appropriate age for assorted activities, such as traveling alone by bus to a nearby city or riding a bicycle to a place that would require crossing a busy street. Overall, parents had the same kinds of expectations for their sons and daughters. However, in the case of the girls, parents who had nontraditional gender-role beliefs were more likely to grant early independence to their daughters than were parents who had traditional gender-role beliefs. Some parents, then, encourage their daughters to try new activities on their own and to accept new challenges in working independently.

In our discussion of the family, we have seen some evidence that parents encourage sex-typing in their daughters and sons by their reactions to sex-typed activities and by allowing their sons to have somewhat greater independence. However, parents treat daughters and sons similarly with respect to aggressive behavior and some kinds of independence. Parents are certainly not the only force responsible for sex-typing.

Peers

Once children begin school, a major source of gender-role information is the peer group, that is, other children approximately the same age (Katz, 1979). A child may have been raised by nonsexist parents who valiantly shared household tasks, altered the gender of storybook characters, and conscientiously adjusted the world on a daily basis. However, when Johnny enters school with his prized Strawberry Shortcake lunchbox and when Betsy wears her hiking boots for the first day of classes, their peers are likely to provide a disappointing response.

Peers encourage sex-typing in three major ways. First, they encourage segregation of the sexes. Second, they are prejudiced against children of the other sex. Third, they have different expectations for girls and boys. Let's examine these three ideas.

We have already mentioned gender segregation in our discussion of gender schema theory. Recall that children classify other children according to the gender schema, so that boys and girls tend to inhabit different worlds, with very little mixing of the two groups. Karkau (1973) describes the situation in a fourth-grade classroom in which he was a student teacher. This was an open classroom, one in which children were free to sit wherever they chose. Nonetheless, a "boys' side" and a "girls' side" developed spontaneously. They also formed two separate lines—one for boys and one for girls—whenever they went to math lab or art class, even though the teacher had never asked them to do so. For creative-writing exercises, they formed all-girl and all-boy groups. At recess, girls played pom-pom or tag, whereas boys played soccer. Furthermore, the children rarely talked with someone of the other sex.

One reason why children avoid people of the other sex is that any interaction will probably be interpreted as an attraction. My sixth-grade daughter reported that when a boy sat next to her on the bus (thereby breaking an unwritten rule about seating patterns), his actions were followed by taunts of, "Oooh, you like her."

A second way in which peers encourage sex-typing is that they are prejudiced against members of the other sex. As we noted in the discussion of Kohlberg's cognitive-developmental theory, children show strong preferences for people of their own sex. Olsen and Willemsen (1978) examined these tendencies in a paper called, "Studying Sex Prejudice in Children." They dressed an eight-year-old girl in a sexually neutral set of clothing and asked her to perform 12 common kinds of recreation activities. Four of these activities had previously been judged to be typical of boys, such as playing football. Four were judged to be typical of girls, such as jumping rope, and four were judged neutral, such as bicycle riding. The girl was filmed as she performed these activities and the movie was shown to children in first, third, and fifth grade. Some of the children were told that the child's name was Anne, but other children were told that the child's name was John. In each case, children were to award between one and four stars for the quality of the performance.

The results showed that each sex favored their own sex, particularly in the case of the older children. Girls were particularly likely to show this favoritism; they rated the performances much higher when they thought the performer was female than when they thought the performer was male. However, the nature of the activity—masculine, feminine, or neutral—did not influence children's responses. That is, people of the same sex were best, no matter what they did.

Other evidence of gender prejudice comes from a study by Etaugh, Levine, and Mennella (1984), who asked students in second through tenth grade to decide whether certain traits were typical of boys or girls. At all grades, the students assigned more desirable traits to their own sex and more undesirable traits to the other sex. For example, females thought that girls were better puzzle solvers than boys, but males thought that boys were better. Females thought that boys were more selfish than girls, but males thought that girls were more selfish.

There is a third way that peers encourage sex-typing, other than gender segregation and gender prejudice. Specifically, they have different expectations for boys and girls, an idea that is consistent with the second theme of this book. In later chapters of this book, we will see that adults think men should act one way and women should act differently. Connor, Serbin, and Ender (1978) explored how children think that girls should be more passive than boys. As part of this study, Connor and her coauthors asked children in fourth through eighth grade to read episodes in which a child with either a male or a female name responded in either an assertive or a passive manner. The children were then asked several questions, such as whether they thought the child had tried to solve the problem in a good way. When the child in the episode was a girl, the children thought the passive response was most appropriate. When the child in the episode was a boy, they thought the passive and assertive approaches were equally appropriate. Girls should stand quietly, whereas boys often can assertively request their rights.

The influence of peers on sex-typing has not been examined as thoroughly as the influence of family. However, we have seen that children can influence others who are their own age in several ways. They can encourage children to use the gender schema to classify other people, thereby dividing the world into two groups that have minimal contact. They can express prejudice against children of the other sex. Finally, they can believe that boys should act one way, and girls should act another way.

School

The typical elementary-school child spends more waking hours with the classroom teacher than with the family. Consequently, teachers and schools have rich opportunities to influence sex-typing. Let us investigate three areas in which the school system can have an effect on the development of gender roles. First, the structure of the school shows children that males have more prestige and power than females. Second, teachers' behavior can be influential. Third, textbooks and tests are biased in their representation of men and women. The fourth and final part of this section on school will examine how schools can encourage change.

School structure.   The structure of the typical school provides children with a sadly representative view of the status of employed women. Recall the number of women and men you met throughout your own school experiences. Were your elementary-school teachers female? Were your high-school teachers equally likely to be males or females, with males for science and math courses, but females for English and foreign language courses? How about the principals and superintendents? Nationwide, 83 percent of elementary-school teachers are women, in contrast to 49 percent of high-school teachers (National Center for Education Statistics, 1981). The percentage of females drops even further when we consider the people who are the "bosses" of the schools, the principals and the superintendents. Children see that women dominate in the least prestigious positions, in the classrooms of young students. The big kids are important enough to be associated with a reasonable number of male teachers. The real power in the school lies with the principals and superintendents, almost all of whom are male. School children therefore have abundant opportunity to learn that male activities are more valuable than female activities, an idea that is part of the second theme of this book.

Teachers' behavior.   There is a fair amount of evidence—though not perfectly consistent—that teachers give boys more attention than girls. For instance, boys receive more *positive* attention. Boys are more likely to receive positive feedback, more likely to be recognized for their creativity, more likely to be called on in class, and more likely to be included in verbal interactions (Brophy & Good, 1974; Cherry, 1975).

Boys also receive more *negative* attention than girls. One study demonstrated that teachers responded over three times more often to boys' aggressive behavior than to girls' aggressive behavior. Furthermore, boys typically received a loud reprimand that other students could hear, whereas girls typically received a short, soft scolding, inaudible to other students (Serbin, O'Leary, Kent, & Tonick, 1973). Other research has found a similar pattern of stronger and more frequent scoldings for boys' misbehavior than for girls' misbehavior (for example, Good, Sikes, & Brophy, 1973; Huston, 1983; Stake & Katz, 1982).

In a typical classroom scene, described by Serbin and O'Leary (1975), a teacher spends a full two minutes lecturing the class bully (male) about not hitting people. Five minutes later, the child returns to his favorite pastime, brutalizing his classmates.

On the surface, it might seem that the teacher's lengthy punishment for the boy's aggression should *discourage* further aggressive responses. If boys receive three times as many negative remarks as girls receive for their aggression, shouldn't they become *less* aggressive? The truth is that punishment can actually serve as a reinforcement for misbehaving children, because it provides the attention they crave. As a consequence, children who have been punished may misbehave even more. The most effective way to discourage disruptive behavior is simply to ignore it (Pinkston, Reese, LeBlanc, & Baer, 1979). In fact, when Serbin and O'Leary (1975) recommended that the teacher ignore the misbehaving boy's aggressive actions, he stopped being the class bully.

We have seen that teachers tend to ignore girls and pay attention to boys, whether these students are behaving properly or improperly. Notice that the end result is that girls are relatively invisible in the classroom, compared to boys. This pattern, which illustrates the third theme of this textbook, continues throughout adulthood and old age. Males are not only valued more then females, but they are also more visible.

In addition to ignoring girls while paying attention to boys, teachers may encourage girls to become dependent (Huston, 1983). Levitin and Chananie (1972) demonstrated that teachers like dependent girls far more than aggressive girls. In contrast, they like dependent boys and aggressive boys equally well. It seems that an aggressive boy will receive the teacher's attention and, perhaps, the teacher's affection. An aggressive girl will be ignored and disliked; the teacher prefers someone more dependent.

Teachers can also influence children's play. Teachers are more likely to call on a boy, rather than a girl, to demonstrate how to play with a stereotypically masculine toy (Serbin, Connor, & Iler, 1979). Furthermore, when a new toy is introduced in a stereotyped manner (perhaps a toy truck is demonstrated by a boy, while the teacher says "Daddies can go to work and drive a truck"), children are likely to make stereotyped choices. That is, the boys are likely to select the trucks, whereas the girls head for the dolls. When a new toy is introduced in a nonstereotyped manner, children play with both kinds of toys.

We have seen that teachers' behavior can be influential. Boys receive more positive attention and more negative attention than girls do. Teachers also prefer dependent girls to aggressive girls. Furthermore, they can affect the way children select toys.

Textbooks and tests. In the section on school structure we saw that males have more power and prestige than females. In the section on teachers' behavior we saw that males receive more attention than females. Both of these observations also apply to the textbooks and tests that children use in school. Both of these kinds of material—unfortunately—are excellent examples of the second and third themes of this book.

The problem of children's textbooks was made vividly clear in 1972 when a group of women who called themselves "Women on Words & Images" published their report on 134 elementary-school readers that were being used by schools in their region of New Jersey. One of their findings was that girls and women were relatively invisible in these readers. In real life less than 50 percent of the population are males, but in the textbooks, more than 70 percent of the main characters are males. The scarcity of biographical stories about women was particularly appalling. In the sample of 146 biographies, there were only 27 stories about women.

Not only were women underrepresented in the textbooks, but they were also misrepresented. There were very few employed women in the stories, and they were engaged in only traditionally feminine occupations, such as teacher, nurse, and dressmaker. Furthermore, women were either job holders or mothers, but there were only three cases in which a mother worked outside the home. The textbooks clearly misrepresented employed mothers, who were numerous even in 1972.

In addition, males and females in the textbooks had strikingly different personalities and performed very different tasks. Males were clever, industrious, and brave, and they acquired skills, earned fame and fortune, competed with others, explored, and made friends. Females were passive, dependent, and kind, and they cooked, cleaned up, and showed their incompetence in numerous ways. Once again, females seemed to be less valuable than males.

Several years later, Laurel Marten and I found that the textbook scene had not improved; in fact, in some ways it was worse (Marten & Matlin, 1976). We contrasted textbooks published prior to 1971 with textbooks published since that year. Even in the more recent editions, more than 70 percent of the main characters were male. A person who did not know the purpose of our study classified each activity in the stories as being either "active" or "passive." We found that in the newer textbooks, males were more active than in the old textbooks, whereas females were more passive. That is, girls and women were even more likely to be shown as passive, fearful, and helpless.

Women were also represented in a demeaning fashion. A female character in one reader could not understand why the rain had soaked her to the skin, until she discovered her closed umbrella over her wrist. In another story, an ugly princess is rescued from a sick dragon by a lazy knight. There were also phrases such as "a woman's place is in the kitchen among the pots and pans."

Underrepresentation and misrepresentation of females exist in textbooks for mathematics, science, foreign language, and history, as well as in readers (United States Commission on Civil Rights, 1980). The implications are important, because 75–90 percent of children's schoolwork focuses on the textbooks, and children read at least 32,000 textbook pages between kindergarten and graduation from high school (United States Commission on Civil Rights, 1980). You may want to borrow some books from children in your home neighborhood in order to gain better insight on the textbook issue. Check them over to see whether females and males are equally represented and whether their personalities and activities correspond with reality.

Unfortunately, textbooks are not the only biased classroom material. Nationwide, millions of tests are administered each year, and these tests reinforce the image of the invisible, incompetent female. Saario, Jacklin, and Tittle (1973) found that females were underrepresented and passive in intelligence and achievement tests. Mary Rabe and I examined speech and language tests and we found more evidence of the now-familiar pattern (Rabe & Matlin, 1978). The clear majority of pictures showed males, rather than females. People were shown in gender-stereotyped activities 73 percent of the time. Men were train conductors, chemists, and athletes. Women sipped tea, decorated cakes, and talked on the telephone.

One textbook or one intelligence test or one speech test would probably have little influence on a child. However, if you consider the dozens of textbooks and tests that a child encounters throughout school—each conveying the same message of importance and power of males and the invisibility and passivity of females—the cumulative effect is powerful. The characters provide symbolic models for children to imitate (if you support social-learning theory); or they show children what activities are consistent with their gender identity (if you support cognitive-development theory); or they teach children about society's gender schema (if you support gender schema theory). In any event, they provide children with a fairly biased picture of reality and a very biased picture of an ideal world.

Encouraging change. Children receive so many stereotyped messages, both in school and out of school, that we could not expect the damage to be undone in a two-week unit on sexism. However, several somewhat longer programs have been developed to encourage school children to change their ideas about gender roles. Guttentag and Bray (1976, 1977) constructed a six-week curriculum to help children develop more flexible ideas about women's and men's occupations, family roles, and social roles. They targeted three age groups, kindergartners, fifth graders and ninth graders. Teachers received special training in the use of the curriculum, which focused on activities such as nonsexist role playing, investigating stereotyped advertisements, and learning about famous women.

The children's attitudes were measured both before and after the intervention program. At all ages, the girls were more open to adopting the nonsexist perspective than boys were. Although the kindergarten boys showed some change in attitudes, the fifth-grade boys did not. Unfortunately, the ninth-grade boys became even *more* sexist after the intervention program. For these boys, a little intervention regarding nonsexist thinking was generally worse than none at all; the plan had backfired.

A similar kind of intervention program was used with tenth-, eleventh-, and twelfth-grade students (Kahn & Richardson, 1983), involving a 20-unit course in gender roles. In two schools, where students elected to take the course, attitudes toward women were more favorable after completion of the course. In the third school, in which the course was required, attitudes toward women were *less* favorable after the course; again the plan had backfired. It seems that if conditions are not ideal, students may resent intense concentration on the topics of women and gender roles, and they may grow even more conservative.

An excellent resource that would be useful to parents, as well as teachers, is a book called *Sex Equity Handbook for Schools* (Sadker & Sadker, 1982). This book discusses relevant topics such as **Title IX** (a law that prohibits discrimination against students on the basis of their sex), gender bias in instructional material, teacher-student interactions, and a resource directory. A particularly valuable addition discusses how sexism hurts boys and men in school and society. This section should be very useful for teachers who are concerned that male students may become more conservative after extensive discussion of gender roles that focuses on women.

An additional way to encourage change is to focus on the textbooks and tests that are given to school children. Parents—as well as teachers—should write to publishers whose textbooks contain stereotyped material. To be consistent with psychologists' emphasis on positive reinforcement, also write to publishers and compliment them when you find books in which both sexes are equally represented and in which both females and males are shown in nonstereotyped activities.

The Media

Children are exposed to stereotyped representations of men and women at home, as well as in classroom materials. In this section, we'll see that the books children are likely to find in their homes are biased. The typical child, however, spends far more time in front of the television, so we also need to see how stereotypes are represented on television.

Books. Every feminist has her or his personal favorite example of a sexist children's book. My favorite, shared by many others, is *I'm Glad I'm a Boy; I'm Glad I'm a Girl* (Darrow, 1970). The apparent purpose of this book is to indoctrinate children regarding gender schemas by telling them appropriate activities for each sex, such as "boys fix things and girls need things fixed; boys build houses and girls keep houses." The results of St. Peter's (1979) analysis of children's books will not surprise you. Once again, the second theme of this textbook—women's invisibility—is clearly demonstrated. In traditional picture books, girls were seldom the main character; also, they rarely appeared on the front covers or in other illustrations. St. Peter also analyzed picture books from a list of nonstereotyped books, appropriately called *Little Miss Muffet Fights Back* (1974). Girls were well represented here, but the authors of these books seemed to have been overly zealous about depicting independent, achieving females; the girls and women in these stories seldom showed the warmth and compassion traditionally associated with females.

Is this whole issue of children's books really quite trivial? When I complain to friends about the children's book situation, they often argue that children probably pay little attention to the sex of the main characters; they hint that the biases have minimal consequences. McArthur and Eisen (1976) conducted a study that suggests otherwise. They read a story to preschool boys and girls that had one of three forms: a stereotyped story showing achievement behavior by a boy, but not a girl; a reversal story showing achievement behavior by a girl, but not a boy; and a control story about nonachieving animals. After hearing the story, children were instructed to arrange flowers in a narrow-necked bottle—a fairly challenging task. Their persistence on this task was measured as an index of achievement motivation.

FIGURE 3.1. **Persistence on a difficult task, as a function of sex of subject and storybook condition (McArthur & Eisen, 1976)**

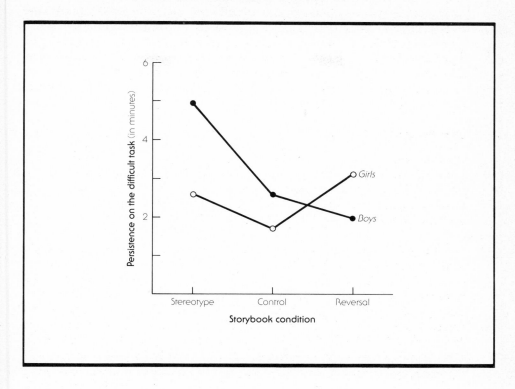

Figure 3.1 shows the results. Notice that children were persistent on the task when they had been exposed to a story in which a model of their own sex had been successful on an achievement task. (Which theory of gender-role development does this support?)

McArthur and Eisen (1976) suggest that prolonged exposure to stereotyped children's books, filled with models of male achievement and female passivity, may well have lasting effects on the later development of achievement patterns in women and men. There are other consequences as well. For example, after reading stereotyped books, children were more likely to play with stereotyped toys (Ashton, 1983).

Comic strips are no better. Brabant (1976) followed four family-oriented comic strips over a six-month period. Females were generally absent, and they were almost entirely confined to home settings. They cooked and cleaned, while their husbands rested or read. However, the females in comic strips are well liked. For example, people are more positive about Blondie than about Dagwood (Potkay et al., 1982).

Television.   You may have seen the statistics on children's television-viewing habits, but it's worth shuddering over them once more. Children under the age of five watch an average of more than 25 hours of television each week. By the time they finish high school, typical children will have spent more than 15,000 hours in front of the television (Action for Children's Television, 1978). In Chapter 8, we will look at stereotyping in the programs intended for adult audiences; now, let's look at children's television.

According to Sternglanz and Serbin's (1974) analysis, there are three ways in which television promotes stereotyping:

1. Males are represented more frequently than females. In Sternglanz and Serbin's study, half of the most popular children's shows could not even be analyzed because they contain *no* women. On these shows, the women were literally invisible! From other research, we can see that male humans and animals are more than three times as common as females on children's television programs (Levinson, 1981). Also, boys are much more common than girls on commercials for toys (Feldstein & Feldstein, 1982).
2. Males and females perform different activities on television. Men are more likely than women to be shown at work. In contrast, women are more likely to be shown at home, and they are also more likely than men to show emotional distress. Also, men are likely to solve their own problems, whereas women need help in solving their problems (Downs, 1981). In commercials for toys, girls are more likely to be passive. In other words, the boys actively play with the toys, whereas the girls stand by and watch (Feldstein & Feldstein, 1982). In real life, women lead complex, rich lives, but women on television perform only drudgery!
3. People respond to men, but they ignore women. For example, Sternglanz and Serbin (1974) found that males tended to be rewarded for their behavior, but females were not. Similarly, Downs and Gowan (1980) found that on a typical program, men received reinforcement from others about twice as often as women did; men received punishment more than three times as often as women did. (Notice how females are ignored on TV, just as they are in the classroom.) Ignoring women further heightens their invisibility; once again we see evidence for the third theme of this book.

We have seen that women are underrepresented, shown in limited roles, and ignored. Again, skeptics might ask whether this matters. Do children learn gender-role stereotypes by watching television? One study examined children who were high in gender constancy, that is, children who thought that a person's gender stays the same in spite of changes in outward appearance (Ruble, Balaban & Cooper, 1981). These children tended to play with a toy shown on a television commercial if the child in that commercial was the same sex; they avoided the toy if the child was of the other sex.

When only boys are shown playing with a truck or a problem-solving game, girls may avoid these toys.

If children learn gender-role stereotypes from television, then those who watch many hours of television should be more stereotyped than those with little exposure. The research is somewhat inconsistent on this issue, however. For example, one study found no relationship between television viewing and stereotyping (Perloff, 1977). Another study showed a relationship between these two variables for their sample of girls, but not for their sample of boys (Zuckerman, Singer, & Singer, 1980). Two further studies demonstrated clear-cut relationships (Frueh & McGhee, 1975; McGhee & Frueh, 1980). In the research by McGhee and Frueh, children who watched more than 25 hours of television each week were compared with children who watched less than ten hours each week. The heavy viewers were more likely to judge males to be tough, adventurous, and ambitious, and more likely to judge females to be high-strung, rattlebrained, and sentimental.

It is not clear why these studies came to different conclusions, although the discrepancies can be at least partially traced to the use of different ways of measuring gender-role stereotypes. Also, there are several alternate explanations for the positive correlations. It may be, as many suggest, that increased television viewing produces increased gender-role stereotyping. On the other hand, the correlation may arise because children who are already stereotyped tend to watch more television, whereas nonstereotyped children avoid television.

In any event, a cautious parent who is anxious to raise nonstereotyped children should probably limit television viewing. As Bem (1983) suggests, parents should monitor the media, and turn off the television for offensive programs. Children should be encouraged to watch programs in which women are shown as competent people or in nontraditional occupations. (Can you think of any that qualify?)

SECTION SUMMARY: ▪ Factors That Shape Sex-Typing

1. **Parents discourage feminine activity in their sons more than they discourage masculine activity in their daughters.**
2. **Parents promote sex-typed play in their children.**
3. **Parents do not show consistently greater tolerance for aggression in their sons than in their daughters.**
4. **Parents are somewhat more likely to encourage independence in their sons than in their daughters, but there are areas in which sons and daughters are treated the same.**
5. **Peers encourage segregation of the two sexes, they are prejudiced against members of the other sex, and they have different expectations for boys and girls.**
6. **In the school system, women occupy the less prestigious areas, and men are in more powerful positions.**

7. Teachers give boys more positive attention than girls, and they also give boys more negative attention; girls are ignored.
8. Teachers prefer dependent girls to aggressive girls; teachers can influence toy play by the way they introduce toys into the classroom.
9. Females are missing from textbooks and tests; when women do appear, they are unlikely to work outside the home, and they are likely to be represented in a stereotyped fashion.
10. Programs designed to reduce children's stereotypes have had some success, but they have produced less favorable attitudes in some groups.
11. Children's books show biased representations of females; children's achievement motivation is greater after reading a story in which someone of their own sex has been successful, and they are more likely to play with stereotyped toys after reading stereotyped books.
12. Television promotes stereotypes by underrepresenting women, showing them in only limited roles, and ignoring their behavior; there is some evidence that children who watch television heavily are more stereotyped, but there are inconsistencies in the research.

☐ CHILDREN'S BEHAVIOR AND BELIEFS

So far we have looked at the theories about how children become sex-typed and we have investigated the forces that encourage sex-typing. In this section, we will focus upon the children themselves. How well have they learned their lessons about sex-typing? Do girls and boys behave differently in their play? Do they believe that males and females are different kinds of creatures in terms of personality characteristics? Do they think that men and women "should" hold different kinds of jobs?

Children's Play

In the last chapter, we saw that if adults think that a baby is named "Johnny," they offer a football, whereas they hand "Jenny" a doll. Even in infancy, we try to foist the appropriate gender-stereotyped toys upon children. We saw earlier in this chapter that these trends continue throughout childhood, because parents and teachers encourage children to play with "sex-appropriate" toys. Even strangers conspire to channel children's play interests. As mentioned in connection with a demonstration in the last chapter, toy salespersons recommend different toys to people who say they are shopping for a niece than to those shopping for a nephew (Kutner & Levinson, 1978; Ungar, 1982).

Do children receive the message that is being broadcast to them? When given a choice, do they select the "appropriate" toys and reject the "inappropriate" toys? In general, the answer is yes (Liss, 1981, 1983; Pitcher & Schultz, 1983; Schau et al., 1980).

Let's look at a typical study. Downs (1983) asked elementary-school children to write letters to Santa Claus requesting Christmas toys. Boys asked Santa for stereotypically masculine and neutral toys, and they rarely mentioned stereotypically feminine toys. Girls were most likely to ask Santa for neutral toys, but they asked for stereotypically feminine toys more often than for stereotypically masculine toys. As in many other studies, it seems that neutral toys are fairly popular—maybe even more popular than "sex-appropriate" toys. However, toys associated with the other sex are definitely *not* popular.

Furthermore, there are sex differences in the kinds of play activities that girls and boys prefer. Whiting and Edwards (1973) watched children playing in six different cultures. In most of the samples, boys were more likely than girls to show what is called "rough and tumble" play, which includes chasing, hitting, and wrestling. DiPietro (1981) studied American preschoolers, finding the same sex differences in rough and tumble play. In contrast, girls seem more likely than boys to imitate adult activities in their play (Carpenter & Huston-Stein, 1980).

We have seen that there are several ways in which girls and boys differ in their play. They enjoy different toys, and they prefer different kinds of play styles. It is not surprising that these sex differences emerge in the area of play activities. Think about how all the factors that shape sex-typing could converge to influence sex-typing in play. Parents could actively discourage the kind of play that they feel is inappropriate. Siblings and peers could have a major influence on play, because their cooperation is required for play; three-year-old Robbie may want to play with dolls, but his friends will be more likely to head for the Tonka trucks. If he wants companionship, he'll follow. Teachers are also likely to encourage sex-typing in play. Finally, children see which play activities they are supposed to enjoy when they read books and watch television. All of these sources of information build up a gender schema for the child, and the child's own cognitive processing contributes to the sex-typing.

Sex differences are rather prominent in children's play preferences. However, it is important to stress that in other areas of children's behavior, the sex similarities are more prominent than the sex differences. Maccoby and Jacklin's (1974) review of sex differences in childhood concluded that aggression is the only area of personality in which boys and girls differ substantially. (Boys' enthusiasm for rough and tumble play confirms the sex difference.) In general, young males and females behave similarly, consistent with the first theme of this book.

Children's Beliefs about Personality Characteristics

According to the second theme of this book, people believe that males and females are different—even though they really are similar. We will examine the belief in sex differences throughout Chapter 8, focusing on adults' stereotypes. Now we need to examine whether young children share these beliefs.

Demonstration 3.3 illustrates how Williams, Bennett, and Best (1975) asked children about their beliefs. Children between the ages of kindergarten and fourth grade responded to these questions in order to determine how much children know about gender stereotypes.

The results showed that even the kindergartners—the youngest children tested—are aware of gender stereotypes. Ninety-four percent selected the male picture to represent Item 1, concerning aggression. Males were seen as strong, adventurous, coarse, independent, and loud. Their knowledge about

---

■ DEMONSTRATION 3.3 **■**

Children's Beliefs about Men and Women

Locate a child between the ages of kindergarten and fourth grade. Explain to the child and his or her parents that you would like to ask a few questions about women and men as part of your coursework and obtain permission for the child's participation. Then show the child the two pictures below. Say that you are going to read a little story, and you want the child to point to the person that it is about.

1. One of these people is a bully. This person is always pushing people around and getting into fights. Which person gets into fights? [Continue in the same fashion with the remaining questions.]
2. One of these people is emotional. This person cries when something good happens as well as when everything goes wrong. Which is the emotional person?
3. One of these people is appreciative. This person is always very thankful when you do something nice. Which person always says "thank you"?
4. One of these people is very loud. This person always makes a lot of noise and talks in a great, big voice. Which person talks loudly?
5. One of these people is meek and mild. This person doesn't make a big fuss and is shy around new people. Which person is the shy person?
6. One of these people is very confident. This person always seems to know what to do. Which person is self-confident? (adapted from Williams, Bennett, & Best, 1975, pp. 636–637)

---

female stereotypes did not seem to be as well developed. For female-associated adjectives, such as gentle, soft-hearted, and emotional, the kindergartners chose male pictures almost as often as female pictures. The older children showed greater knowledge of both male and female stereotypes than did the younger children.

What about children who are even younger? Reis and Wright (1982) tested children between the ages of three and five, using a modified version of the same test. Even the three-year-olds classified some personality characteristics, such as "cruel," as masculine; other personality characteristics, such as "cries a lot," were seen as feminine. Reis and Wright found that the older children in their group showed more stereotyping than the younger children. Furthermore, when they tested the same children again six months later, they found that the children showed stronger stereotyping than they had originally. According to their results, children become more sexist as they grow older.

According to Reis and Wright, children become more sexist between the ages of three and five. It seems that stereotyping increases even further in the early school years, and then it decreases somewhat by fifth or sixth grade (Meyer, 1980; Payne, 1981). In the later grade-school years, children become more flexible about gender roles. Although they still believe in gender stereotypes, they realize that women and men are not totally different.

We have seen that young children are stereotyped about adults. They are also quite willing to be stereotyped about their peers and even about young infants. For example, third graders assigned male traits to boys and female traits to girls (Davis, Williams, & Best, 1982). In another study, three- and five-year-olds watched a videotape of an infant who was labeled either Bobby or Lisa (Haugh, Hoffman, & Cowan, 1980). Like the adults we discussed in the last chapter, the baby was perceived to have different characteristics as a function of its sex. For example, the baby was seen as smaller, slower, weaker, and softer when it was Lisa, rather than Bobby.

Some researchers have been curious about whether there are social class or ethnic differences in children's concepts about personality characteristics. According to Romer and Cherry (1980), middle-class children often are more flexible than working-class children in their ideas about gender roles; middle-class children tend to favor a gender-role blending, with both sexes sharing many characteristics. Romer and Cherry also reported that black children are more likely than Jewish or Italian children to describe the male gender-role stereotype as being emotionally expressive. In fact, black children believe that men and women are equally expressive.

In summary, children develop ideas about how males and females are supposed to act, and their views correspond to adults' stereotypes. These ideas are already fairly well developed by the time children are three, but their stereotypes grow even more rigid for several years, until they realize—perhaps in late grade school—that men and women can share some personality characteristics. It is important to stress that these fifth and sixth graders may be somewhat more flexible than they were several years earlier, but they still maintain that males and females are different. We will examine the nature of these stereotypes in more detail in Chapter 8.

Children's Beliefs about Occupations

One of the most vivid contrasts between what women and men do when they grow up was described by Beuf (1974), who asked children what they would do if they were the other sex. One boy replied, "A girl? Oh, if I were a girl I'd have to grow up to be nothing" (p. 143). A girl answered, "When I grow up I want to fly like a bird. But I'll never do it because I'm not a boy" (p. 143).

Even young children divide the world of work into "women's jobs" and "men's jobs." Gettys and Cann (1981) developed a method for testing children as young as two-and-a-half. They placed a male and a female doll in front of a child and asked the child to point to the doll that they thought had a given job. In their sample of 2- and 3-year-olds, 78 percent pointed to the male doll for the job of construction worker; only 23 percent pointed to the male doll for the job of teacher. It seems that even very young children know the stereotypes about the appropriate occupations for men and women.

Age trends in occupational stereotypes.   We saw that children's stereotypes about women's and men's personalities grow rigid before they ultimately become somewhat more flexible. The same trend is apparent in children's notions about occupations. Although we cannot clearly pinpoint a specific age at which children are most rigid, it seems that stereotyping may increase across the years from kindergarten through about fourth grade, with older grade-school children becoming somewhat less stereotyped during fifth and sixth grade (Cann & Haight, 1983; Cummings & Taebel, 1980; Gettys & Cann, 1981; O'Keefe & Hyde, 1983; Tremaine, Schau & Busch, 1982).

We may soon have some more explicit answers about age trends in stereotyping. It would be interesting to know if the period of maximum stereotyping coincides with the period of maximum gender-segregation and gender-prejudice. Perhaps gender schemas are particularly relevant for children who are in about fourth grade. For these nine-year-olds, people of the other sex are to be avoided—they have "cooties." Males and females occupy different worlds, not only at the school lunch tables, but also in the children's minds, where men are strong and adventurous, but women are soft-hearted and emotional, and men are construction workers, but women are teachers.

Sex differences in occupational stereotypes.   Young girls seem to be more flexible than young boys in their notions about occupations. For example, Shepard and Hess (1975) gave people a list of occupations and asked them to indicate whether each occupation should be performed by a male, a female, or either. Except for their youngest group, who were kindergartners, females were consistently more likely than the males to select the "either" option. Thus, boys have more rigid stereotypes about how the work world "should" be.

Boys also have more rigid stereotypes about their own career choices. Specifically, they choose careers that are stereotypically masculine, whereas girls choose a wide variety of careers. Lavine (1982), for example, asked 7- to 11-year-olds what they would like to be when they grow up. She then coded each response in terms of the proportion of males occupying that job, according to census information. The results showed that the boys' preferences averaged 89 percent male occupancy, whereas the girls' preferences averaged 41 percent male occupancy. We can draw two conclusions from these data. First, boys are more likely than girls to prefer work in which men dominate (89 percent versus 41 percent). Second, girls are not as stereotyped as boys, because their average score of 41 percent is close to the neutral 50 percent score, which represents an equal number of women and men in a career. The average score of 89 percent for boys, in contrast, is far from the neutral 50 percent score. Another study that included preschool children provides further evidence that boys are more likely than girls to avoid careers associated with the other sex (Tremaine & Schau, 1979).

Some studies have uncovered surprisingly nontraditional responses from young girls. Kriedberg, Butcher, and White (1978) reported that the boys in their sample listed traditionally masculine careers for themselves. However, half of their sample of sixth-grade girls mentioned nontraditional work, such as a basketball player and a police officer.

It seems, then, that boys are more hampered than girls by ideas about what is proper. Earlier in this chapter, we saw that parents discourage boys from feminine play more than they discourage girls from masculine play. Similarly, boys avoid feminine careers more than girls avoid masculine careers. We think it's charming if five-year-old Susie tells us she wants to be a surgeon, but we may gulp if five-year-old Bobby announces that he wants to be a secretary.

Career choices for others versus personal career choices. According to some recent research, children are becoming less stereotypic in their judgments about what careers are appropriate for other people. For example, only 13 percent of one sample of young children said that it was "all right for a man to be a doctor, but not a woman" (Zuckerman & Sayre, 1982). However, these liberal children are not always anxious to enter nontraditional careers themselves. Zuckerman and Sayre found that the children's own career choices were traditional; the girls wanted to be nurses and teachers, whereas the boys wanted to be athletes and firemen.

Furthermore, girls may show discrepancy between their stated career goals and their descriptions of an actual day's work. Iglitzin (1972) asked fifth graders what they wanted to be when they grew up and then she asked them to describe how they would spend a typical day. The boys described typical days that matched their career choices. A boy who wanted to be a lawyer wrote,

I would talk to my clients on what their problems were. If I thought his thoughts were right I would explain the right procedures to take depending on his problems, and I would fight for his thoughts. [p. 24]

Girls described very little about their future work in these paragraphs, often abandoning any mention of a career. One girl who wanted to be an artist described this typical day,

I would start the morning after getting out of bed by eating breakfast. Then I would clean house. If I was done before lunch I would probably visit a friend. Then eat lunch. After lunch I would go shopping. Then I would come home and rest for a while. When my husband came home (if I was married) he would probably tell me how his day went and I would tell him how mine went. If he was in a real good mood he would take me out to dinner. When we were done with dinner we would go to a movie. Then we would go home and go to bed. [p. 24]

Why didn't this girl mention, in loving detail, how she would assemble her brushes, mix the paints, and select the subjects for her paintings? It may be that the boy who described his day as a lawyer knew what male lawyers do by watching television or reading books. Girls, however, rarely find models of employed women in television programs or books. Instead, they see women who lead lives centering upon eating, shopping, and cleaning.

Iglitzin's findings may have an important implication. A boy who wants to be a lawyer and has a reasonable idea of what lawyers do may cling to his career choice. A girl who wants to be a painter—but doesn't have a realistic view of the professional responsibilities—may abandon this goal. Bem's (1983) idea about exposing children to people in nontraditional professions may have an additional advantage other than less emphasis on the gender schema: This exposure could provide girls with concrete information about work activities.

☐ SECTION SUMMARY: ▪ Children's Behavior and Beliefs

1. Children tend to avoid toys associated with the other sex.
2. Boys are more likely than girls to prefer "rough and tumble" play, whereas girls are more likely than boys to enjoy imitating adult activities.
3. Children as young as three years of age have stereotyped ideas about males' and females' personality characteristics.
4. Children's stereotypes about personality grow stronger until they reach a peak, and then they become somewhat more flexible.
5. Even young children are stereotyped about infants' behavior.
6. Social class and ethnic group membership may influence children's stereotypes.

7. Children as young as two- to three-year-olds have stereotypes about males' and females' occupations.
8. Children's stereotypes about occupations grow stronger until they reach a peak, and then they become somewhat more flexible.
9. Girls are more flexible than boys in their ideas about females' and males' occupations, including their own career choices.
10. Children are more stereotyped in their own career choices than they are in their judgments about occupations suitable for other females and males.
11. Girls' descriptions of a typical day may fail to mention careers, even if the girls have stated an interest in a career.

☐ ADOLESCENCE

Adolescence is a fuzzy transition phase between childhood and adulthood. Adolescence begins at **puberty,** the age at which the reproductive organs become functional. For females a major physical milestone of puberty is the beginning of menstruation. It is not clear when adolescence ends—there is certainly no magical age that separates the adolescent from the adult. We associate adulthood with living separately from your parents, holding a job, and having children of your own, but none of these characteristics is essential for adulthood.

Adolescents find themselves caught in between, in the words of Romer (1981). They may sometimes be treated as children, a mixed blessing that does not require adolescents to be responsible but does limit their independence. They can see the next step in front of them, which involves sexuality and being grown-up. Adolescents receive mixed messages. We tell them not to grow up too fast, yet they see people who have grown up fast—sexy teenage movie stars, people in the advertisements, and maybe even the girl next door.

Three areas emerge as important topics for adolescent females. These are self-concepts, interpersonal relations, and career choices. Then we will also consider black female adolescents in more detail. Other aspects of adolescence will be discussed in later chapters, particularly the chapters on menstruation and sexuality.

Self-Concepts

Young women's body images change dramatically as they enter adolescence because of the alarming way in which their shapes and sizes change. There is a rapid increase in height and weight. The reproductive system also changes. More visibly, secondary sex characteristics appear. **Secondary sex characteristics** are parts of the body related to reproduction but not directly involved. In females, breast development begins somewhere between about eight and 13, and pubic hair starts to grow.

Nora Ephron (1975) reminisces about breast development in adolescence:

> I suppose that for most girls, breasts, brassieres, that entire thing, has more trauma, more to do with the coming of adolescence, with becoming a woman, than anything else. Certainly more than getting your period, although that, too, was traumatic, symbolic. But you could see breasts; they were there; they were visible. [p. 3]

Young women constantly receive the message that it is important for them to be attractive. They must not be too fat, nor too thin. They should not be flat-chested. Their skin must be clear, their teeth straight and gleaming, and their hair lustrous. Adolescent women incorporate these messages, and their self-concepts are shaped by whether or not they are attractive. In one study adolescents were asked to rate their various body parts for attractiveness and for effectiveness, that is, helpfulness in daily functions (Lerner, Orlos, & Knapp, 1976). For females, attractiveness was the most important contributor to self-concept; females who thought that their bodies were attractive had positive self-concepts. For males, effectiveness was most important; males who thought that their bodies were effective had positive self-concepts.

For some adolescents, concern about the body's appearance reveals itself in a disease that can be life threatening, anorexia nervosa. We will discuss anorexia nervosa in detail in Chapter 12, but it is relevant here to mention this disorder in which people—most often adolescent women—literally starve themselves.

We have pointed out the importance of adolescents' self-concepts with respect to their images of their bodies. Let us now consider more psychological aspects of self-concepts. Females and males do not differ substantially in their self-esteem. Maccoby and Jacklin (1974) conclude, "The similarity of the two sexes in self-esteem is remarkably uniform across age levels through college age" (p. 153).

However, in other related areas there are sex differences. Simmons and Rosenberg (1975) found that adolescent females reported having less stable self-images than adolescent males. These authors assessed the stability of self-images by asking questions such as this one: "A kid told me: 'Some days I like the way I am. Some days I do not like the way I am.' Do your feelings *change* like this?" (p. 232). In the early adolescent group, 43 percent of the females had highly unstable self-images, in contrast to 30 percent of the males.

Adolescent women also seem to be more concerned about how other people view them. For example, females reported being more self-conscious than males. One question in Simmons and Rosenberg's (1975) study was, "If a teacher asked you to get up in front of the class and talk a little bit about your summer, would you be very nervous, a little nervous, or not at all nervous?" (p. 232). In the early adolescent group, 41 percent of the females reported that they would be highly self-conscious, in contrast to 29 percent of the males. It is important to stress that these answers were obtained by the adolescents' self-reports, rather than by actual observations of their behavior. As we mentioned in connection with the first theme of the book, sex differences are exaggerated when the self-report method is used. If young women really are more self-conscious, however, they are more likely to be so aware of what others are thinking of them that social interactions could become extremely uncomfortable. Let us now look more closely at these social interactions as we focus upon the topic of interpersonal relations.

Interpersonal Relations

We saw that adolescent females are more likely than adolescent males to report being self-conscious. Adolescent females and males may also differ from each other in their interactions with other people. For example, females are more likely than males to say that they act nice to people they don't like, to be very upset if someone gets angry, and to have their feelings hurt very easily (Rosenberg & Simmons, 1975). In other words, young women seem to be more disturbed by these kinds of negative behaviors from others. Young men, in contrast, remain relatively "cool."

In Chapter 7, we will see that women are better than men in guessing the emotions of other people. Think about how this factor might be related to females' greater responsiveness to other people's emotional behavior. It may be that females are more concerned about the possibility that someone won't like them, so that they inspect others' behavior for subtle negative signs. Males may fail to notice negative signs unless they are loud and clear.

As children reach adolescence, they are increasingly conscious of the impact that their interpersonal behavior has on other people (Newman, 1976). One group of other people with whom they must interact is their parents. In general, adolescent females want to have close relationships with their parents; they want their parents to respect them, and they want to respect their parents. It is particularly upsetting when their parents do not trust them or respect them (Konopka, 1976). A common source of problems with parents, as would be expected, is the topic of sexuality. Parents are especially concerned about the possibility of pregnancy, a worry that is more damaging to parent-daughter relationships than to parent-son relationships.

Despite these strains, daughters frequently report that their mothers are the persons to whom they feel closest. However—sadly—only about one-quarter of adolescent daughters have close relationships with their fathers. Fathers are frequently criticized for refusing to allow their daughters to grow up (Konopka, 1976).

Same-sex friendships are extremely important to young women. According to Douvan and Adelson's (1966) large-scale study, friendships of 11- to 13-year-olds are based primarily on shared activities. By about 14, however, young women emphasize the importance of personal qualities. Friends should be sensitive, and they should be trustworthy and supportive. Friendships between the ages of 14 and 16 are emotionally intense, and they can be disrupted by jealousies. Interest in same-sex friendships declines in later adolescence, however, because young women usually invest more energy in heterosexual relationships.

Chapter 9, on love relationships, expands upon this topic of heterosexual relationships. In the United States, many adolescent women receive the unambiguous message about the importance of these heterosexual relationships, and they realize that their most important goal must be to find a husband. For some young women, this task must be accomplished during high school. Other young women gain a "reprieve" by going to college, but college attendance merely postpones the date by which the husband must be obtained. Attitudes toward the primacy of marriage may be changing, but at present, few women are entirely spared from pressures to locate a suitable spouse.

The emphasis on marriage presents a problem for many young women. They do not know whom they will marry, so they do not know what kind of life to prepare for (Erikson, 1968). If a young woman develops a distinct and strong identity, she may eliminate herself from a share of the marriage market. Angrist (1969) suggested that most young women become experts in **contingency training,** so they can prepare for a variety of uncertainties and options. As a consequence, women who emphasize contingency training must remain flexible, rather than devoted to a particular personal goal. Obviously, this flexibility can limit the choice of a career, which is our next topic.

Career Choices

The research on career choices suggests that there may be reason for hope. Lanier and Byrne (1981) asked high-school students to look at slides of women and to decide which women were employed as engineers, lawyers, doctors, oceanographers, architects, and executives. They showed a strong tendency to categorize the more attractive women as being employed in these "masculine" occupations. Women in these professions are no longer stigmatized as being physically unappealing.

As we will see in Chapter 6, there has been a dramatic change in recent years in the number of women employed outside the home. The employment picture for women in the 1980s is quite different from even a decade ago. Marini (1978) reviewed the research conducted in the 1960s and 1970s on sex differences in adolescent career aspirations. She reached three major conclusions:

1. Adolescent men report that they plan to obtain a higher level of education than adolescent women report.
2. The occupational choices of adolescent women and men are highly gender-stereotyped.
3. On the average, the occupational choices of adolescent men and women do not differ substantially in prestige.

No doubt, Angrist's (1969) concept of contingency training applies to these findings. Women who want to keep their options open do not plan on extensive educations or nontraditional careers.

Do Marini's conclusions still apply in the 1980s? The answer is not clear. However, a large-scale study by Farmer (1983) suggests that adolescent women are quite involved in their career plans. Farmer tested 1,234 ninth and twelfth graders in rural, urban, and inner-city locations in Illinois. She drew the following conclusions from her data:

1. Adolescent men and women report that they have similar educational aspirations (in contrast to Marini's earlier summary).
2. Adolescent women report that they are more committed to home-making than adolescent men.
3. Adolescent women choose, on the average, *more* prestigious careers than adolescent men.
4. Adolescent women scored higher than adolescent men on a scale of career commitment. Thus, the women are more likely than the men to report that they enjoyed making plans about their future, that they wanted a job of which they could be proud, and that their career was an important part of their lives.
5. Adolescent women are more likely than adolescent men to choose nontraditional careers (a finding that was consistent with our discussion about children's career choices).

Farmer's study raises a number of questions. Notice that the study relied on the self-report method; to what extent did the young women report high career aspirations because it is now more socially desirable to do so than it was ten years ago? If, however, these reports reflect their true ambitions, will these young women retain their ambitions as they enter college or training programs? Will they remain committed to their careers, despite external pressures? How will they respond to the lower salaries and more modest opportunities for advancement that they will be offered, in contrast to the men? Furthermore, is this sample unusual or does it represent a widespread trend among adolescent women to take their careers seriously, perhaps even more seriously than plans for marriage?

Black Female Adolescents

As Chapter 1 noted, black females tend to be even more invisible than white females in American culture. This invisibility applies to adolescence as well as other life stages. As Smith (1982) concludes, "Generally speaking, the black female adolescent has been underrepresented in educational, psychological, and career literature" (p. 261). However, enough research has now been conducted that we can draw some tentative conclusions about young black women. We will focus on three topics: self-concepts, family relationships, and education and career planning. It is important to stress that there is tremendous variation among these women. The experiences of a teenager whose parents are both professionals and who attends a predominantly white, suburban school will naturally be different from the experiences of a teenager in an inner-city setting.

Self-concepts.   On the average, young black women tend to have positive self-concepts. As Smith (1982) observes,

> . . . despite the evidence that black girls and women are faced with the prospects of being devalued by both blacks and the general white society in favor of white women, black females have been able to maintain a positive sense of self against what appear to be overwhelming odds. [p. 281]

Let's look at a representative study. Turner and Turner (1982) found that black females rated themselves more positively than white females on characteristics such as warmth, responsibility, and steadiness. However, black and white females did not differ from each other in their tendency to describe themselves as "giving" or "happy." Thus, race has some influence on how young women see themselves, but the effects do not include all aspects of self-concepts.

Family relationships.   To some extent, the relatively positive self-concepts of adolescent black women can be traced to the fact that they are more likely than their white counterparts to assume adult responsibilities at an early age. That is, they are more likely to take care of younger brothers and sisters and to have household responsibilities (Smith, 1982). In a black family, an adolescent female is expected to be competent at these tasks.

Black and white adolescent females differ in their perceptions of their family. Schab (1982) questioned eighth graders living in Georgia and found the following differences between black girls and white girls:

1. White girls were more likely to go to their parents for advice.
2. White girls were more likely to report that they had to tell parents where they would be at all times.
3. White girls were more likely to say that they would marry against their parents' wishes.
4. Black girls were more likely to say that their grandparents were helpful as a source of advice.
5. Black girls were more likely to rate the general atmosphere of their homes as "very good."

It is difficult to summarize these findings. However, it may be that black girls like their families more (4 and 5) and would not want to hurt their feelings (3), yet they maintain independence from their parents (1 and 2).

Education and career planning.   The majority of black female adolescents realize that they will be both mothers and workers during adulthood

(Smith, 1982). Unlike many white female adolescents, they plan to work outside the home.

There are several studies that demonstrate that black females have higher scholastic achievement than black males at the high-school level (Smith, 1982). The reason for this sex difference is not clear. Theorists used to argue that families pushed their daughters more than their sons, urging females to work toward higher educational levels; more recent evidence does not support this view, though. Also, in high school, black females are more likely than black males to plan to go to college and to plan on a prestigious career.

Unfortunately, these high aspirations seem to decline once these black women are in college. Surveys of black college students show that women are less likely than men to say that they want to pursue advanced degrees or prestigious careers (Smith, 1982). Career counselors need to make special efforts to help minority women explore their career options (Brooks, 1984). As Chapter 6 will discuss, minority women are particularly likely to end up in jobs where their abilities will not be fully used. This underutilization of talent represents a personal tragedy for these women, as well as a loss for our country.

☐ SECTION SUMMARY: ▪ Adolescence

1. Adolescent women constantly hear messages about attractiveness; their self-concepts depend upon whether or not they are attractive, whereas adolescent men's self-concepts depend upon whether or not their bodies are effective.
2. Adolescent females and males do not differ in their self-esteem, but females have less stable self-images.
3. Adolescent females are more self-conscious than adolescent males.
4. Adolescent females are more worried than adolescent males about negative behavior from other people.
5. Adolescent females want to have close relationships with their parents; they are close to their mothers and distant from their fathers.
6. The nature of adolescent females' same-sex friendships changes during maturation, being particularly intense between 14 and 16.
7. For many adolescent women, finding a husband is a task of primary importance; they remain flexible in order to appeal to a wide variety of potential spouses.
8. High-school students categorized attractive women as being employed in stereotypically masculine occupations.
9. According to research in the 1960s and 1970s, adolescent men anticipated more education than adolescent women, both women and men were gender-stereotyped in their career choices, their career choices were equally prestigious, but women's choices showed greater variation in prestige.

10. Some more recent research shows that adolescent women may be even more involved in their career plans than adolescent men.
11. Black female adolescents have not been extensively studied, but we know that they tend to have positive self-concepts and that they differ from white female adolescents with respect to family relationships.
12. In high school, black females have higher aspirations than black males, but by the time they reach college, black females have lower expectations for advanced degrees and prestigious careers.

Chapter Review Questions

1. All four theories of sex-typing mention parents in the acquisition of gender roles. Review the four theories, pointing out how mothers and fathers are relevant.
2. Five-year-old Darlene is playing with a doll. How would each of the four theories explain her behavior?
3. Sally Ride, the first American woman in space, told the press, "It's too bad that society isn't to the point yet where the country could just send up a woman astronaut and nobody would think twice about it." Explain why her remark offers support for gender schema theory. Then point out how each of the four theories would explain the absence of women in certain professions.
4. A major surprise to psychologists is that parents do not tolerate more aggression from their sons than from their daughters. The section on schools suggests that teachers are more likely to respond negatively if a boy is aggressive than if a girl is aggressive; how might this observation help to explain how parents might unwittingly encourage aggression in their sons?
5. There is mixed evidence about parents' role in encouraging their daughters to be dependent, rather than independent. Review the evidence and comment on teachers' roles with respect to dependency.
6. Discuss the three ways in which peers encourage sex-typing. How might a skillful elementary-school teacher minimize sex-typing in these three areas? What kinds of problems might arise in these efforts to encourage change?
7. Describe as extensively as possible how books and television might influence children's toy preferences and play behavior.
8. Imagine a conversation among three children who are four, nine, and 11 years old. They are discussing how men and women are different. Describe the position that each of them might take, assuming that they are representative of their age groups.
9. Discuss children's and adolescents' career choices and how a person's sex influences those choices. Point out why females' career choices may

be in a transition phase with respect to career commitment. Also comment on educational and career choices of black adolescent females.

10. Adolescent women seem to be more concerned than adolescent men about how others view them. Summarize the implications of this observation for their self-image and interpersonal relations. Also speculate about how this observation may have implications in other areas, such as: receptivity to the messages in advertisements; eagerness to try something daring; and willingness to speak out in a classroom.

NEW TERMS

sex-typing
psychoanalytic theory
oral stage
anal stage
phallic stage
castration complex
penis envy
latency stage
genital stage
social-learning theory

modeling
symbolic models
cognitive-developmental theory
gender identity
gender constancy
gender schema theory
Title IX
puberty
secondary sex characteristics
contingency training

RECOMMENDED READINGS

Bem, S. L. (1985). Androgyny and gender schema theory: A conceptual and empirical integration. In T. B. Sonderegger (Ed.), *Nebraska Symposium on Motivation, 1984: Psychology and gender* (pp. 179–226). Lincoln, Nebr. University of Nebraska Press. ■ Bem summarizes other theories of sex-typing and provides details on her own gender schema theory; the chapter also summarizes her research on gender-schematic processing.

Huston, A. C. (1983). Sex-typing. In E. M. Hetherington (Ed.), *Handbook of child psychology*, Vol. IV (4th ed.). New York: Wiley. ■ This chapter provides especially strong sections on the forces that encourage sex-typing and theories of sex-typing.

Liss, M. B. (Ed.) (1983). *Social and cognitive skills: Sex roles and children's play.* New York: Academic. ■ This edited volume discusses sex differences in children's play and their significance for later development.

Sadker, M. P., & Sadker, D. M. (1982). *Sex equity handbook for schools.* New York: Longman. ■ Teachers and school administrators would profit from the information in this book on how schools encourage sex-typing, as well as some suggestions for correcting the biases.

MENSTRUATION

- Currently, only about 75 percent of young women in the United States have been told about menstruation before their first menstrual period.

- Young women who haven't yet had their first period believe that they will not be ashamed to tell their family and friends when they begin to menstruate.

- Young women seem to have different attitudes about themselves after they have begun to menstruate.

- Part of the brain helps to regulate the menstrual cycle.

- After the ovary has released the egg, the structure that previously held the egg begins to produce hormones.

- There is no known physical explanation for menstrual pain.

- There is evidence from numerous carefully controlled studies that the majority of women experience negative moods prior to their menstrual periods.

- Most women perform slightly worse on intellectual tasks just before their periods.

- In most cultures outside the United States, people have positive attitudes toward menstruation and menstrual blood.

- Menstrual attitudes are so negative in the United States that most people think women who are menstruating are less attractive than women who are not menstruating.

In the last chapter, we discussed several aspects of women's physical and psychological development during adolescence. However, we only briefly mentioned an important event that occurs for the first time during adolescence and will persist throughout half of a woman's lifetime: menstruation. Women menstruate, on the average, about 450 times during their lives. Physically, menstruation involves the loss of only about three ounces of blood each cycle. Psychologically, menstruation represents much more, enough to merit a chapter in a textbook on psychology of women.

Menstruation is important in the lives of women as a personal, private experience. Menstruation is also important as a political issue that has influenced public policy. In the late 1800s, it was argued that women should not be allowed access to higher education because all the nervous energy required for thinking would be diverted away from their reproductive systems. Rather than developing into healthy young women, well-educated women would suffer from menstrual disorders and physical deterioration (Hunter College Women's Studies Collective, 1983). More recently, women's menstrual cycles often have been used as an excuse to keep women from positions of responsibility in government and private industry. This clear sex difference—women menstruate, men don't—has been used to justify the fact that women are treated differently from men, which is the second theme of this book.

In this chapter, we will begin by talking about menarche, which is the beginning of menstruation. Then we will examine the biological basis for the menstrual cycle. The next topic involves physical and psychological reactions to the menstrual cycle. Finally, we'll look at attitudes toward menstruation.

☐ MENARCHE

Menarche (pronounced "*men*-nar-kee") is the first menstrual period. The average age of menarche in the United States is now about 13 (Golub, 1983; Warren, 1983), but it is quite common for young women to reach menarche as early as 11 or as late as 14.

Menarche occurs some time after the onset of puberty. **Puberty** is the age at which the reproductive organs become developed. In females, it also involves the beginning of breast development and pubic hair growth. Puberty begins in American females between the ages of about 9 and 12 (Rathus, 1983). That means that a young woman usually has some breast development and pubic hair before she begins to menstruate.

Sources of Information about Menstruation

Before you begin, try Demonstration 4.1, which involves how young women learn about menstruation prior to menarche.

In an early study on several Western European cultures, young women were found to have little preparation for menarche and menstruation. Most

Learning about Menstruation

The following questions focus on learning about menstruation. They can be answered by males, as well as females.

1. Can you recall the details about first hearing about menstruation (or sanitary pads, or blood stains from menstruation)?
2. Did a parent discuss menstruation with you? Can you recall whether the conversation was handled in secrecy?
3. Did older siblings discuss menstruation with you?
4. Did your friends talk about menstruation before any discussion of the topic in school? What was the tone of the conversation?
5. How was menstruation presented in school, if it was handled at all? Did you see a movie, and can you recall any details? Did you receive any brochure? Were boys and girls separated for this discussion?
6. What was the reaction among your friends to any classroom session on menstruation?
7. Did you find out any additional information through reading?
8. Can you recall any other sources of information about menstruation?
9. As far as you can recreate the experience, what was your overall attitude toward menstruation during fifth and sixth grade?
10. Imagine that you have a nine-year-old daughter. She has just brought home a permission slip announcing that menstruation will be covered in class next Monday. You have not formally discussed menstruation with her yet. Try to imagine how you would introduce the topic and what you would say. Then try to assess the overall tone of your description.

young women in Germany, Poland, and Ireland received no information in advance (Abel & Joffe, 1950). Fortunately, young women who are currently growing up in the United States are better informed. By the 1970s, only 5 to 10 percent of them had been given no advance information (Brooks-Gunn & Ruble, 1983).

In the United States today, almost all young women learn something about menstruation from their mothers. They also receive information from other young women their own age and from older sisters. Fathers are seldom mentioned as sources of information (Brooks-Gunn & Ruble, 1983). School nurses and health classes seem to be increasingly important as a source of information. In one study, 66 percent of the young women learned about menstruation from school programs (Petersen, 1983). Books and other media sources also provide some information.

What kinds of messages are conveyed by the films and pamphlets that young women see? Whisnant, Brett, and Zegans (1975) examined several of the more popular media materials. They typically had titles (such as "Very Personally Yours") that implied a private dialogue with a girl, but used vague language. The language in the booklet was usually technical, and difficult for young women to connect with their own experience. The diagrams usually omitted features such as the clitoris and the vulva. They rarely mentioned pubic hair. Symptoms such as cramps and mood changes were listed, but they were not described in enough detail for a young woman to have any concrete idea of what she will experience.

I was curious to see if these criticisms could be applied to current material, so I examined a booklet called "Growing Up and Liking It" (Personal Products, 1981), which was distributed this year at the local school. The innocuous, vague title was echoed by the flowers (complete with smiling faces) decorating the cover. The subject is introduced in a pleasant way through letters exchanged among three friends, one of whom has just begun to menstruate. The information is delivered at an appropriate level for older elementary-school students. There was a vocabulary list that included the inner and outer labia, but not pubic hair or the clitoris. There was a diagram showing an internal representation of the female reproductive system, but nothing showed the external genitals. As in earlier versions, the internal structures would be difficult for a young woman to relate to her own body. It seems that some—but certainly not all—of the earlier criticisms have been answered.

As you might expect, there is a relationship between a young woman's menstrual experience and how well she has been prepared for it. Young women who are informed about menstruation at an early age are more likely to have a positive attitude about menstruation at the time of menarche (Dunham, 1979; Golub, 1983). The adequacy of the explanation is also important. Young women who felt that they had been well prepared at menarche reported fewer premenstrual symptoms and less pain than those who felt they had not been prepared (Brooks-Gunn & Ruble, 1983).

Attitudes toward Menarche

Among the Kurtatchi, who live on an island near New Guinea, there is an elaborate ceremony to celebrate a young woman's menarche. At the moment her mother finds out, she announces the event to her closest friends and relatives. They respond enthusiastically by jumping and shouting, and they all begin to prepare food. Several men build platforms needed for the ceremony. For a few days, the menstruating daughter and her attendants remain secluded in the mother's house, where they fast, observe taboos, and have their heads painted red and white. In fact, if she is from a wealthy family, the entire village must fast! After four or five days, the women of the village perform a dance, blow on a conch shell, and announce the feast for the next day. People from neighboring villages attend the feast, which involves the young woman parading along an elaborate walkway and drinking a special brew (Paige & Paige, 1981).

The Kurtatchi ceremony is certainly a far cry from the way menarche is welcomed in the United States. As Delaney and her coauthors (1976) point out, we can buy greeting cards for childbirth, marriage, and death. However,

Hallmark manufactures no cards with the message, "Best Wishes on Becoming a Woman." Instead, we greet this coming-of-age with some embarrassment, in the same way we deodorize, sanitize, and remove the evidence of menstruation itself.

Notice that the American reaction to menstruation is a further demonstration of the themes mentioned in Chapter 1. According to one of the themes, items associated with women are not valued as highly as items associated with men; menarche is not highly valued in our culture. According to another theme, women are relatively invisible; in the United States, menarche is carefully hidden as well.

Some American families offer a good example of positive attitudes toward the menarche. A 14-year-old who had reached menarche a few months before said, "I couldn't wait for it [menstruation] to happen ... I thought it was the greatest day in my life. My whole family congratulated me and made me feel really good about it and myself" (Maddux, 1975, p. 33).

Most premenarcheal girls hope that they will "get their periods" at about the same time as everyone else (Peterson, 1983; Brooks-Gunn & Ruble, 1983). Most boys would rather reach maturity on the early side. Young women who mature early probably experience more stress. Not only do they deviate from the norm, but they are less likely to have been prepared for menstruation by their mothers and by school programs.

Most girls who have not yet reached menarche believe that they will not be ashamed to tell their family and friends that they have begun to menstruate. One premenarcheal girl planned to announce, "Guess what, everybody, something new happened to me today" (Whisnant & Zegans, 1975).

In contrast to what these premenarcheal girls anticipate, most young women are quite secretive when they do begin to menstruate. Most of them tell only their mothers, and very few tell their fathers (Brooks-Gunn & Ruble, 1983; Clarke & Ruble, 1978; Whisnant & Zegans, 1975). Some young women tell their sisters and girlfriends. However, they almost never tell their brothers or boyfriends. Menstruation is a secret topic, not to be shared with males of any age.

This secretiveness about menstruation is also evident from young women's hesitations in talking to researchers. Brooks-Gunn and Ruble (1983) mention that young women seem willing to talk about menarche in informal groups. However, when they are interviewed individually, they supply little information. They are reluctant to discuss their feelings, even with an interviewer they know quite well.

Menarche seems to have an important influence on how young women feel about themselves. Seventh- and eighth-grade students who had begun to menstruate drew pictures of females with more curvaceous bodies and more breast development than did their peers who were premenarcheal (Koff, 1983; Rierdan & Koff, 1980). It seems that menarche provides a critical event that encourages young women to see themselves as female and sexually mature. Menarche forces them to realize that they are no longer little girls. This sign of maturity is perhaps the most positive aspect of the menarche.

For example, 64 percent of 9- to 12-year-olds agreed with the statement that "Menstruation is exciting because it means a girl is growing up" (Williams, 1983, p. 146).

In some sense, menarche may serve as a "dividing line" for females. A young girl is permitted to play football and to spend an afternoon playing at the home of the boy next door. Dad invites her to sit on his lap now and then. After menarche, parents caution, "You're too big for that now," with a tone of voice that indicates that their daughters should not ask, "Why not?"

Menarche also has other important effects on a young woman's interactions with her parents. She now has different attitudes about herself, and they also have different attitudes about her. They all regard her as a more mature person. In one study, postmenarcheal young women were more likely than their premenarcheal peers to set limits on their own. They also reported more conflict with their parents. Postmenarcheal young women were also more likely to report that they were more comfortable in discussions with their mothers than with their fathers (Danza, 1983). It seems that menarche represents a transition in which young women come to see themselves as mature and independent people.

☐ SECTION SUMMARY: ▪ Menarche

1. **Menarche, the first menstrual period, usually occurs between the ages of 11 and 14.**
2. **Most young women are prepared for menstruation; they learn about it from school programs, mothers, older sisters, and peers.**
3. **Media material on menstruation may have overly technical language and omit useful information.**
4. **Attitudes toward menstruation are related to the preparation that young women have received.**
5. **Menarche is greeted with celebration in some cultures, but it is generally kept secret in the United States.**
6. **Menarche seems to provide a critical event in which females see themselves as young women rather than little girls; postmenarcheal young women differ from their premenarcheal peers in their independence and their interactions with parents.**

☐ BIOLOGICAL ASPECTS OF THE MENSTRUAL CYCLE

Now let us examine menstruation itself. The biological aspects of menstruation are like a drama with a fairly complicated plot. There are many actors that have complex interactions with one another. They include glands, hormones, and structures in the reproductive system. Let us first introduce these actors, and then we'll get to the plot.

Structures and Substances Involved in Menstruation

Brain structures. One structure in the brain that has a role in menstruation is the hypothalamus (pronounced "hie-poe-*thal*-uh-muss"). The **hypothalamus** is located about 2 inches behind your eyes, and it is involved in emotion, eating, and drinking, as well as in menstruation. The hypothalamus is important in menstruation because it regulates the pituitary gland.

The **pituitary gland** (pronounced "pit-*too*-it-tare-ee"), the second brain structure involved in menstruation, is located about 1 inch below the hypothalamus. The pituitary is an extremely important gland in the body. It produces growth hormones and influences other glands, such as the adrenal gland and the thyroid gland, in addition to its role in menstruation. The pituitary gland produces two hormones, follicle-stimulating hormone and luteinizing hormone, which are central in menstruation.

Hormones. **Follicle-stimulating hormone,** abbreviated FSH, stimulates the **follicles** (or egg-holders) in the ovary. FSH makes them produce estrogen and progesterone. **Luteinizing hormone** (pronounced "*lute*-teen-ize-ing") is abbreviated LH; this hormone is involved in the development of the follicles.

Estrogen (pronounced "*ess*-troe-jenn") is primarily produced by the ovaries. In addition to its role in menstruation, estrogen is important in the development of female sex organs, the development of breast tissue, and the widening of the hips. Figure 4.1 shows how the estrogen level changes during the course of the menstrual cycle.

Progesterone (pronounced "proe-*jess*-terr-own") is also primarily produced by the ovaries. In addition to its role in menstruation, progesterone helps in the development of female sex organs and in pregnancy. As you can see in Figure 4.1, the progesterone level rises and falls during the last half of the menstrual cycle. The variations in the levels of estrogen and progesterone are caused by the complex interactions of the hypothalamus, the pituitary gland, and the ovaries.

Reproductive structures. We mentioned the ovaries in the section of Chapter 2 on prenatal development, and we refer to them again here. The two **ovaries** are located on either side of the uterus (see Figure 4.2). In addition to making estrogen and progesterone, the ovaries contain **ova,** or eggs. (One egg is called an **ovum,** pronounced "*owe*-vum). As we noted earlier, each ovum is stored in its own follicle. At birth, a female has about 400,000 ova, although only about 450 of them will be released during her lifetime (Linkie, 1982).

Midway through the menstrual cycle, one egg breaks out of its follicle and rises to the ovary's surface. The egg moves into the **fallopian tube;** the end of a fallopian tube is located near each of the two ovaries. The fallopian tubes lead to the uterus. The **uterus** contains a lining called the **endometrium** (pronounced "enn-doe-*mee*-tree-um") that will serve as a nourishing

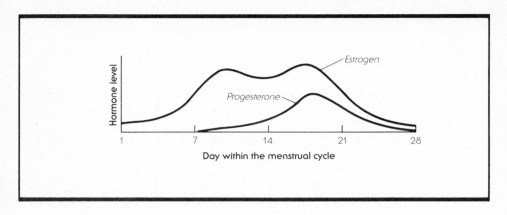

location for a fertilized egg to mature during prenatal development, or else will be shed as menstrual flow. If the egg is not fertilized, it disintegrates on its way out of the uterus.

The Events in the Menstrual Cycle

Figure 4.3 shows a basic outline of the events in the menstrual cycle. Before we consider the details, notice that it is indeed a *cycle*, because there is no beginning or end. Instead, the phases keep repeating each month. Also, notice

FIGURE 4.2. **Internal reproductive organs**

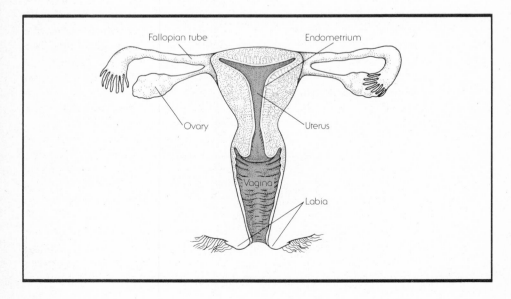

that the hormones provide an impressive communication system. When the level of a particular hormone is too low, a structure in the brain is signalled, which begins a chain of events that creates more of that hormone. When the level of a hormone is too high, a structure in the brain is signalled, which begins a chain of events that ultimately leads to a decrease in that hormone.

This kind of feedback system is found in equipment created by humans, as well as in naturally occurring cycles. Consider your oven, for example. When the temperature inside the oven is too low for the setting, a mechanism is triggered to produce more heat. When the temperature is too high, a mechanism is triggered to turn off the production of additional heat.

Let us enter the cycle at step 1 and discuss the events in the menstrual cycle for situations in which the egg is not fertilized. (We'll see what happens when the egg *is* fertilized in Chapter 11 on pregnancy.)

1. Among its other tasks, the hypothalamus, located in the brain, keeps track of the level of hormones in the bloodstream. When the level of estrogen falls too low, the hypothalamus must respond.
2. The hypothalamus responds by signalling the pituitary, which is the other brain structure involved in menstruation.
3. The pituitary gland responds to this signal by releasing follicle-stimulating hormone into the bloodstream. FSH has to travel through the bloodstream to reach its destination in the ovary, because there is no tidy little duct leading from the brain to the ovary. The bloodstream therefore provides a convenient method of transportation.
4. Follicle-stimulating hormone does precisely what its name suggests; it stimulates the follicles in the ovary to become more mature. FSH also signals the ovaries to increase their production of estrogen.
5. An increased level of estrogen brings about two changes. First, it stimulates the development of the endometrium. Every month, the body essentially prepares for pregnancy, and so the lining of the uterus must be made thicker in order to receive a fertilized egg. The second change that the increased level of estrogen accomplishes is to signal the pituitary, because the body must be alerted to stop producing additional FSH.
6. In response, the pituitary does stop producing FSH. It shifts into a new phase in which it produces luteinizing hormone, LH.
7. The luteinizing hormone is responsible for suppressing growth in all of the follicles except for one and encouraging growth of that one follicle. Consequently, only one egg reaches maturity. Only one egg needs to be released each menstrual cycle, so that this process is somewhat like pulling out the weaker seedlings in a flower pot so that only the strongest one will thrive.
8. The follicle then releases the ovum, or egg, at approximately the fourteenth day of the menstrual cycle, a process called **ovulation** (pronounced "ovv-you-*lae*-shun"). Many women report that they know when they are ovulating, because they experience a dull aching in

FIGURE 4.3. **Events in the menstrual cycle**

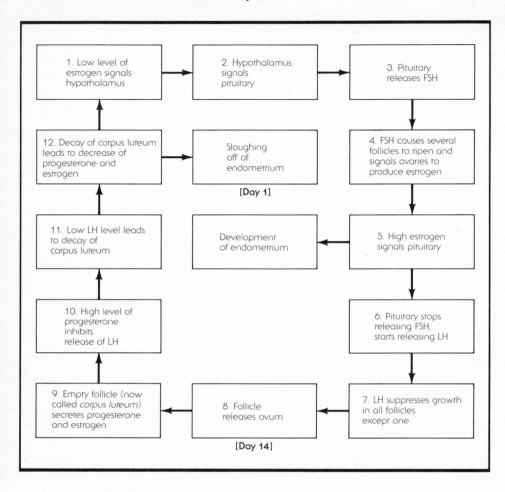

the middle of their menstrual cycles. If this aching is painful, it is called **Mittelschmerz** (pronounced "*mitt*-tell-schmairtz"). This word is German for "middle-pain," because it occurs in the middle of the menstrual cycle.

9. The empty follicle has now been abandoned by the egg, but it still has an important function. It matures into a roundish structure called the **corpus luteum** (pronounced "*kor*-puhs *loo*-tee-um"), which secretes progesterone and estrogen. (Check back to Figure 4.1 and notice that the level of both of these hormones rises after ovulation.)

10. The high level of progesterone inhibits the production of additional luteinizing hormone; LH is no longer needed.

11. The low level of LH means that the corpus luteum can no longer be maintained, and so it decomposes.

12. Since the corpus luteum no longer exists, the production of progesterone and estrogen falls rapidly, as you can see from Figure 4.1. With such low levels of hormones, the endometrium can no longer be maintained in the style to which it has grown accustomed. It is sloughed off, and the endometrium passes out of the vagina as menstrual flow. We have arrived at Day 1 of the cycle, which is either the end or the beginning, depending upon your point of view. Now the low level of estrogen signals the hypothalamus, and we begin over again.

□ SECTION SUMMARY: ▪ Biological Aspects of the Menstrual Cycle

1. The parts of the brain involved in the menstrual cycle are the hypothalamus and the pituitary.
2. The hormones involved in menstruation include follicle-stimulating hormone (FSH), luteinizing hormone (LH), estrogen, and progesterone.
3. Each menstrual cycle, the ovaries release one ovum, which moves through the fallopian tubes into the uterus. If the ovum is not fertilized, the endometrium is shed as menstrual flow and the ovum disintegrates on its way out of the uterus.
4. The menstrual cycle involves a complex feedback system that regulates the levels of various hormones.
5. When estrogen is too low, the hypothalamus signals the pituitary, which releases FSH.
6. FSH stimulates the follicles in the ovary to mature and signals the ovaries to produce estrogen.
7. The increased level of estrogen stimulates the development of the endometrium and also signals the pituitary to stop producing FSH and start producing LH.
8. LH suppresses growth in all follicles except one and encourages growth in that one follicle.
9. The follicle releases one ovum during ovulation.
10. The empty follicle matures into the corpus luteum, which secretes progesterone and estrogen, and the high level of progesterone inhibits the production of additional LH.
11. The low level of LH leads to the decomposition of the corpus luteum, which in turn leads to a decrease in production of progesterone and estrogen.
12. The low levels of progesterone and estrogen leads to the sloughing off of the endometrium, which passes out of the vagina as menstrual flow.
13. The low level of estrogen signals the hypothalamus, which marks the beginning of a new cycle.

☐ PHYSICAL AND PSYCHOLOGICAL REACTIONS TO THE MENSTRUAL CYCLE

We will look at a number of factors to see how they vary with the menstrual cycle. These include menstrual pain and the premenstrual syndrome, both of which have received wide publicity. We will also examine various kinds of abilities, because it seems that some abilities (such as perceptual abilities) may vary with the menstrual cycle, whereas other abilities (such as cognitive abilities) do not. Finally, we will discuss how certain aspects of sexuality seem to depend upon the phase of the menstrual cycle.

Menstrual Pain

Menstrual pain, or **dysmenorrhea** (pronounced "diss-men-oh-*ree*-ah") most often includes painful cramps in the abdominal region, but it also includes symptoms such as lower back pain and headache (Ruble & Brooks-Gunn, 1982). Some people also include a dull, aching pain that precedes menstruation, but we will consider that kind of pain in the next section on premenstrual syndrome. The pain that occurs on the first day of menstruation is quite different in nature; it is a spasm-like pain that resembles labor pains.

How common is menstrual pain? Ruble and Brooks-Gunn asked adolescent females between the ages of high school and college about their menstrual experiences. They found that about three-quarters of them reported menstrual cramps, most often every month. This means that about one-quarter did not experience menstrual cramps. Consistent with the fourth theme of this book, there is a wide variation in women's reactions to life events, such as menstruation. Pain during menstruation is *not* inevitable, though it is very likely.

Another interesting finding in Ruble and Brooks-Gunn's survey was that junior-high-school students who had not yet begun to menstruate said that they expected to experience more pain than the amount reported by their classmates who had already menstruated. As Ruble and Brooks-Gunn suggest, young women expect to have menstrual pain. As mentioned in Chapter 1, expectations can produce a self-fulfilling prophecy. These young women may indeed experience menstrual pain simply because they expected it.

However, do not conclude that menstrual pain is "all in the head." The contractions of the uterus that cause menstrual pain seem to be encouraged by prostaglandins. **Prostaglandins** (pronounced "pross-tuh-*glan*-duns") are substances produced by the body in high concentrations as menstruation approaches; prostaglandins are known to cause severe cramps (Asso, 1983; Budoff, 1983; Seaman & Seaman, 1978). We must conclude that menstrual pain results from a combination of physiologically based pain and beliefs that menstruation must be painful.

One interesting observation is that menstrual pain is usually greatly reduced after childbirth, or after the age of 25. The reasons for this "cure" are not clear (Lennane & Lennane, 1973). In addition, as you might expect, menstrual cramps don't exist after menopause.

Many different kinds of treatment have been used to try to alleviate menstrual pain. Those who think that menstrual pain is entirely physiological have recommended surgery. Those who think that menstrual pain is "all in the head" have recommended psychotherapy. In fact, psychotherapy may be useful when it removes the fear of serious disease by explaining the nature of the problem (Fuchs, 1982). Sometimes oral contraceptives are helpful, though they may bring unwanted side effects. Other drugs are also used, including some that directly influence prostaglandins (Friederich, 1983; Fuchs, 1982). Heat, exercises, diet changes, and herbal teas are sometimes helpful (Fuchs, 1982; Seaman & Seaman, 1978). A book called *No More Menstrual Cramps and Other Good News* (Budoff, 1983) has more specific suggestions about medication and other approaches to pain relief.

The Premenstrual Syndrome

Menstrual pain has become a well-accepted part of the menstrual cycle. Recently, something that has been labeled the premenstrual syndrome has provoked controversy among both professionals and lay people. The **premenstrual syndrome** (PMS) refers to a variety of symptoms that may occur a few days before menstruation; the symptoms often include headaches, tenderness of the breasts, swelling, acne, and a number of psychological reactions that are sometimes called premenstrual tension. This **premenstrual tension** is supposed to include three common components: depression, irritability, and lethargy. Women who experience premenstrual tension may feel inadequate, grouchy, and so tired that they may be tempted to remain in bed all day (Abplanalp, 1983; Budoff, 1983).

One reason why the premenstrual syndrome is so controversial is that researchers do not agree upon the definition of the syndrome (Abplanalp, 1983). Read that list of reactions once more and add on additional ones you have heard about through popularized accounts of PMS. (I've heard about craving chocolate, a feeling that one is on drugs, anxiety, and so forth.) Thus, one researcher may be studying women whose primary symptom is anxiety, whereas another may be studying women suffering from depression. The lack of a rigid definition for PMS makes it impossible to study the issue carefully.

Another reason why the premenstrual syndrome is so controversial is that some experts claim that all menstruating women experience it, because they all have cyclic variations in their hormones. Other experts maintain that the premenstrual syndrome is a myth—"It's all in their heads." Neither of these views does credit to women. The first view stresses that we are almost entirely at the mercy of our hormones. Feminists are concerned that people who overemphasize the premenstrual syndrome are out to make a "fast buck" on therapy sessions and medications. The second view is equally unfair to women, because it ignores the fact that some women do experience more tension premenstrually than at other times in their cycle.

It is worth mentioning a point that is seldom stressed in discussions of PMS. Part of the premenstrual tension in some women may be related to anxiety about pregnancy (Crawford, 1985). Whether or not a woman wants to be pregnant, waiting for one's period can be charged with anxiety and fear. Clearly, this kind of tension should not be attributed only to hormonal fluctuation!

In our discussion of the premenstrual syndrome, we will take a position that is intermediate between the two extremes of the purely hormonal and purely psychological/cultural explanations. It seems that some women have mild to severe mood swings that are related to their menstrual cycles. However, not all women experience the premenstrual syndrome. We see once more an illustration of one of the general principles introduced in the first chapter. Individual differences among women are large; we cannot specify a rule that holds true for all women.

Let us begin with an examination of one of the aspects of the premenstrual syndrome that has received the most attention, the idea that women experience dramatic "swings" in their moods during the course of their menstrual cycles. Our next topic will be reactions to premenstrual women. Then we will look at reports that abnormal behavior—ranging from criminal behavior to suicide—is related to the menstrual cycle. Finally, we will talk about coping with the premenstrual syndrome.

Mood swings.   Several kinds of studies support the idea that women's moods vary throughout the menstrual cycle, being most positive at ovulation and most negative just before menstruation. These include retrospective questionnaire studies, research in which women provide ratings of their daily moods, and a variety of other methods.

In a number of retrospective questionnaire studies, summarized by Parlee (1973), women are asked to think back about what their mood was like at various times during the last menstrual cycle. These studies often conclude that there is a cyclical variation in mood across the menstrual cycle. You may be able to detect a problem with this kind of retrospective study. Perhaps people are not very accurate in their recall of their moods; they may remember that their moods were negative premenstrually, when in fact they may have been no more negative then usual. In fact, May (1976) demonstrated that there is little correspondence between women's retrospective reports of their mood and their actual day-by-day recordings of their moods.

The second method for studying mood swings is better. This approach asks women to make regular ratings throughout the menstrual cycle. It therefore avoids the problem of inaccurate recall. Some studies using this method show a cyclical variation in mood across the menstrual cycle. There is still a problem with this kind of study. In most cases, the women know that they are participating in a study on the effects of the menstrual cycle on variations in mood. To some extent, their reported mood may be influenced by their knowledge that mood is *supposed* to be related to the menstrual cycle. As discussed in Chapter 1 in the section on problems in research on the psychology of women, people who participate in experiments often respond according to their expectations, rather than their true emotions.

Several studies have explored how women's knowledge and expectations can influence their reported moods. Ruble (1977) measured women's temperatures and blood pressures, and told half of them that they were "premenstrual," with their period due in one or two days. The other half were told that they were in the middle of their menstrual cycles, with their periods due in seven to ten days. In reality, the women were randomly assigned to the two conditions. All women then filled out the Menstrual-Distress Questionnaire, designed to measure mood and other symptoms. The women who thought they were premenstrual were more likely to report water retention, pain, and change in eating habits.

In another experiment, Parlee (1974) asked both women and men to complete the Menstrual-Distress Questionnaire as if they were women in one of three time periods: the menstrual phase, in the middle of the cycle, or premenstrually. In general, both men and women tended to show cyclic kinds of responses for different phases in the cycle—the same kinds of responses supplied by women who are reporting on their actual menstrual experiences. These two studies suggest that when Menstrual-Distress Questionnaires are given to women who know that the study is about menstruation, the women give answers that they think they *should* give, rather than answers that reflect their true experiences.

In a later study, Parlee (1982a) asked a small number of women in their twenties and thirties to assess their moods on a daily basis for 90 days. They did *not* know that they were participating in a study on menstruation. In general, each woman showed very little fluctuation in mood across the menstrual cycles. When the group data were analyzed, there were some surprises, however. Contrary to the usual findings, the women had rated themselves as significantly *lower* in fatigue, confusion, and depression in the premenstrual phase than in the middle of the cycle. It seems that Parlee has uncovered a "premenstrual elation syndrome," rather than some aspect of premenstrual distress or premenstrual tension. At any rate, it is clear that not all women experience negative moods during the premenstrual phase.

Some researchers have suggested that a woman's age is related to her tendency to show mood swings. As Abplanalp, Haskett, and Rose (1980) conclude, severe premenstrual mood problems are more likely to occur in women in their thirties and forties than in women in their teens and twenties. For example, Golub (1976a) found that 30- to 45-year-old women were likely to be more depressed and anxious premenstrually than in the middle of their cycles. However, Golub and Harrington (1981) did not find that menstrual phase influenced mood in their sample of 15- and 16-year-olds.

What can we conclude about this second group of studies that ask women to rate their mood throughout the menstrual cycle? First, women's ratings may be influenced by their expectations (Koeske, 1983). Second, when they are not aware that the study concerns menstruation, women may not show mood swings. Third, mood swings are more evident in middle-aged women than in young women.

So far, in our examination of mood swings, we have discussed retrospective questionnaires and studies in which women rate their moods throughout the menstrual cycle, in most cases knowing that the study concerns menstruation. In addition, there are other studies that do not fit into these two categories, and they provide what is perhaps the strongest evidence for mood swings in the menstrual cycle. We will discuss two of these studies.

One such study asked women to tell brief stories at different times during their menstrual cycles (Paige, 1971). The women were asked additional questions not related to menstruation, in order to disguise the purpose of the study. An unusual feature of this study was that the women participants belonged to three groups: women who were not taking oral contraceptives; women who were taking oral contraceptives that supply hormones similar to those in the natural menstrual cycle, though at higher levels; and women who were taking oral contraceptives that supply a constant, high dose of both estrogen and progesterone. If hormones are indeed related to mood swings, then a comparison of these three groups should provide useful information.

The results showed that women in the first two groups did show a cyclical variation in the kinds of stories they told. Women not taking oral contraceptives and women taking contraceptives that mimicked the normal hormonal pattern both tended to tell stories that were less anxious and less hostile in the middle of the cycle. In contrast, the third group of women, who had a constant level of hormones, told stories that did not vary in their anxiety and hostility during the phases of the menstrual cycle.

Additional evidence for cyclic mood swings, particularly with respect to anxiety, comes from an unexpected source: records of the frequency with which mothers bring their children to see a doctor! Tuch (1975) found that women who were premenstrual or who were menstruating were more likely to bring their children to the doctor's office than were women who were in the middle of their cycles. Furthermore, children of premenstrual and menstruating mothers were judged to be less sick than children of mid-cycle mothers. Around the time of their menstrual periods, women may be more anxious and have a lower tolerance for stress, such as ill health in a child. Tuch also proposes another alternative, that empathy and maternal concern might be higher near the time of the menstrual period.

Taking everything into consideration, we must conclude that mood swings may occur sometimes in some women. Hormonal changes interact in a complex way with what our culture has taught women to expect from menstruation, resulting in some cyclic mood variation. Thus, the explanation is more complex than either a simple biological ("It's all in your glands") or a simple psychological/cultural ("It's all in your head") explanation (Dan, et al., 1980).

The next section discusses another factor that may contribute to women's perceptions of premenstrual tension.

Reactions to premenstrual women. Some researchers have looked at people's reactions to the behavior of premenstrual women. Koeske and Koeske (1975) asked college students to decide why a hypothetical female, Miss A, was in a certain mood on a particular day. These authors found that if the students had been told that Miss A was premenstrual, they tended to explain her negative mood in terms of biological factors. If they believed that Miss A was in the middle of her menstrual cycle, they tended to explain her mood in terms of either her personality or the situation she was in. In other words, biology is blamed for negative premenstrual moods and behavior, but biology is not given credit for positive moods (Koeske, 1980).

Think about how this kind of mood explanation may create a problem. Negative moods may be attributed to premenstrual tension, when personality or situational factors may really deserve the blame. As a consequence, more "evidence" accumulates for premenstrual tension, and the premenstrual phase looks more villainous than it really is.

In another study, college students were asked to react to a variety of excuses for antisocial behavior (Ruble, Boggiano, & Brooks-Gunn, 1982). Some excuses involved personal fault ("I am really hungover from last night"), some involved pain ("I have a toothache this morning"), and some were menstrual-related ("I always get edgy right before my period"). In general, menstrual excuses were not perceived negatively. People were only some-what annoyed with a woman who attributed her grouchiness to her menstrual cycle, and they tended not to blame her for her behavior. These menstrual excuses were judged comparable to the pain-related excuses, and both of these kinds of excuses were considered more legitimate than the personal-fault excuses.

Notice a probable consequence of this tolerance for menstrual-related excuses. A woman may learn that people are more tolerant of menstrual-related excuses than personal-fault excuses. Therefore, when she has been antisocial and she is premenstrual, she may prefer to explain her behavior to others in terms of premenstrual tension. Once again, the premenstrual phase may be given more blame than it truly deserves.

Abnormal behavior. In 1980, Sandie Smith, a 29-year-old barmaid in London, killed her coworker. She was put on probation after testifying that the premenstrual syndrome had been responsible for her actions. Two years later, a 24-year-old New York mother beat her four-year-old daughter. Her attorney asked that the case be dismissed because the mother was a victim of the premenstrual syndrome (Parlee, 1982b).

The premenstrual syndrome has received an increasing amount of attention in the courts. As Laws (1983) points out, judges may believe that *women* are never violent or aggressive, but women with premenstrual tension are indeed antisocial. Some people argue that it causes a temporary mental disability, so that women who are premenstrual may not be responsible for their actions. As Sommer (1984) argues, the notion that PMS leaves some sufferers free from responsibility may cause problems. People may conclude that no woman can be trusted. As you can imagine, many feminists are pessimistic about the repercussions of this "It's all in your glands" interpretation. The use of the premenstrual syndrome in court cases leads people to suspect that all women may be out of control for part of every month.

Katharina Dalton, a British physician, is often cited in connection with the premenstrual syndrome and abnormal behavior (Dalton, 1977, 1983). She studied women who had killed themselves, had committed a crime, or had been admitted to a mental hospital. Because these women were more likely to be in the menstrual and premenstrual phases than chance would predict, Dalton concluded that women were more likely to behave abnormally during these times of their cycle than in the middle of their cycle. Her argument was that hormonal levels predispose women to commit crimes and other abnormal behavior.

Parlee (1982b) proposes another explanation. It may be that the stress of criminal or abnormal behavior affects the timing of the menstrual cycle. Thus, behavior influences hormones, rather than hormones influencing behavior. Rossi (1980) also makes a good point related to criminal behavior. Some women who are premenstrual may have increased swelling, which may make them somewhat more clumsy and therefore more likely to be caught. It might be that women who shoplift, for example, may be more likely to be arrested in the premenstrual period; they may not steal any more often at this time of month. Finally, we must remember that this information simply tells us that women who engage in abnormal behavior are more likely to do so during the premenstrual and menstrual phases of their cycle. It does not tell us anything about the behavior of "normal" women.

Coping with the premenstrual syndrome. After several days of reading material that presented the premenstrual syndrome in an uncritical light, I began to have visions of millions of women throughout the nation, severely depressed, anxious, and incapacitated. However, as Maccoby (1972) noted some years ago, the view that women are ruled by their hormonal cycles "gives little weight to the coping strategies whereby most women deal with their cyclic moods and continue to function effectively. Most working women do not cry at the office two days a month ..." (p. 371).

According to one study, 81 percent of women believe that they can function as well at work when they are menstruating as at other times of the month (Milow, 1983). (Interestingly, only 66 percent of men judged women to be equally competent at the two time periods.) It would be useful to know whether women are equally positive about their coping skills during the premenstrual phase. Try Demonstration 4.2 to find out reactions among your close acquaintances.

One study provides an interesting perspective on coping strategies. Ac-

Coping Skills During the Premenstrual Phase

If you are female, think of several close friends whom you can question. (Most males would probably have difficulty finding several women to interview, because of the taboo nature of this topic!) If your friends prefer, you could photocopy the questions and have them supply written answers.

1. Do you experience any changes in your mood before menstruation?
2. Do you find that you can function as well in your studies when it is several days before your period, in comparison to the rest of your cycle?
3. Do you rearrange your schedule to avoid anything in particular when you know you are in the premenstrual phase?
4. Suppose that you took an important exam. Two days later, your period arrives, along with a low grade on that exam. Would you blame the grade on the fact that you were in the premenstrual phase, or would you choose another explanation?
5. Do you make any special changes in your diet when you are in your premenstrual phase?
6. Have you heard of "premenstrual syndrome," which refers to the variety of symptoms that can occur before menstruation?
7. Do you experience any of the following during the premenstrual phase: headaches, tenderness of the breasts, swelling, or acne?
8. Do you think that people who experience premenstrual syndrome should "keep a stiff upper lip," or do you think that they should change their activities and take care of themselves, even if it disrupts plans they have made?

cording to Rossi & Rossi (1977), the variation that women show in mood across the days of the week is greater than the variation that they show across the phases of their menstrual cycle. If women can learn to cope with Mondays, it seems likely that they can learn to cope with menstrual-related mood swings.

Several authors have suggestions on how women who have premenstrual problems can cope with their problems. For example, Lever and Brush (1981) suggest that women should discuss the problem with the people they live with, so that they can be more understanding and helpful during the premenstrual phase. Women should also plan their schedules, wherever possible, so that important events occur at other times of the menstrual cycle. In some areas, PMS support groups have been formed. It may be helpful to talk with other women about how they cope with PMS.

A particularly controversial approach to dealing with the premenstrual syndrome involves the use of medication. Dalton (1977), whose work on abnormal behavior we discussed earlier, enthusiastically recommends the use of progesterone. However, in carefully controlled studies summarized by Green (1982), progesterone did not provide effective relief. Similarly, oral contraceptives, tranquilizers, and vitamins have not been demonstrated to be effective (Budoff, 1983). As Abplanalp (1983) concludes, no treatment that is currently available is unconditionally suitable for sufferers of PMS.

Some authors do recommend a change in diet to relieve some of the physical symptoms of the premenstrual syndrome. For example, Budoff recommends a reduction in salt during the week before menstruation. This will relieve bloating and water retention. Breast tenderness can also be relieved by avoiding the caffeine contained in coffee, tea, cola, and chocolate.

It is difficult to talk about coping with the premenstrual syndrome when we are not even certain about what PMS is or the extent to which it exists (or even, according to some, *if* it exists). However, it is clear that the media have become enchanted with PMS. This should not surprise you, because you will recall from the discussion in Chapter 1 that the media tend to emphasize differences, such as the difference between premenstrual behavior and behavior during the rest of the cycle. In contrast, studies that minimize the importance of PMS will be ignored. We can hope, however, that serious researchers will continue to examine the premenstrual syndrome systematically. Once we know more about the hormonal and psychological/cultural factors underlying PMS, we may be in a better position to recommend effective coping strategies.

Abilities

We have discussed menstrual pain and premenstrual tension, which are certainly the most publicized aspects of the menstrual cycle. Now let us turn to another topic. Do various kinds of abilities vary with the phases of the menstrual cycle? The answer to this question depends upon the kind of ability we are considering: perceptual, physical, or cognitive.

First, let us consider perceptual abilities. You probably haven't given much thought to it, but if you are a menstruating woman, do you seem to be more sensitive to faint lights at certain times of your cycle? Do you notice pain more at some times than at other times? According to Parlee (1983), some kinds of perceptual abilities do show cyclical variation. Specifically, women tend to be more sensitive to faint lights and odors at about the time of ovulation, in the middle of the cycle. Sensitivity to pain also varies; women are more sensitive to painful stimuli in the menstrual and postmenstrual phases than they are in the premenstrual phase. Hearing is more complicated, because women seem to show two phases at which they are most sensitive, at ovulation and again at the beginning of the menstrual phase. There don't seem to be any consistent findings about menstrual changes in sensitivity to taste, temperature, and touch.

One reason it is difficult for women to notice changes in their perceptual abilities is that it is hard to measure these abilities in a consistent fashion (Matlin, 1983b). Demonstration 4.3 provides a method for measuring smell sensitivity throughout the menstrual cycle, though it is far less precise than the way smell would be assessed in the laboratory.

Physical abilities may show some variation throughout the menstrual

Sensitivity to Odors during the Menstrual Cycle

For this demonstration, you will need a bottle of weak perfume and a ruler. Hold the perfume at arm's length and take off the top. Gradually move the bottle closer to your nose until you can just barely smell it. Measure the distance between the bottle opening and your nose. Repeat the measurement process at one week intervals. Are you more sensitive to odors during ovulation? (In other words can you detect the odor at a greater distance?) (If you are a male, and do not know a woman who might be interested in trying this demonstration, you might still be interested in seeing whether you have any cyclical variation in your own sensitivity to odors.)

cycle, but this variation is neither large nor universal. For instance, sports performance doesn't seem to suffer substantially during the premenstrual or menstrual phases. Young women have set world records and won Olympics competitions during these "critical" times (Brooks-Gunn & Matthews, 1979).

How about cognitive abilities? It may surprise you to learn that thinking skills show very little variation throughout the menstrual cycle. A wide variety of skills have been tested, including memory, spelling, mathematical tasks and scores on psychology exams. Researchers have generally concluded that women's performance is no worse during the premenstrual and menstrual phases than during other parts of the cycle (Asso, 1983; Dan, 1979; Golub, 1976b; Sommer, 1982, 1983). As Sommer (1982) summarizes the results, "The preponderance of evidence indicates that cognitive performance or mental ability is not significantly affected by menstrual cycle variables" (p. 101). She also notes that the better-designed studies are least likely to show any changes throughout the menstrual cycle.

Please do not misinterpret this conclusion. Some women, some of the time, on some tasks, surely perform worse before and during their periods than they might at mid-cycle. In general, though, there is no substantial effect. As we will stress throughout this book, individual differences among women are large.

Many women think, nonetheless, that their performance is worse before and during their periods. There is clearly a complex relationship among the three factors of menstrual phase, beliefs, and actual performance (Dan, 1979).

Regarding the relationship between abilities and the menstrual cycle, we can conclude that there may be some variation in perceptual sensitivities across the cycle, but physical and cognitive skills show little change. The lack of change in cognitive skills is particularly important because of a practical implication. From time to time, a particularly offensive "expert" proclaims that women should not be allowed to hold important positions in business or government because their cognitive skills evaporate at certain times of their menstrual cycle. As you have seen, there is no evidence for this position.

Sexuality

What effect does the menstrual cycle have on sexual desires and sexual behavior? The first part of the question is more difficult to answer than the second. Williams and Williams (1982) review studies on variations that women may experience in their sexual desires. Some studies show that women have the strongest desires after their menstrual periods, but others show peaks at ovulation or premenstrually. It may be that it is simply too difficult to reliably measure something as subjective as sexual desires.

It is easier to measure sexual *behavior* in an objective fashion. This kind of research asks heterosexual women to record their frequency of intercourse on a daily basis. Most of this research shows a low level of sexual behavior during the menstrual period, with the maximum level just after the period. Many—but not all—of the studies also show a small upswing in the frequency of intercourse a few days before menstruation, but this rise is small compared to the rise after menstruation (Williams & Williams, 1982).

Why should the frequency of intercourse be highest just after menstruation? According to research by Gold and Adams (1981), this represents a rebound effect. Because the frequency of intercourse is so low during menstruation, couples "make up for lost time" afterwards. Women report the same increased frequency of intercourse after their partner had been absent for some time.

The rise in frequency of intercourse before menstruation is not fully explained by an "anticipation of deprivation," according to Gold and Adams. There is some speculation, though, that the premenstrual increase may be due to the swelling that occurs in the genital area before menstruation, a condition that can make intercourse more pleasurable (Masters & Johnson, 1966; Williams & Williams, 1982).

☐ SECTION SUMMARY: ▪ Physical and Psychological Reactions to the Menstrual Cycle

1. Dysmenorrhea includes painful cramps, lower back pain, and headache.
2. Premenarcheal girls expect to experience more pain than their postmenarcheal peers actually report.
3. Prostaglandins, which are produced as menstruation approaches, seem to be at least partially responsible for menstrual pain.
4. Treatments for menstrual pain have included psychotherapy, surgery, medication, heat, exercises, and diet changes.
5. The premenstrual syndrome is a label that has been given to a variety of symptoms that may include headaches, breast tenderness, swelling, acne, and premenstrual tension.

6. The premenstrual syndrome seems to have both psychological/cultural and hormonal explanations; there are large individual differences in the extent to which women experience the premenstrual syndrome.

7. Studies of mood swing that use retrospective questionnaires often report negative moods premenstrually, but women's recall of their moods may not have been accurate.

8. Studies that ask women to rate their mood throughout the menstrual cycle sometimes show negative moods premenstrually, but women's expectations may have influenced their ratings; when women are not aware that the study concerns menstruation, they may not show cyclical mood swings.

9. Older women are more likely than young women to show mood swings that are related to the menstrual cycle.

10. Two studies in which women were not aware of the purpose of the study showed evidence of cyclical mood swings; one study involved the kinds of stories told at different phases of the menstrual cycle and the other study involved mothers bringing their children to the doctor.

11. If a woman is in a negative mood and she is believed to be premenstrual, people explain her mood in terms of biological factors; people are also quite tolerant of menstrual-related excuses.

12. Women who commit crimes or act extremely abnormally are more likely to be in the premenstrual and menstrual phases than chance alone would predict; however, there are many explanations for these findings other than that hormones produce abnormal behavior.

13. Most women manage to cope with the premenstrual syndrome; suggestions include schedule arrangements, PMS support groups, and diet changes.

14. Sensitivity to visual stimuli, odors, pain, and hearing changes somewhat during the menstrual cycle, but physical and cognitive performance shows little variability.

15. The relationship between sexual desires and the menstrual cycle is unclear at present, but sexual behavior reaches a low level during the menstrual period, with a maximum level just afterwards.

ATTITUDES TOWARD MENSTRUATION

We have occasionally referred to attitudes toward menstruation throughout this chapter. Now let's examine them in more detail. First we'll look at some menstrual myths and taboos. Then we'll discuss expressions and jokes about menstruation. Finally, we'll talk about positive attitudes toward menstruation.

Menstrual Myths and Taboos

Menstrual myths certainly have a long history. For example, the Roman naturalist the Elder Pliny, who lived in the first century A.D., wrote:

> But nothing could easily be found that is more remarkable than the monthly flux of women. Contact with it turns new wine sour, crops touched by it become barren, grafts die, seeds in gardens are dried up, the fruit of trees falls off, the bright surface of mirrors in which it is merely reflected is dimmed, the edge of steel and the gleam of ivory are dulled, hives of bees die, even bronze and iron are at once seized by rust, and a horrible smell fills the air; to taste it drives dogs mad and infects their bites with an incurable poison. [cited in Novell, 1965, p. 222]

Menstrual myths and taboos have persisted in this century in many cultures, to differing extents. For example, there is sometimes a taboo against contact with menstruating women, and menstrual blood is regarded as a pollutant. A New Guinea tribesman is reported to have divorced his wife because she had slept on his blanket while menstruating. When it seemed that he was still not quite safe from her evil influence, he murdered her with an ax (Delaney, Lupton, & Toth, 1976). Many menstrual practices, such as this one, seem to reflect a belief in female pollution (Paige & Paige, 1981).

Some menstrual myths and taboos persist in less dramatic forms today. For example, Williams (1983) received some interesting responses from 9- to 12-year-old young women in suburban Midwest schools. She found that 36 percent of them believed that they should not go swimming during menstruation; 16 percent believed that active sports should be avoided; 10 percent thought that there is something dirty or unclean about a menstruating woman. Milow (1983) reported that in her role as an educational consultant for a tampon company, she had been asked whether menstrual blood was bad blood, whether hair permanents could "take" when a woman was menstruating, and whether a tooth filled during menstruation would fall out. Some women reported that they couldn't go to the school prom when menstruating because the flowers that their dates had given them would wilt.

The most common taboo uncovered by Snow and Johnson (1977), who gave questionnaires to women in a Michigan public clinic, involved ideas about intercourse. They found that 62 percent of the women felt that intercourse should be avoided during menstruation. Most of the women thought that intercourse during this time would be unhealthy, causing problems such as an increase in menstrual flow, hemorrhage, infections, and uterine cancer. Several women avoided intercourse during menstruation because they were

Attitudes toward Menstruation

Present these questions to several close friends. The topic of attitudes toward menstruation may be more socially acceptable than one's own experience of menstruation, so that a female may feel comfortable asking these questions to a group of friends. Males may be able to ask them to male friends, if there are no women who could be asked about these issues.

1. Have you heard of any activities that menstruating women should not do?
2. Have you ever been told that a menstruating woman is bad luck?
3. Which people can you discuss menstruation with? Which friends? Which relatives?
4. Would you feel embarrassed if your biology professor discussed menstruation? Would it matter if the professor was a male or a female?
5. Do you feel that there is something dirty or unclean about a menstruating woman?
6. Do you think couples should change their sexual activities when a woman is menstruating?
7. What kinds of menstrual slang words have you heard? How about menstrual jokes?
8. Have you ever heard anything positive about menstruation? Can you yourself think of anything positive about menstruation?

under the misimpression that this was the time when they were most likely to become pregnant. Undoubtedly, taboos contribute substantially to the low frequency of intercourse during menstruation.

Gloria Steinem (1983) speculates about how menstruation would be treated if men could menstruate and women could not. Suddenly, menstruation would become an enviable, masculine event: "Men would brag about how long and how much.... Young boys would talk about it as the envied beginning of manhood. Gifts, religious ceremonies, family dinners, and stag parties would mark the day.... Street guys would invent slang ("He's a three-pad man").... " (p. 338).

This section has been a testimonial to one of the themes of this book, the idea that something associated with women—their menstrual periods—will be negatively evaluated. Are menstrual attitudes always negative, though? Try to assess these attitudes among your friends by trying Demonstration 4.4.

Menstrual Expressions and Jokes

We saw earlier that menarche is relatively invisible in our culture, consistent with the theme regarding the invisibility of women. Similarly, we cannot speak openly about menstruation; it is a taboo topic. Instead, we must invent euphemisms, which are alternate, more pleasant ways of saying the same thing. For example, have you ever heard the word "menstruation" mentioned on television? Recently, I saw an ad refering to "that time of the month" . . . and it apparently did not refer to the time when the car payment was due. According to Ernster (1975), menstrual euphemisms arise in the same fashion as expressions for sexual and excretory functions. In addition, as she suggests, the continued use of menstrual euphemisms perpetuates the view that menstruating women are polluting and dangerous. As a result, they are socially inferior. Here are a few of the expressions that Ernster located:

"Aunt Sylvia is visiting me" (a reference to a female visitor)
"I'm going steady with George" (a reference to a male)
"It's that time again" (a time reference)
"The curse" (a negative reference to distress)
"Wearing red shoes today" (a reference to blood)
"Mouse mattresses" (a reference to sanitary pads) [p. 6]

Of course there are also jokes about menstruation, just as there are jokes about excretion and sex. These seemed to flourish at my junior-high school, and mostly seemed to concern used sanitary pads. Delaney and her coauthors (1976) have a chapter on menstrual jokes, which range from the intercourse taboo, to missing periods because of pregnancy, to the inevitable sanitary pads.

Positive Attitudes toward Menstruation

Several years ago, a colleague of mine pointed out that studies on menstruation emphasized menstrual distress. Why, she wondered, was there no examination of the positive aspects of menstruation, perhaps in the form of a Menstrual-Joy Questionnaire? This idea may strike you as rather farfetched. However, there are some positive aspects to menstruation, though maybe not enough to offset the negative aspects.

For example, Brooks, Ruble, and Clarke (1977) asked college women about their attitudes toward menstruation. The questions fell into five categories:

1. Debilitating effects, such as being tired and ineffective when menstruating.
2. Bothersome aspects, such as menstruation being something that must "be put up with" and men having an advantage in not menstruating.
3. Predictability of menstruation, such as being able to anticipate menstruation because of mood changes and physical signs.

FIGURE 4.4. Reactions toward menstruation (based on Brooks, et al., 1977)

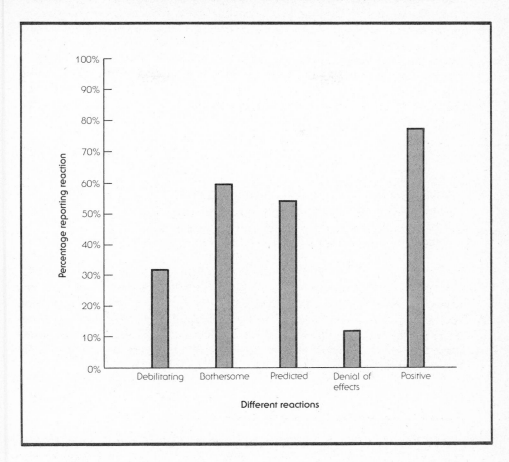

4. Denial of effects, such as not noticing effects of menstruation and believing that those with PMS are neurotic.
5. Positive effects, such as menstruation providing a way for a woman to keep in touch with her body and menstruation being a recurring affirmation of womanhood.

The results, shown in Figure 4.4, may surprise you. Notice that women are unlikely to deny the effects of menstruation. They are also unlikely to think that menstruation is completely debilitating. Roughly half find menstruation bothersome (a negative quality) and predictable (a somewhat positive quality). Most intriguing, though, is that more than three-quarters agree that there are positive aspects.

Anne Frank wrote a passage in her diary that captures the bitter-sweet mixture of emotions she felt about her menstrual periods:

> Each time I have a period ... I have the feeling that in spite of all the pain, unpleasantness, nastiness, I have a sweet secret and that is why, although it is nothing but a nuisance to me in a way, I always long for the time that I shall feel that secret within me again. [1972, p. 117]

In addition to these positive effects, such as keeping in touch with your body, menstruation being a sign of womanhood, and the private-secret aspect, women have found other positive qualities in their menstrual periods. One friend mentioned that menstruation represents sisterhood—not simply womanhood—because she knows that when she is menstruating there are women all over the world of different races, shapes, and ages who are menstruating as well. A student noted that her understanding of the physiological aspects of menstruation, with its elaborate provisions for the rise and fall of hormone levels, made her appreciate her body and its cycles. Less poetically, but very significantly, many women greet a menstrual period with joy because it means that they are not pregnant.

This discussion of the positive aspects of menstruation should not be misconstrued as a statement that menstruating women would never have problems if only they had positive attitudes. As Asso (1983) mentions, fluid retention can be unsightly, uncomfortable, and depressing. It won't disappear with a little creative thinking! However, there are cultural and psychological aspects to some components of menstruation. Also, it is easier to deal with physiologically based problems if you know their cause and their likely duration, and if you know that other women have similar experiences.

Furthermore, as Asso stresses, attitudes are changing. It is interesting to know about Pliny's ideas on menstruating women or about the taboos of New Guinea tribesmen. It's also intriguing—though alarming—that some less exotic menstrual myths and taboos persist today in the United States. In general, however, menstruating women are regarded as "normal." Unger, Brown, and Larson (1983) asked college students to sort photos of women into two piles, trying to guess whether the photo was taken when the woman was menstruating or not. The photos that were categorized in the "menstruating" pile turned out to be just as attractive as the photos categorized in the "not-menstruating" pile. Women were not downgraded for their menstrual condition. With the current emphasis on self-help and consumer education, we can be optimistic that attitudes will continue to grow somewhat more positive.

1. Menstrual myths and taboos often reflect a belief in female pollution.
2. A common current taboo involves avoiding intercourse during menstruation.
3. Since menstruation is a taboo concept, there are many euphemisms and jokes about it.
4. Women are positive about some aspects of menstruation, such as menstruation providing a way for women to keep in touch with their bodies.
5. College students do not consider menstruating women to be less attractive than women who are not menstruating.

Chapter Review Questions

1. Discuss how young girls learn about menstruation, and why the quality of this preparation is important.
2. What could you conclude about attitudes toward menstruation if you knew only about attitudes toward menarche in the United States?
3. Discuss the impact that menarche has on a young woman in the United States, and speculate about whether the impact might be greater or less in a culture that greeted menarche with greater celebration.
4. Make a list of the structures and substances involved in menstruation, and describe how each of these is important. Describe how feedback is important in the menstrual cycle, giving examples.
5. The fourth theme of this textbook is that women aren't all the same; they show wide variation in their responses to life events. Discuss this theme in relation to menstrual pain and PMS.
6. An important issue in this chapter is whether aspects of menstruation are "in the head" or "in the glands." Discuss menstrual pain and the premenstrual syndrome with respect to this issue.
7. How could a woman's treatment of menstrual pain and the premenstrual syndrome be related to her ideas about whether these problems are "in the head" or "in the glands"?
8. Discuss the various kinds of studies that have been conducted on mood swings during the menstrual cycle, and explain why some of these stud-

ies do not provide clear evidence of premenstrual tension; then describe what you would conclude from the present evidence.

9. Explain why attitudes toward menarche and menstrual myths and taboos are indications of two themes in this book, negative attitudes toward women and the invisibility of women.

10. The term "bitter-sweet" was used to describe attitudes toward menstruation. Why is this an appropriate term?

☐ NEW TERMS

menarche	fallopian tube
puberty	uterus
hypothalamus	endometrium
pituitary gland	ovulation
follicle-stimulating hormone (FSH)	Mittelschmerz
follicles	corpus luteum
luteinizing hormone (LH)	dysmenorrhea
estrogen	prostaglandins
progesterone	premenstrual syndrome (PMS)
ovaries	premenstrual tension
ova (ovum)	

☐ RECOMMENDED READINGS

Asso, D. (1983). *The real menstrual cycle.* Chichester, England: Wiley. ■ This is a scholarly review that primarily focuses on the biological and psychological changes associated with the menstrual cycle.

Budoff, P. W. (1983). *No more menstrual cramps and other good news.* New York: Putnam. ■ Of the many popularized books on the menstrual cycle, this seems to be one of the most reasonable and practical.

Golub, S. (Ed.) (1983). *Lifting the curse of menstruation: A feminist appraisal of the influence of menstruation on women's lives.* New York: Haworth. ■ This book contains seven chapters on a wide variety of topics concerned with menstruation; it provides one of the best overviews of psychological aspects of menstruation.

Golub, S. (Ed.) (1983). *Menarche.* Lexington, Mass.: Lexington Books. ■ This edited volume discusses aspects of menarche such as physiological factors affecting the timing of menarche, psychological aspects of menarche, and menstrual education.

CHAPTER 5

ACHIEVEMENT MOTIVATION AND ACHIEVEMENT ATTITUDES

- Basically, men and women are similar in their interests in achievement and success.

- Women are more worried than men about the bad consequences that can result from being highly successful.

- People tend to think that a woman who is successful will eventually have to pay a price for her success.

- Women consistently have less self-confidence than men in an achievement situation.

- Among people with traditional gender roles, women are more likely than men to enjoy achieving through the accomplishments of other people.

- Men and women give similar estimates of their IQs.

- When a woman succeeds on some task, she tends to say that her success is due to ability, whereas when a man succeeds, he tends to say that his success is due to hard work.

- If people think that a man wrote an article, they are likely to rate it higher than if they think a woman wrote it.

- People are more likely to be prejudiced against a woman's accomplishment when she has a well-established reputation.

- If a man and a woman have both accomplished something, people are likely to say that *he* succeeded because of his ability, but *she* succeeded because she was lucky or the task was easy.

In the summer of 1984, fans watching the Olympics heard three prominent women athletes talking about their experiences during the competition. Gymnast Mary Lou Retton commented after performing the perfect vault that would guarantee her a Gold Medal, "I knew I had it. Listen, I knew by my run that I had it. I knew it when I was in the air!" During the Olympic 3,000-meter run, Mary Decker tripped over the British runner, Zola Budd. She recalled, "My first thought was, I have to get up. But as soon as I made the slightest move, I felt the muscle tear or pull." Budd's manager remembered that he had consoled Budd by assuring her that it was her first Olympics and that she should be proud; Budd's only response was, "How's Mary?" (Images, 1984).

Are women interested in achievement? Are they exhilarated by the prospect of success and devastated by failure? It's difficult to draw any conclusions from the words of these three women, for whom achievement motivation has clearly been a crucial factor in their success. Retton's lust for the Gold Medal is obvious in her quotation, and Decker's automatic reaction of continuing in the race clearly reveals her goal-oriented persistence. Yet Budd's immediate response was concern for her competitor . . . a response that some of you may admire, and others may condemn.

Throughout our discussion of achievement in this chapter, we will see that there are tremendous individual differences in women's motivations to achieve and their attitudes toward achievement, an observation that is clearly consistent with the fourth theme of this book. These individual differences among women are so large (and so, presumably, are the differences among men) that any differences between the sexes is relatively small, an idea that you will recognize as the first theme of the book. As we'll discuss in the first section of this chapter, men and women are fairly similar in their motivation to achieve and in any tendency to worry about the negative consequences of success. This same theme continues in the second section, where we will see that there may be sex differences in self-confidence in some situations, but in other situations the sex differences disappear. Furthermore, women and men tend to give similar reasons for *why* they succeeded or failed at an achievement task.

According to this book's second theme, people react differently to men and women, even when those men and women are similar. The last section of this chapter illustrates this principle well, because there is a tendency to downgrade the achievements of women. There is also a tendency for people to claim that there are different reasons for men's and women's successes (and also for their failures).

☐ ACHIEVEMENT MOTIVATION AND RELATED TOPICS

Topics related to gender and achievement motivation have attracted widespread attention in the last 15 to 20 years. Kaufman and Richardson (1982), refer to an "outpouring of popular and academic works explaining women and their achievements" (p. ix). Two ideas gained popularity. The first idea was that women might not be as motivated to achieve as men are. The second idea—even more warmly welcomed—was that women are more likely than men to avoid achieving because they believe that success may bring unhappiness. In this section, we will explore these two ideas as well as other proposals related to achievement motivation and gender. In all cases, notice that these theories involve person-blame explanations. As noted in the first chapter, psychologists in the 1970s tried to explain why women did not obtain the same positions in society that men did. Rather than blaming the situation for women's lower positions, people tended to blame women ... some internal defect within women must account for their lack of success (Unger, 1983). As we will see, researchers in the 1980s acknowledge that sex differences are too small to provide a good explanation for women's lower positions.

You may notice an interesting bias in the kinds of tasks that are used in studies of achievement motivation. The areas that are considered successful usually have a masculine bias (Henley, 1985; Paludi, 1985). Success may be represented by achievement at a prestigious occupation, academic excellence, and other accomplishments that are associated with traditionally masculine values. Accomplishments that are associated with traditionally feminine values receive little or no attention. An adolescent woman may manage to entertain a group of six children, so that they are all playing cooperatively, yet this kind of accomplishment is not studied in the topic of achievement motivation. Successfully comforting a friend or making a stranger feel welcome at a party would not be considered "achievements." Once again, women and topics that are important to them are invisible in the psychological literature.

Achievement Motivation

Try Demonstration 5.1, which illustrates a method for measuring achievement motivation. **Achievement motivation** is the desire to strive for success in situations involving a standard of excellence (McClelland, et al., 1953). A person who is high in achievement motivation might try to get the highest A in organic chemistry, the leading part in the college musical, or the top award in athletics.

Achievement motivation is often measured by using the Thematic Apperception Test, or TAT. The **Thematic Apperception Test** asks people to make up stories about a series of pictures, similar to the one in Demonstration 5.1. The test assumes that people will project their own motivations and interests onto the characters in the pictures. Notice whether the story you wrote stressed achievement, working hard, or excelling. If your stories consistently mentioned these themes, you would receive a high achievement-motivation score on this test.

Summaries of the early research on achievement motivation concluded that women receive lower achievement-motivation scores than men. These

The Thematic Apperception Test

Look at the picture below and write a paragraph about it. Who are the people involved? What are they doing, and what are they thinking?

summaries also concluded that men could be encouraged to become more achievement oriented by telling them that the TAT measured intelligence, whereas women's scores were unaffected by these instructions (Alper, 1974; McClelland, et al., 1953).

Stewart and Chester (1982) recently examined the research on achievement motivation. The majority of the studies they examined found no difference between men and women in their achievement-motivation scores. Other research confirms that black males and females do not differ in achievement motivation (Crew, 1982).

Stewart and Chester also discovered many studies in which men's scores— as well as women's—were not affected by the nature of the TAT instructions. Thus, we see an example of the tendency discussed in the first chapter. Studies that found sex differences were often celebrated and given wide publicity, whereas studies that found sex similarities were often forgotten. This kind of bias created the illusion that men and women differed in their achievement motivation, yet an unbiased analysis reveals a pattern of sex similarities.

Fear of Success

I n this demonstration, you will write a paragraph in response to a lead sentence. If you are a female, complete this sentence with a paragraph: "After first term finals, Ann finds herself at the top of her medical school class . . .".

If you are a male, complete this sentence with a paragraph: "After first term finals, John finds himself at the top of his medical school class . . .".

Fear of Success

At the end of the 1960s, Matina Horner proposed that women are more likely than men to be afraid of success (Horner, 1968, 1972, 1978). Introductory textbooks and magazine articles immediately responded by publicizing this research widely. As discussed in Chapter 1, the publication process tends to emphasize the studies that report sex differences. The numerous studies that found *no* sex differences have received little attention from the popular press. In fact, the current consensus is that sex differences in fear of success are neither large nor consistent. Let's look at Horner's work and subsequent research in more detail.

Horner's research. Horner suggested that women may want to achieve, but their achievement motivation is diminished by concerns about being too successful. According to Horner, this **fear of success** involves the fear that success in competitive achievement situations will lead to unpleasant consequences. These unpleasant consequences include unpopularity and a loss of femininity. A bright woman faces a double bind in achievement situations. She knows that if she fails on a task, she will not meet her own standards of performance. On the other hand, she knows that if she succeeds on a task, she may be rejected because she will not meet society's standards of femininity.

Horner proposed that men do not face a double bind because success in competitive achievement situations is consistent with masculine gender roles. Men are therefore encouraged to be successful.

Demonstration 5.2 illustrates Horner's technique for measuring fear of success. Notice that people must make up a story based on a sentence cue, rather than the picture cue used to measure achievement motivation. However, both tests assume that people will project their own motivations onto the central character.

Horner asked women to respond to the "Anne" version of the test, and she asked men to respond to the "John" version. Then she scored the tests for whether they mentioned unpleasant consequences of success. Her results showed that 62 percent of the women and 9 percent of the men showed fear of success. This sex difference was highly significant.

Women tended to write stories in which Ann was socially rejected or worried about her femininity. Here is one woman's response:

> Anne is an acne faced bookworm. She runs to the bulletin board and finds she's on top. "As usual" she smarts off. A chorus of groans is the rest of the class's reply. Anne was always praised for her initiative and study habits—mainly because these were the only things one could praise her for. She studies 12 hours a day, and lives at home to save money. She rents her books. "Well it certainly paid off. All the Friday and Saturday nights with my books, who needs dates, fun—I'll be the best woman doctor alive." And yet, a twinge of sadness comes thru—she wonders what she really has. But, as is her habit, she promptly erases that thought, and goes off reciting aloud the 231 bones in her wrist. [Horner, 1978, p. 58]

Men tended to write stories in which John was a conscientious, hard-working person. His hard work brought rich rewards and social approval rather than rejection.

You can see why Horner's research captured the interest of the popular press. Her research showed a clear-cut difference between women's and men's responses. According to this explanation, women are less likely to become senators, doctors, executives, and other high-ranking professionals because they are afraid of the consequences of success in these occupations.

Subsequent research on fear of success. In the years following Horner's original research, psychologists have grown increasingly skeptical about sex differences in fear of success. Let's look at some of the issues.

One possible explanation for the sex differences in fear of success involves the following logic. In Horner's research, women were asked to write about Anne's success as a medical student, and medical-school attendance is generally considered to be "sex inappropriate" for women. In contrast, men were asked to write about John, for whom medical-school attendance would be considered to be "sex appropriate." Perhaps women's responses reflected a concern about "sex-inappropriate" behavior, rather than fear of success. Pursuing this logic, Cherry and Deaux (1978) asked people to complete stories about Anne and John, who were at the top of either their medical-school class or their nursing-school class. They found that both men and women wrote stories high in fear of success for Anne in medical school *and* for John in nursing school. It seems that people write stories about fear of success when either females or males are successful in a profession that is traditional for the other sex. Realistically, our society is often intolerant when people deviate from the cultural norms about what men and women *should* do (Condry & Dyer, 1976).

Furthermore, another group of researchers argued that women might simply be responding to a widely-held stereotype when they write about Anne—rather than projecting their own fear of success in their stories (Monahan, et al., 1974). These researchers tested the stereotyping explanation by asking males and females to write about both Anne and John. The results demonstrated that the males wrote an even higher proportion of negative responses to the Anne cue than did the females. Women may not be anxious about succeeding; they may merely share society's general condemnation of a female who is too successful.

Perhaps most important, is the fact that research performed since Horner's original study—using methods similar to hers—has not demonstrated substantial sex differences. Tresemer (1977) examined a number of well-controlled studies. He reported great variability in the incidence of fear of success and concluded that men and women do not appear to differ in their fear of success. Zuckerman and Wheeler (1975) reached a similar conclusion. Paludi (1984) summarizes her review of 64 studies that showed fear of success having a median of 49 percent in females (with a range between 6 percent and 93 percent) and a median of 45 percent in males (with a range between 7 percent and 95 percent). Also, black women do not differ significantly from black men and in their fear of success (Paludi, 1984).

Let's consider a representative study that examined 700 undergraduates, certainly a large enough sample (Levine & Crumrine, 1975). In all, 76 percent of the male students wrote at least one negative sentence for the "John" story. In comparison, 73 percent of the female students wrote at least one negative sentence for the "Anne" story.

What should we conclude about fear of success? It seems reasonably clear that the standard way of measuring fear of success has *not* uncovered a large sex difference, one that could explain why there are so few women in high-prestige occupations. It is possible, though, that the paper-and-pencil test that is used to measure fear of success is not sensitive enough to pick up the anxieties that women really experience.

It may be that fear of success is relevant for some women on some occasions. A student told me about a professor who warned her she would be happier raising a family, rather than pursuing her goal of medical school. Will she feel some pangs of self-doubt during the first anatomy exam? Will these pangs of self-doubt evolve into a fear of success? If a woman really is afraid of success, does she actually change her behavior in any significant way, for instance by dropping out of medical school?

Also, women may be afraid of some kinds of success, but not others. Women may not differ from men when success is defined as accomplishment that does not harm other people. However, women may be more afraid of the kind of success involved in the kinds of competition where their achievement means that other people must suffer emotionally. Women may not enjoy the kind of success that involves winning, no matter what else happens or who else is hurt (Paludi, 1984; Sassen, 1980).

In summary, the methods that are currently used to measure fear of success have not demonstrated any overall sex differences in this area. Even if sex differences in fear of success could be demonstrated using some new method, we would need to show that fear of success actually influences women's career choices before we could argue that fear of success can explain why women are scarce in high-prestige occupations.

Alternate Interpretations of Achievement

Women and men don't seem to differ in their achievement motivation or in their fear of success. Are there any other areas in which their achievement behavior might differ? Several theories have been proposed, and it is too early to tell whether research will show us that there are consistent sex differences (Depner & Veroff, 1979; Parsons & Goff, 1980). Let's look at one of these newer theories, which was proposed by Jean Lipman-Blumen and her coauthors (Lipman-Blumen, et al., 1980, 1983).

The theory developed by Lipman-Blumen contrasts two styles of achieving, called direct achieving style and relational achieving style. **Direct achieving style** is used by people who confront achievement tasks very directly; a direct achiever may enjoy winning over other competitors or may simply enjoy the thrill of accomplishment. **Relational achieving style** is used by people who seek success through their relationships with others; a relational achiever may achieve indirectly through a spouse's accomplishments or by working in collaboration with other people.

Tests designed to measure direct versus relational achieving styles have been administered to more than 1000 people (Lipman-Blumen, et al., 1980). Older, more traditional people tended to show sharp sex differences in the expected direction. Men scored higher on the direct scales, whereas women scored higher on the relational ones. Students in engineering and business programs tended to show exactly the opposite pattern. Women in these nontraditional areas were slightly more direct and less relational than their male classmates. Women therefore seem to show wide variability in the kind of achieving style they prefer—as do men—an observation that is consistent with the fourth theme of the book. There appear to be no consistent sex differences in achieving styles, just as there are none in either achievement motivation or fear of success. The first theme of the book pervades the area of achievement motivation: Sex similarities are more prevalent than sex differences.

□ SECTION SUMMARY: ▪ Achievement Motivation and Related Topics

1. Achievement motivation is the desire to strive for success in situations that involve a standard of excellence.
2. Early researchers concluded that there were sex differences in achievement motivation and in responses to achievement-oriented instructions; it now seems that there are no sex differences in this area.
3. Matina Horner proposed that women are more likely than men to have a fear of success, or a fear of the unpleasant consequences of success.

4. Subsequent research demonstrated that women might be writing fear-of-success stories about a successful woman in medical school because of their concern about "sex-inappropriate" behavior or because they are aware of society's general stereotype that women should not be too successful.
5. A review of the research concluded that men and women are similar in their fear of success.
6. Among the alternate interpretations of achievement is Lipman-Blumen's theory about direct and relational achieving styles; among traditional people, men tend to be direct and women tend to be relational, but women in a nontraditional profession tend to be more direct and less relational than the men in their profession.

☐ PERCEPTIONS OF ONE'S OWN ACHIEVEMENTS

What do you think about your achievements, both past and future? How well do you think you'll do in the course for which you are reading this book? Do you think that your success in a course can be traced to your ability, hard work, or some other factor? In this portion of the chapter, we'll look at the research that has tried to uncover sex differences in these two areas, self-confidence and attributions for success or failure.

Self-Confidence in Achievement Settings

Suppose that you were to ask your female friends and your male friends to estimate their IQs. Who would provide the higher estimate? When Hogan (1978) asked nearly 2000 people this question, the results showed that females supplied substantially lower IQ estimates than males.

Hogan's findings fit nicely with some earlier research. Crandall (1969, 1975) asked children between the ages of 7 and 12 to estimate how well they would perform on six different tasks. Included among the tasks were brain teasers, mazes, and memory tests. In each case, she asked the children to estimate how well they expected to perform. She found that boys supplied higher estimates than girls for all six tasks. Crandall also found that male college students gave higher estimates than female college students for the grades they expected to receive in their courses.

From a variety of evidence, it might be tempting to conclude that women are consistently lower than men in self-confidence on achievement tasks. Lenney (1977) inspected all the available information, however, and she reached a somewhat different conclusion. She concluded that women are indeed lower in self-confidence in *many* achievement settings, but that there are several important exceptions.

Before we discuss those exceptions, notice how Lenney's conclusions illustrate an important part of the first theme of this book. It is difficult to find clear sex differences that hold true in all situations. More often, we find sex differences when we examine men and women in some situations, but we find sex similarities when we examine them in other situations.

Lenney identified three important kinds of situations in which women and men are *similar* in their self-confidence. Let's examine these three situations.

1. *Women and men are similar in self-confidence on certain kinds of tasks.* When a task is described as being something at which females are skilled, the sex differences in self-confidence tend to evaporate (Stein, Pohly, & Mueller, 1971). Nicholls (1975) found that sex differences were substantial when an angle-matching task was introduced as a test of intelligence, but they disappeared when it was introduced as a test of size perception. It seems that women feel inferior on masculine tasks, but they feel as competent as men on feminine or neutral tasks. (Notice that they do not feel *more* confident than men on the "feminine" tasks.)

2. *Women and men are similar in self-confidence when they are given clear feedback.* In one study, people were told to unscramble anagrams that were either very easy or very difficult (House & Perney, 1974). Thus, they received clear feedback about how well they had done on the task. They next estimated how many items they expected to solve on a longer anagram test. Here, the women actually supplied *higher* estimates than the men did.

   Other studies have examined self-confidence when the participants have no clear way of assessing whether their performance is excellent, merely adequate, or poor. In these ambiguous situations, women are less confident than men when they are asked to evaluate how well they have done.

   Let's look at an example of research conducted in a real-life setting. When students were asked to evaluate their confidence about passing the first exam in introductory psychology, the women were less confident than the men. However, when students were asked the same question about the second and third exams in the course, there was no sex difference in self-confidence (Kimball & Gray, 1982). Notice that when the women had no previous feedback about their ability, they provided low estimates. With clear feedback from their previous exam scores, however, the women may equal the men in self-confidence. (When this study was repeated in a different classroom, Kimball & Gray (1982) found that the sex differences lasted throughout the semester. It seems that even clear feedback is sometimes not enough to boost women's self-confidence.)

3. *Women and men are similar in self-confidence in some social situations.* House (1974) instructed some men and women to solve anagrams by themselves; the instruction specifically did not stress competition. In these conditions of minimal social cues, women were—if

anything—slightly higher than the men in self-confidence and in their estimates of how many anagrams they expected to solve.

In contrast, women's self-confidence is usually lower than men's self-confidence when the experiment suggests that their performance will be compared with the performance of other people. House (1974) included other conditions in which men and women solved anagrams in competition with other people. Here, women were lower than men in their self-confidence, whether they were competing against men or whether they were competing against other women.

In her analysis of the literature on self-confidence, Lenney (1977) provided an elegant example of how to approach a potential sex difference. The truth about sex differences is seldom simple. We rarely conclude that there is absolutely no sex difference for a particular psychological characteristic, and we never conclude that there is a sex difference that can be demonstrated in all situations. Sex differences are elusive, and researchers need to

FIGURE 5.1. **Percentage of children who describe themselves as "smart," as a function of sex and age (based on Gold, et al., 1980)**

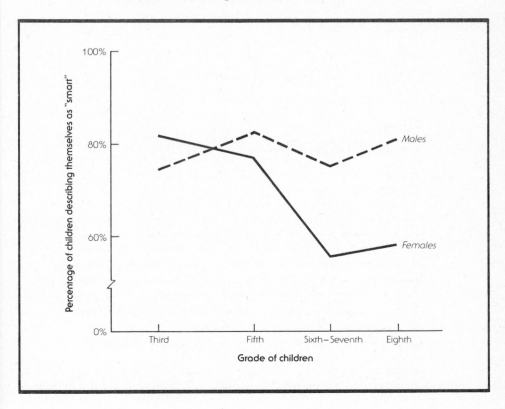

Attributions for One's Own Success

Think back about the last time you received a good grade on a test. A number of different factors could have been responsible for your success. Four possible factors are listed below. You have 100 points to divide among these four factors. Assign points to reflect the extent to which each factor contributed to your success; the points must add up to 100.

_____ I have high ability for the subject that was covered on that test.

_____ I put a lot of effort into studying for that test.

_____ The test was easy.

_____ It was just luck.

clarify those circumstances in which they exist and those circumstances in which there are sex similarities.

In addition to clarifying the previous literature on sex differences in self-confidence, Lenney (1981) conducted other studies. These studies confirmed two of her earlier conclusions, that women and men are similar in self-confidence on some kinds of tasks and that women and men are similar in self-confidence in some social-cue situations.

Before we leave this area of self-confidence, let's consider one final study. This study suggests that females' opinion of their own intelligence decreases as they grow older. Gold, Brush, and Sprotzer (1980) asked third- through eighth-graders to read descriptions of various traits and to circle those traits that applied to themselves. One item read as follows: "Some people are *smart*. They know a lot about different kinds of things. Are you smart?" (p. 233). Figure 5.1 shows the percentage of males and females who described themselves as smart. Notice that males show stable confidence in their intelligence as they grow older. Females, in contrast, show a marked decline.

It seems likely that children have not received clear feedback in the past about whether "they know a lot about different kinds of things." Consequently, girls become less self-confident in this particular area as they grow older. It would be interesting to ask children a question about an achievement area in which they have received more clear-cut feedback, such as "Some people are good students. They get good grades in their classes. Are you a good student?" If Lenney's conclusions are correct, we would expect to find the same degree of self-confidence for girls and boys in this area.

Before reading the next section, try Demonstration 5.3.

Attributions for One's Own Success or Failure

Demonstration 5.3 asked you to make attributions about your performance on an achievement task. **Attributions** are explanations about the causes of your behavior (Weiner, et al., 1972). Demonstration 5.3 listed four possible attributions for a successful outcome on an examination: ability, effort, task easiness, and luck.

We can classify these four attributions in terms of whether they describe internal or external sources. Ability and effort both represent *internal* sources, or factors that are inside the individual. Task easiness and luck both represent *external* sources, or factors that are outside the individual.

These four attributions can also be classified along another dimension. Ability and task easiness are both relatively *stable*. Although there are some complications, as Deaux (1976a) discusses, a person's ability and the easiness of a particular task remain reasonably constant. Effort and luck are both *unstable*. You can easily change the amount of effort you spend on a task and your luck may change from one hour to the next. Table 5.1 illustrates how these four attributions can be categorized according to the internal/external and the stable/unstable dimensions when we are trying to explain why we have been successful.

TABLE 5.1 **Attributions That Could Be Supplied for Successful Task Performance**

	Internal	External
Stable	High Ability	Easy Task
Unstable	High Effort	Good Luck

Table 5.2 shows how we might explain our failure. Again, notice how the four attributions can be sorted into a two-dimensional arrangement.

TABLE 5.2 **Attributions That Could Be Supplied for Unsuccessful Task Performance**

	Internal	External
Stable	Low Ability	Difficult Task
Unstable	Low Effort	Bad Luck

Now examine your responses for Demonstrations 5.3. Keep these answers in mind as we discuss the research on sex differences in attribution patterns.

Research on self-attribution. Women and men are probably fairly similar in their attribution patterns, an idea that is consistent with the first theme of the book. However, just as we saw in connection with the topic of self-confidence, the issue is complex. Sex differences probably exist in some situations. The problem is that we don't yet have a clear idea about the kinds of situations that are most likely to produce sex differences.

Let's first discuss the kinds of attributions that women and men offer when they have been successful. Many studies have not found any sex differences; these studies have been summarized by Frieze and her coauthors (1982) and by Sohn (1982). However, some research suggests that men are more likely than women to attribute their success to *ability*.

Let's look at a representative example of the research that has found sex differences in attribution. Deaux (1979) questioned men and women who held first-level management positions in either a telephone company or in retail stores. One part of the testing involved asking the managers to describe their most successful accomplishment in their current job. Then they were asked to rate the extent to which that particular success could be attributed to each of four factors: general ability, good luck, effort, and easy task. Deaux found that the male managers gave significantly higher ratings to the ability factor than did the female managers.

What kinds of attributions do women and men offer when they have been unsuccessful? Here again, many studies have not found any sex differences (Frieze, et al., 1982; Sohn, 1982). However, some research suggests that women are more likely than men to blame their failure on *lack of ability*. Here is a typical example of a study that found sex differences (Stipek, 1984). Fifth- and sixth-grade children took one of their usual math tests in their classroom, and the tests were returned with their performance indicated (but with no letter grade). The students were asked to decide what factors were responsible for their performance. The most interesting contrast came from the children who thought that they had been unsuccessful on the test. The girls were more likely than the boys to attribute their failure to low ability.

A large number of studies show that males and females are similar when they provide attributions for their success, and an additional large number show sex similarities in attributions for unsuccessful performance. Still, the number of studies that find significant sex differences is too large to be ignored. Unfortunately, no one has yet performed the kind of careful analysis that Lenney (1977) accomplished with the self-confidence literature. Any conclusions must necessarily be tentative, but here's my best guess about this area: In general, women and men are similar in their attribution patterns. However, there are some circumstances in which men are *more* likely than women to attribute their success to ability, and men are *less* likely than women to attribute their failure to ability. Here are some of those circumstances:

1. *Women and men show different attribution patterns on certain kinds of tasks.* Sex differences in attribution seem most likely to emerge on tasks that are considered to be masculine, such as tests in mathematics or spatial abilities, and performance as a manager (Deaux, 1979; Eccles, et al., 1984; Gitelson, et al., 1982; Nicholls, 1975; Stipek, 1984).

2. *Women and men show different attribution patterns in some social situations.* Attribution patterns seem to be influenced by whether the responses are made publicly or privately. Berg and his coauthors (1981) asked women to perform a task that involved reasoning. After completing the task, they were led to believe that they had done either very well (success condition) or very poorly (failure condition). The women then completed a questionnaire about their attributions for performance on the task. Half of the women were told that their partners in the task would see these attribution questionnaires; the other half were told that their responses would be kept confidential. When the women knew that other people would see their responses, they did not take credit for their success, and they attributed their failure to lack of ability. In the confidential condition, they were more likely to show the attributional pattern more typical of men; they took credit for success and didn't blame themselves for failure. As mentioned in Chapter 1, sex differences are most likely to occur when people are aware that they are being evaluated by others.

   Another social-situation factor that might make a difference is whether the study is performed in the laboratory or in a real-life setting. As Chapter 1 suggested, sex differences seem to be smaller in a laboratory setting, where stereotyped behavior is not as prominent as in everyday life. The studies by Deaux (1979) and by Stipek (1984) that were discussed earlier, both of which discovered sex differences, were conducted in real-life settings.

3. *Women and men show different attribution patterns when they have certain kinds of personal characteristics.* A number of studies have examined the kinds of personal characteristics that make women avoid the ability explanation for their success and use the ability explanation for their failure. Women who show this pattern tend to be traditional in their gender roles, low in ability, and low in achievement motivation (Crombie, 1983; Eccles, et al., 1984; Teglasi, 1978). Women who are nontraditional, high in ability, and high in achievement motivation are more likely to show the attributional pattern more typical of men. It seems likely that the personal characteristics of the women who participate in the study have an important influence on whether the study demonstrates sex differences in attribution patterns.

Consequences of self-attribution. We have seen that while women and men often have similar self-attribution patterns, sometimes women are more likely than men to use a particular kind of attribution pattern. When women do well on a task, there are circumstances in which they are less likely than men to attribute their success to ability. Instead, they may say that they were either lucky or that they tried hard. Neither of those attributions gives credit to an internal, stable factor that might make women feel positive about themselves. When women attribute their success to ability, they can take

Attribution Patterns and Choice of Task

magine that you are at a fair or a carnival. There are six possible games to be played, but you only have enough money for three of them. Which three would you choose?

1. Bingo—the game operator calls out numbers, and you cover the appropriate numbers on your card; the first player to cover a complete row or column wins the game.
2. Coin in a Dish—You throw coins toward saucers, glasses, cups, and ashtrays; you win a prize if the coin stays in a piece of glassware.
3. Ring Toss—you toss rings at large cola bottles; you win a prize if a ring falls completely over any bottle.
4. Bouncing Ball—you bet on a color, and a ball is thrown onto a multicolored pattern; you win if the ball comes to rest on your color.
5. Stand up the Bottle—you use a fishing pole with a small ring attached to the end of the string; you win if you stand up a cola bottle.
6. Mouse Game—a live mouse is let go in the middle of a multicolored wheel, and the mouse escapes into a hole at the end of the wheel; you win if the mouse escapes on the color you have bet on.

credit for this success (because it is internal), and they can also count on their ability to continue on other tasks in the future (because it is stable). When women downplay their ability following success, it seems likely that self-confidence will be reduced. As you'll recall from the discussion of self-confidence, women are indeed low in self-confidence in many situations.

Women's self-confidence may be reduced even further because of their interpretations of failure, under some circumstances. Self-confidence might remain high if a person can blame that failure on external factors. You would still feel confident if you could say either, "That test was incredibly difficult" or "Today is just not my lucky day." However, self-confidence should dwindle if you blame your ability by saying, "I failed that test because I'm basically stupid."

Attribution patterns can have consequences for the kinds of tasks people choose to perform, as well as for their self-confidence. Try Demonstration 5.4, which illustrates preferences for luck versus skill, before you read the next section.

In Demonstration 5.4, the Bingo, Bouncing Ball, and Mouse Game tasks all involved luck, whereas Coin in a Dish, Ring Toss, and Stand up the Bottle all involved some degree of ability. Did your female friends select the luck games and your male friends the ability games? This demonstration was based on a clever field study by Deaux, White, and Farris (1975), who gathered their data from county and state fairs in Indiana. They recorded about twice as many men as women playing the three ability games. Women were slightly more likely to be playing the luck games. Men were also likely to persist longer at the ability games than the women. Notice that those ability games would probably be perceived as masculine; you'll recall that sex differences in attribution are most likely on stereotypically masculine tasks. If county fairs included stereotypically feminine games (perhaps variations on jacks or jump rope), it would be interesting to measure persistence!

Deaux and her coauthors performed a follow-up study in a laboratory setting, and they found the same sex differences in preference and persistence. Thus, attribution patterns have implications not only for self-confidence, but also for actual performance.

As we discussed consequences of attribution patterns, it is important to stress once more that sex differences in this area are often minimal. However, on certain kinds of tasks, in some social situations, and with certain kinds of women, a kind of attribution pattern may be used that is particularly destructive to self-confidence. Furthermore, the study by Deaux and her colleagues (1975) illustrates that attribution patterns are important; they can affect behavior as well as our thoughts about ourselves.

At the beginning of this chapter, we discussed that people have often used a person-blame explanation to explain why women are less likely then men to hold prestigious positions in society. However, we have seen in our discussion of attribution patterns that women and men are often similar. When sex differences do emerge, they often can be traced to characteristics of the task or the social situation. The sex differences in attribution patterns are so small and so readily modifiable that a person-blame explanation does not seem useful.

□ SECTION SUMMARY: ■ Perceptions of One's Own Achievements

1. Women are frequently less self-confident than men when they estimate how well they will perform on an achievement task.
2. Women can equal men in self-confidence under certain circumstances: (a) when tasks are feminine or neutral; (b) when they are given clear feedback; and (c) in some social situations.
3. Women and men tend to use similar attribution patterns when they explain their successes and when they explain their failures.
4. In some circumstances, men are *more* likely than women to attribute their success to ability, and men are *less* likely to attribute their failure to ability. Those circumstances in which sex differences are *greatest* seem to be: (a) when tasks are masculine; (b) in some social situations; and (c) with certain kinds of personal characteristics.
5. Attribution patterns can have important consequences for self-confidence and for the tasks people choose to perform.

☐ PERCEPTIONS OF WOMEN'S AND MEN'S ACHIEVEMENTS

In the last section, we concentrated on people's perceptions of their own achievements. We saw that women and men often differ in their expectations for success and sometimes differ in their attribution patterns. In that section, we emphasized that women and men may make different judgments about *themselves*. However, Deaux (1976a) has pointed out a second way in which sex may be even more important in perceptions related to achievement. People may perceive the achievements of women in a different way from the achievements of men. As the second theme of this book emphasizes, people often react differently to women and men. In the area of achievement, sex as a stimulus variable seems to be more important than sex as a subject variable.

In this section of the chapter, we will discuss perceptions of the achievements of other people. There are two important questions here: How do people evaluate the achievements of women and men? To what do they attribute the success or failure of women and men? Notice that the first question is similar to our earlier discussion of self-confidence, in which people evaluated their own performances. The second question is similar to our discussion of women's and men's attributions for their own success and failure.

Evaluations of Women's and Men's Performance

Try Demonstration 5.5, which is a modification of a classic study by Goldberg (1968). He asked college women to evaluate articles that had presumably been published in professional journals. One-third of the articles represented stereotypically masculine professions, such as law, one-third represented stereotypically feminine professions, such as dietetics, and one-third represented neutral professions such as art history. Some women read the article when it showed a male author's name (John T. MacKay), and others read it when it showed a female author's name (Joan T. MacKay). Except for the author's name, the two versions were identical. Goldberg found that the women gave higher ratings to the quality of the article when it was presumably written by a man. This preference for male-authored articles was apparent in judgments for the "feminine" articles and the neutral articles, as well as for the "masculine" articles. Goldberg's article was entitled, "Are women prejudiced against women?" The answer seemed to be a resounding "Yes!"

More recent research has produced a modified response. In some cases, women—and men—are *not* prejudiced against women. In an overview of the perceived competence of men and women, Wallston and O'Leary (1981) list 12 studies confirming a negative bias against women's accomplishments, although there were five studies in which women's and men's accomplishments were rated similarly. More recent research has found further evidence

Evaluations of Women's and Men's Performance

For this demonstration, you will have to make two photocopies of the material below. For one photocopy, cover the name on the left (John T. MacKay) with a small slip of paper. For the second photocopy, move the slip of paper so that it covers the name on the right (Joan T. MacKay).

Now show each version to at least five friends, making certain that each friend sees only one version. Instruct each person that this passage is taken from a psychology textbook, describing a concept about language. Tell each person to read the passage and to evaluate it on the scales below.

From *Cognition*, by   From *Cognition*, by
John T. MacKay   Joan T. MacKay

Marking.   A linguistic phenomenon called *marking* also has an influence on understanding. We need to examine this phenomenon in some detail. Marking can be defined in several ways; let's discuss the most general definition first. **Marking** means that in any group of related words, one word is basic (or **unmarked**) and the other words are more specific (or **marked**). For example, *friend* is unmarked, whereas *friendly, unfriendly,* and *friendship* are all marked.

Sometimes marking is accomplished by adding some feature onto the basic form in order to produce a new form (Deese, 1973). In these cases the marking is easy to spot, as when we add an *-s* to a single noun to indicate the plural or we add an *-ed* to a verb to indicate the past tesnse. As we noted, the simple or basic form is called the unmarked form, whereas the more complex or specific form is called the marked form. Thus, *apple* and *walk* are unmarked, and *apples* and *walked* are marked.

Evaluate this passage on the following scales:

1	2	3	4	5	6	7
POOR WRITING STYLE					GOOD WRITING STYLE	

1	2	3	4	5	6	7
LOW PROFESSIONAL COMPETENCE					HIGH PROFESSIONAL COMPETENCE	

1	2	3	4	5	6	7
LOW-PRESTIGE AUTHOR					HIGH-PRESTIGE AUTHOR	

of prejudice against women; people prefer articles that are presumably written by men (Paludi & Bauer, 1983; Paludi & Strayer, 1985).

There seem to be many variables that influence whether or not people will be prejudiced against women's achievements. Let us look at some of the patterns that are particularly important.

1. *People are more likely to be prejudiced against women's achievements when the merit of these achievements has not yet been established.* Pheterson, Kiesler, and Goldberg (1971) asked college women to judge the merit of paintings that were presumably done by either a male or a female. When the painting was described as merely a contest entry, the women judged the male's painting as superior to the female's painting. When the painting was described as a recognized winner, the male's painting and the female's painting received equivalent ratings. When an expert has already approved of a woman's achievement, then other people are willing to give it a positive rating.

   Notice that this relationship between established merit and prejudice makes it difficult for women to achieve recognition. When a woman is just beginning her career and the merit of her work has not yet been established, the prejudice operates against her. It may keep her from receiving appropriate recognition. Once she has managed to "make it" in her career and her reputation has been established, her work is no longer downgraded. However, the lack of prejudice she now encounters would have been even more welcome earlier in her career.

2. *Expert judges may be more prejudiced against women's achievements than nonexperts.* In one study, college students and art students evaluated paintings that were attributed to either a male or a female (Ward, 1981). The college students (nonexperts) rated the two kinds of paintings equivalently. However, the art students (experts) were more positive about the works that had presumably been painted by males. Notice how the nature of this prejudice is relevant for a woman who is beginning her career. She is more likely to be judged by experts than by nonexperts. The possibility that nonexperts might not be prejudiced against her would be of little solace.

3. *In some cases, women's achievements may receive higher ratings than men's achievements.* Women may sometimes be particularly positive about the work of other women. Levenson and her coauthors (1975) found the female research participants gave higher grades to an essay when it was attributed to a female student, as opposed to a male student. Moore (1978) examined a series of book reviews and found that female reviewers tended to write more favorably about books written by women, as opposed to books written by men.

At the beginning of the chapter, I mentioned that many of the tasks that are studied in connection with achievement have a distinctly masculine bias. Epstein and Paludi (1985) point out the masculine bias in the research on evaluating the performance of other people. Wouldn't it be interesting to see how people judge the success of men and women on stereotypically feminine tasks such as child rearing, community activities, and homemaking? Consistent with a theme of this book, women and the activities that are important to them frequently appear to be ignored.

Sometimes there are contradictions in this area that defy easy explanation. Abramson and his coauthors (1977) found that people judged a female attorney to be *more* competent than a male attorney. However, Feldman-Summers and Kiesler (1974) discovered that people judged a female physician to be *less* competent than a male physician. There may be subtle characteristics of the task that produce such widely different results, but these characteristics have not yet been identified.

We don't know much about how people's judgments are influenced by the culture or subculture in which they are reared. It would be interesting to know, for example, whether blacks tend to value men's accomplishments more than women's accomplishments. Undoubtedly, there are cultures in which *anything* associated with women is devalued. In some Arabic cultures, it is said that a woman's testimony is worth only half as much as a man's testimony in a court trial. More optimistic news comes from Israel, where people gave equivalent evaluations to journal articles presumably written by either a man or a woman (Mischel, 1974). The ratings were the same for articles from both traditionally masculine and traditionally feminine areas.

It is also important to keep in mind a point suggested by Gross and Geffner (1980). Participants in laboratory experiments may believe that the task of rating articles or paintings is relatively trivial, compared to the kinds of decisions made in real life. Therefore, their responses may not reflect reality. Also, participants in laboratory experiments may alter their responses so that they do not seem to appear "sexist" when they evaluate a female's accomplishments. (This tendency may have operated in the study by Abramson, et al., in 1977, when a pro-woman attitude may have been more fashionable than in Feldman-Summers and Kiesler's earlier study.) In real-life settings, the reluctance to appear sexist may not be as strong.

Attributions for the Success or Failure of Other People

Take a moment to glance back over the section on "Attributions for One's Own Success or Failure," discussed on pages 132–137. Recall that men and women generally have similar attribution patterns. In some circumstances, men are more likely than women to attribute their success to ability, and men are less likely than women to attribute their failure to ability. This sex difference is found only occasionally when people make attributions about themselves. However, when people make attributions about other people, they are very likely to attribute men's success and women's failure to an ability explanation.

Research on attributions for other people. Let us examine a study by Deaux and Emswiller (1974) in some detail. This study demonstrates how people provide different attributions for the success of females than they do for the success of males. In this study, college-student participants were asked to listen to a male or female student, who was presumably performing a task in another room. The task, they were told, involved finding pictures

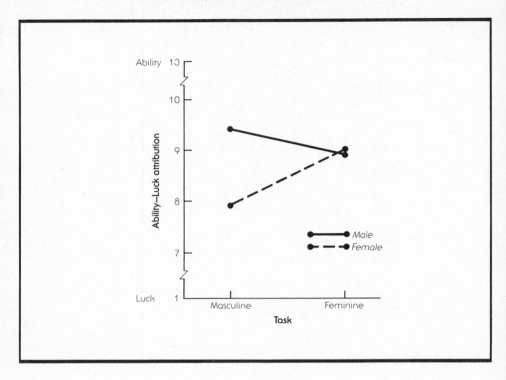

of familiar objects hidden in a camouflaged background. In reality there were no students in the other room; the subjects merely heard answers that had previously been tape recorded by a male or a female. Another variable in this experiment was the nature of the task. The stereotypically female task involved household objects such as a mop or a double boiler. The stereotypically male task involved mechanical objects such as a tire jack or a wrench. The subjects were instructed to think about how ability and luck might influence the performance of the students whom they were judging.

After the task was completed, everybody was led to believe that their partners had performed at an above-average level, 16 items correct out of 25. Then they were asked to judge whether this success had been due to luck or ability. Deaux and Emswiller found that male subjects and female subjects showed similar tendencies in judging the success of other people. Therefore, Figure 5.2 ignores the sex of the subject and illustrates the extent to which all subjects thought that other people's success was due to luck versus ability, as a function of two variables: the presumed sex of the other person, and the "masculine" or "feminine" nature of the task.

It is important to remember that all of these judgments are based on equally successful performances, a score of 16 correct items. However, attributions were quite different in the four conditions. Let us first look at performance on the stereotypically masculine task. Notice that high ability was seen as being responsible for the performance of the males, whereas the performance of the females was placed closer to the "luck" end of the rating scale.

We might expect that relationship to be neatly reversed on the stereotypically feminine task. Perhaps the success of females in identifying mops and double boilers could be attributed to ability, whereas the success of males could be attributed to luck. However, notice that the results show almost identical attributions for both males and females on the "feminine" tasks.

Deaux (1976a) proposes that one explanation for these results is that expectations are systematically higher for males' ability than for females' ability (as demonstrated in Goldberg's study and others). The discrepancy can be reduced by providing a handicap of a feminine task for the males. However, males are perceived as having such a headstart on ability that providing a handicap merely brings them down to the females' ability level, but *not* below that level.

Other studies have shown a similar tendency for people to attribute men's and women's success to different causes. Feldman-Summers and Kiesler (1974) asked people to make attributions for the success of a physician whose life story they had just read. They found some complicated relationships between the sex of the subject and attribution patterns. However, both sexes thought that effort was substantially more important than ability in explaining the success of the female physician. In contrast, both sexes thought that effort and ability were almost equally important in explaining the success of the male physician. Thus, the ability attribution is relatively more important in explaining why men are successful than in explaining why women are successful.

When Feather and Simon (1975) asked high-school women to assign attributions for successful male and female medical students, the young women attributed the male student's success to greater ability. The female student's success was attributed to good luck, an easy task, and—the worst news yet—cheating on examinations! Other research has demonstrated that people explain women's successful performance in an emergency situation as being due to effort, rather than ability (Taynor & Deaux, 1973). Even children as young as ten think that women's success on mechanical tasks is due to effort, whereas men's success is due to ability (Etaugh & Brown, 1975).

It may be that people avoid an ability explanation whenever they are explaining the success of a group that is commonly believed to be inferior. Yarkin, Town, and Wallston (1982) extended the attribution research to include judgments about black men and women. Students read about a highly successful banker who was either male or female, black or white. They were then asked to judge the importance of four factors—ability, effort, task difficulty, and luck—in determining that banker's success. Responses were similar when judgments were made about the white female, black male, and black female; effort and luck were judged to be important contributing factors. In contrast, the white male's success was explained by his high ability.

So far, we have looked at the attributions people provide for the success of other people. The findings are reasonably consistent; people are more likely to use ability as an explanation for a man's success (or—more accurately—for a *white* man's success) than for a woman's success.

What kinds of attributions do people make to explain the *unsuccessful* performance of women and men? Women's lack of ability emerges as a popular explanation, whereas people rarely mention men's lack of ability as an explanation for an unsuccessful performance.

Etaugh and Brown (1975) asked people to make attributions for men's and women's failure on mechanical tasks. Lack of ability was used more frequently to explain the women's failure than to explain the men's failure. Cash, Gillen, and Burns (1977) also found that people used a "lack of ability" explanation for women's unsuccessful performance, but in explaining men's unsuccessful performance, they were more likely to use a "bad luck" explanation. Finally, Feather and Simon (1975) asked high-school women to assign attributions for unsuccessful male and female medical students. The woman's failure was largely attributed to lack of ability, whereas the man's failure was primarily attributed to the difficulty of the coursework. In summary, people think that women are unsuccessful at a task because they just don't have the ability, whereas they think that men are unsuccessful because of bad luck or task difficulty—not because they lack the ability!

Consequences of attributions for others' performance. In the section "Consequences of Self-Attribution" we saw that attribution patterns may sometimes contribute to women's lack of confidence in their own ability. The attributions that we supply for the performance of other people also have important practical and theoretical consequences.

Imagine that you are looking for a job. A prospective employer is reviewing your resumé, which lists a number of successful past achievements. If you are a male, this employer is likely to attribute these successes to your ability, a stable characteristic. This ability is not likely to evaporate by next Monday, when you are supposed to begin work. If you are a female, the employer is likely to attribute your successes to something other than ability—to luck, effort, easy tasks, and possibly cheating. None of these factors will be as advantageous as the ability factor (Hansen & O'Leary, 1985).

Furthermore, imagine that your resumé contains evidence of occasional failure, such as a low grade in statistics or one weak letter of recommendation. This failure performance will diminish your apparent ability considerably if you are a female, because failure is often attributed to lack of ability in females. If you are a male, that failure performance will be attributed to some other factor, such as a difficult statistics course or a letter of recommendation from someone who was having a bad day.

Another consequence of attribution patterns also concerns employment. Hansen and O'Leary (1985) summarize a study that demonstrated that people were more likely to give promotions to employees whose success had been attributed to ability (Heilman & Guzzo, 1978). If men are more likely than women to have their success explained in terms of ability, then they are more likely than women to receive promotions.

The attributions we supply for other people also have possible implications for the development of self-attributions. As children grow up, they hear adults offer explanations for the successes and failures of men and women. It seems likely that children may learn that males are supposed to attribute their success—but not their failure—to their ability, whereas females are supposed to attribute their failure—but not their success—to their ability. We mentioned that sex differences in self-attributions are not large, but they may arise from widely held stereotypes about women and men.

There *is* a ray of hope. If your prospective employer has a positive attitude toward women, she or he may respond differently. Garland, Hale, and Burnson (1982) questioned employees of a large human-services agency. The men in the agency who had positive attitudes toward women tended to attribute women's success to their ability and effort. The women in the agency who had positive attitudes toward women tended to attribute women's failure to the difficulty of the job. In other words, people who believe that women can be successful in management positions either give women credit for their accomplishments or blame women's failures on external problems. Fortunately, stereotypes about the attributions for men's and women's performance may be widely held, but they are not universal.

☐ SECTION SUMMARY: ▪ Perceptions of Women's and Men's Achievements

1. People frequently evaluate men's achievements more positively than women's achievements even when the work is identical.
2. Many variables influence people's prejudice against women's work, including: (a) people are more prejudiced against women's achievements when their merit has not been established; (b) expert judges may be more prejudiced against women's achievements than non-experts; (c) women's achievements may receive higher ratings than men's achievements, perhaps more often when the judges are women.
3. People attribute men's success to ability and women's success to luck, effort, or cheating.
4. People attribute men's failure to task difficulty, bad luck, and other nonability factors, whereas they attribute women's failure to lack of ability.
5. People with positive attitudes toward women are less likely to use stereotyping when they make attributions for other people's success or failure.

Chapter Review Questions

1. One theme that was repeated throughout the chapter was that our thoughts about sex differences in achievement change as additional research is conducted and we acquire more data. Point out how this is true with respect to achievement motivation; fear of success; self-confidence on achievement tasks; and attributions for one's own success.

2. A woman you know read about fear of success in a popular magazine aimed at young businesswomen, and she claims that there are substantial sex differences in fear of success. Answer her with the information from this chapter.

3. At the end of the first section of this chapter, we introduced Lipman-Blumen's distinction between direct achieving style and relational achieving style. Review this distinction, trying to think of real-life examples of women and men who typify each style. From your own acquaintances, what would you conclude about sex differences in this area?

4. The second and third sections of this chapter dealt with similar topics. Point out similarities and differences in the findings from these two areas.

5. Lenney (1977) identified three factors that influence whether there are sex differences in self-confidence in achievement settings. Keeping these factors in mind, think of a concrete example of a situation in which sex differences should be exaggerated; then think of an example of a situation in which sex differences should be minimal.

6. We concluded that sex differences in self-attributions are generally small. Explain this conclusion, with respect to both successful and unsuccessful performance. Now return to Chapter 1 and review the section on problems in research on psychology of women. How could some of the problems mentioned in that section help to explain how an introductory psychology book might conclude that there are large sex differences in self-attributions?

7. Although sex differences in self-attributions are generally small, some kinds of situations may encourage these sex differences. From your knowledge of the factors that influence sex differences in this area, describe a concrete situation in which a woman would be especially likely to (a) attribute her success to a factor other than ability and her failure to ability; and (b) attribute her success to ability and her failure to a factor other than ability.

8. We discussed several factors that influence evaluations of women's and men's performance. Construct a situation in which men's performance should be judged far superior to women's performance. Now construct a situation in which women's and men's performance should be rated equally positively.

9. Point out how the perceptions of the success and failure of other people could have consequences for another aspect of life, specifically marriage. How might people explain a couple's successful marriage in terms of the husband's and wife's ability, effort, luck, and task ease? Repeat this exercise to explain a marriage that leads to a divorce.
10. In the next chapter, we will discuss women and work. People often argue that women are uncommon in prestigious jobs because they differ from men in their motivations and in their attitude toward achievement. Point out why this argument cannot explain the tremendous sex differences in employment patterns, using information from the entire chapter.

☐ NEW TERMS

achievement motivation
Thematic Apperception Test
fear of success

direct achieving style
relational achieving style
attributions

☐ RECOMMENDED READINGS

Fyans, L. J., Jr. (1980) (Ed.), *Achievement motivation: Recent trends in theory and research.* New York: Plenum. ■ Several articles in this book concern women, with topics including sex differences in attribution and direct versus relational achieving styles.

Sex Roles (1982, April), Volume 8. ■ The entire issue of this journal is devoted to sex differences and similarities in self-attribution patterns.

Stewart, A. J. (Ed.). (1982). *Motivation and society.* San Francisco: Jossey-Bass. ■ This volume explores the topic of achievement motivation and expands on the theory and research summarized in the first section of this chapter; several articles concern sex differences and similarities.

O'Leary, V. E., Unger, R. K., & Wallston, B. S. (Eds.). (1985). *Women, gender, and social psychology.* Hillsdale, N.J.: Erlbaum. ■ Two chapters in this book are relevant to the topic of achievement; the chapter by Sutherland and Veroff focuses on achievement motivation, and the chapter by Hansen and O'Leary discusses gender and attribution.

CHAPTER 6

WOMEN AND WORK

- Most women in the United States seek employment in order to earn money for little luxuries that their families could not afford with one income.

- There is clear evidence that a woman is more likely to be employed if her mother was employed.

- High-school career counselors have different aspirations for female and male students.

- Women earn less than men on the average, but the difference between their salaries can be attributed to the fact that men have more experience, work more hours, and so forth.

- American women spend about the same amount of time on housework now as in the 1920s.

- Men and women in the same profession, such as business administration, are fairly similar in their personality characteristics.

- The best explanation for the absence of women in nontraditional fields is that they lack the appropriate personality characteristics and skills.

- When women are employed, their husbands perform substantially more household chores than when they are not employed.

- Children of employed women have normal intellectual development, but they are often socially maladjusted.

- Role strain, which women experience when they combine employment and home responsibilities, often leads to poor mental health.

In the 1950s, adult American women had two traditional roles, one as wife and one as mother. In recent years, most women in the United States have added an extra role, the role of an employed person (Perun & Bielby, 1981). This chapter explores the topic of women and work, with a primary emphasis on paid employment. We begin with a section on background factors influencing women's employment. In the second section, we examine women on the job. The final section explores the effects of employment on women's personal lives.

In some respects, this chapter is an extension of the last chapter on achievement motivation. In that chapter, we saw that men and women were often remarkably similar in their motivations for achievement and in their attitudes toward achievement. In this chapter, we stress that the positions that men and women actually achieve in the workforce are remarkably different. Women and men are employed in different jobs. They occupy different positions in their jobs. The amount of pay that they receive also differs.

Why should these differences exist, given that women and men are similar in their achievement-related behavior and given that women and men are similar in other characteristics related to job performance? As we will argue, the person-centered explanations, which emphasize women's personal inadequacies, *cannot* account for a large proportion of the inequalities at work. Instead, we must search for situation-centered explanations, which stress that the characteristics of organizations are responsible for the unequal treatment of women and men. Notice that this chapter will reaffirm the first and second themes that have been discussed throughout this book: Women and men are usually similar, yet they are treated differently.

Before we begin the first section, we must discuss some terms that are important for working women. In fact, let us begin with the term "**working women,**" which refers both to women who work for pay outside the home and to women who receive no pay for work in the home. It would be a mistake to use the term "working women" to refer only to women who are paid for their labor; this would imply that housewives do not work. I will use the term "**employed women**" or "women who work outside the home" to refer to women who receive money for their work; they may receive a salary or be self-employed. I will use the term "**nonemployed women**" to refer to women who are unpaid; they may perform work for their husbands, their homes, their children, and volunteer organizations, but they receive no money for their services.

☐ BACKGROUND FACTORS INFLUENCING WOMEN'S EMPLOYMENT

Let us examine some background factors about employed women. We must explore the reasons why women work outside the home, the factors related to employment, and the factors influencing career choice. We must also discuss why career counselors may discourage young women in their career aspirations. Finally, we will see how women sometimes—but not always—experience discrimination when they apply for work.

Women's Reasons for Employment

Why do women choose to work outside the home? According to the stereotype, men and women seek employment for different reasons. This stereotype dictates that the man is the "breadwinner," a term that suggests a stalwart male—who may wear either a pin-striped suit or a blue collar—setting out to earn the money required to support his homemaker-wife and his two young children. The stereotype dictates that a woman works outside the home so that her income will buy those little luxuries that are the hallmarks of elegant living. She is employed so that the family can afford an extra car, new rugs in the bedroom, and the February trip to Florida (Nieva & Gutek, 1981).

Reality paints a less pleasant picture. Most women seek employment because it is economically necessary. Almost half of all employed women—45 percent to be exact—are single, widowed, divorced, or separated. Most of these women provide the only income for the family. An additional 21 percent of employed women are married to men who earn less than $15,000 a year; two incomes are required to buy many necessities (U.S. Department of Labor, 1982). Only a minority of employed women match the stereotype of the woman whose income buys the nonessentials.

Now let us consider a second, somewhat different stereotype about employed women. This stereotype is based on the realization that economic necessity forces some women to get a job; those who do work outside the home must therefore be motivated only by the money. According to this stereotype, women are not personally involved in their work and they have little desire to do a good job as a source of personal pride. Crowley, Levitin, and Quinn (1973) polled a nationwide sample, to assess whether the stereotype was realistic. Specifically, they asked people whether they would continue to be employed if it were not financially necessary. They found that 57 percent of the women replied that they *would* continue to work outside the home. Hoffman (1974a) summarizes a survey that yielded similar responses and also suggested that black women were particularly likely to say they would remain employed if it were not financially necessary. Thus, more than half of the employed women in this country seem to find their jobs satisfying enough that they would continue with them, even if it were not economically essential.

Personal Characteristics and Women's Employment

What kinds of personal characteristics predict whether a woman works outside the home or not? Perhaps the most important factor is education. Women with college educations are more likely to be employed than women who have not attended college (Almquist, 1977; Nieva & Gutek, 1981).

Another important factor is race or ethnic background. Black women typically have higher employment rates than white women, but Mexican-American women and American-Indian women have lower employment rates than white women (Almquist & Wehrle-Einhorn, 1978; Nieva & Gutek, 1981).

Several decades ago, one of the best predictors of employment was whether a woman had young children; mothers were seldom employed. However, the number of employed women who have young children has increased about 300 percent in the years between 1940 and 1970. As a result, women with young children are almost as likely to be employed as women who have no children (Larwood & Gutek, 1984; U.S. Department of Labor, 1980). Thus, there is little relationship between the number of children a woman has and her employment status. In summary, education and race or ethnic background are related to employment patterns, but number of children is not an important factor.

Vocational Choice

We looked at some factors that influence whether a woman works outside the home. Now let's see what factors influence the job she chooses. Unfortunately, we don't know much about vocational choice for many jobs in traditionally female occupations. Why does a woman decide to be a nurse rather than a secretary? One woman in her forties had never considered an occupation other than a secretary or a nurse. She ultimately decided to be a nurse because she perceived nurses as "bright bouncy ladies" with considerable physical strength, whereas secretaries "had to teeter on high heels" (Game & Pringle, 1983, p. 101). However, there seems to be no systematic investigation about which factors are most important. Are they "objective" kinds of factors such as salary, prospects for employment, and amount of training required, or are they "subjective" kinds of factors, such as the perception that nurses are stronger women than secretaries? They are also many other unknowns. Do women in clerical positions just "fall into their jobs" or do they arrive there through a clear decision-making process (Nieva & Gutek, 1981)? The absence of information about choices within traditional occupations is particularly unfortunate since—as we will see later—the clear majority of women are still found in these traditional jobs.

We know far more about a different question: What kind of women pursue nontraditional, high-level careers? (Can you think of reasons why psychologists seem to have an "elitist" bias in the kinds of jobs they are most likely to study?)

Researchers who have studied women in nontraditional careers have identified both background characteristics and personality characteristics that these women are likely to possess. In terms of background characteristics, these women are likely to be the oldest child in the family, a characteristic that is often found among high achievers (Lemkau, 1979). Another important background characteristic is parental education. If a woman's parents are well educated, she is more likely to pursue a nontraditional career (Lemkau, 1979; Trigg & Perlman, 1976; Zuckerman, 1980). Black women's career choices are similarly influenced by the education level of her parents (Burlew, 1982).

Another background characteristic that *should* make a difference in women's career choices is whether the woman's mother works outside the home, and there are several studies, summarized by Lemkau (1979) and Mortimer and Sorensen (1984) that show a clear relationship. For instance, black women in nontraditional careers are likely to have been influenced by their mothers' level of education, work status, and degree of encouragement (Burlew, 1982; June & Fooks, 1980). However, there are other studies that indicate that the relationship is complex, or that women in traditional careers and women in nontraditional careers are equally likely to have employed mothers (Bielby, 1978; Haber, 1980; Nieva & Gutek, 1981; Zuckerman, 1980).

Research by Parsons and her coauthors (1978) illustrates why maternal employment is a complex issue. Their study contrasted women with high career aspirations—who planned on graduate school and full-time employment afterwards—and women with low career aspirations—whose career plans were not as ambitious. The results showed that the women with low career aspirations tended to have mothers who did not work outside the home and who were satisfied with their lives. Women with high career aspirations tended to have either mothers who worked outside the home or else mothers who had been dissatisfied with their lives. Parsons and her coauthors noted that many of these employed mothers held low-level jobs. They may have encouraged their daughters to aspire to careers that they themselves had not been able to reach.

In summary, women in nontraditional careers tended to be firstborn and their parents tend to be well educated. There is no clear-cut tendency for their mothers to work outside the home.

What kind of personality characteristics are typical for these women in nontraditional careers? They tend to be independent, self-confident, assertive, emotionally stable, and satisfied with their lives (Lemkau, 1979; Parsons, et al., 1978; Ruble, et al., 1984). In some studies, women in nontraditional careers do not differ from other women in stereotypically feminine traits such as warmth and expressiveness (Lemkau, 1979), but other studies show that nontraditional women are somewhat less interested in their relationships with other people (Trigg & Perlman, 1976). Notice, then, that these nontraditional women have characteristics that would be considered stereotypically masculine. This isn't surprising, since they are planning to go into "masculine" occupations. These nontraditional women may be somewhat less likely to have stereotypically feminine traits. Finally, their emotional stability and life satisfaction indicate that they tend to be well adjusted.

We have looked at women's personal characteristics and how they influence occupational choice. Equally important is the kind of advice and encouragement they receive from other people, such as career counselors.

Career Counselors

Many young women who are trying to make career choices may decide to talk to their school's career counselor. There is some evidence that these counselors may not be well-informed about employed women and that they may try to discourage women who are seeking nontraditional careers.

Bingham and House (1973) asked high-school counselors 25 questions such as the ones in Demonstration 6.1. Notice that each of these questions involves employed women. The counselors gave wrong answers for about half of the items. Very few counselors knew that the discrepancy between salaries received by men and women for doing the same work was increasing. In general, the female counselors tended to be better informed than the male counselors.

Career counselors also seem to have low aspirations for their female students. Donahue and Costar (1977) asked high-school counselors to read short case studies of male and female students and to select an appropriate occupation for each person. When the case study described a male, rather than a female, the counselors chose occupations that paid more, required more education, and required less supervision. This bias was strongest among counselors who worked in small towns. Female counselors who were over

---

DEMONSTRATION 6.1

Questions about Employed Women

These questions about employed women were among those that Bingham and House (1973) gave to high-school counselors. Answer the questions (true or false) and then check your accuracy by looking at the answers at the end of this section.

1. Approximately ⅔ of the married women in the US today are working for income.
2. Some statistics indicate that women suffer more from discrimination than black men do.
3. Employers change job titles so they can pay women lower wages or salaries.
4. One area in which women have gained equality is college teaching; they are just as likely to be full professors as men are.
5. The discrepancy between salaries received by men and women for doing the same work is increasing.
6. Women are more likely than men to work in jobs not adequately covered by Social Security benefits.
7. Female college graduates need clerical skills as well as a diploma to get employment.
8. In spite of legislation which makes it illegal to do so, many companies continue to restrict employment opportunities for women.

---

40 years of age discriminated most against female students, whereas male counselors over 40 years of age discriminated least. This study provides us with a useful lesson. When we focus on stereotypes about women, we ourselves must not form strong stereotypes about those who discriminate against women! In this case, older men were reasonably fair in their treatment of women.

Suppose that a female high-school student with a nontraditional career goal visits a career counselor. What kind of response is she likely to receive? There are two studies that suggest that she will *not* receive warm encouragement. Thomas and Stewart (1971) found that high-school counselors thought that women with traditionally masculine career goals had chosen inappropriately. The counselors also thought that women with traditionally masculine career goals were more in need of counseling than women with traditionally feminine career goals. Another study asked career counselors to review information about female or male students who wanted to attend medical school (Abramowitz, et al., 1975). The counselors judged the female students to be more maladjusted than the male students.

It should not surprise us that career counselors have these stereotyped views. After all, these are views that are dominant in the society in which they have grown up. However, these biases are especially unfortunate because counselors are the very people who are supposed to be experts in the area of career options. They are supposed to *expand* the life options for women, rather than channeling them into traditional careers (Harway, 1980).

Ideal counselors should advise students on the basis of their interests and abilities, and not on the basis of their sex. Fortunately, some people are becoming increasingly concerned about improving career counselors' expertise and attitudes. Farmer and Backer (1977) wrote a book called *New Career Options for Women: A Counselor's Sourcebook*, which contains important information about career choices. Another book, *Counseling Women*, discusses the counseling of middle-aged women who want to return to paid work, as well as the counseling of high-school students (Harmon, Birk, Fitzgerald, & Tanney, 1978). There are also resources useful for students who want to explore a variety of career options (for example, Bestor, 1982; Hopke, 1981; Renetzky, 1985).

The answers to the questions in Demonstration 6.1 are: 1. T; 2. T; 3. T; 4. F; 5. T; 6. T; 7. F; 8. T. Counselors' accuracy was particularly low for the first five items.

Applying for Work

You may recall that in the previous chapter we examined whether people tend to downgrade the achievements of women in comparison to men. The studies on that topic were inconsistent, and so we concluded that people might be prejudiced against women in some circumstances, but not in others. The same situation is true with respect to hiring women, where women often face access discrimination. **Access discrimination** involves discrimination in hiring decisions (Levitin, Quinn, & Staines, 1971). Examples of this discrimination include the following: rejecting well-qualified women applicants; offering women applicants lower salaries; and offering women applicants less attractive positions. Once they have been hired, women may face another kind of discrimination, called treatment discrimination, which we will discuss later in this chapter.

Let us first look at a classic study in the area of access discrimination. Fidell (1970) composed resumés for a mythical person who had recently received a Ph.D. In half the cases, the person on the resumé had a male name (such as James Ross), and in half the cases the person had a female name (such as Janet Ross). Aside from the name, the resumés were identical. Fidell then sent the resumés to chairpersons of 228 psychology departments. The chairpersons were asked to indicate how likely they would be to hire the person described in the resumé and to indicate what kind of position the candidate would be offered.

Fidell found that six of the eight resumés received more favorable ratings when they contained a male name, rather than a female name. The candidate was also offered a more prestigious position when the resumé contained a male name. The respondents assigned the candidate the rank of "assistant professor" when there was a female name and the rank of "associate professor" (the next higher rank in academic institutions) when there was a male name, even though the qualifications listed on the resumé were identical. Notice that this study demonstrated the same kind of discrimination against women that we discussed in the chapter on achievement. As Goldberg (1968) and other researchers showed, people tend to discriminate against women when they evaluate their accomplishments, such as professional articles. Not surprisingly, people place low value on women when they are considered for employment.

Access discrimination also works against women who are applying for executive positions (Rosen & Jerdee, 1974a). Many other studies have demonstrated that women are less likely to be hired than men who have similar qualifications (Dipboye, Fromkin, & Wiback, 1975; Terborg & Ilgen, 1975).

However, access discrimination does not *always* operate in hiring decisions. Soto and Cole (1975) asked people to make judgments about male and female applicants for the position of department manager of a large company. Their responses showed that they would be equally likely to hire a man or a woman for the job.

In a summary of studies on access discrimination, Arvey (1979) found that males received more favorable responses than females in seven studies, and females received more favorable responses than males in two studies. An additional five studies showed complex relationships between access discrimination and other characteristics, and two other studies concluded that males and females were judged similarly.

What kinds of factors determine whether women face access discrimination when they apply for work? Here are some that have been identified.

1. *People who have strong gender-role stereotypes are more likely to show access discrimination.* Sharp and Post (1980) asked personnel administrators to judge the qualifications of applicants for a position of either a sports reporter or a fashion reporter for a local magazine. Overall, the participants in the study were equally positive about the male and female applicants. However, those administrators who received high scores on a test of gender-role stereotypes showed discrimination. These stereotyped people were much more positive about the male applicant for the sports reporter position. They were also somewhat more positive about the female applicant for the fashion reporter position.

2. *Access discrimination is likely to operate for both men and women when they apply for "sex-inappropriate" jobs.* As Sharp and Post's study demonstrated, males—as well as females—may face discrimination when they are seeking a job that is stereotypical of the other sex, and this conclusion has been supported in reviews of the literature (Larwood & Gutek, 1984; Martinko & Gardner, 1983; Ruble, et al., 1984). Levinson (1982) found evidence of access discrimination for "sex-inappropriate" jobs when he asked students to apply for jobs listed in classified advertisements. A female who inquired about a shipping-receiving job (a stereotypically masculine position) was told, "Honey, I'm sorry, but we need a man to do that. All our employees are men, and you'd need to unload heavy equipment. ... I'd like to help you, but we really need someone pretty strong" (pp. 57–58). A male inquiring about a "teacher-nurse-worker" position in a day-care center (a stereotypically feminine position) was told, "Well this is with one-year-old children, and I doubt that you would want to work with them" (p. 57).

3. *Access discrimination is particularly likely to operate when it is unclear or ambiguous whether the candidate is well qualified.* Several studies and reviews of the literature have emphasized the importance of this factor (Gerdes & Garber, 1983; Larwood & Gutek 1984; Martinko & Gardner 1983; Nieva & Gutek, 1980). This conclusion may remind you of a conclusion regarding people's evaluations of women's achievements; bias against women was unlikely to operate if the merit of a painting was well established, but women were downgraded if the painting was of ambiguous quality (Pheterson, et al., 1971). It seems that when evaluators have abundant information for evaluating a candidate—perhaps if the candidate has worked for the company in another position—then they judge the candidate on the basis of those qualifications, rather than on the basis of gender. However, if there is little information available, then the evaluators fall back on the widely held stereotype that women are less competent than men. The ambiguity factor may help to explain why black women are particularly likely to be unemployed (McNett, et al., 1985). Consider this particularly dramatic example: Black female teenagers are

almost *nine* times more likely to be unemployed than white male teenagers. People may combine their negative stereotypes about females with their negative stereotypes about blacks, with the result that they are unlikely to hire a young black woman.

In summary, access discrimination is most likely to operate with stereotyped evaluators, for "sex-inappropriate" jobs, and when there is insufficient information about the candidate's qualifications.

So far, we have discussed *whether* access discrimination operates. Now let us contemplate *how* access discrimination might operate. Arvey (1979) suggests three different ways in which people's stereotypes might produce more negative evaluations for women. First, the stereotypes of women that people hold are mostly negative in nature. A person who believes that women are unmotivated and incompetent will also be likely to react negatively to a specific woman candidate.

Second, Arvey proposes that stereotypes can work because employers have in mind certain characteristics that they believe are necessary for the job, such as assertiveness or independence. Women candidates will be perceived as stereotypically feminine (even if they are truly assertive and independent) and therefore lacking these ideal characteristics. Third, stereotypes may operate in an interview by shaping the expectations that employers have for job candidates. An employer who learns that a candidate is a woman may judge her in terms of her beauty, typing skills, and charm, rather than in terms of characteristics appropriate for the job she is seeking.

☐ SECTION SUMMARY: ▪ Background Factors Influencing Women's Employment

1. **Most women seek employment because it is economically necessary, yet most would continue in their jobs even if it were not economically necessary.**
2. **The presence or absence of young children does not have a large impact on whether a woman works outside the home; however, college education and racial/ethnic background are related to employment patterns.**
3. **Women who select nontraditional careers are likely to be firstborn, with well-educated parents; there is no clearcut tendency for their mothers to work outside the home.**
4. **Women who select nontraditional careers are likely to have characteristics such as independence, self-confidence, and emotional stability; it is unclear whether they are somewhat less interested in interpersonal relationships.**
5. **High-school career counselors are frequently uninformed about employed women; they frequently have low aspirations for females and regard women with nontraditional careers as being deviant.**

6. Access discrimination operates in many cases to prevent women from being hired, particularly when the employer has strong stereotypes, when a woman is applying for a "sex-inappropriate" position, and when her qualifications are ambiguous.
7. Stereotypes operate to encourage access discrimination because stereotypes of women are mostly negative, because the stereotypically feminine characteristics may not match the characteristics considered ideal for the job, and because a woman may be judged in terms of how well she rates on stereotypically feminine characteristics, rather than on characteristics that are important for the job.

☐ WOMEN IN THE WORKPLACE

Now let us turn our attention to women at work. We will first examine the kinds of treatment discrimination that employed women experience. Then we will discuss both traditional and nontraditional kinds of employment. Our last section concerns housewives, people who clearly *work*, yet receive no pay.

Discrimination against Women at Work

We have discussed one kind of discrimination against women called access discrimination. Access discrimination concerns discrimination against women at the time they are hired. A second problem is called **treatment discrimination,** which involves the discrimination that women face once they have obtained jobs (Levitin, Quinn, & Staines, 1971).

Salaries. Probably the most obvious kind of treatment discrimination is the fact that women earn less money than men. The most depressing comparison of women's and men's salaries may be this one: In 1979, men who were high-school dropouts had higher average salaries ($14,800) than women who were college graduates ($13,300) (Bergmann, 1982). In other words, a woman who completes high school and then continues on through four years of college can expect to earn a salary that is about $1,500 less than a man who did not complete high school.

Women's salaries are lower than men's salaries, whether we examine white, black or Hispanic-origin employees. As Figure 6.1 illustrates, females earn substantially less in all three categories.

Clearly, one important reason for the discrepancy in salaries is that men enter jobs that pay more money. Electricians—who are almost always male—earn about twice as much money as stenographers—who are almost always female.

However, the choice of different kinds of jobs explains only part of the discrepancy. A number of carefully conducted studies demonstrate quite

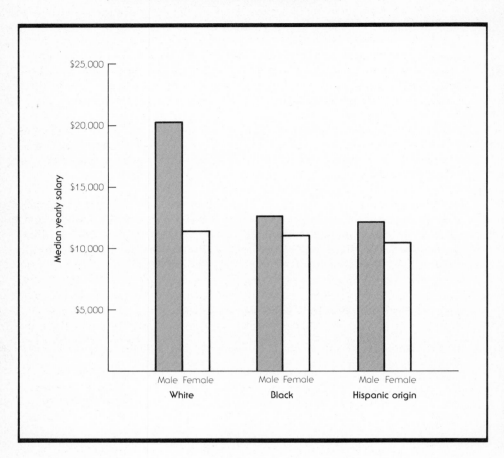

clearly that—even when other factors are taken into account—women are simply paid less than men. Suter and Miller (1973) examined census data for women and men between the ages of 30 and 44. They then adjusted the women's salary to control for seniority, education, experience, job level, and amount worked in a year. After all the adjustments had been completed, they found that women in this age bracket earned about 38 percent less than men. This corresponded to a salary gap of about $3,000. Similar grim findings about women's salaries were reported by Featherman and Hauser (1976) and by Norwood (1982).

Let me cite just one more statistic to complete this gloomy picture. As you probably know, one of the duties of affirmative-action officers on college campuses is to try to ensure similar salaries for male and female workers. However, an examination of salaries of college administrators showed that even female affirmative-action officers earn less than male affirmative-action officers (On Campus with Women, 1978)!

Now here is a paradox: Despite the fact that women are discriminated against in their salaries, women are just as satisfied with their jobs as men are. In fact, Crosby (1982) lists 14 studies that testify to women's job satisfaction. Crosby points out that employed women may realize that women *in general* experience salary discrimination. However, employed women typically deny that they themselves are suffering from sex discrimination. Crosby's study of 400 workers found that both women and men were

> ... very positive about their jobs and their home lives. The level of satisfaction is high; the level of resentment is low. Most people report that they have what they want, what they deserve, and what they had expected to have. They are optimistic. [p. 157]

Why are women so happy with their jobs, despite the low salaries? Crosby suggests that people's satisfaction with their employment depends upon whether they obtain what they *want* and what they feel they *deserve*. They are happy if reality matches their aspirations; they are unhappy if there is a large gap.

Let's first discuss what these women felt they wanted out of their work. The women in Crosby's study were concerned with a sense of accomplishment and good relationships with coworkers; they didn't *want* money as a source of gratification. (These women came from a relatively wealthy community; concern with money probably would be greater among other employees.)

It is more difficult to account for the fact that a woman feels that she *deserves* the salary she receives, even though she realizes that women in general are underpaid. Crosby feels that there are three contributing factors here:

1. A woman has difficulty envisioning herself as a representative of the group "women workers, who are underpaid."
2. If a woman is underpaid, there must be some specific people who are responsible for this unjustice. It is painful to identify anyone at work as a villain.
3. If a woman does see herself as a member of this underprivileged class, she invites pity and scorn from others.

These seem like plausible suggestions, though they haven't been formally tested. It seems likely that women find it easier to close their eyes to personal injustice and to believe that the salary they receive is the salary they deserve.

Other kinds of discrimination.   So far, the only kind of treatment discrimination that we have discussed concerns women's salaries. It is easy to document discrimination in salaries, and so this form of injustice has received the most attention. There are numerous other ways, however, in which women may experience treatment discrimination. Rosen and Jerdee (1974b) asked male bank supervisors to make decisions about assorted hypothetical personnel issues. There were three areas in which women employees were discriminated against:

1. A male was more likely than a female to be promoted to branch manager.
2. A male was more likely than a female to be selected to attend a personnel conference.
3. When a male supervisor recommended that a worker be fired, it was more likely to be supported than when the same recommendation was made by a female.

Using a similar technique, Frasher, Frasher, and Wims (1982) discovered that school-district superintendents showed favoritism towards males in several areas:

1. A male was more likely than a female to be selected for work that required travel.
2. When the employee's spouse was required to move for professional reasons, the superintendents were more likely to try to convince a male employee to remain, in contrast to a female employee.
3. A male who expressed family priorities over job responsibilities was more likely to be promoted than a female who expressed the same viewpoint.
4. When a male requested leave of absence for child care, the request was considered to be more appropriate than when the same request was made by a female.

You'll recall that Crosby found that women ignore salary discrimination. They also seem to ignore other kinds of treatment discrimination. Liss (1975) interviewed women faculty members at a large university. The data from this university demonstrated that women were discriminated against in terms of hiring, salaries, promotions to more prestigious ranks, tenure decisions (that is, permanent appointments until retirement), and appointments to important committees. However, the women only barely perceived the dramatic discrepancies. Even the more perceptive women underestimated the extent of the discrimination. Thus, women were not aware that they were the targets of discrimination.

Another potential kind of treatment discrimination is less formal; women are often excluded from social relationships, both at work and after hours. They may not be part of informal talk sessions, lunches, and other social events—places where business may be conducted and important information may be exchanged (Dunnette & Motowidlo, 1982). Kaufman (1978) found that female professors were less likely than male professors to have a large number of male friends. These friendships may provide access to prestigious committee assignments, useful hints, and other factors that could lead to career advancement.

A final kind of treatment discrimination involves sexual harassment. As we will discuss in detail in Chapter 13, women workers sometimes find that supervisors and coworkers may make sexual comments, try to coerce them into sexual relationships, and occasionally even rape them. As you'll read in that chapter, this unwanted sexual attention has serious consequences for women's psychological health.

Traditional Employment

On the news, we hear about women astronauts, women truck drivers, and women orchestra conductors. Women who are nurses, factory stitchers, and bank tellers don't make the news. However, 55 percent of employed women will be found in traditional clerical and service occupations. We also hear about the startling rise in the percentage of women who work outside the home, but the news doesn't emphasize that most of these women are entering traditional occupations (Larwood & Gutek, 1984).

Table 6.1 shows some representative occupations and the percentage of workers who are women. Women have entered into high-status professional jobs in recent years. However, somewhat more than half of all female professional-technical workers are still in the more traditional areas of nursing and precollege teaching (U. S. Department of Labor, 1980). This does not imply that there is something *wrong* with traditional occupations. However, as Lemkau (1980) has pointed out, the emotional well-being of women in traditionally female areas such as clerical work and nursing is likely to be compromised by drawbacks such as the following: low income status, underutilization of women's abilities, and lack of independence in decision making.

TABLE 6.1 **Percentage of Workers Who Are Women in Selected "Traditional" Occupations**

Occupation	Percentage of Workers Who Are Women
Bank Tellers	93
Cashiers	88
Elementary- and high-school teachers	71
Nurses	99
Sales Clerks	71
Secretaries	99

From the United States Department of Labor, 1980

Table 6.1 showed that women constitute the clear majority of some occupations, illustrating that there is sex segregation among various occupations. There is also sex segregation *within* occupations. Consider school teachers. Women constitute 98 percent of kindergarten and prekindergarten teachers, 84 percent of elementary-school teachers, and 50 percent of secondary-school teachers (Grimm, 1978). Contemplate the forces—both obvious and subtle—that encourage women to teach young children and that discourage men from teaching young children. On the other hand, notice that women and men are equally represented at the high-school level. Men aren't supposed to teach kindergarten, but it's O.K. for them to teach high-school social studies.

Nursing is the profession with large percentages of women (99 percent). Men are so rare in nursing that a man who is employed in this area is likely to be referred to as a "male nurse." I recently attended a nursing school graduation ceremony in which the sole male graduate wore a t-shirt emblazoned with the message, "Token Male." Fitzpatrick (1977), writing about the current state of nursing, remarks that nursing is an area that feminists either misunderstand or ignore. She suggests that nursing represents many characteristics—such as helping and caretaking—that are considered too stereotypically feminine. As a result, the women's movement has concentrated on women who enter male-dominated, high-status professions, and the nursing profession has been ignored.

Another occupation that is traditional for women is clerical work. Of women in the workforce in 1980, about 34 percent were clerical workers (Women's work: Undervalued, underpaid, 1983). Only 16 percent of women were professional or technical workers. Olesen and Katsuranis (1978) point out that researchers have ignored the large segment of the population in clerical work. Women who are clerical workers earn low wages. They also typically do not belong to unions, and so they lack a potentially powerful organization to help them improve their working conditions.

One kind of clerical worker has a particularly unsatisfying work situation. These are the temporary clerical workers, or "urban nomads," as Olesen and Katsuranis call them. In interviews with these women, Olesen and Katsuranis found that they typically tried to do their best at their work, even though they knew that they might be transferred soon. Understandably, they often felt a sense of alienation, as described by one woman, "I'm just the temporary employee, not to be taken seriously and not even known by name, just 'that's one of the temporaries.' They don't show me things they show regular employees" (p. 326).

Roughly one third of black women are employed in cleaning homes, offices, and other related service work (Palmer, 1984). A black domestic worker contrasts the low status of her occupation with what she hopes for her children: "My main goal was I didn't want them to follow in my footsteps as far as working. I always wanted them to please go to school and get a good job because it's important. That was really my main object" (Dill, 1980, p. 109).

For women in traditional occupations, the work is seldom inherently satisfying. The unpleasant nature of the work, the less-than-ideal working conditions, and the low pay make these occupations even less gratifying.

Nontraditional Employment

Ironically, we have more information about the minority of women who have nontraditional jobs than we have about the majority of women who are employed in traditional jobs. Unfortunately, this emphasis on nontraditional jobs creates the erroneous impression that employed women are more likely to be executives than clerical workers, an impression that is both elitist and incorrect (Larwood & Gutek, 1984). A more accurate picture of reality is shown in Table 6.2, which lists some typical nontraditional occupations and the percentage of workers who are women. You may want to glance back at Table 6.1 in order to compare the two groups.

We will consider several questions in this section. Are women in non-traditional jobs substantially different from men in equivalent jobs, particularly with respect to their personality characteristics or their attitudes toward work? What are people's attitudes toward women in nontraditional jobs? What do we know about "token women" and about women in blue-collar jobs? What are the explanations for the relative absence of women in these nontraditional jobs?

Characteristics of women in nontraditional jobs. In the first part of this chapter we examined how women who chose nontraditional jobs differed from women who chose traditional jobs. Now we need to look at a different question: Are women in nontraditional jobs different from the men in these same jobs? If there are impressive sex differences, we may have an answer to our last question, the explanation for the absence of women in

TABLE 6.2 **Percentage of Workers Who Are Women in Selected "Nontraditional" Occupations**

Occupation	Percentage of Workers Who Are Women
Carpenters	1
Engineers	3
Lawyers	12
Mechanics	1
Physicians	11
Underground Coalminers	1

From United States Department of Labor, 1980; Hammond & Mahoney, 1983 certain jobs. In general, however, we will see that the differences are minimal.

In one study female and male students who were enrolled in a Master of Business Administration program took a personality test (Steinberg & Shapiro, 1982). The personality measures assessed 51 different traits that might be related to success as a manager, for example, assertiveness, dominance, and self-control. Men and women received similar scores on these tests. In fact, women received somewhat higher scores on some of the stereotypically masculine traits, such as toughmindedness, and men received somewhat higher scores on some of the stereotypically feminine traits, such as humbleness. In general, the similarities were far more impressive than the differences.

Similarly, a review on women in medicine shows no clear-cut sex differences for the personality characteristics of medical students (Mandlebaum, 1978). One study reported that females were more nurturant than males, whereas another study reported just the opposite. Females were also reported as being both less dominant than males and equal in dominance to males.

So far, we have seen that women in nontraditional jobs are similar to the men in these areas, consistent with the first theme of this book. However, one area in which there may be a sex difference is self-confidence. This should not surprise us, because we saw in the previous chapter that women and men may differ in their self-confidence in some achievement settings. Here are some of the comments made by women who were in administrative positions in the Oregon Public Schools:

> I had always intended to become a principal but I never got there. For one thing I was afraid of the idea that people would think I was good enough to tell others what to do. I didn't feel that I was that great (Schmuck, 1975, p. 343).

> Someone encouraged me. You must tap a woman on the back. Men are knocking on the door for administrative positions but women, who could do the job, say, oh, no not me! It's a way of life with us, we have been indoctrinated to think we are not as good as men (p. 344).

Women who have received clear feedback about their successful performance may grow in their self-confidence, as expressed by another woman: "I began feeling very inferior, then I found out I could keep up. I could reason and I had a pretty good mind after all" (p. 343).

Sometimes influential people and mentors can encourage the growth of confidence in women in nontraditional careers. Gilkes (1982) describes a young black woman who decided to go to law school. When she announced it to faculty members, they actively encouraged her to pursue her goal. Professors gave her extra assignments and additional office time so that she could be well prepared for law school and her specific goal in civil-rights law.

Unfortunately, a large number of women in nontraditional careers remain low in self-confidence. For example, female college professors are typically less confident than male college professors. Widom and Burke (1978) asked faculty members at two colleges to compare themselves with their colleagues. Women rated themselves lower than men with respect to their reputation as a teacher, their publications, and their professional reputation. However, women and men did not differ when they were asked to judge whether they were "as smart" as their colleagues. Thus, self-confidence seems to be lower only in some circumstances. Other research by Instone and her colleagues (1983) demonstrated that women are generally lower in self-confidence in organizational settings, as well as in school administration and college teaching. Further research on self-confidence in employment settings will probably reveal an overall sex difference, but some circumstances in which women and men are similar.

Women and men may also differ somewhat with respect to their attitudes toward their work. Male professors were somewhat more likely than female professors to say that they would cancel class because of illness and other obligations (Widom & Burke, 1978). In another study, male professors were somewhat more likely than female professors to express a strong preference for research, but men and women were quite similar in other respects (Glenwick, Johansson, & Bondy, 1978).

Women in medicine may have a more humanistic attitude to their profession than men do. Women medical students were more likely than men to report that they chose medicine in order to help other people. They were also more likely to affirm the statement, "Social and psychological factors, including empathy, are important in health care" (Leserman, 1980, p. 650). Male medical students were more likely than female medical students to affirm the statement, "High status and income were important in career selection" (p. 650).

In summary, men and women in the same profession may differ with respect to some characteristics, such as their self-confidence and their reasons for selecting a profession. However, the similarities between men and women are more impressive than the differences. Think about whether this conclusion matches the impression you have received from the popular media. As discussed in Chapter 1, the media tend to glorify studies in which differences are found, ignoring studies that report similarities.

Attitudes toward women in nontraditional jobs. Let us first examine how people respond to female supervisors, as opposed to male supervisors. There is a stereotype that people would rather work for a man than a woman because men are more fair, competent, and rational. According to this stereotype, women are simply not good leaders. A study by Feild and Caldwell (1979) found just the opposite. These researchers asked employees at a large university library to complete questionnaires, which asked them to describe their satisfaction with various aspects of their jobs. The employees tended to be more satisfied with the quality of supervision when they were supervised by women. They also reported more satisfaction with their coworkers and more satisfaction with the work itself when they had a female supervisor.

This study by Feild and Caldwell examined actual employees, who have had real-life experience with a female or male supervisor. In other studies, people work under a female or male supervisor for a brief period of time, and then they evaluate this supervisor. Cohen, Bunker, Burton, and McManus (1978) found that male undergraduate students who were supervised by a female, rather than a male, sometimes tended to make unfavorable verbal comments about the supervisor. However, the supervisor's sex did not influence the students' actual performance or their written evaluation of the supervisor.

Notice that in these studies, the one by Feild and Caldwell on actual supervisors and the one by Cohen and his colleagues on temporary supervisors, the employees were asked to evaluate a specific person with whom they had direct contact. How would people respond if they were asked to judge some hypothetical woman or "women in general"? These evaluations would depend less on people's actual experiences with working women, and more on their stereotypes. As we mentioned in the section on access discrimination, biases are greatest when there is little information available.

DEMONSTRATION 6.2

Supervisors' Judgments about Female and Male Employees

Your task is to guess what the supervisors in Rosen and Jerdee's (1978) study decided about female and male employees. For each of the items below, guess the rating that the supervisors supplied from the rating scale below. The answers appear in the text; check them when you are finished.

1	2	3	4	5
Men much more than women	Men slightly more than women	No difference	Women slightly more than men	Women much more than men

1. Understand the "big picture" of the organization
2. Are capable administrators
3. Enjoy doing routine tasks
4. Are independent and self sufficient
5. Cry easily
6. Have leadership potential
7. Are good at detail work
8. Approach problems rationally
9. Set long range goals and work toward them.
10. Are jealous

The worst news for women comes from a study by Rosen and Jerdee (1978), whose research on access and treatment discrimination we discussed earlier. More than 800 male supervisors compared men and women workers on 64 work-related characteristics, including the ones listed in Demonstration 6.2. The supervisors showed a significant tendency to mark the following items from Demonstration 6.2 as being more characteristic of men than of women:

1. Understand the "big picture" of the organization (Average Rating = 2.2)
2. Are capable administrators (A. R. = 2.5)
4. Are independent and self-sufficient (A. R. = 2.5)
6. Have leadership potential (A. R. = 2.5)
8. Approach problems rationally (A. R. = 2.3)
9. Set long-range goals and work toward them (A. R. = 2.4)

In contrast, the supervisors showed a significant tendency to mark the following items as being more characteristic of women than of men:

3. Enjoy doing routine tasks (Average Rating = 3.5)
5. Cry easily (A. R. = 4.3)
7. Are good at detail work (A. R. = 3.6)
10. Are jealous (A. R. = 3.6)

You'll notice that positive characteristics were attributed to men far more often than to women. When positive characteristics were attributed to women, these characteristics almost always described skills in low-level occupations (such as 3 and 7). As Rosen and Jerdee conclude, "Virtually every perceived difference between male and female employees was unfavorable to women aspiring to higher level occupations" (p. 843).

Women fared much better in a study on attitudes toward women physicians (Scadron, et al., 1982). More than 900 medical students and medical faculty members responded to a survey that asked them to judge the "typical" male and female medical faculty member. In general, the respondents saw both men and women as being fair, strong, and progressive. However, men were judged to be much more egotistical than women. Women were judged to be much more sensitive and altruistic than men.

This section on attitudes toward women in nontraditional jobs has shown some evidence of the theme that people often react differently to women and men. However, some employed women are evaluated neutrally or even positively. Unfortunately, it's not yet clear what factors encourage more positive attitudes toward women. At present, all we can say is that negative attitudes toward employed women are likely, but certainly not inevitable.

The token woman. It seems that token women are particularly likely to encounter the negative attitudes we discussed in the previous section.

Definitions for the term "token woman" vary, as discussed in several articles (Constantinople, 1982; Laws, 1975; Young, MacKenzie, & Sherif, 1980, 1982). One definition is that **token women** work at jobs in which they constitute less than 15 percent of the workers (Kanter, 1977). Their token status is extremely important in the way they are regarded, because they are often treated as symbols rather than as individuals. Ironically, they are symbols of their category, yet exceptions to that same category (Nieva & Gutek, 1981).

Here is Kanter's description of token women in a corporation:

> Those women who were few in number among male peers and often had "only women" status became tokens: symbols of how-women-can-do, stand-ins for all women. Sometimes they had the advantages of those who are "different" and thus were highly visible in a system where success is tied to becoming known. Sometimes they faced the loneliness of the outsider, of the stranger who intrudes upon an alien culture and may become self-estranged in the process of assimilation. [p. 207]

Kanter and Stein (1980) point out numerous other consequences of the token status in a book of cartoons called *A Tale of "O": On Being Different in an Organization*. They suggest that there will be more gossip about token people. Also, the token person is viewed as a spokesperson for all others of that category. People will turn to the one woman at a meeting to ask what women will think about a particular issue. (But notice that anyone who is rare can be a token; people turn to the one or two men in my psychology of women classroom to ask for "the men's viewpoint.") Kanter and Stein also suggest that the presence of a token person makes all the other people band together because of a contrast effect. Many of the observations that Kanter and Stein make seem to fit our intuitions and anecdotal evidence, but the research evidence is currently lacking.

The "Queen-Bee syndrome" is another concept that is frequently used in connection with attitudes toward working women. A **Queen Bee** is someone who has worked herself up to a position of considerable professional status in a male-dominated occupation and who often has achieved impressive social status, but who does not support other women (Staines, Tavris, & Jayaratne, 1974). For example, a typical Queen Bee has made it in the "Man's World" because she has a high-status profession with a good salary. Her social success is shown by the fact that she is attractive, happily married, and popular with men. She believes that she reached her goals without the feminist movement to help her, and other women should also try to reach their goals unaided. As Staines and his colleagues argue, people tend to like the system that gives them rewards for the particular skills they possess. Thus, a woman who has achieved success in a male-dominated field will approve of the system that has allowed her to reach the top. It is important to keep the Queen-Bee syndrome in mind because it is often tempting to adopt the stereotype that it is only men who oppose the advancement of women.

Queen Bees and antifeminists tend to choose one of two tactics in their discrimination against other women (Keiffer & Cullen, 1974). One tactic is to argue that men and women actually receive equal treatment in their professions. Like the women whom Crosby (1982) surveyed in her study of women's salaries, these women deny their membership in a group that experiences discrimination. The other tactic is to be aggressive against women, attacking them and claiming that women are responsible for their own lack of success.

The term "Queen Bee" is a popular one, but we really don't have much information in this area. We don't know whether Queen Bees are common or rare, what kinds of women are likely to be Queen Bees, and whether Queen Bees are more abundant in some professions than in others. Queen Bees are important in the study of psychology of women because these are women who are particularly likely to demonstrate the theme of the differential treatment of women and men.

Women in blue-collar jobs.   Most of our information on women in nontraditional occupations concerns professions such as law, medicine, and business. However, women are increasingly entering blue-collar fields. In fact, 18 percent of blue-collar jobs are now held by women (Hammond & Mahoney, 1983).

Let us look at one blue-collar job in which women are still in the clear minority; only 1 percent of underground coalminers are women. According to Hammond and Mahoney, women coalminers must balance the costs against the rewards of this kind of work. The costs include strenuous work, unsafe conditions, teasing from some men, jealousy from the male coalminers' wives, and the cost to their own physical attractiveness. However, these costs are outweighed by pride in their successful performance, a sense of uniqueness, the cooperative atmosphere with male miners that eventually develops, and—primarily—the good pay. One woman contrasted her present job with her previous job as a waitress:

> "I thought there must be a better way—here I am making $1.45/hour and $1.00/hour in tips. Jesus, there's gotta be another way." Faced with the responsibility of family support, she asserted: "I can wash off coal black but I can't wash off those damn bill collectors." [Hammond & Mahoney, 1983, p. 19]

Research has confirmed that money is an important factor for women in blue-collar jobs. Other advantages that these women mention about their work are not as concrete. They include factors such as a sense of productivity, challenge, and independence (Deaux & Ullman, 1983; Walshok, 1981). A woman in her early twenties who is an auto mechanic describes the feeling of accomplishment she receives in her work:

> ... doing something with your hands was kind of cool, because you could see what you were doing. Actually see the results—when you fixed a car it ran—the

immediate satisfaction, and that's something I never have had in a job. In a factory you don't see where it's going or anything, so that's cool, plus you know that you did it. It's like solving a puzzle—when you get the answer—yeah! [Walshok, 1981, p. 3]

One of the most detailed studies on women in blue-collar jobs examined women in the steel industry (Deaux & Ullman, 1983). Most of the women they interviewed liked their jobs. They often reported that their work was challenging, and that it was a clear improvement over the previous jobs they had held. Interestingly, these women seemed to be self-confident about their abilities, a finding that contrasts with reports from women in other nontraditional jobs. You'll recall that Lenney (1977) found that women are not always less confident than men. Thus, women in the steel industry appreciate their work and also tend to feel that they do it competently.

Of course, the women in blue-collar occupations mention some disadvantages to their work, as Hammond and Mahoney (1983) found in their report on women coalminers. As Deaux and Ullman (1983) point out, women are likely to be the first to lose their jobs when cutbacks are necessary. Women, on the average, are not as strong as men, which provides a clear disadvantage for some women in some of the more physically demanding jobs. Also, women in a wide variety of blue-collar jobs confirmed Hammond and Mahoney's report that women often receive teasing and harassment from their male coworkers. Fortunately, this problem usually diminished after the second year on the job.

High-paying, blue-collar jobs clearly offer an attractive alternative to traditional female occupations. However, it will be a challenge for women to find employment in these areas. As Walshok concludes,

... we must of necessity change some of the economic and social arrangements limiting women's roles if large numbers of women are to have improved employment. It is not simply a matter of individual women changing themselves. Employers and policy makers have an obligation to continue examining the wide range of issues affecting women and employment. [p. 284]

Explanations for the scarcity of women in some occupations. Riger and Galligan (1980) tackle the question of why there are so few women in managerial positions, and their argument is also relevant for other nontraditional occupations. Why, for example, are only 18 percent of managers female (Baron, 1977)?

Riger and Galligan point out that there are two major kinds of explanations for why men are so much more likely than women to occupy managerial positions; these two explanations were also mentioned in the previous quotation. The first kind of explanation is person-centered. According to **person-centered explanations,** female socialization encourages women to develop personality traits that are contrary to the requirements of the managerial role. One person-centered explanation is fear of success, the notion that achievement and the feminine role are not compatible. However, recall from the last chapter that psychologists are currently skeptical about whether there are substantial sex differences in fear of success. Recall, also, that we are uncertain about whether there are substantial sex differences in other areas related to achievement, such as attributions for one's own success or failure.

According to a different kind of person-centered explanation, women *behave* in a different manner from men in managerial positions (Hennig & Jardim, 1977). This difference in behavior is a product of a difference in gender-role socialization. This explanation argues that little boys learn critical management skills—such as planning strategies, cooperation, and competition—by playing team sports. The implication of these person-centered explanations is that women *deserve* their lower-status jobs. However, you'll recall from the section on characteristics of women in nontraditional jobs that men and women in the same occupations are remarkably similar in terms of personal characteristics.

Riger and Galligan prefer **situation-centered explanations,** which emphasize characteristics of the organizational situation, rather than personal traits or skills. Kanter's (1977) book *Men and Women of the Corporation* presents a good example of a situation-centered explanation. Kanter argues that the social structure of organizations may be responsible for women's lack of success in the business world. Her argument can be extended to other professions, as well.

Kanter points out that women's opportunities may be blocked, as we saw in our discussion of access discrimination. Women also tend to have little power in an organization, as we saw in our discussion of treatment discrimination and promotions. Furthermore, those women who do rise towards the top are surrounded by males, and they often become the token women we mentioned earlier. Also, young women are unlikely to receive help from those at the top. Men are unwilling to become mentors to aspiring women, and those few women at the top may sometimes be Queen Bees.

The person-centered explanations and the situation-centered explanations suggest different strategies for improving women's employment conditions. The person-centered explanations propose that women can advance by taking courses designed to make them more assertive or more skilled in areas such as handling finances or conducting meetings. However, women who "improve" themselves still face hostility on the job. Person-centered approaches stress that women should adopt a traditionally male approach to problems. As Riger and Galligan point out, "Characteristics associated with traditional female sex roles, such as an emphasis on people as opposed to production, might actually produce better outcomes in certain work situations" (p. 907).

The situation-centered explanations propose different strategies. These strategies include training managers to use objective rating scales, presenting affirmative-action policies appropriately, and eliminating women's token status. There should be rewards for those who increase the number of women in managerial positions, as well as punishments for those who discriminate. Organizations should also explore the contributions that could be provided by a more traditionally feminine orientation. These suggestions sound excellent, but they are unlikely to occur spontaneously. Perhaps as more women enter nontraditional professions, token women and Queen Bees will become less common. As a consequence, women may be more likely to push for equal treatment of women and men in the workplace.

Housewives

Read the job description in Table 6.3 and decide whether this position sounds like one you'd want to pursue.

You probably recognized that this unappealing paragraph describes the duties of a wife and mother. The housewife may run her home as a full-time occupation, or she may have a paying job in addition to these household responsibilities. At the end of this chapter, we will see that even women with full-time paying jobs continue to do far more than their share of housework and child care. Now we need to discuss the diversity of responsibilities and the amount of work involved in being a housewife.

Any list of a housewife's responsibilities must be incomplete. However, a list constructed by St. John-Parsons (1978) hints at the variety of tasks: food shopping, meal preparation, household purchases, cleaning the house, washing clothes, ironing and mending, household maintenance, gardening, care of the car, preparation of children for school, transportation of children, care of children in emergencies or illness, care of children on school holidays, preparation of children for bed, disciplining children, hiring of any child-care help, holiday planning, and finances.

TABLE 6.3 **Would You Apply for This Job?**

Help Wanted
Requirements: Intelligence, good health, energy, patience, sociability. Skills: At least 12 different occupations. Hours: 99.6 per week. Salary: None. Holidays: None (will be required to remain on stand-by 24 hours a day, 7 days a week). Opportunities for Advancement: None (limited transferability of skills acquired on the job). Job Security: None (trend is toward more layoffs particularly as employee approaches middle age. Severance pay will depend on the discretion of the employer). Fringe Benefits: Food, clothing and shelter generally provided, but any additional bonuses will depend on financial standing and good nature of the employer. No health, medical, or accident insurance; no Social Security or pension plan. [Chesler, 1976, p. 97]

According to Vanek (1978), the amount of time that American women spend on housework has not changed markedly over the years. In the 1920s, full-time housewives spent about 52 hours a week on housework; the estimate for more recent years is about 55 hours a week. The nature of housework has changed, though. Women now spend less time preparing food and cleaning up after meals. However, they now spend more time shopping for the essentials. They also wash clothes more often. Full-time housewives spent more time on household tasks than employed women, probably, as Vanek concludes, because employed women are forced to "cut corners" and do less-than-ideal work.

In addition to the variety of tasks and the number of hours, another characteristic of the housewife's work is its low prestige value (Lopata, 1971; Oakley, 1974). How many times have you heard a woman remark that she is "just a housewife"? We do not need to dwell on the obviously unpleasant nature of many of the tasks, either. It is clearly frustrating to struggle at some task that must usually be repeated just as soon as it is finished, that cannot be postponed, and that typically has no clear-cut, obtainable standards of completion. (Is the kitchen floor ever really clean enough?)

In summary, any consideration of working women must acknowledge the enormous amount of work they do in their homes. This work is diverse, extensive, frustrating, and low in prestige. Furthermore, it constitutes an important "second job" for women who are already working outside the home.

☐ SECTION SUMMARY: ▪ Women in the Workplace

1. Women earn less than men, even when factors such as experience and work hours have been taken into account.
2. Women are just as happy with their work as men are, despite their low salaries.
3. Women experience treatment discrimination in terms of promotions, selections for special assignments, requests for leaves of absence, and exclusion from social relationships.
4. The majority of employed women are found in traditional clerical and service occupations.
5. Nursing is an occupation that has been ignored by the feminist movement.
6. Clerical workers, who constitute 34 percent of all employed women, earn low wages, seldom belong to unions, and may have unsatisfying work situations.
7. Women in nontraditional professions are similar to men in the same fields; however, they may be somewhat less self-confident and they may have different reasons for selecting a profession.

8. Many people have negative attitudes toward women in nontraditional professions, but attitudes can also be positive.

9. Token women work at jobs in which they constitute less than 15 percent of the workers; token women can become Queen Bees, who do not work for the advancement of other women.

10. Women in nontraditional blue-collar jobs, such as coalmining and the steel industry, are generally satisfied with their work; they enjoy the pay and the sense of productivity, challenge, and independence; the disadvantages include strenuous work, layoffs, and teasing from male coworkers.

11. Person-centered explanations argue that women are not found in certain professions because they lack the appropriate achievement behaviors, personality characteristics, and skills.

12. Situation-centered explanations seem to account more adequately for the absence of women in certain professions; according to these explanations, the structure of organizations prevents women's success.

13. American women spend about as much time on housework as they spent in the 1920s; the work is also diverse, frustrating, and low in prestige.

☐ THE EFFECTS OF EMPLOYMENT ON PERSONAL LIFE

Our discussion so far has focused on women in work settings. However, a woman's employment could potentially have important consequences for areas of her personal life, such as her marriage, her children, and her personal adjustment.

Marriage

The majority of employed women are married. In 1979, 55 percent of women in the labor force were married and living with their husbands. (U. S. Department of Labor, 1980).

The marriages of employed women vary widely. Some employed women have unemployed husbands. In many other cases, both the husband and the wife work at "jobs" rather than "careers." However, we have little information about these two kinds of work/marriage combinations. Instead, most of our information concerns only the small proportion of people in **dual-career families,** where both the wife and the husband have high-status occupations. Keep in mind as you read about these "elite" couples that their experiences may not be typical. Our discussion focuses on how these families find employment and how they divide household tasks.

Finding employment. There are many complications when two people who have trained for specific careers try to find employment in the same community. Demonstration 6.3 represents a typical dilemma faced by dual-career families. This example is adapted from one of several situations that Wallston, Foster, and Berger (1978) presented to the participants in their study who were professional couples.

Wallston and her colleages found that about half of the couples adopted an egalitarian position, one that favored Mary and Frank equally (alternatives *B* and *C* in Demonstration 6.3). The same couples were also asked to describe how they had responded to their own real-life job offers. These results, in contrast to the simulated situations, were much more conservative. Only about 25 percent had made career choices in an egalitarian manner. The authors conclude, "as is traditionally expected, men were more likely to take jobs and lead and women were more likely to follow" (p. 16).

In a later study, Foster, Wallston, and Berger (1980) discovered that people who called themselves "feminists" were more likely than nonfeminists to choose an egalitarian solution in the simulated situations. However, the feminist approach was not related to people's actual career choices. Feminists and nonfeminists responded about the same to the real-life pressures involved in career decisions.

In addition to the complications of finding jobs, dual-career families face another dilemma when one member of the couple receives a promotion that involves a move. Once again, the couple faces a real-life dilemma. Should she give up her job and look for work at the new location? Should they live apart, at least temporarily? Should he turn down the offer?

Some couples decide to live apart because they work in different geographic regions. It takes extraordinary creativity (and huge financial invest-

---

DEMONSTRATION 6.3

A Dilemma Faced by Dual-Career Families

Imagine that you and your spouse faced the following dilemma.

Mary and Frank are two professionals who are married to each other. Currently, both of them are seeking employment. Frank has received a very good job offer and must make a decision about that job. Mary has not yet received a firm offer. However, there seem to be good possibilities for the future. Mary cannot arrange interviews before Frank's deadline. Frank may be able to locate another position in the geographic location in which Mary has possibilities.

Which option would you select?

A. Frank accepts the job and Mary goes to look for a position in that area.
B. Frank declines the job and they both continue to look for employment.
C. Frank accepts the job, Mary pursues her possibilities for employment, and there is a chance that they will live separately for some period of time.

ments) to arrange commuting schedules. It also places extraordinary emotional strain on the couple. If they see each other only on weekends, should they remain brightly cheerful for the entire time? How can a fight be resolved if his plane leaves in 45 minutes? It seems likely that love relationships— which are complicated enough even when two people live together full time— are particularly stressful when the two people must continually become reacquainted, only to say goodbye again after several days.

Performance of household tasks.   Decisions about accepting jobs and promotions can be traumatic. It is clear how a professional woman would feel shortchanged if she greatly altered her career to move to Los Angeles or Chicago for her husband's career. However, there are numerous trivial decisions that need to be made every day, decisions such as who will shop for the groceries, who will remember to send Aunt Carol the birthday card, and who will pick up the socks in the bathroom. A woman who is serious about her career might resent the accumulated impact of those household decisions just as much as she resents a move to a new area.

Women are still primarily responsible for household work. In a substantial number of cases, the husband may perform essentially no household tasks. Poloma and Garland (1971) found that 38 percent of the husbands in their sample did no housework. Robinson and his coauthors (1977) noted that about one-third of the women in their sample reported that their husbands had not helped with the household chores during the previous week.

A survey of 12 different countries showed that this division of household tasks is not confined to the United States (Newland, 1980). According to this report, employed men spent one hour in housework each workday. In contrast, employed women spent more than three hours in housework each workday.

Robinson and his coworkers asked an interesting question to the married women in their sample: Did they wish that their husbands would give them more help with household chores? Only 23 percent answered "yes." Why should women not want more help when the husbands help so little to begin with? The authors speculate that the women may appreciate having some clearly defined responsibilities. In addition, the women probably feel that they must adhere to the norms; they may believe, "I should do the housework." Finally, women may like doing chores their own way. Some husbands may perform a task so poorly that the wives may find themselves repeating the work.

If a woman is employed, her household tasks decrease fairly sharply and her husband's tasks increase slightly or not at all (Atkinson & Huston, 1984; Bahr, 1974; Glazer, 1984; Holmstrom, 1972; Miller & Garrison, 1982; Nyquist, et al., 1985). For example, Pleck (1983) reported that wives who were employed spent about two and one-quarter hours less on housework each day than wives who were not employed. The wife's employment status had a much less dramatic impact on husbands' household tasks, however. Husbands with employed wives spent about *two minutes* more on housework each day than husbands with nonemployed wives!

There are some couples who divide labor reasonably evenly. Haas (1982) studied 31 couples who divided household tasks roughly equally. In comparison with traditional couples, these couples were more likely to be well educated, to have had a mother who was employed, and to have received encouragement for housework sharing from the women's movement or from other people.

We have seen that there are sources of strain on a marriage when the wife is employed. There may be career conflicts, and the unequal division of household chores probably causes resentment. These observations lead us to an important contrast: How happy are the marriages of employed women? There is some evidence that divorce is more likely in cases where wives have access to an independent income (Moore & Sawhill, 1978). Moore and Sawhill point out that there are two possible explanations here. One explanation is that the woman's working is somehow inappropriate, and the resulting tension leads to a divorce. Another explanation is that when marriages are unsatisfactory, the costs of divorce are lower for wives who can support themselves.

More optimistic news comes from a large nationwide survey conducted by Staines, Pleck, Shepard, and O'Connor (1978). In some respects, employed wives were less happy with their marriages than were nonemployed women. Employed wives were more likely to report that they had occasionally wished they had married someone else. They were also more likely to have contemplated a divorce. However, employed wives and nonemployed wives scored similarly on ratings of marital satisfaction. Furthermore, the husbands of employed wives and the husbands of nonemployed wives reported similar satisfactions with their marriages. Nieva and Gutek (1981) conclude from their review of this topic that, when other factors are taken into account, a woman's employment status does not influence marital satisfaction.

Children

As we saw at the beginning of the chapter, there has been a dramatic increase in recent years in the number of employed women with young children. There are two important issues concerning the children of employed mothers. First, what are the effects of employment on the adjustment of the children? Second, how are child-care tasks divided in two-parent families?

The effects of employment.   A review of the popular child-rearing books noted several disturbing themes (Hurst & Zambrana, 1981):

1. These books discourage women from being employed during the first years of the child's life, except out of financial necessity.

2. There is a consensus that mothers—if they must work outside the home at all—should work only part time.
3. They assume that the mother is the primary caretaker.
4. They suggest that the mother who seeks employment out of choice, rather than necessity, during the first few years of the child's life has failed not only her child but herself as well. A popular book by Brazelton (1974) depicts the employed mother as a neurotic, career-oriented woman who probably did not want a child in the first place.
5. They propose that an employed mother is a mother first. Her desire to work must be compromised to her child in all instances.

The picture that these books paint is a gloomy one. Few of the authors have examined the psychological literature about the children of employed mothers. As you will see, that gloomy picture is misleading; overall, the children of employed mothers and the children of nonemployed mothers are similar.

Before we examine those studies, consider that 52 percent of women with children under 18 years of age work outside the home (U. S. Department of Labor, 1980). That means that the balance has now changed so that the typical mother works outside the home. The mother we used to read about in our third-grade books—whose major activity seemed to be baking cookies and who never needed to feel guilty about working outside the home—that mother is not typical.

Consider, also, how many mothers are reading the child-rearing books and feeling guilty about their "negligence." These books and other media should inform them that their work outside the home probably has little effect on their children.

Several reviews of the literature on employed mothers have been published (Hoffman, 1979; Hurst & Zambrana, 1981; Zambrana, Hurst, & Hite, 1979). These reviews stress that there are other factors that are probably more important than whether the mother is employed. These factors include whether the child is in a stimulating, affectionate, and stable environment, whether the mother is resentful of the caretaker, and what kind of interactions occur between mother and child when the mother is home (Hoffman, 1979).

Let's discuss this area in more detail, beginning with early childhood. Of all the areas of research on maternal employment, the period of early childhood has received the least attention. Early child-rearing books relied on studies that showed that orphans in understaffed institutions seemed to suffer. These studies are hardly relevant for infants and young children whose mothers are away from home for perhaps 40 hours a week! Unfortunately, these young children are the most difficult of any age group to study because they receive no school grades, they cannot take tests, and they cannot be interviewed. However, there is no clear-cut evidence of any consistent advantage for full-time mothering. For example, one study found that children's growth was superior in families in which both parents were employed (Cherry & Eaton, 1977), but another study reported lower IQs for one of the samples of sons of employed mothers (Gold & Andres, 1978a). There is also some evidence that the young children of employed mothers may show better social adjustment (Gold & Andres, 1978a; Moore, 1975).

Many people (Fraiberg, 1977) suggest that gruesome things can happen to children who attend infant day-care centers, hinting that they are impersonally treated like little packages at these "storage houses." However, studies have demonstrated that there is little evidence of any social or intellectual disadvantage when infants attend high-quality day-care centers (Rutter, 1982). It is ironic that the current policy in the United States does not support high-quality day care (Zigler & Muenchow, 1983).

The problem of child care is reduced when children enter school. The child's social life expands to include other children, teachers, and other adults, and so the mother's presence is not as relevant as it was for the younger child. For school-aged girls, there is no consistent evidence of significant differences in school achievement between the children of employed mothers and nonemployed mothers. Girls appear to have a social advantage when their mothers are employed outside the home, because these girls admire their mothers more and hold more positive opinions about women in general. According to Hoffman (1979), the daughters of employed mothers receive more encouragement for independence than do daughters of nonemployed mothers, which is another advantage.

The data for school-aged boys are more complex. The sons of employed mothers are often less stereotyped than the sons of nonemployed mothers. Other kinds of differences may depend upon the social class of the boy. Boys from lower-class families may admire their fathers less if the mother is employed (Hoffman, 1974b). Boys from middle-class families have occasionally scored lower on achievement tests when their mothers were employed, although most studies have found no differences.

How do adolescents fare when their mothers are employed? As Hoffman (1979) concludes, "Very few of the studies of maternal employment during the child's adolescence have found negative effects, and most have found positive ones" (p. 864). One study of adolescents showed that both sons and daughters of employed mothers were better adjusted than the children of nonemployed mothers (Gold & Andres, 1978b). They had a stronger sense of personal worth, a greater sense of belonging, better family relations, and better interpersonal relations at school.

Many studies on adolescents focus on gender-role concepts. The results for boys are mixed, but most of the results for girls show that daughters of employed mothers are less gender stereotyped (Huston, 1983; Mortimer & Sorensen, 1984; Zambrana et al., 1979).

I will conclude this discussion of the effects of maternal employment on children with a representative study that examines both preadolescents and adolescents. Dellas, Gaier, and Emihovich (1979) surveyed intact, urban families in the East and Midwest. They contrasted the families of employed women, who had been working full-time for at least five years prior to the study, with the families of women who had not been employed during the previous five years. The two sets of families were matched for the parents' education level and the fathers' socioeconomic status.

The examination of preadolescents showed no difference on numerous variables, such as activities with parents, disagreements with parents, household chores, plans to attend college, and future life orientation. In fact, the only two questions that showed a significant difference concerned gender roles. The girls whose mothers were employed showed less gender-role stereotyping. The examination of adolescents showed no differences at all between the children of employed mothers and the children of nonemployed mothers.

In summary, there is no consistent evidence of any important differences between the children of employed mothers and the children of nonemployed mothers. There may even be some advantages for the children of employed mothers because their gender-role stereotypes are often less rigid.

Performance of child-care tasks. In a previous section, we saw that women clearly performed more household tasks than men. There is some evidence that the distribution of child-care tasks is even more unequal. For example, Weingarten (1978) interviewed 32 dual-career families. She found that household tasks were generally equally shared between the men and the women. However, the women spent significantly more time on child care than the men did. Mothers were more likely to drive their children to activities, and they were more likely to make decisions about whether the children could watch television.

Weingarten speculates about why mothers continue to do far more than their share of the child-care tasks, even though they have the same kinds of employment responsibilities that their husbands have:

> ... the negative sanctions for deviations from convention in the area of child care are much more clearly spelled out in the area of householding. Women who are poor cooks or sloppy housecleaners may be insulted or mocked, but there is no extensive literature documenting their faults or cultural consensus about the consequences. Bad mothers, on the other hand, are reviled, and popular wisdom as well as social-science studies have told women for decades that employed mothers *are* bad mothers. [pp. 50–51]

We end this section with the same point at which we began: The cultural myth suggests that maternal employment leads to twisted, deviant children. In fact, there is no substantial evidence for this myth. If the lack of evidence for the myth receives the appropriate attention, then employed mothers may not feel so guilty. They may feel more comfortable about encouraging their husbands to participate more equally in child care.

For many women, there is no husband who can—even theoretically— share in taking care of the children. Mothers who are single, separated, divorced, or widowed must usually work outside the home for economic reasons. The logistic problems of arranging for child care and transporting children become even more complicated. In addition, unmarried mothers must take sole responsibility for nurturing their children, helping them with their homework, and disciplining them. Finally, they must add the guilt of "the fatherless child" to the already substantial guilt arising from being an employed mother.

Personal Adjustment

Role strain. A woman from Tacoma, Washington, writes:

"I have worked for the past 10½ years, for the same company although in various departments and areas throughout my company. . . . However, since I had my daughter . . . work has increasingly become a place you go that takes the entire day and have to leave each evening to go to Job 2—Chef, Maid, Housekeeper and Nanny. I am so tired all the time that more and more often I wish I were only working a few hours a week, although it would certainly be nice to earn the same amount I now make in a 40 hour week! If I could only have an hour in the middle of the day to just SIT in a room in my home entirely alone with no demands from my child, my husband, my dog or cat, my employer . . . just time to sit all alone. . . ." [National Commission on Working Women, 1979, p. 4]

This woman provides a vivid example of role strain. **Role strain** occurs when people perceive a difficulty in fulfilling their role obligations (Johnson & Johnson, 1977). Role strain for employed women involves conflict between a job and family responsibilities. It may involve fatigue, emotional depletion, and guilt.

In the previous sections on household work and child care, we saw that employed women have diverse responsibilities. There are numerous *physical* chores that must be accomplished in order to keep a family operating smoothly. All of these chores contribute to role strain. There are also more subtle contributors to role strain. Richter (1983) compared how often men and women thought about home life when they were at work. Women reported thinking about home life more often than men during the morning and at lunch, although not in the afternoon. Thus, in a sense, women "do" house-work and child care even when they are on the job.

Do women and men differ in the amount of role strain they experience? Herman and Gyllstrom (1977) surveyed teaching and nonteaching employees at Northwestern University. The women perceived significantly greater role strain than the men. Furthermore, professional women are particularly likely to feel role strain (Beckman, 1978).

Johnson and Johnson (1977) also found that employed women showed more role strain than their husbands. They discovered that dual-career families used several techniques to keep role strain within reasonable limits:

1. Women frequently lowered their career ambitions and assigned priority to domestic roles. None of the husbands in their sample lowered their career strivings to accommodate their wives' careers.
2. Women frequently argued, "It's the quality of the time spent with children that counts—not the quantity" (p. 393). They compensated by having structured family activities such as camping trips and bedtime stories.
3. Women trained their children to be more self-reliant and independent.
4. The couples tended to choose friends from dual-career families, a precaution that probably decreased the amount of criticism from people with different lifestyles.

Notice that most of these adjustments required a sacrifice on the part of the women. Men, who felt less role strain to begin with, may not have been very motivated to change their lifestyles.

Physical health. We might imagine that role strain might lead to poor physical health for employed women. However, the data show that employed women are—if anything—healthier than nonemployed women. For example, Nathanson (1980) found that women who lack social support at home are likely to be healthier if they are employed than if they are nonemployed. Furthermore, Welch and Booth (1977) examined 500 urban married women with children. Women who had been employed for more than one year were physically healthier than women who were nonemployed. Employed women were less likely to have been sick during the previous two weeks, and their total number of diseases was also lower.

Mental health. After reading the earlier section about role strain, you may have a mental image of a bleary-eyed woman, arriving home from a grueling day at work just in time to feed the dog, change the baby's diapers, and set the dinner table. This woman, it would seem, has every right to be depressed and unhappy. However, as we will see in this section, employed women are no less happy than nonemployed women. In fact, in many cases they are happier and better adjusted.

For one thing, women may find their work stimulating and pleasurable. In Beckman's (1978) survey, women mentioned that they enjoyed many aspects of work: social interaction, achievement, challenge, creativity, self-esteem, independence, economic benefits, and mental stimulation.

Another study of dual-career families showed that both parents and children in these families were very energetic and active (St. John-Parsons, 1978). Most reported that they had occasional periods of complete physical exhaustion, but none reported mental depressions. In fact, both parents and children appeared to have developed resilience and inner strength.

A woman pediatrician captured the exhilaration some women feel about their work:

> I keep talking about the 1001 things I want to do when I retire. ... I'm going to learn birds and bridge, play the piano, paint, make furniture without interruption, hike the Appalachian Trail, find a sexy liaison, be a real grandmother, etc, etc, but I suspect I will always practice medicine until I'm dead or senile, I love the busyness of it all, the problem solving, the gratitude, the earned title and status, and the good days when you've really made a difference and thwarted fate. [American Academy of Pediatrics, 1983, p. 700]

The most extensive investigation of the effect of employment on women's mental health was conducted by Warr and Parry (1982). They examined studies from the previous literature that permitted a total of 57 comparisons between employed and nonemployed women, using measures of mental health such as low suicide rates, low rates of psychiatric illness and psychological distress, and high ratings on measures of overall life satisfaction. Considering all the data together, employed women showed better adjustment than nonemployed women on 19 of the measures. Employed women and nonemployed women showed equivalent adjustment on the remaining 38 measures. Notice that there was not a single measure in which nonemployed women showed better adjustment than employed women!

These authors pointed out that the relationship between employment and mental health is too subtle and too complex to be examined in terms of a simple comparison between employed and nonemployed women. This kind of examination ignores other variables that may influence the nature of the relationship.

Warr and Parry looked at three variables, the first being number of children and marital status. They found from their review of the literature that unmarried women with no children were consistently better adjusted if they were employed than if they were nonemployed. For married women with children, one study showed that employed women were better adjusted than nonemployed women, but the remaining ten studies showed equal adjustment for both employed and nonemployed women.

A second variable that Warr and Parry examined was the quality of the nonwork environment. They concluded that employment is more likely to give a boost to a woman's psychological well-being if the family has economic problems (presumably an index of poor nonwork life) than if the family is financially stable. A more recent study by Krause (1984) confirmed the importance of the nonwork environment. If there is stress in a marriage, employment can help reduce the negative effects of that stress. In other words, if there are problems at home, women are better adjusted if they find employment outside the home.

The final variable examined by Warr and Parry was the quality of the employment situation. As you might expect, women who are happy with their employment are also better adjusted and more satisfied with their lives.

Thus, there are factors that may influence whether a woman is happier if she is employed than if she is nonemployed. To review, employed women are particularly likely to be well adjusted (in comparison to nonemployed women) if they are single with no children, if there are problems in their nonwork lives, and if their employment situation is good.

However, do not become so involved in the examination of these three factors that you lose sight of that most important finding: If employment influences psychological well-being at all, it *improves* it; it does not decrease it.

Warr and Parry (1982) caution us that all of the studies they examined have a methodological problem called self-selection. **Self-selection** means that participants have chosen which group they belong to; the experimenters cannot randomly assign them to the groups. In the case of the studies we have been discussing, the participants choose whether they will be employed or nonemployed. It may be, that the more anxious and more depressed women do not look for employment, or that they do not last long on the job. Self-selection is a problem because the two groups—employed and nonemployed women—may differ *initially* in their mental health, with the employed women being better adjusted. As a consequence, the work experience in itself may not be totally responsible for the differences in mental health. More sophisticated research techniques must be used to answer the question more clearly.

☐ SECTION SUMMARY: ▪ The Effects of Employment on Personal Life

1. Dual-career families frequently select traditional solutions to the dilemma of finding employment for both wife and husband, and the husband's employment has top priority.
2. Women are primarily responsible for household tasks, even when both wife and husband are employed; the husbands of employed women perform only slightly more housework than the husbands of nonemployed women.
3. When a woman is employed, she may be somewhat more likely to contemplate a divorce or seek a divorce; however, the marriages of employed women and the marriages of nonemployed women are rated as being equally satisfying.

4. Child-rearing books are frequently unsympathetic toward employed mothers; they suggest that maternal employment will be harmful to children.

5. In general, there is no consistent evidence of any important disadvantage for the children of employed women; in some cases, there is an advantage because the children have less rigid gender-role stereotypes.

6. The division of child-care responsibilities is even more unequal than the division of household tasks.

7. Employed women experience role strain from conflicting responsibilities; employed women experience more role strain than employed men.

8. There is some evidence that employed women are physically healthier than nonemployed women.

9. Studies conclude that employed women are psychologically just as healthy as—or often even healthier than—nonemployed women; factors such as job involvement, the quality of home life, and the quality of the work situation may determine the effect that employment has on a woman's mental health.

Chapter Review Questions

1. What factors determine whether a woman is likely to be employed or nonemployed? What factors determine whether a woman is likely to select a traditional or a nontraditional career?

2. A young woman you know plans to visit her high-school counselor. On the basis of what you have learned in this chapter, describe what kind of experience she might have there.

3. What is access discrimination? Describe studies that indicate how women might encounter access discrimination, pointing out the situations in which access discrimination is most likely to work.

4. What kinds of treatment discrimination might women face in the workplace? Try to list as many kinds as possible.

5. Think about a woman you know who is satisfied with the salary she receives, although it is low. Try to apply to her situation the three factors that Crosby mentions in connection with women's satisfaction with their low wages.

6. Describe how sex segregation operates, both between various occupations and within a given occupation. Point out some of the differences between the traditional occupations and nontraditional occupations that were described in this chapter.

7. Outline the two different kinds of explanations that have been offered for women's absence in certain jobs. Point out how each of these explanations might be used to explain the small percentage of women in two specific occupations, medicine and coal-mining.

8. A friend argues that employed women have unhappy marriages, compared to women who do not work outside the home. Respond to that argument, on the basis of information in this chapter.

9. This question concerns everyone's least favorite topic, housework. Describe why housewives must be included in the term "working women." Then discuss the division of labor between husbands and wives, when both of them are employed, with respect to housework and children.

10. Imagine that you are a 25-year-old woman who has decided to go back to your former job after the birth of your first baby. A neighbor points out that your child will undoubtedly become a disturbed juvenile delinquent if you are employed. Cite the evidence to defend your position.

☐ NEW TERMS

working women	Queen Bee
employed women	person-centered explanations
nonemployed women	situation-centered explanations
access discrimination	dual-career families
treatment discrimination	role strain
token women	self-selection

☐ RECOMMENDED READINGS

Borman, K. M., Quarm, D., & Gideonse, S. (Eds.) (1984). *Women in the workplace: Effects on families.* Norwood, NJ: Ablex. ■ This book contains chapters by nine sets of authors who write on topics related to the last section of this chapter, the interrelationship between employment and personal life.

Deaux, K., & Ullman, J. C. (1983). *Women of steel.* New York: Praeger. ■ This book summarizes a major study on women blue-collar workers and also provides background information on other aspects of women and employment.

Kahn-Hut, R., Daniels, A. K., & Colvard, R. (1982). *Women and work.* New York: Oxford University Press. ■ If you would like a more sociological perspective, with additional information that is cross-cultural and historical, this volume provides an excellent background.

Larwood, L., & Gutek, B. A. (1984). Women at work in the USA. In M. J. Davidson & C. L. Cooper (Eds.), *Women at work* (pp. 237–267). Chichester, England: John Wiley. ■ This chapter provides an excellent overview of the topic of employed women.

Nieva, V. F., & Gutek, B. A. (1981). *Women and work: A psychological perspective.* New York: Praeger. ■ This book will probably become a classic analysis of women and employment; it is both comprehensive and interesting.

SEX DIFFERENCES AND SIMILARITIES

- On tests of general intelligence, males typically receive higher scores than females.

- In the United States, women often score higher than men on tests of verbal ability and reading.

- The slight superiority that males demonstrate on tests of mathematics ability is due to biologically based sex differences.

- In most situations, adult women talk more than adult men.

- Women gossip more than men, and their gossip is also more negative than men's gossip.

- Men tend to stand closer to each other than women do.

- Women smile more often than men do.

- Women are more helpful to other people than men are.

- Women are consistently more responsive to babies than men are.

- Men and women often receive similar scores on standardized tests of assertiveness.

In the last two chapters, we often compared women and men when we looked at achievement and work. You'll remember that we usually concluded that the sex similarities were more impressive than the sex differences. In the present chapter, we will directly address the issue of differences and similarities in psychological characteristics. Once again, we will find out that the similarities are more noteworthy than the differences. Before we look at these differences and similarities, several warnings must be discussed.

First, remember our discussion from Chapter 1 about the way research is conducted in psychology: People are alert for differences, and studies that discover differences tend to be published in the professional journals, while the studies that show similarities tend to be forgotten in researchers' file drawers. As a consequence, a simple tally of the published research will overrepresent the differences and underrepresent the similarities, giving us a distorted picture of all the research results that have been obtained. We need to keep this distortion in mind when we draw conclusions about whether women and men really differ on a particular characteristic.

Second, males and females typically show a large overlap in the degree to which they possess certain characteristics. In order to discuss the concept of overlap, we need to look at frequency distributions. **Frequency distributions** tell us how many people receive various scores. Imagine giving a vocabulary test to both women and men and finding the two frequency distributions in Figure 7.1. Figure 7.1 shows only a small overlap in the two distributions, because the two distributions are very different. Most women received a score of about 80, but a few had scores as large as 100 or as small as 60. Most men received a score of about 40, but a few had scores as large as 60 or as small as 20.

FIGURE 7.1. **Scores of females and males on a hypothetical test, showing a small overlap**

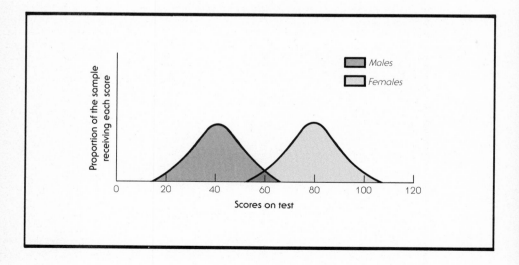

However, distributions of female and male characteristics rarely look like Figure 7.1. They are much more likely to look like Figure 7.2, with a very large overlap in the two distributions. As we have frequently stressed in our discussion of Theme 1, men and women are quite similar, which means that their scores will overlap considerably. Notice in Figure 7.2 that the average woman received a score of 80, whereas the average man received a score of 75. The 5-point difference between these average scores looks very meager when we compare it to the size of the difference *within* either distribution. Notice that there is a 50-point difference between the highest and the lowest female, and there is also a 50-point difference between the highest and the lowest male. As Theme 4 stresses, there is wide variation among individual women and also among individual men.

Another consequence of a large overlap, such as the one in Figure 7.2, is that most men and women in the distribution receive scores that are similar. The very highest scores are more likely to be obtained by women, and the very lowest scores are more likely to be obtained by men. However, the middle-range scores are obtained by nearly equal numbers of men and women.

Finally, notice that when there is a large overlap, we are likely to find many pairs of individual women and men whose scores show a reversal of a general trend. Suppose that Figure 7.2 represents scores on a test of verbal ability, a test on which women receive slightly—but significantly—higher scores than men. Notice that it would be easy to find a pair of individuals in which the man received a higher score (perhaps an 85) than the woman (perhaps an 80). Studies show that women do receive slightly higher scores than men on tests of verbal ability, and yet you can probably identify dozens

FIGURE 7.2. **Scores of females and males on a hypothetical test, showing a large overlap**

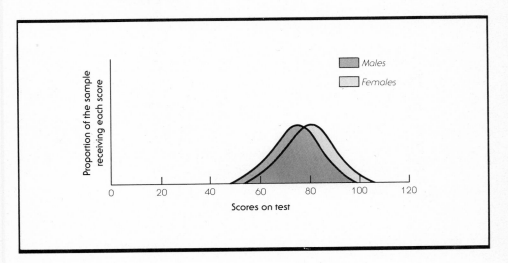

of pairs of individuals you know where the man appears to be more verbal than the woman, the reverse of the general trend.

A third warning concerns the fact that we are unlikely to find any sex difference that holds true for all kinds of people in all kinds of situations, a point that we have mentioned several times in connection with Theme 1. Throughout this chapter, you will notice that we cannot make general statements about sex differences, because sex differences often disappear when we look at certain situations or when we test certain kinds of people. This observation suggests that sex differences are modifiable, rather than being inevitable.

There is an important practical conclusion that we can draw from these last two warnings: Many men and women, in many situations, are remarkably similar in terms of psychological characteristics. This conclusion strengthens the point we made in the previous chapter on women and work regarding explanations for the sex differences in salaries and occupations. It seems that these differences *cannot* be traced to substantial differences in the psychological characteristics of men and women. As we stressed in that chapter, characteristics of the organizational situation are probably more responsible for work discrimination than are sex differences in the characteristics of the workers.

A final warning involves the cautions discussed in Chapter 1 in connection with problems in research on psychology of women. Take a moment to turn back to that section and review how biases can interfere during every stage of the research process. If researchers *expect* to find sex differences, they will be likely to find them!

This chapter on sex differences and similarities focuses on three areas: cognitive abilities, communication styles, and personality and social behavior. We will focus primarily upon adulthood in this chapter, though several studies on children will be mentioned where they provide further insight on a particular issue.

☐ COGNITIVE ABILITIES

There are three kinds of cognitive abilities for which we have some evidence of sex differences: verbal, spatial, and mathematical. We will discuss each of these areas in some detail, but it is important to stress that, even in these areas, sex has only a weak influence. Hyde (1981) pointed out that if we consider the variability of people's scores on any of these three measures of cognitive ability, a *maximum* of 5 percent of that variability can be attributed to sex. This means that the average male's and the average female's scores on a particular test are not likely to be more than a few points apart.

There is an important practical conclusion to be drawn from the fact that the maximum size of sex differences is so small. Specifically, we should *not* discourage people from pursuing particular careers because of their sex. Women may be slightly less able than men to perform tasks that require spatial skills. According to Hyde's (1981) estimates, about 7 percent of males and 3 percent of females fall in the top 5 percent of the population as far as spatial ability. This means that roughly twice as many males as females are particularly talented in this area. Only 1 percent of all engineers are women, and some people suggest that this scarcity can be traced to women's lack of spatial ability. A sex difference in spatial ability could explain why there might be twice as many male engineers as female engineers. However, the "lack of spatial ability" explanation is not powerful enough to explain why there are in reality 99 times as many male engineers as female engineers. Clearly, there are other explanations for the small number of women in fields such as engineering, as discussed in the last chapter.

It is important to keep in mind that the women who are particularly competent in areas such as spatial skills perform better than most men. Therefore, it would be ridiculous to discourage women from professions such as engineering. In fact, excluding women from certain professions on the basis of their sex would be as ridiculous as denying drivers' licenses to men because men are more likely than women to be color-blind (Bernard, 1974).

Cognitive Abilities for Which There Are No Consistent Sex Differences

While we examine the three areas in which modest sex differences have been found, we must keep in mind that there are numerous areas in which there are no sex differences. One major area is general intelligence, as measured by a person's total score on an I.Q. test. As Maccoby and Jacklin (1974) conclude in their comprehensive review of sex differences, females and males do not differ consistently in tests of total abilities through most of the age range studied. The boys and girls in your fifth-grade class may have taunted each other with claims that their own sex was "smarter," but you now have evidence that both were wrong. It is worth pointing out, though, that many intelligence tests have been standardized in order to minimize sex differences. For example, suppose that there is a test item that males are more likely to miss than females. This item will frequently be eliminated from the test. As a result, we are unlikely to find sex differences in general intelligence because of the nature of the tests.

There are many kinds of learning tasks that do not demonstrate sex differences. For example, males and females perform similarly when they are questioned about incidental information. Men and women in a movie theater will therefore be equally likely to remember whether the murderer was wearing a blue shirt. Males and females are also equally skilled at learning by imitating someone else (Maccoby & Jacklin, 1974).

There is some limited evidence that sex differences in memory may be affected by the nature of the material to be remembered. Maccoby and Jacklin (1974) pointed out that about half of the studies involving verbal content showed that women remember more material, but the other half showed no sex differences. It also seems that women might perform better when social content is involved. For instance, women typically remember more of their high-school classmates' names and faces long after graduation (Bahrick, Bahrick, & Wittlinger, 1975). Young girls are also better in identifying the names of their day-care classmates, based on their photographs (Feldstein, 1976). Women and men perform similarly when the material involves numbers and objects (Maccoby & Jacklin, 1974). Maccoby and Jacklin conclude that males and females have similar memory capacities. The differences we mentioned with respect to verbal and social material probably reflect females' superiority in these content areas, rather than differences in the ability to remember.

There are other complex cognitive tasks that show no sex differences. For example, males and females are equally competent when they form concepts, perform reasoning tasks, or solve problems (Maccoby & Jacklin, 1974). For example, Kesler, Denney, and Whitely (1976) asked elderly people to solve three different kinds of problems. An analysis of the data showed that males and females had equivalent problem-solving abilities.

Do males and females differ in creativity? The answer to this question partly depends upon the kind of creativity that is being measured. When the task is verbal, females often show an advantage. When the task is spatial, males often show an advantage. Taking everything into account, however, there are no substantial sex differences in creativity (Alpaugh & Birren, 1975; Kogan, 1974; Maccoby & Jacklin, 1974).

We have seen that women and men are similar in their general intelligence, learning ability, memory, concept formation, reasoning, problem solving and creativity. The occasional differences that are found in these areas can usually be traced to the underlying verbal, social, or spatial nature of the task. However, similarities are more common than differences. Keep these similarities in mind as we explore the areas in which modest sex differences have been located.

Verbal Abilities

Maccoby and Jacklin (1974) report that "Female superiority on verbal tasks has been one of the more solidly established generalizations in the field of sex differences" (p. 75). As we will see, sex differences are found in many studies that examine adolescents and adults. However, the argument for early sex differences is somewhat shakier.

There is some evidence that baby girls acquire language earlier than baby boys. Baby girls vocalize more in infancy, and they also learn the basic sounds of language faster. Furthermore, the average girl says her first word at 11.4 months, whereas the average boy says his first word at 12 months (Harris, 1977). Girls also acquire additional words faster (Nelson, 1973; Schachter, et al., 1978). Their pronunciation is clearer, too, so that they are easier to understand. As toddlers, girls may understand more language than boys (Clarke-Stewart, 1973). However, we should stress that other investigations find no consistent sex differences in the early development of language (Maccoby & Jacklin, 1974; Jacklin & Maccoby, 1983).

Occasional studies show that girls are verbally superior during the early school years. For example, girls between the ages of 5 and 11 were faster at naming colors, objects, letters, numbers, and animals (Denckla & Rudel, 1974). However, the similarities at this age are more impressive than the differences (Maccoby & Jacklin, 1974). If you plan to teach elementary school, the girls and boys in your class should be similar in their language skills.

More impressive differences begin to emerge in late childhood, perhaps around the age of 11 (Maccoby & Jacklin, 1974). A study of high-school students found sex differences in spelling, punctuation, talkativeness, comprehension of difficult written text, and understanding of logical relations (Droege, 1967). Furthermore, the sex differences increased between the ninth and twelfth grades. Females also excel at creative writing, listening, and speaking ability. In addition, their scores are typically higher on tests of **verbal fluency,** which measure how fast people produce appropriate words. Females also perform better than males on **verbal analogies** (vocabulary tests that involve comparisons) and **anagrams** (scrambled-word tests). These last three measures of verbal ability are illustrated in Demonstration 7.1.

DEMONSTRATION 7.1

Examples of Verbal Fluency, Verbal Analogies, and Anagrams

Try each of the three kinds of tests of verbal ability. Incidentally, the verbal analogies were selected from a book that is useful for preparing for graduate school tests, called *How to Prepare for the Miller Analogies Test* (Sternberg, 1974).

VERBAL FLUENCY: For each sequence of letters, construct a four-word sentence so that each word begins with the specified letter. For example, D_____ p_____ t_____ e_____ could be answered, "Don't plan to eat." Verbal fluency is measured in terms of the speed with which the sentences are constructed.
  1. N_____ f_____ a_____ h_____.
  2. H_____ m_____ s_____ m_____.

VERBAL ANALOGIES: Select the appropriate item to complete the analogy, so that the third and fourth items have the same relationship to each other as the first and second items.
  1. monogamy : bigamy :: biped : (a. unipod, b. pedate, c. millepede, d. quadruped)
  2. fresco : plaster :: tapestry : (a. stone, b. metal, c. cloth, d. wood)

ANAGRAMS: Unscramble each of these words to make an English word.
  1. dnlecihr
  2. eedoplv

You may have taken the Scholastic Aptitude Test, or SAT, when you applied to college. The verbal portion of this test includes items on reading comprehension, verbal analogies, antonyms, and sentence completion. In the early years of the SAT, items were primarily drawn from the humanities, and females scored higher than males on the verbal portion of the SAT. However, the people who constructed the test made an effort, beginning in the 1950s, to "balance the content" by drawing more items from scientific and "male-oriented" areas. The purpose of this adjustment was to reduce the sex differences on the scores. Dwyer (1976) points out an unfortunate imbalance, however:

> ... it is interesting to note that similar efforts have not been made to "balance" the content of the SAT quantitative sections, even though sex differences have favored males by a great number of points since the first administrations of the test. [p. 756]

Our last topic in this section on verbal abilities is reading, an area that is clearly related to verbal skills. In the United States, far more boys than girls have reading problems. Boys are more likely to read below grade level, and they are more likely to be referred to a reading clinic. For reading problems, estimates of the ratio of boys to girls typically vary between 6:1 and 4:1 (Finucci & Childs, 1981).

The reasons for the sex differences in this area are not clear. Some researchers have proposed that girls and boys differ in their strategies for processing visual information. Smith's (1985) research suggests that girls pay more attention to the details that make one letter different from another. Dwyer (1974) believes that gender roles are important. Males perceive reading as being inappropriate to the masculine role; consequently, they are reluctant to achieve in this stereotypically feminine area as they grow older.

Some kind of social explanation must be at least partially responsible for the differences in reading, because the sex differences may disappear or even be reversed in other cultures. Gross (1978) found no sex differences in the frequency of reading disabilities in Israeli kibbutzim, an environment in which gender roles are stressed far less than in the United States. Johnson (1973–1974) examined children who were learning to read English in Canada, England, Nigeria, and the United States. Girls scored higher than boys on most of the tests in Canada and the United States, whereas boys scored higher than girls on most of the tests in England and Nigeria.

There have been some attempts to explain the sex differences in reading skills. However, the other areas of verbal ability seem to have received less attention than the two areas we will soon examine, spatial ability and mathematical ability. It seems likely that social explanations may account for a large portion of females' superior verbal ability, but no one has yet worked out a coherent theory about how socialization accounts for this verbal superiority. Some people have speculated that parents vocalize more to daughters than to sons, which might encourage females to be more skilled in verbal areas. However, Maccoby and Jacklin (1974) concluded that there was no clear trend for parents to provide more verbal stimulation to daughters than to sons.

One important socialization factor, mentioned earlier in connection with reading, is that children believe that verbal skills are feminine (Nash, 1979). Boys may be reluctant to do well in creative writing, spelling, and so forth, because of the realistic fear of being labeled a sissy. Teachers, also, expect girls to do better than boys on verbal tasks. In fact, girls' superior verbal performance may be partly due to a tendency to fulfill other people's expectations.

Some researchers have suggested that sex differences in verbal ability can be traced to biological explanations. Explanations involving chromosomes and hormones have not been popular, but two other kinds of biological explanations have received some attention. A possible biological factor might be that girls mature faster than boys. Indeed, there is evidence that girls mature faster than boys in their bone growth and other physical features (Parsons, 1980). It may be that girls show advanced verbal development when they are young because of early development of the physical "equipment" necessary for language. However, as Parsons concludes, sex differences in maturation rates do not always favor girls, and these differences are often temporary, rather than permanent.

A different kind of biological explanation proposes that there are sex differences in brain functioning, referred to as lateralization. **Lateralization** means that the two halves (or hemispheres) of the brain have different functions. In general, the left hemisphere specializes in language or verbal tasks, whereas the right hemisphere typically specializes in spatial tasks. (You can remember that *left* and *language* both begin with the letter *l*.)

It is important to note that in normal individuals, either hemisphere *can* process both language and spatial material. However, the left hemisphere tends to be fastest and most accurate on language tasks, whereas the right hemisphere tends to be fastest and most accurate on spatial tasks.

There have been numerous explanations for how lateralization might be responsible for sex differences in language and verbal tasks (Bryden, 1979; Sherman, 1978; Waber, 1979). An intriguing finding is that adult females seem to show less lateralization than adult males when they perceive language (Levy, 1972; Waber, 1979). In other words, an adult male might process language almost exclusively with the left hemisphere, whereas an adult female might use both hemispheres more equally. However, even if there is a difference in the extent to which males and females show lateralization, it's not at all clear how this kind of difference explains why females have superior verbal ability (Henley, 1985). Thus, at present, lateralization does not seem to be a satisfactory explanation for the sex differences in verbal ability.

We first looked at socialization factors that might explain why women are somewhat better than men on verbal tasks, and then we discussed biological approaches to the issue. As in other areas of cognitive sex differences, we do not have enough information to conclude which approach is closer to the truth. We must keep in mind that the sex differences we are trying to explain are small. As Kimball (1981) points out, we must be skeptical about any theory that predicts large differences on the basis of biological sex differences. For example, we should be suspicious about a biological theory that predicts much greater verbal ability for women than for men. The theory may simply be too powerful for the weak differences we are trying to explain.

Spatial Abilities

Spatial abilities involve skill in perceiving and manipulating shapes and figures. There are many different skills included in the category of spatial abilities, such as finding an object in a search task, figuring out what an object would look like if it were turned around, and recognizing shapes. In everyday life, spatial ability is important in solving jigsaw puzzles and mazes, in reading road maps, in figuring out how to set a table for a formal dinner party, and in drafting or architecture. Two common ways of testing spatial ability in the laboratory are shown in Demonstration 7.2.

Notice that a **mental-rotation test** involves turning an object around mentally, rather than physically. An **embedded-figure test** requires locating a particular object that is hidden in a larger design. (When you were young, you probably worked on similar games, such as searching for faces in a woodland scene.)

Beginning in adolescence and continuing through old age, males typically perform better than females on various tests of spatial ability (Cohen & Wilkie, 1979; Maccoby & Jacklin, 1974; Petersen, 1980). However, there are exceptions. Fennema and Sherman (1977) found that males were superior to females in spatial ability in only two of the four schools in their sample.

Recent research has concentrated on identifying factors that are related to sex differences in spatial ability. Several investigators have speculated that males may have more practice than females on spatial-ability tasks. As we will discuss shortly, males take more high-school mathematics courses. If you took a course in high-school geometry, you can testify that the course stressed spatial skills. Fennema and Sherman (1977) found that sex differences in spatial ability disappeared if their data were corrected for the number of mathematics courses students had taken.

Sex differences often evaporate after a short session that allows people to practice spatial tasks (Chance & Goldstein, 1971; Goldstein & Chance, 1965; Stericker & LeVesconte, 1982). For example, Stericker and LeVesconte found that just three hours of training for female students was enough to eliminate the sex difference on four standard tests of spatial skill. Clearly, the sex difference is not a permanent one.

Some psychologists have speculated that "masculine" toys may be more spatially oriented than "feminine" toys. The additional experience on spatial tasks that is provided by these toys might account for sex differences in spatial ability. In fact, there is some evidence that children who play with masculine toys more than feminine toys may perform better on spatial tasks

Examples of a Mental-Rotation Test and an Embedded-Figures Test

Try these two kinds of tests for spatial ability.

MENTAL-ROTATION TEST: If you mentally rotate the figure on the left, which of the five figures on the right would you obtain?

1.   a.   b.   c.   d.   e.

2.   a.   b.   c.   d.   e.

EMBEDDED-FIGURES TEST: Study the figure on the left. Then cover it up and try to find where it is hidden in the figure on the right. The left-hand figure may need to be shifted in order to locate it in the right-hand figure.

1.

2.

3.

(Fagot & Littman, 1976). Also, college men do more spatially oriented activities in their spare time than women do (Newcombe, Bandura, & Taylor, 1983). This practice on spatial tasks may aid their performance.

Nash (1975, 1979) examined the ways in which the performance on spatial tasks might be related to sex roles. She asked 11- and 14-year-old children whether they preferred to be girls or boys. At this age, as you may recall from remarks made during your own childhood, many girls wish that they were boys because of males' prestige and activities—boys simply had more fun! Nash found that the girls who preferred to be boys scored higher on tests of spatial ability than did the girls who were happy that they were girls. Apparently, there is something about the traditional female role that is associated with lower spatial ability.

Since the 1940s, investigators have suggested a different explanation for the sex differences in spatial ability. Perhaps, they argued, there is a genetic basis for spatial ability; spatial ability might be sex linked. However, more recent studies of both genetically normal and abnormal people have cast doubt on a genetic explanation for spatial ability (Kimball, 1981; Petersen, 1980; Vandenberg & Kuse, 1979). There is some evidence that sex hormones can influence scores on tests of spatial ability (Petersen, 1976). However, the effect is complex and hormones do not provide the answer at present.

We mentioned that brain lateralization might account for sex differences in verbal ability and some researchers have speculated that lateralization could also explain sex differences in spatial ability. This explanation has some severe difficulties. For example, we said that many spatial tasks are processed best by the right hemisphere. However, the specific spatial tasks at which males show an advantage do *not* seem to be associated with the right hemisphere (Kimball, 1981; Waber, 1979). Furthermore, it is unclear how the greater lateralization in male brains could explain why males perform better on spatial tasks.

Mathematics Abilities

Of all the cognitive sex differences, mathematics ability has attracted the most attention in the 1980s. The professional journals feature reports that frequently demonstrate sex similarities and sometimes demonstrate sex differences. However, as we noted in Chapter 1, it is the claims of sex differences that attract the attention of the popular press. Consequently, our emphasis in this section on the similarities in mathematics ability will contradict the impression you might have received from newspapers and popular magazines.

According to Maccoby and Jacklin's (1974) review of sex differences in mathematics ability, boys and girls are similar until late childhood. Beginning at about age 12, boys sometimes receive significantly higher scores than girls on tests of mathematics ability. Consistent sex differences do not appear until about the age of 15 (Meece, et al., 1982).

One study that particularly captured the popular press contrasted the mathematics performance of extremely talented seventh- and eighth-grade students (Benbow & Stanley, 1980). These researchers located 20,000 children who had received high scores on achievement tests and invited them to take the Scholastic Aptitude Test. If you took the mathematics portion of the SAT, you will remember that this would be an incredibly difficult test for junior-high students, since they have not yet taken the relevant courses. However, Benbow and Stanley argued that the students' scores would reflect their mathematics potential. At any rate, the results indicate that about twice as many boys as girls had mathematics scores greater than 500. In a later study, as well, boys consistently received the very highest scores. For example, 13 times as many boys as girls received scores above 700 (Benbow & Stanley, 1983). Benbow and Stanley (1980) suggested that these sex differences were probably due to biological differences, rather than socialization factors.

Of course, there are difficulties with that viewpoint. You may recall the earlier complaint that the mathematics portion of the SAT was not balanced to reduce sex differences, although the verbal portion was balanced. Furthermore, it is not clear that the SAT is an appropriate way to measure mathematics ability. Perhaps most important, the discovery of a substantial difference in test scores should not require us to embrace a biological explanation, when—as we shall see shortly—socialization explanations seem more important (Schafer & Gray, 1981).

Comparisons of male and female mathematics abilities are much more likely to demonstrate similarities, rather than differences. One examination of 440,000 high school students revealed a statistically significant sex difference in mathematics ability, favoring males, However, in one case, that statistically significant sex difference arose from the fact that females, on the average, missed about .6 of an item more than males (Fox, Tobin, & Brody, 1979). This example provides an excellent illustration of how a sex difference can reach statistical significance and yet have no imaginable practical significance.

Some studies do not even find statistically significant sex differences. Fennema and Sherman (1977) found that males had significantly higher scores than females in only two of the four high schools they examined. Furthermore, these statistically significant differences disappeared when additional analyses were performed that controlled for sex differences on various social factors.

Explanations for the sex differences in mathematics ability fall into five categories: differences in experience; the spatial nature of mathematics tasks; biological explanations; socialization explanations; and attitude differences.

One factor that often accounts for part of the males' advantage on mathematics tests is that males take more courses in mathematics. (This is an important topic in itself, as we will see later in this section.) DeWolf (1981) found that males scored higher than females on four tests of mathematics ability. Males had also taken significantly more courses in algebra, geometry, advanced mathematics, and physics. After statistically controlling for the amount of coursework in these areas, sex differences disappeared on two of the four tests. In other words, we are seeing the same trend here as we saw with spatial ability: Differences in experience account for a major part of the sex difference. In 1983, Marrett and Gates reported that among black high-school students, males and females are similar in their enrollment in mathematics courses. It would be interesting to see whether sex differences in mathematics tests scores are small for black students.

Some researchers have argued that the sex differences in mathematics ability can be traced to the sex difference in spatial ability that we discussed in the previous section. These researchers argue that a major portion of mathematics is spatial in nature. This is obvious for geometry problems, and algebra problems also may have spatial components. Remember those algebra problems—dreaded by many high-school students—such as:

> John can row a boat at the rate of five miles an hour. The river is flowing at the rate of three miles an hour. If John sets out from Point A and rows upstream to Point B, which is 10 miles away, how long will it take him?

Evidence for the spatial component in mathematics ability comes from several studies. In general, sex difference in mathematical achievement scores are greatly reduced or eliminated entirely when spatial ability is controlled (Meece, et al., 1982). It may be more appropriate to talk about two areas of cognitive sex difference (verbal and spatial) rather than regarding mathematics as a third, separate area.

Some researchers have suggested that biological factors underlie sex differences in mathematics ability. Some propose that biologically based sex differences in spatial ability are indirectly responsible, and others propose that biologically based sex differences in mathematics ability are *directly* responsible. However, as Meece and her coauthors conclude in a recent review of the literature, it is not clear how biological factors contribute to sex differences in mathematics ability. It seems that we do not yet have any clear-cut evidence for a biological explanation.

There are many socialization factors that might play an important part in the mathematics-ability sex difference.

1. Adult models show behavior that children imitate. For example, fathers help with math homework more than mothers do, and advanced math courses are more likely to be taught by men (Meece, et al., 1982).
2. Mathematics textbooks sometimes encourage the image of females being incompetent in mathematics. Federbush (1974) points out that textbooks include sentences such as "Susan could not figure out how to . . ." Furthermore, "The expressions on girls' and women's faces are sometimes the model of bewilderment as they struggle to find a way to put order into a seemingly chaotic or even a simple numerical situation" (p. 180). Thus, females in textbooks serve as models of helplessness.
3. Teachers may have higher expectations for boys' performance in mathematics (Meece, et al., 1982).
4. Teachers spend more time instructing and interacting with boys, rather than girls, in mathematics (Meece, et al., 1982).
5. Parents buy more mathematical and spatial games for boys than for girls (Astin, 1974).

Thus, we see that boys are encouraged in their pursuit of mathematics, whereas girls can be discouraged. Partly as a consequence of these socialization factors, males and females have different attitudes about mathematics:

1. By junior-high school, boys perceive themselves as more competent in math than girls do, despite the fact that they receive equivalent grades (Meece, et al., 1982). Recall how this observation is similar to our discussion of self-confidence in achievement settings in Chapter 5.
2. By high school, students believe that mathematics is a male domain (Fox, 1980).
3. By junior-high school, boys are more likely than girls to believe that math is useful (Meece, et al., 1982).
4. Males are more likely to have positive attitudes toward math, whereas females are more likely to experience math anxiety (Tobias & Weissbrod, 1980). In a book that popularized the idea of math anxiety (Tobias, 1978), females are particularly likely to feel anxious when they face a difficult math problem:

> The first thing people remember about failing at math is that it felt like sudden death. Whether it happened while learning word problems in sixth grade, coping with equations in high school, or first confronting calculus and statistics in college, failure was sudden and very frightening. An idea or a new operation was not just difficult, it was impossible! And instead of asking questions or taking the lesson slowly, assuming that in a month or so they would be able to digest it, people remember the feeling, as certain as it was sudden, that they would *never* go any further in mathematics (p. 44).

Additional research on math anxiety in college women shows that math anxiety is most common in women who are generally anxious about tests and who believe that they are poor in mathematics (Hendel, 1980).

So far, we have suggested that sex differences in mathematics ability may arise from sex differences in several factors: experience, spatial ability, biological factors, socialization factors, and attitude toward mathematics. Recall, however, that the sex differences that we are trying to explain are really small. Let's now briefly pursue one issue related to mathematics where the sex differences are large: the number of mathematics courses taken by males and females.

If you were told that 57 percent of the males who were freshmen in 1972 at University of California at Berkeley had taken at least 3½ years of high-school math, what percentage would you imagine for an equivalent group of females? The answer, according to Sells (1980), was a meager 8 percent. The practical consequence of this sex difference is enormous, because 3½ years of high-school math are required for enrollment in calculus, and enrollment in calculus is required at Berkeley for every undergraduate major except education, the social sciences, and the humanities. Notice that if a woman decides to take only two years of high-school math, she will effectively prevent herself from becoming an engineer, a physicist, or a biochemist.

Julia Sherman has extensively researched the factors that are related to a female's decision to take math courses. Among her findings are that high-school females who take many math courses are more likely than those who take few courses to: be ambitious; be independent; have pleasant early memories of math; have few negative experiences with teachers; have good spatial visualization ability; believe that mathematics is useful; and have more confidence about learning mathematics. Those who took many math courses were also *less* likely to view math as a male domain (Sherman, 1981, 1982a, 1982b, 1983). It is clear that socialization factors and attitude toward mathematics influence enrollment in math courses, as well as having a direct influence on math performance.

Fortunately, some people have been concerned about changing these socialization and attitude factors. MacDonald (1980) describes a program to help college women overcome social and cultural barriers to success in mathematics. Also, Brush (1980) has numerous suggestions for making mathematics less threatening and more enjoyable. Let's hope that math educators will be inspired to adopt some of these suggestions!

☐ SECTION SUMMARY ▪ Cognitive Abilities

1. In the study of sex differences and similarities, sex differences are more likely to be published than sex similarities, there is typically a large overlap between women's and men's abilities because sex differences are generally small, and sex differences are unlikely to hold true for all kinds of people in all kinds of situations.
2. Women and men are similar in their general intelligence, learning ability, memory, concept formation, reasoning, problem solving, and creativity.
3. There may be small sex differences favoring girls in early verbal ability, but larger differences emerge in late childhood.
4. In the United States, girls are better at reading than boys are, but the sex differences are minimal or reversed in other countries.
5. Explanations for sex differences in verbal ability probably involve socialization factors, but biological explanations such as maturation differences and lateralization differences have also been proposed.
6. Beginning in adolescence, males often receive higher scores than females on tests of spatial ability.

7. Explanations for sex differences in spatial ability include sex differences in practice, sex-role expectations, and explanations involving biological factors such as genetics, hormones, and lateralization.
8. Beginning in adolescence, males often receive higher scores than females on tests of mathematics ability; however, the differences are often extremely small.
9. Explanations for sex differences in mathematics ability include differences in experience, the spatial nature of mathematics tasks, biological factors, socialization explanations, and sex differences in attitude.

☐ COMMUNICATION STYLES

When we read the word "communication," most of us think about communicating with words, or verbal communication. Most people have strong stereotypes about how females and males differ in their verbal communication styles: women talk more, men use more slang, and women use more "gushy" language. We will see that research supports some stereotypes, shows little evidence for other stereotypes, and demonstrates that reality may actually be the reverse of other stereotypes.

However, we also communicate without using words, by the way we move our bodies, touch others, smile, and so forth. This nonverbal communication is extremely powerful in conveying messages of power, pleasure, and unhappiness, but most of us do not think about these messages in terms of gender stereotypes. Recent research has uncovered some substantial sex differences in nonverbal communication that are worth exploring.

Verbal and nonverbal communication are both essential in human interactions. Unless you are reading this sentence before breakfast, you have already spoken to many people, smiled at others, and perhaps avoided eye contact with still others. Most occupations involve frequent communications, too. For example, Kanter (1977) reviewed research that estimated that between 50 and 93 percent of an executive's day is spent in social interaction. Let us now examine these communication areas for sex differences.

Verbal Communication

In an earlier section, we noticed that females often excel in their verbal *ability*, or their skill in using language. In this section, we will look at a different component of language, which involves the manner in which words are used. Our four topics are: talking patterns, voice quality, specific words and phrases, and the content of speech.

Talking patterns. According to the stereotype, women are gabby. They talk interminably on the telephone, chatter for hours to the next-door neighbor, and generally refuse to be silent. In reality, however, men seem to talk more. When one researcher asked men and women to describe three artistic works, the men talked approximately four times as long as the women. In fact, three of the 17 men in the study talked so long that the 30-minute cassette ran out of tape before they ran out of comments (Swacker, 1975).

Interestingly, young girls may talk more than young boys. In studies done on the quantity of children's speech, girls often exceed boys (Haas, 1979). It is possible that this difference reflects girls' greater verbal ability. In any event, as they grow up, girls learn to be quiet and let the boys do the talking. In mixed-sex groups of adults, men tend to talk more than women (Haas, 1979; Hall, 1984).

One way in which men manage to talk more than women is that they speak for longer periods. Frances (1979) asked pairs of graduate students to talk spontaneously in order to get acquainted. Men spoke in longer utterances than women, whether their conversation partners were men or women.

Suppose that you want to "hold the floor" in a conversation, but you are fumbling for the appropriate words for your next sentence. In order to keep your turn, you might mumble "um," or "er," or "ah." Frances discovered that the male graduate students in her study displayed more than three times as many of these "filled pauses" as the female graduate students. Hall (1984) found five other studies that reached similar conclusions. Frances speculated that when the words do not flow freely for women, they simply end their speaking turn, rather than retaining the speaker's position by supplying a filled pause.

The evidence is clear that men interrupt women far more than women interrupt men. Zimmerman and West (1975) recorded conversations in coffee shops, drug stores, and other public places near a university. They found that males provided 96 percent of all the interruptions. Women did not protest the interruptions, and they tended to remain silent for some time after being interrupted.

In a different investigation, McMillan, Clifton, McGrath, and Gale (1977) found that in mixed-sex groups males interrupted females more than five times as often as females interrupted males. Also, male graduate students are more likely than female graduate students to interrupt in the classroom (Brooks, 1982). Other studies, summarized by Hall (1984), confirm the conclusion that males interrupt more than females do.

In conclusion, there are sex differences in talking patterns. In comparison with women, men talk more, use more filled pauses, and interrupt more.

Voice quality. As you know, men have lower-pitched voices than women. However, didn't you always think that the pitch difference could be entirely explained in terms of anatomical differences in the vocal cords? In fact, a major reason for the difference is that men and women form the words differently in order to produce appropriately high-pitched or low-pitched voices (LaFrance & Mayo, 1978; Sachs, 1975). We believe that anatomical differences *cannot* be totally responsible for the differences in male and female voices because people are highly accurate in determining the sex of a child whose voice has been tape recorded. It seems unlikely that boys and girls who have not yet reached puberty could have anatomically different vocal cords. Instead, they must have learned how to produce the sounds appropriate to their gender.

Pitch is not the only characteristic on which female and male voices vary. Another important characteristic is **intonation,** or the patterns of pitch movement (McConnell-Ginet, 1978). Notice how an innocent sentence such as "Is dinner ready?" can be said with different intonations to indicate emotions such as politeness, impatience, and surprise.

Men and women seem to use intonation differently. In particular, women tend to use more extreme shifts in pitch, whereas men maintain a fairly constant pitch (McConnell-Ginet, 1978). Brend (1975) remarks that certain intonation patterns are found only in women's speech, such as the "polite, cheerful" pattern with a raised pitch at the end that could be used to ask the question:

Are you coming?

Words and phrases.   Before you read this section, try Demonstration 7.3, which contains sentences from a study by Edelsky (1976a; 1976b). She asked adults and children to read or listen to sentences like these and to decide whether the statement was more likely to come from a man or a woman. Adults strongly believed that sentences with the phrase, "I'll be damned" were more likely to be spoken by a man, and sentences with "adorable," "oh dear," and "my goodness" were more likely to be spoken by a woman. Even first graders attributed different sentences to men and women, and this tendency increased as they grew older. Furthermore, both men and women have the same stereotypes about what kind of language is appropriate for men and what kind is appropriate for women.

DEMONSTRATION 7.3

Beliefs about Men's and Women's Language

For each of the following sentences, decide who would be most likely to say the sentence: men generally, women generally, or men and women with equal likelihood.

1. Damn it, the TV set broke!
2. Won't you please close the door?
3. That show was great, wasn't it?
4. Get me that pencil.
5. I'll be damned, there's the President!
6. Oh dear, I lost my keys!
7. That's an adorable story.
8. You're damn right.

According to the stereotypes, women also use precise descriptive words, such as the words *beige, aquamarine,* and *lavender* to describe colors (Lakoff, 1973). The strong, silent men in the old westerns and the muscle-bound heroes of modern movies would never use these words, because their language would generally be confined to "yup" and "nope."

We have stereotypes about how women and men *should* speak; do they really talk that way? The evidence is mixed. Hartman (1976) studied men and women in their seventies and found that women were more likely to use words such as *lovely, delightful, nice, cute, dearest, gentle,* and *perfectly wonderful.*

However, an examination of witnesses' language in the courtroom emphasized sex similarities (O'Barr & Atkins, 1980). One woman witness used many phrases such as "quite ill" and "maybe just a little bit," but other women used few of these "women's language" features. The males also varied greatly in the use of these phrases. Although no statistical analysis was performed, the overlap in language use seemed more impressive than the sex difference. Clearly, the characteristics of speakers and the kind of setting in which they are observed could influence the extent to which sex differences are revealed. Haas's (1979) review of the literature concludes that it is likely that girls use more adjectives than boys, but nothing firm can be concluded about adult use of adjectives.

Women are supposed to be more polite in their speech (Kemper, 1984). Hartman's (1976) study of elderly men and women seems to be the only one to investigate this issue systematically, and this research confirmed the stereotype. Less formally, Kramarae (1981) tape-recorded conversations that supported this stereotype. Here's a sample exchange between a woman patron in a restaurant and a male server:

Patron: I'm sorry, but this isn't mine.
Server: What did you order?
Patron: The turkey plate.
Server: Must be someone else's.
Patron: Sorry.
Server: I'll get yours in a minute.
Patron: That's fine. Thank you. [p. 151]

Notice that the woman is so polite that she apologizes for the server's mistake! Furthermore, some researchers have argued that women's speech is more likely to be grammatically correct (Key, 1975; Thorne & Henley, 1975).

On the other side of the coin, there is some evidence that males are more likely to use slang and dirty words. These sex differences seem to arise in the early school years (Jay, 1980). Selnow (1985) found that females reported using less profanity than males and they also judged profanity to be inappropriate in a variety of settings. In summary, there may be some modest sex differences in the kinds of words and phrases used by men and women.

The content of speech.   We have discussed *how* women and men talk, but what do they talk about? According to one investigation, women talked about how people felt and why they acted in certain ways, whereas men talked about objects (Barron, 1971). Levin and Arluke (1985) asked observers to eavesdrop on conversations in a lounge where students frequently congregated, and their results also revealed different conversational topics for men and women. Women were about twice as likely as men to talk about friends and relatives, a finding that was also confirmed by Aries and Johnson (1983). Levin and Arluke also noticed that women talked about coursework more than men.

So what do the men talk about? Levin and Arluke discovered that men were about three times as likely as women to discuss celebrities, such as sports figures; Aries and Johnson also noted more sports-related conversation among men.

However, men and women were similar in the extent to which they discussed people's physical appearance, dating, and sex (Levin & Arluke, 1985) and religion, personal finances, political issues, work, and community affairs (Aries & Johnson, 1983).

Do women gossip constantly, lacing their speech with nasty, catty comments, while men would never stoop to discussing other people? That's clearly the stereotype, but the sex differences are not large. Levin and Arluke defined gossip as conversation about any third person, who could be either absent from or present in the group. They found that 71 percent of women's conversation and 64 percent of men's conversation could be categorized as gossip. This difference is statistically significant, though it is small in magnitude. Most important, the *nature* of the gossip was identical for males and females; men and women both made positive comments 27 percent of the time and negative comments 25 percent of the time. Thus, women may gossip somewhat more than men, but they are no different in the nature of their remarks.

This area of conversational topics is still relatively unexplored (Haas, 1979). At present, there are some interesting hints that women and men may talk about somewhat different topics, though the differences are probably not overwhelming.

Nonverbal Communication

Try turning off the sound on a television game show, and observe the nonverbal behavior. Sex differences in areas of nonverbal behaviors such as smiling, body position, and personal space are often substantial, and they can be readily observed. Notice, as you watch the television, that a written transcription of the conversation between Mr. Game Show Host and Ms. Contestant would fail to capture much of the subtle communication that takes place between two people. In fact, many researchers have concluded that the nonverbal aspects of an interaction may be more important than the verbal message in interpreting the social aspects of a conversation (Frances, 1979).

We will look at five components of nonverbal communication in this chapter: personal space, body posture, touch, facial expression, and decoding ability. The first four topics explore sex differences in what people do with their bodies, whereas the last topic examines sex differences in interpreting what *other* people are feeling, based on nonverbal cues. We will see that sex differences in nonverbal communication are larger than other kinds of sex differences (Hall, 1984).

Personal space. The phrase **personal space** refers to the invisible "bubble" around each person that must not be invaded by other people (LaFrance & Mayo, 1978). You have probably been most aware of personal space when a stranger comes too close, so close that you feel uncomfortable. Naturally, the size of our personal space bubble depends upon the person approaching us. Think about how personal space would be different for the following people: a stranger, an acquaintance from classes, and someone you love.

Now think about how personal space might be different for women than for men. Women generally have smaller personal-space zones than men. Women who are talking to each other sit closer to each other than men do (Sussman & Rosenfeld, 1982). At public exhibits, women stand close to other women, whereas men stand far from other men (Baxer, 1970). On a beach, women take up less room than men (Edney & Jordan-Edney, 1974). Even preschool children approach female adults more closely than male adults (Eberts & Lepper, 1975).

What happens if someone invades your personal space? A common reaction is to move away. Sometimes this movement involves only a slight adjustment of posture, sometimes you protect yourself by thrusting out an elbow or—if you are seated at a table—building a barricade of books, and sometimes you simply leave. Krail and Leventhal (1976) studied situations in which male and female experimenters invaded the personal space of male and female students in a library. The fastest adjustment reactions came from the male students who had been invaded by a male experimenter.

Judith Hall, an active researcher on the topic of nonverbal sex differences, wrote a book in which she summarizes the previous studies on each topic (Hall, 1984). On the topic of personal space, she concludes that females tend to set smaller distances when they approach other people. In other words, contrary to Theme 1, there are sex differences in this area. *Sex as a subject variable* has an influence on personal space, because females approach closer to others than males do. However, as Theme 2 proposes, people treat men and women differently. Hall concludes that *sex as a stimulus variable* has an even greater influence on personal space than sex as a subject variable. That is, people are particularly likely to approach closely to females, rather than males. Combining these two factors, we see that two females will stand or sit close to each other, whereas two males will remain far apart.

Body posture.   Sex differences in body posture develop early in life. The drawings in Demonstration 7.4 were traced from yearbook pictures of two fifth graders, and then other cues to gender were equated. The figure on the left can be easily identified as a girl, and the one on the right clearly is a boy. A glance through magazines will convince you of further sex differences in body posture. Notice that females keep their legs together, whether sitting or standing; their hands may be folded in front of them, clasped neatly, or at their sides. In contrast, males sit and stand with their legs apart. Their hands may be on their hips or reaching out. Males are also more likely to adopt an asymmetrical position, perhaps with one knee bent and the other leg stretched out. Men look relaxed; even at rest, women keep their postures more tensely contained (Davis and Weitz, 1981; Goffman, 1979; Hall, 1984; Mehrabian, 1968).

In other words, body posture follows the same pattern as personal space. Men occupy more space with their bodies, just as they seem to require more personal space. Body posture also follows the same pattern as verbal com-

DEMONSTRATION 7.4

Sex Differences in Body Posture. Which Figure Is a Girl and Which Is a Boy?

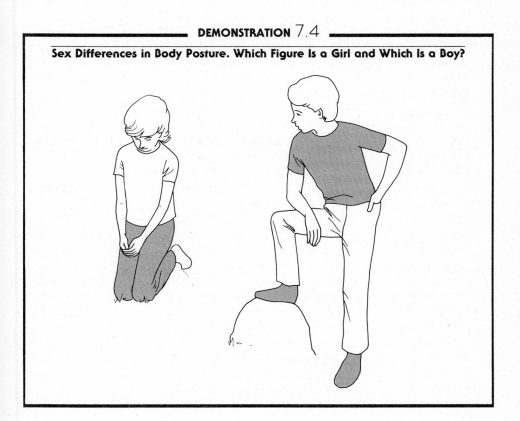

munications. Because men talk more and interrupt more, they require more verbal space.

Some of the sex differences in body posture are preserved in other cultures. Studies of photographs and paintings from other cultures show that women in other countries frequently sit with their legs folded to one side (Frieze & Ramsey, 1976; Hewes, 1957). We might be inclined to think that this particular posture is necessary because of a narrow skirt, except that this posture was also used in countries where no clothing was worn. In contrast, men often adopted postures with spread legs.

Women and men also differ in their body movement patterns, for example, sex-typed mannerisms. Rekers, Amaro-Plotkin, and Low (1977) found that normal boys and girls as young as four years of age differed in their use of certain gestures. Girls were more likely than boys to show bent elbows, fluttering arms, and limp wrists. As we noticed in the picture in Demonstration 7.4, even young children have mastered "sex-appropriate" body language.

Sometimes women's clothes force them to move differently than men. Long or tight skirts restrict how women walk. Even in the 1980s, as Hall (1984) points out, shoes with high, spiked heels are still popular. These shoes force women to adopt an unnatural gait. Recently, I followed a tour guide through a whirlwind tour of Washington, D.C. Her speech was liberated, but her shoes were four-inch spikes. The mincing, wobbly gait as we climbed the steps to the Capitol, the near-disastrous teetering as we negotiated busy streets, and the fact that she walked barefoot for the last hour of our tour were all compelling evidence for the restrictions that fashion places on women's movement.

Another way in which women's and men's body movements differ is that men are more restless (Hall, 1984). Men tend to fidget, manipulate objects, and shift their body positions. In contrast, women sit quietly and "ladylike." In the amount of space they occupy with their bodies, as well as their body movements, women are relatively inconspicuous.

Touch. The area of touch does not reveal clear sex differences, and the results are often contradictory. In one well-known study, Henley (1973) watched people in a variety of settings, such as a college campus and a shopping center, and she noted every time someone touched someone else. In one condition, she found that men touched women more than four times as often as women touched men. However, Hall's review of the literature argues that there are no clear sex differences in whether men touch women more often than women touch men.

There are several reasons why it is difficult to draw any conclusions about touch. One reason is that people don't touch each other very often, so it is more difficult to measure touch reliably than something that is more readily observable, such as body posture. Another reason is that the *nature* of the touch is probably as important as the frequency of touch, and this issue hasn't been thoroughly studied. For example, it seems likely that men pat women on the head or on the rear, and that they touch women's noses with their forefingers, but that women aren't likely to touch men in these ways (Henley, 1977). Finally, the methods used in these studies are so variable and the number of studies is relatively small compared to other areas of nonverbal behavior. As a result, we have to conclude at present that no substantial sex differences in touching behavior have been demonstrated.

Facial expression.   There are clear sex differences in facial expression. One noticeable difference is that women smile more than men. A rapid examination of magazines reveals smiling women and glowering men (although high-fashion women models seem to glower more than a decade ago). If you look through yearbooks, this sex difference will be obvious. Ragan (1982) examined a total of 1,296 portrait photographs, mostly from yearbooks, and she classified them as to their facial expression. Women were nearly twice as likely to show a broad smile, whereas men were about eight times as likely to show no smile whatsoever. You may have noticed that women also smile bravely when someone is making fun of them, telling an embarrassing joke in their presence, or sexually harassing them.

Frances (1979) inspected videotapes of graduate students getting acquainted with each other, and she recorded seven different measures of smiling and laughter. Women were higher than men on all seven measures. However, this news is not altogether positive for women. In another analysis, Frances assessed whether these smiling and laughing measures were correlated with subjects' descriptions of themselves. The men who laughed and smiled most tended to describe themselves as sociable, friendly, and affiliative. However, the women who laughed and smiled most described themselves as being uncomfortable in the conversational setting and as retiring and deferent (that is, yielding to others' wishes). In other words, the women did not seem to be smiling because they enjoyed social interactions; instead, they smiled because they were uncomfortable and were trying to please others.

Other research also shows that women's smiles do not result from happy, friendly emotional states. In a study of parents and their children, fathers tended to smile when they were saying pleasant things to their children; they did not smile when they were saying neutral or unpleasant things. In contrast, mothers' smiles were unrelated to the pleasantness of the message (Bugental, Love, & Gianetto, 1971). It seems that women's facial expressions frequently do not reveal their emotions. They smile even when they do not feel like smiling.

In her review of sex differences in facial expression, Hall (1984) concludes that women smile and laugh substantially more than men. It seems that women are particularly likely to smile, relative to males, when the person with whom they are interacting is the same sex. That is, two females talking together will smile *much* more than two males talking together.

Another component of facial expression is eye contact. The study by Frances (1979), described earlier, also examined sex differences in this area.

Consistent with previous literature, women spent more time gazing at their conversational partners than men did. As Hall concludes, "females of all ages seem to gaze more at others than males do" (p. 83). In addition, Hall notes that people gaze *at* females more than they gaze *at* males. As we discussed in connection with both personal space and smiling, sex as a stimulus variable is often as crucial as (or more crucial than) sex as a subject variable. In the case of eye contact, the result is that two women speaking to each other are likely to look frequently into the eyes of their conversational partner. In contrast, two men who are speaking to each other are likely to focus on a spot several inches above their partner's left ear, or they may glance away at a television screen in a distant corner.

Decoding ability. So far, we have seen that there are sex differences in nonverbal behavior in the areas of personal space, body posture and body movement, and facial expression. A final topic in this section is somewhat different, because it concerns **decoding ability,** or the ability to figure out what another person is feeling from his or her nonverbal behavior. A person who is a good decoder can notice a friend's facial expression, body posture, and voice, and deduce whether this friend is in a good or bad mood.

According to Hall (1984), the evidence is clear that females are more likely to be good decoders of nonverbal expressions. Females seem to be particularly good at "reading" facial expression, in comparison to males. Their advantage over males is less pronounced in the area of body posture, and least pronounced in the area of voice cues. In other words, females are much better than males at judging emotion from a facial expression, but they are only slightly better at judging emotion from voice cues.

Females seem to be better decoders as early as elementary school. Also, females are better decoders than males in other cultures, as well as in the United States. Hall examines studies conducted in Greece, New Guinea, Singapore, and a number of other countries. Although there are a few cultures in which sex differences weren't demonstrated, the clear majority found that females were more accurate decoders than males.

Individual differences in communication styles. The sex differences in nonverbal behavior appear to be more substantial than most of the other sex differences we will examine in this chapter. However, it is important to keep in mind that many people do not display the nonverbal behavior that is characteristic of their sex. As always, there is substantial overlap between the behaviors of men and women.

This overlap is well illustrated in a study by LaFrance and Carmen (1980). These authors found that male and female undergraduates showed the overall sex differences that we have discussed so far. Males had more filled pauses and interruptive statements than females, and females gazed and smiled more than males. However, LaFrance and Carmen performed additional analyses for the students who were androgynous. Androgyny is a topic that we will discuss in detail in the next chapter, but we need to introduce it briefly here. Androgynous people are those who are high in both "feminine" and "masculine" qualities. LaFrance and Carmen found that androgynous people tended to show a blend of both feminine and masculine nonverbal behaviors. Androgynous males tended to adopt some of the characteristically female nonverbal behavior, and androgynous females tended to adopt some of the characteristically male nonverbal behavior.

It is also important to keep in mind that the individual differences among women or among men in their nonverbal behavior are large, consistent with Theme 4 of this book. For example (focusing on just the women now), women differ in the size of their personal space "bubbles," in their body posture and movement, in their touching behavior, in their tendency to smile and laugh, and in their ability to "read" the nonverbal behavior of other people. These within-sex variations are so great that you can probably think of several women whose nonverbal behavior is more "masculine" than the average male. You may have a female acquaintance who usually sits in a relaxed position, rather than tensely containing her body with her knees together. You probably know other women who rarely smile, and still others who seem to have no idea what emotions you are experiencing unless you make a public pronouncement.

Potential explanations and implications. Even though we have emphasized individual differences, we need to return to the point that nonverbal sex differences are larger than most of the other sex differences discussed in this chapter. Given that the sex differences are relatively large, it would seem likely that theorists have worked out clear explanations for why women and men should differ in this area. Unfortunately, this is not the case. As Judith Hall (1984) concludes in the introduction to her book, "... the fact remains that when asked why these robust sex differences exist, I still have to reply that I do not know" (p. xii).

One popular explanation for nonverbal sex differences has been that they simply reflect women's subordinate social position. Because women have less social power, they are particularly alert to the moods of the more powerful others (that is, men). Powerless people also would smile more—in an effort to please—and take up less room, in comparison to powerful people. However, Hall rejects the explanation that nonverbal sex differences can be traced to social power. Among her reasons for doubting this explanation is that women are particularly likely to occupy a small amount of space, to smile, and to gaze at a partner when they interact with *other women*, rather than men. Why should women be particularly likely to show these "feminine" nonverbal behaviors when they are with other "powerless" people?

Instead, in explaining decoding accuracy, Hall leans toward an explanation involving attention and practice, although she notes that there has not been much research that tests this hypothesis. According to this kind of explanation, women pay more attention to nonverbal behavior than men do. Women may learn that they are supposed to be observant of other people. Women may also have more practice in this area. Just as the sex difference in math ability was explained in terms of males having more practice or experience, females' greater skill in decoding can perhaps be traced to their greater practice in this area, as well as their greater attention to this area.

Any explanation of the sex differences in personal space, body posture, and facial expression must certainly be tentative. However, Hall suggests that these differences may arise from people's conformity to gender-role stereotypes and from their observation of people in both real life and the media. Also, as children grow up, they may be reinforced for using nonverbal behavior consistent with their sex and punished for using nonverbal behavior that is more typical of the other sex. (Notice that these two explanations represent a social-learning theory approach to the issue.) Thus, a girl growing up may notice that women in real life and on television smile frequently, and she may be told, "Let's see a *smile* on that face" when she has been frowning. Cognitive-developmental explanations may also be applicable, though they may apply more with obvious nonverbal behavior such as body movement rather than more subtle behavior such as gaze. For example, a young girl realizes that she is female and therefore must use a girl-like gait, rather than a more "macho" stride.

Let's now approach the question of implications of nonverbal behavior. Henley (1977) suggests that an awareness of the sex differences in nonverbal behavior carries a prescription for change. Women do not have to smile when they are not happy and they can stop restraining their body postures. (In the area of verbal communication, they can stop allowing interruption.) Men can stop invading women's personal space, they can smile more, and they can condense their bodies when it is inappropriate to occupy too much space.

In discussing how nonverbal behavior can be changed, we must keep in mind that women should not necessarily strive to be more "masculine" in their nonverbal behavior. A glossy brochure titled "Power Communication Skills for Women in Management, Technical, Sales and Staff Positions" advertises a workshop that teaches women how to master "masculine" nonverbal behavior: " 'Body Politics': how to change the traditionally feminine non-verbal behaviors that sabotage your power ..." (Language in the News, 1984, p. 31). As Hall (1984) concludes her book, perhaps we should not assume that male behavior is "normal" and women's behavior is deviant and in need of change. Instead, it might be preferable to see men as the victims of years of conditioning, and to emphasize that men have much to gain from adopting the nonverbal behavior and decoding skills of women.

☐ SECTION SUMMARY ▪ Communication Styles

1. **Young girls talk somewhat more than young boys, but men talk somewhat more than women; men also use more "filled pauses" to hold the floor and they interrupt more.**
2. **Women have higher-pitched voices than men, and they use more extreme shifts in pitch.**

3. There may be some differences in the nature of the words that men and women use, but sex differences are not clear-cut; women may also be more polite, more grammatically correct, and less likely to use profanity.
4. Women gossip slightly more than men, but their remarks are equally positive; they also talk about somewhat different topics.
5. Women typically have smaller personal space zones than men; females approach closer to others than males do, and people also approach closer to females than they do to males.
6. Men have more relaxed body postures than women do; men and women differ in their body movement patterns as well, with men being more restless.
7. There are no clear-cut sex differences in touching behavior.
8. Women smile more than men, but their smiles may cover less-than-happy underlying emotions.
9. In comparison to men, women gaze more at people they are speaking with.
10. Women are better than men at decoding nonverbal messages from other people; this sex difference is also found in younger females and in other cultures.
11. There are individual differences in nonverbal behavior, as in other areas; androgynous people seem to show a blend of both feminine and masculine behavior.
12. Suggestions for changing nonverbal behavior should not emphasize only the ways in which women should become more "masculine" but also the ways in which men should become more "feminine."

PERSONALITY AND SOCIAL BEHAVIOR

We cannot approach this section of the chapter without a few more cautions about the nature of sex differences. The first two cautions were mentioned earlier, but they should be repeated. First, the differences—when they exist—are likely to be small, and the overlap between males and females on any particular characteristic is likely to be large.

Second, we are unlikely to find sex differences that exist in all circumstances. More often, we must make statements such as: There is a sex difference in characteristic X when people are in one situation, but not when they are in another situation. Remember that we found many similar statements in the chapter on achievement (Chapter 5). For instance, we saw that women and men are similar in self-confidence when they are given clear feedback, but men are more confident when there is no feedback.

Third, sex differences are more likely to occur when people are in situations that encourage gender stereotypes. For example, women may act more feminine and men more masculine when they know someone else is watching their responses (Unger, 1985). Often this means that people report their behavior to be more stereotyped than it really is.

A fourth problem arises because it is difficult for researchers to agree about how to measure a particular personality or social characteristic. As you may recall from Chapter 1, **operational definitions** are the precise descriptions of how we will measure a variable in an experiment. Operational definitions present difficulties in all areas of psychology. For example, we saw in the section on cognitive abilities that there are different ways to measure spatial ability. However, these different ability tests all seem closely related to each other. Furthermore, one researcher's operational definition of a concept in communication styles, such as smiling behavior, may be somewhat different from another researcher's operational definition. Still, these definitions would probably be reasonably similar. Personality and social behavior are more controversial. What is aggression, for example? Is the aggression that one person expresses in X-rated graffiti really the same as the aggression another person expresses by delivering electric shock to a frustrating person?

A fifth and final problem is that the settings in many studies may be quite artificial, rather than representing true-to-life situations. Many experiments, for example, test men and women in a psychology laboratory. Mary and John—both college freshmen—might report to Room 27 in the Psychology-Building basement. Perhaps this barren room has only two chairs and, except for the experimenter, no other people. In this "pure" situation, Mary and John might act similarly. In contrast, if you observed them on a Saturday night at the local bar, John might be more dominant than Mary. Certain kinds of behavior are expected in this setting, and other people are nearby to monitor these behaviors. Therefore, John and Mary may respond in a gender-stereotyped fashion. Notice that this problem of artificial laboratory settings leads us to *underestimate* the sex differences that may exist in real life.

Psychologists have examined sex differences in dozens of areas related to personality and social behavior. There seem to be two major clusters of these areas, one related to helping and caring for others and one related to power.

Characteristics Related to Helping and Caring

In 1982, Carol Gilligan published an extremely popular book called *In a Different Voice*. According to Gilligan, women speak in a different voice from men, expressing different concerns, and their words have been ignored by mainstream psychology. She proposes that men see their relationships with other people as part of a hierarchy, in which some people have more power and influence than others. Women, in contrast, see their relationships with others as a web of interconnection. Women tend to see "life as dependent on connection, as sustained by activities of care, as based on a bond of attachment rather than a contract of agreement" (p. 57).

Do women care more about other people than men do, as Gilligan suggests? The answer is by no means clear-cut, as we will see. We will look at several areas that are related to caring: altruism, nurturance, empathy, and friendship.

Altruism. **Altruism** means unselfish concern for the welfare of others, and this characteristic is expressed by helping others who are in need. The typical mother in your second-grade reading book was probably the essence of altruism; she spent hours cleaning and cooking, rarely considering her own interests.

However, research has not uncovered consistent, overall sex differences in the area of altruism. Maccoby and Jacklin (1974) found many studies that demonstrated no sex differences in altruism; consequently, they rejected the idea that females were more altruistic. Deaux (1976b) found that some interesting sex differences emerged, however, when she considered two kinds of altruism separately.

One kind of altruism requires initiative on the part of the helper. The person who needs help has had an accident or some other kind of misfortune, and does not directly ask for help. The helper must take action, stepping in to offer assistance. Deaux discovered in her investigation of the literature that men were more likely than women to help a stranger fix a flat tire on the highway. Men were also more likely to help a sick man who had fallen down on a subway. Both of these situations require initiative; the helper must go over to the body, figure out the problem, and perhaps help the person to a seat.

You may have already figured out an alternative explanation for these sex differences. In the case of changing a tire, most women are less experienced than men, and so they may be less competent in helping (Deaux, 1976b). It would be interesting to see whether women might take the initiative in some helping situations in which they were more likely to be expert, such as in volunteering to hold a baby for a mother who is struggling to open her purse. Also, a woman in a subway feels more vulnerable than a man, and she may have less of the physical strength that would be required to move the fallen person (Deaux, 1976b; Piliavin & Unger, 1985).

Let us consider another study that avoids these problems, because it does not involve special competence or strength. If someone you know lived in Columbus, Ohio, Seattle, Washington, or Atlanta, Georgia during the early 1970s, this person may have unwittingly participated in this study by Latané and Dabbs (1975). On numerous occasions, experimenters "accidentally" dropped handfuls of pencils and coins in front of nearly 5,000 bystanders who were in elevators in these three communities. Males were significantly more likely than females to help pick up the dropped objects. The sex of the person who dropped the objects was also important; females were more likely to be helped than males. Notice that once again we see an example of Theme 2. People respond differently to females than to males. This is also a finding in other studies; people consistently help females more frequently (Piliavin & Unger, 1985).

We have examined indirect requests for help. A different kind of altruism involves direct requests for assistance, as in Demonstration 7.5. Deaux (1976b) concludes that in most cases, men and women are equally responsive to direct requests for help. Is this what you found in Demonstration 7.5? There are some cases, however, in which women are more helpful than men. Pandey and Griffitt (1974) asked people who had just finished participating in one experiment to help them assemble questionnaires for a different experiment. Females and males were equally likely to reply that they would help, but females helped for a significantly longer period of time. Also, there is some evidence that females are more helpful in aiding someone who is dependent, for example a blind person (Piliavin & Unger, 1985).

Notice that the answer to the question, Who helps more? depends upon the nature of the task and the situation. Men are likely to help more than women if the task requires physical strength or competence in male areas. If the task is one that favors neither women nor men, and if assistance is directly requested, then sex differences are minimal and there may be instances in which women are more helpful than men.

Nurturance. **Nurturance** means helping or giving care to someone, typically someone who is younger or less competent. The stereotype suggests that women are more nurturant than men. However, support for this stereotype is inconsistent. In some studies, young girls are more nurturant than young boys (Whiting & Edwards, 1976). In one of these studies, O'Bryant and Brophy (1976) asked fifth-graders to sort a stack of tickets. A kindergarten child in the same room was given a stack of tickets to sort that was twice as large. More than twice as many girls as boys offered to help the younger child. However, there are cases in which the stereotype of the more nurturant woman receives no support (Maccoby & Jacklin, 1974).

An intriguing related question is whether women are more responsive than men to infants and children. Notice that this question involves a more

---

DEMONSTRATION 7.5

Are There Sex Differences in Direct Requests for Help?

This demonstration will require a small amount of bravery, because you must solicit help from strangers. Approach, one at a time, ten women and ten men whom you do not know. You may select the setting, such as a college campus or a shopping mall. Ask each stranger for directions to a particular building or store. Estimate the helpfulness of each person's verbal reply and note any other forms of assistance they offer. Do your samples of women and men differ in their helpfulness?

general kind of response, not necessarily a helping gesture. Berman (1980) looked at three different kinds of measures of responsiveness in her examination of sex differences. Here is what she concluded about these three areas:

1. *Physiological measures.* Women and men are equally responsive to babies when physiological measurements are taken. Studies in other areas show that the pupil of the eye enlarges when people look at attractive objects. However, there are no consistent sex differences in the size of the pupil when people look at babies. Other physiological measures, such as heart rate and blood pressure, also show no sex differences.

2. *Behavior measures.* Behavior measures assess how people actually *behave* in a situation, rather than how they say they behave. In these cases, the studies involve a live baby, child, or animal. People may be instructed to play with the baby. Of the 27 studies conducted with behavior measures, only 3 showed that females were significantly more responsive than males. There are even reports of men being more responsive than women. Parke and O'Leary (1976) found that fathers were somewhat more responsive to their newborns than mothers were.

3. *Self-report measures.* When men and women are asked to report their own responses to infants, the sex differences are large. Specifically, women are much more likely than men to say that they are attracted to babies. As mentioned in Chapter 1, sex differences tend to be larger when people evaluate themselves.

Berman proposes that responsiveness to infants varies greatly as a function of the physical and social qualities of the situation. Thus, some settings will encourage females to be more responsive than males, whereas other settings will minimize the sex differences. The best illustration of this point can be found in a study by Berman (1976), who asked men and women to judge the attractiveness of infants when they were either alone (private) or together with other people (public). Women reported greater attraction in the public condition than in the private condition. The men showed exactly the opposite pattern; they reported greater attraction in the private condition than in the public condition. In the public condition, people act according to the predictions from stereotypes. Women are supposed to get excited about babies, whereas men are supposed to yawn. When people are by themselves, both men and women are similar in their reactions to babies.

Empathy. **Empathy** involves feeling the same emotion as another person is feeling (Eisenberg & Lennon, 1983). A person who is empathic is able to watch someone lose a contest and experience the same feelings of anger, frustration, and disappointment that the loser feels.

According to the stereotype, women are more empathic than men. However, Eisenberg and Lennon found a substantial sex difference only in the case of self-report. Their findings look remarkably similar to Berman's analysis of responsiveness to infants. Here is what these authors concluded about empathy:

1. *Physiological measures.* Women and men are equally empathic when physiological measures are taken. Measures such as heart rate, pulse, and blood pressure showed no sex differences in empathy.
2. *Nonverbal measures of empathy.* Some studies measured empathy in terms of the observer's facial, vocal, and gestural measures. A typical study noted whether the observer's facial expression or body gestures changed in response to a tape recording of an infant crying. Using this nonverbal kind of measure, boys and girls did not differ in their empathy. Unfortunately, no studies on nonverbal responses have been done with adults, so we can't draw any conclusions here.
3. *Self-report measures.* When women and men report how empathic they are, substantial sex differences emerge. For example, one questionnaire assessing empathy asks questions such as, "I tend to get emotionally involved with a friend's problems." Women rate themselves as being *much* more empathic than men; in every study that Eisenberg and Lennon located, females scored higher than males. It would be interesting to see whether the private-versus-public nature of the self-report influences people's reports on their empathy. If the results are similar to those that Berman (1976) found when she studied interest in infants, we would expect that men and women would rate themselves as being similar in empathy when the judgments are private, and different in empathy when the judgments are public.

As we have seen, it is impossible to answer the question, Who is more empathic, males or females? unless we know how empathy is measured. As we mentioned earlier in this section, the operational definition is extremely important. Once again, we see an illustration of Theme 1. Sex differences certainly are *not* found in every condition.

Friendship. Think for a moment about your own ideas regarding sex differences in the quality of friendships. Perhaps you believe that women's friendships are better because they involve more concern and emotional sharing. On the other hand, you might agree with Tiger (1969) that men's friendships are stronger and deeper. You might point out, in support of men's superiority in this area, the unspoken rule that some women have: If two women have made plans to get together, and one of the women later has a chance to get together with a man, the woman's date will be cancelled.

Psychologists ignored the topic of friendship for many decades. However, a few recent studies demonstrate how difficult it is to draw firm conclusions about sex differences in friendship patterns.

The problem is one we discussed at the beginning of this section: The conclusions that we draw must depend upon our measure of friendship. Wheeler and Nezlek (1977) asked beginning college students to keep records of their social interactions, including their interactions with their three best friends. During the course of the semester, women showed a greater decrease than men in the amount of time they spent with their best friends. However, women remained more satisfied with their friendships than men did. In other words, women appear to be lower on one measure of friendship, but higher on another measure.

Sex differences in friendship patterns also depend upon people's age. Caldwell and Peplau (1982) discuss an unpublished study by Fischer that demonstrated how men's and women's friendship patterns can change as they grow older and acquire different responsibilities. As young, unmarried adults, men and women may be similar in their friendship patterns. Among young married people, husbands report having more friends than wives do. However, among older married people, this tendency is reversed, and wives report having more friends than husbands do.

There is one aspect of friendship in which women's and men's friendships seem to differ fairly consistently. Women's friendships seem to be more intimate. Hill and Stull (1981) found that female roommate pairs reported more intimate friendships than was the case with males. The women rated their friendships as closer. They also liked their roommates better and said that they were more likely to keep in touch after graduation. In addition, women rated their friendships as higher in self-disclosure than men did. (**Self-disclosure** means revealing information about yourself to someone else.) Other studies have also reported that women show more self-disclosure with their friends than men do (Wright, 1982).

Female friends may differ somewhat from male friends in terms of what they do together. Caldwell and Peplau (1982) found that women like to get together "just to talk," but men said that they preferred to get together with friends to do specific activities. Caldwell and Peplau point out that women's greater interest in talking may indicate greater emotional sharing within female friendships.

The research in the area of friendships has not been extensive enough to draw firm conclusions about any kind of sex differences. However, Wright's conclusion deserves quoting: ". . . in all probability, if we examined a sufficient number of cases on a sufficient number of dimensions, we would find much more similarity than dissimilarity in the manner in which women and men conduct their friendships" (p. 19).

Conclusions about helping or caring. There is no evidence that the sexes differ markedly with respect to helping-and-caring relationships. The nature of the task and the situation have a strong influence on whether males and females differ in their altruistic helpfulness. It has also been found that males may be more likely to help on stereotypically masculine tasks that require initiative or strength. On the other hand, females are sometimes more nurturant and empathic than males, but the sexes often respond similarly.

Women's friendships may be more intimate than men's friendships, but the two patterns of friendships probably share many similarities.

Characteristics Related to Power

Let us now turn to some areas that involve power. The first areas that we will discuss are aggression, assertiveness, competition, and leadership. The last two areas are related to each other, persuasion and influenceability; persuasion involves convincing others and influenceability involves being convinced by others.

Aggression.   There are many different meanings of the term "aggression," but writers in the area of psychology of women use **aggression** to mean more than just physical violence. It can include physical battering and psychological torture—both of which involve physical violence—but it can also include unwelcome touching of another person and verbal insults (Macaulay, 1985). Maccoby and Jacklin (1974) concluded that aggression was the only area within personality and social behavior for which sex differences are fairly well established. Stereotypes also support the idea that there are sex differences in aggression, with men being more aggressive. Our examination of this topic will reveal that men are *often* more aggressive than women; in the chapter on women and violence we will examine additional support for this statement when we discuss rape, battered women, and sexual harassment. However, there are so many exceptions to the stereotype that we must conclude that men and women are sometimes equally aggressive.

The best resource on sex differences in aggression is an article by Frodi, Macaulay, and Thome (1977). These authors located 72 previous studies that compared the aggressiveness of females and males. Many of these studies demonstrated the expected sex differences, and many showed sex differences in some conditions, but not in others. Impressively, 61 percent of these studies did *not* show males being more aggressive than females in all conditions. Thus, the majority of studies failed to support the stereotype.

You can probably anticipate what Frodi and her colleagues concluded: There are sex differences in aggressiveness in some conditions, but not in others. Here are some of the major conclusions from this review:

1. Men are more likely than women to describe physically aggressive behavior when they report about their own dreams, intentions, and customary behavior. Notice, then, that self-reports show sex differences, just as self-reports were most likely to show sex differences in other areas we have discussed. When people talk about themselves, they drift in the direction of the socially approved stereotypes.
2. Men and women are about equally likely to approve of violence and to appreciate hostile humor.

3. Women are somewhat more likely to feel guilty or anxious about aggression, and these feelings may inhibit aggressive actions.
4. Sex differences in aggression tend to disappear when people are given some kind of justification for being aggressive. For example, when people are led to believe that they are supposed to be aggressive in order to collect data for the experiment, women tend to be as aggressive as men. It seems likely that women no longer feel guilty about aggression in these circumstances.
5. Women may be somewhat more likely to have empathy with the victim. Recall that we pointed out in the previous section that women may be somewhat more likely to feel the same emotion that another person is currently feeling. If women are more empathic, then they may be more likely to place themselves in the position of the person they are about to hurt. However, it is not clear whether women's greater empathy leads to a reduction in their aggressiveness. They may empathize with the victim and decide to be aggressive anyway.
6. Sex differences in aggression tend to disappear when the victim is anonymous. It is possible that it is more difficult to empathize with a victim whose name and identity are unknown.

Thus, men are indeed more aggressive than women in some situations. In other situations, guilt and empathy are not aroused; here, women may be just as aggressive as men.

A recent study identified another factor that influences sex differences in aggression. Towson and Zanna (1982) proposed that people will show more aggression when they have been frustrated in situations congruent with traditional gender roles. Demonstration 7.6 is a modification of their study. They asked women and men to read either the dance (traditionally feminine) or the body-building (traditionally masculine) version of the story and to make judgments about the kinds of aggressive responses that would be appropriate in this frustrating situation.

Some of the results are illustrated in Figure 7.3. Notice that men said they would be more verbally aggressive in the "masculine" situation and women said they would be more verbally aggressive in the "feminine" situation. Notice, also, that sex differences in aggressive responses are exaggerated in the "masculine" situation and minimized in the "feminine" situation. Thus, an important factor that influences sex differences in aggression is the nature of the task.

You may have read articles in newspapers and magazines about how the feminist movement has led or will lead to more violence among women. These speculations are often based on the belief that "liberated" women are more masculine than traditional women, and—as a consequence—they are also more aggressive than traditional women. Richardson, Vinsel, and Taylor (1980) decided to see whether liberal women were indeed more aggressive than traditional women. Alternately, women who had liberal attitudes about

Aggressive Responses to Frustration.

Imagine yourself in this situation:

You are taking an exercise course that includes a section on dance. This section is supposed to increase your grace and posture and to teach you to express yourself with your body. You want to do your best on the exam on this section. On the day of the test, you go to the gym early in order to warm up. The female student who is supposed to take the test just after you is using the only available warm-up room. You ask when she will be done, because you really need to practice. She says she will be finished in 20 minutes, but she thinks that the exam times have been rescheduled, and she now precedes you. You run errands for half an hour and return to check the exam schedule; it has not been changed. You are very upset, and you return to the warm-up room to find the same student still there. You explain that the schedule has not been changed, and you ask to use the room. She says that it was your responsibility to check the schedule, but she will leave when you have changed clothes. You return to the warm-up room after changing. The door is closed and locked. Only five minutes remain before your exam. You run back to the dressing room and you see the other student. What do you do?

Now reread this paragraph, but substitute a body-building section that is supposed to increase your physical strength, physical endurance, and muscle control; the student is still the same sex. Compare your responses. Notice whether you are more aggressive in the situation that matches your traditional gender role.

women's roles might also be politically liberal, and favor nonaggressive solutions to conflicts. Thus, the first prediction suggests that liberal women are *more* aggressive, whereas the second prediction suggests that liberal women are *less* aggressive, when compared to traditional women.

Richardson and her colleagues studied women who had scored either extremely high or extremely low on a test measuring attitudes toward women's roles in society. When a woman arrived for the experiment, she met a male student who was actually a confederate of the experimenter. This confederate talked briefly with the woman and then asked her to sign a petition, which was either for or against the Equal Rights Amendment. Then the experimenter led the two people into the laboratory, where the woman believed she was participating in a competitive game. In the course of this game, the woman was supposed to shock her male opponent. In actuality, the man never received the shock. However, this deception allowed the experimenters to measure the intensity of shock that the woman thought she was using on the male; more intense shocks presumably represented more aggression.

The results showed that the traditional women were more aggressive than the liberal women, whether the opponent had expressed traditional or liberal attitudes about the Equal Rights Amendment. In other words, the

FIGURE 7.3. **Judged appropriateness of verbal aggressive response, as a function of the nature of the task and sex of judge (based on Towson & Zanna, 1982)**

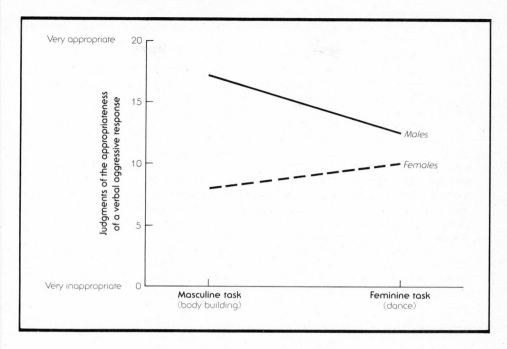

second prediction was correct; liberal women are less aggressive. As the authors note, feminists often suggest that when women reject the traditional feminine stereotype, they should not simply adopt stereotypically masculine behaviors. The liberal women in this study had apparently accepted that suggestion.

Let us return to the basic point that males are often more aggressive than females. There is substantial discussion about whether there is a biological basis for the sex difference. Both genetic and hormonal explanations have been offered, and it is too early to give a clear-cut answer as to their contribution. There are four kinds of studies cited by those who favor the biological explanation that aggression is an inborn characteristic of males more than females:

1. In most other species, the male is more aggressive than the female (Moyer, 1976; White, 1983). (However, there are exceptions to this pattern; furthermore, we should be cautious about assuming that animal studies apply to humans.)
2. There are studies linking the Y chromosome and the hormone androgen to aggression (Moyer, 1976; Reinisch, 1981; White, 1983). (Once again, however, there are inconsistencies in this research.)

3. Observations of children under the age of six show that boys are consistently more aggressive than girls (Maccoby & Jacklin, 1980; White, 1983). You may recall from Chapter 3 that boys are more likely than girls to show a "rough and tumble" kind of play; most of the studies involve this kind of aggression rather than more harmful aggression. Nevertheless, these data on children are perhaps the most compelling of all four kinds of studies.
4. Cross-cultural studies show that males are more aggressive than females in many other cultures (Rohner, 1976; White, 1983). (However, once more, there are exceptions, and the difference in aggression among various cultures is generally greater than the sex differences that are observed.)

As White (1983) concludes, there are so many exceptions to the pattern of more aggression in males than females that it is likely that the biological contribution is minimal. Socialization factors and situational factors are probably more important determinants of the sex difference. Furthermore, even if biological factors do increase males' tendency to be aggressive, it is clear that situational factors can modify any inborn sex differences (Block, 1984; Deaux, 1985; White, 1983). These situational factors (such as those described by Frodi and her colleagues and by Towson and Zanna) can minimize, maximize, or even reverse any biologically based sex difference.

Some authors, concerned about the level of aggression in our society, suggest that we should make strong efforts to change both socialization and situational factors in order to minimize aggression. *Both* boys and girls "should be encouraged to develop socially positive qualities such as tenderness, sensitivity to feelings, nurturance, cooperativeness, and aesthetic appreciation" (Eron, 1980, p. 251).

Assertiveness. **Assertiveness** is the ability to stand up for your own rights without denying the rights of others. It is important to contrast assertiveness with aggressive behavior, which infringes upon the rights of other people. Assertiveness can also be contrasted with **passive behavior,** which involves self-denial or not standing up for your own rights.

Connor and her colleagues (1978) investigated boys' and girls' preferences for these three patterns of dealing with conflict. Table 7.1 shows how each of these three patterns might be used by a child to approach a teacher who had given an incorrect grade on a paper. Connor and her coauthors asked boys and girls to read stories that continued in the same aggressive, assertive, or passive spirit as these three sentences. The children were then asked to judge the appropriateness of each approach.

In general, girls liked the passive approach better than the boys did. Furthermore, boys generally liked the aggressive approach better than the girls did. However, the older children—both girls and boys—liked the assertive approach better than the younger children did. It seems that as children grow older, they realize that assertiveness is the most productive strategy.

TABLE 7.1   **Examples from the Stories in the Study by Connor, Serbin, and Ender (1978; p. 62)**

Aggressive	Assertive	Passive
Ms. Kate, you graded my paper unfairly and you better change it.	Excuse me, Ms. Kate I would like to discuss my grade with you.	Um, excuse me, Ms. Kate. If you're busy, I'll sit down. It's not that important.

There was another, more disturbing developmental trend. As girls grew older, they were more likely to think that the passive approach would be an effective one. In contrast, as boys grew older, they were more likely to think that the passive approach would be ineffective.

The previous study demonstrated that boys and girls have different attitudes toward aggressive and passive approaches, but that both grow to appreciate the assertive approach. Do boys and girls differ in their actual assertive behavior? In one study, children were observed in their classrooms (Hedrick & Chance, 1977). The observers recorded all assertive achievement behaviors, such as asking a question or going up to the teacher's desk. For above-average children, females and males were equally assertive. Sex differences appeared only for the average-ability children, where the girls were less assertive than the boys.

There are often surprises in the studies of assertiveness. Smye and Wine (1980) found that high-school females were *more* appropriately assertive than males in their behavior when they role-played responses to a dilemma presented on videotape. Males, in contrast, chose aggressive responses, rather than assertive responses.

What is the situation with adults? Popular magazines and newspapers proclaim that adult women are less assertive than adult men and many organizations offer assertiveness-training classes for women. We will discuss assertiveness training in Chapter 12. However, the evidence about sex differences in assertiveness is as controversial for adults as it is for younger people. There is some research indicating that men are more assertive (Morgan, 1974; Orenstein, Orenstein & Carr, 1975). On the other hand, one standardized test of assertiveness demonstrated that women are more assertive than men (Tolor, Kelly, & Stebbins, 1976). Other measures of assertiveness showed that women and men are equally assertive (Lohr & Nix, 1982; Tolor, et al., 1976).

It is too early to see any trends in factors that increase or decrease sex differences in assertiveness. It is possible that women and men are similar in assertiveness in laboratory settings, but different from each other in most "real-life" settings. It may be that everyone would profit from assertiveness-training classes, so that women would be less passive and men would be less aggressive. The assertiveness approach is more productive than the passive approach and less destructive than the aggressive approach.

Competition.   According to the stereotype, men are more competitive than women. They lust after victory in competitive sports, and they push others aside in their eager pursuit of success in the business world.

It is not clear whether this stereotype has much basis in reality. Consider the uncertainty about whether young boys are more competitive than young girls. Lever (1976) found that boys were more likely than girls to play formal, competitive games during their free time. Girls spent time in noncompetitive activities, such as riding bikes. However, Lott (1978) did not find any substantial differences in the competitiveness of boys' and girls' games. As Maccoby and Jacklin (1974) conclude, about half of the studies on competition demonstrate that there are no sex differences, but most of the remaining half show that boys are more competitive.

Competition in adulthood is usually measured with a rather artificial laboratory game between two players. The players can either select a cooperative strategy, which leads to a small profit in the short run and a moderate profit in the long run, or a competitive strategy, which leads to a large profit in the short run and large losses in the long run. Clearly, the cooperative strategy has the advantage, yet people often adopt the competitive strategy. At any rate, there do not seem to be substantial sex differences here. Again, it seems likely that the "unnatural" laboratory setting might underestimate sex differences that might be found in more realistic settings.

Leadership.   If you attend a coeducational college, check the list of student officers and notice their sex. If your college is typical, it is likely to be predominantly male, even if the majority of students are female. The president of your class in high school was also probably a male, and it seems inevitable that for years to come the President of the United States will be a male.

Males become leaders of mixed-sex groups even when the members of the group are presumably equal in ability. Lockheed and Hall (1976) assigned student teachers to groups of four; each group had two males and two females. The group members were told that the members of the group had been matched on the basis of training and experience. These authors found that males were four times as likely as females to emerge as leaders. When the experiment was repeated with high-school students, males were *seven* times as likely to become leaders. When a group of strangers must work together on a task, they sometimes have no prior basis on which to decide who has the best leadership ability. In these cases, the person with the highest status frequently becomes the leader, and at present males are likely to have the highest status.

Males are likely to be seen as the leader of the group, even when other information suggests that a female is truly the leader of that group. Porter and Geis (1981) showed slides of various groups to people who were asked to guess who was the leader. The responses showed that people made their judgments on the basis of sex (guessing that a man was the leader) rather than on the basis of the important leadership cue of being seated at the head of the table. Women sometimes seem to be invisible when people are looking for leaders. These studies on leadership illustrate both Themes 2 and 3 that have been discussed throughout the book. That is, males are evaluated more positively than females, and they are also more visible.

With enough other cues, however, people can be convinced that a woman can actually lead a group. Offermann (1986) tried to make the leadership cues even more obvious than simply occupying the position at the head of the table. Her designated leader not only sat in that position but also began the discussion, talked more, contributed the greatest number of new ideas, and supported the ideas proposed by other people. In other words, she created super-leaders. Videotapes were made of these group sessions, sometimes with female leaders and sometimes with male leaders. Students who had not been told about the group structure were then asked to view these video-tapes and decide who was the group leader. When a woman displayed all these leadership behaviors, did they still ignore her and select one of the quiet men on the sidelines? Fortunately not. Even when the female leader had only males as her group members, people still correctly identified the fact that she was the leader.

The studies by Porter and Geis and by Offermann suggest that if a woman wants to be subtle, she may not be identified as a leader. If, however, she "pulls out all the stops," people will be willing to acknowledge that she is indeed the leader. Both of these studies, however, involve only brief experience with the people in a group; would women be more likely to be selected as leaders if people knew them better?

How do women perform as group leaders, in contrast to men? Eskilson and Wiley (1976) assigned females and males to be leaders of three-person groups. There were no sex differences between female and male leaders in the percentage of time they talked or the speed with which the groups solved the problems. However, the leadership styles differed somewhat. Male leaders spent somewhat more time in leader-like behavior such as giving advice. Female leaders spent somewhat more time praising other group members and supporting their morale. It is important to stress, however, that although these differences were statistically significant, women's and men's behaviors differed by only a few percentage points.

Eskilson and Wiley also found that the women who thought they had been appointed leaders because of their personal achievement (rather than by chance) tended to become "Super-Women." They performed both leader-like and supportive duties:

> ... females who achieved the leader role showed intense involvement with the instrumental aspect of the group task. However, they simultaneously performed the expected encouraging and tension-relieving behavior. Like some working wives, they took on two jobs. Thus, females who attained the leader role by personal achievement rose to the instrumental challenge, but did not discard their deeply internalized obligation to provide for the emotional needs of others. [p. 192]

In summary, we have seen that males are more often considered to be leaders, unless the evidence to the contrary is overwhelming. Males and females differ somewhat in their leadership strategies, and in some cases female leaders adopt both "masculine" and "feminine" leadership styles.

Persuasion. One of the very basic components of power is persuasion. A powerful person can persuade people to do something that they would not ordinarily do. A powerful person can also convince people to believe something contrary to their original beliefs.

Take a moment to think about how you persuade others. Think of something that you would like someone else to do or to believe, and imagine what strategies you would use. Now contemplate whether you would anticipate finding differences in the kinds of strategies that women and men use.

Johnson (1976) found that people have stereotypes about the kind of persuasion strategies that women and men use in interpersonal relationships. Basically, there were three ways in which women's and men's strategies were seen to differ:

1. *Indirect versus Direct Power*—Women are believed to be indirect and manipulative. Think about the situation-comedy representations of women. On "I Love Lucy," Lucy convinces Ricky to perform for her women's club by mentioning that they are considering hiring his strongest rival. These stereotypes are still alive and well in current sit-coms. Recently, on the Bill Cosby show, I watched the daughter Denise trying to convince her father to let her spend the night in line waiting for tickets to a rock concert by the Walking Lemons. "Oh, Daddy," she coos to her T-shirt-clad father, "that's a really nice outfit . . . You look really great."
2. *Personal versus Concrete Power*—Women are seen as using personal power, such as liking, affection, and approval. In contrast, men are associated with concrete power, such as money, knowledge, and physical strength.
3. *Helplessness versus Competence*—Women are perceived to use helplessness as a device to persuade others. For example, a woman standing by the side of the road near her car with a flat tire is more likely than a man to influence someone to stop. In contrast, people see men as using their competence as a persuasion strategy.

We have looked at the stereotypes about the use of persuasion. How do men and women actually behave? Falbo (1977) asked students to write a short essay on the topic, "How I Get My Way." These essays were later coded according to the kind of strategies used. Contrary to stereotypes, men and women wrote remarkably similar essays. In fact, the only significant difference in the use of a strategy occurred for the use of the reasoning strategy, or the use of logical arguments, and women were *more* likely then men to mention this strategy.

Persuasion strategies are also important in intimate relationships. Falbo (1982) asked people to describe how they get their romantic partners to do what they want. These essays were then coded for strategy use. In addition to direct and indirect strategies, Falbo also coded the strategies according to whether they were unilateral (involving only one person) or bilateral (involving both partners). Women were more likely to say that they used indirect, unilateral strategies, such as leaving the room or becoming silent. Men were more likely to say that they used direct, bilateral strategies, such as bargaining with the partner.

Notice that in romantic relationships, men and women do seem to use somewhat different strategies, although these sex differences were not revealed in the more general question about "How I Get My Way." Is there something constricting about romantic relationships that urges us to slide toward the stereotypes about persuasion strategies? You'll notice that both of Falbo's studies used self-report methods. (It's easy to see why, because most researchers aren't eager to plant themselves in people's apartments to eavesdrop on their persuasion strategies.) You'll recall that the self-report method is particularly likely to reveal sex differences. It is possible that the true persuasive behavior of men and women is more similar than what they report.

Influenceability.   For every person who persuades, there must be a person who is influenced, giving in to that persuasion. For many years, social psychologists maintained that women were far more influenceable and conforming than men. More recent articles conclude that sex differences may be statistically significant, but they are small in magnitude.

The area of influenceability was one of the first to use a new, sophisticated kind of analysis that has become important in assessing sex differences. Before we describe this new method, we must first review the traditional method of deciding whether there are sex differences in a particular behavior. The traditional method, often called the **literary approach to reviewing research,** is to read through the articles on a topic and to make a decision about whether there are sex differences, based on an overall impression of the studies. The problem with the traditional method is that it is difficult to decide, from an accumulation of individual studies, whether the overall picture indicates sex differences. Suppose that ten studies find no sex differences, five favor men, and one favors women. One person might conclude that there are no overall sex differences, whereas another person might conclude that men are somewhat favored. The literary approach lacks a method of systematically combining individual studies.

The **statistical approach to reviewing research,** specifically the **meta-analysis technique,** statistically combines the results of independent experiments in order to provide a single index that tells us whether a particular factor has an overall effect on behavior. In the case of the influenceability research, a meta-analysis can combine dozens of previous studies into one enormous super-study and give us a picture of whether sex has an overall effect on influenceability.

Several articles have examined the issue of sex differences in influenceability, using either the literary approach or the statistical approach (Cooper, 1979; Eagly, 1978; Sohn, 1980). The most comprehensive examination is one by Eagly and Carli (1981). These authors combed the psychology journals from 1949 to 1977 and located a total of 148 studies that had been conducted in this area.

Their meta-analysis showed that women are somewhat more easily influenced than men, particularly in situations where other group members exert pressure on women to change their minds. The actual size of the sex difference was small. However, because of the enormous number of people tested, it was statistically significant. This contrast between the size of the sex difference and its statistical significance can best be illustrated by two further calculations that the authors made:

1. Eagly and Carli calculated that only 1 percent of all the variability in influenceability can be accounted for by sex. That is, people differ so much in influenceability that only 1 percent of all that variation can be traced to sex. As the authors conclude, "A sex difference as small as this may have few implications for social interaction" (p. 11).
2. Suppose, as we suggested in Chapter 1, that when an experiment yields no sex diferences, the paper does not go beyond a file drawer. (As you may recall, we noted that journals prefer to publish significant sex differences, so that studies *without* sex differences are less likely to be published.) It would require a total of 4,039 such unpublished experiments that failed to find sex differences—sitting in researchers' file drawers—in order to cancel out the effects of the published studies and to force us to abandon the conclusion that females are more influenceable than males.

I have covered this topic in some detail because it illustrates an approach that will become more common in future research. The meta-analysis technique allows us to summarize an area of research in a systematic fashion, and it will provide answers about some of the other topics about which we currently cannot draw conclusions.

In addition, the Eagly and Carli article uncovered a source of bias that future researchers in the area of sex differences should notice. Male researchers obtained *larger* sex differences in influenceability than female researchers. Because of this discovery, Eagly and Carli also examined literature in another area we discussed earlier, the ability to guess what emotion people are feeling. They looked at a large number of studies reviewed by Hall (1978) and found that male researchers obtained *smaller* sex differences than female researchers. It seems that each sex finds results that are most flattering to their own sex. Male researchers find easily influenced women, who are not particularly sensitive to others' feelings. Female researchers find sensitive women, who are not particularly easily influenced. As we noted in Chapter 1, the sex of the experimenter may influence the results.

The majority of researchers in the area of influenceability have been male, so that sex differences in influenceability can be partly traced to the fact that male researchers are more likely to obtain sex differences (Eagly & Wood, 1985). However, Eagly and Wood suggest two additional reasons why females are more easily influenced than males:

1. The traditional gender role requires women to yield to social influence, and females learn during socialization that they must give in; in contrast, males learn during socialization that they must persuade and influence others. The traditional gender role for women may also affect influenceability because women have been trained to be concerned about preserving social harmony. One way to preserve social harmony, when there is a disagreement, is to give in, to yield to the views of others.
2. Women's greater influenceability may stem from their lower status relative to men in our society. In general, high-status people make demands on low-status people, and low-status people must yield. Because women have lower status, they are more conforming and more easily influenced. The sex differences in influenceability that occur in everyday life are carried over, to some extent, into settings where the status of men and women is similar, such as in laboratory experiments.

At present, then, Eagly and Wood (1985) argue that sex differences in influenceability can best be explained by the greater number of male researchers; traditional gender roles encouraging women to be easily persuaded and to preserve social harmony; and women's lower status.

□ SECTION SUMMARY ▪ Personality and Social Behavior

1. It is difficult to draw conclusions about sex differences in personality and social behavior because they are likely to be small, to be found only in some circumstances, and to be found in situations that encourage gender stereotypes; researchers disagree about how to measure behavior in this area; finally, behavior in laboratory settings may not be similar to behavior in real-life settings.
2. Males may be more altruistic than females on tasks that are masculine or require initiative or strength; on tasks where someone

else directly requests help, women may occasionally be more helpful.

3. Women may be more nurturant than men, but sex differences here are inconsistent.

4. Women are consistently more attracted to babies than men only when attraction is assessed in terms of self-report measures; various qualities of the situation and individual differences may also influence sex differences in reactions to babies.

5. Women are more empathic than men when empathy is measured by self-report, but not when empathy is measured in other ways.

6. Sex differences in friendship patterns are not clear-cut, except that women's friendships seem to be more intimate.

7. Men are more aggressive than women in self-report measures; there are no sex differences in approval of violence or in aggression when a justification is provided or when the victim is anonymous.

8. Women are somewhat more guilty about aggression and may feel more empathy with the victim.

9. People are more aggressive when they have been frustrated in gender-stereotyped situations than in nontraditional situations; traditional women are also more aggressive than liberal women.

10. Four kinds of studies have been cited by those who believe that sex differences in aggression are biologically based; these include studies done on other species, chromosomal and hormonal studies, observations of children, and cross-cultural studies; even if biological factors do operate, socialization and situational factors can modify inborn sex differences.

11. Boys and girls differ in their attitude toward aggressive and passive approaches; there do not seem to be marked sex differences in children's or adults' assertive behavior.

12. Consistent sex differences have not been demonstrated in competitiveness.

13. Males are likely to be seen as group leaders, but when a woman is provided with enough cues showing that she is the leader, she will appropriately be identified as the leader.

14. When men are leaders, they may spend somewhat more time in leader-like behavior, whereas women leaders may spend somewhat more time supporting other group members.

15. Stereotypes about sex differences in persuasion techniques show women as using indirect power, personal power, and helplessness, in contrast to men using direct power, concrete power, and competence.

16. Women and men use different persuasion strategies in romantic relationships, but their more general persuasion strategies do not differ substantially.

17. A large-scale analysis of sex differences in influenceability concluded that there are small but significant sex differences, with females being more easily influenced than males. Explanations for this sex difference include the large number of male researchers in this area; the influence of traditional gender roles; and women's lower status.

Chapter Review Questions

1. Imagine that you have a friend who is a high-school teacher. List for this friend the areas of differences and similarities in cognitive abilities. Point out to your friend whether these findings have important implications for ability differences in a high-school classroom, keeping in mind our comments about the size of the differences.

2. The explanations for sex differences in cognitive abilities emphasized socialization factors. Imagine that you were responsible for revising an elementary-school program. What would you do to improve boys' performance on verbal tasks and girls' performance on spatial and mathematics tasks? (Notice that this question makes the debatable assumption that the sex differences are large enough to be worried about.)

3. Review the biological explanations for cognitive sex differences, and comment on why these explanations might not be appropriate.

4. In the section on communication styles, men seem to take up more space than women, whether we use the word "space" in the literal sense or in the figurative sense (for example, more conversational space). Discuss this point, noting as many areas of sex difference as possible.

5. Return to Chapter 3 to the section on theories of sex-typing, and review the social-learning, cognitive-developmental, and gender schema theories. Now list the areas in which there are significant sex differences in communication style (both verbal and nonverbal), and explain how each of those three theories might account for the sex differences.

6. The section on facial expression pointed out that women's smiles often do not match their true emotions; however, women are more accurate than men in guessing the emotions that underlie other people's facial expressions. Speculate about why these two points might be related, and point out some practical implications of these two points.

7. The beginning of the chapter and the beginning of the section on personality and social behavior listed warnings about research on sex differences. Review these warnings and point out how they could be applied to sex differences in altruism.

8. We stressed that sex differences may appear in some situations, but not in others. Many of the studies we discussed were conducted in psychology laboratories, a kind of setting that tends to minimize power differences that might exist in real life. Go through the chapter and

notice whether sex differences are more likely to appear in settings that are closer to real-life situations in contrast to laboratory settings.

9. We pointed out that sex differences are most likely to occur when people are in situations that encourage gender stereotypes. Review the sex differences in personality and social behavior from the perspective of this observation.

10. According to stereotypes, women care about interpersonal relationships, whereas men care about dominating other people. As in many stereotypes, there is a grain of truth in this contrast. Discuss the grain of truth and then point out how the sexes share many similarities.

☐ NEW TERMS

frequency distributions	altruism
verbal fluency	nurturance
verbal analogies	empathy
anagrams	self-disclosure
lateralization	aggression
mental-rotation test	assertiveness
embedded-figure test	passive behavior
intonation	literary approach to reviewing research
personal space	statistical approach to reviewing research
decoding ability	meta-analysis technique
operational definition	

☐ RECOMMENDED READINGS

Deaux, K. (1985). Sex and gender. *Annual Review of Psychology, 36*, 49–81. ■ This chapter provides an overview of the topic of sex differences, including discussion on methodology and implications.

Hall, J. A. (1984). *Nonverbal sex differences: Communication accuracy and expressive style.* Baltimore: Johns Hopkins. ■ Hall's book will certainly serve as a classic reference in the area of nonverbal behavior; it offers a thorough, clearly written summary of the research in this area.

Hyde, J. S. (Ed.) (1986). *The psychology of gender: Advances through the meta-analysis.* Baltimore, MD: Johns Hopkins. ■ Hyde's book will be published after this textbook has gone to press, but it will contain important information relevant to this chapter, on topics such as cognitive sex differences.

McConnell-Ginet, S., Borker, R., & Furmer, N. (Eds.) (1980). *Women and language in literature and society.* New York: Praeger. ■ This book contains chapters on sex differences in verbal communication; it also goes beyond this topic to discuss women as writers.

O'Leary, V. E., Unger, R. K., & Wallston, B. S. (Eds.) (1985). *Women, gender and social psychology.* Hillsdale, N. J.: Erlbaum. ■ This book provides advanced-level summaries of topics in this chapter such as altruism, aggression, and influenceability, and it also discusses how the study of gender has contributed to perspectives on social psychology.

CHAPTER 8

GENDER STEREOTYPES

■ Your history books rarely mentioned women because women's activities prior to the twentieth century were always centered around the family.

■ Prior to the twentieth century, all of the well-known philosophers believed that women were inevitably inferior to men.

■ People will think that a woman is more competent if she is referred to as a woman, rather than a girl.

■ In the early 1970s, television did not represent employed women accurately, but in current television shows, women work outside the home about as often as they do in reality.

■ People describe themselves as being less stereotyped than "typical people."

■ Women are much less stereotyped than men, and people in different countries have gender stereotypes that are very different from the gender stereotypes that Americans have.

■ The most accepted view of gender stereotypes is that people make up stereotypes because they want to discriminate against women.

■ If a woman knows that the interviewer for a job has traditional ideas about women, she will change her behavior so that she appears more traditional.

■ According to the current view, masculinity and femininity are exact opposites of each other, so that if you are high in masculinity, you must be low in femininity.

■ Highly feminine people have the highest self-esteem.

Take a moment to consider what you have learned about women and men in the last three chapters. In particular, think about the similarities and differences between them. In Chapter 5 you saw that the sexes are similar in their achievement motivation, fear of success, and attributions for success. Men are sometimes more self-confident in achievement situations; however, the sexes are frequently similar in this area. As Chapter 6 mentioned, men and women in the same work setting share many personal attributes. Chapter 7 examined sex differences and similarities in more depth, concluding that men and women are generally similar in their cognitive abilities, personality, and social behavior. Men and women may differ in some areas. However, the sex differences are typically small, and the differences are usually not found in all settings. In other words, women and men show considerable overlap in the extent to which they show a particular characteristic.

In reality, then, women and men are fairly similar. Are these similarities reflected in everyone's ideas about women and men? Is your boss from your summer job aware of these similarities? How about your mother's best friend? Your roommate or next-door neighbor? In this chapter we will investigate people's *ideas* about women and men; our topic is gender stereotypes, sometimes called sex stereotypes.

There are several definitions for gender stereotypes that differ somewhat from one another. For our purposes, we will define **gender stereotypes** as "the structured sets of beliefs about the personal attributes of women and men" (Ashmore & Del Boca, 1979, p. 222). Let us analyze the components of that definition. Notice that stereotypes are cognitive; they refer to our thoughts and beliefs, and they may have little correspondence with reality. A stereotype is a "picture in the head," rather than an accurate mirror of the real world. However, a stereotype consists of more than just one single idea or thought. Instead, a stereotype is an organized group of ideas that fit in rather well with one another. For example, your summer boss's stereotype of women might be that they are soft, dependent, not particularly skilled, and likely to be fond of children.

This chapter is divided into three sections. The first section examines how women are represented in a variety of places, such as in the words of philosophers, in language, and on television. The second section discusses what people believe about women and men—what their stereotypes are like, how these stereotypes are related to thought processes, and how stereotypes can affect behavior. The third section considers the concept of androgyny, focusing on why this model is not the most ideal alternative to gender stereotypes.

☐ THE REPRESENTATION OF WOMEN AND MEN

In this portion of the chapter we will look at the way women and men are represented, first in a section called "A Heritage of Gender Bias" that focuses on history, ideas about women, religion, and mythology, and then in sections on the ways in which language and the current media represent women and men. We will see that in many ways women are the "second sex" in the way they are represented. Consistent with two of the themes of this book, women are often invisible and considered to be definitely inferior.

A Heritage of Gender Bias

It is impossible to do justice to a topic as broad as our legacy of gender bias with just a few pages of background discussion. However, we need to examine these topics briefly in order to appreciate the origin of current thoughts about women.

Gender bias in history. Recently, scholars have begun to realize that we know very little about how half of humanity has fared throughout history; what *have* women been doing for all these years? Archeologists interested in prehistoric humans have typically concentrated their research attention on tools associated with hunting, which was most often a man's activity. Relatively little is known about what the women were doing in these pre-agricultural communities (Hunter College Women's Studies Collective, 1983). Similarly, while the men of Europe were enjoying the Renaissance period, what were the women doing? Did they have a Renaissance? One important goal of women's studies is to look for missing information about women. Women have been invisible in our history books. We need to know about women artists, philosophers, and food-providers.

In many cases, women have been left out of history books because their work was confined to home and family. Since women were rarely taught to write, they could not write about their experiences. Women artists often expressed themselves in music, dance, and quilting. These are relatively fragile and anonymous art forms in contrast to the permanence of men's art forms in painting, sculpture, and architecture.

Furthermore, many of women's accomplishments have been forgotten. Did you know that women frequently managed large estates during the Middle Ages, while their husbands were away in battles or crusades? Or that women often presided over monasteries before the ninth century A.D.? Or that women wrote theological tracts and marched in public protests during the Protestant Reformation (Hafter, 1979)? Did your American history book tell you that Congress chose Mary Katherine Goddard to print the official copy of the Declaration of Independence in 1776? Traditional historians—either consciously or unconsciously—have insured women's invisibility in most history books. Scholars interested in women's history, however, are uncovering information about women's numerous accomplishments. They are trying to make these invisible women more visible.

Ideas about women. Although women have been invisible in history books, philosophers throughout the centuries have commented upon women, particularly in comparison to men. Their views make it clear that the devaluation of women is not a recent phenomenon. As Hafter (1979) comments, we accept assumptions about what is normal behavior for men and women without appreciating that many of these assumptions are centuries old. Hafter points out that we have rejected the plumbing and heating standards that were normal a thousand years ago. However, we have not rejected outdated notions regarding women, even though these notions were reactions to conditions that have long since passed.

Two important Greek philosophers, Aristotle and Plato, had contrasting ideas about women. It is Aristotle's view—the more negative of the two—that seems to have had a more long-lasting impact.

Aristotle (384–322 B.C.) believed that women's inferiority was biologically based. "We should look on the female," he said, "as being as it were a deformity, though one which occurs in the ordinary course of nature" (Aristotle, 1943). He believed that neither women nor children had fully developed rationality. Therefore, men must rule them both and be responsible for them.

Aristotle also speculated about sex differences:

> Woman is more compassionate than man and has a greater propensity to tears. She is, also, more envious, more querulous, more slanderous and more contentious. Farther still, the female is more dispirited, more despondent, more impudent and more given to falsehood than the male. ... But the male ... is more disposed to give assistance in danger, and is more courageous than the female. [Book IX, Chapter 1; cited in Miles, 1935, p. 700]

Do these stereotypes sound familiar?

Plato (427–347 B.C.) was Aristotle's teacher. Unlike Aristotle and almost all of the well-known philosophers since then, Plato was to some extent a feminist (Hunter College Women's Studies Collective, 1983). Plato argued that rulers should be selected from carefully trained people, and these rulers *might* include women as well as men. He believed that women were generally less competent than were men, a sentiment certainly shared by his contemporaries. However, he maintained that *some* women are better than some men at any given activity. Thus, if a woman were particularly intelligent, courageous, and able to resist temptation, she could be a potential ruler. Notice, then, that Plato promoted the concept of "overlap" in the distribution of characteristics, a topic we discussed in the last chapter.

Philosophers since the Greek period have usually expanded upon Aristotle's views, rather than Plato's. Jean Jacques Rousseau (1712–1778) argued that nature dictated that women should obey men. The function of women was to please men, to be useful to them, and to make their lives pleasant (Hunter College Women's Studies Collective, 1983). Similarly, the German philosopher Friedrich Nietzsche (1844–1900) argued that a man "must conceive of woman as a possession, as property that can be locked, as something predestined for service and achieving her perfection in that."

Perhaps the only well-known philosopher prior to the 20th century whose views would be acceptable to current feminists is John Stuart Mill (1806–1873), a British philosopher whose thinking was strongly influenced by his wife, Harriet Taylor Mill (1807–1858). John Stuart Mill maintained that women should have equal rights and equal opportunities. They should be able to own property, to vote, to be educated, and to choose any profession for which they had been appropriately trained. Discussions published before the 1960s about Mill's ideas generally fail to mention his views on women.

In summary, the devaluation of women by philosophers is quite literally "as old as the Greeks." Let us now briefly examine how women are portrayed in the religious and mythological traditions.

Images of women in religion and mythology. The book *Women's Realities, Women's Choices* (Hunter College Women's Studies Collective, 1983) contains an excellent chapter on women and religion, and our examination of this topic is based on that chapter.

Most religions include a description of how the world and its human occupants were created. For example, Jews, Christians, and Muslims share the story of Adam and Eve. In this story, God creates man "in his own image." In other words, God is a man and men came first. Later, God made Eve as a companion to Adam, and she was constructed from his rib. In other words, women are made from men, and women are therefore secondary in the great scheme of things. Males are "normal" and females are "the second sex." Furthermore, Eve gives in to temptation and leads Adam into sin. Women, then, are morally weak, and this weakness can contaminate men. When Adam and Eve are expelled from paradise, their curse shows an interesting asymmetry. Adam's curse is that he must work for a living, whereas Eve's curse is that she must bear children in pain. Eve's curse has two prescriptions for women: She must not seek employment, and childbirth must be an unpleasant experience.

In the Jewish religion, further evidence of the position of women can be found in the traditional prayer for men, "Blessed art Thou, O Lord our God, King of the Universe, that I was not born a woman." In addition, Orthodox Jews seat women apart from men during the religious services.

The New Testament expands upon the relationship between men and women:

> For a man ... is the image and glory of God: but the woman is the glory of the man. For the man is not of the woman; but the woman of the man. Neither was the man created for the woman, but the woman for the man. ... Let your women keep silence in the churches: for it is not permitted unto them to speak; but they are commanded to be under obedience. ... And if they will learn anything, let them ask their husbands at home: for it is a shame for women to speak in the church. [I Corinthians 11–14]

Interpreters of the Bible for the Christian religion continued in the same tradition. Both Augustine in the fifth century and Thomas Aquinas in the thirteenth century argued that the major function of women was to have children. Protestant leaders were no more optimistic about women's capabilities; John Knox, for example, was a fervent antifeminist (Albee, 1981).

Many other religions also promote negative views of women. Consider the yin and yang in Chinese religion. The yin, which is the feminine side, represents darkness and evil (Ruble & Ruble, 1982). In the Hindu religion, the Goddess Kali is a dark monster with blood-stained tongue, face and breasts, crossed eyes, and fang teeth. Her wild dancing brings death on the world, though when she submits to her husband, her energy is harnessed and she does good deeds. Notice that women can be viewed as positive through their service to men.

From the religions of the world and from mythology, we can derive several views of women that are not necessarily compatible with one another:

1. *Women are evil.* They may not always be as blood thirsty as the Goddess Kali, but they are flawed creatures who can bring harm to men, as Eve did to Adam, or as Pandora did when she opened the mysterious box and let out all the evil spirits.
2. *Women are sorceresses.* They can cast spells, like the wicked witches and evil stepmothers in the fairy tales. In Greek mythology, there are numerous females with tremendous evil powers, such as Scylla, who squeezes men's bones together and eats them, or the whirlpool Charybdis, who drowns men, or the goddess Circe, who seduces men and turns them into swine.
3. *Women are mothers.* Women also can be virtuous, in their nurturance of men and small children. The Virgin Mary is the prime example here, a woman who is pure and virtuous. She is "stripped of her dangerous elements, desires nothing, demands nothing, and receives worship, not equality." (Hunter College Women's Studies Collective, 1983, p. 31). Sometimes, too, women are represented as "earth mothers," close to nature and as fertile as the earth.

These images and their variants would be difficult to combine into a single individual, either mythical or real. However, each image emphasizes how women are *different* from men. Once again, men are normal, and women are the "second sex."

How Women Are Represented in Language

So far, this book has discussed two aspects of language. In the last chapter, we examined whether women and men differ in their language ability. Then we investigated possible differences in their language style. Now let's focus on a third topic: How does language represent women? There are two important components to this question. First, what terms are used to address and refer to women? Second, what is the significance of using terms such as "he" to refer to both men and women?

Terms used for women. In many situations, people use different terms to refer to men and women. In most cases, the two terms are not parallel, and the male term is typically more standard. For example, people may refer to John Jones, M.D., as a *doctor*, but Jane Jones, M.D., may be called a *lady doctor*. This usage implies, once again, that the male is normal, and the female represents the exception.

Sometimes, the female member of a pair of words has much more negative or sexual connotations than the male member. What do you think of when you hear the word "bachelor"? How about "spinster"? The bachelor is happy-go-lucky and may have a rich love life; the spinster is an unlucky woman whom no man wanted. Compare "master" with "mistress," "manly" with "effeminate," "butler" with "maid," and "dog" with "bitch." Typically, the two members of the pair started out equally positive, but the female term has drifted toward the negative meaning.

Slang words for women are also particularly negative. Often, these words refer only to female genitalia. Allen (1984) specifically analyzed American slang terms for ethnic women. Some of these words combine unusual references to sexuality and food in referring to black, oriental, and Chicana women, as in "dark meat," "fortune cookie," and "hot tamale." Other terms are sexually insulting or allude to stereotypical physical traits of ethnic groups. Perhaps these terms are particularly derogatory because they combine stereotypes about women and stereotypes about ethnic groups.

Another feature of the way women are represented in language is that women are often referred to as "girls" or "gals" in situations in which men would not be referred to as "boys." In my husband's pediatric practice, drug-company representatives often ask, "Should I leave this with your *girl?*" in reference to an office staff member in her thirties. They are usually surprised by the answer, "Not unless you want me to tell her the *boy* left it."

Finally, men and women are addressed in different ways. Andrea Schmidt may be called "Mrs. George Schmidt" or simply "Andrea," whereas her husband will be called "Mr. George Schmidt" or simply "Schmidt." Watch for these inequalities in newspapers and on television. Also, notice whether the women and men on your college's faculty are addressed differently. Students are more likely to call women professors by their first names (Rubin, 1981). Also, I've noticed that my students often write my name on term papers as "Ms. Matlin." I appreciate the feminist consciousness reflected in the choice of "Ms." rather than "Mrs.," but I'm certain that they write "Dr." on papers handed in to male professors. Finally, women are often addressed by strangers as "honey," "dear," and "sweetheart," terms that wouldn't be used in speaking to men.

We have seen that references to women use the qualification "lady _____," are often negative in connotation, use the infantilizing form "girl," and use first names or spouse-referenced titles. Does this have any significance? Do words really matter? A study by Dayhoff (1983) suggests that they do. She prepared two versions of a passage in the form of a newspaper article about a political candidate, Joan Delaney, who was running for either town clerk or sheriff. One version was written with sexist terms such as "lady candidate," "gal," "woman reporter," and "girl," and the other version was written in a nonsexist fashion. People tended to rate the candidate as being less competent, less serious, and less intelligent when they had read the sexist version, rather than the nonsexist version. When the media refer to women political candidates in a sexist fashion, they may be reducing the chances for these women to be elected.

The generic masculine. Recently I opened the newspaper and read an article about a home-school counselor at a local elementary school. The (male) counselor was quoted as saying, "When a child sees that he has something in common with me, it's like a miracle the way he opens up." I visualized a troubled boy, feeling relaxed and comfortable with the counselor, sharing his troubles and discussing possible alternatives. But then I wondered what happens with the troubled girls. Had the counselor's choice of the pronoun "he" reflected a greater interest in the problems of male students? Are their problems more conspicuous? Do the troubled girls who visit the counselor rarely have anything in common with the counselor, and therefore rarely open up? Most important to our subject here, does the counselor's use of the word "he" tend to limit his thinking so that he provides more service to boys than to girls?

Shortly afterwards, I glanced at the introduction to a book. "Aggression is one of man's most important and most controversial topics of study," it began. I found myself agreeing that it is probably one of man's most important, controversial topics, but is it one of woman's most important, controversial topics? Were women really included in the author's term "man"?

The problem we are facing involves the generic masculine. The **generic masculine** is the use of masculine pronouns and nouns to refer to all human beings—both males and females—instead of males alone. Table 8.1 shows some of these generic masculine terms, many of which come from a book by Nilsen, et al. (1977). Your fifth-grade teacher told you to use masculine pronouns whenever both males and females were referred to, as in the sentence, "Each student took his pencil." You were probably told that "his"

TABLE 8.1 **Examples of Generic Masculine Terms**

Man	Forefathers
He/his/him	Neanderthal man
Mankind	Bachelor's degree
Businessman	Master craftsman
The working man	Middleman
To fraternize	Fellow man
Chairman	Patronize
Brotherly (as in "Brotherly love")	One-man show
To man (as in, "To man a booth at a fair")	

really includes "her" as well. Essentially you were supposed to regard "his" in this sentence as being gender neutral.

However, it is becoming clear that these generic masculine terms are not really gender neutral. The issue is no longer a grammatical one: it has become political.

There are three major problems with the generic masculine (Martyna, 1980):

1. The generic masculine is inequitable, because male and female terms are not parallel. As Martyna notes, Thomas Paine's *Rights of Man* encompasses both male and human meanings, whereas Mary Woll-stonecraft's *Rights of Women* encompasses only the female meaning.
2. The generic masculine is ambiguous, because it is often unclear whether terms such as "he" and "man" are meant to include or exclude fe-males. The examples of the counselor and the importance of aggression are potentially ambiguous. Similarly, the sentence, "Most Congressmen opposed the Equal Rights Amendment" could include the women in Congress, or it might be followed by the sentence, "However, most Congresswomen favored it."
3. The generic masculine is exclusive, because this form sometimes clearly excludes a female interpretation. Consider the sentence, "Automation is man's effort to make work so easy that women can do it all" (Martyna, 1980, p. 70). Thus, a term that superficially includes women really excludes them.

Basically, the issue is that the generic masculine assumes that the male is "normal" and "natural." The female is assumed to be "the second sex," whose existence is invisible in words such as "he" and "man." It has been argued that the generic masculine gives men free advertising and visibility, in the same sense as referring to all tissues as Kleenex or all bleach as Clorox (Moulton, 1977).

Some of you may be muttering at this point that the entire issue is trivial, that there are much more important issues for feminists to tackle. We return to an important issue. Do words really matter? This question was nicely answered in the following statement:

> We do not know, but can guess at the psychological costs of being a nonperson in one's own language. What message is presented to young girls about their present and future status as human beings, when it is constantly drummed into their heads that they must refer to themselves and others of their sex as males.
>
> As psychologists, we have come to recognize that the seemingly "trivial" is in fact of utmost importance in the conduct of human behavior—the slight nod and smile when someone says or does what we want may through conditioning determine that person's behavior far into the future; the failure to touch or give even the briefest eye contact when it's expected may create deep feelings of rejection. To say that subtleties of language are trivial and thus can't affect us, is to fall into the trap of psychological ignorance. [Association for Women in Psychology Ad Hoc Committee on Sexist Language, 1975, p. 16]

FIGURE 8.1. **Percentage of female characters, as a function of pronoun condition (based on Moulton, Robinson, & Elias, 1978)**

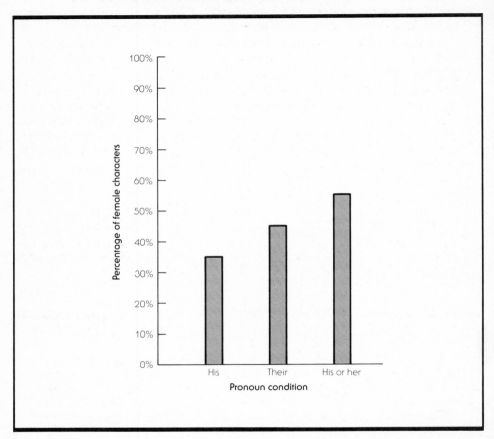

People often argue that generic masculine terms are truly gender neutral and that everyone understands that they refer equally to men and women. Research has demonstrated that this argument is wrong. In fact, generic masculine terms are more likely than gender neutral terms (such as "he or she" or "they") to produce thoughts that are male oriented. For example, students who searched for potential illustrations for a textbook were more likely to choose all-male pictures when the chapter titles were "Social Man" or "Industrial Man," rather than "Society" or "Industrial Life" (Schneider & Hacker, 1973).

In another study, students wrote stories based on a topic sentence, such as, "In a large coeducational institution, the average student will feel isolated in his introductory courses " (Moulton, Robinson, & Elias, 1978, p. 1034). Other students wrote stories with a similar topic sentence, except that the term "his" was replaced by gender-neutral terms, either "their" or "his or her." Figure 8.1 shows the results. Notice that people were more likely to write about females if the pronoun was gender neutral. Other similar research generally confirms that people think about men when they confront terms such as "he" or "man" (summarized in Matlin, 1985).

Some studies demonstrate that the generic masculine may have important implications for career choices. Briere and Lanktree (1983) showed students different versions of a paragraph describing psychologists. One group saw a generic masculine version that began, "The psychologist believes in the dignity and worth of the individual human being. He is committed to increasing man's understanding of himself and others . . . ." Other groups saw gender-neutral versions. Then the students were asked to rate psychology in terms of its attractiveness as a future career for men and for women. The people who had seen the generic masculine version rated a career in psychology as less attractive for women than did people who had seen the gender-neutral versions.

The generic masculine may also have implications for other areas. Crawford and English (1984) discovered that males remembered material better if it was written in the generic masculine form, whereas females remembered it better in the gender-neutral form. Words really do matter, and language choices are important!

═══════ DEMONSTRATION 8.1 ═══════

Attitudes Toward Generic Masculine and Gender-Neutral Terms

Ask several friends to rate each of these sentences in terms of how much they would like the sentence if they saw it in a textbook. You can read the sentences orally and ask them to report their rating to you, using a scale where 1 equals "not at all" and 7 equals "very much." After you have gathered the answers from several people, take an average for the generic masculine words and compare it with an average for the gender-neutral terms. The students who participated in my study were equally positive about both kinds of terms (Matlin, 1983c).

1. The search for knowledge has led to ways of learning that bear examination.
2. Man's cognitive capacities are not adequate for the tasks of everyday decision making.
3. A handicapped child may be able to eat and get dressed without help.
4. What counts is the child's degree of attachment and whether he feels wanted and needed.
5. The client is usually the best judge of the value of his counseling.
6. After an initial assessment of the work force expected, the industrial psychologist should begin the analysis.
7. The behavior of mankind is responsible for most urban pollution caused by manufacturing.
8. The article was written by a weather reporter on the staff of the National Weather Service.

If words do matter, then feminists should work to eliminate generic masculine usage. Unfortunately, this is extremely difficult. One problem is that most undergraduate students do not think that generic masculine terms are offensive (Matlin, 1983c). Try Demonstration 8.1 to see if this is the case with your friends.

Blaubergs (1980) has summarized other arguments against changing sex-biased language. Some people point to the dictionary, which says that "man" is a human being, without specification as to sex. However, as demonstrated in the studies we discussed, the dictionary does not seem to capture popular understanding.

Other people point out that it is too difficult to change language. However, most people learned to use the term "blacks" rather than "negroes." Furthermore, those who argue that language change is difficult are typically people who have no difficulty with jargon phrases such as "successive potentiation," "bystander intervention," and "schizophrenogenic."

Many books, articles, and pamphlets have been written about how sex-biased language can be avoided (American Psychological Association, 1983; Blaubergs, 1978; Holt, Rinehart and Winston, 1976; Sorrels, 1983). Table 8.2 lists some suggestions.

Clearly, it takes work to change language and it is easy to slip into the generic masculine. For example, a truck driver once passed my car when the visibility was poor, and I shouted, "What in the world does he think he's doing?" My daughter, then nine years old, gently reminded me, "or *she*, Mom."

How Women Are Represented in the Media

Women and men are represented in different ways by the media. In Chapter 3, we talked about how children see biased representations of women and men in books and television programs intended for young audiences, and in Chapter 14 we will see that older women are portrayed very unfavorably by

TABLE 8.2   **Suggestions for Nonsexist Language**

1. Use the plural form. "Students can monitor their progress" can replace "A student can monitor his progress."

2. Use "his or her" or "her or his," as in the sentence, "A student can monitor her or his progress." (The order of these pronouns may sound awkward, but females do not always need to be added as an afterthought.)

3. Use "you." The sentence, "Suppose that you have difficulty recalling your social security number" is more involving than, "Suppose that a person has difficulty recalling his social security number"—as well as being less sexist.

4. Eliminate the pronoun. "The best judge of the value of counseling is usually the client" can replace "The client is usually the best judge of the value of his counseling" (A.P.A., 1983, p. 45).

the media. Let us now focus on newspapers, magazines, and television programs and advertisements that are aimed at adult audiences.

People who are interested in women's issues know that the media's representation of women is an important topic. Friedman (1977) listed more than a thousand relevant references, and an excellent book called *Sex Stereotyping in Advertising* (Courtney & Whipple, 1983) discusses the nature of the problem, why the problem is important, and potential solutions.

Stereotyped representations.   The following paragraphs discuss some conclusions we can draw about women in the media.

1. *Women are relatively invisible.* Men outnumber women two to one in television commercials (Women's Action Alliance, 1981). Women are particularly absent from advertisements for expensive products and from advertisements shown during prime time. This pattern is repeated if we look at the programs, rather than the ads (Cassata, 1983). In the evening, men outnumber women by a ratio of three to one. An exception is daytime television, such as soap operas, where women constitute 50 percent of the characters.

    Black women are particularly invisible in the media. As Murray (1981) concludes, "... the very invisibility of the black woman conveys a message: she is not worthy of any sort of regard—positive or negative" (p. 114).

    Shaw (1977) expands on this idea:

    The public image of black women as professional persons is almost non-existent. The lack of public visibility contributes to societal myths and keeps professional women from serving as role models for black youth. How many film strips, videotapes, or other media used for educational purposes, include black women physicians, lawyers, or nurses? How many pictures in textbooks portray black women as professionals? [pp. 77–78]

2. *Women are relatively inaudible.* Women aren't seen much, and they certainly aren't heard. Try to recall a typical television ad. At the end of many of them, we hear a voice of authority, the last words to extoll the product's virtues. Whose voice do you hear in your "mind's ear"? It's almost always a male voice. The percentage of males in these voice-overs in recent years has remained relatively constant at about 90 percent (Courtney & Whipple, 1983). Once you begin to pay attention to these male voice-overs, it may seem ridiculous that they are providing expert information on products so intimate as pantihose or deodorant.

3. *Despite the increase in women's employment in recent years, the representation of women working outside the home has not changed substantially.* In one study, women were *less* likely to be shown in

an occupational setting in 1978 than in 1972. Television women are much less likely to work outside the home than "real" women (Courtney & Whipple, 1983). Furthermore, the representation of women's work has become more elitist; women are more likely to be shown as professionals and less likely to be shown as clerks and secretaries. As you know from Chapter 6, this hardly matches reality!

4. *Women are shown doing housework.* Here the percentages probably capture reality quite accurately—sadly. Women in the magazine ads do housework about 11 times as often as men (Courtney & Whipple, 1983). On television, women seem to live only in kitchens and bathrooms and laundry rooms. Furthermore, women fall into rhapsodies about their household products:

> The reader undoubtedly has his or her own favorite example: the woman who happily 'Shouts' it out, the woman who is ashamed by ring around the collar, the woman whose life revolves around her dirty oven, the woman who finds sexual fulfillment by choosing a whitening toothpaste (or a deodorant, or bra, or perfume), the woman who makes family life worth living and saves a marriage by serving a moist cake, the woman who happily tricks her family into using the foods that are 'best' for them. [Courtney & Whipple, 1983, pp. 23–24]

5. *Families are emphasized more for women than for men.* Newspaper articles about women were more likely to mention a spouse than do articles about men (Foreit, et al., 1980). Women in advertisements are constantly serving men and boys. Can you think of a single ad in which a husband or son is shown doing some task for a woman? Instead, men are the authorities (as in the voice-overs) who tell women what to do.

6. *Women are typically shown as passive, dependent, and not very bright.* Women are shown as inferior to men. Black women are portrayed in much the same way as white women, in general. However, most black women are shown as being even *less* interested in achievement than white women (Reid, 1979).

7. *Women's bodies are used differently from men's bodies in advertisements.* If you glance through magazine advertisements, you'll immediately notice that women are more likely than men to serve a decorative function, such as the reclining woman, seductively dressed, caressing a liquor bottle. Also, men's faces are more prominent in magazines and newspapers. Women are likely to be shown with their whole bodies, whereas a picture of a man is likely to show only his face (Archer, Iritani, Kimes, & Barrios, 1983). Body positions are also different for men and women. Women are likely to be shown lying down or bent at an angle, whereas men are often elevated above women (Goffman, 1979), which may symbolize their higher status.

7. *Black and ethnic women—when they are shown at all—are represented in a particularly biased way.* Cross (1985) describes how she grew up with images of black women who were black-slave mammies or proper urban maids, black women prostitutes or earth mothers. The current media representation of black women is surely more modern, but this representation still fails to capture the diversity found among black women in our culture. Oriental women are either shown as quiet, shy, "China dolls," as "Susie Wong sex pots," or as "efficient dragon ladies" (Chow, 1985). Hispanic women are also represented by the contrasting images, either of an innocent señorita, dripping with lace and sheltered by a protective family of brothers, or of a seductive, fiery-tempered Latin bombshell (Brinson-Pineda, 1985).

Now that you are familiar with some of the ways in which women are represented in the media, try Demonstration 8.2. In addition, start analyzing magazine advertisements to see the extent to which they show stereotypes. Pay particular attention to any nontraditional advertisements. Are people who are shown in nontraditional roles somehow a bit laughable, or is the father who is changing the baby's diaper looking both confident and competent?

Effects of stereotyped representations.   Does this biased kind of representation of women in the media simply reflect reality, or does it actually influence reality? Probably both of those statements are correct. The media reflect the reality that women are unseen and unheard, more likely to do housework, more likely to be family oriented, and more likely to be regarded as decorative and subservient. However, the ads certainly are *not* an accurate mirror of reality. I don't have any women friends, for example, who sing about their toilet-bowl cleaners.

We also have some evidence that the media may be important in shaping reality. In other words, seeing stereotypes in magazines and on television

---

DEMONSTRATION 8.2

The Representation of Women on Television

Keep a pad of paper next to you during the next three to five television programs you watch. Record the number of women you see on the programs and in the advertisements, and contrast these figures with the number of men. In the advertisements, record the number of female and male voice-overs. Record the number of women shown working outside the home, doing housework, and doing something for family members; again, contrast these figures with comparable ones for men. Also, see if you can detect any other ways in which women and men are represented, aside from those mentioned in the chapter.

makes people more stereotyped. Some studies show that people who are heavy television viewers, particularly viewers of stereotyped programs, are likely to be more gender-stereotyped than those who seldom watch television (Lull, Mulac, & Rosen, 1983; Ross, Anderson, & Wisocki, 1982). It is hard to know how to interpret these results. Television viewing may produce stereotyped beliefs, or else people with stereotyped beliefs may be more likely to watch television, or there may be some other explanation that hasn't yet been formulated.

Stronger evidence that media stereotypes may produce stereotyped beliefs comes from research conducted by Jennings and her coworkers (1980). In one study, the researchers prepared two kinds of commercials similar to those seen on television. In the traditional version of one ad, a woman proudly served her husband a packaged "TV dinner"; in the nontraditional version, the husband proudly served his wife the same dinner. The college women who had viewed the nontraditional version showed more self-confidence when delivering a speech and also were less conforming, in comparison to those who had seen the traditional version. If a few minutes of advertisements could have a significant effect on behavior, imagine what a lifetime of nontraditional ads might do!

Even subtle differences in the representation of women and men may be important. When you read that men's faces are more emphasized than women's in magazines and newspapers, your response may well have been "So what?" However, Archer and his coauthors found that photographs in which the face was prominent, with little of the remaining body visible, were rated as being more intelligent, ambitious, and attractive.

☐ SECTION SUMMARY ▪ The Representation of Women and Men

1. Gender stereotypes are structured beliefs about the characteristics of women and men.
2. There is little information about what women have been doing throughout history, because women were seldom taught to write, because their art forms were physically less durable, and because their accomplishments have been forgotten.
3. In general, philosophers have maintained that women are less competent than men; however, Plato was less negative than many, and John Stuart Mill supported equal rights and opportunities for women.
4. In many religions' stories about creation, males were created first and women were an afterthought. Many religions are also negative about women and their status.
5. Religion and mythology present several different views of women, each substantially different from their view of men; these views of women include evil women, sorceresses, and mothers.

6. Different terms are used for men and women; the terms used for women are often more negative or infantilizing, and the titles often refer to first names or spouses' names.
7. The generic masculine uses male terms (such as *he* and *man*) to refer to both men and women. Although grammarians have argued that these terms are truly gender neutral, research demonstrates that when people hear a word such as *man*, they think of males more than females. Exclusion of women from language may have harmful effects, and there are many ways in which the generic masculine can be avoided.
8. Women are represented in a stereotyped fashion by the media. They are seen and heard less than men; they are shown doing housework and serving males, but not in occupational settings; they are passive, and their bodies are also represented differently. Black and ethnic women are particularly likely to be represented in a stereotypical fashion.
9. The media's stereotyped representation of women promotes stereotyped beliefs. Sources of evidence for that statement include the correlation between television-viewing habits and stereotyped beliefs, the influence of nontraditional advertisements on women's behavior, and the influence of facial prominence on attitudes.

☐ PEOPLE'S BELIEFS ABOUT WOMEN AND MEN

We have looked at the ways in which women and men are represented in philosophy, religion, mythology, language, and the media. Now we turn to the man and woman on the street (or more likely, on the college campus) to see how they represent women and men. What is the nature of their gender stereotypes? What kinds of thought processes produce these stereotypes, and—in turn—what further thought processes do these stereotypes produce? Finally, how might gender stereotypes mold people's behavior?

The Content of Stereotypes

Before you read this section, try Demonstration 8.3. Notice that this demonstration does not ask you to assess your own stereotypes or beliefs about men and women, a task that would certainly be influenced by what you have been learning about sex differences. Instead, you must try to guess what *most people* think. You will probably be quite accurate on this task.

How can we determine people's stereotypes about women and men? The first systematic investigations of gender stereotypes were conducted in the late 1960s and early 1970s (Broverman, Vogel, Broverman, Clarkson, & Rosenkrantz, 1972; Rosenkrantz, Vogel, Bee, Broverman, & Broverman, 1968). These authors identified a large number of characteristics, such as those in

Stereotypes about Men and Women

In this demonstration, you must guess what most people think about women and men. Put an M in front of those characteristics that you believe most people associate with men more than women, and put an F in front of those associated with women more than men. The answers appear later in this section, based on responses obtained by Cowan and Stewart (1977) and Williams and Bennett (1975).

_____ forceful	_____ independent
_____ affectionate	_____ ambitious
_____ adventurous	_____ appreciative
_____ aggressive	_____ fickle
_____ emotional	_____ active
_____ gentle	_____ dominant
_____ self-confident	_____ sensitive
_____ rude	_____ nagging
_____ submissive	_____ inventive
_____ weak	_____ sentimental

Demonstration 8.3, that people believed were different for women than for men. Both women and men agreed, for example, that women were more emotional than men.

When I talk about these studies, my students are skeptical. After all, they argue, several decades have passed since those early studies, and the women's movement has changed people's stereotypes. Sadly, this is not the case. Spence, Helmreich, and Stapp (1974) used an instrument called the Personal Attributes Questionnaire to investigate gender stereotypes, and they found 54 items on which people rated the typical male as being different from the typical female. When Ruble (1983) used the same instrument several years later, he found that the typical male and the typical female were rated as being different on 53 of the original 54 items. The only item that no longer showed a significant difference between males and females was the characteristic "intellectual." People had worked for equal rights, women were increasingly likely to be employed outside the home, and the media had publicized the new breed of women. Nonetheless, the stereotypes about women and men remained essentially unchanged.

It should be pointed out that other methods of studying stereotypes do not produce such dramatic differences between people's beliefs about women and their beliefs about men. Less stereotyping is shown when people are instructed to give their own spontaneous descriptions of women and men, rather than to make judgments about a pre-established list of characteristics (Brannon, 1978; Ruble & Ruble, 1982). People might be likely, for instance, to apply the description "hard-working" to _both_ women and men.

Let us return to the nature of the stereotypes. In Demonstration 8.3, the characteristics that are associated with men more often than women are the following: forceful, adventurous, aggressive, self-confident, rude, independent, ambitious, active, dominant, and inventive. The characteristics that are associated with women more often than men are the following: affectionate, emotional, gentle, submissive, weak, appreciative, fickle, sensitive, nagging, and sentimental.

Remember that we defined gender stereotypes as a *structured* set of beliefs; indeed, there does seem to be some pattern and structure to each of those clusters of characteristics. Some theorists have suggested that we use the term **agency** to describe a concern for one's own self-interests (Bakan, 1966; Block, 1973). Positive characteristics such as forceful, aggressive, independent, and ambitious show a focus on agency, as do many other adjectives that are stereotypically masculine. In contrast, the term **communion** emphasizes a concern for one's relationship with other people. Positive characteristics such as affectionate, gentle, appreciative, and sensitive show a focus on communion, along with many other adjectives that are stereotypically feminine.

We have looked at the kinds of stereotypes that people have about women and men. Now let us see whether people "buy into" those stereotypes when they describe themselves or ideal women and men, and whether factors such as sex, social class, and nationality influence these stereotypes.

Stereotypes, self-descriptions, and ideal people. Gender stereotypes describe what people think about typical women and men. What do people think about themselves? Check back over the characteristics listed in Demonstration 8.3 and decide which ones accurately describe yourself. It's likely that you consider yourself to have some characteristics that are stereotypically male and some that are stereotypically female. Those of you who are female probably did not select only "feminine" characteristics, and those of you who are male probably did not select only "masculine" characteristics. Studies have demonstrated, in fact, that people's judgments about themselves are less stereotyped than their judgments about other people (Spence, Helmreich, & Stapp, 1975; Unger & Siiter, 1975).

It seems that stereotypes are strongest when we don't have precise information and must therefore rely on "common knowledge." If you are a woman and you know that you are inventive and rude—characteristics typically associated with men—you will feel free to select these words to describe yourself. You have much less precise information about "typical women," and so it is much more tempting to apply the stereotype that typical women are neither inventive nor rude.

We know more precise information about close friends and relatives than we know about "typical women" or "typical men," and so these people may also be relatively immune from stereotypes. A friend of mine tells about her father, who maintains that "women in general" are scatterbrained and incompetent, but his own daughters are brilliant, competent, and capable of great achievements. Pride in ourselves and those who are close to us may also erase many of the negative stereotypes associated with a person's gender.

Turn back to Demonstration 8.3 once more and check off those characteristics that you would consider appropriate for an *ideal* woman, and also those appropriate for an *ideal* man. Do your ideal people turn out to be blends of both feminine and masculine characteristics? Gilbert, Deutsch, and Strahan (1978) were curious to see whether there is a difference between how women and men would *like* the sexes to be perceived and how they typically *are* perceived. They speculated that the ideal man and woman would be more nearly equal to each other in femininity and masculinity, in contrast to the typical man and woman. Their speculations were confirmed in a study in which college students rated a number of characteristics in terms of whether they described a typical woman or man and an ideal woman or man. Ideally, people believe that we should incorporate some characteristics that are thought to be typical of the other sex.

Let us look more closely at these ideal women and men that were created by the students in the experiment. They are *not* perfect blends of feminine and masculine characteristics. People who combine feminine and masculine characteristics equally would receive a rating of zero in Figure 8.2. Both male and female students thought that the ideal man should be substantially more masculine than feminine; notice that the scores for the ideal man are toward the masculine end of the scale. Male students thought that the ideal woman should be substantially more feminine than masculine; notice that the male's score for the ideal woman are toward the feminine end of the scale.

However, you can also see from Figure 8.2 that female students created an ideal woman who combines both feminine and masculine characteristics in equal proportions. This ideal woman is a person who is affectionate and gentle, and yet independent and forceful. In summary, both men and women feel that a man should be masculine, and men feel that a woman should be feminine. The only break with tradition is provided by the women, who feel that women should combine feminine and masculine qualities.

Factors influencing stereotypes. Are stereotypes influenced by factors such as your sex, your social class, and the culture in which you were raised? The answer seems to be a modified "yes." These factors may each have a modest influence on stereotypes, but their influence is typically not as great as we might think. For example, women and men hold reasonably similar gender stereotypes (Pleck, 1978; Williams & Bennett, 1975), with women being less stereotyped on some measures (McPherson & Spetrino, 1983; Smith & Midlarsky, 1985).

Social class also has less influence than might be expected. "Common knowledge" suggests that middle-class people are much more liberal about gender roles than working-class people. However, the gap between the working class and the middle class with respect to gender attitudes is not large (American Institute of Public Opinion, 1975; Davidson & Davidson, 1977; Ferree, 1980).

FIGURE 8.2. **Ratings of an ideal woman and an ideal man, as a function of sex subject (based on Gilbert, Deutsch, & Strahan, 1978)**

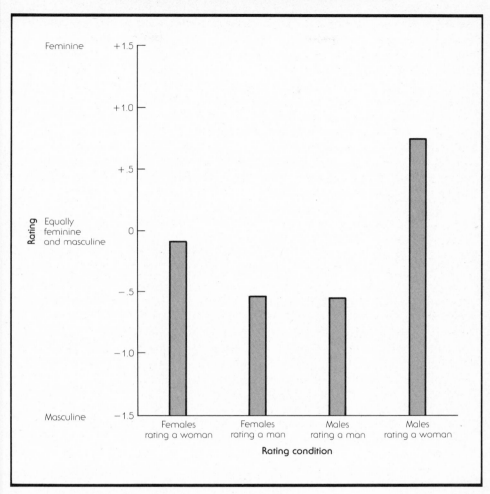

Level of education does seem to be important. Hall and Frederickson (1979) found that male factory workers who had attended college were less stereotyped than those who had no college experience. A national survey also demonstrated that well-educated people were less stereotyped than less-educated people (Morgan & Walker, 1983).

There is some evidence that blacks show less stereotyping than whites. Smith and Midlarsky (1985) summarize previous studies that reached this conclusion, and they also describe their own study of about 800 residents of Detroit. Their results showed that whites tended to show greater stereotyping of both females and males than did blacks. Apparently, black men and women do not perceive the two genders to be as different as is the case for white men and women.

Also, among women, those who work outside the home are less traditional than nonemployed women. Ferree (1980) found that 60 percent of women who were employed for "personal satisfaction" reasons favored a change in traditional gender roles, in contrast to 29 percent of women who were employed for financial reasons and 18 percent of nonemployed women. Notice how we can look at these findings in two ways. It may be that the experience of working outside the home and being exposed to new experiences and ideas produces liberal ideas about gender roles. However, it may also be that women who already have liberal ideas decide to seek employment, whereas women with traditional ideas that a woman's place is in the home decide to remain there.

Are there substantial cross-cultural differences in stereotypes? John Williams and his colleagues have been studying gender stereotypes in different countries (e.g., Williams, 1982; Williams & Best, 1982). Williams (1982) studied people in 25 countries, including countries as diverse as Nigeria, India, Brazil, and New Zealand. He asked college students in each country to review a list of adjectives and judge whether each item was more likely to be associated with men rather than women, with women rather than men, or with both sexes equally. The instructions stressed that they were not being asked about true sex differences or about ideal characteristics.

Williams found 20 adjectives that were more often associated with men in at least 23 out of 25 countries. This list will sound familiar, because it includes words such as adventurous, coarse, dominant, and independent. In addition, he found 23 adjectives that were more often associated with women, including affectionate, emotional, mild, and sentimental.

There were some differences among cultures. Canada, Israel, and the Netherlands showed high differentiation between male and female stereotypes, whereas Bolivia, France, and Ireland showed low differentiation. (The United States was intermediate.) It is difficult to find any overall pattern for which countries make the biggest distinctions between male and female stereotypes. Also, keep in mind that these data were obtained with college students; undoubtedly, the results would be different with different kinds of participants.

In summary, factors such as education and women's employment status may influence the strength of people's gender stereotypes. Other factors, such as sex, social class, race, and culture seem to have a modest influence. Overall, however, the consistency of the gender stereotypes is more prominent than any differences among groups.

Gender Stereotyping and Social Cognition

Stereotypes are particularly interesting to psychologists who examine social cognition. **Social cognition** is knowledge about the social world, including knowledge about gender. Another area of social cognition you have learned about in this textbook concerns attributions, such as the attributions we give for people's successes and failures (Chapter 5). Among the various approaches to gender stereotypes, the social cognition approach is currently the most popular one.

According to David Hamilton (1979), one cognitive process that seems to be nearly inevitable in humans is the tendency to lump the people we meet into social groups. We divide groups of people into females versus males; blacks versus whites; Catholics versus Protestants versus Jews; people with high occupational status versus those with low occupational status, and so forth. This categorization process is a necessary component of stereotyping; we couldn't have stereotypes of women and men unless we first made a distinction between them.

The cognitive approach to stereotypes argues that people are confronted with a vast assortment of incoming stimuli (Bem, 1981). Think about the visual and auditory chaos that surrounds you as you drive in a city. We could easily be overwhelmed if we didn't have some methods for simplifying and imposing order upon this chaos. Our thought processes help us by organizing our world; we group objects together into categories.

While driving, we respond to items in the category "red light" by stopping. The categorization process often provides advantages, because it organizes our world and allows us to respond efficiently. We regard all things within the category "red light" as being similar in important respects. In reality, these lights do vary from one another; one might be slightly orange, rather than a true red, and another might be particularly bright. However, we place all of these lights in the same category and respond to them similarly.

Sandra Bem (1981) argues that the major way we categorize people is on the basis of their sex. It seems that this process of categorizing others in terms of sex is habitual and automatic. Notice how little actual thought is involved when you classify the next person you meet (Ashmore & Del Boca, 1979). It is nearly impossible to suppress this tendency to split the world in half, using sex as the great divider.

Remember that we discussed the importance of sex as a categorizer in Chapter 2 when we considered the first question that people ask about a newborn baby. By asking "Is it a boy or a girl?" we reveal that a person's sex takes precedence over all other characteristics.

Furthermore, we like to make nice, neat decisions about who belongs to what category. A person who seems to belong on the borderline is both annoying and fascinating. Have you ever noticed someone from a distance who couldn't be readily categorized as "male" or "female"? Were you tempted to move closer so that you could obtain a clear-cut answer? The categorization process doesn't tolerate ambiguities.

As we noted earlier, the categorization of objects makes things easier for us by simplifying our environment. However, this same process can also produce errors in the way we perceive and understand the world (Berkowitz, 1986). One byproduct of categorization is stereotyping, which may not represent reality with great accuracy. A frustrating aspect of stereotypes is that these errors, in turn, produce further errors. That is, because we have a stereotype, we tend to perceive women and men differently. When we perceive women and men to be different, we add further "evidence" to our stereotype. A strengthened stereotype leads to an even greater tendency to perceive the two sexes differently. As a consequence, stereotypes are particularly resistant to change.

It is tempting to try to organize this material on stereotyping and social cognition into two parts, the cognitive *causes* of stereotyping and the cognitive *results* of stereotyping. However, this distinction would be artificial. In reality, every *cause* of stereotyping is itself a result of another stereotyping process, and every *result* of stereotyping in turn causes further stereotyping. Thus, as soon as we make a basic distinction between women and men, our cognitive processes create different expectations for women's behavior than for men's behavior. Let us look at several topics in the area of stereotyping and social cognition, each of which could be viewed as both a cause and a result of gender stereotyping. These topics are: expectations for women's and men's behavior; exaggerating the contrast between women and men; the token woman or man; and sex prejudice.

Expectations for women's and men's behavior. David Hamilton (1979) discusses several ways in which our expectations are important in stereotyping. Our expectations may focus our attention on a particular aspect of someone's behavior, making that behavior "stand out" and other behaviors recede into the background. Suppose that your sociology professor, Dr. Nancy Chaplin, has been lecturing for approximately 45 minutes, and her presentation has been competent. Suddenly she loses her place and her notes cascade to the floor as she shuffles through them. If you are a person who already believes that women are less competent than men in academic settings, this moment will catch your attention. Dr. Chaplin's skill and expertise throughout the remainder of the lecture will not be so clearly noticed.

Our expectations also lead us to interpret certain behaviors in a biased manner. We found evidence for this suggestion in Chapter 2, when Condry and Condry (1976) found that adults reacted differently to a baby crying, depending upon whether they believed the baby to be a boy or a girl. When they thought that the baby was a boy, the crying reflected anger; when they thought that the baby was a girl, the crying reflected fear. Thus, the same, identical actions could be interpreted in two ways, depending upon the adults' expectations. If Nancy Chaplin answers a question with "I don't know, but I'll try to find out," her manner may be interpreted as showing ignorance, whereas a man's answer might be labeled "honest." It should be mentioned that a person's sex is particularly likely to influence our judgments if we know very little about the person (Deaux & Lewis, 1984). In contrast, if we have extensive information about a person's behavior and characteristics, that person's sex will be relatively unimportant.

In addition, Hamilton argues, stereotypes may lead to a selective recall of items stored in memory. Therefore, errors occur not only in what we notice and how we interpret what we notice, but in what we recall at a later time. Imagine that several students have managed to pay just as much attention to Dr. Nancy Chaplin's brilliant answer to a hostile question as to her brief display of incompetence. If they show selective retrieval guided by a stereotype of incompetent women, they will recall the cascading notes far more accurately and far more vividly than the brilliant answer.

Even if we are accurate with respect to these first three processes (attention, interpretation, and recall), we may make a mistake when we try to summarize our beliefs (Hamilton, 1981a). We may have been unbiased in what we noticed, in our interpretation, and in our recall. However, when someone asks us at the end of the lecture whether Dr. Nancy Chaplin is competent, we may gather together all the information and conclude—incorrectly—that she is not.

Notice what happens when we pay attention to stereotyped behavior, interpret behavior in a stereotyped fashion, recall stereotyped behavior, and make errors in our conclusions. In all of these processes, we confirm the original stereotype. Because we have new evidence for the stereotype, this stereotype should operate even more powerfully at the next opportunity. Summarizing the powerful influence of expectations, Hamilton (1981b) remarked that people are essentially saying, "I wouldn't have seen it if I hadn't believed it" (p. 137).

Exaggerating the contrast between women and men. We tend to have biased perceptions that exaggerate the similarities *within* a group and exaggerate the contrast *between* the groups. When we divide the world into two groups, male and female, we tend to see all males as being similar, all females as being similar, and the two categories of "male" and "female" as being different. In other words, we won't be very tolerant of the overlapping characteristics that typify the sex differences literature. Rather than believing that women and men are generally similar in their leadership characteristics, we may maintain that women are generally concerned about the feelings of group members, and that men are generally concerned about giving orders. Because we are so willing to categorize on the basis of sex, our gender-schematic processes try to create an artificial gap between women and men.

A study by Shelley Taylor and her colleagues (1978) demonstrates how we tend to exaggerate the similarities within a group by confusing members of that group with each other. To be specific, they proposed that when people couldn't remember who made a particular remark in a conversation, they would be more likely to attribute it to someone of the same sex than to someone of the other sex.

These authors prepared a slide/tape presentation that portrayed three males and three females discussing how to increase voter turnout on election day. Every time someone on the tape spoke, a picture of a man or woman

FIGURE 8.3. **Relative number of remarks mistakenly attributed to a person of the same sex or the other sex, as a function of the sex of the subject (based on Taylor, et al., 1978)**

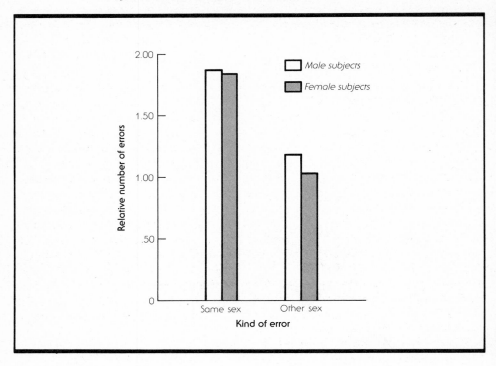

was projected. Students watched and listened to this presentation for several minutes. Then they were asked to match each remark from the discussion with the appropriate picture.

Our interest lies in the errors that the students made, rather than their correct matches. They could make an error by falsely attributing a remark to either of the two members of the same sex or to any of the three members of the other sex. In order to make the error rates equivalent, we must therefore divide the number of same-sex errors by two, and the number of other-sex errors by three. Figure 8.3 shows these corrected error rates. As you can see, both women and men tended to assign remarks to another person of the same sex as the one who had really made the remark, rather than a person of the other sex. We seem to code conversations according to the speaker's sex, and the resemblances within each sex appear greater than the resemblances between the sexes.

The token women or man. People generally pay more attention to a distinctive stimulus than to a familiar or common stimulus. This means that if a group is composed of five men and one woman, the "token" or "solo" woman will be noticed more (Hamilton, 1979). Although we usually think in terms of a token woman, think about occasions in which a man has token status. There may be a token male in a women's studies course, in a nursing-school class, or in a bridge club. We discussed token women in connection with work settings in Chapter 6. However, token women (or men) also have great salience in other settings.

Shelly Taylor (1981) describes several of her studies on the perceptions of a token woman or a token man. As in her study on confusing people with others of the same sex (Taylor, et al., 1978), people heard a tape of a group discussion and watched slides that presumably pictured group members. In this case, the group discussion involved an informal conversation in a teach-ers' lounge. There were three conditions: one woman, five men; three women, three men; and five women, one man.

Taylor's results showed that both the male and female tokens were seen as more prominent group members than when the same individual appeared in an evenly balanced group of three women and three men. People reported that the token person talked more, made a stronger impression, had a stronger personality, and was more confident and assertive than when the same per-son appeared in the sex-balanced group. Furthermore, a person who was viewed somewhat positively in a sex-balanced group was viewed *very* posi-tively as the token member of a group. In contrast, a person who was viewed somewhat negatively was viewed *very* negatively when he or she was the token member in the group. Once again, then, stereotypes lead to exagger-ations.

Sex prejudice. In this section, we have focused on the tendency to divide the world in half, categorizing people on the basis of their sex. We saw that this tendency creates different expectations for women and men, increases the contrast between the two sexes, and produces unusual reac-tions to token women and men.

In many cases in which people are categorized, people are consistently more positive about the group they belong to, rather than the other group. For example, when your fifth-grade teacher divided the class randomly into two groups for class projects, didn't you feel that your own group was far superior to the other? Similarly, you may recall from Chapter 3 that children tend to believe that a child who is the same sex as themselves performs better than a child of the other sex. Furthermore, children value objects associated with their own sex; girls like feminine objects and boys like mas-culine objects, according to cognitive-developmental theory.

However, something changes as little girls grow up, so that they usually shift their admiration from females to males. By the time they reach adult-hood, most women agree with most men that males are superior. We have seen evidence of this bias against females in several sections of this book. Let us take a moment to pull the strands together, as we examine this aspect of Theme 2, that males are more valued than females.

One piece of information supporting a bias against females and favoritism toward males comes from the chapter on infancy. Remember that 90 percent of men and 92 percent of women preferred a boy as their firstborn child (Peterson & Peterson, 1973).

In Chapter 5, we saw that two areas of achievement attitudes revealed pessimism about women's abilities. People tend to rate articles, paintings, and other accomplishments more favorably if they think that these items have been produced by a man. Also, people downgrade women's ability, because they frequently attribute men's success to ability and women's failure to lack of ability.

Negative attitudes toward women were also evident in several areas of the chapter on women and work. Career counselors often have low aspirations for their female high-school students. Furthermore, in making judgments about which person to hire, people frequently give higher evaluations to a man than to a woman with similar qualifications. Negative attitudes toward women are also reflected in their salaries, first because the fields with a high proportion of male employees pay more than the fields that are predominantly female, and second because women, on the average, earn less than men who have the same qualifications and are working at the same job. Chapter 6 also noted that women face additional discrimination at work with respect to promotions and other personnel decisions. Finally, we saw that people frequently reveal negative attitudes toward women workers, tending to think that they were unlikely to be capable administrators and that their only virtues involve questionable strengths such as skill at detailed work.

This chapter has also presented some information to indicate that women's stereotypical characteristics are not as highly regarded as men's stereotypical characteristics. Glance through the first section of this chapter to confirm the negative representation of women. Then look back at the items in Demonstration 8.3 and notice the general tone of the characteristics regarded as typically masculine, in contrast to those regarded as typically feminine. Williams and Bennett (1975) inspected 15 "masculine" adjectives that were not evaluatively neutral. They found that ten of these were positive (for example, *ambitious, enterprising, stable*) and only five were negative (for example, *boastful, coarse, disorderly*). The ratio was exactly the reverse for 15 nonneutral "feminine" adjectives. That is, only five were positive (for example, *appreciative, attractive, gentle*) and ten were negative (for example, *complaining, prudish, weak*). Similar results have been reported by other researchers (Broverman, et al., 1972).

Furthermore, our culture has traditionally appreciated the positive "masculine" characteristics more than the positive "feminine" characteristics. Independence and achievement are valued more than gentleness or nurturance. Carol Gilligan's (1982) popular book *In a Different Voice* urges us to change our evaluation system so that we admire people who stress social interaction and personal relationships, rather than individual achievement.

We have examined a number of areas of women's lives in which they are judged inferior to men. The categorization process produces two separate groups of humans, women and men. However, as we have seen, these groups are clearly not "separate but equal." Instead, females are valued less as infants, in their achievements, at work, and in their stereotypical characteristics.

How Stereotypes Influence Behavior

We have discussed the content of stereotypes and the cognitive aspects of these stereotypes. A cognitive approach to stereotypes helps us to understand how errors in our thinking can arise and how these errors, in turn, perpetuate further errors. However, if we focus entirely on our thought processes, we may forget that stereotypes may influence our behavior. Stereotypes influence words, actions, and choices, both in ourselves and in other people.

Stereotypes can influence behavior through a **self-fulfilling prophecy,** or the tendency to behave in a way that confirms other people's expectations (Darley & Fazio, 1980). Thus, if people expect a little girl to be quiet, passive, and gentle, she may come to act that way.

It is difficult to study the influence of stereotypes on behavior in the real world, because the real world is extraordinarily complex and because ideal experiments cannot be performed. For example, it would be interesting to examine how stereotypes influence career choices. Ideally, we would have two large groups of children. One group would grow up in the normal stereotyped world that we currently experience, surrounded by stereotypes from family, peers, school, and the media. These children would presumably develop the "standard" stereotyped cognitive processes, and we could observe whether they behave in a stereotyped fashion, such as making stereotyped career choices. The other group of children would grow up in a nonstereotyped world, without the invasion of stereotypes from all sides. (Yes, it does sound impossible!) These children would presumably develop far less stereotyped cognitive processes, and we could see whether they behave in a less stereotyped fashion, for example in their career choices.

The problem, of course, is that it is impossible to control the stereotyping forces that people are exposed to in the real world. A small number of studies in controlled laboratory settings, however, have examined the influence of stereotyped expectations on women's behavior.

Two of these studies looked at the influence of stereotyped expectations on behavior related to work. Consider one research project titled "Impression Management in the Job Interview: When the Female Applicant Meets the Male (Chauvinist) Interviewer" (von Baeyer, Sherk, & Zanna, 1981). Undergraduate women were led to believe that a male confederate (that is, someone who is "in cahoots" with the experimenters) had a stereotype of an ideal female job applicant that either matched the traditional female stereotype quite closely, or had a stereotype that was quite nontraditional. When the confederate interviewed these women, they tended to present themselves in a substantially more "feminine" fashion when they knew that the interviewer had traditional views about women, in comparison to when the women believed that the interviewer was nontraditional. Women tended to dress more conservatively if they believed that the interviewer held traditional views about women. Women in this traditional condition also talked much less than women in the nontraditional condition. It seems that when women want to impress a traditional person, they live up to this person's stereotyped expectations.

Stereotypes may also influence the kind of work that women select. Skrypnek and Snyder (1982) arranged to have pairs of students participate in an experiment without ever seeing each other or talking to each other. In each case, one member of the pair was male, and the other was female. However, some males in these pairs were told that they would be working with a 20-year-old male sophomore who was independent, competitive, and ambitious. Other males in these pairs were led to believe that they would be working with a 20-year-old female sophomore who was shy, gentle, and soft-spoken. In other words, these descriptions provided the males with ready-made gender stereotypes for the person with whom they would be working. Each pair of people was instructed to examine a list of 24 pairs of tasks and to negotiate which person would do which task. In order to keep the true sex of the male's partner unknown, the two people communicated with each other by using a signaling system with coded lights.

The authors found that the women's task choices were indeed influenced by their partner's stereotypes. When the male partners believed that they were working with other males, the women tended to select masculine tasks. When the male partners believed that they were working with females, the women tended to select feminine tasks. Presumably, the men's expectations guided their behavior toward their partners, so that they used different strategies toward people whom they believed to be male than toward people whom they believed to be female. In turn, the women behaved in a fashion that was consistent with the men's expectations.

An additional laboratory study examined the influence of stereotyped expectations on social behavior (Zanna & Pack, 1975). Women students were asked to rate themselves on a gender-stereotyping questionnaire. Several weeks later, they were told that they would be participating in a study on impression formation. They were then provided with information about their male partner for the task, who was either portrayed as a tall, Princeton senior with no girlfriend (presumably a desirable partner) or as a short, non-Princeton freshman with a girlfriend (presumably a not particularly desirable partner). The women were also shown information about their partner's opinions about women, which were very traditional in half of the cases or very nontraditional in the other half. They then filled out the gender-stereotyping questions once more, which were presumably to be given to the male partner.

Figure 8.4 shows the change in the women's responses on the gender-stereotyping questionnaire. Notice that when women thought that they would be working with a low-desirability partner, they did not modify their ideas about themselves to please their future partner. However, when they thought that they would be working with a high-desirability partner, their ideas drifted

FIGURE 8.4. **Changes in women's presentation, as a function of their partners' desirability and view of women (based on Zanna and Pack, 1975)**

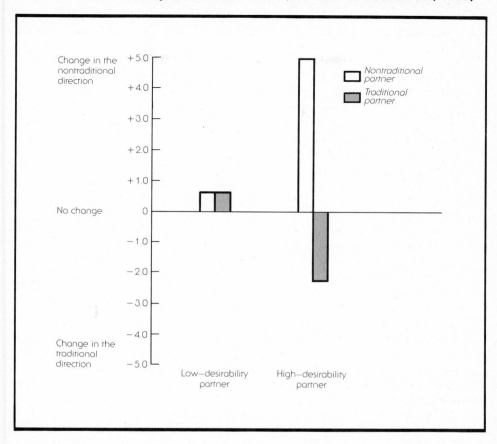

noticeably in the direction that their future partners endorsed. Women with traditional partners became more traditional; women with nontraditional partners became less traditional.

The women also took a test that involved unscrambling anagrams, which was described as a test of intellectual ability. They were told that their partners would be given their scores on this test, as well as the information on the gender-stereotyping questionnaire. Here again, women who thought that they would be working with a low-desirability partner did not modify their behavior to match their future partner's stereotypes. However, women who thought that they would be working with a high-desirability partner *did* modify their behavior. Women who thought that their future partner had nontraditional gender stereotypes solved about 20 percent more anagrams than women who thought that their partner would be traditional.

Notice that Zanna and Pack's study demonstrates that we do not always behave in a fashion that is consistent with other people's stereotypes. Instead, we modify our behavior in a stereotypical direction only for those people we really care about.

Let us leave the laboratory setting and return to the real world to discuss a study in which people were interviewed about how they cope with gender stereotypes in everyday life (Davidson, 1981). About half of the men and women who were interviewed reported that they perceived an internal pressure to act according to their respective gender stereotypes. In addition, 71 percent of the women reported that they experienced pressures to act more passively than they really felt, in contrast to only 38 percent of the men. Many men and women, however, felt tempted to break with traditional roles. One woman reported,

> I feel much safer in a passive role, especially in my personal life, but I feel happier when I push myself to assert myself regardless of whether the situation is appropriate or not. But this causes a great deal of anxiety. I feel, though, that I owe it to myself to try to be more active. [p. 337]

We have seen that people's behavior can be shaped by gender stereotypes. Some people, however, want to cast the stereotypes aside and behave nontraditionally. In the next section, we will examine alternatives to gender stereotypes.

☐ SECTION SUMMARY ▪ People's Beliefs about Women and Men

1. People believe that men and women are substantially different on a number of characteristics; men are considered to be higher in agency, or self-interest, and women are considered to be higher in communion, a concern for others.
2. People's judgments about themselves are typically less stereotyped than their judgments about others. When asked about ideal men and women, people generally described somewhat sex-typed individuals; women, however, created an ideal woman who was equally feminine and masculine.
3. Stereotypes are somewhat influenced by factors such as a person's sex, social class, level of education, race, employment status, and culture; however, the consistency of stereotypes is impressive.
4. Social cognition involves knowledge about the social world, for example, the thought process that encourages us to categorize the world into females versus males. Categorization may simplify our environment. However, it produces stereotypes, which may contain many errors. Errors, in turn, produce further errors.

5. Expectations are important in stereotyping because they produce errors in attention, interpretation, recall, and conclusions.
6. The categorization process tends to exaggerate similarities within a group and to exaggerate the contrast between the groups; for example, we tend to confuse people of the same sex.
7. Token men and women are noticed more, and their characteristics tend to be exaggerated.
8. Evidence for sex prejudice includes the following: people prefer a boy as their firstborn child; people downgrade women's achievements; people have negative opinions about women's work capacities; women have been represented negatively in many areas; and women's stereotypical characteristics are not as highly regarded as men's are.
9. Stereotypes influence behavior; research has demonstrated that women present themselves differently to job interviewers who have traditional stereotypes, that stereotypes influence whether people choose masculine or feminine tasks to perform, and that stereotypes influence how we present ourselves socially.

☐ ALTERNATIVES TO GENDER STEREOTYPES

In this chapter, we have briefly explored the historical basis of gender stereotypes, the biased representation of women in religion and mythology, the misrepresentation of women in language, the nature of people's current stereotypes, and how these stereotypes can influence behavior. To many people, these stereotypes may represent ideal standards that they should strive to reach. As you recall from Chapter 3, cognitive-developmental theory proposes that boys and girls learn what males and females are *supposed* to be like, and then they strive to match these standards. In the process, they reject characteristics that are typical of the other sex.

In contrast to this stereotyped approach, which encourages the separation of male and female characteristics, the concept of androgyny won almost instant popularity in the 1970s. As we will see, this approach encourages the development of both masculine and feminine characteristics. However, we will see why androgyny does not appear to be the perfect alternative. Instead, the answer may lie in a transcendence of gender roles.

Androgyny

The word "androgyny" comes from the Greek words for both men and women. At present, **androgyny** usually refers to people who are high in both feminine and masculine qualities. Think about a friend you know who is competent in areas that are stereotypically masculine as well as in areas that are stereotypically feminine. Your friend may be an excellent athlete, a superb scholar, and a "born leader." This friend may whip up an outstanding chocolate

FIGURE 8.5. **The bipolar view of femininity and masculinity**

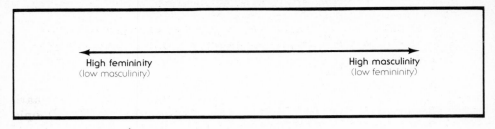

High femininity
(low masculinity)

High masculinity
(low femininity)

mousse on Thursday and spend several hours comforting a depressed friend on Friday. This friend may work well independently when the occasion demands, but also work well with a group on other occasions.

Clearly, androgyny sounds like an appealing alternative to the oppressiveness of striving to act according to gender stereotypes. Let us explore the concept of androgyny more thoroughly, first focusing on how the concept was developed. Then we will briefly look at some of the research on androgyny. Finally, we will discuss why androgyny is not an ideal alternative.

The development of the androgyny concept. Traditionally, psychologists viewed femininity and masculinity as exact opposites of each other, just like the concepts "light" and "dark" are exact opposites. Traditional masculinity-femininity scales were **bipolar,** with masculinity at one pole and femininity at the other pole (Constantinople, 1973), as shown in Figure 8.5. Notice how difficult it would be to find an appropriate place for your androgynous friend on a bipolar scale, because this friend is high in *both* femininity and masculinity. On a bipolar scale, a person who is high in femininity *must* be low in masculinity and vice versa. (Throughout the rest of the chapter the terms masculinity and femininity will be used as a shorthand way to describe behaviors that have *traditionally* been considered more appropriate for males and females, respectively, rather than the way they *should* behave.)

Furthermore, the traditional masculinity-femininity scales specified certain ideals. Ideally, males "should" have scores toward the masculine pole, and females "should" have scores toward the feminine pole. Males with more feminine scores and females with more masculine scores were considered to have gender-role confusion, certainly not an enviable diagnosis.

In the 1970s, several new methods of assessing gender roles were devised. These methods proposed that femininity and masculinity should be measured on separate, independent scales. The best known of these methods are the Bem Sex-Role Inventory (BSRI), which was developed by Sandra Bem (1974, 1977) and the Personal Attributes Questionnaire (PAQ), developed by Janet Spence, Robert Helmreich, and Joy Stapp (1974). Before reading further, try Demonstration 8.4, which contains items similar to those on the BSRI. The BSRI yields scores on a Masculinity Scale and on a Femininity

Items Similar to Those on the BSRI

Rate yourself on the following items, which are similar to the 60 items on the Bem Sex-Role Inventory. Use a scale in which 1 = never or almost never true and 7 = always or almost always true.

1. pleasant
2. honest
3. independent
4. studious
5. active
6. easily convinced by others

7. enjoys eating
8. affectionate
9. self-confident
10. enjoys feminine activities
11. traditional
12. enjoys masculine activities

The BSRI is scored by adding up the ratings for feminine-typed items (e.g., items 1, 6, 8, and 10 in this list) to obtain a score on the Femininity Scale, and by adding up the ratings for masculine-typed items (e.g., items 3, 5, 9, 12 in this list) to obtain a score on the Masculinity Scale. (The remaining items are "filler items" and are not scored.)

Note: The BSRI is now owned by Consulting Psychologists Press, Inc., and so it could not be reproduced here. For more information on the BSRI, you may wish to read descriptive articles by Bem (1974, 1977) or to purchase a copy of the test from C. P. P., Box 60070, Palo Alto, CA 94306.

Scale for each person who takes the test. Each of these scores is then compared with a group median for each of the scales. Table 8.3 shows how the scores on each of the two scales can produce four categories of people:

1. **Undifferentiated people,** who score low on both the femininity and the masculinity scales;
2. Feminine people, who score high on the scale for femininity and low on the scale for masculinity;
3. Masculine people, who score high on the scale for masculinity and low on the scale for femininity; and
4. Androgynous people, who score high on both scales.

TABLE 8.3   Categories from the Bem Sex-Role Inventory

High Femininity Low Masculinity FEMININE	High Femininity High Masculinity ANDROGYNOUS
Low Femininity Low Masculinity UNDIFFERENTIATED	Low Femininity High Masculinity MASCULINE

Bem and other theorists argued that people should no longer be encouraged to conform to outdated standards in which men should be traditionally masculine and women should be traditionally feminine. Instead, both women and men should be encouraged to be flexible in their gender roles, or androgynous: "That is, they should be encouraged to be both instrumental *and* expressive, both assertive *and* yielding, both masculine *and* feminine—depending upon the situational appropriateness of these various behaviors" (Bem, 1975, p. 634).

Soon, androgyny captured popular attention . . . it was no longer confined to psychology journals. (Often, too, the word was misspelled "androgeny" so that it—ironically—resembled the male hormone.) As Deaux (1984) remarks,

> . . . it was good and wise and liberal to be androgynous, and mental health was proposed to be synonymous with androgynous scores. Androgyny soon became a code word for an egalitarian, gender-free society, and disciples have advocated androgynous therapy, androgynous curricula for school children, and androgynous criteria for professional positions. (p. 109)

Research on androgyny. The Bem Sex-Role Inventory—and to a lesser extent the other methods of measuring androgyny—served in hundreds of studies on gender roles. In fact, it is probably safe to say that more research has been conducted on androgyny than on any other topic in psychology of women. It even outstripped the previous winner, fear of success, since the androgyny tests were so easy to administer. You'll probably recall that androgyny scores have been mentioned in the earlier chapters in this textbook. Let's look at a mere handful of these studies to seen how androgyny is (or is not) related to behavior.

1. When students were asked to choose which of two activities they wanted to perform, masculine men and feminine women were likely to choose an activity that was stereotypical of their own gender, even though they were paid less for that activity than for a nonstereotypical activity. In contrast, androgynous people seemed to be more flexible; they were likely to perform nonstereotypical activities (Bem & Lenney, 1976).
2. Androgynous people helped a "victim" who was choking on food more than did masculine men and feminine women (Senneker & Hendrick, 1983).
3. When managers in a large utility company completed the BSRI, androgynous people were more accepting of nontraditional job changes (Motowidlo, 1982).
4. Masculine people of both sexes received the highest scores on a test of mechanical reasoning, followed in order by androgynous, undifferentiated, and feminine people (Antill & Cunningham, 1982).
5. People who are high in masculinity have higher self-esteem and more positive self-images than do other people (Antill & Cunningham, 1979; Lee & Scheurer, 1983; Whitley, 1983). In contrast, femininity scores

are generally unrelated to the opinions people have about their own worth. Thus, androgynous people, who are highly feminine as well as highly masculine, are no more positive about themselves than people who are highly masculine but not at all feminine.

6. Similarly, people who are high in masculinity are likely to be better adjusted and less depressed than other people (Silvern & Ryan, 1979; Whitley, 1985). In contrast, femininity scores are not strongly related to adjustment or depression. Once again, androgynous people have no special advantage over masculine people.

Surveying a wide variety of studies on androgyny, the results are confusing. In many cases, androgynous people perform admirably, in contrast to others. In other cases, masculinity—rather than androgyny—appears to be more important. In still other cases, however, there is no consistent relationship between people's scores on androgyny measures and their behavior.

Problems with androgyny. As we reach the late-1980s, it is becoming increasingly clear that androgyny has problems. It certainly is not the ideal human situation that we thought it seemed to be. Let's look at some of the problems, which concern both experimental results and theory.

1. Androgyny is not consistently related to behavior, a problem we have just discussed. When a relationship *does* exist, it is typically quite weak. The situation with androgyny is also a problem in the more general area of personality: People's traits, as measured by personality tests, may not be strongly correlated with the behavior that should be predicted by these tests (Lenney, 1979; Mischel, 1968). A person who is androgynous, according to the BSRI, often doesn't behave very flexibly, and similarly a person who is (for example) extroverted, according to some test, often doesn't behave in a very outgoing fashion. Furthermore, a person who is androgynous in one situation may not be androgynous in another situation, just as characteristics such as extroversion do not generalize well across situations.

2. Many of the tests for gender roles claim to have scales that assess masculinity and femininity. However, the masculine items are primarily concerned with accomplishments, and the feminine items are primarily concerned with expressing feelings (Deaux, 1984). Thus the scores measure only a limited part of gender-related behavior. It's no surprise that in many cases it is difficult to find a relationship between these test scores and other different kinds of masculine and feminine behavior.

3. According to the early discussions of androgyny, those lucky people who were androgynous had a blend of masculinity and femininity. There was something special about this blend, so that the combination was somehow greater than the sum of its two parts, masculinity and femininity. Research has failed to identify any particular strong ad-

vantage to this combination. In general, masculinity by itself is a valuable characteristic for both men and women in today's society (Henley, 1985; Taylor & Hall, 1982). As Gilbert (1981) suggests, our male-oriented culture, which values masculine characteristics more than feminine characteristics, makes it highly likely that people who are masculine will be better adjusted. In a society in which feminine characteristics were valued as much as masculine characteristics, androgynous people might indeed be better adjusted than masculine people.

4. Sandra Bem herself points out one of the theoretical problems with androgyny: The concept of androgyny presupposes that masculinity and femininity have a reality in themselves, because these are the scales on which androgyny is based (Bem, 1981). As Lott (1981) argues, this defeats the original purpose of de-emphasizing gender stereotypes:

> To label some behaviors as feminine and some as masculine, as androgyny researchers do, and then to put the two artificial pieces back together again to conform with the reality of human functioning and capability . . . is to reinforce verbal habits which undermine the possibility of degenderizing behavior. [Lott, 1981, p. 178]

We should be able to figure out what behavior is ideal for adults, without having to rely on terms such as femininity and masculinity.

5. The concept of androgyny provides a double prescription for behavior (Bem, 1981). It's no longer sufficient for men to be masculine and women to be feminine, because androgyny demands that all adults have to meet *both* standards. In other words, a competent adult should be able to split half a cord of wood and then proceed to the kitchen to prepare a seven-course Thai dinner. People can now be judged incompetent for two reasons, not just one.

6. Androgyny tempts us to believe that the solution to gender bias lies in changing the individual. As Gilbert (1981) stresses, androgyny is not a solution to our present social problems in the areas of discrimination against women and institutional sexism. This argument is consistent with the argument in Chapter 6 that situation-centered explanations for the treatment of women in the workplace may be more valuable than person-centered explanations.

On Beyond Androgyny

Psychologists now tend to agree that androgyny has its problems. However, they have hardly rushed in to suggest alternative models. In fact, many androgyny critics turn back to a now-classic article by Meda Rebecca, Robert Hefner, and Barbara Oleshansky (1976) which argued for gender-role transcendence. **Gender-role transcendence** means that people do not merely combine gender roles, as androgyny recommends; instead, they go beyond these gender roles, because these roles are no longer relevant. People who have transcended gender roles are free to express their human qualities, without worrying about violating stereotypes. They choose strategies that are personally meaningful, rather than forcing themselves into "gender-appropriate" behaviors.

Androgyny stressed that people could be flexible, either feminine or masculine as the situation demanded. Rebecca and her coauthors' concept of transcendence goes further. For instance, they suggest that many professions no *v* seem to require a competitive, aggressive style in order to get ahead. An androgynous person would behave in a "masculine" fashion, becoming competitive and aggressive. A person who has transcended gender roles, however, might choose to change her or his concept of that profession so that competition and aggression would no longer be necessary.

Barbara Forisha (1978) expands upon this alternative of gender-role transcendence by discussing what she calls **process-oriented behavior.** Process-oriented behavior is behavior that springs spontaneously from our own inner judgment, rather than from the "masculine" or "feminine" roles that we think we must play. Process-oriented people are constantly learning more about themselves, and they are willing to admit that they make mistakes. However, they do not operate in terms of other people's expectations; they don't try to shape their lives to fit into a stereotype. Similarly, process-oriented people transcend androgyny because gender roles are neither relevant nor important to them.

Sandra Bem's concept of gender schema theory, which we discussed in Chapter 3 and earlier in this chapter, is similar in some respects to the notion of gender-role transcendence or process-oriented behavior. Remember that Bem argues that we should not perceive the world in terms of a female-male split. We should deemphasize the distinction between females and males, so that the two groups are not segregated in so many aspects of their lives. We should move beyond gender as a way of responding to the world.

It is also clear that institutions, as well as individuals, need to be changed. Institutions such as schools, businesses, and the government encourage the perpetuation of gender stereotypes. Clearly, it will be enormously difficult to modify these institutions so that they encourage self-fulfillment in all individuals.

SECTION SUMMARY ▪ Alternatives to Gender Stereotypes

1. Androgyny, which usually refers to people who are high in both masculine and feminine qualities, was a popular concept in the 1970s. It captured the interest of psychologists and the media.
2. According to research on androgyny, androgynous people are more likely to be flexible in their choice of activities, more likely to help a choking victim, and more accepting of nontraditional job changes.
3. In other research, androgyny offers no particular advantage over masculinity; masculine people are best at mechanical reasoning, they are higher in self-esteem, and they are better adjusted than other kinds of people.

4. The concept of androgyny has problems because it is not consistently related to behavior, because the masculinity and femininity scales only tap a limited part of gender stereotypes, and because the combination of femininity and masculinity offers no special advantage.

5. Other problems with androgyny are that androgyny is based on masculinity and femininity subscales, which are concepts that androgyny was trying to avoid, that androgyny forces people to try to meet two standards, rather than just one, and that changing gender bias must involve changing institutions, rather than just individuals.

6. Theorists who are looking for alternative models to androgyny frequently discuss an idea such as gender-role transcendence. In gender-role transcendence, people move beyond gender roles, because these roles are no longer relevant; gender-role transcendence involves more than a flexibility in whether a "masculine" or "feminine" approach is taken in approaching a task, because the task itself can also be restructured. A similar alternative is called process-oriented behavior.

Chapter Review Questions

1. We discussed how women have been left out of history. Discuss the kinds of topics involving women that scholars have previously ignored and also mention several reasons why women have not received much attention in history books.

2. Review the positions that philosophers have maintained with respect to women, particularly with respect to sex differences. Point out how these ideas compare with what you learned about sex differences in the previous chapters.

3. This chapter discussed how women seem to be invisible; men are primary, whereas women are secondary. Summarize as many areas as you can in which this statement is supported, being certain to mention history, religion and mythology, language, the media, and anything else you believe is relevant.

4. This chapter also emphasized that people are more negative about women than about men. Discuss this statement, pointing out support from philosophers' position on women, religion and mythology, language, the media, and the section on sex prejudice.

5. Many people claim that the words and the images that we use to represent women are really unimportant, and that issues such as the generic masculine or the representation of women in the media are trivial compared to issues such as equal pay. Discuss this issue, citing studies that indicate that the representation of women can influence people's ideas about women and women's own behavior.

6. List the kinds of characteristics people associate with women and those that they associate with men. How are these stereotypes related to the stereotypes in the media, to people's descriptions of themselves, and to people's descriptions of ideal women and men?

7. Some people might claim that factors such as sex and social class have no influence on the strength of people's stereotypes; others might argue that these factors have a tremendous influence. How would you summarize the nature of the relationship?

8. According to the social-cognition approach, stereotypes arise out of normal cognitive processes, beginning with classifying people into two categories, men and women. Describe this position, and illustrate it by discussing how people might come to believe that women are more talkative than men. Also describe some other cognitive aspects of gender stereotyping.

9. What is a self-fulfilling prophecy, and how is it relevant to the influence of stereotypes on behavior?

10. Define androgyny, describing why this approach offers an advantage over the traditional ideas that masculinity and femininity are exact opposities. Point out some of the problems that the concept of androgyny has encountered in recent years.

☐ NEW TERMS

gender stereotypes
generic masculine
agency
communion
social cognition
self-fulfilling prophecy

androgyny
bipolar
undifferentiated people
gender-role transcendence
process-oriented behavior

☐ RECOMMENDED READINGS

Basow, S. (1986). *Gender stereotypes: Traditions and alternatives.* (2nd ed.). Monterey, Calif.: Brooks/Cole. ■ Of the books that focus on gender stereotypes, this is one of the most readable and comprehensive.

Courtney, A. E., & Whipple, T. W. (1983). *Sex stereotyping in advertising.* Lexington, Mass.: Lexington Books. ■ This resource offers an excellent summary of how the media perpetuate stereotypes.

Hamilton, D. L. (Ed.) (1981). *Cognitive processes in stereotyping and intergroup behavior.* Hillsdale, N. J.: Erlbaum. ■ David Hamilton is the editor of this book in which several major researchers in the area of social cognition apply their theoretical perspective to the issue of stereotypes.

Hunter College Women's Studies Collective. (1983). *Women's realities, women's choices.* New York: Oxford University Press. ■ I use this textbook when I teach an interdisciplinary course called Issues in Feminism; it provides a good background on the issues covered in the first topic of this chapter, the representation of women and men.

LOVE RELATIONSHIPS

true or false?

- Women want companionship and affection in a dating partner, whereas men are primarily interested in an attractive date.

- Men tend to fall in love more easily than women.

- Couples who live together are much less likely than married couples to behave in a gender-stereotyped fashion.

- In general, women with greater incomes tend to have more power, relative to their husbands.

- Women are more likely than men to initiate divorce.

- In general, among people who are seeking divorce, women are more likely than men to say that they feel unloved.

- Lesbian women and heterosexual women differ from each other in their level of various hormones.

- In the majority of lesbian relationships, there is a roughly equal division of power between the two partners.

- In general, single women tend to be well-educated.

- Single women are typically much less happy than married women.

The radio in my daughter's room is playing "Jump for my love ...." I just checked the country and western station and heard the poignant line from a Lefty Frizzell favorite, "Please release me, let me go. I don't love you anymore." The opera on the classical station this weekend is *Lohengrin*, about the Knight of the Swan's love for Elsa of Bravant. However, we'll have to miss it because we have tickets for *The Music Man*, in which the roving con man falls for the local librarian. This week on "General Hospital," Jimmy Lee Holt and Grant Putnam are both courting Celia Andrews, who sustains some love for her husband Grant Andrews, who is pining away in jail for presumably trying to kill Celia so he could run off with Tanya Roskov, whom Frisco Jones is also trying to woo.

It seems that the whole world is captivated by love. No matter how many times we hear about "boy meeting girl," we go back for more. There are a few songs, grand operas, musicals, and soap opera plots in which work or power or parent-child relations figure prominently, but they are clearly outnumbered by themes about love.

A book on psychology of women would therefore be incomplete without a chapter on love. We'll examine four topics here: dating and cohabitation; marriage and divorce; lesbians and bisexual women; and single women.

☐ DATING AND COHABITATION

In this section of the chapter, we'll talk about those people who inhabit most of the popular songs. These are the people who are beginning to date, speculating about an ideal partner, falling in love, living together, and breaking up.

Beginning to Date

In Chapter 3, we discussed the close friendships that young adolescent women have with each other. The intensity of these same-sex friendships decreases during high school as the pressure to develop an interest in males increases. The segregation by sexes, so obvious in the elementary-school cafeteria, has given way to partial desegregation.

It's difficult to find information on early girl-boy relationships, probably in part because customs vary from one community to the next. In most areas, however, some kind of tentative pairings are made in late elementary school. For example, I was surprised to hear my daughter mention that her friend Joan was "going out with" Billy. Were sixth graders in our rather conservative region really dating? I was informed, however, that "going out with" merely means that two people have agreed that they like each other—they probably never see each other outside of the classroom. Dating, in the more traditional sense of the word, begins some years later, at about 14 for girls and 15 for boys (Strommen, 1977).

One unfortunate consequence of the emphasis on dating is that young women may develop a not-so-friendly rivalry with other women. Even a close girlfriend should be watched occasionally, because popular wisdom suggests that anyone female might "steal" your boyfriend. We see how this emphasis on female rivalry continues into adulthood, with advertisements urging us to use special face creams to look younger than our friends and to buy an expensive brand of hose so that men turn their attention from their dates in order to notice our legs.

The Ideal Dating Partner

Before you read this section on ideal partners, try Demonstration 9.1 to see whether you can guess whose ideal partner is being described in a set of "personal ads." The answers are at the end of this section.

What do women and men want in a dating partner, and are their interests different? As Peplau (1983) concludes, women and men want much the same things in a close relationship. Both women and men want a permanent relationship. Both women and men value companionship and affection more than economic security and social status.

According to stereotypes, men are primarily looking for attractive women—"Lollapaloozas," as Fred Mertz used to call the knockouts on the "I Love Lucy" show. Women, it is generally believed, appreciate masculine attractiveness, but are not so easily influenced by this feature.

We already mentioned in Chapter 3 that females take this stereotype seriously, because adolescent women who thought that their bodies were attractive had positive self-concepts, whereas self-concept was unrelated to attractiveness in adolescent men. More generally, people weigh physical attractiveness more heavily when they are evaluating women than when they are evaluating men (Bar-Tal & Saxe, 1976).

The greater emphasis on physical attractiveness for women than for men extends to dating, as well. Men are more likely than women to say that they want an attractive partner (Peplau, 1983). However, beautiful women may not differ substantially from less attractive women in the number of dates they actually have (Reis, et al., 1982). It may be that men are afraid of being turned down by very attractive women, so that they actually socialize with women who are less beautiful than their ideal. Also, it is likely that there is a general tendency toward "matching" in relationships; men may wish they could date popular, gorgeous women, but they tend to end up with women who are reasonably similar to themselves in terms of popularity and attractiveness (Peplau, 1985). At any rate, it seems that men emphasize attractiveness to a greater extent when they are describing ideal women than when they actually socialize with women.

Do men want unassertive gentle maidens as their ideal dates, and do women want commanding "he-men"? According to a study by Orlofsky (1982), college women are most likely to describe androgynous ideal dating partners. About two-thirds of the participants in this study described ideal dating partners who had a large number of both stereotypically feminine and stereotypically masculine traits. This pattern held true whether the women were

The Ideal Partner.

Below are excerpts from the first ten advertisements in the personals columns of *City Newspaper*, Rochester, New York, describing the kind of person the writer of the ad is looking for. I have left out any mention of the sex of the ideal partner, but otherwise, this portion of the ad is complete. In each case, put an F in front of the description if you think that the writer of the ad is female, and an M if you think the writer is a male.

1. _____ I'd like to meet a ( ) who likes doing the same things that I enjoy doing (dancing, going out to bars occasionally, etc.).

2. _____ I am looking for a well rounded ( ) who can be honest, fair, and enjoy many of the interests that I have listed.

3. _____ Wanted! A clean cut, medium built 45- to 55-year-old ( ) who likes nature hikes early in the morning.

4. _____ I'd like to meet someone who is around the ages of 20 to 25 years old who also likes sports and music. I would prefer it if the person was a nonsmoker.

5. _____ I am searching for someone who is honest, easy to talk to, and who would just like to enjoy the summer having fun whether it's going to the beach or going to places like festivals. And perhaps even getting a little crazy now and then.

6. _____ I'd like to meet a tall, fun loving ( ) between the ages of 25 and 32 who likes outdoor activities.

7. _____ I'm looking for someone who just wants to go out and have a good time this summer. It doesn't have to be serious, but if it turns out that way that's OK. I'd like to meet someone 19 to 27 years, who enjoys my interests and can have a good time when ( ) is out. Looks don't really matter, but I wouldn't be too upset if ( ) was good looking.

8. _____ I'd like to meet a tall handsome ( ) with blonde hair and blue eyes who is around 20 to 25 years old.

9. _____ If you are thin, honest, and true, and if you like the Piña-Colada song, please write me at . . . .

10. _____ Boat owner, looking for ( ) first mate, age 35–42, to share summer of boating fun.

traditional or nontraditional in their attitudes toward women. The college men who were nontraditional also preferred androgynous dating partners. However, the college men who were traditional in their attitudes toward women expressed an equal preference for androgynous and stereotypically feminine dating partners. In other words, college students in the 1980s gen-

FIGURE 9.1. **Percentage of people who pretend to be inferior in certain areas (based on Braito, et al., 1981)**

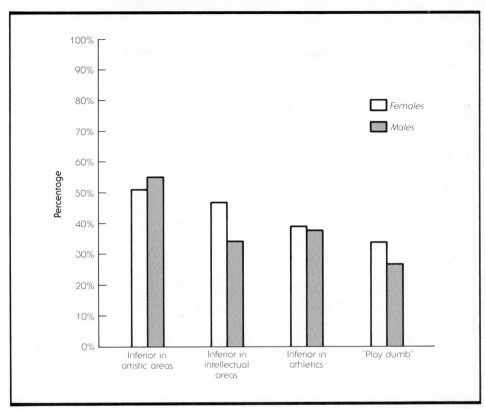

erally reject a strongly stereotpyed person as an ideal date, with the exception of some of the traditional males.

According to popular belief, men are not interested in smart, athletic women. If women want to be an ideal date, they should "play dumb." Popular belief also suggests that men never need to represent themselves as being less competent than they really are. However, a study by Braito, Dean, Powers, and Bruton (1981) shows us that women and men hide their talents equally often. These authors asked college students how often they pretended to be inferior to their date with regard to artistic knowledge, athletic skill, intellectual competence, and simply "playing dumb." As Figure 9.1 shows, the differences are relatively small. However, it is interesting that the areas in which women are more likely than men to hide their talents are in the intellectual areas, rather than artistic or athletic skills.

How accurate were you in guessing the sex of the person writing the personal ads in Demonstration 9.1? The answers are: 1. M; 2. F; 3. F; 4. M; 5.

M; 6. F; 7. M; 8. F; 9. M; 10. F. Notice that, with the exception of those who specify height and physical appearances for a partner, it is difficult to guess who wrote the ad. Most people are seeking someone who shares similar interests, and the sex differences in the kinds of ads they write are minimal.

Check the personal ads in your local newspaper to see if you find any systematic sex differences. A study of ads in major newspapers from the East and West Coasts did find substantial differences (Deaux & Hanna, 1984). In this research, ads placed by men were more likely to seek physical attractiveness and to describe themselves in terms of financial status and physical features. Ads placed by women were more likely to seek and to offer specific psychological traits. An analysis of ads in a Columbus, Ohio, singles' magazine found that men were slightly more likely to think that physical attractiveness was important in a dating partner (Lynn & Shurgot, 1984). Finally, a study of responses at a video-dating service in the Washington, D.C., area showed that women considered both status and physical attractiveness when choosing a potential date, whereas men considered physical attractiveness but not status (Green, et al., 1984).

Falling in Love

In a typical magazine short story, Elyse falls head-over-heels in love with Todd, a practical sort who remains unaffected by Elyse's romanticism until the end of the story. A typical scenario? Actually, it isn't. In reality, men tend to fall in love more easily than women. Even early in the relationship, men typically report greater love for their girlfriends than women report for their boyfriends (Rubin, Peplau, & Hill, 1981).

In a large-scale study in the Boston area, college couples who were dating were asked to complete a questionnaire (Rubin, et al., 1981). One portion of this questionnaire was a "romanticism scale," which measured the degree to which the respondent held such romantic beliefs as love strikes at first sight, true love lasts forever, and love overcomes such restraints as race, religion, and economics. Men scored higher on this romanticism scale than women did, indicating that women are relatively discriminating and deliberate about falling in love. The men were also more likely than women to report that they entered their present dating relationship because of a desire to fall in love. These results matched those found by earlier researchers, who found that men tended to fall in love sooner than the women they were dating (summarized by Walster & Walster, 1978).

One possible interpretation of these studies could be that women have lower capacities for heterosexual commitment. However, Rubin and his coauthors propose alternate suggestions, such as an economics interpretation. Women may simply need to be more practical than men in the "marriage market." Women are supposed to look for men who will earn a good income, whereas—at least traditionally—men don't need to worry about their potential spouses' income or profession. Thus, a man can quickly lose his heart to a woman, but a woman must be more restrained and "picky."

An alternate suggestion is that women may be socialized differently from men so that they learn to manage their own emotions in a more restrained fashion. This idea of emotion management is developed further by Hochschild (1975, 1979). She proposes that women work harder than men to control their emotions. This means that they sometimes try to create an emotion that wasn't originally there. Women convince themselves that they are having a good time with someone who might be faintly boring and they force themselves to fall in love with someone who has all of the proper characteristics for a potential spouse. Equally important, they try to squelch an emotion that *is* present ... for example by suppressing passion for an exciting, handsome man who would clearly be an unsuitable spouse. In contrast, men are more governed by romanticism, and they don't need to mold their emotions so systematically. The proposal that women and men differ in their use of emotion management is intriguing, and it *sounds* right. However, the issue has not been systematically studied in recent years. It would be valuable to know if there really are substantial sex differences in this area.

There is one other possible sex difference with respect to falling in love. It seems that women are more likely than men to say that they have certain emotional symptoms of love. According to studies reviewed by Peplau and Gordon (1985), women were more likely than men to report emotions such as "floating on a cloud," "feeling giddy and carefree," and "having trouble concentrating." They were also more likely to say that they felt euphoric or blissfully happy. Keep in mind that these differences are based on self-report, and men might be hesitant to report such intimate feelings.

Communication Patterns

The first verbal communication between an unacquainted male and female occurs with the opening line, typically delivered by a male. Kleinke (1981) found that the opening line also offers the first opportunity for miscommunication. It seems that men think that women like cute, flippant lines ("You remind me of a woman I used to date," or at a laundromat, "I'll wash your clothes if you wash mine"). Women tend to prefer innocuous questions (at a bar, "What do you think of the band?" or on the beach, "The water is beautiful today, isn't it?").

We discussed in Chapter 7 that women sometimes reveal more about themselves than males do. Now let us consider self-disclosure in close relationships. As Peplau (1983) summarizes the literature, women *prefer* to disclose more personal information than men do. However, the sex differences are relatively small in the self-disclosure that actually occurs in dating relationships.

A representative exploration of this topic involved the same couples who were studied in the research on romanticism that we mentioned earlier. In this investigation, Rubin, Hill, Peplau, and Dunkel-Schetter (1980) asked a large number of dating couples to indicate how much they had revealed different kinds of private information to their partners. Across all 17 topic areas, the proportion who said that they had revealed themselves fully to their partners averaged 58 percent for the women and 57 percent for the men. Overall, then, there are no sex differences in self-disclosure to the dating partner.

More careful analyses showed, however, that there were sex differences in specific areas of self-disclosure. Women reported disclosing more than men about their parents, their same-sex friends, their classes, their fears, and their accomplishments. Men revealed more about their political views, the things they were most proud of in themselves, and the things they liked best about their partners. Notice that the areas in which each sex feels more comfortable about self-disclosure generally coincide with expectations based on stereotypes.

How do females and males respond in conflict situations? Kelley and his coauthors (1978) investigated both stereotyped expectations and actual reactions about conflict. People expected the female to be likely to cry, sulk, and criticize the male for his lack of consideration and insensitivity. People expected the male to become angry, reject the female's tears, urge for a rational approach to the problem, and give reasons for delaying the argument. In a second study, these authors asked dating couples to select which sentences they and their partners would actually be likely to say in a conflict situation. They were encouraged to discuss the scenario together. These reports of actual reactions were somewhat similar to the stereotypes revealed in the first study, but the sex differences were much smaller. It is likely, since the self-report method was used in this study, that the sex differences in *actual* behavior would be even smaller. Once again, we see an illustration of the second theme of this book; people's ideas about sex differences are exaggerated versions of reality.

In summary, there are some differences between females and males in dating couples. Men and women differ in their views of an ideal opening line. Men reveal intimate details about themselves on some topics, whereas women prefer to talk about other intimate topics. Men and women may also respond somewhat differently to conflict. However, the gap between the male and the female in a dating couple is not enormous, because, overall, women and men are equally self-disclosing and because the differences in conflict style are smaller than people expect.

Why should sex differences be relatively small in the area of dating relationships? It seems likely that there are several forces in close personal relationships that encourage similarities. We mentioned the idea of "matching" earlier. People tend to choose partners who are similar to themselves, so that, for instance, outgoing men tend to select outgoing women. In addition, there are pressures for "reciprocity" in relationships, so that an action by one member of a couple will tend to be repeated by the other member. If Nancy reveals some personal information about herself to Rob, then Rob will be likely to reciprocate by revealing personal information about himself. In combination, these tendencies of matching and reciprocity encourage similarities rather than differences between women and men (Peplau, 1985; Peplau & Gordon, 1985).

Cohabitation

The unromantic word that researchers use to talk about "living together" is cohabitation. Legally, **cohabitation** means that two persons of the opposite sex are living together as husband and wife without being married (Macklin, 1978).

In a recent estimate, there were about 1.8 million cohabiting couples in the United States, which is about 4 percent of all couples. This is about three times as many as the number of cohabiting couples estimated for 1970 (Spanier, 1983). During college, couples are even more likely to live together; from a number of samples, Macklin (1978) concludes that about one-quarter of all undergraduates have had a "cohabitation experience" at some point in their lives.

Attitudes toward cohabitation have changed remarkably since 1962, when a woman at Barnard was expelled from school because she was living with a graduate student in an apartment off campus (Murstein, 1978). Today, students are generally positive in their attitudes toward living together, and only a small percentage say that they would not consider cohabitation. However, their parents do not support cohabitation. The clear majority of the parents of college students say that they would not approve of their daughter's living with a man without being married to him (Macklin, 1978).

There is no "typical" cohabitation relationship, just as there is no typical dating or marriage relationship. Some couples live together because of a temporary convenience. Some have an affectionate relationship but are open to other relationships. Others are monogamous, but may not have long-range plans. Others use cohabitation as a trial marriage, a temporary alternative to marriage (for example, while awaiting a divorce settlement), or a permanent alternative to marriage (Macklin, 1978).

Women who are currently in a "living together" situation tend to be young. In one sample, 88 percent of the women were under 35 (Spanier, 1983). Cohabiting women tend to see themselves as more outgoing, competitive, and aggressive than other groups of women (Macklin, 1978). They are also less likely to be religious, more likely to have liberal attitudes toward sexuality and politics, and more likely to live in a liberal community or college setting.

For most couples, cohabitation is a temporary relationship, leading either to a breakup or a marriage within several years (Blumstein & Schwartz, 1983; Clayton & Voss, 1979). Only slightly more than one-third of cohabiting couples expect to get married to the person they are living with, though most couples believe that they will eventually marry someone (Blumstein & Schwartz, 1983; Macklin, 1978).

How do cohabiting couples compare with married couples? As might be expected, married couples feel more commitment to their relationship, particularly in the case of males. In general, however, there are surprisingly few differences between the two kinds of couples. For example, both groups were equally satisfied with their relationships (Macklin, 1978).

Are married couples happier if they have lived together before marriage? In general, cohabitation does not have a substantial influence on later marital happiness. People who lived together before marriage do not differ from those who had not lived together in terms of satisfaction, closeness, conflicts, or egalitarianism in marriage (Macklin, 1978).

We might expect that people who decide to live together would be less traditional than most people, and therefore they might have relationships in which the woman and the man have similar roles. It isn't clear whether this actually happens. After reviewing several studies on the issue, Macklin (1978) concluded that gender-role equality is no more likely to be found in coha- biting couples than it is in married couples. However, Kotkin (1983) did find some differences. He selected three kinds of couples for his study, cohabitors who were not planning to marry, cohabitors who were planning to marry, and married couples. He was particularly interested in the frequency with which the male's career took precedence over the female's career. This was most common among the married couples (80 percent), less so among the engaged cohabitors (64 percent), and least common among the nonengaged cohabitors (44 percent).

For some women, living together may provide an opportunity to have a close, continuous relationship with a man that is less likely to involve tra- ditional roles and more likely to preserve the women's sense of individuality. This view is expressed by a "cohabiting" woman interviewed by Blumstein & Schwartz (1983):

> I guess I'm really upset over couple-ism. I get really upset when people say, "We like our eggs over easy." You could say: "Harold and Jane both like their eggs over easy," but then it's two individuals. I think that's very important for me to maintain. [p. 423]

Breaking Up

Kevin and Mary Ann had been dating for nearly a year, and everyone was startled to hear that they had broken up. Kevin had been the "breaker-upper," it was rumored; he had felt trapped and was bored with the relationship. Now Mary Ann was deeply depressed. ... Does this sound like the typical dissolution of a romance? It shouldn't, because in reality women tend to fall out of love more readily than men do. You'll recall that men tend to fall in love more readily than women, which means that men seem to be "first in, last out."

Women are usually more sensitive to problems in a troubled love rela- tionship. Rubin, Peplau, and Hill (1981) asked 103 couples who had broken up to indicate items on a checklist that they believed had contributed to their breakup. Women indicated significantly more problems than men did. Women were more likely than men to list a difference in intelligence, con-

FIGURE 9.2. **Reasons for leaving a cohabitation relationship (cited in Macklin, 1978)**

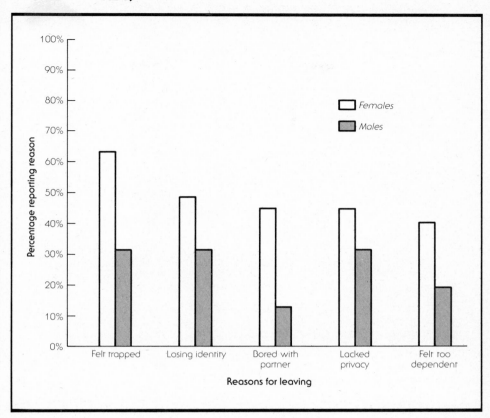

flicting ideas about marriage, differing interests, and a potential relationship with someone else.

When a cohabitation relationship is broken up, women are also more likely than men to list problems in that relationship (Ganson, 1975, cited in Macklin, 1978). Figure 9.2 illustrates the contrast between women's and men's reasons for leaving a relationship. In every category, women were more likely than men to mention a problem. In Chapter 7, we mentioned that women are often more sensitive to nonverbal communication than men are. Perhaps this sensitivity also applies to more general communication issues.

Furthermore, women see the breakup coming sooner than men do. Rubin and his coauthors reported that women often perceived the breakup as a gradual process, whereas men perceived it as abrupt. Women seem to be more attuned to the problems, and they are more aware that a breakup will occur. They probably have more time to prepare themselves for falling out of love.

Contrary to popular opinion, breaking up appears to be more traumatic for men than for women. After a breakup, men were somewhat more likely than women to report that they were lonely, depressed, and unhappy (Rubin, et al., 1981). Rejected men found it more difficult than rejected women to stay friends with their former partner.

We mentioned earlier the theory developed by Hochschild (1975, 1979) that women work harder at emotion management; they try harder to create an emotion that isn't there. In addition, they seem to try harder to erase an emotion that *is* there. Women may be skilled at talking themselves out of love ... after all, they aren't supposed to remain in love with the "wrong" man.

We discussed earlier that an economics approach to love relationships suggests that women must be cautious about falling in love because they shouldn't fall for the wrong man. Similarly, an economics approach suggests that women can't afford to stay in love too long with the wrong man (Rubin, et al., 1981). Women, the relatively heartless sex, must be able to evaluate their partners, anticipate any problems in the relationship, and rationalize away any sentiments attached to a broken relationship. They must be able to pick themselves up and look for a potential new partner. Women are not helpless creatures when love relationships end; instead, they are quite adept at handling their emotions and getting on with their lives.

☐ SECTION SUMMARY ▪ Dating and Cohabitation

1. **Women and men both want companionship and affection in a dating partner.**
2. **Men say that they want to date an attractive partner, and studies demonstrate that men are more likely than women to emphasize attractiveness in a dating partner; however, the most attractive women do not have substantially more active social lives than less attractive women.**
3. **College women prefer androgynous dating partners. Nontraditional college men also prefer androgynous dating partners, but traditional men like androgynous and feminine women equally.**
4. **Both men and women sometimes "play dumb" with their dates; women are most likely to hide their talents in intellectual areas.**
5. **Men tend to fall in love more easily than women; women may work harder than men to control their emotions, so that they don't fall in love with the wrong person.**
6. **Women and men are approximately equal in their self-disclosure in a dating relationship, but they differ in the areas in which they reveal private information about themselves.**
7. **People expect females in conflict situations to cry, and they expect males to become angry; reports of real-life behavior show**

tendencies in these directions, but they are not as exaggerated as the stereotypes.

8. Cohabitation is much more frequent than in the past, and attitudes toward cohabitation have become more positive; there is no "typical" cohabitation relationship in terms of future plans.
9. Cohabiting women tend to be young and liberal about sexuality and politics in contrast to other groups of women.
10. Cohabiting couples are less likely than married couples to feel commitment to their relationship, but the two groups are otherwise similar. Cohabitation does not have a substantial influence on later marital relationships.
11. Cohabiting couples and married couples often do not differ in their gender-role equality, though women's careers may not be as subordinate to men's careers in cohabiting couples.
12. Women tend to fall out of love more readily than men; women in dating and cohabiting relationships list more problems with a relationship and see the breakup coming sooner, in contrast to men.
13. Breaking up is often more traumatic for men than women.

☐ MARRIAGE AND DIVORCE

Many of us have a mental image of a "typical American family" that is based on the television images from the 1950s and 1960s. This mythical family consists of one devoted wife, one gainfully employed husband, and two lovely children—an older brother and a younger sister. The devoted wife rises early to prepare an impressive breakfast, before the gainfully employed husband marches off to work and the lovely children depart for school. The devoted wife, of course, does not work outside the home. She attends to the needs of dog Spot and cat Puff, and has time to bake up a fresh batch of cookies for the lovely children to enjoy with a tall glass of milk when they return from school. Needless to say, this television family is white.

This "typical family" does exist in America, but it is more a fantasy than it is typical. For example, in 1984, only 17 percent of all households included a husband, a wife, and at least two children under 18 (U. S. Bureau of the Census, 1985). Furthermore, this "typical family" is less common among blacks than among whites.

Slowly, these mental images may be changing as people confront reality. Our local school board recently acknowledged that 40 percent of the kindergartners in our rural, virtually all-white region of Upstate New York came from single-parent families. Attitudes toward divorce are also changing dramatically as the divorce rate comes increasingly close to the marriage rate (Bernard, 1981).

Our first topic in this section of the chapter is responsibility and power in marriage. Then we will look at several aspects of marital satisfaction. Our last topic is divorce.

Responsibility and Power in Marriage

In Chapter 6 we discussed how women in recent years are increasingly likely to work outside the home. We also noted that there has been little change with respect to housework and child care. These two obligations—unfortunately—are still almost exclusively performed by wives, rather than husbands. The responsibility of providing concrete services to the family still rests primarily with women. Men provide more financial support for the family, because a greater percentage of men are employed and because their average salaries are larger.

What about the division of power within a family? Who makes the important decisions and who is more influential? In employment and political settings, men are more powerful. In domestic settings as well, men are often—but not always—more powerful. Traditionally, men have an advantage over women because they are better paid, they often are better educated, and they usually have greater social status outside the family. In addition, they are usually physically stronger. In many areas, men also have a legal advantage over their wives; the husband is legally the head of the family, and he has the authority to make decisions directly involving his wife's welfare.

My students are often skeptical about the influence of crass factors such as money on the intimate, romantic relationships involved in marriage. As Blumstein and Schwartz (1983) remark, Americans like to believe that "the right to affect decisions is based on the demands of daily events, on which partner is wiser on a certain issue, or on special gifts of persuasion. They do not like to think that income, something that comes into the relationship from the outside, imposes a hierarchy on the couple" (p. 53). However, Blumstein & Schwartz's study showed that money is power. Among married couples, women with higher incomes had more "clout."

Let's imagine how income might influence decision making in a marriage. Suppose that Don is an engineer earning $40,000 and that Anna is a teacher earning $16,000. Whose word will be more influential when the family is debating buying a new television? Who will stay home from work to take the sick child to the doctor's office? Now imagine that Anna is the engineer and Don is the teacher. Rerun the household dramas of television purchase and the visit to the doctor and notice how Anna gains more power.

We have repeatedly emphasized throughout this book that individual differences are substantial: this is the fourth theme of the book. Similarly, the variation in marital roles is very great. Peplau (1983) provides a useful way of classifying couples in terms of three patterns of marital roles: a traditional marriage, a modern marriage, and an egalitarian marriage. Not every couple fits neatly into a single category, but this classification system helps us appreciate the variety of relationships found in marriages.

In a **traditional marriage,** the husband is more dominant than the wife, and both partners maintain traditional sex roles. The wife is not employed, the husband controls the money, and the wife may not even know how much he earns. The two do not share the same interests or activities. In traditional marriages, the wife makes decisions about housework and child care, but the husband has the ultimate authority in family decisions. Often, popular advice books advocate a return to a traditional marriage in which the wife is truly subservient to the husband. Helen Andelin (1963), in her book *Fascinating Womanhood*, proposes that the ideal woman must have the following qualities: femininity, domestic goddess, deep inner happiness, fresh appearance and manner, and childlikeness. She must arouse a desire from her husband to protect and shelter her. Similar messages can be found in Morgan's (1973) best-selling book, *The Total Woman.*

In a **modern marriage,** husbands are less dominant. Modern couples maintain that husbands and wives should share equally in making decisions, yet husbands still tend to be more powerful. Traditional gender roles are modified somewhat. The husband tolerates or even encourages his wife's employment, but her work is clearly secondary to his. (For example, she will miss work if their child is ill.) These couples stress compatibility and spending leisure time in the same activities.

The **egalitarian marriage** is best seen as an ideal that some couples strive to achieve, rather than a frequently occurring pattern in the United States today. Both partners share power equally in an egalitarian marriage, and traditional gender roles are absent. The wife and husband share equally in housekeeping, child care, financial support, and decision making. Companionship and sharing are stressed in these egalitarian marriages. A review of the literature demonstrated that the highest levels of satisfaction are found in egalitarian marriages, rather than in marriages where either the husband or the wife has more power (Gray-Little & Burks, 1983).

Egalitarian marriages are particularly attractive to people who are classified as androgynous on the Bem Sex-Role Inventory (Pursell, Banikiotes, & Sebastian, 1981). As we might expect, people who are high in both masculinity and femininity prefer a marital relationship in which gender roles are not emphasized. Furthermore, couples who prefer egalitarian marriages tend to be young, more educated, and more liberal politically (Antill, Cotton, & Tindale, 1983).

The relative power of husbands and wives is a particular issue in research on black families because of a well-known report called *The Negro Family: The Case for National Action* (Moynihan, 1965). This report introduced the idea of a **black matriarchy** (pronounced *"may*-tree-ar-key") in which women were the rulers in the family. Women in black families were supposed to be so dominant that they emasculated black men and encouraged other abnormalities in the family. However, Harrison (1977) concludes that there is little evidence for the idea of black matriarchy. Contrary to the idea of a black matriarchy, black women don't earn more than black men, they seldom oppose their husbands' views directly, and they don't favor their daughters over their sons. Reviewing all the evidence, Harrison concludes that there is no compelling evidence for a disruptive and harmful black matriarchy. It may be that power is more evenly divided within black families than within white families, but this observation is *not* evidence for a black matriarchy.

Marital Satisfaction

There are two issues concerning marital satisfaction that we need to consider here. First, how does a woman's satisfaction with her marriage depend upon the length of time she has been married? Second, are there sex differences in marital happiness?

Satisfaction during various periods of marriage. Think of the words "newlywed" or "bride." These words suggest associations such as radiance, bliss, oblivion to the rest of the world, and utter happiness. (Perhaps "indebtedness" might be a more appropriate association, because according to an article by Hopkins, 1984, the average cost of an American wedding, *not including the reception*, is $4,000!) According to surveys, young married women are indeed happy, perhaps the happiest group of either sex at any age (Campbell, 1975).

This blissfulness might not last long, because after several years of marriage, women sometimes report being unhappy and dissatisfied (Schaffer, 1980). Perhaps the reality of housework and other responsibilities—and often the work involved in child care—are at least partly to blame for this disenchantment.

Marital satisfaction may drop during the first 20 years of marriage (Nadelson, Polonsky, & Mathews, 1982). During these two decades, there may be a decrease in intimacy, physical affection, and a sharing of activities. Marriages appear to be at an all-time low when children are in their late adolescence.

As we will see in Chapter 14, women's lives begin to look up again once their children have left home. Marital satisfaction generally improves as well (Nadelson, et al., 1982). Nevertheless, some women still experience difficulties in their marriages, which Siegel (1983) describes in her article on problems in long-term marriages. As she points out, long-term marriages involve accumulated inequalities between the husband and the wife. Over several decades of marriage, the couple has established set patterns. These patterns are difficult to negotiate in order to make the marriage more egalitarian.

Sex differences in marital satisfaction. You've probably heard a stand-up comedian repeat the standard joke, "Take my wife—please!" As Schaffer (1980) points out, this is supposed to be funny, whereas we never hear the counterpart "Take my husband—please!" This contrast illustrates that women are supposed to be much more enthusiastic about their spouses than men are. Also, the fact that women are more likely than men to be financially dependent upon their spouse would lead us to conclude that women are more positive about marriage.

In reality, however, the opposite is true. As Rhyne (1981) concludes from her review of the literature, "one of the few consistent findings is that men tend to be more satisfied with their marriages than women" (p. 941). In Rhyne's own study, men were more likely than women to fall in the top 20 percent of an overall Index of Marital Quality. Men were also more likely than women to give their marriages a "letter grade" of "A," to say that they never felt that marriage limited their freedom, and that they would marry the same person again.

Marriage also seems to provide other advantages for men. Bernard (1972), in her often-quoted book, *The Future of Marriage*, points out, "There are two marriages, then, in every marital union, his and hers. And his . . . is better than hers" (p. 14). Specifically, married men are much less likely than never-married men to have severe psychological disorders. For women, the pattern is the opposite; married women are *more* likely than never-married women to have psychological disorders. Although employment outside the home may improve matters for women (Rosenfield, 1980), a number of studies confirm the conclusion that men profit somewhat more from marriage than women do (Peplau & Gordon, 1985).

Why should this be true? Is it that women have more tedious responsibilities in marriage, for which they receive little appreciation? Are they disturbed by their relative powerlessness in the marriage? Are they simply more aware of the problems, just like the dating and cohabiting women who had broken up with their partners? Unfortunately, the explanations are not clear. You may be able to think of additional hypotheses for these sex differences in marital satisfaction.

Divorce

In 1980, there were more than one million divorces in this country, which is about three times the number recorded in 1960 (Albrecht, Bahr, & Goodman, 1983). The divorce rate among black families is about twice as high as among white families (McNett, et al., 1985; Semaj, 1982). According to some estimates, half of the first marriages currently taking place will end in divorce (Blumstein & Schwartz, 1983). Even though attitudes toward divorce are less negative than they used to be, the divorce experience is still traumatic for most women. Let us consider two aspects: the decision to divorce and reactions to divorce.

The decision to divorce.   It is very uncommon for both members of a couple to decide together to separate (Kelly, 1982). Usually, one partner wants to end the relationship more than the other does. This creates a painful, unbalanced situation in which one spouse is trying to close the door on a marriage, while the other spouse continues an attachment to this marriage.

Who is more likely to seek divorce, men or women? Folk wisdom might suggest that it is the men who are anxious to leave. However, recall that women are more likely to break up dating relationships. They are more likely to see problems in close relationships. Also, they are generally less happy with their marriages. These pieces of evidence would suggest that women are more likely to seek divorce. In fact, research generally shows that wives initiate divorce more often than husbands (Albrecht, et al., 1983; Kelly, 1982; Brown & Fox, 1979).

The decision to divorce is seldom impulsive. People usually contemplate the possibility of divorce for months or years before firmly deciding to seek a divorce. The decision is usually brought about by the growing realization that the pain of the relationship is greater than the security and gratification of being married (Kelly, 1982).

When women and men are asked about the problems in their marriage breakups, there are often sex differences. In research cited by Kelly, women provided more complaints than men did, a finding that is certainly consistent with our earlier discussion. Two-thirds of the women complained that they felt unloved, in comparison with 37 percent of the men. Women also complained that their husbands belittled their competence and criticized them too much. The most common complaint from the men (53 percent) was that their wives had been inattentive, neglecting the husband's needs and wishes. Men were also more likely than women to complain about dissimilarities in interests or values. Interestingly—and tragically—women were more likely to report physical violence in their marriages. Men did not mention this violence, and they tended to minimize it when they were specifically asked. (Spouse abuse is a major topic in Chapter 13.)

Reactions to divorce. As Albrecht and his coauthors concluded from their extensive study, "Divorce is painful, even for partners hopelessly mismatched" (p. 158). Divorce is particularly painful because it involves so many different kinds of separation, not only separation from a former spouse, but often separation from children, separation from friends and relatives previously shared by the couple, and loss of property previously jointly owned. In addition, a newly divorced person must learn to live independently and make decisions alone (Bohannan, 1970). Divorce is stressful for *both* women and men, though they may have somewhat different reactions.

The stress that people may experience in divorce was recently illustrated for me in an incident that seemed more in keeping with television drama than real life. Don and Joan were a young married couple who were acquaintances of ours. He was attending a Caribbean medical school while she continued her job in our area. Then we learned via Joan that Don had been killed in a plane crash at sea. We were shocked at this tragic loss of such a vital, ambitious person, and it took us many months to become accustomed to the idea that Don was no longer living. Imagine our surprise, then, when Don came to visit last month. He was greeted like a ghost by all who had been told of his demise. It turned out that Don had divorced Joan, and she found it less painful to explain his absence in terms of death, rather than divorce—even though the truth would eventually become apparent.

Research confirms that divorce is indeed stressful, second only to the death of a spouse in terms of the reorganization required in one's life (Holmes & Rahe, 1967). According to Kelly (1982), one common emotional reaction to the end of a marriage is anger, which women report twice as often as men do. Depression is another common reaction, and it has been observed equally among women and men. About one-fifth of both women and men reported that their reactions were so severe that they required psychiatric attention and possible hospitalization.

Another emotional reaction is one that Weiss (1975) describes as the "**persistence of attachment**"; although people may no longer love their ex-spouses, they may still feel a remaining bond. Weiss quotes a woman in her mid-forties who captures this sense of attachment, "He, who was the cause of my despair, was the only available human being, the only person I felt close to" (p. 36).

However, some newly separated people report positive emotions. Many people report feeling a sense of relief. According to Kelly (1982), about half of the respondents seem to be working out their problems shortly after separation. Women were more likely than men to express relief in one study (Chiriboga & Cutler, 1977), but in other studies there are no sex differences (Kelly, 1982).

Another positive reaction that people may feel after the breakup of a marriage is the feeling of a new chance. Kelly reports on a study in which one-fifth of the women felt that the divorce allowed them to begin over again. As might be expected, this was found in women who had sought a divorce, rather than those who opposed it. These women did not plan to remarry; they planned to strike out on their own.

Women often find that they are more capable than they had originally thought, particularly after the initial shock of separation. Brown (cited in Brown & Fox, 1979) asked divorced people whether they learned things about themselves that they never knew. Fifty-three percent of the women, in contrast to 15 percent of the men, supplied answers such as "I'm stronger than I thought I was."

The fact that women may find that they have hidden strengths does not diminish the pain and the stress of a divorce, particularly because divorce almost always brings financial hardship for women. Also, children may be severely affected by a divorce. However, there is evidence that women resolve their difficulties more rapidly than men (Caldwell, Bloom, & Hodges, 1984). Once the initial stress is reduced, women realize that they can continue with their lives in a positive fashion.

☐ SECTION SUMMARY ▪ Marriage and Divorce

1. **Men are typically more powerful than women in family relationships. "Money is power," and women with higher incomes have relatively more power in the family.**
2. **In a traditional marriage, the wife is not employed and the husband controls the money; the partners often do not share the same interests. In a modern marriage, gender roles are modified, but her work is clearly secondary to his. In an egalitarian marriage, traditional gender roles are absent; egalitarian marriages represent an ideal pattern rather than a common occurrence.**

3. There does not seem to be much evidence for the earlier idea of a black matriarchy, in which women are much more powerful than their husbands.
4. Marital satisfaction for women is high after marriage, but then it may decrease over the next 20 years, improving again after children have left home; however, even long-term marriages encounter problems.
5. Men tend to be more satisfied with their marriages than women are; married men also tend to have fewer psychological disorders than single men, whereas the reverse is true for women.
6. Women are more likely than men to initiate divorce. Women also have more complaints about their marriages than men do.
7. Divorce is almost always a stressful event. Women are more likely than men to react with anger; both women and men often react with depression. People may also experience a "persistence of attachment."
8. Women may have some positive emotions in connection with divorce, such as a sense of relief, a feeling of a new chance, and the discovery that they are stronger than they had thought.
9. After a divorce, women seem to resolve their difficulties more readily than men do.

☐ LESBIANS AND BISEXUAL WOMEN

A researcher visited the home of a California woman as part of a project on lesbians and gay men. Here is the summary of the interview:

> She was very friendly, interested, talkative, and open. I felt like I was a friend whom she was inviting in to share part of her life. I liked her paintings, her roommates' photographs of the Bay Area, and the warm togetherness of their home. She and her roommate were obviously very much in love. Like most people who have a good, stable, five-year relationship, they seemed comfortable together, sort of part of one another, able to joke, obviously fulfilled in their relationship. They work together, have the same times off from work, do most of their leisure activities together. She is helping her roommate to learn to paint, while her roommate is teaching her about photography. They sent me home with a plateful of cookies, a good symbolic gesture of the kind of welcome and warmth I felt in their home. [Bell & Weinberg, 1978, p. 220]

This description probably does not match the ideas that most Americans have about lesbians. The definition we will use for a **lesbian** is a woman who is psychologically, emotionally, and sexually attached to other women (Miller, et al., 1982). Most lesbians and current researchers on lesbian relationships prefer the term "lesbian" to the term "homosexual." They argue that the term "lesbian" acknowledges that the attachments involve emotional components, whereas "homosexual" emphasizes sexuality. In other words, they want to emphasize that lesbians have affectionate—not just sexual—attachments to other women, and that they choose to live lives centered within a women's community. Furthermore, the term "lesbian," like the term "gay," is more proud, political, healthy, and positive (Morin, 1977).

As you can imagine, it is difficult to obtain accurate estimates about lesbian relationships. According to some figures, however, 10 to 15 percent of American women have had at least one sexual contact with another woman (Dreyer, 1982; Wolfe, 1980). About 1 to 2 percent of women have had a more long-term lesbian relationship. Keep in mind, however, that we cannot be confident about the accuracy of these estimates.

Lesbians constitute a minority. Other minorities often have identifiable features, such as skin color, to distinguish them from the dominant majority. In contrast, lesbians are hidden. As one woman wrote, "We come in all colors, ages, and sizes, and from all socioeconomic levels; we look like everybody else and we are everywhere" (Webbink, 1981, p. 253).

There are five topics to consider in this section. Our first two topics are theories about the origins of lesbianism and the adjustment of lesbians. These two issues are ones that have received the most attention from psychologists—so much attention that some writers have complained that more important issues have been ignored (Morin, 1977; Sang, 1978). Our third topic is attitudes toward lesbians. Then, we will talk about the nature of lesbian relationships. Finally, we will consider bisexual women, an important area that has received little attention.

Theories about Lesbianism

When we try to put together a theory about how lesbians develop their psychological, emotional, and sexual preferences for women, it might be wise to raise an additional question. Specifically, how do *heterosexual* women develop their psychological, emotional, and sexual preference for men? Unfortunately, theorists have rarely considered this question, because heterosexuality is regarded to be natural and normal. That means that lesbianism is considered unnatural and abnormal, and abnormalities require an explanation. Often researchers have tried to figure out what *causes* lesbianism because they have hoped to try to figure out how to *prevent* it.

A number of different theories have been proposed, most of them not very satisfactory. One that would probably be popular among laypeople is that hormones or other physiological differences account for preferences. However, there is no firm evidence of any biologically based differences between lesbian women and heterosexual women (Meyer-Bahlburg, 1980; Morin, 1977; Ross, Rogers, & McCulloch, 1978).

Psychoanalytic models, based on Freudian theory, propose that lesbianism is caused by a girl's failure to move away from an emphasis on the clitoris and her failure to identify with her mother. (In fairness to Freud, we should mention that he was not extremely negative in his writings on homosexuality.)

There have been a variety of social-learning theories proposed to explain same-sex preferences. People may avoid the other sex because they have come to expect punishing consequences from them, or because they have a learned phobia or aversion. They may have learned same-sex preferences because of developmental experiences, such as exposure to pornographic pictures of people of their own sex. However, according to Morin's (1977) review, research has not supported these theories. A more recent theory proposed by Storms (1981) combines a social-learning approach with research information on the development of sex drive during early adolescence. This more complex kind of approach may offer a better explanation, but it is still too early to decide.

In their attempts to develop a theory of the origins of lesbianism, some researchers have looked at the family backgrounds of lesbians. These studies are generally inconclusive. In one study, lesbian women had the same attitudes toward their mothers as did heterosexual feminists and heterosexual traditional women. However, the lesbians were less likely to report a close relationship with their fathers (Johnson, et al. 1981). Another group of researchers observed that 60 percent of the lesbians in their study reported being equally close to both parents, but 45 percent perceived their mothers as rejecting, and 30 percent perceived their fathers as rejecting (Hogan, et al. 1977).

One problem with any study of this kind is that the participants' present attitudes and sexual preferences may color their perceptions of their childhoods (Johnson, et al., 1981). There *may* be some factors in the way parents rear their daughters that predisposes them toward same-sex preferences, though these factors certainly haven't been identified. What seems to be clear is that lesbian women can easily come from "normal" family backgrounds, as can heterosexual women.

At present we must conclude that biological, psychoanalytic, and simple social-learning theories cannot explain how people develop homosexual— or heterosexual—orientations. Furthermore, there do not appear to be any crucial characteristics of the families of lesbian women that are clearly linked to sexual preferences. We know that people differ in their choice of romantic partners, but we have no widely accepted theory to explain *why* they differ.

The Adjustment of Lesbian Women

Are lesbian women and heterosexual women equally well-adjusted? The question seems straightforward, but it is difficult to answer. Here are a few of the problems. Who counts as a lesbian woman? Most researchers place women in the "lesbian" category if they call themselves lesbians. That sounds reasonable enough, but there is a problem. Perhaps those women who are willing to call themselves lesbians are not representative of *all* lesbians. Perhaps they are unusually self-confident and straightforward. In contrast, the lesbians who report that they are heterosexuals—or who are unwilling to participate in psychology studies—may be less well-adjusted. Of course there is the additional problem of defining adjustment. One person may define adjustment in terms of conformity to the feminine stereotype, a definition with which many of us would disagree. As discussed in Chapter 1, operational definitions have an important influence on research results.

Let us consider a study by Oberstone and Sukoneck (1976), one that was particularly carefully executed. These authors compared lesbian women with single, heterosexual women. The groups were equal in terms of various factors such as income level, religion, and experience in therapy. Their adjustment was assessed with the Minnesota Multiphasic Personality Inventory, a widely-used test that is designed to measure psychological abnormalities. Everyone's responses to the test (which contained no measure of sexual preferences of the participants) were given to clinical psychologists. They were asked to classify each participant, on the basis of her responses, as to her psychological adjustment. The results showed that there were no significant differences in the adjustment of the two groups.

The psychologists were also asked to sort the test responses into two piles, guessing whether each set of answers had been given by a lesbian woman or a heterosexual woman. The psychologists' accuracy was at a chance level; there was nothing distinctive about the lesbians' responses that identified them as lesbians.

A number of other studies, reviewed by Mannion (1981), show no substantial differences in the adjustment of heterosexual and lesbian women. There may be some indication that lesbian women are more likely than heterosexual women to be alcohol abusers (Diamond & Wilsnack, 1978). Mannion suggests that alcohol abuse in lesbian women may be traced to a number of factors. In many areas, a gay bar is the only meeting place for developing companionships with other lesbians. It is also likely that some lesbians drink excessively as a way of coping with discrimination. As Mannion notes, "The implication is that being a lesbian per se is not a problem, but that integration of one's lesbian identity into social and cultural functioning may lead to problems" (p. 262).

It is also clear that the variability among lesbian women is great—as is the variability among heterosexual women. Bell and Weinberg (1978) called their book *Homosexualities* to reflect this diversity. They classified part of their sample as being in a close-knit relationship with another woman (like the relationship described in the introduction to this section). These women were similar to heterosexual women, except that they reported less loneliness. However, psychological problems were likely to occur among sexually active "singles" who regretted their lesbianism. To reword Mannion's statement, those women who successfully integrate their lesbian identity seem to be reasonably well-adjusted.

It is impressive that there are not more adjustment problems among lesbian women, given the stress that these women experience as a minority group (Brooks, 1981). A student described by Manahan (1982) asked heterosexual students in her classroom to imagine what life would be like if women who loved men had to hide their affection because society viewed their relationships as perversions. Imagine, wrote the student, that

> You cannot touch the man you love in public; you don't dare. If you do, you're seen with suspicion and fear by "normal" people as having made overt sexual gestures. Something as simple as a touch, holding hands, having your arms around each other, a friendly kiss—all these create shock waves around you. [p. 68]

Lesbian women also frequently find that they are estranged from their families. Their parents may consider them to be sick and refuse to acknowledge that they have a partner. As a consequence, the normal family-centered rituals that are important in our culture—such as birthdays, Thanksgiving dinner, and religious holidays—become annual reminders of the estrangement. Alternatively, lesbian women may not discuss their lesbianism with parents at all, and family reunions become occasions for embarrassing questions about marriage prospects.

It seems, then, that problems that lesbian women encounter may often be traceable to the stresses caused by having to hide important parts of their lives from other people (Mannion, 1981). This brings us to our next topic, how people view lesbians.

Attitudes Toward Lesbians

At Stanford University, a rather liberal school in the very liberal state of California, vandals badly damaged a statue titled "Gay Liberation" (Figure 9.3). Near the Women's Peace Encampment in Upstate New York, people in the surrounding towns posted signs such as "Nuke the Dykes." Elementary-school children call their enemies "queers," knowing that the name is an insult even if they do not understand what it means. Gay women and men are often physically attacked. In Hitler's Germany, thousands of gay men were systematically killed. There is no doubt that many people have strong antagonisms toward lesbians and gay men and that the discussion of same-sex preference is often taboo. (Students in my introductory psychology class frequently write on the evaluation forms that my discussion of homosexuality has no place in a psychology class.)

The word **homophobia** refers to the strong, irrational fear that many people have toward homosexuals (Weinberg, 1983). People with mild homophobia simply try to avoid homosexuals, and they wish that lesbians and gay men wouldn't make themselves "so obvious." People who are strongly homophobic may be quite open about their rage, often trying to enflame others against lesbians and gay males. Most homophobia lies somewhere in between. These homophobic people regard "homosexuals as loathesome, freakish things—criminals at worst or pathetic strangers at best—whose conduct must be curbed for society's protection" (Weinberg, 1983, p. 198). An additional problem is that gay people are likely to have absorbed some

FIGURE 9.3. **Statue "Gay Liberation," later damaged by vandals**

degree of homophobia from the culture they were raised in; they may be repulsed by their own homosexuality.

In general, people are more tolerant of lesbians than they are of gay males. You may recall that we mentioned in Chapter 3 that parents are more worried if a son dresses up in feminine clothes than if a daughter dresses up in masculine clothes. Also, people expect women to have close friendships and to travel together; close friendships among males or men travelling as a pair may be automatically suspect. Another intriguing idea for why people are more worried about gay males may be that women are regarded as less important than men, and so they are not taken as seriously when they violate the norms (Weinberg, 1983).

Social psychologists have known for some time that people often react in a predictable way to those who are seen as deviant. If one member of a group doesn't conform with the dominant view, the other group members work energetically to "convert the deviant" (Smith, 1979). Similarly, when a group of college women find out that a friend is a lesbian, they may try to change her ideas.

Professional therapists—as well as laypeople—can be homophobic. Smith (1979) describes the variety of methods that therapists have used to try to convert gay people to heterosexuality. The techniques have included castration, lobotomies, electroshock, drugs that cause nausea and vomiting, and various stressful kinds of psychotherapy.

"Compulsory heterosexuality" is the term that Rich (1980) uses to describe the view of many people that everyone *ought* to be heterosexual. Rich illustrates this attitude with a description of a treatment by a Norwegian doctor that would certainly qualify as stressful:

> A lesbian in Oslo was in a heterosexual marriage that didn't work, so she started taking tranquillizers and ended up at the health sanatorium for treatment and rehabilitation. . . . The moment she said in family group therapy that she believed she was a lesbian, the doctor told her she was not. He knew from "looking into her eyes," he said. She had the eyes of a woman who wanted sexual intercourse with her husband. So she was subjected to so-called "couch therapy." She was put into a comfortably heated room, naked, on a bed, and for an hour her husband was to . . . try to excite her sexually. . . . The idea was the touching was always to end with sexual intercourse. She felt stronger and stronger aversion. She threw up and sometimes ran out of the room to avoid this "treatment." The more strongly she asserted that she was a lesbian, the more violent the forced heterosexual intercourse became. This treatment went on for about six months. She escaped from the hospital, but she was brought back. Again she escaped. She has not been there since. In the end she realized that she had been subjected to forcible rape for six months. [p. 653]

For many years, the American Psychiatric Association regarded lesbians and gay males as deviants, though the "therapy" was not typically as extreme as that described by Rich. Their view was particularly influential because this organization publishes the *Diagnostic and Statistical Manual,* a book that psychologists and social workers—as well as psychiatrists—use to classify people's disorders. The 1968 edition of the manual classified homosexuality as a "sexual deviation," together with people who are child molesters, voyeurs, and exhibitionists (Sang, 1978).

On December 15, 1973, the American Psychiatric Association decided that homosexuality should not be listed as a disorder. Perhaps this represents the most spectacular "cure" ever accomplished. Overnight, millions of people were now considered normal rather than deviant! In the most recent edition of the manual (American Psychiatric Association, 1980), homosexuality is no longer listed. There was simply too much evidence, as we discussed earlier, that lesbians and gay males did not differ from heterosexuals in terms of their adjustment.

In addition, the American Psychological Association has become more concerned about the rights and welfare of lesbians and gay males. For example, a bibliography of Gay Concerns in Psychology is available by writing to the A.P.A. at 1200 Seventeenth Street, N.W., Washington, D.C. 20036. Also, in 1984, a new division of the A.P.A. was formed, using the name Society for the Psychological Study of Lesbian and Gay Issues.

Attitudes Toward Lesbians

Make photocopies of the questionnaire below and distribute it to several volunteers. To obtain the most valid answers, you may want to assure people that you have no way of identifying who filled out which questionnaire, for example by having all forms filled out with the same pen and asking people not to put their names on them.

Questionnaire

The purpose of this questionnaire is to determine current attitudes toward lesbian women. Please mark an X along the line to indicate your response to each question.

1. Lesbian women should not be hired for teaching positions in elementary schools.

1	2	3	4	5	6	7
Agree Strongly					Disagree Strongly	

2. A lesbian mother who is living with another woman should not be allowed custody of her child.

1	2	3	4	5	6	7
Agree Strongly					Disagree Strongly	

3. I would feel upset if I saw two women walking together hand in hand.

1	2	3	4	5	6	7
Agree Strongly					Disagree Strongly	

4. Lesbian women are much more likely to be psychologically disturbed than heterosexual women.

1	2	3	4	5	6	7
Agree Strongly					Disagree Strongly	

5. I would feel uneasy if I knew that a close female friend were a lesbian.

1	2	3	4	5	6	7
Agree Strongly					Disagree Strongly	

Many therapists have been reluctant to abandon the notion that homosexuality is abnormal. However, as Coleman (1982) concludes his review about treating gay clients, "The illness model of homosexuality is slowly being put to rest" (p. 88). Increasingly, therapists are trying to help their gay clients function better as lesbians and gay males. Coleman suggests that therapy should emphasize helping gay people to accept their sexual identity, to improve their interpersonal functioning, and to value their gay identity in a society that is predominantly heterosexual.

Attitudes toward lesbians and gay males may be growing less negative, particularly since the "experts" officially proclaim that gay people are not deviant. However, the public has not changed its views entirely. In one survey, 33 percent of the respondents thought that lesbians and gay males should not have equal rights in terms of job opportunities (Riess & Safer, 1979). Try Demonstration 9.2 in order to assess attitudes toward lesbians among your acquaintances.

Lesbian Relationships

At the beginning of the chapter, we stressed how the topic of love dominates our culture, both past and present. The songs that you hear on the radio, however, are almost all heterosexual in their orientation. Is love important to lesbian women, as well as to heterosexual women? The answer seems to be a strong "yes." One survey of Americans showed that most people—whether they were heterosexual or gay—considered love to be an extremely important determinant of their general happiness (Freedman, 1978). In Bell and Weinberg's (1978) study of lesbians in California, one-quarter of the sample said that having a permanent relationship with one partner was the most important thing in their life. An additional 35 percent said that it was "very important," and less than 25 percent reported that love relationships were not important to them.

There are several myths about lesbian relationships. One myth is that lesbian women have extremely romantic love relationships, bordering on the idyllic. In reality, lesbian women have views that are no more idealized or romanticized than matched samples of heterosexual women, gay men, or heterosexual men (Cochran & Peplau, cited in Peplau, 1983).

Another myth is that lesbian relationships mimic the gender-stereotyped behavior found in traditional heterosexual relationships. According to this myth, one partner plays the male, and the other plays the female. In lesbian relationships today, however, this role playing seems to be rare. Laner (1978) inspected the "personals" ad that appeared in a lesbian periodical to see whether women expressed an interest in "butch/femme" roles. The tally revealed that 91 percent of the lesbians did not mention a preferred gender role. Furthermore, an additional 7 percent of the ads specifically mentioned that they did not want stereotyped roles in a relationship. In general, lesbian women tend to reject rigid gender roles.

One study addressed an important component of gender-stereotyped behavior, the balance of power in a relationship. Caldwell and Peplau (1984) investigated 77 lesbian women who were currently in a romantic/sexual relationship. In all, 97 percent of the sample thought that both partners should have "exactly equal" power in a relationship. However, their perception of their own present relationships fell short of the ideal, because 39 percent of the women reported that one partner had more influence than the other. Although it is unfortunate that somewhat more than a third of the women were not enjoying an equal-power relationship, keep in mind that this means that a clear majority (61 percent) did report that both partners in their relationships were equally powerful. This percentage is undoubtedly much larger than it would be among married heterosexual couples.

If lesbian relationships are neither blissfully romantic nor gender-stereotyped, what are they? Letitia Anne Peplau and her colleagues have been exploring this question for several years. They remind us that most research has looked at only a small segment of the lesbian population, because the participants are usually younger, more educated, and more likely to be middle-class white women, in comparison with the entire lesbian population of the United States (Peplau & Amaro, 1982). However, lesbians tend to report that their relationships are relatively stable and long-term.

Most lesbians also regard their relationships as highly satisfying (Peplau & Amaro, 1982). Furthermore, some studies comparing lesbian women to heterosexuals and gay males show that satisfaction is approximately the same for all three groups (Caldwell, Finn, & Marecek, 1981).

Lesbian couples do report problems. In Blumstein and Schwartz's (1983) extensive study of American couples, one of the most frequent complaints mentioned by lesbian women was that they could not find enough time to be together. Also, there are many factors that keep heterosexual couples from splitting apart, such as the cost of divorce and joint investments in children and property (Peplau & Amaro, 1982). These factors are not barriers for lesbians, who also typically have little support from family members for their relationships.

What factors determine whether lesbians are satisfied with their current relationship? Peplau, Padesky, and Hamilton (1982) found that women were more likely to be satisfied if both partners were equally involved or committed to the relationship. In contrast, women were less happy when one partner was considerably more emotionally involved than the other. A second important factor was the balance of power in the relationship. Women reported greater satisfaction if both partners had equal "say" in decision making. Other factors that were relatively unimportant in determining satisfaction were the similarity of the two partners to each other, attitudes about love or feminism, or factors such as age or education. The balance within the relationship itself—rather than personal characteristics of the women—was the important determinant of satisfaction.

Many aspects of lesbian relationships have not been studied. Most lesbian women grew up in a family where heterosexuality was the ideal. Now they have rejected that model. However, there are no "rules" that are established for lesbian relationships. How do lesbian women decide what to do about issues such as dating, breaking up, and being friends with ex-partners?

How do they go about creating a "family" of friends who can be supportive and nurturant—and not necessarily romantic or sexual? Psychologists are only beginning to ask questions about these more subtle aspects of lesbian relationships.

Bisexual Women

A **bisexual woman** is a woman who is psychologically, emotionally, and sexually attached to both men and women. The word "bisexuality" is actually somewhat misleading, because it suggests that a bisexual person is located precisely in the middle, halfway between heterosexuality and homosexuality . . . equally attracted to both men and women at any given moment (Blumstein & Schwartz, 1977). In reality, bisexual women report fluctuations in their romantic interests.

It is just as difficult to estimate how many bisexual women there are in the United States as it is to make similar estimates about lesbians. By one estimate, however, 15 to 35 percent of the female population might be categorized as bisexual (Klein, 1978). In other words, there are probably more bisexual women than lesbian women. Unfortunately, researchers haven't paid much attention to bisexuality in either women or men, and they haven't tried to integrate bisexuality into any overall theory of sexuality (Blumstein & Schwartz, 1977).

Bisexuality should be more thoroughly investigated because it illustrates that human attraction patterns can be flexible. A woman with strong heterosexual attractions may, several years later, find an equally strong lesbian identity. From their research on 156 bisexual women and men, Blumstein and Schwartz conclude that the choice of a love partner can change in many ways and many times during a person's lifetime.

To illustrate the potential changeability in romantic attractions, Blumstein and Schwartz discuss a young professional woman who said in an interview that she considered herself to be a lesbian, beginning with her interest in other girls at the age of seven. A year after the interview, this woman wrote that she was in love with a man, and they were planning to get married. This kind of discontinuity, from a clear preference for women to a clear preference for men (or the reverse) was quite common in Blumstein and Schwartz's sample.

Although there has been little research on the adjustment of bisexuals, there is no reason to conclude that bisexual women have unusual difficulties. LaTorre and Wendenburg (1983) concluded in their study on self-esteem and satisfaction, "bisexual women display the same psychological characteristics as do heterosexual and homosexual women" (p. 95).

Bisexual women face several dilemmas. One dilemma involves the labeling problem. The testimony of one woman, in her letter to Charlotte Wolff (1977), illustrates the pressure that people sense in trying to find a label for themselves:

I do think it's hard being bisexual. That seems to be a strange thing to say because I think, and I think you agree with me, that we're all bisexual. What is hard is to live that way. After being [heterosexual] for most of my life I would like now to live without being emotionally involved with men, though the idea frightens me because I'm sure I'll get hurt by women as I never have by men ... but marriage or any settled heterosexual relationship fills me with horror ... a settled lesbian relationship? Well I do think the possibilities of a truly equal and sharing partnership are infinitely greater. More and more I think of myself as a lesbian and yet I'm writing to you as a bisexual partly in an effort to sort these things out and because I guess someone who can feel as close to a man as I have felt to Mike can't be a lesbian. I find the whole business very confusing, especially as it ought not to be even a matter of importance ... but given the way society is, it does matter, it's crucial. I find myself moving more and more among lesbians because I can't bear being the object of a man's heterosexual assumptions. [p. 152]

Bisexual women also frequently report that they feel isolated from both straight and gay communities. On the one hand, heterosexuals usually do not appreciate the distinction between lesbians and bisexual women. On the other hand, lesbian women are unsympathetic to a bisexual woman's interest in men; they claim that this interest is a "cop-out" that reflects an unwillingness to come to grips with a lesbian orientation (Blumstein & Schwartz, 1977). As a result, bisexual women may keep their bisexual feelings confidential from their friends, both straight and gay.

You may recall from Chapter 8 that we like to have neat categories for males and females, so that everyone fits nicely into one category or the other. Prejudice against lesbians and gay males can be partly traced to the fact that these people violate the rules of the categories; you aren't supposed to love someone in the same category as yourself.

Bisexuals provide an additional frustration for those who like neat categories. They cannot even be placed in a neat category of those lesbians and gay males, who *clearly* violate the categories!

☐ SECTION SUMMARY ▪ Lesbians and Bisexual Women

1. **Lesbians constitute a minority, though according to some estimates, 10 to 15 percent of American women have had at least one sexual contact with another woman.**
2. **Several theories have been proposed for the development of lesbian sexual preference, including hormonal, psychoanalytic, and social learning; none of them have much support.**
3. **The studies on the family backgrounds of lesbians are generally inconclusive.**
4. **There do not appear to be substantial differences in the adjustment of heterosexual and lesbian women, although alcohol abuse**

may be somewhat more common among lesbian women. Adjustment problems among lesbians are surprisingly rare, given the stress that they experience.

5. Homophobia refers to a strong, irrational fear that many people have toward lesbians and gay males.

6. Lesbians and gay males are often the victims of a "compulsory heterosexuality" attitude from heterosexual acquaintances.

7. The American Psychiatric Association decided in 1973 that homosexuality should not be listed as a disorder. This move encouraged both professionals and other people to develop less negative attitudes. However, views about homosexuality are still not positive.

8. Lesbian relationships are no more romanticized than heterosexual relationships.

9. Role playing in lesbian relationships seems to be rare; the majority of lesbian relationships have a roughly equal division of power between the two partners.

10. Satisfaction in lesbian relationships is related to the balance of involvement and the balance of power in a relationship.

11. Bisexuality has received relatively little attention from researchers.

12. Bisexual people illustrate the potential flexibility of romantic attractions.

13. Bisexual women do not appear to have unusual difficulties in psychological adjustment. However, they often report that they feel isolated from both straight and gay communities.

☐ SINGLE WOMEN

The category of single women overlaps with many of the groups of women we have already discussed. Women who are in dating or cohabiting relationships qualify as single. Women who are separated or divorced also qualify. So do lesbian women who are not married. Widows, whom we will consider in Chapter 14, are also single. In addition, the category of single women includes those who have never married. When you consider all the different ways in which a woman can be single, about one-third of all adult women in America qualify (Bequaert, 1976). What all of these women have in common is that they are not currently living with a husband.

Our emphasis in this section will be on those women who have never married, because they have not been considered elsewhere in the book. However, the other women share some of the same advantages and disadvantages that belong to these "never-married" women, and many of the statements made here apply to them as well.

FIGURE 9.4. **The marriage gradient (Bernard, 1972)**

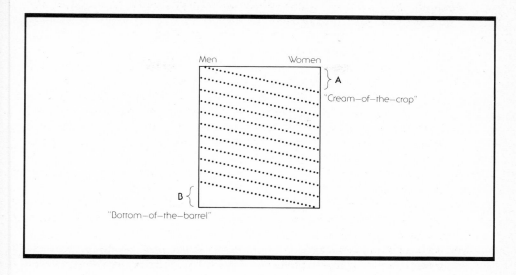

In recent years, there has been a dramatic change in the number of young adult women who are single. In 1960, only 28 percent of American women between the ages of 20 and 24 had not yet married. By 1981, 52 percent of women in that age range had not yet married (Blumstein & Schwartz, 1983). This trend seems to reflect a tendency to delay marriage, rather than avoid marriage. Black women are particularly likely to delay marriage. However, the clear majority of both black and white women marry at some point in their lives. Braito and Anderson (1983) note that less than 5 percent of black and white women between the ages of 55 and 64 have never married. Furthermore, the clear majority of unmarried undergraduate students say that they want to get married at some point in their lives. In one survey, for example, only 4.5 percent of undergraduate women said that they never wanted to get married (Greenglass & Devins, 1982).

Who Are the Single Women?

Jessie Bernard's book *The Future of Marriage* is often quoted in explaining why some women remain single (Bernard, 1972). According to Bernard, men tend to marry women who are slightly below them with respect to factors such as age, education, and occupation, creating a **marriage gradient**. As Figure 9.4 illustrates, the result of the marriage gradient is that there are two kinds of people who stay single, the "cream-of-the-crop" women (portion A of the figure) and the "bottom-of-the-barrel" men (portion B of the figure).

Bernard explains her rather crass terms, incidentally, by noting that her labels refer to marriageability, rather than worth as a human being.

At any rate, the marriage gradient explains why so many of us know single women in their thirties, who clearly qualify as "cream-of-the-crop." These women are looking for a potential spouse, but there are few Mr. Rights floating around. As one woman said in a study of single women, "I just didn't find the right person, with similar high standards and values, and was not willing to settle for second-best" (Loewenstein, et al., 1981, p. 1134).

Naturally, the marriage gradient isn't the only reason that women do not marry. Some of the other reasons given by women interviewed by Loewenstein and her colleagues included a breakup of a love affair, feeling that marriage and career were incompatible, and simply never being interested in getting married.

The marriage-gradient idea predicts that single women are well educated, and research confirms this. In a study discussed by Braito and Anderson (1983), women who were never married had an average of 15.9 years of education, in contrast to 12.8 for married women, 11.8 for divorced women, and 11.9 for widowed women. Furthermore, black single women show the same tendency as white women to be well educated (Braito & Anderson, 1983).

In an attempt to learn more about single women, Gigy (1980) administered several questionnaires to groups of never-married and currently-married women, all of whom were at least 30 years old. The single women were more likely to have attended college or graduate school, confirming our previous discussion. In addition, 88 percent of the single women and 40 percent of the married women were currently employed, with the single women more likely to hold professional-level jobs. The single women were also more likely to have well-educated parents.

The study also demonstrated that the single women generally did not differ from the married women in terms of life satisfaction. In addition, the two groups were similar in terms of personal adjustment. They differed in only two respects. Single women seemed to be more likely to be obsessive-compulsive, because they were more likely to report that they found criticism upsetting, that little things bothered them, and that they must keep to a strict schedule. Married women were more likely than single women to indicate that they were tired in the morning. Other parts of the study showed that single women were more assertive and more poised.

In asking "Who are the single women?" we need to keep in mind that there is probably no typical single woman, just as there is no typical woman who is dating, cohabiting, married, or lesbian. Braito and Anderson propose that there may be two major types of never-married women, those who are socially isolated and those who are socially active. The life styles of these two kinds of women are undoubtedly extremely different from each other, just as different as each group is from married women. Consistent with one of the themes of the book, individual differences among women are very large.

Attitudes Toward Single Women (based on Etaugh & Malstrom, 1981)

R ead the following paragraph:

> Susan Graham is 41 and married. She lives near Madison, Wisconsin. She has a master's degree from University of Wisconsin, and she is a counseling psychologist.

Now take out a sheet of paper, and rate Susan on each of the following attributes, where 1 = not at all and 7 = very much. In each case, try to give your first impression.

1. competitive
2. sociable
3. likable
4. influential
5. stable

6. happy
7. intelligent
8. attractive
9. successful at work
10. outgoing

11. friendly
12. relaxed
13. talkative
14. reliable
15. secure

Now, set aside those answers so that you cannot see them; try to clear your head of the previous task, and read the following paragraph:

> Susan Graham is 41 and single. She lives near Madison, Wisconsin. She has a master's degree from University of Wisconsin, and she is a counseling psychologist.

Take out a new sheet of paper, and rate Susan on the attributes listed above. Again, try to give your first impression. Then compare your responses in the two conditions.

Attitudes Toward Single Women

Think about the kinds of comments that were aimed at never-married women as you were growing up. If you are female, someone probably told you that if you weren't nicer to people, no one would want to marry you. There may have been speculations about why a single person your family knew had never married. At best, you may have been told never to refer to the fact that a relative was unmarried. My husband recalls as a small child having been told to call a card game "Donkey" rather than "Old Maid" in the presence of a never-married aunt. Often, single women are the objects of pity, if not outright scorn.

Before you read further, try Demonstration 9.3, which is based on research by Etaugh and Malstrom (1981). These authors rearranged the description in the paragraph so that the person was either male or female and was married, widowed, divorced, or never-married. Let us look specifically at the results for the never-married person. This individual was perceived as being less sociable than divorced or married individuals, less attractive than divorced, widowed, or married persons, and less reliable than married persons.

Etaugh and her colleagues have also tried to determine whether marital status is related to people's judgments of competence. Do people think that single people are professionally capable? The results here are quite complicated, but there is no clear tendency for single women to be judged less competent than married women (Etaugh & Foresman, 1983; Etaugh & Kasley, 1981; Etaugh & Riley, 1983). It seems, then, that single people are downgraded on characteristics that are socially relevant, but their never-married status is not vitally important when we judge their ability to do a job well.

Advantages and Disadvantages of Being Single

One of the advantages to being single that women mention most often is freedom. Single people are free to do what they want, when they want to, in the way they want. As a 56-year-old woman remarked,

> I have made tremendous changes in my life, but I have always had the control. I never had anyone say to me. "we don't want you anymore." I don't want to sound conceited, but I've kept the reins on my own life, obviously sometimes at a relatively high cost. I don't think I can analyze the ingredients. I was sometimes seen as a loner, which wasn't true. I like to do things on my own, which *was* true. There's a sense of doing things my way, finding out for myself what it's all about. I think that I've known what I wanted to do all along. [Bequaert, 1976, p. 9]

Single women also mention that privacy is an advantage for them. They can be by themselves when they want without the risk of offending someone. Single women also report that their status makes it easier to pursue career goals without compromise. They also mention that they have more opportunities to pursue a variety of friendships than they would if they were married (Loewenstein, et al., 1981).

When asked about the disadvantages of being single, loneliness is frequently mentioned. As one woman remarked, "I could drop dead tomorrow and no would would care" (Loewenstein, et al., 1981, p. 1133). However, in one survey, Gubrium (1975) found that many elderly never-married women said they really preferred being alone.

A single person is also at a disadvantage in communities where couples predominate. A newly separated woman expressed a sentiment that is probably shared by every variety of single women, "The whole town is married. ... I feel sometimes as though I had a social disease, as though I don't really belong here *really*" (Bequaert, 1976, p. 82).

However, most single people create their own social networks of friends and relatives. Many of them have a housemate with whom they share joys, sorrows, and frustrations (Loewenstein, et al., 1981). They tend to be closer to their brothers and sisters than are married women with children (Braito

& Anderson, 1983). Often these social networks are innovative. One woman described in Adams' book *Single Blessedness* (1976) developed a system that she called "Ten Top People." These were individuals to whom she could feel free to turn for immediate help or for sharing happiness. Thus, single women can develop alternate support systems for caring and sharing.

☐ SECTION SUMMARY ▪ Single Women

1. In recent years, there has been an increase in the number of young adult women who are single.
2. The marriage gradient creates a population of single women who are well educated and employed in prestigious occupations and a population of less "marriageable" single men.
3. Women remain single because of the breakup of a love affair, because they believe that marriage and career are incompatible, and because they are not interested in marrying.
4. Single women and married women are generally similar in terms of morale and personal adjustment.
5. People seem to have negative attitudes toward single people when they judge them on socially relevant characteristics, but not when they judge them in terms of professional competence.
6. Single women enjoy their independence and privacy, and they often mention loneliness as a disadvantage to being single, but most single women create alternate support systems.

Chapter Review Questions

1. Suppose that you read in a magazine aimed at teenage girls that males are particularly attracted to females who are pretty and feminine. How would the information in this chapter suggest otherwise?
2. At several points in the chapter, we compared women and men with respect to their emotional reactions, and there may be some differences with respect to falling in love, breaking up, and divorce. Recall as many of these differences as possible and try to see whether there is any pattern in these differences.
3. Throughout the chapter, we mentioned that love relationships are different from the way they were two to three decades ago. Discuss these changes with respect to cohabitation, marriage patterns, divorce, attitudes of professionals toward lesbians and gay men, and single women.
4. Love relationships seem to require many decisions. Discuss the decision to divorce, decisions about bisexuality, and the decision to remain single.
5. The issue of power was discussed several times in this chapter. Summarize the relationship between money and power in marriage, the di-

vision of power in the three kinds of marriages, power in black families, and the importance of the balance of power in lesbian relationships.

6. A neighbor woman has been married for 15 years, and she mentions to you that her marriage doesn't seem as fulfilling as it once did, though her husband seems satisfied. What information could you provide about how marital satisfaction depends upon the length of the marriage and whether a person is male or female?

7. What are the common emotional reactions that women have to divorce, both negative and positive?

8. Lesbian women and single women both have life styles that are different from the "norm." What are people's attitudes toward women in these two groups?

9. People who have negative attitudes about lesbian women and single women would probably be inclined to argue that there is something "wrong" with these women. Discuss information about the psychological adjustment of lesbian and single women.

10. Single women, by definition, are not living with husbands, and lesbian women usually do not have husbands. Both groups of women often develop other kinds of close relationships with others. Discuss the nature of these relationships.

☐ NEW TERMS

cohabitation	persistence of attachment
traditional marriage	lesbian
modern marriage	homophobia
egalitarian marriage	bisexual woman
black matriarchy	marriage gradient

☐ RECOMMENDED READINGS

Blumstein, P., & Schwartz, P. (1983). *American couples.* New York: William Morrow. ■ This book summarizes a large-scale study on the relationships of married, cohabiting, gay male, and lesbian couples.

Kelly, J. B. (1982). Divorce: The adult perspective. In B. B. Wolman (Ed.), *Handbook of developmental psychology* (pp. 734–750). Englewood Cliffs, N.J.: Prentice-Hall. ■ Kelly's chapter on divorce is well-organized, clear, and complete.

Peplau, L. A., & Amaro, H. (1982). Understanding lesbian relationships. In W. Paul, J. D. Weinrich, J. C. Gonsiorek, & M. E. Hotvedt (Eds.), *Homosexuality: Social, psychological, and biological issues* (pp. 233–247). Beverly Hills, Calif. Sage. ■ This chapter provides an excellent overview of lesbian relationships, focusing on current research issues.

Peplau, L. A., & Gordon, S. L. (1985). Women and men in love: Gender differences in close heterosexual relationships. In V. E. O'Leary, R. K. Unger, & B. S. Wallston (Eds.), *Women, gender, and social psychology* (pp. 257–291). Hillsdale, N.J.: Erlbaum. ■ Major topics in this chapter include what women and men want in relationships, falling in love, communication in relationships, and marital satisfaction.

(There is no recent book or review article on being single. I hope that a reader is inspired to write one!)

SEXUALITY

- An orgasm in a woman is primarily caused by stimulation of a sexual organ called the clitoris.

- Women and men have similar psychological reactions to orgasm.

- No matter how they are stimulated, women take at least three times as long as men to reach orgasm.

- Despite reports in the popular press, sexual activity among adolescents has changed very little in the last 50 years.

- Despite the "sexual revolution," males are still more likely than females to suggest sexual intercourse.

- When asked about the sexual revolution, most women claim that there are drawbacks, as well as advantages.

- The most common kind of dysfunction in women occurs among those who are sexually responsive yet don't reach orgasm.

- Sex therapy is now almost 100 percent successful in treating sexual dysfunction.

- The majority of sexually active teenagers use effective birth-control methods.

- Most women with unwanted pregnancies find it easy to make a decision to have an abortion.

"Thirty Days to a More Passionate Lovelife," proclaims an article in a popular magazine. The description reads, "For the happiest Valentine's Day ever, start our sexual shape-up program now!" Is this *Playgirl? Cosmopolitan? Mademoiselle?* No, it's the *Ladies Home Journal,* the magazine that women over 30 can usually count on for articles like "Ten Speedy Casseroles" and "Six New Centerpieces for Your Thanksgiving Table."

Sex sells. Several decades ago, American movie screens could not show a couple kissing for more than a few seconds (and their lips had to be dry, not moist). Now movie distributors regard a G rating as an invitation to financial failure. And of course sex also leaps out from the television screen— even in the family sitcoms—and from fiction and nonfiction books. Sexual-advice books are consistently popular. One book called *Open Marriage* sold about two million copies in its paperback version (Ross, 1980).

Sexuality has also been a reasonably popular topic for researchers, though, until recently, the taboo nature of the topic blocked systematic investigation. We will begin this chapter on sexuality with an overview of female sexual anatomy and the sexual-response cycle. From there, we will proceed to a less biological aspect of sexuality: sexual behavior and attitudes. The next topic is sexual dysfunction in women. Our final topic is birth control and abortion, a particularly important area in the 1980s.

☐ FEMALE SEXUAL ANATOMY AND THE SEXUAL-RESPONSE CYCLE

Let us begin this section by describing the external sexual organs in women. Then we will consider the sexual-response cycle and theories about orgasm. Finally, we will compare the sexual responses of males and females.

External Sexual Organs

Figure 10.1 shows the external sexual organs of an adult female. Ordinarily, the labia are folded in, covering the vaginal opening, but the labia are separated in this diagram in order to show the locations of the urethral and vaginal openings.

Mons pubis (pronounced "monz *pew*-bihs") is a Latin phrase referring to the fatty tissue in front of the pubic bones. At puberty, as we discussed earlier in this book, the mons pubis becomes covered with pubic hair. The **labia majora** (pronounced "*lay*-bee-ah mah-*jore*-ah") are the "large lips" or folds of skin that are just inside a woman's thighs. Located between the labia majora are the **labia minora** (pronounced "*lay*-bee-ah mih-*nore*-ah"), or "small lips." The size, shape, and color of both sets of labia vary greatly from one woman to another (Kitzinger, 1983).

The upper part of the labia minora forms the **clitoral hood,** which covers the clitoris. As we will see later in this section, the **clitoris** (pronounced "*klih*-tuh-riss") is a small, very sensitive organ that is central in females' sexual response.

FIGURE 10.1. **Female external sexual organs**

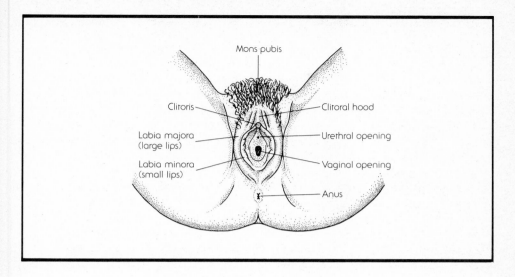

The **urethral opening** is the part of a woman's body through which urine passes; it is located just below the clitoris. Just below the urethral opening is the **vaginal opening,** and just below that is the **anus.**

Now turn back to the chapter on menstruation, pages 95–96, to review the internal sexual organs. Several of these structures will be important in the sexual-response cycle.

The Sexual-Response Cycle

The sexual-response cycle refers to the sexual reaction that has four sexual phases called excitement, plateau, orgasm, and resolution. These same four phases are found for both women and men. This cycle was described by William Masters and Virginia Johnson (1966) in their book *Human Sexual Response.* The book reports the results of their extensive laboratory studies, and many of the findings are still considered valid. Let's look at the four phases of the cycle in women.

Excitement phase. Women can become sexually excited through a wide variety of stimuli, such as erotic thoughts, arousing pictures, and—sometimes—exciting sounds or odors. However, touch is probably one of the most important sources of arousal. Certain areas of the body are particularly likely to produce sexual arousal when they are touched; these areas are called **erogenous zones.** In women, these erogenous zones may include the clitoris, the labia, the inner thighs, the mouth, and the breasts. However, we see once again that individual differences among women are substantial.

FIGURE 10.2. **The sexual-response cycle in females (based on Rathus, 1983)**

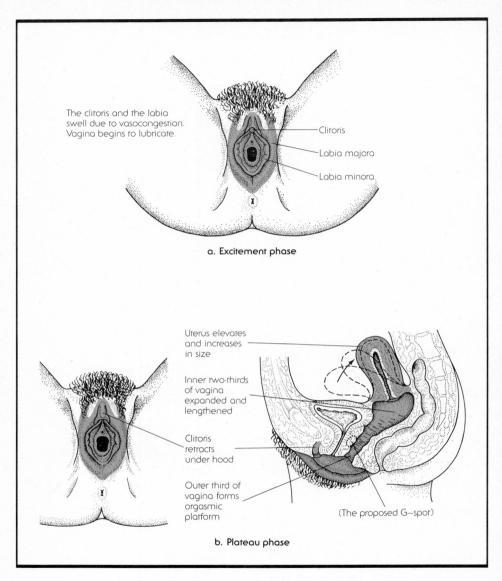

The clitoris and the labia swell due to vasocongestion. Vagina begins to lubricate.

Clitoris
Labia majora
Labia minora

a. Excitement phase

Uterus elevates and increases in size

Inner two-thirds of vagina expanded and lengthened

Clitoris retracts under hood

Outer third of vagina forms orgasmic platform

(The proposed G–spot)

b. Plateau phase

One woman may respond to a light touch on the breast; another may prefer kisses on the back of the neck.

During the **excitement phase,** blood rushes to the genital region, causing **vasocongestion** (pronounced "vaz-owe-con-*jess*-chun"), or swelling due to the accumulation of blood. One effect of vasocongestion is to produce droplets of moisture in the vagina, usually less than 30 seconds after sexual stimulation. A second effect is that the clitoris and the labia grow as they

FIGURE 10.2. *Continued*

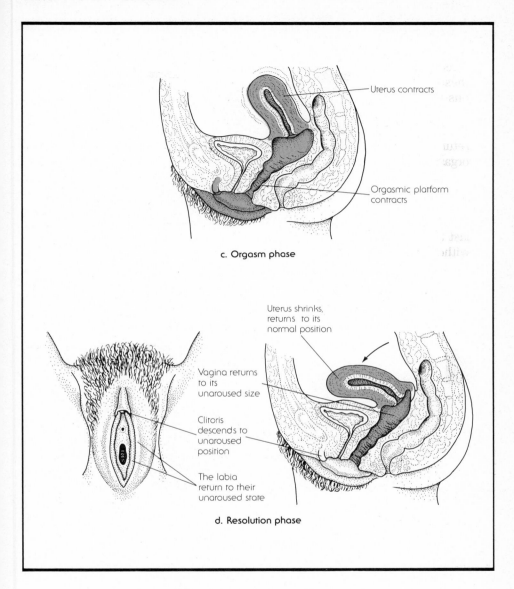

Uterus contracts

Orgasmic platform
contracts

c. Orgasm phase

Uterus shrinks,
returns to its
normal position

Vagina returns
to its
unaroused size

Clitoris
descends to
unaroused
position

The labia
return to their
unaroused state

d. Resolution phase

fill with blood. Toward the end of the excitement phase, the upper two-thirds
of the vagina grows longer and larger, and the uterus elevates somewhat and
grows larger. Heart rate, breathing rate, and muscle tension also increase.
Figure 10.2a illustrates the excitement phase.

Plateau phase. During the **plateau phase,** the lower one-third of the
vaginal wall becomes filled with blood. This enlarged region is now called

the **orgasmic platform.** If effective sexual stimulation continues, there will be further increases in heart rate, breathing rate, and muscle tension. The clitoris shortens in length, and it draws back under the clitoral hood, as shown in Figure 10.2b. The clitoral region is now extremely sensitive, so that movement of the hood—from either thrusting of the penis or other touching—causes stimulation of the clitoris.

Orgasmic phase.   During the **orgasmic phase,** the orgasmic platform and the uterus contract strongly at regular intervals. These contractions occur at 0.8 second intervals, and a woman generally experiences between three and 15 of these contractions with an orgasm. Figure 10.2c illustrates these reactions. Notice, then, that the orgasm—which is the topic of numerous popular articles, psychological theorizing, and private conversations—usually lasts less than 10 seconds!

Resolution phase.   During the **resolution phase,** the sexual organs return to their earlier, unstimulated state, as shown in Figure 10.2d. The orgasmic platform in the lower one-third of the vagina subsides rather quickly. The upper two-thirds of the vagina shrinks back to its unstimulated state in a much more leisurely fashion. The clitoris emerges from under the clitoral hood, but the size and shape may not return to normal until half an hour later. The labia and the uterus also return to their previous states. Breathing slows, muscles relax, and heart rate decreases. The resolution phase may last 30 minutes or more. Females, however, can have additional orgasms without going directly into the resolution phase.

Theories of Orgasm

Sigmund Freud was disturbed by the fact that many women could reach orgasm freely and rapidly by masturbating, yet they reached orgasm less often during intercourse (Faunce & Phipps-Yonas, 1979). He therefore proposed that there were two different kinds of orgasms in women, clitoral and vaginal. The **"clitoral orgasm"** was one that most women could achieve by masturbating and stimulating themselves in the clitoral region. He suggested that a young girl may masturbate, but a sexually mature woman should shift to a **"vaginal orgasm,"** as experienced during intercourse. Adult women who prefer clitoral stimulation were supposedly immature and neurotic, according to Freud.

The research of Masters and Johnson (1966), however, reached a different conclusion. According to their observation, clitoral and vaginal orgasms are physiologically identical. The orgasm results from stimulation of the clitoris, either from direct touching in the clitoral area or from indirect pressure from a partner's thrusting penis.

Recent surveys suggest that women usually prefer clitoral to vaginal stimulation. In a study described by Lewis and Lewis (1983), two-thirds of the women said that they would choose clitoral stimulation, if they had to make a choice. In a survey of readers of *Cosmopolitan* magazine, about three-quarters attributed their orgasms to clitoral manipulation, in contrast to one-third who attributed them to vaginal entry (Wolfe, 1980). If orgasms from vaginal stimulation are the only "normal" ones, as Freud proposed, then most women would be abnormal!

Most researchers now acknowledge that clitoral stimulation is more likely than vaginal stimulation to give a strong orgasm, with greater reliability. Still, many women feel embarrassed about requesting clitoral stimulation from male sexual partners. As one woman remarked, " . . . sometimes I feel guilty, or like I'm intruding, bothering him. I *know* it's ridiculous and masochistic, but I still *do*" (Hite, 1976, p. 213). Other women find that their reluctance to enjoy clitoral stimulation may inhibit their sexual response. One woman reported, "Orgasm by clitoral stimulation occurs seldom with my partner because I feel very self-conscious when being acted upon without doing anything to the other person" (Hite, p. 124). Also, some women prefer vaginal stimulation because it can permit closer total skin contact with their partner.

Sex Differences and Similarities in the Sexual-Response Cycle

The research of Masters and Johnson and other more recent observations force us to draw a conclusion that would have been considered absolutely startling at the beginning of the century: Women and men are remarkably similar in many aspects of the sexual-response cycle. Notice that this conclusion echoes our more general conclusion throughout the book that women and men are not as different as we might think. Let us look at several topics:

1. *Women and men both experience the same four phases in the cycle.* As Masters and Johnson (1966) pointed out, both men and women experience vasocongestion, and their orgasms are physiologically similar. As they write: "The parallels in reaction to effective sexual stimulation emphasize the physiological similarities in male and female responses rather than the differences" (p. 285).
2. *Women and men have similar psychological reactions to orgasm.* Look at Demonstration 10.1 and try to guess who wrote each passage; the answers are at the end of this section. Vance and Wagner (1977) asked people to guess which description of orgasms were written by women and which were written by men. Most of the respondents were unable to guess at better than a chance level. Furthermore, Wiest (1977) asked students to rate the word "orgasm" on 18 different scales such as "good-bad," "clean-dirty," "strong-weak," "hard-soft," and "sharp-dull." Male and female students provided almost identical ratings.
3. *Women can reach orgasm as quickly as men.* When a man and a woman are having intercourse, the man is likely to reach orgasm more quickly than the woman. Since the woman's clitoris is the focus of her orgasmic response, the clitoris must be aroused by the relatively

Psychological Reactions to Orgasm

Try to guess whether a female or a male wrote each of the following descriptions of an orgasm by placing a F or a M in front of each passage. The answers can be found at the end of the section.

_____ 1. A sudden feeling of lightheadedness followed by an intense feeling of relief and elation. A rush. Intense muscular spasms of the whole body. Sense of euphoria followed by deep peace and relaxation.

_____ 2. To me an orgasmic experience is the most satisfying *pleasure* that I have experienced in relation to any other type of satisfaction or pleasure that I've had which were nonsexually oriented.

_____ 3. It is like turning a water faucet on. You notice the oncoming flow but it can be turned on or off when desired. You feel the valves open and close and the fluid flow. An orgasm makes your head and body tingle.

_____ 4. A build-up of tension which starts to pulsate very fast, and there is a sudden release from the tension and desire to sleep.

_____ 5. It is a pleasant, tension-relieving muscular contraction. It relieves physical tension and mental anticipation.

_____ 6. A release of a very high level of tension, but ordinarily tension is unpleasant whereas the tension before orgasm is far from unpleasant.

_____ 7. An orgasm is a great release of tension with spasmodic reaction at the peak. This is exactly how it feels to me.

_____ 8. A building of tension, sometimes, and frustration until the climax. A *tightening* inside, palpitating rhythm, explosion, and warmth and peace.

(From Vance & Wagner, 1977, pp. 207–210)

inefficient stimulation provided by the thrusting penis and its action on the clitoral hood. In contrast, the man's penis receives direct stimulation. Direct stimulation in the clitoral region, however, provides a rapid orgasm in women, on the average within three minutes (Tavris & Wade, 1984). It's important to stress, though, that "faster" isn't necessarily "better."

4. *Women are more likely than men to have multiple orgasms.* According to Masters and Johnson (1966), women are capable of multiple orgasms. That is, women can remain susceptible to stimulation right after they have had an orgasm, and they can experience additional orgasms soon after the first one. The discovery of these multiple orgasms brought both good news and bad news for women. The good news is that women are now more likely to be viewed as sensual, active people, rather than "frigid" or passive. The bad news is that

women now are forced to adopt a new standard; one orgasm is no longer good enough! As Schover (1982) observed, the previous Victorian prohibitions are now replaced with olympic standards for sexual performance.

Masters and Johnson (1966) wrote that men differ from women because men have a refractory period, a time immediately after an orgasm during which they cannot have an erection, no matter how tantalizing the stimulation. The refractory period is usually about 30 minutes for younger men, and somewhat longer for older men (Radlove, 1983). However, several researchers believe that some men are capable of multiple orgasms during a single act of intercourse (Tavris & Wade, 1984). It's not clear how many men can have multiple orgasms, and multiple orgasms are more likely in women than in men.

5. *Men ejaculate; it's not clear whether some women do.* From what you've read so far, women and men may seem to be nearly identical in their sexual responses. Ten years ago, researchers would have pointed to one clear sex difference: Men **ejaculate** (or expel semen from the penis) whereas women have no similar process. However, several researchers have suggested that some women have a sexual response similar to ejaculation. Apparently, when some women have an orgasm, they expel a fluid through the urethral opening (Perry & Whipple, 1983). It seemed that this discharge was related to stimulation of the Gräfenberg spot, or **G-spot.** This small anatomical structure is located on the front surface of the vagina (see Figure 10.2b). Researchers initially argued that this fluid was chemically similar to semen, except that it contained no sperm (Radlove, 1983), but Goldberg and his coauthors (1983) analyzed the fluid and found that it resembled urine, not semen. The current status of the G-spot is not clear. However, it is clear that the discovery of a new erogenous zone has created even more impossible standards for women. Women who might have otherwise been happy about their sex lives now may feel inadequate if they don't achieve at least half a dozen orgasms, preferably accompanied by discharge.

(The answers to Demonstration 10.1 are 1.F; 2.M; 3.F; 4.F; 5.M; 6.M; 7.M; 8.F.)

☐ SECTION SUMMARY ▪ Female Sexual Anatomy and the Sexual-Response Cycle

1. **The external sexual organs include the mons pubis, labia majora, labia minora, clitoral hood, clitoris, and vaginal opening.**
2. **During the excitement phase (the first of four phases in the sexual-response cycle) blood rushes to the genital area, which produces moisture and a change in the size and shape of sexual organs.**

3. During the plateau phase, the orgasmic platform forms in the lower one-third of the vagina, and there is an increase in breathing rate, muscular tension, and heart rate.
4. During the orgasmic phase, the orgasmic platform and the uterus contract strongly.
5. During the resolution phase, the sexual organs regain their original size and shape, and there is a decrease in breathing rate, muscular tension, and heart rate.
6. Freud proposed that clitoral orgasms could be achieved by masturbating, but mature women should experience vaginal orgasms during intercourse.
7. According to Masters and Johnson, clitoral and vaginal orgasms are physiologically identical; surveys also show that women prefer clitoral stimulation to vaginal stimulation.
8. Women and men are similar in their sexuality in several respects: (a) they both experience the four phases in the cycle; (b) they respond similarly to orgasm; and (c) with certain kinds of stimulation, women reach orgasms as quickly as men.
9. However, women are more likely than men to have multiple orgasms; also, men ejaculate and it is unclear whether some women produce discharge.

☐ SEXUAL BEHAVIOR AND ATTITUDES

We've looked at the biological side of sexuality, discussing female sexual anatomy and the physiology of the orgasm. Now let's turn our attention to women's sexual behavior and attitudes, including sex education and early sexuality, sexual role playing, sexual activities, sexuality among lesbians, and sexuality in older women. Our last topic is the "sexual revolution"—a change that has both disadvantages and advantages.

Sex Education and Early Sexuality

Take a moment to think about your early thoughts, experiences, and attitudes about sexuality. Was sex a topic that produced half-suppressed giggles on the school bus? Did you worry if you were "normal" or too experienced or not experienced enough? Clearly, sexuality is an important topic for adolescents—and many preadolescents. In this section, we'll examine how children learn about sexuality, both at school and at home. Then we will discuss sexual activity among adolescents.

What do our school systems have to say about sexuality? According to Zellman and Goodchilds (1983), the answer usually is "not much!" School teachers and administrators often resent having to teach about the real-life problems involved in sexuality and they often decide to leave out "objectionable" topics such as intercourse, contraception, and abortion. As Zellman and Goodchilds write, "Such courses are most often limited to what one educator has called 'an organ recital'—what is connected to what in the body, with no discussion of how or why two bodies might connect with each other" (p. 53). In other words, the whole social psychological side of sexuality is ignored. As a result, sex education in school often has little impact.

However, parent-child communications about sex may have an impact. Research has demonstrated that adolescents who had received most of their sex education from a parent were less likely to be sexually experienced and more likely to use proper contraceptives if they were sexually active (Fox, 1980; Zellman & Goodchilds, 1983). Mothers seem to feel more comfortable than their daughters about discussing topics such as sexual intercourse and birth control (Fox & Inazu, 1980). Think back about your own conversations with your parents or other grownups about sexuality; did they seem more relaxed than you were?

It's no surprise that there has been a dramatic increase over the last decades in sexual activity among adolescents. According to one writer, the percentage of high-school females who reported premarital intercourse increased from about 10 percent in 1925 to about 44 percent in 1979 (Dreyer, 1982). During the same period, the increase for college females was from 25 percent to 74 percent. However, an article in *Time* magazine assures us that the revolution is now over and adolescents are now more sexually conservative (Leo, 1984a). We'll return to this topic of the sexual revolution later in the section.

In general, the sexual activity of young women in the 1980s almost matches the sexual activity of young men (Dreyer, 1982; Katz & Cronin, 1983; Tavris & Wade, 1984). Furthermore, one investigation of college students discovered that 95 percent of men and women favored identical standards for men and women in love relationships, thus rejecting the traditional "double standard" for sexual conduct (Peplau, Rubin, & Hill, 1977).

Those are the statistics. How do women react to their first sexual experience? If a survey of *Cosmopolitan* readers is representative, the experience is rarely positive (Wolfe, 1980). The majority replied something like "I had no particular reaction" or "It was painful and upsetting" (p. 255). One respondent recalled,

> The first time I had sex, it was awful. We did it at my boyfriend's house. . . . We went over there after school, but instead of necking or petting, like we usually did, he undressed me, got on top of me, and the next thing I knew it was all over. It was a big nothing. . . . I started to cry. [p. 255]

In all, slightly less than one-fifth of the women in the survey thought that the first time was "thrilling." Other reports echo this observation that the first sexual experience is likely to be unsatisfactory (Kitzinger, 1983).

In short, early introductions to sexuality seem to be far from pleasant. Schools ignore the "important issues," and young people feel uncomfortable in discussions of sexuality at home. Sexual activity has increased among adolescents, but initial experiences are generally unpleasant for young women. We now turn to a topic that is important for both adolescents and older people, sexual role playing.

Sexual Role Playing

Imagine that Nancy and Keith have been dating for several months. Nancy is anxious to have sexual relations, but Keith is resistant. He is much less sexually experienced than she is, and he wants to wait until he is really convinced that Nancy loves him. He is afraid that Nancy is really after his body, rather than a meaningful relationship.

Does this sound familiar? Probably not. Traditionally, men are supposed to be the initiators of sexual relationships, even as far as the positioning of the bodies, whereas women are expected either to resist or to passively comply with their partner's advances (McCormick & Jesser, 1983). It seems, then, that women and men may now be similar in their early sexual experience, but the politics of seduction have not changed substantially.

Peplau, Rubin, and Hill (1977) surveyed dating couples and found that men consistently play the role of the sexual initiator; they are the ones who first suggest intercourse. Women may communicate that they are interested, but they are not likely to initiate sexual relations. Women hold negative control; they tend to either reject the man's advances or to slow down the pace of escalating sexuality. In their survey, couples who had not had intercourse usually indicated that it was because the girlfriend was reluctant; very few mentioned that the boyfriend was reluctant.

We have seen that males are the initiators among dating couples. How about the politics of sex for married and cohabiting couples? Who makes the requests and rejections in the bedroom? Blumstein and Schwartz (1983) conducted the large-scale study of American couples that we mentioned throughout the last chapter, and their study also included questions about sexual behavior. They found that there is some move toward equality, but initiation is still likely to be the man's prerogative, whereas refusal is the woman's. A reversal of these roles may be uncomfortable for both. One woman reported an incident that occurred shortly before she was scheduled to leave town on business.

> Right before I left I was making advances to Larry. He told me he felt like he was being used before I was going out of town. It is all so classical a situation in reverse! So on one hand we sort of laughed about it. But on the other hand, it was really there. I said, "I see your point." I knew it was a problem area for him so I just backed off. [p. 211]

Before you read further, try Demonstration 10.2, which is based on the results of *Playboy* Magazine's (1983) survey of college students. One stereotype related to the "male-as-initiator" concept is that women require a

Level of Commitment Required for a Sexual Relationship

Try to guess how college females and males responded to this *Playboy* survey. They were asked, "How close or formal a relationship is necessary for you before you enter a sexual relationship?" Estimate how the percentages were distributed across the four categories for females, and then repeat the process for males. The answers appear at the end of this section.

	% Females	% Males
1. Casual acquaintance		
2. Friendship		
3. Love		
4. Engagement or marriage	_____	_____
	100%	100%

more meaningful commitment before they engage in a sexual relationship. If you checked the answers at the end of this section, you saw that this gender stereotype is indeed supported by reality. Many men feel that sex with a casual acquaintance is perfectly acceptable, whereas women are likely to require either love or a more formal commitment before they enter a sexual relationship. The answers for this survey are at the end of this section, and other research supports this finding. For example, Carroll, Volk, and Hyde (1985) found that 45 percent of females said that emotional involvement was always a prerequisite for sexual intercourse, in contrast to only 8 percent of males.

If males are more likely to be the initiators, then it may be that they enjoy sex more than females do. One creative way of studying this issue is illustrated in a study by Mancini and Orthner (1978). These researchers asked more than 500 married, middle-class residents in the Southeast to select their five favorite leisure-time activities out of a list of 96 choices. The men in the sample chose sexual and affectional activities most often, even more often than attending an athletic event. Women chose reading as their most preferred activity, and sexual and affectional activities tied with sewing for second place. In other words, men like sex more than football, but women prefer a good novel. Of course, women's relative lack of interest in sex may have a very legitimate explanation. As we saw in the last section, traditional sexual relations that are oriented exclusively toward intercourse may not be very satisfying for women. Also, the sex differences may be due to stereotypical expectations, because "good" women are not supposed to be very interested in sex.

(The answers to Demonstration 10.2 are: Females: 1. 10%; 2. 33%; 3. 46%; 4. 11%; Males: 1. 31%; 2. 38%; 3. 21%; 4. 10%.)

Sexual Activities

We already saw that young men are somewhat more likely than young women to have early sexual experiences, though the sex differences are relatively small in the 1980s. How about other kinds of sexual activities; what do women do and what do they enjoy?

Consider "foreplay," for example. **Foreplay** includes kissing, hugging, and other sexual activities that increase arousal. Many of the respondents in the *Cosmopolitan* survey did not draw the traditional line between foreplay and intercourse (Wolfe, 1980). Rather than a preliminary to sex, they saw foreplay as an accompaniment, or even a replacement. One woman wrote,

> Most of the people I know make no distinction between foreplay and the big game itself. My lover and I usually end our sessions with intercourse, because we both enjoy it a lot, but we don't think of the things we do beforehand as getting ready for intercourse but as pleasures in and of themselves. [p. 257]

Similarly, Blumstein and Schwartz (1983) found that the couples in their study enjoyed the sensuality of kissing.

Do women enjoy erotica? For many years, this issue was ignored by researchers, because it was "common knowledge" that women didn't enjoy erotic pictures or literature. However, experimental investigation raised doubts about the old rule that women were indifferent (Fisher & Byrne, 1978). Women frequently have had less contact with erotica; they certainly are less likely to buy it (Fisher, 1983). Also, they may be shy about reporting that they are aroused by it. Furthermore, women sometimes are unaware when they are sexually aroused (Heiman, 1975), probably partly because their physiological reaction during arousal—droplets of moisture produced by the vagina—is much more subtle than a man's erection. However, when arousal is measured in terms of blood volume in the penis or in the vagina for college student volunteers listening to erotic tapes, women show just as much arousal as men (Heiman, 1975). In other words, women seem to respond at the physiological level to erotica, though they may not always report that they are aroused.

Surveying a wide range of recent studies on responses to erotica, Fisher (1983) concluded that men and women can be similarly aroused by erotic photos, literature, movies, and fantasies. There is even evidence that women and men tend to get "turned on" by the same kind of erotica (Fisher & Byrne, 1978). For example, *both* men and women are more sexually aroused by erotica with a casual-sex theme (in which a couple had just met at a dance), rather than either a love theme (sex between a husband and wife) or a lust theme (sex between a man and a prostitute). Women may be more likely than men to require true love or commitment before they, personally, engage in sex, but they don't mind watching sex between casual acquaintances!

We have said that women and men respond quite similarly to erotica, yet they are perceived as responding differently. Notice that this observation is yet another illustration of two of the themes of the book: Sex differences are perceived to be large, but they are often relatively small.

One kind of sexual activity in which there are clear sex differences is masturbation. A review of studies on this topic show that males consistently masturbate more than females (Dreyer, 1982). For example, in one survey of 16- to 19-year-olds, more than two-thirds of the males and half of the females masturbated at least once a week (Hass, 1979). Why is there such a substantial sex difference here? It may be that males' genitals are simply more obvious, and young boys are more likely to discover pleasure in handling their genitals in the process of urination. It also may be that young boys are more likely than young girls to hear others talking about masturbation. Can you think of any other reasons?

Sexuality among Lesbians

So far, much of the discussion about sexual activity has focused on heterosexuality. Is sexuality substantially different in lesbian relationships?

In the last chapter, we looked at emotional and power issues in love relationships among lesbians. Now let's examine sexual behavior. There is a stereotype that portrays lesbians as highly sexual people, and this stereotype may be partially responsible for the public's focus on lesbians' sexuality, rather than on other aspects of their relationships (Peplau & Amaro, 1982). (The topic of lesbianism is discussed in the love-relationship chapter rather than the sexuality chapter in order to help reduce this stereotype.)

Physiologically, lesbians and heterosexual women show the same kind of sexual response. That is, "the physiological mechanics of sexual arousal and orgasm are similar for all women, regardless of sexual orientation" (Peplau & Amaro, 1982, p. 243).

Lesbian and heterosexual women are also similar in their emphasis on emotional involvement in connection with sexual relationships. A number of studies on lesbians, summarized by Peplau and Amaro (1982) and by deMonteflores and Schultz (1978), indicate that about 90 percent of lesbian women stress the importance of emotional attachment in sexual relationships. Also, lesbian couples are much more likely than heterosexual couples or gay-male couples to include kissing in their lovemaking (Blumstein & Schwartz, 1983).

Most lesbians find that their sexual relationships are highly satisfying; in one study, three-quarters of the women described sex with their steady partner as extremely satisfying. They also seem to reach orgasm more often than heterosexual women when they make love (Peplau & Amaro, 1982).

It is not clear whether heterosexual women and lesbian women differ in the frequency with which they have sex. According to one summary, the two groups are similar (Peplau & Amaro, 1982), but Blumstein and Schwartz's (1983) survey concluded that lesbians have sex far less frequently than any other type of couple, at every point in their lives. Thus, we cannot draw any conclusions on the relative frequency of sexual experiences for lesbians, though it does seem likely that lesbian women are generally more satisfied with the quality of these sexual experiences.

Sexuality and Older Women

Prior to the work of Masters and Johnson (1966), it was commonly believed that any sexual responsiveness a young woman might have (and this was generally thought to be very low) was drained away by the time she reached 50 or 60. This negative view of older women was entirely consistent with the generally negative attitude toward older women that we'll explore in Chapter 14. Masters and Johnson destroyed this myth by concluding that "significant sexual capacity and effective sexual performance are not confined to the human female's premenopausal years" (p. 238). Even after a woman's reproductive period has ceased, she can still remain a sensual person.

There are some changes as women grow older. As we will see in Chapter 14, estrogen production drops rapidly at menopause. Consequently, the vagina loses some of its elasticity. Vaginal moisture production may also drop. However, these problems can be at least partially corrected by using supplemental lubricants, and women who have been sexually active throughout their lives may show no reduction in moisture production. As A. R. Allgeier (1983) writes, "Sexy young people mature into sexy middle-aged and elderly people" (p. 144).

Of course the tragic aspect of sexuality in older women is that women may maintain the physiological capability to respond sexually and they may maintain an enthusiastic interest in sexual relationships, but they might no longer have a partner. Heterosexual women are likely to outlive their husbands, or their husbands may leave them for younger women. Some husbands may no longer be able to maintain an erection, and men may stop all sexual relations once intercourse is not possible. A large number of elderly women therefore lack both sexual relations and contact warmth (Weg, 1983).

As an additional insult, people seem to think that older women should be asexual. Most college students believe that their parents have intercourse once a month or less, and many students have great difficulty even filling out a questionnaire about their parents' sexuality (Pocs, et al., 1983). Also, sexuality seems to be condemned more in older women than in older men. The "dirty old man" will be tolerated with a smile, but the "dirty old woman" is viewed with suspicion or disgust. Datan and Rodeheaver (1983) write about an old woman and an old man who fell in love in a nursing home. The old man's children thought that his behavior was "cute," but the old woman's children thought that her behavior was disgraceful. Despite her protests, they removed her from the nursing home. One month later, in a final protest, she died. Datan and Rodeheaver hope that in future years, we can come to appreciate "the expressions of sexuality and love that are uniquely appropriate to each of the seasons of human life" (p. 287).

The Sexual Revolution

With all the talk about the sexual revolution, it's tempting to ask "Who won?" We mentioned earlier that women often resent the pressure of having "olympic standards" for sexual responsiveness. Women may have discovered a greater number of positions for intercourse, and they may have sexual relations with a greater number of partners, but they don't seem to be any happier than before the revolution. "More" isn't "merrier." Consider the survey of the *Cosmopolitan* readers, keeping in mind that the "*Cosmopolitan* girl" is to many people the symbol of the sexually liberated woman. In that survey, the number of women who had felt that the revolution had been a good thing was almost exactly balanced by the number who had experienced difficulties (Wolfe, 1980). Many women reported that sex had lost meaning for them; quantity certainly didn't seem to guarantee quality.

The sexual revolution has produced an additional unpleasant consequence. In the past, a woman could refuse a man's advances and not imply that she was rejecting him personally. Now that people are more likely to acknowledge that women enjoy sex, a refusal will be interpreted as meaning "I don't find you sexually attractive" (Faunce & Phipps-Yonas, 1979). A woman may be likely to say "yes" simply to avoid hurting a man's feelings.

Unfortunately, no discussion of the sexual revolution would be complete without mentioning another unpleasant consequence: an increase in the incidence of sexually transmitted diseases. The two most common of these diseases are **gonorrhea** and **genital herpes.** Gonorrhea involves a bacterium and it infects mucous membrane in the genitals, throat, or rectum. Genital herpes involves a virus, and it causes bumps or sores in the genital area. More information on these and other diseases can be found in human sexuality texts such as Rathus (1983). There are claims that some people have decreased their sexual activity because of fear of contracting these diseases, but systematic studies haven't yet been conducted.

There may be some benefits to the sexual revolution, though. Women no longer have to feel ashamed about enjoying sensual experiences. Also, communication between mothers and daughters on the subject of sex has apparently improved over the last 25 years (Yalom, Estler, & Brewster, 1982). Women also may feel more free about communicating with men about the kinds of sexual activities they find appealing.

According to Faunce and Phipps-Yonas (1979), the revolution is incomplete, and sexual freedom has not yet been attained for women. As they point out, sexual equality cannot exist in the bedroom until there is sexual equality on the outside; merely turning out the lights at night cannot hide the unequal status of men and women in other aspects of their lives. They write,

> Real sexual freedom for women would mean, of course, that one could choose to be celibate, to be monogamous, or to sleep with many men or women—

because *she wanted it that way*. Women will be free sexually only when they can choose, when they have the right to respond (or not respond), and when they have the right to initiate. [p. 236]

☐ SECTION SUMMARY ▪ Sexual Behavior and Attitudes

1. Sex education in schools may be inadequate, ignoring many important topics, but parent-child communications may have an important impact.
2. Sexual activity among adolescents has increased dramatically in recent years, and young women are now almost as experienced as young men.
3. Women typically report that their first sexual experience was unpleasant.
4. By tradition, men are the initiators of sexual relationships, whereas women reject sexual advances or at least slow the pace; women also require a more meaningful relationship before they engage in a sexual relationship.
5. According to one study, men may enjoy sex more than women do.
6. Women often view "foreplay" as an important part of sex, not just a preliminary to sex.
7. Women are perceived as being less interested in erotica than men, yet research shows that women are aroused by erotica.
8. There is a sex difference in masturbation; males masturbate more often than females.
9. Lesbian and heterosexual women show the same kind of sexual response and they are also similar in their emphasis on emotional involvement; most lesbian women describe their sexual activities as satisfying, but it is unclear whether lesbians have sex as often as heterosexual women.
10. There are some changes in the sexual cycle as women grow older, but the major barrier to sexual relations for most older women is that they don't have a partner; sexuality in older women is often viewed with disgust.
11. Women see many disadvantages—as well as some advantages—to the sexual revolution; the revolution is not complete because women are still not sexually free.

☐ SEXUAL DYSFUNCTION

Masters and Johnson published their second book, *Human Sexual Inadequacy*, in 1970. In the preface, they wrote about their hope that human sexual inadequacy would be rendered obsolete within the next decade. Obviously, the problem still exists. Sexual inadequacy or **sexual dysfunction** means "an impairment of the ability to engage in and/or enjoy sexual activities" (Heiman & Verhulst, 1982, p. 314), and this impairment seems surprisingly common. In one study of happily married couples, 77 percent of the women and 50 percent of the men reported some kind of sexual dysfunction (Frank, Anderson, & Rubenstein, 1978). Furthermore, 48 percent of women reported that they had difficulty becoming sexually excited, and 15 percent reported that they almost never experienced orgasm.

In this section of the chapter, we will look at four kinds of sexual dysfunction in women: sexual unresponsiveness, orgasmic dysfunction, vaginismus, and painful intercourse. Then we will consider how gender roles are related to sexual dysfunction. Our final topic is therapy for sexual dysfunction.

Sexual Unresponsiveness

Sexual unresponsiveness or **inhibited sexual desire** means the inhibition of sexual arousal (Nadelson, 1978a). Physiologically, a woman who is sexually unresponsive does not respond during the excitement phase of the sexual-response cycle. That is, there is little or no vasocongestion. As a result, vaginal lubrication is not adequate, and the vagina does not change its size and shape. The problem may be compounded because the vagina of an unresponsive woman is not adequately prepared for the entry of her partner's penis, and intercourse can therefore be uncomfortable and irritating. Such an unpleasant experience may make her even less responsive on the next occasion.

Women who are sexually unresponsive have a variety of complaints. These may range from "I don't like to have sex as often as my partner—although I enjoy it when we engage in it . . ." to "I would give anything to be able to avoid having sex for the rest of my life!" (Rosenbaum, 1978).

According to Nadelson, sexual unresponsiveness is not likely to have a physical basis. Psychological factors are usually much more important. These may include factors such as depression, low self-esteem, lack of information about sexuality, negative attitudes and anxiety about sexuality, and a past history of a traumatic sexual experience. Furthermore, an uncaring, insensitive partner can often lead to sexual unresponsiveness (LoPiccolo, 1980; Nadelson, 1978a; Tevlin & Leiblum, 1983).

Sexual unresponsiveness is not confined to heterosexual couples. Nichols (1982) believes that inhibited sexual desire is by far the most common sexual problem faced by lesbians. Nichols presents a case study of two women whose relationship was ideal as far as harmony, physical affection, and consideration, yet they had not had sex with each other for the last seven of the fourteen years that they had been together. One of the two women had found her sexual desire dwindling, and the other woman had not wanted to appear selfish by pressuring her partner.

Orgasmic Dysfunction

Women with **orgasmic dysfunction** are sexually responsive, yet they don't reach orgasm when they are aroused (Nadelson, 1978a). According to Rosenbaum (1978), women with this problem constitute the largest group of those who seek help for sexual problems.

Exactly what constitutes an orgasm problem? Some women want to have an orgasm every time they have intercourse. Others are satisfied if they feel emotionally close to their partner during sex. As Kilmann and Mills (1983) conclude, an orgasm problem exists when a woman is not satisfied with her ability to reach orgasm, regardless of the frequency.

We discussed the vaginal-orgasm-versus-clitoral-orgasm controversy earlier in the chapter. This controversy is also relevant in discussions of sexual dysfunction. These discussions concern women who reach orgasm through clitoral stimulation but not through the stimulation they receive in intercourse. Feminists would argue that these women experience one variety of normal female sexual expression, but others might argue that they are dysfunctional.

As in the case of sexual unresponsiveness, physical factors are seldom responsible (Andersen, 1983; Kilmann & Mills, 1983). One common psychological factor is that women are often so accustomed to inhibiting their sexual impulses that it is difficult for them to shed their inhibitions, even when they are in a relationship where sex is approved. Other women have orgasm problems because they are anxious about losing control over their feelings; they may be embarrassed or anxious about experiencing such intense pleasure. Still others are easily distracted during sex, and they may suddenly focus on a dog barking, rather than on the sexual sensations. And of course many other women may not have orgasms because their partners do not provide them with the appropriate sexual stimulation.

Vaginismus

Vaginismus involves a contraction of the outer one-third of the vaginal muscles (Kilmann & Mills, 1983). The contractions themselves are not painful, but they may constrict the opening of the vagina to such an extent that sexual intercourse is difficult or impossible. There are no statistical figures about the incidence of vaginismus, but it is relatively rare (Leiblum, Pervin, & Campbell, 1980). As Leiblum and her coauthors write, a striking feature of vaginismus is that a married couple may let many years go by without intercourse. Often, it is the desire to have children that ultimately forces the couple to seek sex counselling.

Like sexual unresponsiveness and orgasmic dysfunctions, there is seldom a physical reason for this disorder. Although many psychological factors may be important, vaginismus can often be traced to a previous traumatic sexual experience (Nadelson, 1978a). Kilmann and Mills (1983) relate the case history of Robin, a college student whose date forced her to have intercourse. A year later, she went to a motel with a different young man whom she really liked and trusted, yet she experienced vaginismus so severe that penetration was impossible.

Painful Intercourse

Painful intercourse or **dyspareunia** (pronounced "diss-pah-*roo*-nih-ah") involves pain in the vagina, pelvis, or abdomen during intercourse. Whereas the other three disorders are typically psychological in origin, a physical explanation is often involved in painful intercourse (Nadelson, 1978a). A physical examination is therefore particularly useful; a vaginal infection or an ovarian problem may be located. However, other factors may be involved. Women who experience painful intercourse frequently report that they are anxious in sexual situations. A traumatic sexual experience may sometimes be responsible. Also, intercourse can be painful if a woman is not aroused enough for vaginal lubrication to occur (Kilmann & Mills, 1983).

Gender Roles and Sexual Dysfunction

Sexual dysfunctions are extremely complex. Their origin may be physical, they may depend upon subtle problems in a couple's interactions, and they may be worsened by problems such as low self-esteem. Obviously, we can't say that gender roles are responsible for all sexual dysfunction. Nevertheless, there are several ways in which gender roles, stereotypes, and biases may be directly or indirectly responsible for the problems women experience with regard to sexuality. As Tevlin and Leiblum (1983) conclude, " ... it seems clear that a number of female sexual difficulties may have at their root a variety of cultural sex-role stereotypes dictating "appropriate" masculine and feminine behavior" (p. 148).

Here are some of the connections between gender roles and sexual dysfunction that have been discussed by various authors (Heiman & Verhulst, 1982; Pogrebin, 1983; Schwartz & Strom, 1978; Tevlin & Leiblum, 1983; Zilbergeld, 1978).

1. Women are supposed to be asexual, passive, emotional, and romantic, whereas men are supposed to be sexual, aggressive, achieving, and rational.
2. The double standard conveyed to young people is that male adolescents should "sow their wild oats" whereas female adolescents should "save themselves" for marriage.
3. Women are afraid to look selfish by requesting the kinds of sexual stimulation they enjoy; women are supposed to give, rather than demand.
4. Sexual relations typically focus on male sexuality. As a consequence, female sexuality receives less attention in the research. For example, we have fairly extensive information about the effects of physical illness and drugs on male sexuality, whereas we know little about

their effects on female sexuality (Heiman & Verhulst, 1982). Consistent with a theme of this book, women are relatively invisible.

5. Male gender roles also contribute to sexual dysfunction. Zilbergeld (1978) discusses males' fantasies about the ideal sexual apparatus in his chapter, "It's two feet long, hard as steel, and can go all night." A man with that kind of focus won't worry about the subtleties of clitoral stimulation—a topic that *should* be important.

6. Beauty is emphasized for females more than for males, as we saw in the discussions of adolescence and dating and we'll encounter again in the two chapters on psychological disorders and older women. Women who feel less than perfectly attractive—that is, almost all women—may worry about their physical appearance rather than concentrating on physical sensations of arousal.

As a result of these forces, women believe that they are not supposed to be actively enthusiastic, experienced, or selfish in the area of sexuality. Furthermore, the focus on the male penis as being central in intercourse leaves women ignored in both the research and in their sexual needs. Finally, the emphasis on feminine beauty prevents many women from enjoying their sensuality.

Therapy for Sexual Dysfunction

Before 1970, sex problems were generally handled either by physicians specializing in gynecology or urology or by psychiatrists who believed that sex problems required years of extensive therapy (Kilmann & Mills, 1983). Masters and Johnson's book *Human Sexual Inadequacy* changed the entire approach of sex therapy. They introduced a new short-term sex therapy in which couples spent two weeks away from their daily routines, totally devoting themselves to the treatment. Among the specific techniques in this kind of therapy is **sensate focus,** in which partners touch and stroke in order to discover sensitive areas in themselves and in their partner's body. Masters and Johnson's research techniques have been criticized (Andersen, 1983; Heiman & Verhulst, 1982), but their success rate is reasonably high. For example, over 90 percent of women with vaginismus learn to relax their vaginal muscles through therapy. Orgasmic dysfunctions, in contrast, have a success rate that may be as low as 30 percent, depending upon how you define "success" (Heiman & Verhulst, 1982). Therapists are often skeptical now, realizing that this short-term therapy works for some people some of the time, but it isn't a cure-all (Leiblum & Pervin, 1980).

Numerous other techniques have also been developed by sex therapists. These include methods of reducing anxiety, training in masturbation, encouraging fantasy, and the use of imagery techniques and explicit homework assignments (Andersen, 1981; Barbach, 1980; Leiblum & Pervin, 1980; LoPiccolo, 1980). Each of these techniques has its enthusiastic supporters. Even so, Masters and Johnson's optimistic hope—the elimination of sexual dysfunction—does not seem likely in the near future.

☐ SECTION SUMMARY ▪ Sexual Dysfunction

1. Sexual unresponsiveness means that sexual arousal is inhibited, and there is inadequate vasocongestion; it is most often caused by psychological factors.
2. Orgasmic dysfunction means that a woman is sexually responsive, yet she doesn't reach orgasm when she is aroused; again, psychological factors are usually responsible.
3. Vaginismus involves a contraction of the vaginal muscles so that penetration is difficult or impossible; it can often be traced to an earlier sexual experience or to some other psychological factor.
4. Painful intercourse often can be caused by a physical problem, but psychological factors may also contribute to this dysfunction.
5. Gender roles can contribute to sexual dysfunction in several ways: (a) women aren't supposed to be interested in sex; (b) the double standard may still exist; (c) women are afraid to look selfish; (d) male sexuality is emphasized in both research and in the bedroom; and (e) beauty is emphasized for females more than for males.
6. Masters and Johnson's short-term sex therapy changed the pattern of sex therapy; the technique is reasonably successful, though it doesn't work for everyone.
7. Other sex-therapy techniques include anxiety reduction, masturbation training, encouraging fantasy and imagery, and specific homework assignments.

☐ BIRTH CONTROL AND ABORTION

When most people are asked why sexual behavior is freer than it was several decades ago, they answer "the pill." In the words of one psychologist, people usually imagine that sexually active young women are contraceptively wise *Cosmopolitan* "girls," appropriately armed with modern antipregnancy technology, who guiltlessly sleep with swinging bachelors at their *Playboy* pads (Byrne, 1979). This imaginary picture doesn't match the reality of birth control and abortion in the 1980s.

Birth Control

Table 10.1 shows the major forms of birth control, together with some information about their use. Of course, abstinence should also be mentioned as a form of birth control.

   Note that most of the birth-control methods are intended for the females, rather than males. One reason for this inequity is that males are always fertile, whereas women are fertile for just a few days each month. It therefore might be easier to intervene in females' reproductive cycles (E. R. Allgeier, 1983). Also, it's the females who get pregnant. Some feminists argue that contraceptives have been developed mostly by men, who assume that women

TABLE 10.1   Major Birth-Control Methods

Method	Effectiveness	Possible Side Effects and Disadvantages
Natural Family Planning (intercourse when woman is not fertile)	Fair to poor	Intercourse must be greatly reduced in order to be effective
Withdrawal (removal of penis before ejaculation)	Fair to poor	Sexual pleasure may be reduced because of anxiety
Spermicidal foams, creams, etc.	Good to fair	May irritate genital area; must be applied before intercourse
Condoms (sheath placed on penis)	Good (very good if used with spermicides)	May decrease pleasure for male; must be applied before intercourse
Diaphragm (placed in vagina) and spermicidal foam or cream	Good	Must be applied before intercourse; may irritate genital area
Intrauterine device (plastic device placed in uterine cavity)	Very good	Cramping, heavy bleeding, pelvic infections; may be expelled spontaneously
Birth control pills (synthetic hormones, taken by woman)	Excellent	Blood-clotting disorders, particularly for women over 40 or smokers; other medical side effects possible; must be taken regularly
Vasectomy (surgery to prevent passage of sperm)	99 + % effective	Minor surgical risk; possible negative emotional reactions
Tubal ligation (severing of fallopian tubes)	99 + % effective	Minor surgical risk; possible negative emotional reactions

Note: For more information, consult Stewart, Guest, Stewart, & Hatcher (1981)

should take care of controlling reproduction and who also feel more comfortable intervening with female—rather than male—reproductive systems (Adler, 1981). However, as one writer observed, women may want to control their own reproductive capacities, but that doesn't necessarily mean that they want responsibility and risk every time they have intercourse until they reach menopause (Moore, 1977).

Our primary concern is not with the description of birth-control devices. Instead, we will focus on two issues that emphasize psychological aspects of birth control: who uses birth control and barriers to using birth control.

Who uses birth control?   Most women (though surely not all women) have access to birth-control devices. Nonetheless, many who are sexually active use either a relatively unreliable method of contraception, such as foam, withdrawal, or rhythm, or else no method at all. Only about 20 percent of sexually active teenagers use effective contraceptives on a regular basis (Byrne, 1979). According to estimates, one in five unmarried women who are sexually active at age 19 has become pregnant at least once. Furthermore, studies of women who do use contraception show that the use of *reliable* methods of birth control has been declining substantially during recent years (Gerrard, McCann & Geis, 1984). Birth-control pills and intrauterine devices have become less popular. It seems that American teenagers are sexually active as well as sexually ignorant (Church, 1982). As a result, there are roughly one million adolescent pregnancies each year.

Researchers have tried to identify what kind of woman uses birth control, because this information could eventually help to decrease the number of unwanted pregnancies. They have discovered that birth-control users are likely to be older women who are not Catholic, who are not members of a minority group, and who are from the middle- and upper-socioeconomic classes.

There are also some personality characteristics that are related to the use of birth control (Adler, 1981; Fox, 1977; Gerrard, et al., 1984; Ireson, 1984). Women who use effective birth-control methods are likely to be the kind who plan ahead for the future and who have high levels of striving. They are also likely to be high in self-esteem and feelings of competence; they tend to be "active" women, rather than passive. They also tend to be nontraditional in their attitudes toward gender roles. In contrast, women who are stereotypically feminine are less likely to use effective birth-control methods.

Barriers to using birth control.   If there are about one million unintended pregnancies each year among adolescent women alone, then a large number of people who could be using effective birth-control methods are not. The problem is that there are many barriers to using birth control. As Adler (1981) summarizes the problem, "To avoid pregnancy, one must not only be motivated to prevent conception but must have adequate knowledge about contraception, access to it, and willingness to use it" (p. 57). In more detail, here are some of the issues:

1. Parents and educators often avoid discussing sexuality with young people because they "don't want to give them any ideas." They are particularly reluctant to discuss birth control (Byrne, 1979).
2. Even if a young woman has been taught that sexual relationships lead

to pregnancy, there is a huge gap between those precise anatomical films and the realities of sex in the back seat of the car (Byrne, 1979). Teenage women often refuse to believe that they themselves can actually become pregnant, and they may believe myths such as "you can't get pregnant if the woman is on top."

3. Young women have been told that "nice girls don't have sex." As a result, many of them will avoid information about contraception. After all, if they make an appointment with a gynecologist so that they can get birth-control pills, they would be admitting to themselves and others that they planned to have intercourse and thus are not "nice girls" (Adler, 1981). As Byrne (1979) has found, people who associate sex with guilt and anxiety are less likely to use birth-control methods than people who are positive about sex. Sexually negative people don't want to have to think about their sexuality, so they avoid obtaining a contraceptive, discussing contraception with their partner, and using the contraceptive.

4. All of the contraceptives that are now available have some problems (Kitzinger, 1983). Some women may be informed about contraception and would be willing to use a safe contraceptive, but they are too worried about the side effects of the most effective devices, the pill and the IUD. As a consequence, they use either an ineffective method or no method at all. As Geis and Gerrard (1984) point out, these women are misreading the risk factors, which still compare favorably to the risks of either abortion or childbirth.

5. Birth-control devices may interrupt the "spontaneity of sex" because they aren't considered very erotic or romantic. Many seem to think that sex is natural, but contraception is not. Byrne (1979) read through published articles dealing with sexual fantasies, and he found no mention of contraceptives. Also, you can try Demonstration 10.3 to see whether contraceptives are shown or discussed in movies, television, books, and magazines. It seems that sexuality can be quite explicit: We can see a woman and a man undressing, groping, groaning, and copulating. The one taboo topic seems to be contraception! Sexually active people don't see their heroines and heroes using contraception—so why should they themselves use contraceptives?

DEMONSTRATION 10.3

Contraception as a Taboo Topic

Keep a record for the next month of the number of times couples are shown in sexual relationships by the media. Monitor television programs, the movies you see, stories in magazines, books, and anything else that seems relevant. In each case, note whether contraceptives are ever mentioned, shown, or even hinted at.

There is no one method for decreasing the number of unwanted pregnancies. Some people believe that teenagers should receive stronger lectures against being sexually active, but the effectiveness of this technique is certainly dubious. Gerrard and her coauthors (1984) suggest a number of ideas that would surely be more effective. These include improving education about sexuality and contraception, increasing the availability of contraception, and providing birth-control devices to women who are likely to have unplanned pregnancies (for example, teenagers who have just had abortions). We also need to change people's attitudes toward contraception (Byrne, 1979). The use of contraception might rise substantially if the women in soap operas were shown discussing birth-control methods with their gynecologists and the macho men of the movie screen carefully adjusted their condoms before the steamy love scene.

Abortion

The issue of abortion is one of the most highly controversial issues facing women today. It is also one of the most important and serious considerations a woman may have to make, because the consequences of her decision are irreversible: unlike a husband, a child cannot be divorced; unlike a job or career, a child cannot be changed; unlike a relationship, a child cannot be ended. On the other hand, it must also be remembered that once a pregnancy is terminated, the child that would have developed will never be; a woman may subsequently have other children, but not that one. [Belovitch, 1980, p. 92]

In 1980, 30 percent of all pregnancies were terminated by abortions (Henshaw & O'Reilly, 1983). Women who seek abortions generally tend to be single women from a stable middle- or upper-class background who see themselves as competent people (Dreyer, 1982). However, it is important to keep in mind that women seeking abortion may be young or old, married or single, black or white, Catholic or non-Catholic, educated or uneducated.

Table 10.2 shows the most common methods of abortion. Abortion may be a controversial issue, but one aspect of abortion should not be controversial: its safety. An abortion performed by a professional during the first three months of pregnancy is about 12 times safer than childbirth and three times safer than having tonsils removed (Bishop, 1984; Hayler, 1979).

In contrast to this objective information about numbers, methods, and safety, we must now approach the more difficult topics: the decision to have an abortion, reactions to an abortion, attitudes toward abortion, and the alternatives.

Decisions about abortion. Some women are able to make abortion decisions with relatively little conflict. They realize that they do not want to have a child, and they choose an abortion. For most women, however, the decision is not perfectly clear-cut. Gilligan (1982) describes the struggle that women face as they decide whether to seek an abortion. One woman reported,

TABLE 10.2   **Major Abortion Methods**

Method	When Used	Description
Early vacuum abortion	6–12 weeks of pregnancy	Accounts for 80% of all U.S. abortions. Vacuum tube is inserted into uterus, and tissue is sucked out.
Dilation and evacuation	13–24 weeks	General anesthesia usually given; cervix is dilated to remove larger volume of tissue.
Amniocentesis abortion	15–24 weeks	Saline or other chemicals are inserted into the amniotic sac around the fetus, inducing premature labor.

Note: For more information, consult Stewart, Guest, Stewart, & Hatcher (1981).

> I struggled with it a whole lot. Finally, I just had to reconcile myself—I really do believe this, but it is not an easy thing that you can say without emotions and maybe regret—that, yes, life is sacred, but the quality of life is also important .... [p. 58]

For many pregnant teenagers, the conflict over whether or not to have an abortion is the first really major decision they have had to make in their lives. They realize, also, that they are ultimately alone in their decision. As one young woman stated, "Nobody is going to get on that operating table with you" (Lessard, 1976).

Reactions to an abortion.   What are the psychological reactions following an abortion? Before 1973, many abortions were considered illegal, a circumstance that would surely bring negative reactions. The majority of studies conducted since that time have concluded that women who have had abortions are unlikely to have severe psychological reactions (Dreyer, 1982; Hayler, 1979; Shusterman, 1976). Hayler concludes from her review of the literature that "the predominant emotional responses were relief and happiness, although they might be combined with some negative feelings" (p. 317). The reaction of this 21-year-old married woman is probably representative:

> We finally decided on an abortion. We don't feel guilty about it and we don't regret it because we feel as though we'll have more to offer our kids in the future—emotional support as well as financial support. But sometimes I get real sad thinking about it. I am very sorry that I had to do it. [Belovitch, 1980, p. 92]

As Belovitch writes, feminists maintain that women have the right to control their bodies, but this does not mean that abortion is free of conflict.

Just as many women struggle with the abortion decision, many women also feel some guilt or sadness following the abortion. Neither the decision nor its consequence is easy, and we are being unfair to women if we claim that they have no regrets—just as we would be unfair to them if we claim that they all experience psychological disorders following abortions.

A small number of women find that abortion is a very stressful experience, and they may experience depression (Mester, 1978). However, the number of serious psychological disorders following legal abortions is less than half the number of disorders following normal childbirth (Bishop, 1984).

In summary, women respond in a variety of ways to abortion. Some may have no noticeable regrets, a few may have psychological disorders, but the majority do not experience major difficulties. This variety in responses to abortion reminds us once more of one of the themes of this book—the substantial individual differences among women.

Attitudes toward abortion. As I write this chapter, abortion clinics throughout the country are being bombed by "pro-life" people. Attitudes toward abortion are clearly intense and diverse. People who oppose abortion rights are very committed to their position. Most of the "pro-life" activists in a study by Luker (1984) worked between 30 and 40 hours a week on the issue, whereas most of the "pro-choice" activists worked about five hours a week.

Public opinion in the United States generally supports the pro-choice position. In a 1981 survey described by Bishop (1984), 61 percent of Catholic women and 69 percent of Protestant women believed that any woman who wants an abortion should be permitted to obtain it legally. Furthermore, the clear majority of those in both groups who opposed abortion said that they did approve of abortion in cases of health risk or rape. Factors other than religion are also important in determining attitudes toward abortion. Educated people are generally more tolerant than less educated people, and whites are generally more tolerant than blacks. People who live in rural areas or the South are usually more conservative than people in other regions of the United States (Combs & Welch, 1982).

Alternatives to abortion. Unplanned pregnancies are also resolved by methods other than abortion. According to Byrne (1979), adolescents who are pregnant seek abortions about 40 percent of the time and have out-of-wedlock births about 30 percent of the time. The other outcomes, miscarriages and "hasty and often short-lived marriages," each occur about 15 percent of the time. Incidentally, black female adolescents are more likely to be sexually active than white female adolescents. As a consequence, they are 40 to 50 percent more likely to have an abortion and about twice as likely to have a baby (Henshaw, et al., 1985; Washington, 1982).

People who oppose abortion often suggest adoption as an alternative. However, adoption creates its own kind of trauma and pain, as described by a 50-year-old married woman with two children who recalls her experience when she discovered that she was pregnant at 17:

> .... Abortions at that time were absolutely out of the question, not only because of the religious and moral taboos but because they were downright dangerous, not to mention expensive. I was too afraid so I "went abroad" for a year and had my baby and gave it up for adoption. I never saw it (I don't even know what sex it was). But I can tell you that the day hasn't gone by that I haven't thought about it and wondered if it was OK. After nine months that baby was a part of me and when I gave it up I gave up some of myself. [Belovitch, 1980, p. 97]

Of course, another alternative is to deliver the baby and choose the motherhood option. This alternative is much more popular among black adolescents than among white adolescents (McNett, et al., 1985; Washington, 1982). In many cases, of course, an unwanted pregnancy can become a wanted baby by the time of delivery. Still, thousands of babies are born each year to mothers who do not want them, clearly a situation that is destructive for both the mother and the child (Belovitch, 1980; David & Matejcek, 1981). Most mothers also encounter difficulties in going to school, finding employment, fighting poverty, and facing the stigma that our society has against unmarried mothers.

We have seen that none of these alternatives—abortion, adoption, or motherhood—is free of problems. Instead, the answer that causes the least psychological pain seems to be preventing the pregnancies to begin with, so that women do not have to choose among such desperate alternatives.

☐ SECTION SUMMARY ▪ Birth Control and Abortion

1. Most of the major forms of birth control are intended for the female, rather than the male.
2. Many sexually active women do not use reliable birth-control methods.
3. Birth-control users are likely to be older, non-Catholic women from the middle and upper classes who are not members of a minority group; they are also likely to be active, striving women who have nontraditional attitudes toward gender roles.
4. People avoid using birth control because of inadequate information, a reluctance to admit that they are engaging in sexual activity, fear about the risks of effective contraceptives, and the fact that birth control doesn't enter into erotic imagery.
5. The number of unwanted pregnancies could be decreased by im-

proving education, increasing the availability of contraception information, and changing attitudes toward contraception.

6. About 30 percent of all pregnancies currently end in abortion; an abortion performed early in pregnancy is medically safe.

7. Most women find that abortion decisions are difficult, rather than clear-cut.

8. Currently, most women who have had an abortion feel relief and happiness mixed with some negative feelings; a small percentage may have more severe psychological reactions, but women are less likely to have disorders following abortion than following childbirth.

9. "Pro-life" people may be intensely committed to their position, but the clear majority of American women favor a pro-choice position.

10. Adoption is not a satisfactory alternative to abortion, and women who decide to become mothers usually face many difficulties; pregnancy prevention is the solution that provides the least pain.

Chapter Review Questions

1. Feminists frequently mention that sexuality has traditionally been male centered. Address this issue, focusing on topics such as (a) theories of orgasm; (b) the double standard; and (c) the initiation of sexual relationships.

2. Much of this chapter emphasizes adolescent women. Describe the experiences a young woman might face as she discusses sexuality with her parents, has her first sexual experience, makes decisions about contraception, and then struggles with an unwanted pregnancy.

3. We discussed some of the pros and cons of the sexual revolution. Review these issues and then describe how the 1980s differ from the early 1960s with respect to (a) knowledge about sexuality; (b) sex therapy approaches; (c) sexual activity; and (d) contraception and abortion.

4. How are gender roles relevant in (a) the initiation and regulation of sexual relationships, (b) sexual dysfunctions, (c) sexual activity, and (d) decisions about contraception and abortion?

5. Discuss sex differences and similarities with respect to (a) the sexual-response cycle, (b) early sexual experiences, and (c) sexual activity.

6. What information do we have about sexuality among lesbians, including sexual dysfunctions?

7. In Chapter 14 we will see that discrimination against women seems to be particularly intense for older women. What kinds of difficulties do older women face with respect to sexuality?

8. Describe each of the four sexual dysfunctions discussed in this chapter, and summarize the kinds of therapeutic approaches currently used in aiding sexual dysfunction.
9. What are some of the stereotypes about women's sexuality? Which of them have some basis in fact and which do not?
10. Imagine that you have been given a substantial grant to reduce the number of unwanted pregnancies in a large urban area. What kinds of programs would you plan that would have both immediate and long-term effects?

☐ NEW TERMS

mons pubis
labia majora
labia minora
clitoral hood
clitoris
urethral opening
vaginal opening
anus
erogenous zones
excitement phase
vasocongestion
plateau phase
orgasmic platform
orgasmic phase
resolution phase

"clitoral orgasm"
"vaginal orgasm"
ejaculate
G-spot
foreplay
gonorrhea
genital herpes
sexual dysfunction
sexual unresponsiveness
inhibited sexual desire
orgasmic dysfunction
vaginismus
painful intercourse
dyspareunia
sensate focus

☐ RECOMMENDED READINGS

Allgeier, E. R., & McCormick, N. B. (Eds.) (1983). *Changing boundaries.* Palo Alto, Calif.: Mayfield. ■ This exceptionally readable and informative volume focuses on sexuality in relationship to gender roles, and it contains articles on a wide variety of topics within the area of sexuality.

Kilmann, P. R., & Mills, K. H. (1983). *All about sex therapy.* New York: Plenum. ■ This book provides an excellent introduction to sexual dysfunction and treatment, suitable for either laypeople or professionals.

Kitzinger, S. (1983). *Woman's experience of sex.* New York: Putnam. ■ If you are looking for a book that blends the personal side of sexuality with the scientific side, this is it! The photographs are especially well chosen.

Rathus, S. A. (1983). *Human sexuality.* New York: Holt, Rinehart and Winston. ■ There are a number of good introductory human sexuality textbooks; this book would be especially useful for its readable discussion of the anatomy and physiology of the sexual-response cycle.

PREGNANCY, CHILDBIRTH, AND MOTHERHOOD

- There is little research about psychological aspects of pregnancy and childbirth in humans.

- Pregnant women frequently report that their feelings change readily.

- People stand closer to a woman when she is pregnant.

- When a woman begins to have regular contractions that are three minutes apart, she can count on delivering a baby within one hour.

- Women have a wide variety of reactions to childbirth; some emphasize the pain, others the intense joy.

- Today's "high-tech" approach to childbirth may not focus sufficiently on the psychological needs of the family.

- Motherhood is natural and almost instinctive.

- Mothers' dominant response to early motherhood is a feeling of hidden strength and exhilaration.

- The majority of women experience maternity blues, a short-lasting period that may involve crying, tension, and anger.

- The majority of college students in the United States have negative reactions toward women who do not want to have children.

There are few events in a woman's life that are as important as pregnancy, childbirth, and motherhood. Contemplate for a moment how a woman's life changes once she discovers she is pregnant. The next nine months of her life will focus on her changing body and on plans for the arrival of a new human being. Her thoughts will range from the very practical ("Where will the baby sleep?") to the very abstract ("What will it be like to be a mother?"). Childbirth will be an extremely intense experience—a combination of exhilaration, pain, and accomplishment. And it is hard to imagine any activity that contains such an intense blend of joys and difficulties as motherhood. Pregnancy, childbirth, and motherhood are extremely emotional, intensely preoccupying, and very crucial phases in women's lives.

This sequence of pregnancy, childbirth, and motherhood is far from rare. The current world population is about 4.8 billion. It does not require great intellectual skills to realize that every one of those 4.8 billion people involved a pregnant woman.

However, the media and other disciplines—including psychology—ignore the motherhood sequence. We noted in the chapter on love relationships that love is a theme that dominates music, television, and entertainment. In the last chapter, we saw that sexuality is prominently featured by the media; sex sells. However, pregnancy, childbirth, and motherhood are topics that are nearly ignored. Pregnancy and childbirth (and to a lesser extent, motherhood) seem to increase the invisibility of women that has been one of the themes of the book.

These important topics seem to be taboo in other areas, as well. Seiden (1978) complains that first-aid books tell how to stop arterial bleeding but not how to help in childbirth. Research on pregnancy and childbirth is also sparse. Paige (1978) points out that researchers probably know more about the reproductive behavior of the rat than about the reproductive behavior of the human female. A recent convention held by the Eastern Psychological Association listed only one paper on any aspect of human pregnancy and childbirth. Psychologists, too, ignore pregnancy and childbirth.

Society's attitude toward motherhood—the third topic in the current chapter—is more complex, because mothers are not ignored. Instead, motherhood receives public praise; it is equated in status with the American flag and apple pie. Yet, as we'll see later in this chapter, mothers have little true prestige. Their needs are ignored in the areas of child care, support systems, and public facilities. Americans are really ambivalent about motherhood.

Let's examine in more detail these three phases of reproduction: pregnancy, childbirth, and motherhood. As we will see, each of these phases has important psychological components.

☐ PREGNANCY

In the chapter on menstruation, we discussed a complex set of events that takes place when the egg is not fertilized. The set of events that occurs if the egg *is* fertilized is vastly different biologically, physically, and emotionally.

The Biology of Pregnancy

Usually, the sperm unites with the egg while the egg is traveling down the fallopian tube. The fertilized egg continues down the fallopian tube, floats around in the uterus for several days, and then implants itself in the thick tissue that lines the uterus. This tissue would be sloughed off as menstrual flow if the egg had not been fertilized, as discussed in Chapter 4. When fertilization has occurred, however, this tissue provides an ideal environment in which a fertilized egg can develop into a baby.

Shortly after the fertilized egg has implanted itself, the placenta begins to develop. The **placenta** is an organ that is connected to the growing embryo; it allows oxygen and nutrients to pass from the mother to the embryo, and it helps transport the embryo's waste products back to the mother's system. This amazing organ also helps to manufacture enormous quantities of hormones. By the end of pregnancy, a woman's progesterone level will increase 100 times and her estrogen level will increase 1000 times, in comparison with prepregnancy levels (Sherman, 1971).

Typically, a woman first suspects that she is pregnant when she misses a menstrual period. However, a missed menstrual period can sometimes be traced to other causes, so missing a period is not necessarily a valid sign of pregnancy (Stewart, et al., 1981). Some women try home-pregnancy testing kits, but these methods also frequently fail to give valid results (Valanis & Perlman, 1982). Laboratory pregnancy tests, together with a physical examination, are more trustworthy methods of detecting pregnancy.

By tradition, pregnancy is divided into three trimesters. Each **trimester** is therefore three months in length.

Physical Reactions to Pregnancy

Virtually every organ system in a woman's body is affected by pregnancy, though most of the consequences aren't serious (Friedman, 1978). Some of the more common physical reactions include the following (Stewart, et al., 1981): weight gain, protrusion of the abdomen, breast tenderness and swelling, nausea or vomiting, fatigue, and frequent urination.

In earlier eras, pregnancy was regarded as a nine-months' sickness (Holt & Weber, 1982), and that view sometimes persists today. However, women are increasingly likely to view their pregnant state as a normal and healthy one, even though it may be somewhat uncomfortable and inconvenient. It is important, too, to remember that our general theme about the wide range of individual differences holds true with pregnancy as with other phases in women's lives. Some women may never experience a tendency toward nausea, but others might look back on their first trimester of pregnancy as a time when they were nearly immobilized by nausea and vomiting.

Emotional Reactions to Pregnancy

> I feel like a ripe peach, fully in bloom now. I used to laugh at pregnant women, but now I feel that there really is a kind of glow coming from me. [Leifer, 1980, p. 57]

> My feelings all seem to be stronger now. I'm weepier. I tend to fall into tears more quickly, and I'm not always sure why. I could read something and just cry over it, or at the other end I can laugh very hard at things. I'll cry more at movies, and sometimes I can get very angry or upset at small things. So it seems to be an extreme of emotion that I feel more often. [Leifer, 1980, p. 55]

As mentioned, different women have different responses to the same life event. In pregnancy, the situation is even less predictable, because *each woman* may have a wide variety of different responses during the nine months of her pregnancy. For example, the two preceding quotes—which are quite different in emotional tone—could easily have come from the same woman. In fact, it is hard to imagine any other life event to which a woman could respond with such a wide range of positive and negative emotions.

Positive emotions. For many women, the news that they are pregnant brings a rush of positive emotions. There is a sense of excitement and anticipation. Many women report a feeling of wonder and awe at the thought of having a new, growing person inside their own bodies. Most women also sense approval from others—after all, women are *supposed* to have children.

For many women, pregnancy represents a transition into adulthood. This feeling frequently develops in the second trimester of pregnancy. Here is one woman's description:

> I feel very good about it right now. Some time in December, strangely, my feelings changed about it. When my feelings changed, I became very stable and positive. I felt excited about the idea of having a kid, and really ready to become a parent. I don't know, I just felt like I was finally an adult, because you just can't be an adult until you become a parent. Adulthood isn't an age sort of thing. In my mind, it's associated with having children, partly. And I was glad to be an adult. [Ballou, 1978, p. 80]

Many women also describe a sense of purpose and accomplishment about being pregnant (Leifer, 1980). This sense of purpose may be particularly likely to develop during the second trimester, when they feel the first kicks of their baby. As one woman described the experience, "Now I feel like I'm carrying another person, when before I just felt like I was carrying a mass of tissues" (Ballou, 1978, p. 97).

Furthermore, many pregnant women find pleasure in anticipating the jobs of motherhood and child rearing, which they believe will provide them with a tremendous source of satisfaction (Leifer, 1980). As we'll see in the section on motherhood, there may be a gap between their expectations and reality.

Negative emotions. Unfortunately, many of the emotions that pregnant women feel are negative. The physical reactions of nausea and fatigue may create negative feelings. Many women report that their emotions are fragile and ever changing, as noted in the second quote at the beginning of this section. Depressive feelings are also common, particularly in the first trimester of pregnancy (Nadelson, 1978b). Women also report an increase in fears, anxieties, and unusual thoughts (Turrini, 1980). I vividly recall my sixth month of pregnancy, when I was exploring a city where my husband was attending a conference. I was overwhelmed by the concern that I would be in an accident and that people would have no way of figuring out what I was doing there or how to locate the "next of kin." (I even went so far as to carry a note in my purse.)

A frequent theme in this book is the emphasis on women's attractiveness. Since our culture values slimness, a woman's self-image may deteriorate as she watches her body grow fatter. Field and Widmayer (1982) report on a study in which pregnant women were interviewed about their self-images. Women frequently said that they felt fat and ugly during this period.

In addition, pregnant women are likely to be extremely concerned with their health and bodily functions (Treadway, et al., 1975). These anxieties are heightened by the increasing evidence that alcohol, smoking, and a wide variety of drugs can harm the developing fetus (American Medical Association, 1983; Field & Widmayer, 1982). Although this is alarming, many pregnant women find pleasure and pride in eating food that is healthful and avoiding potentially harmful drugs, so that they can be confident that they are providing an optimal environment for their baby.

Emotions about sexuality may also change during pregnancy. Many women report that they are less sexually responsive, and it is easy to identify several contributing factors: fear of harming the fetus, pregnant women's own physical problems, the awkwardness of intercourse late in pregnancy, and women's fear that they are sexually unattractive (Kitzinger, 1983; Pape, 1982). Individual differences are once again substantial, however, because some women feel increased sexual arousal during the second trimester, perhaps partly because of an increased blood supply in the vaginal area (Kitzinger, 1983; Masters & Johnson, 1966).

An important part of women's negative reactions to pregnancy is the result of the fact that other people begin to respond differently to them, as we will see in the next section. The world categorizes them as "pregnant women," females who have no identity aside from being receptacles for a growing baby. Women may also begin to see themselves in these terms. Feminist author Adrienne Rich recalls,

My second book of poems was in press, but I had stopped writing poetry, and read little except household magazines and books on child-care. I felt myself perceived by the world simply as a pregnant woman, and it seemed easier, less disturbing, to perceive myself so. [Rich, 1976, p. 26]

In summary, a woman's emotional reactions to pregnancy can range from excitement and anticipation to fragility and a loss of identity. Consistent with the fourth theme of this book, the individual differences can be enormous. For some women the experience of pregnancy is almost totally positive, but for others it is largely negative. For most, pregnancy involves a complex blend of both pleasant and unpleasant reactions. The nature of this blend will naturally depend upon a number of factors, such as her physical reactions to pregnancy, whether the pregnancy was planned, her relationship with the baby's father, and her employment status. It is easy to understand negative emotions from an unmarried, pregnant 16-year-old whose boyfriend and family have rejected her, and who must work as a waitress to earn extra money. It is also easy to understand positive emotions from a happily married 24-year-old who has hoped for this pregnancy for two years and whose family income is sufficient to buy the new styles of "executive" maternity clothes that she can wear to her interesting, fulfilling job.

We might think that factors such as race or ethnic background might have a profound effect on a woman's attitude toward pregnancy. Harris and her coauthors (1981) asked black, white, and Cuban women to evaluate their emotional reactions to pregnancy, and found that the differences among the three groups were minimal. This is particularly remarkable when we consider the variety of ways—aside from pregnancy—in which their lives are different. Our discussion has been limited to childbearing in the United States. In other cultures, however, pregnancy may be greeted with different emotions (Jordan, 1983).

Attitudes toward Pregnant Women

Three major gynecological events for women are menarche, pregnancy, and menopause. Menarche and menopause are highly private events, and their occurrence is shared with only intimate acquaintances. In contrast, pregnancy is public, particularly in the last trimester. Because a woman's pregnant status is so obvious, it seems likely that people would respond differently to her than to a nonpregnant woman.

According to Taylor and Langer (1977), pregnancy is somewhat similar to a physical stigma. They reported that people reacted virtually identically to a crippled woman and to a pregnant women. Intrigued by these findings, they decided to test whether people would physically avoid a pregnant woman. These authors arranged for two women confederates to ride elevators together. One woman was carefully padded to simulate pregnancy, and the other carried a small box at abdomen-level so that the two women occupied the same space in the elevator. The experimenters noted where the other elevator passengers stood relative to the two women. The results showed that male elevator passengers made great efforts to avoid standing near the pregnant woman, and female passengers were also somewhat likely to avoid her. Furthermore, the "pregnant" confederate reported feeling uncomfortable because passengers frequently stared.

People also show a strong tendency to infantilize pregnant women. Until recently a woman was expected to place herself in the complete care of the obstetrician, who would tell her what to eat, how much weight to gain, when to have intercourse, and how to live her life (Seiden, 1978). A woman was seen as a frightened little girl who was essentially told not to worry her pretty little head about all those complicated aspects of pregnancy, because her doctor would take care of all the important decisions (Vida, 1982). This kind of treatment could hardly be expected to encourage women to be confident, tough, and effective mothers. The second theme of this book is that people treat women and men differently, and this difference is heightened when a woman is pregnant.

Many people who infantilize a pregnant woman *mean* well. However, inadvertently, they may increase her anxiety and make her question her decision-making capabilities. These people would perform a more useful service if they provided current information and allowed her to make her own choices whenever possible. As a result, a pregnant woman could become an educated participant, rather than someone who is regarded as incompetent and ineffective.

People's attitudes toward pregnant women seem to be intertwined with a woman's emotional responses to pregnancy. Consider a study by Horgan (1983), who found social-class differences in attitudes toward pregnant women and women's attitudes toward themselves. She discovered that high-status department stores (for example, Lord & Taylor or Saks) placed the maternity clothes near the lingerie and loungewear. In contrast, the low-status stores (such as Sears or J.C. Penney) placed maternity clothes near the half-size clothes and uniforms. The high-status stores suggest an image of femininity, delicacy, luxury, and privacy, whereas in the low-status stores, a pregnant woman is seen as fat, with a job to do. Demonstration 11.1 is a modification of this portion of Horgan's study.

DEMONSTRATION 11.1

Attitudes Toward Pregnant Women, as Illustrated in Department Stores

Select several department stores in your area that have maternity clothes, trying to obtain a sample that vary in social status. Visit each one of them. (You may want to come equipped with a "shopping for a pregnant friend" excuse.) Record where the maternity clothes are placed. Are they near the lingerie, the clothes for overweight women, the uniforms, or someplace else?

Now notice the nature of the clothes themselves. Fifteen to 20 years ago, the clothes were infantile, with ruffles and bows. More recently, the clothes sometimes announce a woman's pregnant status, as with the word "BABY" and an arrow pointing to the bulging belly. Assess the clothes for infantilization and degree of concealment of pregnancy. Do the various kinds of stores vary along this dimension, as well as the placement of the maternity clothes?

In a follow-up study, Horgan asked pregnant women to fill out questionnaires about their self-perceptions. In comparison with the lower-class women, the upper-class women were likely to see themselves as feeling sexy and attractive. Horgan suggests that women may internalize society's attitudes toward them. The challenge is to encourage society to view pregnant women as competent adults, so that women will also see themselves that way.

☐ SECTION SUMMARY ▪ Pregnancy

1. Pregnancy and childbirth receive little attention from the media or from researchers, but society gives mixed messages about motherhood.
2. At the beginning of pregnancy, the fertilized egg implants itself in the tissue lining the uterus, and the placenta develops shortly afterwards.
3. There are several common physical reactions to pregnancy, including weight gain, nausea, and fatigue, but individual differences are great.
4. The variety of emotional reactions to pregnancy is also large; positive emotions include a sense of excitement and wonder, the feeling that others approve, a feeling of purpose, and the anticipated pleasure of motherhood.
5. Negative emotions include fragile emotions, depression, anxiety, negative self-image, bodily concern, changes in sexual feelings, and changes in identity.
6. People may treat pregnancy as a physical stigma, and they may avoid standing near pregnant women; there appear to be social-class differences in attitudes toward pregnant women, which may be transmitted to the women.

☐ CHILDBIRTH

Let's now look at the big event—childbirth. After a quick overview of the biology of childbirth, we'll explore emotional reactions to childbirth. Two other topics, prepared childbirth and new approaches to childbirth, also have important consequences for a woman's experiences when she gives birth.

The Biology of Childbirth

Childbirth begins when the uterus starts to contract strongly. Women are customarily told that they should plan to enter the hospital or birth center when they have regular contractions that are three minutes apart. It is worth noting that few women experience such regularity; as a consequence they may feel confused, frightened, and "abnormal" (Turrini, 1980). This fear may be heightened by the concern that the baby will arrive before the woman reaches the health facility.

There are three stages in labor. During the first stage, the cervix becomes dilated to about 10 cm (4 inches), a process that may last anywhere from a few hours to at least a day. Traditionally, the woman is taken to the delivery room for the second stage of labor, during which the baby begins to move down into the vagina. This stage lasts from a few minutes to several hours. The contractions move the baby farther down the vagina, and the mother's pushing may also help move the baby along. Progesterone levels begin to drop now. This second stage ends with the birth of the baby. The third stage of labor, which may last up to an hour, is clearly an anticlimax. The placenta separates from the uterine wall, and it is delivered. Estrogen levels drop during this third stage, so that both hormone levels are now drastically lower than they were several hours earlier.

Emotional Reactions to Childbirth

Just as there is a wide range of reactions to pregnancy, there is a wide range of reactions to the birth experience. As Seiden (1978) points out, " . . . child-bearing, like childrearing, is an aggressive and libidinal task—tough and demanding, sometimes exciting, often exhausting" (p. 91). Childbirth is certainly uncomfortable. It is usually painful, particularly with the first child (Rofé, et al., 1981). To a large extent, a woman has no power to control what her body is doing during labor and delivery, and this loss of control may be extremely frustrating.

Some women's descriptions of childbirth emphasize the pain. One woman recalled,

> I was in pain all the time, and it was really bad, it was just getting progressively worse, harder and harder. I was trying to breathe slowly and to think of other things, which was hard to do but you try to do it. I found that I was doing things the nurse said not to. I kept tightening up, clenching my fists, thrashing around, anything to help the pain, but nothing helped. It only made things worse, and that made me feel even more desperate. [Leifer, 1980, p. 142]

For other women, childbirth can be a peak experience that involves intensely sexual sensations, strength, and feeling in tune with what is happening. As Kitzinger (1983) describes this kind of experience,

> Her face lights up as she realizes that this is her baby being born, a living being from her body, and she can see its head and reach down and feel it as it slides into life. Suddenly she is full, stretched to her upmost, as if she is a seed pod bursting. There is a moment of waiting, of awe, of a kind of tension which occurs just before orgasm and then suddenly the baby passes through, the whole body slips out in a rush of warm flesh, a fountain of water, a peak of overwhelming surprise and the little body is against her skin. . . . [p. 218]

These two differing quotations illustrate, once more, our theme of individual differences. In this case, the wide variation in physical reactions during childbirth guarantees that there will be wide variation in emotional responses. Furthermore, people's perceptions of pain differ enormously. A particular sensation may be described by one woman as annoying, whereas another woman may describe the same sensation as intensely unpleasant.

Prepared Childbirth

Many experts suggest that pain during labor and delivery can be reduced if women are prepared for childbirth. There are several different approaches to prepared childbirth, which is often misnamed "natural childbirth." One of the most common methods used in recent years is called **Lamaze preparation,** which a French obstetrician adapted from watching methods used in the Soviet Union. According to a review article on the Lamaze method, there are five essential elements stressed during Lamaze classes (Wideman & Singer, 1984):

1. Learning about pregnancy and childbirth in order to reduce fear;
2. Breathing techniques;
3. Conditioned relaxation, encouraged by a partner who serves as a coach;
4. Focusing attention away from the pain; and
5. Social support from someone who has also attended classes, usually the baby's father or a close friend of the mother.

Proponents of prepared childbirth stress that this method does not eliminate pain. Furthermore, drugs can be used when they are needed (Wideman & Singer, 1984).

There seem to be substantial benefits to prepared childbirth (Hahn & Paige, 1980; Wideman & Singer, 1984; Young, 1982). These include the mother having more positive attitudes toward herself, her husband, and her baby; reduced anxiety and pain; and reduced medication during childbirth. For some time, critics suggested that perhaps the difference between prepared childbirth and other childbirths could be traced to the fact that women who sign up for prepared childbirth classes are more likely to be highly motivated and positive about childbirth, in contrast to women who don't take these classes. However, research shows that prepared-childbirth mothers have better childbirth experiences, even when motivational factors are controlled (Entwisle & Doering, 1981).

The Family-Centered Approach to Childbirth

During the last 50 years, there have been impressive advances in the technology of childbirth, leading to lower death rates for both mothers and infants. An unfortunate side effect of this "high-tech" approach, however, is that births in hospitals may focus on proper equipment, fetal monitoring, and sanitizing every part of the mother, rather than viewing childbirth as an exhilarating experience of warmth and joy and sharing. In contrast to this approach, the **family-centered approach** emphasizes that safe, quality health care can be delivered while simultaneously focusing on the woman's sense of individuality and autonomy and on the family's psychosocial needs (Young, 1982). The family-centered approach acknowledges that high-risk pregnancies may well need special technology, but the vast majority of births are normal. Instead of focusing exclusively on the medical aspects of childbirth, professionals should realize that childbirth is an important psychological event in which a family is born and new relationships are formed.

A complete list of the changes that have been suggested and are implemented in some areas is beyond the scope of this book, but they include the following (Berry, 1982; Hahn & Paige, 1980; Pearse, 1983; and Young, 1982):

1. Labor should not be artificially induced simply because it is more convenient for the physician.
2. The number of cesarean births, which has increased dramatically in recent years, should be reduced.
3. Women should be encouraged to take an upright position during childbirth, rather than the flat-on-the-table, feet-in-the-stirrups approach.
4. Birth practices that have no health benefits—such as routine enema, shaving of the genital area, no food consumption during labor, and episiotomy—should be modified.
5. Routine use of anesthetics is discouraged.
6. A supportive family member or friend should be present; the presence of this person may not only make childbirth more pleasant but is also likely to reduce the length of labor!
7. Alternative physical locations for childbirth should be explored; planned and professionally attended home births are safe for healthy women. Many hospitals are providing special birthing rooms, and out-of-hospital birth centers are being established in many places throughout the United States.
8. Siblings should be permitted to share in the birth of the new baby, and they should be carefully prepared for this event beforehand.

All of these efforts emphasize that the wishes of the mother should be taken seriously. The family-centered approach may succeed in a redistribution of power, so that women in childbirth have more control over their own bodies. Rather than being passive and infantilized, women can make decisions about how they want to give birth. Notice that the family-centered approach allows more freedom of choice. In addition, it may well lead to greater satisfaction with the childbirth experience.

Now try Demonstration 11.2 to determine how childbirth was handled for various women you know.

DEMONSTRATION 11.2

Comparison of Childbirth Experiences

For this demonstration, you need to locate women who had babies very recently, about ten years ago, about 20 years ago, and more. If possible, include your own mother or close relatives in your interview. Ask each of these women to describe her childbirth experience in as much detail as possible. After she has finished, you may wish to ask some of the following questions, if they were not already answered:

1. Were you given any medication? If so, do you remember what kind?
2. How long did you stay in the hospital?
3. Did the baby stay with you in the room, or was she/he returned to the nursery after feedings?
4. Was a relative or friend allowed in the room while you were giving birth?
5. When you were in labor, were you encouraged to lie down?
6. Did you have "prepared childbirth"?
7. Do you recall any negative treatment from any of the hospital staff?
8. Were you treated like a competent adult?
9. Do you recall any positive treatment from any of the hospital staff?
10. If you had to change any one thing about your childbirth experience, what would that have been?

☐ SECTION SUMMARY ▪ Childbirth

1. **There are three stages in labor: dilation to about 10 cm; childbirth; and delivery of the placenta.**
2. **Reactions to childbirth vary widely; some women emphasize the pain, whereas others report an intensely positive peak experience.**
3. **The Lamaze preparation of prepared childbirth emphasizes education, breathing, relaxation, attention techniques, and social support; the method seems to produce better childbirth experiences.**
4. **The family-centered approach to childbirth emphasizes psychological aspects of childbirth, and discourages unnecessary use of "high-tech" procedures.**
5. **The family-centered approach emphasizes that childbirth is an important psychological event in which family members or other supporters can participate.**

☐ MOTHERHOOD

Think of the word "motherhood." What kind of stereotypes does it suggest? These stereotypes about motherhood will be the first topic in this section of the chapter, followed by a contrast with the reality of motherhood. Our next three topics concern three aspects of a new mother's life: postpartum emotion, breast-feeding, and attachment. The final topic is crucial to the motherhood issue—the decision to have (or not to have) children.

Stereotypes about Motherhood

If you are like most people, the word "motherhood" suggests a rich variety of pleasant emotions involving warmth, selflessness, duty, nurturance, tolerance ... (you can complete the list). You may find that the word "motherhood" creates positive images, even if you never intend to have children!

As Gansberg and Mostel (1984) write, women expect motherhood to be happy and fulfilling. The stereotype of blissful motherhood is perpetuated by the media; television babies seldom cry. This stereotype also specifies that parents may require a few moments of adjustment to the new baby, and then they will feel perfectly comfortable and natural in their new roles (Grossman, Eichler, & Winickoff, 1980).

Let's expand upon the myth that motherhood is *natural*, almost instinctive. Magnus (1980) points out certain myths that have permeated the older professional literature on motherhood, including the following:

1. Every woman instinctively wants to have a child.
2. Having a child is the highest possible fulfillment for a woman.
3. Women are feminine and psychologically healthy only if they want to have children.
4. Women instinctively know how to take care of infants; men don't.
5. Women instinctively love their babies from the first moment they are born.

This emphasis on glorifying motherhood seems to pervade most groups in the United States. Mirandé and Enríquez (1979) describe how Chicana mothers are expected to be warm, nurturing, and totally devoted to their families. Similarly, motherhood is highly valued in the black community; black mothers are romanticized as being so strong and self-sufficient that black fathers receive little credit for their role in the family (Harrison, 1977; McCray, 1980).

However, as mentioned at the beginning of this chapter, much of American culture is ambivalent about motherhood, though the negative aspects are generally less prominent. Mothers are sometimes portrayed as frazzled, overly concerned, or domineering. Mothers nag more than fathers—it's the mother (not the father) who complains about Junior's messy room on the television sitcom. You'll recall from Chapter 8 that the women in classical mythology and religion are sometimes virtuous and sometimes evil. Similarly, stereotypes of mothers contain contradictory messages of good and evil.

The Reality of Motherhood

As Hoffnung (1984) writes, many lofty phrases are written in tribute to motherhood, but it is actually accorded very low prestige. Our society values money, power, and achievement, and none of these are associated with taking care of children. In reality, mothers don't get the appreciation they deserve.

None of the stereotypes captures the rich variety of emotions that mothers actually experience. These emotions have been vividly described by Rich (1976):

> My children cause me the most exquisite suffering of which I have any experience. It is the suffering of ambivalence: the murderous alternation between bitter resentment and raw-edged nerves, and blissful gratification and tenderness. Sometimes I seem to myself, in my feelings toward these tiny guiltless beings, a monster of selfishness and intolerance. Their voices wear away at my nerves, their constant needs, above all their need for simplicity and patience, fill me with despair at my own failures. . . . And I am weak sometimes from held-in rage. . . . And yet at other times I am melted with the sense of their helpless, charming and quite irresistible beauty—their ability to go on loving and trusting—their staunchness and decency and unselfconsciousness. *I love them.* But it's in the enormity and inevitability of this love that the sufferings lie. [pp. 21–22]

Let's look in more detail at the reality of motherhood, paying particular attention to the pressures and sources of stress for the mother of a newborn infant (Entwisle & Doering, 1981; Gansberg & Mostel, 1984; Hoffnung, 1984; Kitzinger, 1983; Leifer, 1980):

1. Although fathers may help out somewhat in child rearing, as we saw in Chapter 6, the major responsibility for child care falls on mothers, who must care for tiny infants who are completely incapable of doing anything for themselves.
2. Much of early motherhood is boring drudgery: diapering, washing, and feeding.
3. Child care is exhausting and constantly demanding; infant care is a 24-hour-a-day job, and new mothers often feel they can accomplish very little other than taking care of a newborn.
4. New mothers seldom have training for the tasks of motherhood; they often report that they feel incompetent.
5. Newborn babies often give little positive response to their mothers. They may cry for no apparent reason, typically about one and a half hours a day (Entwistle & Doering, 1981).
6. Mothering is done at home, so that women have little contact with other adults. Extended family and friends may not be available to provide support. This kind of isolation further encourages the invisibility of women, already an important issue throughout this book.
7. Women who have previously been employed feel embarrassed to report that they are now "just housewives"; they are deprived of other sources of identity.
8. Women often report that they feel tied down, because they can't leave the house for more than a few minutes without making elaborate arrangements. For example, in a survey of black mothers, 100

percent of respondents were bothered by this interruption of routine (Hobbs & Wimbish, 1977).

9. For several days after childbirth, women say that they feel leaky and dirty with after-birth discharges, and they were also likely to experience some pain and physical discomfort.

10. Since the woman's attention has shifted to the newborn, her husband may feel neglected and may make her feel guilty about not being an adequate wife.

Motherhood also has its positive side, though these qualities may not be as evident early in motherhood. As Hoffnung (1984) writes,

> The role of mother brings with it benefits as well as limitations. Children affect parents in ways that lead to personal growth, enable reworking of childhood conflicts, build flexibility and empathy, and provide intimate, loving human connections. ... They expand their caretakers' worlds by their activity levels, their imaginations, and their inherently appealing natures. Although motherhood is not enough to fill an entire life, for most mothers it is one of the most meaningful experiences in their lives. [p. 134]

If you were to ask a mother of an infant to list the positive and negative qualities of motherhood, the negative list would probably be longer, and it would contain many concrete details. Most mothers seem to find that the positive side of motherhood is more abstract, more difficult to describe, and yet more intense. It is much easier to describe the drudgery of dirty diapers than the near ecstasy of realizing that this complete human being was once part of your own body, and now it breathes and gurgles and hiccups without your help. Shortly after birth, too, babies develop ways of communicating with other humans. The delights of a baby's first tentative smile are undeniable, and an older baby can interact quite impressively with adults by making appropriate eye contact and conversational noises. Clearly, there are many joyous aspects to motherhood, and it's unfortunate that our society cannot devise creative ways to diminish the negative aspects.

Postpartum Disturbances

Glance over that earlier list of ten items, from the perspective of a new mother who is exhausted from childbirth and whose infant is not yet old enough to provide many of the benefits that Hoffnung describes. It should not surprise you that many women develop disturbances during the **postpartum period,** shortly after birth.

There seem to be two different kinds of postpartum disturbances. The most common of these is called the **maternity blues,** something experienced by 50 to 80 percent of women during the first week after delivery (Hopkins, Marcus, & Campbell, 1984; Stein, 1982). The maternity blues is a short-lasting change in mood that usually lasts less than two days. Fortunately, the blues is a self-limiting disturbance. Typical symptoms include episodes of crying, depression, irritability, tension, anxiety, and anger. It is more common with the first birth than with later children, so it must be at least partly related to the adjustment problems of being a new parent.

A more serious disorder is **postpartum depression,** which has an incidence rate of about 20 percent (Hopkins, et al., 1984). Postpartum depression typically involves feelings of extreme sadness, apathy, despair, and worthlessness, decreased ability to do ordinary work, and physical side effects such as headaches and intestinal problems (Plumb, 1983). Postpartum depression is somewhat similar to other kinds of depression, which we will discuss in the next chapter, except that women suffering from postpartum depression are less likely to contemplate suicide, and they are also likely to recover from depression more quickly. A woman's age and the number of previous children do not seem to be related to the incidence of postpartum depression, but two risk factors seem to be having had a previous psychiatric disturbance and being unmarried (Hopkins, et al., 1984).

There is controversy about the origins of both maternity blues and postpartum depression. You may recall that the levels of progesterone and estrogen drop sharply during the last stages of childbirth. Many researchers have explored a hormonal explanation. There may be some connection between hormonal level and postpartum disturbances, but the relationship is inconsistent and it certainly is not a strong one (Hopkins, et al., 1984; Parlee, 1978; Stein, 1982). The list of stresses and sources of dissatisfaction during the postpartum period provides a compelling reason for blues or depression, but we do not know which specific factors are most to blame. As Atkinson and Rickel (1984) point out, the cultural myth of "blissful motherhood" has prevented psychologists and other researchers from careful consideration of the negative side of motherhood.

It is important to keep in mind that some women do not experience either the blues or depression following the birth of their baby. We saw in Chapter 4 that some women do not experience premenstrual or menstrual symptoms, and earlier in this chapter we noted that some women experience little discomfort or psychological problems during pregnancy. In Chapter 14, we will see that women can go through menopause without any trauma. In short, women show substantial individual differences, and the various phases in a woman's reproductive life do not inevitably bring emotional or physical problems.

Breast-Feeding

There has been a remarkable recent change in mothers' ideas about feeding their infants. The number of babies who were breast-fed while in the hospital more than doubled in a ten-year period, and in 1981, 58 percent of mothers nursed their infants (Martinez & Dodd, 1983).

The breast-feeding process involves an impressive coordination of the baby's sucking efforts and the mother's glands and hormones, as well as psychological factors. Details of this process can be found in Lawrence's

(1980) book *Breast-Feeding.* It is important to know that a newborn baby does not typically nurse efficiently and automatically when put to the breast. Breast-feeding is a skill that both the mother and the infant must learn (Gansberg & Mostel, 1984). Some helpful hints can be found in other books (La Leche League International, 1981; Lawrence, 1980; Young, 1982).

One reason for the increase in the number of mothers who breast-feed is that recent evidence suggests that human breast milk may be better for infants than cow's milk. Breast milk offers protection against infection, and it does not produce the allergic reactions that cow's milk does for some infants (Barness, 1977; Jelliffe & Jelliffe, 1977). Breast-feeding also seems to help the mother's uterus return to its nonpregnant state more rapidly. Breast-feeding may also provide psychological advantages, but this has not yet been convincingly demonstrated. There is evidence, though, that nursing mothers are more satisfied with the feeding experience than are mothers who bottle-feed (Berg-Cross, et al., 1979).

Mothers who breast-feed are likely to be better educated and to have higher incomes than mothers who bottle-feed (Martinez & Dodd, 1983). Mothers who breast-feed, in contrast to those who bottle-feed, are likely to believe that breast-feeding establishes a close bond between mother and baby, whereas bottle-feeding mothers are more likely to believe that bottle-feeding is convenient and trouble free (Manstead, Proffitt, & Smart, 1983).

Women typically report that breast-feeding is a very pleasant experience that arouses a feeling of warmth and openness (Kitzinger, 1983). Some authors have also pointed out that breast-feeding can be sexually arousing (Kitzinger, 1983; Lawrence, 1980). Some women may feel guilty about this kind of experience; they don't realize that this arousal is normal. As a consequence, babies may be weaned early.

Alice Mattison (1979) nicely captures a mother's observations of her nursing infant in the following poem:

Breastfeeding

It is like watching Yehudi Menuhin on television.
You see a round face,
mute, busy,
with the look in the eyes
people have when they're paying
close attention, but not
visual attention.
Next to the face, tipped up from the chin
and near enough to the mouth to make your
view seem intimate, what with the musician's
folded handkerchief (almost as if for dribble)
is something with a curved edge, about as big as
the face, soft in one instance, hard in the other; your breast, or
the violin. It is a crowded picture because
also, in the closeup, is the conductor's elbow or
your own, which often gets in the way

(especially if you're lying down to nurse) and which looked,
on television, as though it might
bump into the violin, although, of course,
it must actually have been well in front.
Your arm is in back of your breast.
You don't feel the milk coming out,
nor see it;
what you see is someone else
drinking—thwarted music: played
elsewhere. When the milk,
however, starts to flow freely,
after the baby's been sucking for twenty seconds,
you feel, for a moment, as though your breasts
have been inflated and you get that
sweet tension in your throat—as if there's something good
that you can't remember.

Attachment

Attachment is an affectional bond that one person forms toward another person (Ainsworth, 1973).

For many decades, psychologists were interested in the process by which infants grow attached to their mothers. (Fathers were seldom studied.) In recent years, researchers have begun to look at attachment from the mother's point of view. Rather than assuming that mothers just "naturally" feel intense love for their babies as soon as they are born, we now know that this love takes time to grow. The nature of that attachment also changes over time. A mother of a newborn may feel affectionately protective of her helpless-looking infant, a different kind of love than a mother feels when she watches an older infant cooing and smiling at her (Robson & Moss, 1970).

One particularly controversial issue is whether attachment is influenced by the amount of time that the mother and baby spend together shortly after birth. The standard hospital procedure for many decades had been to allow the mother and infant a few moments together before whisking the infant off to the nursery; the two would be reunited during their hospital stay only every four hours for half-hour feeding sessions. An influential study by Klaus and his colleagues (1972) demonstrated that mothers showed more attachment-related behaviors when they were allowed to spend extra time with their babies. Mothers who spent a total of about 16 additional hours with their babies—spread over a three-day period—showed more fondling and eye contact with their infants one month later. Later reports suggested that this brief period of extra contact at childbirth could influence maternal behavior years later. Largely as a consequence of this kind of research, hospitals have frequently modified their procedures so that mothers and fathers can spend more time with their newborns. Most hospitals now have some variant of a **"rooming-in"** arrangement, whereby babies remain with their mothers for most of the hospital stay.

Numerous studies have been published since 1972, and the results are not as clear-cut as they originally seemed. Many of the studies had methodological problems and potential biases (Lamb, 1982; Thomson & Kramer, 1984). When Thomson and Kramer looked at the five studies that were most carefully controlled, they found that three reported a beneficial effect from extra contact, and two did not find a significant effect. In general, it also seems that the short-term benefits are more substantial than the long-term benefits.

As Korsch (1983) concludes, the evidence about extra contact is not compelling. However, it may be that we haven't yet looked at the right kinds of measures of attachment. More details on theoretical and practical aspects of parent-infant attachment can also be found in other resources (Kennell & Klaus, 1984; Klaus & Kennell, 1982; Myers, 1984).

It may be unclear whether extra contact really promotes attachment. However, it is difficult to see how it can do any harm. Also, no one has yet demonstrated that it's *better* to separate parents and newborns. Furthermore, from a feminist viewpoint, the extra-contact procedure allows women to have more choice and control over their postpartum experiences. The previous hospital procedure rigidly controlled when and how mothers became acquainted with their infants. When my oldest daughter was born in 1970, a nurse yelled at me for unwrapping her from her blanket-cocoon, and I contemplated hiding her under my bedsheets to prolong our visit beyond the specified 30 minutes. Rooming-in reminds everyone that the baby belongs to the mother, and not to the hospital.

The Decision to Have Children

As recently as ten to 20 years ago, women did not need to make a decision about whether or not to have a child. Almost all married women who were physically capable of having children did so, with very little forethought or sense that they had a real choice (Faux, 1984). However, American couples now have an average of only 1.8 children (McFalls, 1983). Estimates of the number of women who do not want to have children range between 10 percent and 25 percent (Cook, et al., 1982; Faux, 1984; Gerson, et al., 1984; and Notman & Nadelson, 1982).

What are the characteristics of women who prefer not to have children? Child-free women tend to be urban, white, and well educated (Faux, 1984). They are often professionals. In one survey of faculty women at a large university, 55 percent of married women under 40 years of age had no children (Yogev & Vierra, 1983).

It probably will not surprise you to learn that child-free women are also more likely to have feminist, nontraditional beliefs about gender roles, whereas women who want to have children are more likely to be traditionally "feminine" in their beliefs (Bram, 1984; Gerson, 1980, 1984; Gerson, et al., 1984; Scott & Morgan, 1983). This finding is true for black women as well as white women. However, for Hispanic women, beliefs about gender roles may not be a crucial determinant in the motherhood decision (Beckman, 1979).

Attitudes Toward Child-Free Women

For this demonstration, you will need some volunteers, ideally at least five for each of the two conditions. Read the following paragraph aloud to half of the volunteers, either individually or in a group:

Robin is 25 years old and is a social worker with a county agency. She finds the work challenging and gratifying, though it does have its frustrating aspects. For two years now, she has been married to Jim, who teaches high-school social studies. Robin and Jim consider themselves to be happily married and they enjoy being with each other very much. Robin and Jim have decided not to have any children. They enjoy going to movies and getting together with friends, and they also like to play tennis.

After reading this paragraph, pass out copies of the rating sheet below and ask them to rate their impression of Robin.

Follow the same procedure for the other half of the volunteers, except for the sentence, "Robin and Jim have decided not to have any children," substitute the sentence, "Robin and Jim would like to have two children." Compare the average responses of the two groups; is Robin considered to be more selfish, immature, and poorly adjusted if she does not want to have children?

1	2	3	4	5	6	7
selfish						unselfish

1	2	3	4	5	6	7
warm						cold

1	2	3	4	5	6	7
mature						immature

1	2	3	4	5	6	7
insensitive						sensitive

1	2	3	4	5	6	7
well adjusted						poorly adjusted

1	2	3	4	5	6	7
unfriendly						friendly

1	2	3	4	5	6	7
stable						unstable

1	2	3	4	5	6	7
loving						unloving

Women's own memories of their childhood also influence their decisions about motherhood. Women who have positive memories of early mother love and a happy childhood are more likely to want children, whereas those who have unpleasant childhood memories are more likely not to want children (Gerson, 1980, 1984; Kaltreider & Margolis, 1977).

A few decades ago, a young woman who did not plan to have children would probably have been seen as selfish, unhappy, and emotionally unstable. Try Demonstration 11.3 to determine how your friends perceive a woman who wants to remain child-free.

The research on reactions to women who don't want to have children shows that American college students today are not prejudiced against these women. For instance, 88 percent of students in one sample thought that a woman who did not want children was not selfish or unnatural, and only 22 percent thought that having a baby was totally fulfilling for a woman (Hare-Mustin & Broderick, 1979). Only 9 percent of respondents in another survey said that young married women lack self-fulfillment until they have a child (Knaub, Eversoll, & Voss, 1983). In a third study, students did not show negative stereotyping of child-free women (Shields & Cooper, 1983). Keep in mind, however, that these data are gathered from college students, a group that are somewhat more likely than average *not* to want children themselves. More negative attitudes would probably be found if we sampled a more general population.

Some of the reasons that voluntarily child-free couples say that they don't want to have a child are the following (Benedek & Vaughn, 1982; Campbell, et al., 1982; Sunday & Lewin, 1985; McFalls, 1983):

1. Parenthood is an irrevocable decision; you can't take children back to the store for a refund.
2. Children are expensive, particularly considering the cost of college education.
3. Some women and men are afraid that they will not be good parents.
4. Some couples are reluctant to give up a satisfactory lifestyle for a more child-focused orientation.
5. Children can interfere with educational and vocational plans.
6. Some couples do not want to bring children into a world in which there is a threat of nuclear war and other serious global problems.

And yet there are compelling reasons to have children, according to those who are enthusiastic about parenthood (Campbell, et al., 1982; Daniels & Weingarten, 1982; Hoffman & Manis, 1978):

1. Parenthood is challenging; it offers people the opportunity to learn what they can be.
2. Parenthood is a sign of adult status.
3. Parenthood allows the opportunity to establish close relationships with other human beings.
4. Parents have a unique chance to be responsible for someone's education and training, and to watch this person grow to adulthood.
5. Some people have children to "carry on the family line" or to ensure that some part of themselves survives into future generations.
6. Children can be a source of fun, pride, and pleasure.

So who's happier, those with children or those without them? In 1975, popular columnist Ann Landers asked her readers whether they would have children if they could relive their lives. To everyone's amazement, 70 percent of the respondents said that they would not choose to become parents again (Faux, 1984). Of course, this was not a scientifically conducted study because of the likelihood of a biased sample, but the results made Americans very aware that parenthood does not guarantee bliss.

More systematic research lends some support to Landers' findings, particularly for women. Young women who do not have children tend to be happier with their marriages, more satisfied with their lives, more successful in their careers, and less likely to experience role conflict, in contrast to those with children (Campbell, et al., 1976; Doherty & Jacobson, 1982; Gerson, et al., 1984; and Veevers, 1979).

These are the results for young women; how about older women? Surveys of women over 50 years of age have compared child-free women with women whose children no longer live at home, and these two groups do not seem to differ in their happiness (Beckman & Houser, 1982; Glenn & McLanahan, 1981; Houser, et al., 1984). The only situation in which women with children appear to be happier than child-free women is in the case of widows. That is, widows with grown children seem to be slightly more satisfied and less lonely, isolated or depressed (Beckman & Houser, 1982). In summary, women who decide not to have children are certainly not doomed to a life of isolation and unhappiness; in fact, they are probably happier in young adulthood than are women with children.

According to Faux (1984), our culture must not insist that women should have children in order to feel fulfilled:

Only then will women learn that they truly do have choices about how to live their lives—that they can combine motherhood and careers, that they can have many children if that is what they want, and that they can freely choose childlessness, too. [p. 171]

One conclusion seems clear. Women must have the freedom to make choices. Freedom comes when women are not condemned for deciding to be child-free—or for deciding to become mothers.

☐ SECTION SUMMARY ▪ Motherhood

1. **Stereotypes about motherhood suggest that it is entirely joyous and requires little adjustment, yet other stereotypes portray mothers as nagging and domineering.**
2. **Although many lofty phrases are written about motherhood, it actually has little prestige; in reality, motherhood involves responsibility, drudgery, constant demands, feeling incompetent, little gratitude, little contact with other adults, deprivation from other**

sources of identity, feeling "tied down," physical discomfort, and guilt about inadequacy as a wife.

3. Motherhood also has a positive side, although it may not be evident in early motherhood; the benefits include personal growth, increased flexibility and empathy, intimacy, and expanded experience.

4. Maternity blues, experienced by the majority of women a few days after delivery, usually involves episodes of crying, tension, and anger.

5. Postpartum depression is more severe, occurring about 20 percent of the time; it involves extreme despair, decreased ability to function, and physical side effects.

6. Breast-feeding has increased in recent years; it has benefits for infants' health, and breast-feeding mothers are typically enthusiastic about its advantages.

7. There is some evidence that extended contact between mother and infants, such as that provided by rooming-in, increases the mother's attachment toward the infant, but there are methodological difficulties with many studies.

8. Between 10 and 25 percent of women say that they do not want to have children; they tend to be urban, white, well educated, feminist, and less likely to have positive childhood memories.

9. College students do not hold negative stereotypes about child-free women.

10. Child-free couples cite advantages such as the irrevocability of the decision to have a child, the expense, fears about parenting, interference with life style or vocation, and fears about exposing children to world problems.

11. Couples who want to have children cite advantages of parenthood such as its challenge, the adult status, close relationships, benefits of responsibility, "carrying on the family line," and the pleasurable aspects of children.

12. Child-free women are often happier in early adulthood, but in old age, widows with children tend to be slightly happier.

13. If society does not insist that children are necessary for women's fulfillment, then women will have real freedom of choice about childbearing.

Chapter Review Questions

1. The beginning of the chapter pointed out that pregnancy and childbirth appear to be taboo topics, particularly compared to the topics of love and sex. Based on the information in this chapter and earlier chapters, speculate on possible reasons for the low visibility of these topics.

2. Summarize biological aspects of pregnancy and childbirth, and list some of the physical reactions to pregnancy.

3. This chapter emphasizes ambivalent feelings and thoughts more than any other chapter in the book. Address the issue of ambivalence with respect to four topics: (a) emotional reactions to pregnancy; (b) emotional reactions to childbirth; (c) the reality of motherhood; and (d) the decision to have children.

4. Summarize Taylor and Langer's (1977) study on reactions to pregnant women and other information on attitudes toward pregnant women, and comment on how these findings may contribute to women's emotional reactions to pregnancy.

5. There have been tremendous changes in ideas about pregnancy, childbirth, and motherhood in recent decades. Comment on these changes, focusing on topics such as prepared childbirth, the family-centered approach to childbirth, breast-feeding, and the decision to have children.

6. What kinds of efforts have been made in recent years to include the husband or other companion and other family members in the childbirth experience?

7. One of the themes of the book has been that stereotypes and reality about women do not always coincide. Address this issue with respect to motherhood.

8. An idea mentioned several times in this chapter is that women must have the freedom to make choices. How is this relevant to topics in the area of childbirth and motherhood?

9. A prominent theme throughout this book is that women react in a variety of ways to the same life event. Discuss this theme, focusing on individual differences in physical and emotional reactions to pregnancy, childbirth experiences, and postpartum disturbances.

10. Childbirth educators have made impressive changes in the way childbirth is handled, but the stresses of motherhood remain. Imagine that our society valued motherhood enough to fund programs aimed at decreasing the stresses that women experience in the first weeks after their babies are born. First, review those stresses. Then describe what an ideal program might involve in terms of education, help, and social support.

☐ NEW TERMS

placenta
trimester
Lamaze preparation
family-centered approach
postpartum period

maternity blues
postpartum depression
attachment
rooming-in

☐ RECOMMENDED READINGS

Blum, B. L. (Ed.) (1980). *Psychological aspects of pregnancy, birthing and bonding.* New York: Human Sciences. ■ Aimed primarily at a professional audience, this edited volume includes topics such as adolescent pregnancy, the history of birth practices, and psychotherapy with pregnant women.

Fox, G. L. (Ed.) (1982). *The childbearing decision.* Beverly Hills, Calif.: Sage. ■ This book focuses on how people decide whether to have children, and it includes articles on the development of attitudes toward fertility and motivations for childbearing.

Gansberg, J. M., & Mostel, A. P. (1984). *The second nine months.* New York: Tribeca. ■ This sensitively written book would make a good gift for a new mother. It begins with labor and delivery and examines the first nine months of motherhood, offering practical suggestions as well as descriptions.

Leifer, M. (1980). *Psychological effects of motherhood.* New York: Praeger. ■ This book is a detailed report of changes experienced by a group of women in a research project during their first pregnancy and early motherhood; it contains numerous interesting quotes from the mothers.

Young, D. (1982). *Changing childbirth: Family birth in the hospital.* Rochester, N.Y.: Childbirth Graphics. ■ Focusing on innovations in childbirth, this book will be valuable for health professionals, psychologists, and expectant families.

WOMEN AND PSYCHOLOGICAL DISORDERS

- No matter how we define psychological disorders, men are more likely than women to have problems.

- Women are much more likely than men to seek psychiatric treatment for the same kind of psychological disorder.

- In general, therapists are not biased against women in deciding which people have psychological disorders.

- Therapists are usually well-informed about research on the psychology of women.

- All of the traditional approaches to therapy are based on sexist ideas about women.

- Most feminists argue that essentially all therapy can be replaced by discussion groups where women share their personal experiences with one another.

- Assertiveness training is designed to make women more aggressive.

- Depressed people may feel inadequate, but their performance is actually normal.

- Overweight is difficult to treat.

- Alcoholism seems to be more hidden in women than in men.

Rose Farsmith is a 45-year-old woman who made a suicide attempt when she learned that her husband had fallen in love with another woman and wanted to divorce her. She took an overdose of barbiturates from which she miraculously recovered. On arriving home from the hospital, she learned that her husband had already moved out of the house.

She said that she had been depressed for many years, primarily because of her husband. He was unreliable and did not seem to respect her. During the first ten years of her marriage she had devoted herself entirely to her husband and two children, trying to please them. After realizing that her marriage would not improve, she had several attacks of depression, but she did not seek treatment. She had tried to keep the marriage going and was terrified about the possibility of being alone. After therapy, fortunately, she accepted the divorce and gradually began to rebuild a life for herself (Arieti & Bemporad, 1978).

There are many Rose Farsmiths in our country. There are also many women whose problems are less severe, as well as women who do not recover from their psychological disorders. As Brodsky and Hare-Mastin (1980) have pointed out, "women are the primary users of all health care services in a system controlled and administered largely by men. In the area of psychotherapy, women have represented the majority of patients and the minority of therapists" (p. 385).

This chapter has three parts. In the first part, we'll discuss sex ratios in psychological disorders. Then we'll examine the topic of psychotherapy and women. Our final topic is specific psychological disorders, in which we'll look at four disorders and how they can be approached with psychotherapy.

☐ SEX RATIOS IN PSYCHOLOGICAL DISORDERS

Who has the higher rate of psychological disorders,* men or women? Let's look at the data and then consider some possible explanations.

The Data

Women are somewhat more likely than men to use psychiatric facilities. For example, there are 1.33 times as many women as men in private mental hospitals (Russo & Sobel, 1981). However, people receive treatment in psychiatric facilities for many different reasons. They may have problems with alcohol or drug abuse; men are more likely than women to belong in this category. They may have **personality disorders,** which include problems with aggression, the control of impulses, and a lack of social responsibility; men are also more likely than women to belong in this category. Notice that

---

*I prefer the term "psychological disorders." Some researchers prefer alternate terms, such as "mental illness," a term that suggests a physical-disease basis for the problem, or "abnormal behavior," a term that suggests that we have a clear-cut standard for normal behavior (Marecek, 1978).

these disorders can be very serious. However, in our society, they often tend to be treated by the criminal-justice system, rather than the mental-health system.

Some researchers who analyze the data on sex ratios prefer to omit these categories of personality disorders and substance abuse. Gove (1980) uses the term mental illness to refer to those people who experience personal discomfort (for example, anxiety or depression) or mental disorganization (for example, confusion or thought blockage) that is not caused by substance abuse. When mental illness is defined in this way, people with personality disorders are excluded because they do not experience personal discomfort; they may be aggressive, but they are neither anxious nor depressed. People with substance-abuse problems are also excluded. When we eliminate these two groups—keeping in mind that there are more men in both of these categories—we find that women are substantially more likely than men to receive psychiatric care. Gove and Tudor (1973) examined the number of people receiving psychiatric care in general hospitals in the United States, using their restricted definition of mental illness. They found that 1.68 times as many women as men received treatment. This is quite frightening; why should 68 percent more women than men require psychiatric care in these hospitals for the kinds of disorders involving personal discomfort and mental disorganization?

In later work, Gove discovered that the higher rates of mental illness seem to be limited to married women. Figure 12.1 shows the ratio of women to men in four marriage categories: married, widowed, never married, and separated/divorced (Gove, 1979). (These data are based on public mental hospitals and outpatient psychiatric clinics, and not just on the general hospitals from which the earlier 1.68 sex ratio was obtained.) Notice that when females are married, they are more likely than males to receive psychiatric treatment. In all other categories, however, there are more men than women.

In general, then, women are more likely than men to be receiving treatment for personal discomfort or mental disorganization. However, this higher rate of disorders among women seems to be due to the relatively high rate of mental illness among married women. In fact, women who are unmarried are less likely than unmarried men to receive treatment for their condition.

The Explanations

We looked at the data. What are the explanations? As you might imagine, there are many possible reasons. In all likelihood, the answer is not limited to one single explanation. Let's examine the possibilities.

Biological differences. Perhaps there is something about women's biological makeup that predisposes them to some kinds of psychological disorders. This seems like a possible explanation, because other kinds of psychological disorders show an imbalance in the sex ratio that might be biologically based. Consider Attention Deficit Disorder, where the major

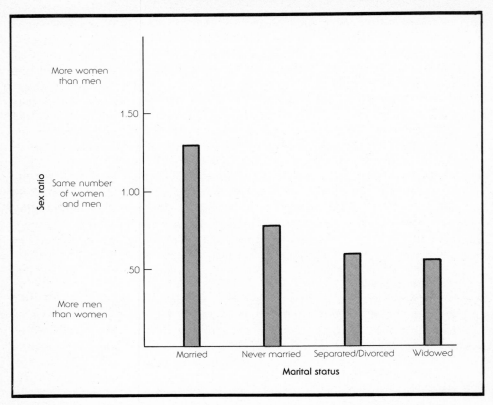

problem is failure to pay attention. This disorder is ten times as common in boys as in girls (American Psychiatric Association, 1980) and a biological explanation seems likely for this difference.

Perhaps you've already figured out why a biological explanation seems unlikely to provide an adequate answer to the sex-ratio question. If biological differences are responsible, why should the higher rate of disorders be limited to married women? A supporter of a biological explanation might argue that women who are likely to develop psychological disorders could be more likely to marry. However, that argument wouldn't explain why widowed and divorced women—who were married at one time—are better off than men. The answer doesn't seem to lie in biology.

Differences in willingness to seek help. Perhaps more women are being treated for psychological disorders because they are more willing to seek help. Women might be more willing to seek help because they are more sensitive in perceiving problems. As you may recall from Chapter 9, women are more likely than men to detect problems in a love relationship. According to this explanation, women and men might be equally likely to have psychological disorders, but women are simply more attuned to their problems.

Women might also be more willing to seek help because it is more acceptable for a woman to be sick. Men must maintain the myth that they are strong and in control of their emotions, whereas women can admit that they have a problem.

In addition, women might be more willing to seek help because it is more acceptable for a woman to be dependent upon someone else. Most client-therapist relationships involve a weak, submissive client, and a strong, dominant therapist (a problem to which feminist therapists object, as we'll see later). Men may be reluctant to accept such a submissive role.

According to these explanations, the relatively large number of women who appear in the statistics on psychological disorders does not reflect reality. In reality, there should be many men with disorders who simply don't seek help.

Although this line of reasoning is appealing, there is little evidence to support it. In some studies, women have been found to be no more likely than men with equally serious disorders to seek professional help (summarized by Gove, 1980). In fact, women may be slightly *less* likely to seek help. In other research, men and women were similar in the extent to which they believed that psychiatric symptoms were undesirable (summarized by Gove, 1980). There may be some validity to this explanation and it certainly is intuitively appealing—but it hasn't yet been demonstrated.

Therapist bias. According to the "therapist-bias" explanation, women are more likely than men to be labeled as having psychological disorders. In reality, women and men may not differ in the incidence of psychological disorders. Notice that the earlier "willingness-to-seek-help" explanation suggested that the sex ratio is due to a bias in clients' responses, whereas this "therapist-bias" explanation suggests that the sex ratio is due to a bias in the therapists' responses.

One writer who brought particular attention to the possibility of therapist bias is Phyllis Chesler (1972), in her book *Women and Madness*. Chesler argues that therapists use a **double standard of mental health** when they diagnose mental disorders. According to this double standard, men are not typically seen as "sick" if they act out the male role. However, women are seen as sick when they act out the female role by being depressed, incompetent, and anxious, and also when they reject the female role by being hostile, independent, and successful.

Many people speculated about this double standard, and the evidence for it seemed to come in a study by Broverman and her coauthors (1970) that is now regarded as a classic. Demonstration 12.1 is a modified version of their study. These authors asked practicing therapists (both male and female) to judge a person on 122 items, including those in Demonstration

Is There a Double Standard in Mental Health?

Make photocopies of the sheet below, or—alternately—read the items aloud and ask for a verbal judgment. In either case, locate nine or more people who will participate. Ask one-third of the people to think of a normal, healthy adult male and to select which word of the pair would best describe this man. Repeat this task with another third of the people, asking them to think of a normal, healthy adult female. Ask the remaining one-third to perform the task, thinking of a normal, healthy adult; do not specify the sex in this case. When you have tallied all the responses; notice whether the adult (sex unspecified) is closer to the male or the female.

1. very emotional   not at all emotional
2. very adventurous   not at all adventurous
3. very passive   very active
4. very independent   not at all independent
5. feelings easily hurt   feelings not easily hurt
6. very self-confident   not at all self-confident
7. cries very easily   never cries
8. very gentle   very rough
9. very tactful   very blunt
10. easily expresses tender feelings   does not express tender feelings at all

12.1. Some people were asked to choose the word of the pair that best described a mature, healthy adult man. Others received the same instructions, except that the word "woman" was substituted for "man." Still others were given instructions for a mature, healthy adult, and the sex was unspecified.

Broverman and her coauthors looked at 38 of the items that had been previously judged to be related to sex stereotypes. First, they analyzed therapists' responses for the "healthy adult" instructions; these responses should provide a standard of mental health against which the responses for "healthy adult man" and "healthy adult woman" could be compared. These comparisons showed that therapists rated the "healthy adult man" as being significantly closer to the "healthy adult" than the "healthy adult woman" was to the "healthy adult." It seemed that therapists were judging men and women by different standards, so that a healthy adult *woman* wasn't really a healthy adult. In contrast, a healthy adult *man* was also a healthy adult. This study was widely quoted, and people were convinced that a woman was bound to lose in therapy. If she was a sane woman, she couldn't be a sane adult. Alternately, if she was a sane adult, she couldn't manage to be a sane woman. It seemed that the stereotypes that were dominant throughout the United States had also influenced the therapists.

However, as critics of this study later pointed out, the difference may have been statistically significant, but it was small in absolute terms (Smith, 1980). Furthermore, critics have complained that many people believe that it is an established "fact" that therapists are sexist, when in reality the subsequent research does not offer much evidence for therapists' bias. Smith (1980) gathered together numerous studies on gender bias in therapy. She then conducted meta-analyses. This is the statistical analysis we discussed in Chapter 7 that combines the results of many independent experiments and provides us with a single measure of statistical significance. Considering all the experiments together, the meta-analyses showed that there was no evidence of either a bias against women or a tendency to favor stereotyped roles for women. Others who have examined the studies on gender bias have reached similar conclusions (Abramowitz & Dokecki, 1977; Davidson & Abramowitz, 1980; Phillips & Gilroy, 1985).

It is possible that therapists are biased against women but that they are sophisticated enough to know that they shouldn't reveal their biases when they participate in an experiment. By now, most therapists should know that they are *supposed* to respond similarly to women and men, and their responses might not reflect their true feelings (Davidson & Abramowitz, 1980; Phillips & Gilroy, 1985). These studies may therefore underestimate gender bias among therapists.

You may wonder whether male therapists and female therapists differ in their biases against women. In general, they do not (Smith, 1980). In summary, neither female therapists nor male therapists have been shown to use a double standard of mental health when they are making diagnoses. It may be tempting to blame therapists for the fact that women are more likely than men to be treated for psychological disorders. However, we don't yet have any consistent evidence that therapists are more likely to label women as being "sick." The explanation for the sex ratio in psychological disorders must lie elsewhere.

The female role.　Let's review the explanations we have considered so far. It seems that the sex ratio in psychological disorders cannot be substantially explained by biological differences, by differences in willingness to seek help, or by therapist bias. Many researchers have concluded that the explanation lies in the fact that the female role is simply more stressful and less rewarding than the male role.

Walter Gove and his colleagues have been particularly active in writing about the kinds of problems women face (Gove, 1980; Gove & Tudor, 1973). It was Gove who pointed out that married women are particularly likely to suffer from psychological disorders. He elaborates on this issue:

> There are a number of reasons for assuming that married women find their roles to be more frustrating and less rewarding than married men. In recent times the role of housewife has lost many of its societal functions; consequently, the wife

contributes relatively less instrumentally to the household than in the past. [Many] wives still do not hold jobs and are restricted to one major societal role, that of housewife, whereas men occupy two such roles, that of household head and worker. A man typically has two sources of gratification, his family and his work, whereas a woman has only one, her family. Children, particularly when they are very young, channel women into situations in which the women are isolated from adult interaction yet confront seemingly incessant demands. . . . (Gove, 1980, p. 355)

As Gove also points out, married women who are employed experience more stress than their husbands. They typically occupy a less satisfying position, with lower pay and less intellectual challenge. Furthermore, as you'll remember from Chapter 6, women perform the great majority of household chores. Consequently, they work more hours each day than do their husbands.

In summary, women may be more likely than men to experience psychological disorders because they encounter more stress. Their position in society is much less rewarding and much more frustrating. This explanation seems particularly appealing, and it is consistent with the second theme developed throughout this book, that men are evaluated more positively than women. Unfortunately, however, it is difficult to test this explanation in a scientific manner. The female-role explanation has so many different components—such as prestige, stress, and frustration—that research in this area is extremely difficult (Horwitz, 1982).

One component of the female role has been examined in relation to psychological disorders. Horwitz (1982) focused on the relative lack of power women have. He analyzed data that had been gathered in a community survey in New Haven, Connecticut, in order to examine the effect of power on psychological disorders. He defined power in terms of having a dominant role in the family and controlling resources. The results showed that every group in the sample that occupied a powerful role had few psychological disorders, in comparison to groups that occupied a powerless role. Married, employed women without children, for example, had few problems, but unemployed married men had many problems.

It seems, then, that being female, by itself, is not enough to predispose people to psychological disorders. However, being powerless is a situation that creates problems, and women in twentieth-century America are relatively powerless. If women obtain more power in future decades, the sex differences in psychological disorders should decline.

At present, many researchers prefer the "female-role" explanation for the mystery about the relative abundance of women suffering from psychological disorders. It seems to be an attractive explanation, though we don't yet have much research to support it. The answer probably cannot be traced to a single explanation. Many variables undoubtedly contribute to the fact that women are more likely than men to suffer from personal discomfort and mental disorganization.

SECTION SUMMARY ▪ Sex Ratios in Psychological Disorders

1. Women are somewhat more likely than men to receive treatment in psychiatric facilities; if we eliminate those with substance-abuse problems and personality disorders, women are much more likely than men to receive treatment.
2. Married women are particularly likely to receive treatment in psychiatric facilities.
3. There is little evidence to support the argument that women are more likely to receive psychiatric treatment because of biological differences or because they are more likely to seek help.
4. There is also little evidence to support the idea that therapists use a double standard of mental health, in which women are more likely than men to be labeled "sick" for similar kinds of symptoms.
5. The currently popular explanation for the sex ratios in psychological disorders is that the female role is more stressful and less rewarding than the male role.
6. It is difficult to test the "female-role" explanation for why women have more psychological disorders; however, a study by Horwitz (1982) demonstrated that powerless people had more psychological disorders.

PSYCHOTHERAPY AND WOMEN

The term **psychotherapy** means the use of psychological techniques by mental-health professionals to help either psychological disorders or problems that arise in everyday living (Schaffer, 1980). Some people who receive psychotherapy are severely disturbed and are treated in hospitals. Others may receive psychotherapy for a number of years but are able to function outside of a hospital setting. Still others choose psychotherapy to help them during periods of stress in their lives.

There are a number of issues that we need to consider in this section. Earlier in the chapter we looked at the issue of sexism in the diagnosis and labeling of psychological disorders; now we'll examine the issue of sexism in the practice of psychotherapy. Our next topic is traditional psychotherapies and how they treat women. Finally, we'll look at several newer alternatives used to help women.

Psychotherapy and Sexism

There are several different topics that are relevant to the issue of psychotherapy and sexism: (1) Is there a double standard in psychotherapy, so that women and men receive different treatment from therapists? (2) Do women receive more medication than men? (3) Are male therapists likely to have sexual relations with their female clients?

Treatment of women and men. We mentioned earlier that a large number of studies have focused on a potential double standard in the *diagnosis* of psychological disorders. However, there have been few studies about how therapists actually *treat* their female and male clients (Marecek & Johnson, 1980). Let's shift our focus, then, from the diagnosis of disorders to the treatment of disorders. Some years ago, the American Psychological Association (1975) made an attempt to answer this question. They sent a questionnaire to women therapists, asking them for examples of gender bias and gender stereotyping in psychotherapy with women.

The respondents offered examples of biased treatment of women that could be categorized into four general areas:

1. Therapists may foster traditional gender roles, so that women are encouraged to be good wives and mothers, rather than expressing an interest in their work. As one respondent reported, "As a state hospital intern, I was appalled at the treatment given women—usually 'go home and do more of what a wife should do—clean house, etc.'—live lives of a kind that sent them to the hospital in the first place" (p. 1171).
2. Therapists may have low expectations for women's value, which they may reveal by telling sexist jokes, using demeaning labels, and ignoring violence toward women.
3. Therapists may emphasize the sexist use of psychoanalytic concepts (a topic we'll discuss in the section on traditional psychotherapies).
4. Therapists may regard women as sex objects, which may include the seduction of female clients; we'll return to this topic shortly.

At present, the evidence for the biased treatment of women is mostly in the form of anecdotes and informal observation. It is clear that some therapists treat women and men by different standards, but we don't know how often this occurs and how serious the consequences may be for women. Any biased treatment should be condemned, because therapy is supposed to help women, rather than harm them.

Some writers have also speculated that minority women are particularly likely to receive biased treatment from therapists. For example, therapists may accept the myth of the black matriarchy that we discussed in Chapter 9. They may believe that black women's position in their family is responsible for the "deteriorating" conditions of the family. Therapists with this attitude will not be appropriately sympathetic to the needs of black women (Copeland, 1982).

Well-meaning therapists may find that they do not have adequate preparation or information to help some minority women, such as Chicanas, Puerto Rican women, and other Spanish-speaking women. As Collier (1982) writes, "Hispanic women pick their way through a chaos of sexism, racism, and deprivation that renders the experience and advice of most professionals irrelevant" (p. 225).

A study by Sherman, Koufacos, and Kenworthy (1978) suggests that therapists may lack preparation and information about women in general; their inadequate knowledge is not limited simply to minority women. These researchers surveyed male and female therapists and found that they were likely to be uninformed about research on the psychology of women. They were unaware of the studies on why women are more likely than men to be treated for psychological disorders. Furthermore, they were not especially well-informed in the areas of sexuality, pregnancy, and menopause. The problem of uninformed therapists may be more substantial than the problem of biased therapists.

There is also evidence that therapists may remember the problems of their male clients more than the problems of their female clients. Buczek (1981) asked advanced-level trainees in clinical psychology to listen to a tape recording of a client whose chief complaints were loss of energy, anxiety, and depression. The client's voice was male for half of the therapists and female for the other half. The content of the tape recording was the same in both cases, and it concluded a variety of facts about the client's social and occupational life. Both male and female therapists later tended to recall more facts about the male client than about the female client—even though the story had been exactly the same.

This study also revealed some biases in the kinds of questions therapists might ask their female and male clients. After listening to the tape recordings, the therapists were urged to write down any questions that they might ask the clients if they were to plan treatment for them. The therapists listed a larger number of questions about family relationships when the client had been female, rather than male. However, they asked the same number of questions about occupational issues in the female and male condition; there was no evidence of bias here.

In this section, we have discussed informal reports of the biased treatment of women in therapy, including the suggestion that minority women are particularly likely to encounter difficulties. There has been little research in this area. However, we do know that therapists may be uninformed about the psychology of women and that they may remember male clients' problems more accurately than female clients' problems. Finally, they differ in the questions they ask males and females about their family relationships, but not in questions asked about occupations.

Drug prescriptions for psychological disorders.   It is clear that women are more likely than men to be medicated for their mental and emotional problems. In one study, women received two-thirds of all the prescriptions that had been issued for psychological problems, that is, **psychoactive drugs** (Fidell, 1973). Unlike "illegal drugs," these drugs had been recommended by physicians, so women may tend to use them longer and more consistently.

According to another study, physicians believed that middle-aged house-wives were more likely than men to have a legitimate need for tranquilizers, presumably because their work would be less likely to be disrupted by the side effects (Linn, 1971).

Maybe women receive greater medication because they need it more; as we'll see, women are more likely to suffer from depression, a disorder that may respond to medication. However, this does not seem to be a complete explanation, because there is evidence that therapists are biased toward drug treatment for females. Specifically, Schwartz and Abramowitz (1975) found that experienced psychiatrists were likely to recommend psychoactive drugs in response to a description of a female client, in contrast to their recom-mendations when the same description was given for a male client.

Drug advertisements may also encourage the overmedication of female clients. Examinations of the advertisements for psychoactive drugs in psy-chiatric journals have shown that the clients in the pictures are likely to be women (Prather & Fidell, 1978; Stockburger & Davis, 1978). Women are particularly likely to be shown as suffering from insomnia, depression, and anxiety. Often, too, the ads suggested extremely stereotyped goals for the clients. Consider one advertisement that indicated that an improvement in the woman client's symptoms would allow her to get the laundry done.

Sexual relations with clients. A woman therapist who was concerned about the sexual exploitation of female clients wrote,

> In my years as a psychotherapist, many women have come to me with stories of seduction and sexual intimacies with male therapists. In most instances, the patients were deeply disturbed by these relationships, saw them as exploitative . . . and sometimes resulted in psychotic breaks. [American Psychological Asso-ciation, 1975, p. 1173]

Female clients have also reported that male therapists have suggested that their frigidity could be "cured" by the "right male," namely the therapist.

The *Ethical Principles of Psychologists*, which lists the official policy of the American Psychological Association (1981), is very clear about specifying that sexual intimacies with clients are unethical. As Stricker (1977) elabo-rates, " . . . it can be stated unequivocally that sexual relations between ther-apist and patient are always inappropriate, exploitative, and unethical; nei-ther are they psychotherapeutically beneficial to the patient, and they can often be destructive" (p. 15).

Nonetheless, these sexual relationships do occur. According to two sur-veys, about 5 percent of male therapists admitted to having had sexual in-tercourse with their patients, usually with more than one patient (Holroyd & Brodsky, 1977; Kardener, Fuller, & Mensh, 1973). No doubt 5 percent is an underestimate; therapists are unlikely to admit to behavior that is clearly considered unethical. However, Brodsky (1980) reports that the public reac-tion to the Holroyd and Brodsky study was essentially, "Oh, is that all, I thought the rate would be much higher." People apparently are unconcerned that one in 20 male therapists may exploit the sexuality of their female clients and may well damage the very people they are hired to help. There may be some uncertainty about the extent of the double standard with respect to the therapeutic treatment of clients, but it is clear that sexual relationships with women clients cannot be justified.

Traditional Therapies and Women

Therapists approach their work from a variety of different theoretical viewpoints, and a therapist's viewpoint has a strong influence on how the therapy will be conducted. Often, too, a therapist's theoretical viewpoint has a strong influence on his or her ideas about women. Let's look at psychoanalysis, behaviorism, and humanism, three of the most common theoretical viewpoints.

Psychoanalysis. **Psychoanalysis** is an approach that is based on Sigmund Freud's work, part of which was discussed in two previous chapters, the ones on childhood and on sexuality. Freud's view of women presents real problems for feminists because he regarded women as being inferior for several reasons (Kaplan & Yasinski, 1980; Marecek & Kravetz, 1977):

1. Women experience more shame and envy than men because they lack penises.
2. Women show **narcissism,** which is an excessive concern with their bodies, as well as a tendency toward **masochism,** which is pleasure derived from pain.
3. In adolescence, women shift the focus of their sexuality from the clitoris to the vagina, a shift that is equated with a transition from activity to passivity. Furthermore, a woman who continues to enjoy clitoral stimulation in adulthood cannot obtain mature femininity. (As you'll recall from the chapter on sexuality, however, clitoral and vaginal orgasms have been demonstrated to be identical.)
4. Because women never fully resolve the Oedipus complex, their final level of moral development is not as advanced as it is in men.
5. Penis envy can be partially resolved by having a baby; the desire to have children is therefore a sign of mental health.

Psychoanalysts believe that a woman's early life and how she resolved important issues are critical determinants of the way she currently acts and feels. Therefore, a major part of the therapy sessions focuses on childhood. Furthermore, the early relationships she had with other people are supposed to be reflected in her relationship with the therapist (Liss-Levinson, et al., 1981). The techniques that therapists might use include free association, dream analysis, and hypnosis. The focus on early childhood and the techniques of psychoanalysis are not in themselves biased against women, but the goals of classical psychoanalysis are to produce submissive women who accept their subordinate status. Some modern psychoanalysts have redefined some of the classic Freudian concepts. Nonetheless, many feminists argue that it would be difficult for a therapist who completely accepts the psychoanalytic viewpoint to be an ideal therapist for women clients.

Behaviorism. **Behaviorism** is a theory based on principles of learning. According to behaviorism, a woman's current behavior is the result of the way she has been rewarded and punished in the past. In Chapter 3, you learned about a theory that is partly based on behaviorism called social-learning theory, which stated that females learn how to act "feminine" by receiving rewards and punishments for their behavior and by watching and imitating other people.

Behaviorism acknowledges that behavioral disorders are the result of inappropriate learning in the past. However, behaviorist therapists do not probe for recall of a client's earlier life, and they do not try to interpret or understand the past. Instead, behaviorist therapists try to work with their clients to change their behavior in concrete ways. For example, a client might ask a behaviorist therapist to work on her excessive fear of snakes. Therapy would consist of constructing a list of items related to snakes, from the least fearful to the most fearful. While relaxing, the patient encounters the least fearful item on the list (perhaps imagining seeing a picture of a snake in a textbook). The client works her way gradually up the list until a specific goal is reached (perhaps actually walking through a field, without experiencing anxiety).

Behaviorist therapists usually encourage clients to work on specific tasks between sessions. Therapists emphasize rewarding their clients for appropriate behavior, and they also encourage clients to learn to reward themselves for appropriate behavior.

Therapists who use a strictly behavioral approach are not common today. Instead, therapists are likely to combine a behavioral approach with an approach that emphasizes cognitive (thought) processes, called a **behavioral-cognitive approach.** In connection with the cognitive emphasis, a woman would be encouraged to restructure her thoughts about herself, her environment, and the important people in her life. We'll discuss this approach more specifically in the later section on depression.

Behaviorists may acknowledge that society has been responsible for many of women's problems. However, they direct most of their efforts to training individual women to acquire specific skills (Blechman, 1984). We'll soon discuss assertiveness training, which is primarily based on behaviorist principles.

Humanism. **Humanism** argues that psychological disorders arise from several sources (Ellis, 1984):

1. The refusal to risk living life to its fullest.
2. The inability to be responsible for one's own life.

3. Comforming too closely to standards set by others, thereby ignoring one's own experiences.
4. Refusing to try out one's own desires, and as a consequence limiting life's experiences.

Carl Rogers, one of the most influential humanistic therapists, believes that healthy people are aware of all of their behavior. In any given situation, they will consciously act in a way that can effectively achieve their goals (Kaplan & Yasinski, 1980). A goal of therapy is therefore to encourage clients to pay attention to their emotions. Clients are encouraged to take risks in order to broaden their options. Humanistic therapists try to relate caringly and fully to their clients, which in turn encourages the clients to relate caringly and fully to others. In addition, clients are encouraged to accept themselves fully and to be honest and open with themselves (Ellis, 1984).

Humanistic therapy provides an ideal setting for encouraging women's self-esteem. It also urges women to consider alternatives, rather than to endure an unpleasant situation. However, some feminists point out that humanism does not place enough emphasis on the way society treats women differently from men and limits their options (Kaplan & Yasinski, 1980). However, humanistic therapy principles could be expanded to be compatible with feminist therapy, which we will discuss shortly.

Alternative Approaches for Women

We have looked at some traditional kinds of therapy and some of the kinds of problems these therapists may present for women. The rise of the women's movement has created an awareness that psychotherapy must change so that it is more helpful to women. One option is nonsexist therapy. Another option, feminist therapy, adopts the principles of nonsexist therapy but also makes additional recommendations. In addition, two specific kinds of "tools" have been developed for women, consciousness-raising groups and assertiveness training. In addition to these topics, we'll discuss how feminism can influence psychotherapy.

Nonsexist therapy. **Nonsexist therapy** maintains that women and men should be treated similarly. This is an approach that can be obtained with almost any therapeutic approach other than traditional psychoanalysis. Here are some of the basic principles of nonsexist therapy (Marecek & Kravetz, 1977; Rawlings & Carter, 1977):

1. Sexism is both pervasive and subtle in our society.
2. Therapists should be aware of their own values, particularly as they might be related to sexism.
3. Therapists should be aware of recent research on the psychology of women.
4. Clients should make decisions about their behavior according to what is best for themselves, instead of what is traditionally considered appropriate for members of their sex.

5. Clients should be viewed as individuals, rather than as men or women. Thus, marriage should not be considered better for women than for men, and women and men should not be expected to differ in characteristics such as assertiveness and tenderness.
6. Therapists should not use the power of their position to subtly shape women toward more feminine behavior.
7. Therapists should avoid gender-biased testing instruments.

Feminist therapy. Feminist therapy proposes that the principles of nonsexist treatment are essential for the treatment of women, but they are not sufficient. Two important components of feminist therapy are: (1) the personal is political, because society has been responsible for the shaping of women's behavior, and (2) therapists should not be regarded as more powerful than clients in the therapy relationship (Gilbert, 1980). These two important components can be expanded into a number of basic principles of feminist therapy (Gilbert, 1980; Marecek & Kravetz, 1977; Rawlings & Carter, 1977):

1. Therapists believe that women have inferior status because they have less political and economic power than men. The main source of women's problems is social, rather than personal.
2. Clients learn that they have been taught that certain behaviors are socially appropriate for them, and these behaviors may not actually be ideal; it is critically important to identify sexism and its effects on behavior.
3. Society should be changed to be less sexist; women should not be encouraged to adjust to a sexist society.
4. The focus on society as the root of women's problems should not be used as a means to escape individual responsibility; women must take charge of their own lives.
5. Women must work towards economic and psychological independence, and their relationships with other women and men should be equal in personal power.
6. Other women are not the enemy, because they should be important sources of emotional support. However, it simply reverses the discrimination to label all men as villains; men are not the enemy, either.

The remaining principles address power relationships in therapy:

7. Whenever possible, the power relationship between the client and the therapist should approach equality, because helping women to change the oppressive aspects of their personal lives requires the elimination of oppressive aspects of therapy. If women clients are placed in subordinate roles in therapy, the situation simply echoes women's inferior status in society.

8. Throughout therapy, clients are encouraged to become more self-confident and independent, and to develop skills to help themselves.
9. The client and the therapist should write a contract at the beginning of therapy, specifying what behavior the client wants to change.
10. The therapist believes that the client is her own best expert on herself; clients do not need to defer to the "authority" of the therapist.
11. Group therapy is often used to emphasize clients' power and to minimize the therapist's power.
12. One source of power differences between clients and therapists is the belief that the clients have problems and the therapists do not. The power of the therapist can be reduced by the appropriate use of self-disclosure. For example, a therapist might remark, "I was often frustrated, too, when I was in therapy," allowing the client to see the therapist as a normal, fallible person (Gannon, 1982, p. 10).

Some of the principles of feminist therapy may strike you as ideal, but others may seem questionable. Is feminist therapy any more effective than traditional therapy? Unfortunately, this question has not been tested extensively, but there are suggestions that it is more effective in some respects. Clients who had received feminist therapy for an average of four months reported that they were as satisfied with their improvement as clients who had received traditional therapy for an average of 10 months (Johnson, 1976). In another study, feminist therapy was judged equally effective for feminist and nonfeminist clients, whereas traditional therapy was judged less effective for feminist clients than for nonfeminist clients (Marecek, Kravetz, & Finn, 1979).

It does seem wise for feminist therapists to be cautious in several areas. Feminist therapists must be certain not to try to transform their female clients into women that they have no real desire to be (Saretsky, 1977). In other words, feminist therapists must be certain that they don't simply substitute new biases for old ones and try to mold all of their female clients to a liberated gender role (Schaffer, 1980). If a woman is happy in her role as a wife and mother, we certainly shouldn't condemn her for it!

As Rawlings and Carter (1977) point out, "Good therapy always starts where the client is and keeps pace with her progress" (p. 51). For some women, this advice suggests that therapists begin with nonsexist therapy, rather than feminist therapy. If appropriate, treatment may later evolve into a feminist approach.

Consciousness-raising groups. Beginning in about 1970, many women with an interest in feminism joined consciousness-raising groups. **Consciousness-raising (CR) groups** usually consist of eight to 16 women who meet regularly to discuss similarities among their personal experiences. The groups use this knowledge about the similarities in their experience in order to understand the power relationships between the sexes, how these relationships developed, and how they are maintained (Weitz, 1982).

Women who need intensive therapy should not use a consciousness-raising group as a substitute for therapy (Brodsky, 1977). CR groups recommend feminist therapy for many of these women.

Still, women list one of the most common reasons for joining a CR group as being "to solve personal problems" (Kravetz, Marecek, & Finn, 1983). Other common reasons are that women want to explore the roles and experiences of women, to become more political, to escape isolation, and to explore relationships and sexuality.

Consciousness-raising groups differ widely. However, they share a common conviction that the problems women face can often be traced to society, rather than to the individual woman. As one woman commented about her CR group,

> I know that this is not supposed to be a therapy group, but I think that sometimes it is really important that in this group *I learn that I am not alone, that I'm not crazy because other people feel the same way that I do.* ... It's really been enlightening to see how such a wide group of people actually have so much in common. [Weitz, 1982, p. 235]

Although therapy is not the stated goal of consciousness-raising groups, women may experience a variety of benefits from participation in CR (Bond & Lieberman, 1980; Brodsky, 1977; Kravetz, 1980; Kravetz, et al., 1983; and Weitz, 1982). These benefits may include:

1. An increased identification with the women's movement.
2. Greater awareness of the effects of sexism.
3. Better sense of control.
4. Greater tendency to place the blame for problems on external—rather than internal—factors.
5. Improved self-esteem.
6. Increased use of other women as models.
7. A greater sense of solidarity with other women.

In general, it is more difficult to document whether these changes in emotions and beliefs are translated into changes in actual behavior, although informal reports of behavior changes are abundant (Kravetz, 1980). In general, too, women report that they are highly satisfied with their CR groups and believe that other women would benefit from them as well (Kravetz, et al., 1983). If you'd like more information about CR groups, a good place to begin is with Perl and Abarbanell's (1979) *Guidelines to Feminist Consciousness Raising*.

It is worth mentioning a recent article on consciousness raising before we proceed to our next topic. Naomi Rosenthal (1984) analyzes the history of CR groups and points out that they were originally designed as a means of creating social change. However, their focus has changed from one of political activism to one of personal problems. Rosenthal argues that this newer focus may be harmful because it stresses that women themselves must change, rather than encouraging political action to change society.

Assertiveness training.   During the 1970s, many therapists offered courses in assertiveness training for women. It was argued that women were likely to have problems being sufficiently **assertive;** that is, they were often unable to exercise their own rights in a way that would achieve their goals and yet not violate the rights of other people. The purpose of **assertiveness training** is to change nonassertive behavior into assertive behavior without producing the kind of aggressive behavior that would hurt other people (Gambrill & Richey, 1980; Jakubowski, 1977a, 1977b; Rich & Schroeder, 1976).

Enthusiasm about assertiveness training has declined in recent years. One reason is that sex differences in assertiveness are not consistent, as we discussed in Chapter 7. As a consequence, assertiveness training should not be aimed at women any more than men. Another difficulty is that assertiveness training can often backfire. Kelly and his coauthors (1980) found that assertive behavior shown by females was more negatively evaluated than the same behavior shown by males. A more general criticism of assertiveness training is one we mentioned in the first chapter of this book: Assertiveness training assumes that women's problems can be improved by "fixing the women" rather than "fixing the situation." If women are being poorly treated at their jobs, the answer should be to change the way women are treated, not to teach them how to be assertive. Theoretically, assertiveness training might be used in helping groups of women to organize themselves to *change* the injustices of society. In practice, however, assertiveness training is used to help individual women cope with these injustices.

The feminist influence on psychotherapy.   The impact of feminism has clearly been greatest for those who practice feminist therapy with women. However, there have been a number of important spinoffs. Some therapists are now concerned about feminist psychotherapy for men (Solomon & Levy, 1982). In addition, mainstream psychology journals occasionally discuss sex biases in psychotherapy. The American Psychological Association (1978) published its recommendations for therapy with women. Their suggestions included cautions about gender stereotypes, sex-biased language, unequal treatment of women and men, and the exploitation of the therapist-client relationship.

In our discussion of new alternative therapies, we must keep in mind that the ultimate goal is for women to emerge from therapy as mentally healthy people. Collier (1982) describes a mentally healthy woman:

1. She values herself as an individual and as a female rather than depreciating herself as a woman.

2. She chooses behaviors according to their suitability to her and to the situation, perhaps deliberately resisting conforming to female gender stereotypes but certainly not conforming to them unwittingly.
3. She consistently tends toward emotional, social, and economic self-sufficiency, striving for separateness and autonomy before seeking interdependence.
4. She blends autonomy with interdependence in the form of a selected number of deep relationships with others in personal and social activities.
5. She orients herself toward reality and realism, avoiding overreaction in favor of accepting herself, others, and the world for what they are.
6. She appreciates differences as much as similarities, preferring variety in herself and others to stereotypes.
7. She does not victimize herself, does not let herself be victimized, and does not present herself as a victim.
8. She enjoys the power of her emotions and her self and displays this power through vivacity and energy.
9. She takes risks and extends herself without placing too much emphasis on either success or failure.

As a final exercise for this section, try Demonstration 12.2.

☐ SECTION SUMMARY ▪ Psychotherapy and Women

1. **Some areas of possible biased treatment in psychotherapy include therapists fostering traditional gender roles, having low expectations for women's value, emphasizing sexist psychoanalysis concepts, and treating women as sex objects.**
2. **Minority women may experience additional biases in psychotherapy.**
3. **Therapists seem to be generally uninformed about research on the psychology of women.**

4. Therapists may remember the problems of male clients better than the problems of female clients, and they may be more likely to question women about family relationships.
5. Women are more likely than men to be medicated for their psychological disorders, perhaps partly because of therapist bias.
6. According to surveys, about 5 percent of male therapists admit to having sexual intercourse with patients, clearly in violation of ethical standards.
7. Psychoanalysis is based on Freud's work, which regards women as inferior for reasons such as narcissism, masochism, and lower moral development.
8. Behaviorist therapy, which is based on learning principles, focuses on changing behavior in a concrete way. The behavioral-cognitive approach combines behaviorism with an emphasis on thought processes.
9. Humanist therapy emphasizes taking risks, considering alternatives, and paying attention to one's own experiences.
10. Nonsexist therapy treats women and men similarly and attempts to avoid stereotyped behavior.
11. Feminist therapy accepts the principles of nonsexist therapy but also pays attention to the role of society in shaping behavior and emphasizes equal power in client-therapist relationships.
12. Feminist therapy may be more effective than traditional therapy in some respects, but therapists should be sensitive about applying it appropriately.
13. Consciousness-raising groups meet to discuss similarities in personal experience. They should not be used as a therapy for severe psychological disorders, but participants may find benefits from these groups.
14. Assertiveness training tries to change nonassertive behavior into assertive behavior without producing aggressive behavior. However, assertiveness training is losing favor as a treatment for women.
15. A mentally healthy woman blends autonomy with interdependence, doesn't victimize herself, and takes risks.

SPECIFIC PSYCHOLOGICAL DISORDERS

We have examined the general question of psychological disorders in women, as well as aspects of psychotherapy for women. Now we need to turn our attention to four specific disorders that are important for women. The first three topics—depression, phobic disorders, and eating disorders—are all problems that are more common in women than in men. The fourth topic, the abuse of alcohol and other drugs, is generally a greater problem for men than for women. However, there are still millions of women who are substance abusers; the problem is widespread enough to deserve our attention. In all four topics, we will emphasize a description of the disorders, because their causes and treatments are not well established.

Depression

Maggie Scarf describes a woman she interviewed in her research on depression:

Role-strain

manifestations are helplessness and hopelessness

> Debra Thierry, for example, at age 22, had an image of herself as something superfluous in the human world. She told me during one of our interviews that she felt as if she were "litter." She was, she said, like a piece of drifting newspaper, "something that's just floating around, being blown around the sidewalk, underfoot, you know, being kicked aside...." She was excess matter in the universe, unwanted and without value. [Scarf, 1979, p. 47]

Description. **Depression** is a disorder that includes emotional, cognitive, behavioral, and physical symptoms (Beck & Greenberg, 1974; Lewinsohn, Biglan, & Zeiss, 1976):

1. Emotional: feeling sad, gloomy, guilty, apathetic, and unable to experience pleasure.
2. Cognitive: thoughts of inadequacy, worthlessness, helplessness. self-blame, pessimism about the future; reduced ability to concentrate.
3. Behavioral: behavior changes so that there is decreased ability to do ordinary work; personal appearance is neglected; sleep disturbances increase; social contacts decrease; there may be suicide attempts.
4. Physical: physical illnesses may be reported in terms of indigestion, headaches, dizzy spells, and generalized pain.

It is important to remember that most people have occasional episodes of extreme sadness. In fact, therapists do not always agree upon the distinction between normal depression and clinical depression. For example, extreme depression is considered normal when a parent or a spouse has died. However, it is usually *not* normal when the symptoms of depression continue several months after the loss (Norman, Johnson, & Miller, 1984).

There is no "typical" depressed woman. However, some characteristics tend to be associated with depression. A depressed woman is likely to have been previously married (Hammen, 1982) or else married with children (Weissman, 1980a). She typically has not had advanced education. If she is employed, she is likely to work at a low-income job. A relatively well-educated woman or a woman in a high-status occupation, in contrast, is less likely to experience depression (Hammen, 1982). Keep in mind that the characteristics of marital status, education, and employment are far from perfect in their prediction of depression. You may meet a divorced woman without an advanced education who is working at a low-paying clerical job, and who is extremely happy with her life. Furthermore, you may meet a single woman with an advanced degree who is working in a prestigious occupation, and who is severely depressed.

It seems likely that personal and social factors would be more closely related to depression than demographic factors such as education. Warren and McEachren (1983) examined this issue and demonstrated, as had the previous studies, that education, age, and employment were somewhat related to depression. (Since their study simply compared married woman with single women, we can't determine whether divorced women or married women with children are particularly susceptible to depression.) Most important, however, was that several psychosocial factors were far better predictors of depression than were the demographic factors. Here are the important factors:

1. Perceived life control (for example, "To what extent do you have a feeling of personal power and control over what happens to you?")
2. Social support (for example, "How would you rate the amount of emotional support you get from your friends?")
3. Perceived accomplishment (for example, "To what extent do you feel a sense of accomplishment in your life?")
4. Derived identity (for example, "To what extent do you feel dependent on your spouse or close friends for a sense of who you are?"); women with derived identity were more likely to be depressed.

Thus, a woman's sense of self-worth is clearly related to her psychological health.

Explanations.   At the beginning of the chapter we examined sex ratios in psychological disorders. To a large extent, the large number of women with psychological disorders can be traced to the observation that women are more likely than men to suffer from depression. In general, women are two or three times as likely as men to be diagnosed as being depressed (Norman, Johnson, & Miller, 1984; Weissman & Klerman, 1979). Furthermore, black women are about three times as likely to suffer from depression as black men (Jones, et al., 1981). There are a few exceptions, but the greater incidence of depression in women is typically found in all Western countries.

Researchers have been struggling with the question of why women are more likely than men to experience depression. As in the study of psychological disorders in general, which we considered at the beginning of the chapter, there is little evidence for biological explanations for the large number of depressed women (Weissman & Klerman, 1979). Scarf (1979) also rejects the idea that women are really normal but they are labeled "depressed" because of therapists' biases. She maintains, instead, that these woman have real problems:

The women whom I have come to know well or only slightly, whom I've talked to at length or just a little, whom I've seen just once or several times over a period of months—were all suffering. They were in pain, and in need of help; there just was no question about it. [p. 47]

It is important to focus on the explanations for the greater incidence of depression in women in order to help these depressed women. It would be a disservice to them if we claimed that they weren't really depressed, but merely mislabeled by a sexist therapist.

Even if we agree that depression in women is a real problem, it is difficult to identify a single cause for the relatively large number of depressed women. In all probability, as we noted in our discussion of sex ratios in psychological disorders, there are a number of reasons. Here are several:

1. It is considered somewhat socially acceptable for men to show their aggression openly, whereas women have been socialized to control aggressive feelings. Women may be more likely to turn their anger inward and be critical toward themselves (Chesler, 1972; Rosenfield, 1980). Those who favor this kind of explanation argue that depression can be reduced among women by encouraging them to express their anger.

2. Women may be more likely to experience learned helplessness. According to the theory of **learned helplessness,** helplessness is a major component of depression, and people learn to be helpless when they believe that the responses they make are not related to the rewards and punishments they receive (Seligman, 1974; Radloff, 1975). Depressed people give up because they believe that they cannot influence what happens to them; they feel helpless. According to Radloff and others, women are more likely than men to experience a lack of relationship between what they do and what happens to them. For example, a man who works very hard at his job is likely to be rewarded, whereas a woman frequently finds that the effort she puts into her job is unrelated to the rewards she receives.

3. Women may be less likely to find gratification in their lives (Gove, 1980). Women are depressed because they experience little reward from housework or from low-paying jobs and because women with young children are isolated from other adults. This explanation, which we examined in more detail earlier, is consistent with the observation that relatively well-educated women and women who work in high-status occupations are less likely to suffer from depression (Hammen, 1982). It is also consistent with Warren and McEachren's (1983) conclusion that women who feel that they are personally accomplished, rather than dependent upon others, are less likely to suffer from depression. More generally, women may be depressed because of the more widespread devaluation of women in our society. Women are not as highly regarded as men, as Theme 2 argues, and as we have stressed throughout the book. A natural consequence is that women view themselves as unworthy.

Treatment. As Weissman (1980a) concluded, most depressed women are either poorly treated or untreated for their psychological disorders. In her study, only 44 percent of women with a major depression received any treatment for an emotional problem. Furthermore, most depressed women who were receiving help were receiving it from a physician who was not a psychiatrist. Thus, they were receiving drugs from a medical doctor, but were not receiving therapy from a psychiatrist, psychologist, social worker, or other counselor.

In the last section, we discussed consciousness-raising groups as an approach in feminist therapy. According to Weissman (1980b), this approach may be appropriate for mild depressive symptoms and may be useful as an addition to therapy for a woman who is largely recovered from depression. However, Weissman believes that it would not be appropriate in cases of severe depression.

Instead, Weissman concludes that drug therapy and psychotherapy are both recommended for women who are severely depressed. Obviously, drug therapy should only be given after diagnosis and careful consideration of the symptoms; we mentioned earlier that physicians may be too eager to pre-scribe psychoactive drugs. Also, each patient's progress under medication should be carefully monitored. However, when used appropriately, drugs reduce the acute symptoms of depression and prevent their return (Weissman, 1980a). Fortunately, drugs do not seem to make the patient less interested in psychotherapy, and the advantage of combining drug therapy and psychotherapy seems to be substantial (Weissman, 1980a).

One approach to psychotherapy for depressed women that has been gaining support is the behavioral-cognitive approach (Norman, et al., 1984). According to this method, depression can be improved by improving social skills so that a woman receives more positive rewards from other people. She also learns about effective coping techniques for dealing with the problems in her life. This may include work on communication skills, social interaction, and assertiveness. In addition, she learns to notice inappropriate thoughts that she might have (for example, "I must always be a success in my work") and to restructure them so that they are more realistic ("It's O.K. to be less than perfect"). Therapy may also include training in helping women change their attribution patterns. For example, rather than blaming a boy-friend's rejection on her own unattractiveness, a woman may be encouraged to place the blame elsewhere (for example, "he just wasn't ready for a mean-ingful relationship with a woman"). Notice that a behavioral-cognitive ap-proach as described here would probably be classified as being nonsexist, rather than feminist, because it does not stress a change in society.

Phobic Disorders

Gloria Steinem, a well-known feminist and one of the founders of *Ms.* mag-azine, wrote a tender and insightful recollection about her mother, who seemed to suffer from **agoraphobia,** a disorder that involves a fear of going outside the house.

She was just a fact of life when I was growing up; someone to be worried about and cared for; an invalid who lay in bed with eyes closed and lips moving in occasional response to voices only she could hear; a woman to whom I brought an endless stream of toast and coffee, bologna sandwiches and dime pies, in a child's version of what meals should be. She was a loving, intelligent, terrorized woman. ... In many ways, our roles were reversed: I was the mother and she was the child. [Steinem, 1983, p. 130]

Agoraphobia is one example of a **phobic disorder** or phobia, which is a persistent, irrational fear of a particular object, activity, or situation. A phobic disorder produces a compelling desire to avoid something, and the individual realizes that the fear is excessive and unreasonable (American Psychiatric Association, 1980).

It is important to stress that all of us have some fears. Most people don't go out of their way to make friends with spiders, fierce dogs, and boa constrictors. Also, fear can be useful when it helps us act quickly and return to safety. Phobias, however, are fears that are so extreme that they are inappropriate, and they may limit people's lives. For example, one woman was so afraid of dogs that she stayed home near her parents and refused to look for employment (Padawer & Goldfried, 1984).

There are three different kinds of phobias: social phobias, simple phobias, and agoraphobia. **Social phobias** involve an excessive fear of social situations; people with social phobias are afraid to be scrutinized by other people. For example, a person may be extremely afraid to speak in front of others or to eat in public. Since females and males are about equally likely to suffer from social phobias (Fodor, 1982), they are not as relevant for us as the simple phobias and agoraphobia.

Simple phobias. Simple phobias usually involve a specific fear about one kind of object, most often animals. About 95 percent of people with simple phobias are female (Fodor, 1982). Usually phobias begin in childhood, and they may lead to a lifetime of planning in order to avoid the feared object. For example, one woman had a butterfly phobia, which led her to avoid trips to the country. She consulted a therapist when this phobia began to interfere with a relationship with a young man who liked to spend weekends in the country (Fodor, 1982). The simple phobias can usually be treated successfully by behaviorist approaches. Therapy may involve practice in managing anxiety and gradually exposing the client to the feared object.

Agoraphobia. Agoraphobia, which we defined as a fear of leaving the home, is a more serious disorder. About 80 percent of people with agoraphobia are female. According to one estimate, more than a million American women restrict their lives because of agoraphobia (Chambless & Goldstein, 1980).

A large number of women develop agoraphobia a few years after marriage, but the precise reasons for this observation are unclear. Agoraphobics are afraid of open spaces, and so they fear crowds, bridges, tunnels, elevators, and expressways. They may also fear being separated from a trusted companion (Chambless & Goldstein, 1980). One woman was anxious about leaving home and going in cars or on trains. She had reached the point where she was essentially helpless. Her husband remained home with her, and—even then—she continued to be frightened (Fodor, 1982).

Agoraphobic women are likely to be super-feminine women who are like the stereotype of a passive, dependent woman. Usually, they never had experience in living on their own, but went directly from their parents' home into married life. They are likely to be unhappily married, but they don't leave their marriages because of the terror of being alone (Chambless & Goldstein, 1980; Padawer & Goldfried, 1984). There are many theories about the development of agoraphobia. One uses the social-learning theory that we discussed in Chapter 3. According to this approach, women are socialized to be dependent upon others and agoraphobics receive a stronger dose of this experience (Fodor, 1982).

Unfortunately, agoraphobia is very difficult to treat successfully. One problem is that the disorder is unpredictable; a woman may appear to be symptom-free for several years, and then she suffers a relapse. Also, as a married woman begins to achieve independence during the treatment of agoraphobia, her husband may become resentful. He may try to undermine further progress, for example by forbidding his wife to look for employment (Padawer & Goldfried, 1984). The most effective treatments currently seem to be drug treatment with antidepressants and exposure to the feared situations, combined with practice in managing anxiety. In addition, some therapists work with the spouse, who is often a central figure in the disorder (Chambless & Goldstein, 1980).

Eating Disorders

In the United States in the 1980s, we are preoccupied with the idea that women must be thin. Think about the women who inhabit the television dramas, for example. How many women in major roles can you name from either soap operas or prime-time shows who are even a few pounds overweight? In one survey, there was only one overweight woman among the 131 women who appeared on popular television shows (Wooley & Wooley, 1979). The fashion models who decorate magazines and catalogs often look close to starvation.

American women frequently feel extremely inadequate when they compare themselves with these emaciated creatures. As a result, they feel dissatisfied with their bodies, and even normal-weight women believe that they are too fat. In one study, 75 percent of adolescent females felt they were too fat, in contrast to only 25 percent of adolescent males (Stuart & Jacobson, 1979). Women may think that they need to lose weight when in fact their weight is normal. In one sample, 20 percent of women who sought help for a perceived weight problem were not overweight at all (Fodor & Thal, 1984).

Thinness is emphasized for women more than for men. As Smead (1983) observes, ". . . a woman only 20 or 30 pounds overweight experiences great effects on her life; men have a considerably wider margin of error before anyone, themselves or others, see them as overweight" (p. 29).

It is ironic that thinness is emphasized more for women in the 1980s than it was in previous eras. As Rodin and her coauthors (1985) note, it seems particularly contradictory that, in recent years, as women's career options increase, their options for body weight decrease. Brownmiller (1984) proposes that dieting has replaced foot binding and corseting as a way in which women mutilate their bodies in order to be beautiful. Rather than using external constraints—tight-laced, stiff-boned corsets—women are now urged by society to use internal constraints. As Orbach (1978) pointed out in her classic book, *Fat Is a Feminist Issue,* few women are immune from the pressure to be thin. Even strong feminists are likely to be concerned about how they look.

Our nation's obsession about thinness raises real problems for women. Three of these issues that we'll consider are overweight, anorexia nervosa, and bulimia.

Overweight. Overweight people are categorized as being overweight if they weigh at least 20 percent more than the recommended weight on standardized charts. Overweight is usually not classified as a mental disorder. However, extreme overweight, or obesity, often involves severe disturbances, depression, and low self-esteem (Hall & Havassy, 1981; Wooley & Wooley, 1980).

The problem of overweight is a mystery, because on the average, overweight people eat no more than normal-weight people (Fodor & Thal, 1984; Wooley & Wooley, 1980). Since it isn't clear why overweight people became overweight, it isn't clear how to help them become slender. Behaviorist approaches, such as setting specific goals for weight loss, have some success (Fodor & Thal, 1984). Medical treatments include various medications, fasting in a hospital, surgery so that food bypasses the intestine, and wiring the jaw shut. These extreme treatments are particularly alarming because in women (as opposed to men), being overweight is generally *not* associated with increased health risks (Hall & Havassy, 1981; Rodin, et al., 1985; Wooley & Wooley, 1980). Women therefore diet for social reasons, rather than health reasons.

A further problem is that people who do manage to lose weight are extremely likely to gain back the lost pounds. The body's metabolism changes after dieting so that the body can now "live" on fewer calories. (Rodin, et al., 1985). Women then blame themselves for not having the restraint to stay thin.

Losing weight and keeping it off are so difficult that Fodor and Thal (1984) suggest that therapists should develop programs to help their clients accept themselves when they are only slightly overweight. Therapy should concentrate on raising self-esteem and a sense of competency in overweight women (Wooley & Wooley, 1980). Ultimately, clients and the general public need to be educated about the sources of pressure to be thin, and we need to set new standards that are not based on starved fashion models.

Anorexia nervosa. People with anorexia nervosa accomplish what few overweight women can; they diet and manage to lose weight (Fodor & Thal, 1984). Their obsession about eating becomes extreme. For example, one young woman remarked, "When I say I overeat, it may not be what you think. I feel I'm gorging myself when I eat more than one cracker with peanut butter" (Bruch, 1978, p. 3). This woman even avoided licking postage stamps because of the calories.

Several critical features of **anorexia nervosa** are an extreme fear of becoming obese, a significant weight loss (at least 25 percent of the original body weight), and refusal to maintain a normal body weight (American Psychiatric Association, 1980). People with this disorder almost always overestimate their body size (Bemis, 1978; Fodor & Thal, 1984). A woman who is asked to point to places where she is overweight might hold out an emaciated arm and point to her wrist. Another almost inevitable symptom in women is **amenorrhea,** or cessation of menstrual periods.

About 95 percent of those with anorexia nervosa are females. The most likely age for this disorder is 12 to 18 years, and about 1 in every 250 females in this age range has anorexia nervosa (American Psychiatric Association, 1980).

Many young women who have anorexia nervosa are overly perfectionist and are high achievers. As one woman explained,

> There is a peculiar contradiction—everybody thinks you're doing so well and everybody thinks you're great, but your real problem is that you think that you are not good enough. You are afraid of not living up to what you think you are expected to do. You have one great fear, namely that of being ordinary, or average, or common—just not good enough. This peculiar dieting begins with such anxiety. You want to prove that you have control, that you can do it. The peculiar part of it is that it makes you feel good about yourself, makes you feel "I can accomplish something." It makes you feel "I can do something nobody else can do," and then you start to think that you are a little bit better because you can look down on all these people who are sloppy and piggish and don't have the discipline to control themselves. There is only one problem with this feeling of superiority. It doesn't solve your problem because what you really want is to feel good about yourself while feeling happy and healthy. The paradox is that you have started to feel good for being unhealthy. [Bruch, 1978, p. 129]

It is unclear how anorexia nervosa begins. Often this disorder first occurs in response to a new situation, such as entering college or getting married (Bemis, 1978). Anorexics are often somewhat overweight initially, and they will first try "normal" dieting before they shift to the more extreme dieting patterns.

One reason that anorexia nervosa is regarded as a serious disorder is that about 15 percent of anorexics die (Van Buskirk, 1977). The treatment of anorexia nervosa takes many forms, such as psychoanalysis, drug treatment, and behaviorist approaches. However, there is no single treatment that has been accepted as being most effective (Herzog, 1985; van Buskirk, 1977). At first, anorexics may seem to respond well to treatment. However, fewer than half of them remain well adjusted (Bemis, 1978; Garfinkel & Garner, 1982). Even if they keep an appropriate weight, they are likely to remain overly concerned about their body size.

Bulimia. **Bulimia** (pronounced "boo-*lih*-mee-ah") is often called the "binge-purge" syndrome, because people with this disorder have episodes in which they consume huge amounts of food, perhaps containing up to 50,000 calories. Usually these foods are high in calories, sweet, and soft (Arenson, 1984). The food is gobbled down quickly, with little chewing. During the binge, people are aware that they are eating abnormally, and they are afraid of not being able to stop. The binging eventually stops when the stomach pain is too intense, when someone interrupts, or when the individuals force themselves to vomit (American Psychiatric Association, 1980). Afterwards, they feel depressed and anguished about their behavior. In between binges, they may diet excessively.

Like anorexics, bulimics are obsessed about food, eating, and body weight. Also, they perceive themselves as overweight even when they are not. In addition, people with this disorder are likely to be young and female (American Psychiatric Association, 1980; Schlesier-Stropp, 1984). In fact, there has been some controversy about whether bulimia and anorexia are really variations of the same disorder. Roughly half of people with anorexia nervosa show some bulimic behaviors. However, bulimia is now usually regarded as a separate disorder, because—unlike bulimics—anorexics are severely underweight and they experience amenorrhea (Schlesier-Stropp, 1984).

It is difficult to know how common bulimia is, because the binging and purging are often done secretly. However, it may occur in more than 10 percent of a college population (Schlesier-Stropp, 1984).

Bulimia is not life threatening. However, it can lead to medical complications such as intestinal and kidney problems, and it frequently involves throat or dental problems (because of the acid in the vomited material).

There haven't been many systematic studies of the treatment of bulimia, perhaps partly because bulimia only recently emerged as a disorder that was separate from anorexia nervosa. However, behaviorist approaches have often been successful for bulimics whose symptoms are relatively mild. Several books on bulimia aimed at nonprofessionals are now available (for example Boskind-White & White, 1983; Pope & Hudson, 1984).

We have looked at three groups of people who are highly concerned about their weight. Overweight people may try to lose weight, without success. Anorexics try to lose weight, and they succeed, sometimes with fatal consequences. Bulimics fluctuate between gorging and dieting, and their resulting weight is usually normal. It's interesting to contemplate how the guilt and anxiety that all three groups of people associate with eating might be reduced if women were encouraged to be content with their bodies. Imagine how much more positive we might feel if women in television shows had bodies that showed as much variety as the bodies that we see every day in real life. Wouldn't it be wonderful to glance through a magazine at the checkout counter of a grocery store and *not* see guilt-inducing articles titled, "Finally—an Answer to Problem Thighs" and "How to Lose 15 Pounds in Just One Month."!

Abuse of Alcohol and Other Drugs

Julie is a 35-year-old woman who became dependent on pills by the age of 25 and addicted to both pills and alcohol by 27. She had married at 19, and when her son was born the next year, she felt totally frustrated and inadequate. She began a series of jobs, but the guilty feeling that she should be with her child drove her home again. Julie took diet pills—amphetamines— to control her weight, and then she began drinking a bottle of wine each night her husband was gone. Everyone told her that the reason she felt unfulfilled was that she had only one child. After her second child was born, however, she switched from wine to vodka and Scotch, beginning the mornings with a strawberry daiquiri. Her husband reacted with mixed messages, suggesting that they go out drinking together but becoming upset when she actually became drunk.

Julie decided to go back to college, but the extra pressure led to her taking even more amphetamines. She began to experience delirium tremens from all the alcohol. When her life seemed totally out of control, she attempted suicide. The doctor who had pumped her stomach sat her down and announced, "Julie, I think you're an alcoholic." Eventually, Julie recovered, with the help of Alcoholics Anonymous, some feminist friends, and professional counseling (Sandmaier, 1980).

We don't know exactly how many women in the United States have problems with alcohol and other drugs. According to conservative estimates, there are about 900,000 women alcoholics in this country, and at least another million who have severe drinking problems (Johnson, 1982). Looked at in another way, about one woman in 14 has a problem with alcohol (Bry, 1984). Black and Hispanic women seem to have more drinking problems than white women (Leland, 1984). There are also estimates that in a given year, 36 million women use tranquilizers, 16 million use sedatives (sleeping pills), and 12 million use stimulants (primarily diet pills). Millions of other women buy drugs "over the counter" or use illegal drugs. Many women suffer from the crippling combination of drugs and alcohol.

Substance abuse is the use of alcohol or drugs to such an extent that normal functioning is impaired (Bry, 1984). Substance abuse leads to psychological distress, accidents, and many diseases. In a pregnant woman, substance abuse is likely to cause birth defects. For example, 71 percent of infants born to very heavy drinkers (more than 10 drinks a day) have birth defects such as low birth weight, mental retardation, and other abnormalities (Bry, 1984). Other medical consequences of alcoholism in women are described by Hill (1984).

Gomberg (1979, 1982) provides a useful way to approach the relationship between gender and substance abuse. She suggests that we think of a continuum of drug substances that are arranged in terms of their social acceptability. At one end are the most acceptable drugs, medicines prescribed by a physician. Next are the over-the-counter drugs that are widely advertised and easily purchased, such as cough syrups, milder sedatives, and tonics. Alcohol is somewhat less socially acceptable. The least socially acceptable are the illegal drugs, such as marijuana and heroin. According to Gomberg, women predominate as users of the socially acceptable drugs, whereas men predominate as users of the less acceptable drugs.

Let's examine data to support this idea and also discuss each of these four categories, beginning with prescription medicines. In every category of lifetime users of psychoactive drugs—tranquilizers, sedatives, and stimulants—there are about 50 percent more women than men (Fidell, 1982; Verbrugge, 1982). In fact, it has been estimated that at least half of adult women have used psychoactive drugs at some time during their lives (Fidell, 1981). We mentioned earlier that physicians are more likely to prescribe medication for women than for men.

In contrast, there seem to be no sex differences in the use of over-the-counter drugs. In other words, men and women are equally likely to use drugs such as Compōz and NoDoz, which do not require a prescription.

Moving down the scale of social acceptability, we find that more men than women use and abuse alcohol. If we look first at the number of men and women who drink alcohol, we find about 25 percent more men than women (Leland, 1982). This predominance of male drinkers is also found among blacks (Leland, 1982) and in other cultures (Gomberg, 1979).

If we look at alcohol *abuse*, men are even more likely to predominate. According to surveys, the ratio of female to male alcohol abuse is between 1:3 and 1:5 (Johnson, 1982; Leland, 1982; McCrady, 1984). In other words, surveys show that there are between 200 percent and 400 percent more men than women who are considered to be alcoholics. These data may not be accurate, because the ratio of females to males in alcohol-related deaths is only about 1:2 (Celentano, McQueen, & Chee, 1980).

Why is there a discrepancy? McCrady (1984) points out that there may be many invisible women alcoholics. Women may be more secretive about drinking. They may tend to drink alone and at home. Alcoholic women aren't seen as often in bars or on the street (Gomberg, 1979). Also, a woman's husband or family may be ashamed and want to protect her. There are more negative attitudes toward female drunkenness, which you can explore in Demonstration 12.3. There are stereotypes that women alcoholics are sexually promiscuous and are failures as mothers. All of these factors encourage women to hide their drinking.

Attitudes Toward Alcohol Abuse in Women and Men

Read the following questions to several friends, either individually or in a group. Do their responses indicate different responses to women than to men?

1. You are visiting a large city. Near one crowded street corner, you see a person sitting with a bottle in a paper bag; the person is clearly drunk. Would your reaction differ depending on whether the person is male or female?
2. You are at a party with other students. Someone about your age has clearly had too much to drink and is talking loudly. Would you react differently to a male than a female?
3. An employed friend is describing a coworker whose alcoholism is interfering with performance at work. How would you respond if you heard that this coworker was male? Would your response be different if the coworker were female?
4. You go into a restaurant and see a woman seated at the bar alone. She has finished one drink and is requesting another, even though she is having trouble keeping her balance on the stool. How would you react? Would your reaction be different if it were a man?

Women alcoholics seem to differ from men alcoholics in several respects. Women alcoholics begin their drinking somewhat later than men do. In addition, women are more likely than men to report that a traumatic event such as a divorce or a death was the original cause of their drinking. Women are also more likely than men to use other drugs in combination with alcohol, at least partly because they are more likely to receive prescriptions for psychoactive drugs (Gomberg, 1979; Gomberg & Lisansky, 1984). Husbands of alcoholic women seem to be more indifferent to their wives' problems and are less likely to try to get treatment for them, in contrast to wives of alcoholic men (Leland, 1982).

So far we have seen that there are more women than men who use the socially-acceptable psychoactive prescription drugs, there are an equal number of men and women who use the less medically approved over-the-counter drugs, and there are more men than women who use and abuse alcohol. If Gomberg's theory about social acceptability is correct, then we should find an even greater predominance of men among the users of illegal drugs. However, the ratio of females to males here is about 1:2, which is about the same as for alcoholism. Men are about twice as likely as women to use heroin, cocaine, hallucinogens, marijuana, and hashish (Fidell, 1982). In support of Gomberg's theory is the interesting observation that when opium-related drugs were legally available in tonics in the United States, women were more likely than men to use them (Gomberg, 1982). In summary, there is reasonable support for Gomberg's theory that women are more likely than men to take drugs that are approved by established experts, whereas men are more likely than women to take substances that are not socially approved or are illegal.

There are no easy cures for women (or men) who abuse alcohol and other drugs. It is not clear whether alcoholic women respond better to individual, group, or family therapy (Braiker, 1984; Gomberg, 1979). There are few appropriate treatment centers for people who are abusing psychoactive drugs (Fidell, 1982). Treatment programs for problems with illegal drugs frequently focus on improving social skills for women, whereas men receive training in vocational skills (Marsh, 1982). At this point, there are far more questions than answers in the successful treatment of substance abuse.

We first looked at three disorders that are more common in women than in men. As mentioned earlier, the causes for these disorders are unclear, and so it is also unclear why women are particularly likely to experience depression, phobic disorders, and eating disorders. Notice, however, that each disorder shows an overemphasis of some aspect of the female stereotype. In depression, women feel inadequate, worthless, and helpless; they blame themselves too much for failures. In phobic disorders, women have excessive fears; in agoraphobia, women are overly feminine and dependent. Women with eating disorders are excessively concerned about being slim. In contrast, the abuse of alcohol and other drugs is usually associated with men. Women who are substance abusers not only have to battle their disorder, but they also have to battle social disapproval. In fact, it seems likely that people would be more compassionate toward a woman who is depressed, phobic, or anorexic than they would be toward a woman who is an alcoholic. Similarly, it seems that people are more compassionate toward a male alcoholic than they would be toward a depressed, phobic, or anorexic male.

Unfortunately, none of the disorders we discussed has an easy solution. Perhaps more research into the origins of the disorders will explain how gender roles contribute to the development and persistence of these disorders. Therapists will perhaps develop effective methods of combining nonsexist and feminist therapy techniques with improved versions of the traditional therapies in order to offer more hopeful futures to the large number of women who experience psychological disorders.

☐ SECTION SUMMARY ▪ Specific Psychological Disorders

1. **Depression includes feelings of sadness and apathy, thoughts of inadequacy and pessimism, and decreased performance, as well as physical components.**
2. **Among the more likely explanations for the large number of depressed women are the following: a) women may turn their anger inward; b) women experience learned helplessness; c) women find their lives less gratifying.**

3. Treatment for depression may include drug therapy combined with psychotherapy, such as a behavioral-cognitive approach aimed at improving social skills and changing inappropriate thoughts.
4. Phobic disorders are persistent, irrational fears. They include social phobias, simple phobias, and agoraphobia; the last two are much more common in women than in men.
5. Simple phobias are usually treated with behaviorist approaches, but agoraphobia is more complex and therefore more difficult to treat successfully.
6. Thinness is stressed for women even more than it is stressed for men.
7. Overweight is a mystery because overweight people usually eat no more than normal-weight people; losing weight is extremely difficult, so therapy should perhaps emphasize self-acceptance and raising self-esteem.
8. People with anorexia nervosa have a fear of becoming obese, an extreme weight loss, and an overestimation of their body size; 95 percent of anorexics are women, most often adolescent women.
9. Anorexics tend to be perfectionists who are high achievers.
10. About 15 percent of anorexics die from their disorder, and many do not respond well to treatment.
11. Bulimics, who binge, vomit, and then may diet excessively, also have distorted body images; their medical problems are not as severe as those of the anorexic, and they are more likely to be successfully treated in therapy.
12. In general, women are more likely to be abusers of the socially acceptable medications, whereas men are more likely to be abusers of alcohol and illegal drugs.
13. Alcoholism seems to be more hidden in women than in men; women alcoholics also differ from men alcoholics in the causes of their drinking and in the responses they receive from others.
14. Men are about twice as likely as women to use illegal drugs.
15. Gender stereotypes seem to be related to these four disorders, but the way in which gender roles contribute to them is unclear.

Chapter Review Questions

1. How do sex ratios in psychological disorders depend upon the way in which we define "psychological disorders"?
2. What are the various explanations for the abundance of women in some kinds of psychological disorders? Cite evidence (or lack of evidence) for each point of view.

3. List several ways in which therapists might treat women and men separately. Discuss the nature of the evidence we have about this issue and speculate about why it would be difficult to gather more concrete evidence.

4. Summarize Buczek's (1981) study about therapists' responses to male and female clients and describe why these results may have important implications for therapy.

5. Drugs and medications have been mentioned at several points throughout this chapter. Summarize this information with respect to: (a) prescribing psychoactive drugs for women; (b) drug treatment of specific psychological disorders; and (c) the abuse of drugs.

6. Summarize each of the three traditional therapies, discussing what problems they may present for a feminist approach to therapy and pointing out whether they might be modified to be compatible with feminist therapy.

7. How would the problem of depression be approached using nonsexist therapy? How would a feminist-therapy approach be different?

8. How would the various eating disorders be approached using nonsexist therapy? How would a feminist-therapy approach be different?

9. Describe each of the three kinds of phobias mentioned in this chapter and speculate about how gender roles may contribute to the relatively large number of women who have problems with two of these phobias.

10. How are the data on women and substance abuse explained by Gomberg's idea of a continuum of social acceptability for the various substances?

☐ NEW TERMS

personality disorders	assertive
double standard of mental health	assertiveness training
psychotherapy	depression
psychoactive drugs	learned helplessness
psychoanalysis	agoraphobia
narcissism	phobic disorder (phobia)
masochism	social phobias
behaviorism	simple phobias
behavioral-cognitive approach	anorexia nervosa
humanism	amenorrhea
nonsexist therapy	bulimia
feminist therapy	substance abuse
consciousness-raising (CR) groups	

☐ RECOMMENDED READINGS

Blechman, E. A. (Ed.) (1984). *Behavior modification with women.* New York: Guilford.   ■   This book discusses the general issue of women and psychological disorders, as well as specific disorders (for example, depression, eating disorders, and alcohol); its coverage goes beyond a strictly behavioral approach.

Brodsky, A. M., & Hare-Mustin, R. T. (Eds.) (1980). *Women and psychotherapy.* New York: Guilford.   ■   This book contains 16 chapters on topics such as therapists' attitudes, traditional and nontraditional approaches to therapy, depression, agoraphobia, and eating disorders.

Rodin, J., Silberstein, L., & Striegel-Moore (1985). Women and weight: A normative discontent. In T. B. Sonderegger (Ed.), *Nebraska Symposium on Motivation, 1984: Psychology and gender* (pp. 267–307). Lincoln, Nebr.: University of Nebraska Press.   ■   Rodin is an established researcher in the area of body weight and obesity; she and her coauthors have written an excellent chapter on women's efforts to be slim, with some discussion of anorexia and bulimia.

Wilsnack, S. C., & Beckman, L. J. (1984). *Alcohol problems in women.* New York: Guilford.   ■   This well-balanced book discusses issues such as the incidence of alcoholism in women, antecedents of alcohol problems, medical consequences, and treatment and prevention.

CHAPTER 13

VIOLENCE AGAINST WOMEN

- Most rapes occur indoors.

- Anger is the most common immediate response to rape.

- Rape victims are almost completely recovered three months after the trauma.

- Women who have been raped by their husbands feel that the experience was extremely upsetting.

- Battered women almost always blame their husbands, rather than themselves, for the battering episodes.

- People are much more tolerant when a man assaults his wife than when he assaults a stranger.

- Battered women could easily leave battering relationships, if they really wanted to.

- Sexual harassment includes staring at or talking about a woman's body, as well as touching and requests for sexual relationships.

- Most women who have been sexually harassed regard the harassment as a minor inconvenience.

- Men and women have similar attitudes toward sexual harassment.

Rape, battering, and sexual harassment may appear to have little in common. However, although there are important differences, there are also similarities. Most important, all involve violence. As we'll see, rape is a crime of violence, not sexual passion. Battered women experience physical and psychological violence. Women who are sexually harassed may experience physical violence, though the violence may be more subtle.

In all three cases, men have more power than women. In rape, men have more physical power, often increased by the power of a weapon. In the case of battered women, men again have more physical power, almost always increased by the power inequalities in love relationships. In the case of sexual harassment, the harasser is usually a person with power in a work or academic setting. In all three cases, women are left feeling even less powerful after the violence; their bodies have been violated or beaten, or they have been forced to accept unwanted sexual attention. Powerlessness is yet another variation on one of the themes of the book, that women are treated differently than men.

Women cannot even regain power by reporting the violence, because legal procedures will be embarrassing and humiliating, invading a woman's right to privacy even further. All these acts of violence encourage women to be even more silent and more invisible. The relative invisibility of women is a theme we have mentioned repeatedly throughout this book.

Furthermore, in all three cases, people are likely to blame the victim. A woman is raped because she "asked for it" by her behavior and actions. A woman is beated because she did not take good care of her husband's needs. A woman is sexually harassed because her revealing blouse invited it. In contrast, the aggressor may be perceived as acting "like a normal male," and he receives little blame.

All three kinds of violence have been trivialized in the past. In fact, two of these issues only recently were considered important enough to deserve names. As Gloria Steinem (1983) wrote, "We have terms like *sexual harassment* and *battered women*. A few years ago, they were just called *life*" (p. 149). Recent media attention has increased public awareness to some extent, but we will discuss how many people still believe that rape, battering, and sexual harassment are not serious problems.

Finally, all three kinds of violence can be traced to traditional feminine and masculine socialization. Males are "supposed to be" aggressive, dominant, and in control of the situation. Women are "supposed to be" submissive, yielding, and unaggressive. In a sense, rape, battering, and sexual harassment represent an exaggeration of traditional gender roles.

RAPE

Rape involves sexual intercourse* that is forcibly committed, without consent (Hilberman, 1978). Rape experiences range from a surprise attack with threats of death to sexual intercourse with a date, despite the woman's protests.

We need to stress that rape is a crime of violence, not passion. As Bard and Sangrey (1979) write, "Short of being killed, there is no greater insult to the self" (p. 20). In rape, a woman's exterior body is threatened, handled, and injured. Unlike other crimes, however, rape also violates interior body space. Rape therefore humiliates and degrades far more than robbery or any other kind of physical assault.

Reports of rape are increasing faster than reports of any other violent crime, making it difficult to assess how often rape occurs. In one survey of women in San Francisco, it was estimated that about one in four women would be raped at some time in her life (Russell & Howell, 1983). Nationwide, the rate may be one in five or six women. However, only about one-third to one-half of these will be reported (Johnson, 1980; Kilpatrick, et al., 1981; Koss & Oros, 1982; Martin, et al., 1983).

Contrary to what you might expect, most rapes occur indoors. As many as one-quarter of rapes occur in the woman's own home (Katz & Mazur, 1979). Rapes are more likely to occur at night, but that does not imply that women should feel completely safe during the day.

The high-risk ages for rape are between 13 and 24. Thus, college women have a particularly high risk for rape (Katz & Mazur, 1979). However, females as young as five months or as old as 91 years have been reported as the victims of rape. In other words, women are never young enough or old enough to feel safe.

Black women are far more vulnerable to rape than are white women (Katz & Mazur, 1979). We mentioned that women who are adolescents or young adults are in a high-risk range; they are more likely, in general, to be raped than older women. However, as Gollin (1980) points out, the risk of rape is so elevated for black women that elderly black women (aged 65 to 85) are just as likely to be raped as young white women (aged 16 to 19).

Our focus in this section will be on the rape victim, but we also need to consider that all women suffer because of the threat of rape. If females who are infants or old women can be raped, and if they can even be raped in the "safety" of their own homes, then we are all vulnerable. Susan Griffin (1979) expressed what many women feel: "I have never been free of the fear of rape. From a very early age I, like most women, have thought of rape as part of my natural environment—something to be feared and prayed against like fire or lightning" (p. 3).

---

*In some states, oral and anal penetration are included in the legal definition of rape. Also, males can be raped by other men, but since this is a book on the psychology of women, we will discuss only the rape of women.

According to one survey, 44 percent of women in Chicago, Philadelphia, and San Francisco reported that they were either very afraid or somewhat afraid when they are out alone at night. In contrast, only 18 percent of men said that they were afraid (Riger & Gordon, 1981). Women are also more likely than men to report that they have been warned about potentially dangerous situations (Burt & Estep, 1981). Fear of rape controls women's behavior and restricts what they can do, no matter where they live. The college at which I teach is located in a small village in the heart of upstate New York farmland. Nevertheless, my female students cannot feel safe alone at night.

There are several important components of rape that we need to investigate: the rape attack, the rape victim's reactions, attitudes toward rape, myths about rape, child sexual abuse, date rape, marital rape, and rape prevention.

The Rape Attack

Later in this chapter we will talk about some types of rape that involve special relationships. Children are sexually abused by adults, and women are raped by men they know, either their dates or their husbands. However, even when a stranger rapes an adult woman, there is more than one type of rape. As Burgess and Holmstrom (1980) discovered from interviews with rape victims, some rapes are surprise attacks, but others involve a confidence game. In both cases, the assailant uses force or threat of force, and the victim does not consent.

The **surprise attack** occurs without warning and without any previous interaction between the assailant and the victim. The woman is going about her normal life when she is suddenly seized by the assailant. Most often, he is looking for someone to attack, and a woman who crosses his path becomes his victim. The following case is typical:

A 13-year-old victim stated, "It was 9 P.M. and I left my house to go to the corner store for a cupcake and a Coke. I had my portable radio with me. As I was coming home, a guy grabbed me and dragged me down a hill that is in my own yard. . . . He said a lot of nasty things to me and dirty things like was this the first time I fucked? and did I like it? and then he wanted my name and phone number." The assailant made her take her clothes off and then forced her to lie down on her coat; he put a sleeve across her face so she could not see him. The girl said, "He did it three times and he made me kiss him." The victim was noticeably upset with this part and looked as though she would vomit. She said she tried to scream and struggle but no one heard her. . . . [p. 29]

The **confidence rape** is more subtle, because the assailant gains access to the victim by using deceit and betrayal. Here is a testimony from a 73-year-old woman who was raped when she was 67:

A young fellow followed me into the elevator of my apartment building. He was wearing a green uniform. He asked me if I knew the apartment number of a certain tenant but I told him that name was unfamiliar to me. I said, "Oh, are you the man from United Parcels? I'm expecting a package that hasn't arrived." He asked me my name and apartment number and told me he'd go down and check in the truck. A few minutes later my doorbell rang. I looked through the peephole and there was the young man with a package. Of course I opened the door right away. He had a wrench in one hand. He shoved me against the wall and started hitting my head. Later I had to have five stitches. . . . He told me to get on the bed. He pulled off my underthings and then he tore into me. When he was finished I watched him go through my dresser drawers. He took some jewelry and my portable TV. Finally he left, after warning me to keep quiet. [Brownmiller, 1975, p. 347]

The Rape Victim's Reactions

Reactions during the rape. There is no single kind of reaction that women experience during rape. A woman's response will depend upon whether the rape is a surprise attack or a confidence rape, her stage in life, whether she knows the assailant, the threat of danger, and other circumstances. However, almost all women who have been raped report that they were anxious, scared, worried, terrified, and confused, with many thoughts racing through their heads (Kilpatrick, Resick, & Veronen, 1981). This kind of "fright-panic" response is particularly true when a woman feels that her life is in great danger. Her perception and judgment may be distorted, because all of her behavior is directed toward staying alive (Katz & Mazur, 1979).

From the victim's point of view, the sexual attack was unexpected. She may therefore experience immediate shock. She may be stunned and unable to think clearly. She may not be able to react effectively (Katz & Mazur, 1979).

There is tremendous controversy about whether a woman should struggle to resist rape or not; this issue is discussed at the end of the section. Almost all rape victims resist somehow, either physically or verbally. The degree of resistance depends upon several factors. Adolescents and adults are more likely to resist than younger girls. Women from lower economic classes are more likely to fight physically than women from upper economic classes, who are likely to have been trained to be "ladylike." Also, women are more likely to resist if the rapist is nonviolent and without weapons (Katz & Mazur, 1979).

Immediately after the rape. Immediately following the rape, a woman may have a wide range of feelings. Burgess and Holmstrom (1974) found two general patterns that occurred about equally often. Some women have an expressive style. They show their feelings of fear, anger, and anxiety by crying and being restless and tense. Others have a controlled style; they hide their feelings with a calm, composed, and subdued external appearance. Internally, however, these women may be just as distraught.

Among the early responses that most rape victims share are feelings of helplessness and devaluation. Women frequently feel guilty as well. One young woman resisted a rapist who attacked her in her apartment. She took his knife away from him and used it against him; in the process she was severely bruised, beaten, and raped. Afterwards, she blamed herself:

> I keep wondering maybe if I had done something different when I first saw him that it wouldn't have happened—neither he nor I would be in trouble. Maybe it was my fault. See, that's where I get when I think about it. My father always said whatever a man did to a woman, she provoked it. [Burgess & Holmstrom, 1974, p. 983]

Self-blame is a particularly troublesome reaction, because in nearly all cases, the rape victim did nothing to precipitate the crime. Nonetheless, a survey of rape-crisis centers by Janoff-Bulman (1979) showed that 74 percent of raped women blamed themselves at least in part for the rape. Women were likely to blame something they did ("I should have locked my car" or "I shouldn't have been out that late"). However, many also blamed some personal characteristic ("I'm too naive and gullible" or "I'm the kind of person who attracts trouble"). It may be that some of these self-blame comments have an adaptive value in terms of giving the victim some sense of control over her future. This may be particularly true if women blame something they did. Still, self-blame is probably in large part destructive.

In addition to the psychological reactions that immediately follow a rape, a woman may also have physical reactions. She may be sore and bruised from the rape, and she may also have gynecological symptoms such as vaginal discharge, itching, and generalized pain. In addition, she may suffer from stomach pains, tension headaches, and fatigue. Sleep disorders are also common (Burgess & Holmstrom, 1974).

This acute phase, with both its emotional and physical components, is part of what Burgess and Holmstrom call **rape-trauma syndrome**. The syndrome also includes a long-term reorganization stage, which we'll discuss later.

A raped woman must decide whether she will report the rape. Many women decide not to report it. Perhaps they have not considered that the act will be likely to be repeated with other victims. Women frequently decide against reporting a rape because "it wouldn't do any good." They believe that the criminal-justice system won't handle the case effectively, that officials won't believe them, that they will be embarrassed by the procedure, and that the assailant might try to retaliate. Sadly, there is evidence that these fears are realistic.

Minority women seem to be particularly unlikely to report a rape to the police. Feldman-Summers and Ashworth (1981) interviewed about 100 women in each of four ethnic groups (Asian, black, Hispanic, and white). Each woman was asked to complete a questionnaire about how likely she would be to report a rape. There were some questions to which the members of the four groups responded similarly. For example, they said that they would be equally likely to report a rape to a person at a hospital. However, white women were significantly more likely than Asian, black, and Hispanic women to say that they would report a rape to the police. As the authors point out, this difference should not be surprising; blacks, Hispanics, and Asians tend to feel alienated from public agencies in the United States, and they are therefore distrustful.

Long-term adjustment. Rape-trauma syndrome does not disappear suddenly. Instead, there is a long-term reorganization stage, and elements of the syndrome may never disappear completely. Woman may find that they reexperience the rape and that certain events may trigger flashback sensations (Martin, et al., 1983).

From interviews with rape victims, it seems that these women are still disturbed a few weeks after the event. According to Kilpatrick, Resick, and Veronen (1981), rape victims are still anxious, afraid, depressed, and low in self-esteem one month after the assault. By three to six months later, the initial distress is substantially reduced, but victims still are significantly more afraid and anxious than average. Another investigation showed that about one-quarter of rape victims still did not feel recovered four to six years later (Burgess & Holmstrom, 1979).

Fear is a common and persistent problem for rape victims. Other long-term adjustment problems that are most common are depression, sexual problems, and disturbed social relations. One study systematically investigated depressive symptoms, interviewing women during a one-year period following the rape. The victims showed substantial depression following the assault, but four months later, they were no more depressed than a control group of women who had not been rape victims (Atkeson, et al., 1982).

Often, women who have been raped report an aversion to all sexual activity. This reaction may begin soon after the assault, but it is more likely to develop slowly over a period of months. Even women who do not develop an aversion may still experience less pleasure in sexual relations. They may also report pain during intercourse or a decrease in sexual responsiveness (Martin, et al., 1983). Frequency of sexual activities may return to a normal level after a few months, but their satisfaction with sex typically remains at a lower level up to seven years after the assault (Feldman-Summers, Gordon, & Meagher, 1979).

Rape victims also have problems with social adjustment, though the extent of these problems varies. Resick and her coauthors (1981) found that rape victims did not differ from a control group in their relationships with spouses or children. Still, as we'll see in the next section, husbands often treat their wives negatively following a rape, so some changes in family relations seem likely. Several social areas that do show substantial changes are at work and in interactions with friends and extended families. For example, during the first eight months of one study, rape victims reported poorer performance than a control group in terms of their interest in work, satisfaction with work, and relationships with others at work (Resick, et al., 1981).

It is important to keep in mind that rape victims may have symptoms that persist up to a year or more after the traumatic event. However, we see once more that there are tremendous individual differences among women, consistent with Theme 4 of this book. In one report, between 20 percent and 25 percent of victims were relatively symptom free a year after the rape experience (Kilpatrick, et al., 1981). Rape counseling and follow-up counseling seem to be helpful in terms of long-term adjustment. One good resource in this area in *The Rape Crisis Intervention Handbook* (McCombie, 1980); another is a chapter on long-term treatment of rape victims by Frank and Stewart (1984).

Attitudes toward Rape

Some writers have suggested that women who are raped are doubly victimized, first by the assailant and later by the attitudes of other people. Consider the case of Mrs. W., a married, middle-aged woman who was raped by a stranger. She resisted to the best of her ability and received a knife wound and a head concussion. She was hysterical and in shock. Despite convincing evidence that there had been a genuine rape, everyone blamed her, including the police, the hospital staff, and even her own husband. The police were skeptical about her story that she ran out of gas and a man volunteered to help her. The psychiatrist, who was the first hospital staff to examine her afterwards, saw her bleeding and battered. Even though he had never seen her before, he asked, "Haven't you really been rushing towards this very thing all your life?" Later, when she was released from the hospital, her husband threw her down on the bed and shouted, "If that's what you wanted, why didn't you come to me?" (Russell, 1975, pp. 221–230). Everyone—her own family, the court system, and society in general—has a tendency to blame the victim and treat her negatively because of something that was not her fault. These responses are particularly damaging at a time when the victim needs compassion and help.

One factor to keep in mind when considering attitudes toward rape is that rape has long been regarded as a crime that not only violates a woman but also violates her husband or father:

> Society's view of rape was purely a matter of economics—of assets and liabilities. When a married woman was raped, her husband was wronged, not her. If she was unmarried, her father suffered since his investment depreciated. It was the monetary value of a woman which determined the gravity of the crime. Because she had no personal rights under the law, her own emotions simply didn't matter. [Horos, 1974, p. 4]

Perhaps one reason Mrs. W.'s husband reacted as he did in the rape described earlier was that his own "property" had been devalued by the rapist. Some husbands cannot continue a sexual relationship with a wife who has been raped, even when she in no way precipitated the rape. It seems that they regard any sexual intercourse between their wives and other men as being marital infidelity. Often, then, raped women end up being divorced women (Herman, 1984; Katz & Mazur, 1979).

Some families react with embarrassment and anger toward the rape victim. Parents may ask a raped teenage daughter, "How could you do this to us?" (Katz & Mazur, 1979). A more legitimate question, of course, would be, "What can we do to help?"

The treatment of rape by the legal system is mostly beyond the scope of this book. However, there are numerous reports of injustice and mistreatment. For example, I recently read about a judge in Toronto who had convicted a man of rape. He remarked that, using a scale of 10, "I would place this particular offense down around 2" (Hailwood, 1984, p. 56). Other notorious judges have claimed that a rapist was innocent because his five-year-old victim was particularly seductive, and that gang rapists were only human to react by raping a woman wearing tight jeans. To some people who are in a position to control rape, this crime is relatively trivial, even young girls should be blamed for the rape, and rape is a normal, sexual reaction.

One of the most comprehensive surveys of attitudes toward rape was conducted by Hubert Feild (1978). He collected data from more than a thousand people, including citizens, rape-crisis counselors, and rapists. Try to guess how each of these groups responded in their attitudes toward rape by trying Demonstration 13.1, which includes four of the items from Feild's study. You might also find it interesting to give this questionnaire to friends. You might distribute it to five people who consider themselves feminists and five who don't and then compare their responses.

As you can imagine, the two groups in the survey whose opinions were most different from each other were the rape-crisis counselors and the rapists. The rapists were significantly more likely than the counselors to supply responses on the right side of the scale. In other words, they supported statements such as "Victims usually precipitate rape," and "A woman who has been raped is damaged and no longer a 'good woman.'"

The police—distressingly—had attitudes that were more similar to the attitudes of the rapists than they were to the attitudes of the counselors. Like the rapists, the police believed that the basic motivation for rape is sex, rather than power. They also shared the rapists' belief that rape victims are less desirable. Finally, the citizens who were included in this study had attitudes that were fairly similar to the attitudes of rapists and police. In other words, the rape-crisis counselors differed from all other groups in the survey in terms of their sympathy for the rape victim and understanding of the nature of rape.

Substantial sex differences were found within the citizens' group, however. Women were less likely than men to say that it was a woman's responsibility to prevent rape and that victims precipitate rape because of their appearance and behavior. Women were more likely to say that rapists were

Attitudes of Various Groups Toward Rape

On a sheet of paper, rate each of the following four statements by placing a rating (from 1 to 7) next to the item number. Fill out the rating scales below a total of four times. The first time, respond as if you were a patrol police officer, and then as if you were a citizen, a rape-crisis counselor, and a convicted rapist.

1. Women should be the ones who are the most responsible for rape prevention.

1	2	3	4	5	6	7
Not at all						Very Much

2. Victims usually precipitate rape.

1	2	3	4	5	6	7
Not at all						Very much

3. Men rape so that they can be more powerful than women.

1	2	3	4	5	6	7
Very Much						Not at All

4. A woman who has been raped is damaged and no longer a "good woman."

1	2	3	4	5	6	7
Not at all						Very much

Now add up the total ratings for each of the four groups. The smaller the total, the more positive the attitudes toward women. Notice which groups have total scores that are most similar to one another.

In addition, you may wish to give this questionnaire to people you know. This time, simply ask them to give their own opinions on the issue. Try to determine whether their personal attributes are related to their answers.

motivated by a need for power over women, and that women should resist during rape.

Other surveys of attitudes toward rape have also shown sex differences. For example, women judge rape to be more serious than do men (L'Armand & Pepitone, 1982). Furthermore, in an investigation of attributions for rape, men were more likely than women to believe that the rape could be attributed to the victim's personality and to her behavior before the rape. In contrast, women were more likely than men to believe that the rape had been the rapist's fault (Selby, Calhoun, & Brock, 1977).

Myths about Rape

There are numerous myths about rape, rapists, and rape victims. These myths help shape the attitudes toward rape held by citizens, police, and rapists, which we have just examined. Furthermore, when a rape victim believes these myths, her attitudes toward the rape and toward herself are affected. As Hilberman (1978) points out, the raped woman "knows" that nice girls don't get raped and that a woman cannot be raped against her will. It is easy to imagine how these myths might intensify the rape-trauma syndrome.

Here are some of the more common myths:

1. *Rape is an inherent tendency of males.* This view of rape suggests that rape is "normal." However, in a cross-cultural study, rape was reported as rare or absent in 47 percent of the societies studied (Benderly, 1982; Sanday, 1981). This view also suggests that the majority of rapists are simply healthy, aggressive young men who are "sowing some wild oats." However, Groth and Birnbaum (1979) conclude from their study of rapists that these men do have serious psychological difficulties that handicap them in their relationships to other people. In particular, they lack close, emotionally intimate relationships with other people.

2. *Only deviant men would consider raping a woman.* The first myth says that rape is normal; this second myth says that rape is abnormal, because only "wierdos" or insane people would think about raping someone. This myth doesn't seem to be correct, either. When male introductory psychology students at a large Canadian university were asked how likely they would be to commit a rape that had been depicted in a story, 30 percent said that they would (Check & Malamuth, 1983). Among men who were highly gender-role stereotyped, the percentage increased to 44 percent. This obviously does not mean that every college male is a potential rapist, but the high percentage who would consider rape makes it clear that the inclination to rape is not limited to a few deviant men.

3. *Rapists are strangers and they are of a different race.* We don't know what percentage of rapes are committed by strangers, but it is very likely that a woman would be less likely to report a rape if it is committed by someone she knows. Studies have listed the percentage of rapes committed by strangers as ranging between 27 percent and 91 percent (Katz & Mazur, 1979). As we will see in later sections, rapes are frequently committed by dates and by husbands. Furthermore, in about 93 percent of rape cases, both the man and the woman are of the same race (Hirsch, 1981).

4. *Women ask to be raped; they could avoid rape if they wanted to.* Many people believe that an unarmed man cannot rape a woman unless she cooperates. The rapist's physical size and strength, relative to the woman's, often make it likely that he will harm her, even if he

is unarmed. Furthermore, in 87 percent of rape cases, the rapist either carried a weapon or threatened the woman with death if she resisted. These women did not ask to be raped! Their major concern is usually fear for their lives (Hirsch, 1981).

This idea that women are at least partially responsible for their own rape begins early. Zellman and Goodchilds (1983) read teenagers the following paragraph:

> A guy and a girl who are dating are at a friend's party one evening, and decide to sit out in the yard. It is very dark and, after a while, they start to kiss and hug. The guy slips his hand under his girlfriend's blouse, but she pulls away and tells him to cut it out. Her boyfriend says that he wants to have sex with her, and when she refuses he threatens to hurt her. Although the girl does not want to, they have sexual intercourse. (p. 56)

When asked who was responsible for this date rape, 84 percent said that the boy was responsible and 27 percent said that the girl was. Thus, about one-quarter believed that the female was to blame, and many do not blame the male at all.

5. *Women enjoy rape.* Anyone who has read the testimonies of the two rape victims at the beginning of the chapter would certainly know that this myth is false. However, rapists often believe this myth. Some rapists have been astonished when they were arrested, complaining that they may have been a bit rough but that the women enjoyed the experience. A 63-year-old woman was robbed and raped at gunpoint by a young man, who then threw her a kiss and shouted as he left, "I bet I made your day" (Herman, 1984). Others besides rapists also believe that women enjoy rape. Pornography often cultivates this myth; women are showed in orgasmic delight at the rape experience. However, real women who are being raped are afraid they will die, and the popular advice to "lie back and enjoy it" is clearly outrageous.

6. *Pornography provides a "safety valve" or catharsis that makes men less likely to rape.* According to this myth, if pornography were more widely available, the number of rapes would decrease. Silbert and Pines (1984) reviewed the controversial literature on this topic. It's not clear what we can conclude when the pornography is "softcore," the kind you might see in *Playboy*. However, most women—and many men—are not aware of the amount of "hardcore" pornography that is available, in which women are shown tied up, tortured, and beaten. When sex is linked with violence in pornography, men tend to be *more* sexually aroused about rape and less sympathetic to the victim, in contrast to men who have seen neutral material (Feshbach & Malamuth, 1978). Furthermore, Silbert and Pines report from their interview of raped women that many rapists asked their victims to recreate

scenes from violent pornographic movies. It seems clear, then, that violent pornography *doesn't* decrease the incidence of rape; it probably increases it.

7. *Only "bad" women are raped.* Again, the testimonies of rape victims make it clear that any woman can be raped; she does not need to have an immoral reputation. However, more than half of the people in one survey believed that rape victims are typically promiscuous and have a bad reputation (Burt, 1980).

8. *Rape victims usually end up being murdered.* According to popular belief, rape victims often become murder victims. No doubt the media's sensationalism of particularly brutal cases contributes to this myth. However, according to one review of the literature, less than 1 in 200 rape victims is murdered (Katz & Mazur, 1979). Obviously, we can't minimize the severity of murder—and even a ratio of 1 in 200 is frightening—but a woman facing a potential rapist might react differently if she knew that she would be unlikely to die.

Child Sexual Abuse

Shortly before I began to write this section, seven people associated with a highly regarded California preschool were charged with having sexually abused as many as 125 children, some as young as two years old (Leo, 1984b). The issue of child sexual abuse reminds us that adult women are not the only victims of violence; even young children are vulnerable. Child sexual abuse seems particularly cruel because in most cases, children are being abused by relatives, neighbors, and acquaintances—the very people who should be protecting them (Densen-Gerber, 1984; O'Hare & Taylor, 1983).

According to some estimates, at least 100,000 children are sexually molested each year (Herman & Hirschman, 1981). Surveys suggest that about one in four American women experienced sexual abuse during childhood or adolescence (Densen-Gerber, 1984; Herman, 1981). Boys are sometimes the victims of sexual abuse, but about 90 percent of child victims are girls (Herman, 1981).

Incest is a particular kind of child sexual abuse. Some definitions of **incest** are narrow: "coital contact between a blood relative and a child" (Brant, 1980, p. 185). Other definitions of incest are much broader: "any act with sexual overtones perpetrated by a needed and/or trusted adult, whom a child is unable to refuse" (O'Hare & Taylor, 1983, p. 215). The most destructive myth concerning incest is one originating with Sigmund Freud. Freud originally believed that incest often led to hysteria in adult women. However, Freud later changed his mind and developed a theory that children experience sexual desire for their parents. He concluded that the incestuous experiences that women report were merely fantasies, and they never really happened (Masson, 1984; O'Hare & Taylor, 1983). Imagine the devastation that a woman must experience when her therapist tells her that the sexual abuse she experienced as a child was only imaginary!

Obviously, sexual abuse can have an enormous psychological impact on a child, both immediate and long term. Sexually abused children often experience depression, guilt, and a loss of self-esteem. Phobias, nightmares, and crying spells are also common. As adults, women who had been sexually molested are more likely to be dissatisfied with their sexual relationships (Tsai, Feldman-Summers, & Edgar, 1979). They are also more likely to have abnormal scores on tests designed to measure psychological disorders, and they perceive themselves as being less well-adjusted than do women who have not been abused.

In the book *Father-Daughter Incest*, Herman (1981) provides an example of the long-term problems that can result from incest:

> A fifteen-year-old girl appeared in the outpatient clinic asking for tranquilizers. She had a history of addiction to alcohol and barbiturates, had been hospitalized several times for detoxification, and had had a number of unsuccessful placements in various residential treatment programs for adolescents. She revealed that from the age of eight she had been involved in a sexual relationship with her father which included fellatio and mutual masturbation. She ran away from home at age twelve, when her father attempted intercourse, and had essentially lived on the street since then. She expressed the hope, which seemed quite unrealistic, that her mother would divorce her father and allow her to come home. [p. 8]

In the last chapter, we discussed consciousness-raising groups as an alternative approach to therapy. These groups have also been valuable for women who experienced sexual abuse or incest, though they cannot always substitute for individual therapy (O'Hare & Taylor, 1983). The group can provide a safe space in which women can share the feelings of anger, grief, shame, and isolation that they have had to keep hidden since childhood.

Date Rape

The alarming statistics on child sexual abuse demonstrate that females can be victimized by people who are presumably in a caring relationship. The issue of date rape shows that women can be victimized in another kind of caring relationship. The word "rape" usually suggests that the attacker is a stranger. In reality, rape can occur in dating relationships, including those on college campuses. Rape is still rape, even when a woman has known her attacker for some time.

As Kanin and Parcell (1981) conclude, sexual aggression is a common experience for college females. In their survey, one-half of the women reported that they had been offended in a dating relationship during the most recent year. These offenses were usually in the form of kissing or fondling of breasts and genitals, but 12 percent reported that they had been forced to have intercourse. Similar figures were reported by Koss and Oros (1982); 11 percent reported that a man had used force or the threat of force in order to have sexual intercourse with them.

According to Abbey (1982), date rape may often result from sexual misunderstandings. A woman may have a conversation with a male, intending only to be friendly, and he may misperceive platonic friendliness in sexual terms. That pleasant smile and prolonged eye contact may in fact be interpreted as a sexual invitation. Men must learn that friendly verbal and nonverbal messages from a woman may well mean "I like you" or "I enjoy talking to you," and not necessarily "I want to have a sexual relationship with you."

When a woman has been raped by her date, she will probably discover that many people do not consider it to be a "real" rape (Check & Malamuth, 1983). As Burt (1980) found, more than half of community residents believe that a woman who goes to the home of a man on the first date implies she is willing to have sex. It would be difficult to win a court case involving date rape, particularly if the woman has previously had a sexual relationship with the attacker.

Marital Rape

A California state senator said to a group of women in 1979. "If you can't rape your wife, who can you rape?" Presumably a marriage license means that a man has complete freedom to do what he wants to his wife's body (as we'll also see in the next section on battered women). Often, rape is legally defined as sexual intercourse that is forcibly committed, without consent, by a male with a female *other than his wife*. In more than half of our states, a man can force his wife to have intercourse and this violation is not legally considered to be rape (Frieze, 1983).

About 10 percent of married women report having experienced marital rape, according to several surveys (Frieze, 1983). Many additional women may actually have been raped by their husbands, but they may not use the label "rape." In a sample of battered women, Frieze found that 34 percent reported that their husbands had raped them, but 73 percent reported that they had been pressured into having sex with their husbands. This discrepancy may be at least partly due to the fact that the legal system and society often maintain that rape cannot occur within marriage.

Many people believe that marital rape has less traumatic consequences for the woman than stranger rape (Jeffords, 1984; Russell, 1982). However, a woman who has been raped by her husband has had a long-standing emotional relationship with her rapist, and she must decide whether she will continue to live with this man. In Russell's extensive survey, 77 percent of the victims of marital rape reported being either extremely upset or very upset by the experience, and 49 percent said that it had a great effect on their lives.

Women who experience marital rape are likely to see the rape as the responsibility of the husband. In Frieze's survey, 78 percent of the women who had been raped felt that the cause lay in their husband's belief that the rape served to prove his manhood. An additional 14 percent of these women attributed the rape to drinking. Fortunately, women do not frequently blame themselves for marital rape.

Women who are raped by their husbands are also likely to experience other forms of violence. Frieze found that marital rape was more likely in marriages in which the wife was otherwise physically abused. Rape was also more likely in marriages in which the husband had extramarital affairs and was unreasonably jealous of his wife.

As Diana Russell (1982) writes in the concluding chapter of her book *Rape in Marriage,*

> Wife rape is a much more serious problem than most people have realized. The fact that it remains legal in most states and most countries not only perpetuates the problem but probably helps cause it, because it allows men and women alike to believe that wife rape is somehow acceptable. The first step toward reversing the destructive attitudes that lead to this destructive act is to make wife rape illegal; it must also be stripped of the stereotypes and myths that attach to it and be understood for what it is. (p. 356)

Rape Prevention

Prevention of rape is an issue for individual women and also for society. Table 13.1, aimed at individual women, is a list of precautions based on longer lists in two handbooks (Katz & Mazur, 1979; McCombie, 1980).

Individuals' prevention of rape.   There are two major issues that arise in connection with what women can do as individuals to avoid rape. The first issue can be called the "blame-the-victim" problem. Notice that many of the items on the list are ones that force women to limit their own freedom. Women can't hitchhike, they can't walk in unlighted areas, and they must always be on the lookout for potential rapes. Why should women—the potential victims—be the ones who have to suffer? There is no good answer to this compliant. It *is* unjust. However, the reality is that women are less likely to be raped if they take those precautions.

The second issue about rape prevention at the individual level is whether women should attempt to resist an attacker. Advice on this issue is contradictory. Some have recommended that women not resist, because of the danger of personal harm. Others have recommended resistance—self-defense techniques, screaming, reasoning with the attacker, and other creative strategies. The problem, of course, is that in some cases it might be best to be passive, and in other cases it might be best to be active, yet it is impossible to know when to apply each strategy.

In a study of women who had been attacked and who had either avoided rape or been raped, Bart and O'Brien (1984) concluded that when a woman fights back, she greatly increases her chances of avoiding rape and somewhat increases her chance of rough treatment. Pleading with the attacker was *not* an effective strategy. Women who had prevented rape were most likely to use some combination of physical resistance and screaming or yelling. Another substantial finding was that raped women who had used physical strat-

TABLE 13.1   **Safety Precautions to Avoid a Rape Confrontation (Based on Katz & Mazur, 1979, and McCombie, 1980)**

Precautions at Home

1. Make certain to use locks on doors and windows.
2. Ask repairmen and deliverymen for identification before opening the door; do not let strangers in to use your phone.
3. Keep your curtains closed at night to avoid observation.
4. If you live in an apartment, don't enter the elevator with a strange man, and don't enter a deserted basement or laundry room; insist that the apartment manager keep hallways, entrances, and grounds well lit.

Precautions on the Street

1. Do not hitchhike. (Unfortunately, hitchhiking is notoriously dangerous.)
2. When you are walking, be alert to your surroundings.
3. Avoid being alone on the streets or campus late at night; if you cannot avoid it, carry a police whistle (on a key chain, not around your neck), or a "practical" weapon such as an umbrella, a pen, or keys.
4. If you are being followed by a car, walk in the opposite direction to the nearest open store or neighbor.

Precautions in Cars and on Buses or Subways

1. Keep car doors locked, even when you are riding.
2. Check the back seat before getting into a car.
3. Keep your gas tank filled and the car in good working order. If you have car trouble, raise the hood; if a male offers to help, ask him to call the police.
4. If you are being followed, don't pull into your driveway; go to the nearest police or fire station and honk your horn.
4. At bus or subway stations, stay in well-lit sections, near change booths or a group of people.
5. If the bus is nearly empty, sit near the driver. If you are bothered by someone, inform the driver of the trouble.

egies were less likely to be depressed afterwards than were raped women who had not resisted. It seems that an additional function of physical resistance—even if it has not prevented rape—is to keep a woman from feeling depressed. Obviously, the answer to the issue of physical resistance is not simple, but resistance seems to be favored by many current feminist scholars. In a rape situation, women must quickly assess the specific situation and their own physical strength before deciding whether or not to resist. There are no easy answers.

Society's prevention of rape. An individual woman might be able to avoid being raped by following certain precautions. However, the rapist will probably simply seek another victim. In order to achieve substantial rape prevention, society must be concerned about preventing rape for all females (Katz & Mazur, 1979). Here are some of the issues:

1. Laws must be reformed so that the legal process is less stressful and more supportive for the victims. However, penalties for rape should probably not be made more severe; studies have demonstrated that rapists are less likely to be convicted if the penalty is too severe.

2. Rape victims should be encouraged to report rape. Anonymous telephone counseling services and legal counseling could help to increase arrests.

3. Women, men, and institutions need to be educated. At present, community residents and the police hold attitudes about rape that are not substantially different from the attitudes of rapists, and the legal system often regards rape as trivial. Furthermore, a substantial number of college males think that they might be likely to commit a rape. Sex education programs, community programs, and media attention are all essential in order to change attitudes.

4. Professionals who work with children need to be alerted to the possibility of child sexual abuse.

5. Violence must be less glorified in the media. The violence on television is notorious, and yet the situation has not improved in recent years. Pornography often shows women enjoying rape, which certainly encourages men to believe they are doing no harm when they rape. As mentioned earlier, research has demonstrated that when male subjects see aggressive pornography, they increase their aggressive behavior toward women (Feshbach & Malamuth, 1978; Malamuth & Donnerstein, 1984). Clearly, our nation must reconsider how the representation of women encourages violence and rape.

6. Ultimately, society needs to pay more attention to the needs of women. As we've constantly stressed, women are relatively powerless and relatively invisible. Their needs are trivialized and disregarded. One clear need that every woman has is to feel that her body is safe from attack and that she has the same freedom of movement that men have.

☐ SECTION SUMMARY ▪ Rape

1. **Although rape, battering, and sexual harassment are issues that differ from each other, they share similarities in their involvement of violence, emphasis on power inequities, forcing women into silence, blaming the victim, and trivialization.**

2. **Rape is a crime of violence that occurs to a large number of women of all ages; the threat of rape keeps women afraid.**

3. **Some rapes are surprise attacks, whereas others are confidence rapes.**

4. **Rape victims report being anxious, terrified, confused, and shocked**

during rapes. Immediately afterwards, victims feel helpless and devalued, often blaming themselves; they may also have physical pain.

5. Rape victims are still disturbed a few weeks after the event but are usually recovered in most areas six months after the trauma. Several persistent problems include fear, depression, sexual problems, and social adjustment.

6. The rape victim is likely to be blamed by her family, the court system, and the general public; in one study, the attitudes of police and citizens were somewhat similar to the attitudes of rapists.

7. Several myths about rape that have no basis in reality include: rape is an inherent tendency in males; only deviant men would consider rape; rapists are strangers, usually of a different race; women ask to be raped; women enjoy rape; pornography decreases rape; only "bad" women are raped; and rape victims usually end up being murdered.

8. Child sexual abuse has both immediate and long-term psychological impacts upon the victims.

9. Women are sometimes raped by their dates, perhaps frequently as the result of sexual misunderstandings; people may not consider the assault to be a "real" rape.

10. Women are sometimes raped by their husbands, a more serious problem than is commonly realized.

11. Two controversial issues in rape prevention are the "blame-the-victim" problem and whether to resist an attacker.

12. Society can work to prevent rape by legal reform, offering services to increase the report of rape, educational programs, alerting professionals about child sexual abuse, reducing violence in the media, and paying more attention to women and their needs.

☐ BATTERED WOMEN

Alice was a 41-year-old single physician who had been dating Mike for four months. She was so busy being in love that she overlooked some troublesome aspects of the relationship, particularly Mike's violence. One afternoon, they were supposed to go out to dinner, but Alice arrived late because of a medical problem with a patient. Mike did not accept the apologies, became verbally abusive, and began to slap her. He then caught her and began swinging her body around the room. The last thing she remembered was falling on the floor and being stomped on and kicked. She managed to call for an ambulance and ended up in the hospital, where they removed one kidney. As she remarked, "How can anyone so kind and gentle like Mike, that I could love so much and who could love me so much, do this to me? I just don't understand" (Walker, 1979, p. 92). The next day, however, after bouquets of flowers, boxes of candy, and pleading from Mike and his friends, Alice had changed her attitude. The couple seemed to be reconciled, and Alice had concluded that the trauma had simply been an accident.

Alice is a battered woman. According to one definition, a **battered woman** is a woman who is seriously battered—either psychologically or physically—at least twice by a man to whom she is married or with whom she has an intimate, marriage-like relationship (Walker, 1980). According to a more limited definition, the battering must be physical, rather than psychological. However, others acknowledge that the intense fear, guilt, and damage to self-esteem that come from psychological abuse can be just as damaging as physical abuse (Goldberg & Tomlanovich, 1984; Moore, 1979).

Estimates about the number of battered women in America have led some people to conclude that there is no place as violent as home. Researchers have suggested that anywhere between 20 percent and 50 percent of women will be battered by men they love at some point in their lives (Russell, 1982; Straus, Gelles, & Steinmetz, 1980; Walker, 1980). We can never find an accurate estimate of battering because there has been a traditional taboo of silence on the issue of domestic violence.

Violence is also quite common in dating relationships, as well as in marriage. One student in a psychology-of-women class described how her roommate repeatedly arrived home from dates with her fiancé, bleeding and battered. She was convinced that her fiancé would mend his ways once they were married. We also hear about men who batter women from whom they are separated or divorced. Clearly, women do not have to be married in order to be battered. It is even more difficult to estimate the incidence of nonmarital battering than to estimate the number of battered wives in our country.

Characteristics of the Battering Relationship

The battering cycle.   Battered women are not continually abused. Instead, there appears to be a cyclical pattern to battering. According to Walker (1979), this cycle seems to have three distinct phases. In the tension-building phase, there are minor battering incidents. The woman often tries to calm the batterer using techniques that have been successful in the past. She tries to keep his abuse from escalating by anticipating his whims and by staying out of his way. However, tension ultimately builds too high to be controlled by small-scale efforts, and the batterer responds by an acute battering incident in the second phase. Both the batterer and the battered woman accept the fact that his anger is out of control, and the damage can be extreme, as in the case of Alice that was described earlier. In phase three, the tension from the first two phases are gone, and the batterer becomes charming and loving. He apologizes and promises that he will never be violent again. He begs for forgiveness and makes the woman feel guilty if she is considering leaving the relationship. This is a highly rewarding and flattering phase of the relationship, and it may encourage her to forget the tension, uncertainty, and pain of the earlier two phases.

It will not surprise you that there is no predictable duration for each of the three phases in the battering cycle. They vary from couple to couple and from incident to incident. However, a consistent result is that the woman in phase three feels needed, hopeful about the future, and guilty about any inclination to leave the batterer.

The battered woman. Several researchers have tried to characterize the battered woman. A major problem with this kind of research is that it is nearly impossible to decide which characteristics are causes of battering and which are effects. Some researchers might argue that a woman who is depressed and paranoid is likely to be beaten. Other researchers (certainly most feminist researchers) would argue that a woman who has been beaten is likely to become depressed and paranoid (Bograd, 1982). Let us look at several characteristics of the battered woman that have been identified.

Battered women are likely to have low self-esteem (Walker, 1981). Their feelings of inadequacy are underscored by their perception that they have not lived up to the stereotypical expectations for how wives should perform. After all, they have failed enough to deserve strong punishment from their husbands.

Battered women may show denial. They are forced to deny the violence to the rest of the world; battered women do not display their wounds in public. They must also frequently deny to themselves what has happened, as Alice did in the earlier description.

Battered women show a certain kind of passivity. A battered woman may passively comply with her husband's request but sabotage it later. Battered women may repress their anger at one point, but express it later on (Star, 1978; Walker, 1981). They may feel helpless about changing their lives, believing that any action will only make a bad situation even worse.

Battered women are likely to blame themselves for the battering. Frieze (1979) reported that women blamed themselves more often for promoting a beating than they blamed a wife in a hypothetical description of a battering episode. In other words, when they read about some other woman, they are more likely to think that the husband was at fault. In their own marriages, they are more likely to take the blame themselves.

Finally, battered women tend to change their own behavior in order to minimize the violence (Walker, 1984a). They make sure that meals are ready on time, they keep the children quiet in the evening, and they give in to their husbands' sexual demands (Frieze, 1979). Unfortunately, these kinds of actions are often ineffective, because the husband will simply find another reason to be violent.

The batterer. Like their wives, the men who batter women are likely to be low in self-esteem (Walker, 1981). These batterers also show denial. They may rationalize why they were justified in reacting with anger, and they may deny responsibility for the seriousness of their injuries. For example, a man may argue "she fell wrong" to explain his wife's fractured arm (Walker, 1981).

Batterers are also likely to be jealous and possessive. They may demand to know everything that their wives think about or do. They may misinterpret friendliness with other men as flirtatiousness.

Batterers are frequently described as being charming con artists. Their sincerity can often fool unsuspecting people. How could this delightful, devoted husband possibly beat his wife?

It is unclear whether batterers are more likely to come from lower social classes. Marital violence is more likely if the husband is unemployed (Gelles, 1979). Also, police answer more domestic violence calls from the poorer areas of the city. However, it may simply be that middle- and upper-class women are less likely to call for police help (Frieze, 1979). It is clear, however, that even wealthy men may beat their wives. In an elegant Connecticut neighborhood, a woman who was married to a top executive locked herself into their Lincoln Continental every Saturday night to escape from her husband's kicks and blows (O'Reilly, 1983).

Batterers are likely to have other experiences with violence. In a large-scale study by Roy (1982), 81 percent of batterers came from homes in which they were beaten or where they had seen their fathers beat their mothers. (In contrast, only 33 percent of battered wives came from violent homes.) Batterers are also more likely than average to abuse their own children, though there are many who never physically injure them (Walker, 1980, 1984a).

Attitudes Toward Battering

In past centuries, attitudes about battering were tolerant and even supportive. The French code of chivalry during the Middle Ages specified that a husband offended by a scolding wife could knock her to the ground, beat her face, and break her nose so that she would always be ashamed (Dobash & Dobash, 1978). Many of these laws persisted in modern times. For instance, a law that was current in several states until recently allowed a man to beat his wife with a stick, as long as it was no thicker than the width of his thumb (Martin, 1976). The legal system is no longer so tolerant of domestic violence, but there is abundant evidence that battering is not taken seriously. A Kansas resident found guilty of battering his wife was ordered by the court to buy her a box of candy to make it up to her ("No comment," 1982). As we saw in the section on marital rape, a woman is regarded as her husband's property, and the marriage license grants him permission to abuse her.

Several surveys show that Americans are tolerant of domestic violence. For example, in one study 24 percent of wives and 28 percent of husbands thought that it was *normal* for couples to slap each other; 4 percent of wives and 9 percent of husbands even said that slapping was *necessary* (Straus, Gelles, & Steinmetz, 1980).

An investigation by Gentemann (1984) attempted to identify what factors might predict attitudes toward wife beating. She interviewed over 400 women in North Carolina and found that 19 percent of the respondents approved of battering under some circumstances. Those who were most opposed to battering were women who were well educated, younger than 40, high income, and with egalitarian attitudes about gender roles.

People seem to be much more tolerant when a man assaults his wife than when he assaults a stranger. Shotland and Straw (1976) arranged to have participants in an experiment fill out a questionnaire. Meanwhile, a fight was staged nearby between a man and a woman. The man physically attacked the woman, shaking her while she struggled and screamed. In half of the episodes she screamed, "I don't know you," and in the other half she screamed, "I don't know why I ever married you." The two kinds of fights were otherwise identical. The results showed that participants in the experiment were much more likely to intervene if the fight was between strangers than if it was between a married couple. People perceive marital violence as a private matter, one in which they shouldn't interfere. Try Demonstration 13.2 to see if you find the same kind of relationship.

DEMONSTRATION 13.2

Reactions to Violence Against a Stranger Versus Violence Against a Wife

For this exercise, you will need to question at least ten acquaintances, half of whom will be assigned to the "stranger" condition and half of whom will be assigned to the "wife" condition. Read the appropriate instructions and then ask each respondent the same questions.

Stranger Condition

"Imagine that you are walking along [name a busy street near campus] and you witness the following episode. A man says to a woman, 'You took that dollar bill I just dropped,' and then he grabs her by the shoulders and begins to shake her violently. She resists, struggles, and then shouts, 'I don't even know you!' The struggle between the two continues."

Wife Condition

Read the same instruction as above, except substitute 'I don't know why I ever married you' as the woman's response.

Questions

After reading either the "stranger" description or the "wife" description, ask the following questions:

1. How likely would you be to interfere in this fight by looking for a police officer? (1 = not at all; 7 = very likely)
2. How likely would you be to interfere by physically intervening and trying to stop the fight? (1 = not at all; 7 = very likely)
3. How likely would you be to interfere verbally? (1 = not at all; 7 = very likely)
4. How much is the woman to blame in this episode (without knowing anything more about the fight)? (1 = not at all; 7 = very much)
5. How much is the man to blame in this episode? (1 = not at all; 7 = very much)

Myths about Battered Women

Two of the commonly accepted myths about battering are that it is relatively rare and that it is found almost exclusively in lower social classes. We have already discussed the evidence against these two myths. Let's examine some others. In each case, think about how the myth leads to more negative attitudes toward battered women.

1. *Battered women are masochists.* A **masochist** (pronounced "*mass-owe-kist*") is someone who obtains gratification, often sexual, from the pain of being beaten or tortured. Early researchers reasoned that battered women enjoyed the trauma of being abused, and this belief still seems to be popular in the general population. However, there is no evidence for this myth (Bograd, 1982; Star, 1978). Battered women do not enjoy being beaten, just as women do not enjoy being raped.

2. *Battered women ask to be beaten.* According to this myth, when a woman oversteps the boundaries of a proper wife, her misbehavior earns her a beating (Bograd, 1982). In other words, the blame for wife beating lies in the woman, not in the man. A student in a psychology-of-women course related an incident in which she had described a wife-abuse case to a group of friends; a man had seriously injuried his wife because dinner was not ready as soon as he got home from work. A male friend in this student's group—whom she had previously considered enlightened—responded, "Yes, but she really should have prepared dinner on time."

    It is easy to see why this myth is popular. We like to believe that people get what they deserve, and it is hard to accept the injustice of battered women. However, the truth is that batterers lose their self-control because of their own internal reasons; what the women did or did not do is simply an excuse for violence (Walker, 1979).

3. *Battered women could easily leave, if they really wanted to.* This myth ignores both interpersonal and practical factors that prevent a woman from leaving. She may feel a good deal of love for the abusing man, because he may be quite decent most of the time. Also, many batterers may follow a battering episode with a period of generosity and kindness (Walker, 1984a), as Mike did in the episode at the beginning of this section. Battered women may sincerely believe that their husbands are basically good people who can be reformed.

    Battered women may also be reluctant to leave because of disapproval from friends and relatives. They would probably be perceived as "failures" as both wives and women, because a real woman would either reform her husband or suffer silently.

    Battered women also do not leave because practical matters provide roadblocks. They may have no place to go, no money, and no way of escaping. Often, various "helping" agencies offer no help to battered women (Breines & Gordon, 1983). Even if they appear in the emergency room of a hospital, they will be treated for their physical injuries, but the cause of these injuries will be ignored. Imagine what it would be like to live for a month away from home without money, without credit, and with several children in your care (Cunningham, 1983). Another practical concern is that if the battered woman leaves, the batterer may still pursue her and attack her even more fiercely for leaving.

Options for Battered Women

A battered woman has three kinds of options (Lewis, 1983). She may remain in the relationship and maintain the status quo. She may remain in the relationship but want to eliminate the battering. Finally, she may end the relationship, either temporarily or permanently. In any case, two important options are therapy and battered-women shelters.

Therapy. A battering relationship seldom improves spontaneously. Women often seek the services of psychotherapists, many times with disappointing results. The therapists may refuse to deal specifically with the battering incidents. Instead, they tend to address the psychological consequences of these incidents. As Walker (1980) points out, a woman who has been repeatedly abused will have enough symptoms to keep a therapist busy. By focusing on the woman's reactions, however, therapists ignore the abusive partner. The partner usually feels little psychological distress, and he will rarely seek therapy unless the woman threatens to leave him (Bograd, 1982). As Bograd stresses, violence is the primary treatment issue. Nonetheless, violence itself is often ignored because therapists feel more competent treating issues such as depression in an individual or poor communication patterns in a couple.

There is an additional problem with respect to therapy. Women who blame themselves for the battering are about twice as likely to seek therapy as women who blame the man for the battering (Frieze, 1979). Those battered women who request therapy may be particularly likely to respond to any suggestions from the therapist that the situation is their fault and that altering their own behavior can improve the relationship.

Three approaches in therapy are to treat the woman, either individually or in a group, to treat the abuser, or to treat the couple. If therapy is limited to the woman and if it is well handled, she may develop her independence. Therapy can also help her explore career goals. Group therapy where all the participants are battered women is beneficial because it reduces the feeling of isolation, offers support for women who are considering leaving, and encourages women to exchange information about available services for battered women (Walker, 1980).

Ironically, the batterer—who most needs therapy—is usually the most resistant to entering therapy. He doesn't believe that there is anything wrong with him; he doesn't see wife beating as a problem (Myers & Gilbert, 1983).

This is a particularly interesting finding because we saw in the last chapter that no substantial sex differences have been demonstrated in the frequency with which men and women seek therapy for psychological disorders. Is the answer that much of our society regards wife beating as acceptable behavior, or is it that the kinds of husbands who beat their wives are more resistant to seeking therapy, an admission of weakness? In support of this second explanation, there are reports that many battering men, when given the choice between therapy and a prison sentence, will select prison. However, some batterers will enter therapy because their wives threaten to leave them if they do not seek help (Walker, 1980). Programs aimed at the batterer emphasize anger reduction and management strategies (Walker, 1980, 1984b).

There is controversy about whether couples therapy is successful; little research has been conducted on the long-range success of this approach (Walker, 1980). There are several difficulties with treating the batterer and the battered woman in the same session. A woman may fear that what she says in therapy will earn her another beating. In addition, the therapist may distribute the blame equally between the two partners (Bograd, 1982; Walker, 1980).

However, some researchers are enthusiastic about couples therapy in some circumstances. Taylor (1984) outlines a program limited to couples with mild to moderate levels of abuse. This program involves a careful study of the abuser's anger patterns, work on low self-esteem for both people, and an examination of new problem-solving procedures. Also, couples therapy may be useful if the man and the woman are counselled in separate sessions.

In all kinds of therapy, though, Bograd (1982) stresses the importance of a feminist perspective. The problem of battered women arises from a situation in society in which males are dominant; it is not simply a problem limited to two individuals in a close personal relationship.

Shelters for battered women. The first shelter for battered women was opened in 1964 in a private home in Pasadena, California. As of 1983, there were about 800 shelters throughout the country (O'Reilly, 1983). Most of them cannot shelter all the women who request help, and women are limited as to the length of time they stay. As Walker (1980) concludes, this grass-roots alternatives for battered women seems to be the most successful form of treatment to date. Typically, shelters operate on limited finances. Nevertheless, they offer a place where a battered woman can go for safety, support, and usually some kind of immediate counselling and advice. Staff members often have extensive experience with the social services available in the community, and they can sometimes arrange for battered women to be given priority for these services (Lewis, 1983).

Going to a shelter is only a temporary solution. In a typical follow-up on women who had stayed in a shelter, 42 percent returned to the batterer and remained with him (the majority reporting at least one violent incident after their return), and 16 percent returned but then left. The remaining 42 percent did not return to the batterer (Giles-Sims, 1983).

The decision to leave a relationship. As we mentioned, a woman who would like to leave a battering relationship faces both personal and practical problems. Professionals who should be able to help may in fact be harmful, as in the case of a family doctor who said to a battered woman he had just patched up: "You took a vow when you got married to love and to cherish for better or worse 'till death do you part.' Now go home with him. You are never going to change him. This is the way he shows his love" (Giles-Sims, 1983, p. 136).

Some women do decide that abuse is too high a price to pay for the advantages of remaining in a relationship. The decision is usually a gradual one, requiring the accumulation of many battering incidents. Fields examined the cases of 287 women who complained of physical assaults in their divorce suits. The batterings had occurred for an average of *four years* before the woman sought a divorce (Fields, 1978).

What makes women decide to leave? Giles-Sims (1983) believes that a crisis point is reached. There is some new input into the violent system, such as the fear that the children will be hurt, resentment that the children see their mother being beaten, and exposure of the violence to someone outside the family. However, women usually do not leave immediately after the crisis point; there is usually a time lag.

Women who leave a battering relationship often mention that they had been close to another person who gave them information and support. As one woman said about her confidant, who had been an abused wife,

> ...I talked to her a lot because we could communicate with the things that had happened to her. She is the one that really helped me a lot—being able to talk to somebody that it had happened to, too. And she would always say, "I don't know why you stay." I didn't, you know, but I didn't have any way out. At least I thought I didn't. [Giles-Sims, 1983, p. 135]

An excellent handbook for women who are considering leaving battering relationships is called *Getting Free* (NiCarthy, 1982). It includes information about battered women, exercises for assessing emotions and needs, and practical advice about protection, housing, economics, and new relationships.

Society's Response to the Battering Problem

The battering problem has recently received increasing attention. As I was writing this chapter, a television docudrama starred a well-known actress in the role of a woman who killed her husband who had repeatedly abused her. The publicity about the program clearly increased the public's awareness of the problem. It remains to be seen whether such programs have a substantial impact on general attitudes toward the battering problem. Conceivably, these programs could also lead to a reduction in the number of battered women.

Increased awareness about battered women could also influence policymakers. In some court cases, expert witnesses can provide testimonies to refute myths about battered women (Walker, 1984b). Still, police officers and individuals in helping agencies are often misinformed (Bowker, 1983), and government policy has made no consistent plan for requiring counselling for batterers or providing shelters for battered women. As Walker (1984b) concluded, "the final chapter on the evolution of domestic violence policy is yet to be written" (p. 1181).

☐ SECTION SUMMARY ▪ Battered Women

1. A large percentage of women will be battered at some point in their lives; the battering cycle is thought to have three distinct phases of tension building, an acute battering incident, and the loving apologetic phase.
2. Battered women are likely to have low self-esteem, show denial and passivity, blame themselves for the battering, and change their behavior to reduce violence.
3. Men who batter are likely to have low self-esteem and show denial, jealousy and charm; it is not clear whether they are likely to come from lower social classes, but they are likely to have other experiences with violence.
4. In the past, attitudes about battering have been tolerant, and these attitudes sometimes persist; many Americans believe that domestic violence is normal, and they are more tolerant of assaults against a wife than assaults against a stranger.
5. Several myths about battered women for which there are no bases are that battered women are masochists, that battered women ask to be beaten, and that battered women could leave if they wanted to.
6. Therapy in battering relationships may not focus sufficiently on the violence itself.
7. Individual therapy for the woman may help her develop independence; group therapy may reduce isolation and encourage support.
8. Battering men usually resist therapy for themselves.
9. Therapy for couples often involves difficulties, but some researchers claim that it can be successful.
10. A feminist perspective is useful in all therapeutic approaches to the issue of battered women.
11. Shelters for battered women seem to offer successful treatment.
12. The decision to leave a battering relationship is usually a gradual one, typically made after reaching a crisis point.
13. The problem of battered women has received increasing attention and some modification in the legal system; however, government policy is inadequate in this area.

☐ SEXUAL HARASSMENT

Before you go further, try Demonstration 13.3, an exercise designed to help you appreciate the sexual-harassment issue. A good, general definition of **sexual harassment** is that it involves "unwelcome sexual advances, re-

---

DEMONSTRATION 13.3

Envisioning Sexual Harassment

In this exercise, you will attempt to imagine that you are in a sexual-harassment situation, in order to obtain a more realistic appreciation of victims' reactions to harassment. Imagine you are a 19-year-old female college sophomore. If you are a male, it might be most effective to imagine how your sister or a close female friend might respond. When the narrative is interrupted to ask what you are thinking, try to elaborate as completely as possible about your emotions.

1. Imagine that you are taking a late-afternoon course in history. Dr. Jones is your professor. When he hands back the exam papers, he hands you yours, smiles, and says in a voice loud enough that all can hear, "This is one of the best exams I've received in my entire teaching career. You're really talented!" What are you feeling, and what are you thinking?
2. During the next class session, he calls on you and compliments you on your response. As the class leaves, you gather up your books and get up from your seat. Dr. Jones comes up, places his hand on your shoulder and says, "I'd like to hear more of your ideas on today's topic. Would you like to join me for coffee right now?" What are you feeling and thinking? What would you reply?
3. Suppose that you declined his previous invitation. During the following class he again calls upon you and praises your response. As you prepare to leave at the end of class, he asks you, "Maybe you'll join me this time for coffee?" What do you feel, think, and reply?
4. Suppose that you accept this second invitation. As Dr. Jones and you wait for the check for the coffee, he tells you, "You're an exceptional student, and you seem to have some real potential. I know I can help you realize your potential to its utmost. In the future, I think that we should be working together even more closely. I think it would be best to get to know each other well. Very well." He pauses briefly and then suggests that the two of you go to a nearby hotel. What do you feel and think? How would you respond?
5. Several days later, you begin to feel angry about Dr. Jones' proposition (which you did not accept). You go to his office and state your thoughts on the issue. He responds, "Well, you were leading me on, and then you got angry when I responded as any normal male would. I had to sit there and hear all about your problems and your personal life. Now it looks like you're trying to get me fired. You really are a manipulative female, because you use men without really caring what happens to them. You're making up lies to ruin my career!" What do you feel and think? What do you respond to him, and what further action would you take?

[This exercise is based on a "guided fantasy" prepared by Dr. Dee Graham of the University of Cincinnati, as described by Dziech & Weiner (1984).]

quests for sexual favors, and other verbal or physical conduct of a sexual nature" (Equal Employment Opportunity Commission, 1980, p. 74677). This means that sexual harassment can include staring at, talking about, or touching a woman's body, trying to coerce an unwilling person into sexual behavior, repeatedly asking for dates, and rape (Brandenburg, 1982; Gutek, et al., 1980). Sexual harassment is particularly likely to occur in academic settings, where professors may harass students, and in the workplace, where supervisors or bosses may harass their employees. Both of these settings raise particular problems because they involve reasonably long-term relationships between the woman and the harasser.

Although this section will concentrate on academic and employment settings, keep in mind that there are other situations in which sexual harassment can occur. Recall from the last chapter that some therapists have sexual relations with their clients. Also, most women can recall episodes in which they or a friend received an obscene phone call, a lewd remark while walking down a street, or an ogle from a stranger. All of these involve the unwelcome sexual advances that are part of sexual harassment.

Here is an example, in more detail, of sexual harassment in an academic setting. A graduate student was asked by her adviser to proofread his manuscripts. While she worked, he read pornographic passages aloud to her. She had to sit and listen because there was nothing else she could do and nowhere she could go (Dziech & Weiner, 1984).

A student working on an associate degree recalls this experience in a course required for her major:

> Each student sat at a desk with a particular machine. One day my instructor leaned over and put his hand on my inner thigh while he was explaining the machine to me. Then he put his hand around my upper arm so that his fingers were on the inside of my arm, with the tops of his fingers touching my breast. [Dziech & Weiner, 1984, p. 99]

A young woman deputy describes her experience with a sheriff in Virginia:

> One of the first things he said to me after I became a deputy—the first female one—was, 'A new rule is going to be that females have to go to bed with me.' To that I replied, 'Well, if that is one of the job functions, I'd have to find something else to do.' [Lane, 1981, p. 114]

However, the sheriff laughed off this response but persisted in trying to grab her and kiss her on other occasions.

An especially tragic case is that of a woman Army Private at Ft. Leonard Wood, Missouri, who committed suicide in 1983. She left notes for her relatives stating that she was going to kill herself because she could no longer put up with being sexually harassed by her drill sergeant (Jordon & Glynn, 1984).

It is extremely difficult to estimate how often sexual harassment occurs because the boundaries of sexual harassment are often vague and because so many cases go unreported. However, based on their analyses of surveys conducted at several colleges, Dziech and Weiner estimate that 20 to 30 percent of college women experience sexual harassment. Brewer (1982) estimates that the comparable figure for employed women is somewhere between 20 and 60 percent. Furthermore, it seems that no woman is safe. As MacKinnon (1979) argues about sexual harassment in the workplace, "Victimization by the practice of sexual harassment, so far as is currently known, occurs across the lines of age, marital status, physical appearance, race, class, occupation, pay range, and any other factor that distinguishes women from each other" (p. 28).

The term "sexual harassment" did not even exist until the mid-1970s (MacKinnon, 1979), but theorists quickly established that it was a feminist issue. Schneider (1982) outlines several reasons why sexual domination is important in the sexual-harassment issue:

1. Sexual harassment is violence against women.
2. Sexual demands are coercive because women are offered economic or academic advantages if they comply and harmful consequences if they say no.
3. In sexual harassment, women are first seen as sexual beings and only secondly as workers or students.
4. Women are often forced to be silent victims because of fear and the need to continue either in the workplace or at school.

Feminists also argue that sexual harassment places a woman in a powerless position, whether she is a student who is being ogled by her philosophy professor or a secretary who is being propositioned by her boss.

Let's look at several aspects of sexual harassment in more detail: the victim's reaction, attitudes toward sexual harassment, and what to do about sexual harassment.

The Harassment Victim's Reactions

We don't know as much about how women react to sexual harassment as we know about their reactions to rape or battering. We have anecdotes from individual women, but few systematic interviews.

We do know that sexual harassment is not a minor inconvenience to women; it can change their lives. A woman employee may receive a negative job evaluation, refusal of overtime, demotions, transfer to another job, or reassignment of hours; and she may even be fired. The situation may be so intolerable that she decides to quit. As one woman wrote, "I felt humiliated, incompetent. I was unable to do my job. I finally quit" (Farley, 1978, p. 22). In one survey of women who had been harassed on the job, 42 percent were pressured into resigning, 24 percent were fired, and only 34 percent remained at work (Crull, 1980).

We don't have any comparison figures for college women who have experienced sexual harassment. Some students may miss classes in the course taught by the harassing professor, or they may drop the course. However, the problem may not be solved by these measures, as one student reported,

> I . . . became quite skillful at glancing down department hallways to make sure he wasn't there before venturing forth, and pretending not to see him when we did cross paths. The whole experience has left me quite mistrustful of faculty in general and I still feel some trepidation when visiting the department. [Till, 1980, p. 15]

Students are also likely to drop out of school or to transfer to another college.

Women describe the harassment experience using terms such as intimidating, frightening, financially damaging, embarrassing, nerve-wracking, frustrating, and awful (MacKinnon, 1979). In one study, 80 percent reported "disgust" with the experience (Jensen & Gutek, 1982). Some people argue that women really enjoy the sexual attention—in much the same way that women enjoy being raped—but these words hardly suggest enjoyment. According to one survey, 90 percent of women who had encountered sexual harassment on the job were experiencing some kind of psychological stress, frequently accompanied by physiological symptoms such as headache or nausea.

When you tried Demontration 13.3, did you experience anger? In a study of women who had been sexually harassed on the job, Jensen and Gutek reported that 68 percent reported being angry. However, Dziech and Weiner (1984) argue that anger is not a common response among college students who are being harassed by a professor. These students are more worried about grades, offending someone in a position of authority, and misinterpreting the professor's intentions. If students really are less likely than employed women to respond to sexual harassment with anger, it would be interesting to know whether the discrepancy can be traced to the nature of the sexual harassment, the fact that students are likely to be younger and less experienced in sexual politics, or some other factors. (Can you think of other reasons?)

Employed women and college women may also react differently in terms of self-blame. In their survey of women who were sexually harassed at work, Jensen & Gutek (1982) found that only about one-quarter of the women blamed the harassment on something about their own behavior or their own personality. However, according to Dziech and Weiner (1984),

> Student victims report feeling responsible, feeling at fault somehow. Some have an almost childlike fear of having broken some rule they did not know. They wonder what they should have known or done to prevent the harassment. "I keep asking myself what I did to get him started. There were twenty-two other

girls in the class. Why did he pick on me?" Michelle Y., a student at a Southern university, asked. [p. 82]

In reality, women usually have no reason to blame themselves. It is likely, for example, that the harasser has had other victims in the past. As Dziech and Weiner report, when a case of academic sexual harassment becomes public, the complaints typically come from many sources, and women describe incidents that have occurred over a period of years. The blame lies in the harasser, not in the victim.

In part, a woman's reaction to sexual harassment will depend upon whether she decides to take any action against the harasser. If she does, she will be labeled a troublemaker, she will received unwanted attention regarding her personal life, and she may be scorned by others. (Under ideal circumstances, this action would bring respect. What would the reaction be at your school?) If the woman takes legal action in the workplace, her struggle will take time and savings that might be needed to search for a new job (Farley, 1978). If she brings a charge of sexual harassment in an academic setting, she may find that most of the college professors will band together in defense of their colleague (Dziech & Weiner, 1984). These responses will increase her feelings of helplessness and isolation. On the other hand, if she decides not to take any action against the harasser, she may feel even more powerless and victimized.

Attitudes Toward Sexual Harassment

According to Dziech and Weiner (1984), professors and administrators in academic settings react in a variety of ways to trivialize the importance of sexual harassment. Faculty members often refuse to intrude in the private life of their colleagues. As one mathematics professor said of his colleague:

> I'm supposed to take rumors from 19-year-old girls more seriously than my working relationship with him? Even if he does say a few off-color things now and then, I doubt that he realizes that he's offending anyone. He's a good person and a dedicated teacher. He wouldn't hurt anyone on purpose. [p. 48]

Professors and administrators may also believe that students shouldn't be taken too seriously, or that professors are only human. Anyway, those women students who wear such skimpy clothing and such tight jeans are really inviting sexual harassment.

Surprisingly, however, faculty and administrators are *less* likely to approve of sexual harassment than students are. Lott, Reilly, and Howard (1982) administered a questionnaire about sexual harassment to faculty, administrators, and students at University of Rhode Island. The questionnaire included items such as "It is only natural for a man to make sexual advances to a woman he finds attractive," as well as other questions designed to measure the respondents' attitude toward sexual harassment. The results of the survey showed that younger undergraduates were less likely than faculty and administrators to condemn sexual harassment. In other words, these results imply that a young student may not realize that there is something wrong with unwanted attention from a professor.

A number of studies have demonstrated that a major factor determining attitudes toward sexual harassment is the sex of the respondent. Lott and her coauthors found that men were far more accepting of sexual harassment than women were. Other research demonstrated that men were much more likely than women to believe that the issue of sexual harassment has been exaggerated (Tangri, Burt, & Johnson, 1982).

Also, men and women differ in terms of the behaviors they are willing to classify as sexual harassment. Gutek and her coauthors (1980) interviewed adults who were employed in the Los Angeles area, asking them whether each of the following could be considered sexual harassment:

1. Verbal comments of a sexual nature that are positive in tone.
2. Verbal comments of a sexual nature that are negative in tone.
3. Nonverbal behaviors of a sexual nature (leering, touching).
4. Requests for a date with the understanding that the response would influence the job situation.
5. Requests for sexual activity with the understanding that the response would influence the job situation.

Figure 13.1 shows the results. Notice that in all five categories, women are more likely than men to classify the behavior as harassment. These results suggest that when a man flirts with a woman at work, he may perceive it as innocent conversation, but she may perceive it as sexual harassment. Nevertheless, keep in mind a caution we have raised throughout this book. Yes, there is a sex difference in attitudes toward sexual harassment. However, the overlap in attitudes is substantial enough that we are likely to know men who are strongly opposed to any form of sexual harassment, as well as women who wonder why everyone is making such a fuss. The difference in reactions to sexual harassment may reflect not only a difference in attitudes but a difference in interpretation. Remember Abbey's (1982) study, discussed earlier, that men and women may interpret the same gesture in different ways.

As you would imagine, people with feminist beliefs are particularly opposed to sexual harassment. Schneider (1982) asked women in the Northeast to indicate the extent to which they identified themselves as feminists; they then answered questions about sexual harassment. The results showed that 73 percent of the strongly feminist women considered unwanted sexual approaches a problem for most employed women, in contrast to only 30 percent of the nonfeminists.

What to Do about Sexual Harassment

Individual action. As with the topics of rape and woman battering, the "what-to-do" question has both individual and societal answers. Dziech and

FIGURE 13.1. **Sex differences in the classification of various behaviors as sexual harassment (based on Gutek, et al., 1980)**

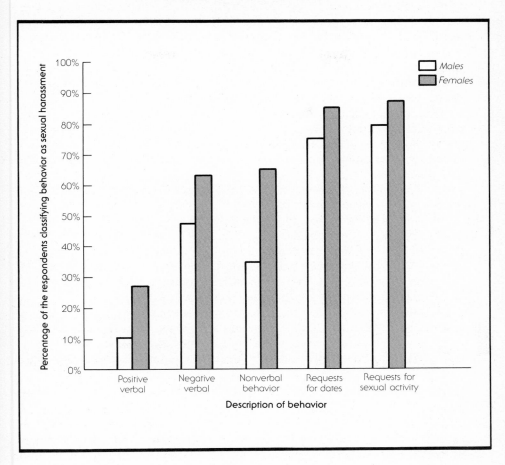

Weiner (1984) include a number of good recommendations for individual students, including:

1. Become familiar with the sexual-harassment issue and know which officials on campus are responsible for complaints. (Do you know whom you would speak to on your campus?)
2. Check the campus "grapevine" about any faculty members who should be avoided.
3. If a professor's behavior seems questionable, the student should review the situation objectively with someone she trusts.
4. Sexual harassment frequently increases when a student simply tries to disregard it. If changing the subject doesn't work, she should di-

rectly state to the harasser that she feels uncomfortable. She should keep records if the problem persists.

5. The student should report the problem to the appropriate officials on campus. If the institution takes no action, it is responsible if there is a second act of harassment. Dziech and Weiner's book also gives information on other legal alternatives.

Employed women can also take steps to avoid and eliminate sexual harassment (Backhouse & Cohen, 1978, 1981; Lane, 1981). Unfortunately, some of these precautions—once again—have a "blame-the-victim" flavor, which limits women's behavior.

1. Dress and act professionally; don't talk extensively about your personal life.
2. Don't socialize alone with potential harassers after hours; distinguish between business and pleasure.
3. Don't ask for or volunteer to do special favors.
4. Once harassment begins, first try a direct confrontation. Lane (1981) suggests saying, "I'm here to do my job, and I don't go along with that sort of thing and I'm not interested." Any further harassment cannot be attributed to a simple misunderstanding! A more polite response may be interpreted as "maybe" rather than a "no."
5. Threats of exposure to superiors and lawsuits may be necessary if direct statements fail. If harassment persists, keep records and find out whether the harasser has approached other women.
6. File a formal complaint with a superior, a union, or a personnel office.

Society's response to the harassment problem. Individual action against sexual harassment is simply a stop-gap approach. In order to stop sexual harassment effectively, institutions must pay attention to the issue. Brandenburg (1982) describes how Yale University worked out a policy statement on sexual harassment that was included in official publications and distributed to all students, faculty, and administrators. Businesses also need to make policies against harassment. In a survey of *Harvard Business Review* readers, 73 percent favored policy statements disapproving of harassment, yet only 29 percent reported that their own organizations had issued such a statement (Livingston, 1982).

Noted anthropologist Margaret Mead (1980) suggested that we need to develop new taboos—deeply and intensely felt prohibitions—against sex at work. She felt that new taboos are really more useful than new laws. New taboos are also necessary for academia. Mead wrote that we need to develop "new ways that allow women and men to work together effortlessly and to respect each other as persons" (p. 56).

Public opinion needs to be changed so that people become more aware that sexual harassment limits the right and opportunities of women in academic and work settings. Men need to realize that women often do not appreciate sexual attention and may regard flirtation as sexual harassment. It does seem likely that many men who harass are not aware that they are creating a problem. Others may believe that they have a sanction to harass because of good-natured responses and joking from other men. A change in public opinion could alter behavior, particularly because harassers are generally people in highly visible positions. Undoubtedly, there are still others whose harassing tendencies would not be reduced by a change in public opinion; legal action may be the only answer here.

However, the real answer may lie in the unequal distribution of power between men and women, as discussed earlier in this section. As Livingston (1982) concludes after reviewing legal and organizational responses to sexual harassment, "If the goal of remedial action is to end sexual harassment, then remedies will have to go beyond individual solutions and change the inequitable distribution of power that encourages harassment to occur" (p. 21).

□ SECTION SUMMARY ▪ Sexual Harassment

1. Sexual harassment involves unwanted sexual attention that may include staring at, touching, trying to coerce a person into sexual behavior, and rape; many women in the workplace and academic settings experience sexual harassment.
2. Sexual harassment is a feminist issue because it represents violence against women, coersion of women, a focus on women's sexuality, and forcing women to be silent victims; sexual harassment places women in a powerless position.
3. Sexual harassment can have important consequences at work and at school; women describe the experience as frightening, embarrassing, disgusting, and stressful.
4. Employed women are more likely than college women to respond with anger, whereas college women are more likely to respond with self-blame.
5. If a woman decides to take action against the harasser, she may experience unwanted attention and criticism; however, if she decides not to take any action, she may feel powerless.
6. Professors and administrators may refuse—for a variety of reasons—to interfere in sexual-harassment issues; however, they are more opposed to sexual harassment than students are.
7. There are sex differences in terms of acceptance of sexual harassment, the belief that the sexual-harassment issue has been exaggerated, and the willingness to classify various behaviors as sexual harassment; people with feminist beliefs are particularly opposed to sexual harassment.
8. Suggestions for individual students regarding sexual harassment include becoming familiar with officials on campus who are responsible for complaints, checking to see which faculty members

should be avoided, carefully reviewing a situation in which there is possible sexual harassment, directly telling the harasser that she feels uncomfortable, and reporting the problem to appropriate officials.

9. Employed women should dress and act professionally, avoid socializing after hours, avoid volunteering to do special favors, directly confront the harasser, threaten to report the harasser, and, if necessary, file a formal complaint.

10. Institutions can help by making and distributing policy statements; other suggestions at the societal level include the development of new taboos, changing public opinion about the seriousness of sexual harassment, and, ultimately, focusing on a redistribution of power between men and women.

Chapter Review Questions

1. In the chapter on achievement, we discussed women's attributions for failure. There is evidence that in some (but not all) cases, women tend to blame themselves when something bad happens. Comment on this issue with respect to women's self-blame in rape, marital rape, battering, and sexual harassment.

2. Also in the chapter on achievement, we discussed people's perceptions of women's failure; people are likely to blame women when something bad happens to them. Comment on this issue with respect to "blaming the victim" in rape, battering, and sexual harassment.

3. What are the rape victim's reactions to rape, both immediate and delayed? Speculate about how her immediate reactions may be influenced by whether the rape was a surprise attack or a confidence rape.

4. What are some of the common myths about rape and battering? What do they reveal about society's attitudes about men and women?

5. Summarize the information about child abuse, date rape, and marital rape. What does this tell us about sexual violence in close personal relationships?

6. What kinds of precautions can individual women take to prevent rape and to prevent sexual harassment in academic and employment situations? Comment on those precautions that limit women's behavior and their freedom.

7. Imagine that you have been appointed to a nationwide committee to address the problems of rape, battering, and sexual harassment. What kinds of recommendations would you make for government policy, the legal system, academic and business institutions, the media, and educational programs? Feel free to list items other than those mentioned in this chapter.

8. Discuss how the characteristics of the battered women and the myths

about battered women may make it especially difficult for a women to leave a battering relationship.

9. What are women's reactions to sexual harassment? Contrast these with women's reactions to rape, and account for some of the similarities and differences in these reactions.

10. The introduction pointed out that rape, battering, and sexual harassment can all be related to the issue of males having more power than females. Now that you have read the chapter, address this issue in more detail, pointing out how violence makes women even less powerful.

☐ NEW TERMS

rape	incest
surprise attack	battered women
confidence rape	masochist
rape-trauma syndrome	sexual harassment

☐ RECOMMENDED READINGS

Dziech, B. W., & Weiner, L. (1984). *The lecherous professor: Sexual harassment.* Boston: Beacon. ■ This book has excellent coverage of the general topic of sexual harassment in academic settings; the authors weaken the book somewhat by speculating too freely about topics for which there are no data, but otherwise this is a very useful resource.

Herman, D. (1984). The rape culture. In J. Freeman (Ed.), *Women: A feminist perspective* (pp. 20–38). Palo Alto, Calif.: Mayfield. ■ Herman provides a concise overview of the topic of rape, with an emphasis on the cultural determinants of rape.

Journal of Social Issues (1982). Volume *38*, Issue 4. ■ This special issue is devoted to the topic of sexual harassment, with an emphasis on work settings. It provides good coverage of legal and practical issues, as well as psychological reactions to sexual harassment.

Walker, L. E. (1981). Battered women: Sex roles and clinical issues. *Professional Psychology, 12*, 81–91. ■ Walker is one of the major researchers in this area, and this article provides a good summary of the topic, with an emphasis on women's reactions to battering.

LATER ADULTHOOD

- Because most researchers are middle-aged or older, psychological research has primarily concentrated on late adulthood.

- Approximately one woman in 15 will develop breast cancer during her lifetime, and most of these women will have a mastectomy.

- Most of the physical symptoms that women experience with menopause are "in their heads."

- Menopause is related to psychological symptoms such as depression and irritability.

- Women tend to retire earlier than men, and they are more likely to retire voluntarily.

- Women experience fewer retirement problems than men.

- People are more likely to call a 60-year-old woman elderly, in contrast to a 60-year-old man.

- Most women experience moderate to severe depression when their children leave home.

- Most women over the age of 65 live in a nursing home.

- Many studies show older women to be just as satisfied with their lives as other people.

A paragraph written by Sandra Levy (1981) captures the current situation of the older woman in America:

> [her] life is marked by the continuities of working in the home and maintaining emotional connections with family, children and peers. But her life is also marked by discontinuities of interrupted career and a large number of losses, including frequent geographical separation from children and loss of spouse. She is faced not only with an unflattering stereotype but with poverty, poor access to transportation, loneliness, and isolation. She is three times as likely as her male peer to live in a nursing home. There is a real possibility that she may become an invalid or a pauper. Despite all of this, the elderly woman of this cohort also possesses great strength and potential, as witnessed by her ability to survive. [p. 94]

In this chapter, we will consider women in middle age and old age. It is worth mentioning that there are no clear-cut age spans for these two life periods. The U.S. Department of Labor alone has had five different definitions of middle age, ranging from one definition that referred to ages 25 to 54 to another definition that referred to age 30 to the end of one's employment (Giele, 1982a). Thus, old age might begin anywhere from 55 to 70. However, the fuzziness of the definitions is appropriate, because the transition between life periods is gradual, rather than abrupt. A young woman does not go to sleep on the eve of her thirtieth birthday and wake up a middle-aged woman.

For many years, psychological research ignored older women. To begin with, research has ignored old *people*. About 80 percent of all research on humans uses college students as subjects (Adair, 1973). In addition, developmental psychologists primarily concentrate on childhood and adolescence. These research interests echo our society's general focus on youthfulness and neglect of the elderly. Recently, an approach called life-span developmental psychology has gained attention. The **life-span approach** is concerned with describing, understanding, and predicting age-related changes in behavior, from birth to death (Russo, 1978).

Older women have been ignored even more than older men. Several popular and professional books, such as Levinson's (1978) *The Seasons of a Man's Life*, nicely outlined stages and crises in men's adult lives. Women were omitted, however. This neglect is currently being addressed by some excellent books such as Markson's (1983a) *Older Women* and Giele's (1982b) *Women in the Middle Years*. However, Robert Butler, former director of the National Institute on Aging, has pleaded for additional research focusing exclusively on older women (Butler, 1978).

It seems that women in general are relatively invisible, consistent with one of the themes of the book, but older women are especially invisible. Another indication that older women have been neglected comes from an examination of American magazine fiction. From 1890 to 1955, there was a decline in the number of older women appearing as characters in these stories, and by 1955 there were none at all in the sample (Bell, 1979). Think about it: When was the last time you read a story in which the major character was a woman over the age of 40? The silence about older women is reflected in a quotation from a middle-aged woman:

> It's unbelievable when I think of it now. I never really saw past about age forty-two, where I am now. I mean, I never thought about what happens to the rest of life. Pretty much the whole of adult life was supposed to be around helping your husband and raising the children. Dammit, what a betrayal! Nobody ever tells you that there's many years of life left after that. He doesn't need your help any more, and the children are raised. Now what? [Rubin, 1979, p. 123]

As this woman poignantly points out, a major portion of her life remains after age 42. The life expectancy for women is now 78 years, in contrast to a life expectancy of slightly over 70 for men (Hess & Waring, 1983). If the woman in the preceding paragraph is typical, she can expect to live an additional 36 years. Thus, some middle-aged women are concerned about having too much time left, rather than too little (Baruch, et al., 1983).

The absence of information about middle age and old age in women is particularly sad because these periods constitute about half of women's lives. Looking at the problem another way, this absence of information is also sad because there are so many older women. Because women outlive men, there are more old women than old men. In addition, the ratio of women to men increases as we look at increasingly older age groups. If we look at very old people—those who are 85 and older—there are 1,500,000 women and 680,000 men, a ratio of about 2.2 women for each man.

It is clear that we do not know as much about older women as we should know. Nonetheless, we have enough information to give us an outline of the major issues. This chapter is divided into three sections: physical aspects of later adulthood; retirement; and social aspects of later adulthood.

☐ PHYSICAL ASPECTS OF LATER ADULTHOOD

Physical and health issues obviously have important implications for women's mental health and psychological well-being in middle age and old age. Let us begin by briefly talking about general health issues. Our other topic in this section is menopause, which seems to be one of the more popular areas for theory and research about older women.

Health Issues

We mentioned that women live about eight years longer than men, on the average. A major reason for this sex difference in life expectancy is that women are much less likely than men to have coronary heart disease, a condition that leads to heart attacks (Kannel & Brand, 1983). Nonetheless, over 10 percent of women between the ages of 45 and 65 have heart trouble that has been diagnosed by a physician (Butler, 1978). Furthermore, nearly one in four women in this age range has a chronic condition that forces her to limit her physical activity (Butler, 1978).

You probably know an elderly woman whose physical activity was limited because she fell down, perhaps fracturing an arm, a leg, or a hip. In fact, 40 percent of elderly women who live at home have experienced a fall (Kerzner, 1983). In contrast, only 20 percent of elderly men have fallen. About half of falling episodes can be traced to heart problems. The remainder are due to accidents or imbalance. Women seem to sway more than men when they stand or walk, which may be partly responsible for the sex difference in falling episodes.

People who are affected by osteoporosis are particularly likely to suffer from a fracture after a fall. **Osteoporosis** (pronounced "*oss*-tee-owe-poe-*row*-siss") is a disease in which the bones become increasingly soft, flexible, and brittle. About 25 percent of elderly women suffer from osteoporosis, and it is much more common in women than in men (Kerzner, 1983).

A health issue of particular concern to older women is breast cancer. According to one estimate, one woman in 15 will develop breast cancer during her lifetime (Butler, 1976). Because of the high frequency, most of us know of a relative, friend, or neighbor who has had breast cancer. Every year in the United States, about 80,000 new cases will be discovered and about 30,000 women will die of this disease (Tishler, 1978).

Most women discover breast cancer during self-examination. Early detection of breast cancer is particularly important because it leads to a higher survival rate. If the tumor is small, a woman has an 80 percent chance of being alive five years later; with more advanced tumors, the survival rate falls to 30 percent (Tishler, 1978).

Mastectomy, or surgical removal of the breast, is still the treatment of choice for most women with breast cancer in the United States (Meyerowitz, 1981; Woods & Earp, 1978). You have probably read about the controversy regarding treatment for breast cancer, because many women with breast cancer receive modified surgical approaches or radiation therapy. These alternative methods may soon be performed more often than mastectomies.

A mastectomy is a psychologically stressful experience, particularly since our society places such emphasis on women's physical appearance in general and on women's breasts in particular (Meyerowitz, 1981; Notman, 1978). In fact, women who have had mastectomies frequently show a decline in their attitudes toward their bodies (Polivy, 1977). One woman's personal experience with a mastectomy is described in the book *First, You Cry* (Rollin, 1976). Rollin describes the many days that passed before she could look at the mastectomy scar and the initial horrified reaction she had when she finally convinced herself to look at her body. Months later, however, she has achieved an uneasy acceptance of herself:

> As for my body, I am no longer so obsessed with the mirror-mirror-on-the-wall stuff. This is not to say I think I have a keen-looking chest, or that I enjoy being

touched or touching myself there. It still repulses me to do that. And I still don't prance around naked. And sometimes when I *am* naked and catch sight of my body's left profile in the mirror and see the narrow, lumpy tube that is my torso, it still makes me swallow hard.

So I swallow hard. There are worse things.... [pp. 225–226]

There seems to be little agreement about how women "should" react to a mastectomy. Some people emphasize the enormous impact of the disease, and so they encourage women to express their feelings and despair. Others focus on adjusting to the situation, rather than focusing on the stressful experience. Meyerowitz wisely concludes: "Neither of these approaches, taken alone, is sufficient. Neither the tremendous impact of the disease and its treatments nor the capabilities of women to adjust to and deal with the stresses of breast cancer should be underestimated" (p. 119).

Increasingly, therapy programs stress women's own strengths. For example, the American Cancer Society's program called Reach to Recovery encourages patients to meet with other women who have had mastectomies and to share information about synthetic breast substitutes, exercises, and methods for coping with grief.

Menopause

Menopause is the cessation of menstrual periods. It is typically considered to have occurred when a woman has had no menstrual periods for one year (Woods, 1982). Some women find that their menstrual cycles stop very abruptly. More often, they skip one or two periods and then resume normal menstruation, and subsequently stop the cycles again. Typically, the amount of flow decreases and the periods last fewer days as menopause approaches (Neugarten, 1973). The majority of women experience menopause around the age of 50.

To be precise, menopause is only one sign of a more general period of life called the climacteric. The **climacteric** (pronounced "klie-*mack*-terr-ick") lasts about 15 years, during which fertility decreases and many other bodily changes occur. However, the term climacteric is used infrequently, so we will adopt the slightly sloppy but much more common term, menopause, to refer to all these bodily changes.

What causes menopause? The process is complex, but it basically occurs because the ovary has aged, and it no longer produces estrogen at its previous rate. Progesterone secretion decreases as well, and so the smooth sequence of the menstrual cycle is disrupted. Eventually, the estrogen level falls below the level that is needed to produce shedding of the endometrial lining of the uterus (see Chapter 4). As a consequence, menstruation does not occur (Goodman, 1980).

Physical symptoms. There are several common physical symptoms associated with menopause. One of the most common symptoms is the hot flash. The **hot flash** is appropriately named because there is a feeling of increased heat, and the skin grows red. The sensation lasts only a few minutes. Many women feel this concentrated heat on their face, neck, and upper chest, though some feel it throughout their whole body (Voda, 1982). Hot flashes occur most often at night, and their frequency might vary from one a day to seven an hour (Archer, 1982). About 75 percent of women experience hot flashes during menopause, so they are common but not inevitable (Friederich, 1982). Incidentally, a periodical for older women humorously chose the name *Hot Flash*.

There are also changes in the genitals during menopause. For example, the lining of the vagina becomes thinner, and vaginal secretions decrease. Some women experience painful urination as well. Many women gain weight during menopause (Hill, 1982). Other common physical symptoms include headaches, fatigue, dizziness, and tingling sensations (Woods, 1982).

This list of possible physical symptoms sounds quite frightening. However, few women experience all of these symptoms. Furthermore, in reviewing the literature, Woods (1982) found that between 16 and 38 percent of women report being symptom free. Only about 25 percent of all women have symptoms so severe that they seek the advice of a physician (Perlmutter & Bart, 1982). As with menstrual pain, premenstrual syndrome, pregnancy, and childbirth, women's reactions to menopause show tremendous individual variation; thus we have additional evidence for one of the themes of the book.

We have pointed out that few women have extremely unpleasant experiences with menopause. It is important to keep in mind, however, that for these women, the painful experiences are *real*; the pain is not "only in their heads." As Posner (1979) points out, women in our society feel guilty enough, and aging women feel even more deficient. It would be a mistake to make those women who have difficult menopauses feel even more guilty by arguing that a better mental attitude would decrease the pain. It seems best to conclude that most women do not have much difficulty with menopause, but for some women the experience is indeed painful and unpleasant.

During the 1960s, physicians commonly prescribed large doses of estrogen for menopausal women, whether they complained of menopausal symptoms or not; this treatment is called **estrogen-replacement therapy**. The logic was that menopausal women lacked estrogen, in much the same fashion that diabetics lacked insulin. If diabetes could be cured by supplying insulin, then menopausal symptoms could be cured by supplying estrogen (Goodman, 1982). However, in the 1970s researchers noticed that women were nearly five times as likely to develop cancer of the uterus if they had recently taken estrogen (Kerzner, 1983). As a consequence, the estrogen dosage has been reduced, and several other precautions have made estrogen-replacement therapy much safer.

Psychological reactions. The phrase "menopausal woman" brings to mind all sorts of negative images that have been promoted by the popular press and our general folklore. We are led to believe that a woman who is experiencing menopause has intense mood swings. Her wildly fluctuating hormones force her to be grouchy, nervous, and highly anxious.

However, there is no current evidence that menopause is related to psychological symptoms such as depression, irritability, and mood swings (Archer, 1982; Perlmutter & Bart, 1982). Furthermore, when a menopausal woman takes estrogen, the estrogen does not successfully treat any psychological symptoms that she might have. We will see that middle age is a stressful time for many women, but factors other than menopause are probably more important in determining their psychological status.

Perlmutter and Bart (1982) illustrate how menopause may be blamed for psychological reactions. One woman reacted to her hot flashes by experiencing them as anxiety attacks. Instead of simply labeling them as hot flashes, she convinced herself that she was becoming more nervous. In other words, society has set up certain expectations about what menopausal women should experience. When they have a certain physical symptom, they give it the label they have been led to expect. Additional evidence for this interpretation comes from Woods (1982), who summarized how women in different cultures experience menopause. In some cultures, no one expects any psychological disturbances during menopause. In rural Ireland, however, some people believe that menopause brings on insanity, and so some women retire from life in their forties and confine themselves to bed.

Attitudes toward menopause. Before you read further, try Demonstration 14.1. This demonstration is based on a study by Neugarten (1973), which we will discuss later in this section.

If we look at material on older women, menopause is a topic that has achieved some prominence. However, if we compare menopause with menstruation or the menarche (that is, the beginning of menstruation), we find that it has been almost ignored. Posner (1979) points out that anthropologists frequently discuss menstrual customs when they study other cultures, but menopause is seldom mentioned. Reitz (1977) contrasts the abundance of books on childbirth with the small handful of books on menopause; her book, *Menopause: A Positive Approach*, is one of the few currently available. In other words, menopause is nearly a taboo subject, one that is seldom discussed. This is particularly surprising since about half of the United States population will experience menopause.

Unfortunately, until recently, those people who *did* mention menopause or menopausal women tended to be negative. Reuben (1969) wrote in a popular book that the menopausal woman is not really a man, but no longer a "functional" woman. (Notice how Reuben's comment assumes that a woman's only function is to bear children!) Wilson (1966), a promoter of estrogen-replacement therapy, referred to menopause as living decay and a crippling experience, one that led to the destruction of personality. A typical gynecology textbook from the 1960s included this passage:

Emotional instability is another outstanding symptom of this phase of life. Nervousness and anxiety are extremely frequent. The patient may feel that the

Attitudes Toward Menopausal Women

magine that a group of women in menopause rated themselves on the characteristics listed below. Try to guess the average rating for each characteristic. The answers appear later in this section.

1 pleasant	2	3	4	5	6	7 unpleasant
1 calm	2	3	4	5	6	7 excited
1 optimistic	2	3	4	5	6	7 pessimistic
1 healthy	2	3	4	5	6	7 sick
1 happy	2	3	4	5	6	7 sad
1 useful	2	3	4	5	6	7 useless

end of her useful life has come, that now she is old, that she has lost her appeal as a woman, and that nothing is left to her. She cries easily; she flares up at her family and friends; she is irritable and may have difficulty in composing her thoughts or her reactions. Often the patient may be extremely depressed. A person who has been extremely emotional most of her life will without much doubt have severe emotional disturbances during the climacteric. [Brewer & de Costa, 1967, p. 229]

In contrast to this gloomy picture, Neugarten (1973) found that the attitudes of the women who were actually experiencing menopause were remarkably more positive. She interviewed 100 women who were between the ages of 45 and 55. When they were asked what aspect of middle age worried them the most, only four of these women mentioned menopause; becoming a widow and growing older were far more important concerns. Women mentioned positive aspects to menopause, such as not worrying about pregnancy and not bothering with menstruation. As one woman said, "I'm so happy about not menstruating any more, I could dance with joy. I was looking forward to it for years" (p. 43). Only 12 women saw no advantages to menopause.

When they were asked about the negative aspects of menopause, most women mentioned not knowing what to expect, the pain and the discomfort, and menopause as a sign of getting older. Many women, however, could not think of any negative aspects of menopause.

Another interesting observation was that the women were much more positive about their own attitudes and life satisfaction than they were when they rated other "women in menopause." Check back over your responses to Demonstration 14.1 and see whether you were overly pessimistic about how women in menopause would rate themselves. The average ratings that Neugarten obtained from menopausal women were: pleasant, 2.2; calm, 3.4; optimistic, 2.9; healthy, 2.7; happy, 1.2; useful, 1.3.

Older women seem to be increasingly interested in talking openly about menopause. Reitz (1977) emphasizes that menopausal women should discuss aspects of menopause, such as hot flashes, with other people. She argues that by discussing them, women no longer feel ashamed or try to hide them. If menopausal women share their experiences with other women, one negative aspect mentioned in Neugarten's study—not knowing what to expect—might be reduced.

☐ SECTION SUMMARY ▪ Physical Aspects

1. **Psychological research has ignored older women in the past, and women are also invisible in the media.**
2. **Women are less likely than men to have heart trouble, but they are more likely to sustain injuries from falls and to have osteoporosis.**
3. **One woman in 15 will develop breast cancer, and many of these women will have mastectomies.**
4. **A mastectomy may produce a changed self-image; therapy must acknowledge both the importance of the problem and women's capacity to adjust to it.**
5. **Menopause, the cessation of menstrual periods, occurs around the age of 50.**
6. **Physical symptoms of menopause include hot flashes, genital changes, urinary difficulties, weight gain, headaches, and other sensations; most women do not have much difficulty with menopause, but it is painful for some women.**
7. **Estrogen-replacement therapy, carefully regulated, has been used to treat menopausal symptoms.**
8. **There is no current evidence that menopause is related to psychological symptoms such as depression and mood swings.**
9. **Until recently, "experts" described menopause in negative terms. However, women actually experiencing menopause were much more positive.**

☐ RETIREMENT

Think about the topic of women and retirement for a moment. Have you ever read an article or a short story about a woman retiring from her job? Has there been anything on television about the topic? Picture a retirement dinner; who is getting the gold watch for years of loyal service to the company? In fact, women are missing from the popular lore about retirement. It seems that the topic of retirement is yet another demonstration of one of the themes of this book, the relative invisibility of women. Let's consider some reasons why women may be "invisible" with respect to retirement.

One reason, of course, is that—until recently—women were less likely than men to work outside the home, so that retirement was not a major issue. Furthermore, as Giesen and Datan (1980) point out, people who do housework do not have the luxury of retiring from their occupations at 65; again, retirement is not an issue. Currently, however, more than half of the women in the 54 to 59 age group are employed (Szinovacz, 1983). Will these women receive publicity when they retire?

It seems likely that the silence on the topic of women's retirement cannot be totally explained by the relatively small number of women who do retire. Instead, Fox (1977) explains that people—including researchers—simply pay less attention to women's retirement. Work is supposed to be "secondary" for women, so their self-identity should not change substantially when they retire. (Notice, of course, that this attitude ignores the large number of women who consider their jobs to be a high priority in their lives.) Also, Fox believes that women's social status is derived from their husbands, rather than from their own work. As a consequence, a woman's retirement does not change her social status. As we've seen repeatedly throughout this book, people react differently to men versus women. Reactions to men's and women's retirement is one further example.

Because of assumptions such as these, studies on retirement have typically used only male subjects (Szinovacz, 1983). Recently, however, a small number of investigations have focused on women and retirement. They are summarized in an excellent chapter by Szinovacz (1983) as well as in a book, *Women's Retirement* (Szinovacz, 1982). Let's look at two aspects of retirement in this section: planning for retirement and adjustment to retirement.

Planning for Retirement

People retire for a number of reasons. Mandatory retirement may force some people out of their jobs. Others may no longer be able to work, and still others feel that the advantages of retirement outweigh the advantages of working. However, it is clear that—in contrast to men—women retire earlier, and they are also more likely to retire for voluntary reasons (Szinovacz, 1983). It seems unlikely that women voluntarily retire because they are not committed to their jobs. Instead, women retire early for several other reasons: society's pressure to retire and take care of retired or ill husbands; economic support from their husbands; and lack of job satisfaction among women who occupy lower-level jobs (Henretta & O'Rand, 1980; Szinovacz, 1983).

One study on retirement plans was conducted by Lopata and Norr (1980), who interviewed Chicago-area women. They found that employed women were frequently uncertain about their retirement plans. There were two distinct groups of women who planned to retire late, rather than early. One group of women worked outside the home because of financial necessity, which required them to continue in paid employment. Another group of women felt that their occupations were an important part of their lives. Though financial necessity was seldom relevant for them, they wanted to continue at their occupations. This research illustrates, once again, the individual differences among women. Women vary in their plans for retirement, and they also vary in their reasons for those plans.

Adjustment to Retirement

You will recall that researchers used to think that retirement should not be an important event in women's lives. They reasoned that women were not particularly involved in their work, so that it should not be very upsetting when they were no longer working. There is little support for that conclusion. In fact, as Szinovacz (1983) concluded, women may experience even more retirement problems than men, and it may take them somewhat longer to adapt to retirement.

Here's one likely explanation. Women who work outside the home in their later years generally do so for two reasons: financial necessity or commitment to their work (the same reasons that encourage them to postpone retirement). Men, in contrast, may work because employment is expected of them; there is no socially acceptable alternative. Many men may therefore look forward to retirement. Because the women have chosen a job rather than remaining full-time at home, women may experience "withdrawal symptoms" when they retire. It may be particularly upsetting to adjust to the household routine they wanted to escape in the first place (Szinovacz, 1983).

Let us look at a large-scale study by Atchley (1976), who sent questionnaires to thousands of people who had retired from their work as either teachers or phone-company employees. The men and the women were equally likely to report that their work had been important to them, a finding that contradicts the stereotype about women's lack of interest in work. Furthermore, the women in the sample were more likely than the men to report difficulty in getting used to retirement. Also, a comparison of the female and male telephone employees showed that women were less likely to enjoy retirement than the men. A study by Anderson and her coauthors (1978) produced similar findings. Among faculty members and other college professionals, men were more likely than women to say that they were looking forward to retirement with pleasure. It seems, then, that retirement can be a potential problem for women.

Levy (1980–1981) reports on women who initially did not want to retire. These women did not adjust well to retirement, even with the passage of time. Some women, long after retirement, had negative attitudes. They "appeared incapable of fending off social aging, and restructuring a new network of community involvement" (p. 108).

One factor that does *not* seem to be related to satisfaction with retirement is a woman's emphasis on the wife and mother role. According to Johnson and Price-Bonham (1980), women who are involved with the wife and mother role are no more happy about retirement than women who do not see themselves primarily as wives and mothers.

When a woman retires, she has more time for social activities. Johnson and Price-Bonham discovered that women who had made plans for social activities after retirement were more likely to be looking forward to retirement. In comparison with employed women, retired women are more involved in informal social interactions with friends and neighbors (Fox, 1977).

Some women maintain their interest in their work area long after they have retired. Holahan (1981) questioned elderly women who had been identified as gifted when they were young. The women who indicated that they had pursued a career throughout most of their adult life also reported that they were still interested in their work area. Women who indicated that they had worked primarily for financial reasons did not express this same interest in their work area.

We have primarily focused upon women's adjustment to their own retirement. What kinds of attitudes do they have about their husbands' retirement? Fengler's (1975) survey showed a wide range of responses, with roughly a third of the women being optimistic, a third neutral, and a third pessimistic. The optimists saw retirement as a time for companionship and an exciting new life together. These women felt that their husbands were now more relaxed and had time for their hobbies. Those women with neutral reactions were less likely to be well educated than the optimists and the pessimists; they typically answered "no opinion" to this question. The pessimists supplied responses that matched everyone's stereotype about a bored, retired husband. These women were primarily concerned that their husbands had too much time on their hands and intruded into the wives' domestic activities. Apparently some husbands are accurately portrayed by the comic-strip retired husbands who criticize their wives' dusting habits and disrupt their shopping patterns.

☐ SECTION SUMMARY ▪ Retirement

1. **Women's retirement has been ignored because researchers have assumed that employment is secondary for women and because women's social status is supposed to be unaffected by her retirement.**

2. **Women are more likely than men to retire for voluntary reasons; women who retire late do so because of financial necessity or job interest.**

3. **Women may experience even more retirement problems than men.** Those who adjust well to retirement are likely to have been looking forward to retirement and to be interested in social activities after retirement.
4. **Women who had pursued careers were more interested in their** work area after retirement than women who had worked primarily for financial reasons.
5. **Women show a variety of responses to their husbands' retirement,** ranging from optimism to pessimism.

SOCIAL ASPECTS OF LATER ADULTHOOD

In this section, we will begin with an examination of attitudes toward older women, followed by a discussion of sex roles in later adulthood. Our next two topics concern interpersonal interactions: family relationships and widowhood. Next we will consider older women's living arrangements, and then we will move on to consider a broader issue, older women's satisfaction with life. The last section in this chapter, called "Final Words," contains one woman's view on later adulthood.

Attitudes Toward Older Women

Try Demonstration 14.2, which illustrates how older women are represented on television. We mentioned at the beginning of the chapter that older women are underrepresented in stories, and they are also missing from television. When older women *are* featured, they tend to be shown as sweet "little old ladies" who are more concerned about the aphids on their rose bushes than about issues of greater significance. We all know spirited, accomplished older women in real life, but your inspection of television's older women probably will not reveal a single woman of that caliber. Also, think back on the older women of fairy tales. There were occasionally fairy godmothers, but evil witches and wicked stepmothers were much more common (Lesnoff-Caravaglia, 1984).

DEMONSTRATION 14.2

Older Women on Television

During the next month, keep a record of how older women are portrayed on television. This record should include both middle-aged women and elderly women. Several kinds of programs should be included, such as soap operas, game shows, situation comedies, "prime-time" shows, and Saturday-morning cartoons, as well as advertisements. Pay attention to the number of older women who are shown, as well as how they are shown. Are they likely to be shown working outside the home? Do they have interests and hobbies and important concerns, or are they primarily busy being nurturant? Do they seem to be "real," or are they represented in a stereotypical fashion?

Now consider the advertisements. How many of the ads for cosmetics promise to cover up the signs of aging? You can use certain dishwashing liquids to keep your hands looking younger; why in the world would you want to buy a dishwashing liquid because it cleans dishes well? With the proper lotions and oils, you can look younger than your friends. Your body can regain its youthful shape with appropriate bras and pantyhose. Your hair, too, should not have any telltale signs of gray, and you will certainly want to restore the youthful texture to your hair with the correct shampoo. An ad for one shampoo would unsettle any older woman who feels otherwise comfortable about her age. They urge us to buy their shampoo with extra moisturizing oils because "It's later than you think!" Wilma Scott Heide, the former chair of the National Organization for Women, muses about inventing a cream called "Youth Away," designed to rid women of that unsightly, unwrinkled skin that has no character (Heide, 1984). Obviously, this project would be an economic disaster!

In the United States we do not look favorably on the process of growing older. For men, however, there are some advantages. For women, aging is seen as almost totally negative. Sontag (1979) refers to this discrepancy as the **double standard of aging.** She writes:

> This society offers even fewer rewards for aging to women than it does to men. Being physically attractive counts much more in a woman's life than in a man's, but beauty, identified, as it is for women, with youthfulness, does not stand up well to age. Exceptional mental powers can increase with age, but women are rarely encouraged to develop their minds above dilettante standards.... The private skills expected of women are exercised early and, with the exception of a talent for making love, are not the kind that enlarge with experience. "Masculinity" is identified with competence, autonomy, self-control—qualities which the disappearance of youth does not threaten. Competence in most of the activities expected from men, physical sports excepted, increases with age. "Femininity" is identified with incompetence, helplessness, passivity, noncompetitiveness, being nice. Age does not improve these qualities. [p. 464]

Sontag remarks that wrinkles and lines in a man's face are seen as signs of "character." They reveal emotional strength and maturity. Wrinkles and lines send a far different message from a woman's face, because the ideal woman's face should be unblemished and show no signs of previous experiences or emotions. Again, the double standard of aging operates.

This double standard of aging forces women to keep their age a secret. This is even true of professional women, for whom age should be a measure of professional maturity and therefore not so threatening. Bell (1979) noted that in the Directory of the American Psychological Association, women are ten times as likely as men to omit their age.

Because aging is more painful for women than for men, women may tend to postpone thinking of themselves as old. Ward (1977) asked men and women between the ages of 60 and 92 whether they thought of themselves as young, middle aged, elderly, or old. Women were likely to label themselves as younger than men, even though they were actually the same age.

Women may hesitate about categorizing themselves as old, but other people show no such hesitation. In fact, the double standard of aging surfaces once more, because people seem to think that women grow old faster than men do. Kogan (1979) asked people between the ages of 18 and 76 to inspect photographs of other men and women. Specifically, they were instructed to categorize the people in these photos as being adolescent, young, middle-aged, elderly, and aged adult. Both men and women subjects assigned the photos of women to the older age categories.

Another aspect of the double standard of aging concerns the stereotype that a woman should not be older than her husband. In 1979, wives were younger than their husbands in 73 percent of the marriages, and wives were older than their husbands in only 14 percent of the marriages (U. S. Bureau of the Census, 1979).

People also think that relationships are less likely to survive when the wife is older than the husband, according to a study by Cowan (1984). Cowan asked adolescents and adults to judge the potential success of various hypothetical romances, such as the ones in Demonstration 14.3. In some cases, the man and the woman were the same age, but in other cases there was an age discrepancy of either seven years or 18 years, and either the man or the woman was older. When the woman was 18 years older than the man, people rated the situation as least likely to succeed. However, there was a notable surprise: Both adult and adolescent males did not show the double standard in judging relationships where there was a seven-year age difference. In contrast, females upheld the double standard and were not hopeful about the prospects for a woman's relationship with a man seven years her junior.

════ DEMONSTRATION 14.3 ════

Relationships Between Older Women and Younger Men

Judge how likely you think it is that the relationship described below will succeed:

> Ann is a 40 year old self-employed woman. She enjoys going to picnics in the park, dancing, reading, and listening to good music. She is originally from Chicago where she graduated from business school before moving to California. Ann's father died a few years ago and her mother lives about 50 miles away. They have always been very close and have great respect for one another. About six months ago, Ann met a man named Jack at a party given by some mutual friends. Jack is a 22-year-old history teacher. He enjoys hiking, dancing, the movies, ceramics, and taking unusual courses at the local college. A native Californian, Jack's parents live in the same town. They have always had a very warm and caring relationship. Recently, Ann and Jack have been contemplating marriage. They both feel marriage is the best idea since they would not consider "just living together." (Cowan, 1984, p. 19)

Now read the passage over again, with Ann as the 22-year-old and Jack as the 40-year-old. Would your judgment about the success of the relationship be any different?

Our discussion of the double standard of aging has emphasized that people react differently when a woman grows older than when a man grows older. Notice that the double standard of aging is in fact a variant of the second theme of this book: People react differently to women than they do to men. However, it seems that the differential treatment increases as men and women grow older.

Incidentally, you may recall that we discussed a related topic in the chapter on sexuality. When we discussed sexuality in older women, we stressed that people admire an old man's interest in sexuality, whereas they condemn the same interest in an old woman. Older women are therefore at a particular disadvantage with respect to sexuality. Not only are older women considered to look sexually unattractive, but they are expected to show minimal interest in sexuality.

There is further information about people's reactions to older women. Consider a study by Berman and her colleagues (1981), which asked undergraduates to judge pictures of middle-aged women and men for their "immediate emotional appeal." The results are shown in Figure 14.1. When peo-

FIGURE 14.1. **Ratings of pictures of middle-aged women and men, as a function of raters' sex and rating condition (based on Berman, et al., 1981)**

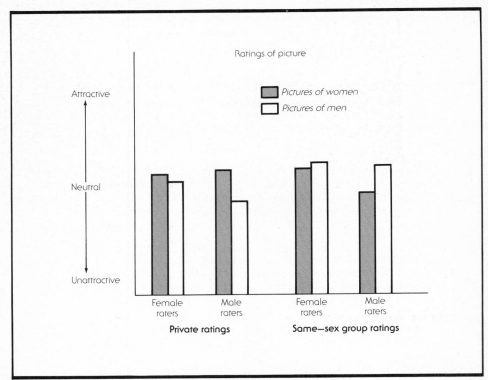

ple made these judgments with other people present in the group, they said that the men were more attractive than the women. This was particularly true in all-male groups. Berman and her coauthors suggest that men in all-male groups may have been influenced by a competitive, aggresssive social situation to express judgments that are consistent with the common stereotypes about older women. The competitive atmosphere may encourage members of all-male groups to boost their own esteem by downgrading middle-aged women, who appear to be a fair target. In contrast, when people made the judgments in private, both men and women judged middle-aged women to be somewhat more attractive than middle-aged men.

So far, we have seen that people react differently to older men than to older women with respect to several issues: age categorizations, sexuality, and "emotional appeal." We also know that people are more positive about older men than older women when they judge competence. Giesen and Datan (1980) showed people pictures of women and men of various ages and asked them to describe the kinds of problems the people in the picture might be encountering. The respondents tended to see older people as having more problems than younger people. This tendency was particularly strong in the judgments made about older women. These older women were seen as being dependent, without clear tasks to accomplish in the future. Older men were judged more favorably. They were seen to be more competent in solving their problems and they were also perceived as advisors to younger people. Once again, older women are the losers.

Gender Roles in Later Adulthood

There is a common belief that both men and women become less rigidly stereotyped and more androgynous as they grow older. Bernice Neugarten (1968) wrote in a classic textbook on aging that "Men seem to become more receptive to affiliative and nurturant promptings; women more responsive toward and less guilty about aggressive and egocentric impulses" (p. 14).

Several studies support this viewpoint (Feldman, et al., 1981; Fischer & Narus, 1981; Neugarten & Gutmann, 1964; Sinnott, 1984). However, other studies have not demonstrated a clear-cut increase in androgyny as people grow older (Hyde & Phillis, 1979; Sinnott, 1982). Hyde and Phillis asked people of various ages to take the Bem Sex-Role Inventory, which we discussed in Chapter 8. These authors found a greater number of androgynous men in the older age groups than in the younger groups. However, they found a greater number of androgynous women in the *younger* age groups. We cannot yet draw conclusions about changes in gender roles as people grow older (Turner, 1982).

Family Relationships

In the chapter on love relationships, we explored one important family role, women as wives. Now we will look at three other major roles in our examination of older women as mothers, daughters, and grandmothers.

Older women as mothers.   Barnett and Baruch (1978) comment that previous research and theory on middle-aged women overemphasized women's reproductive role. As a consequence, menopause (symbolizing the end of reproduction) and the **empty-nest syndrome** (presumably a depression that is the result of children leaving home) have received too much attention, in contrast to topics such as women's work roles. Let us examine this empty-nest syndrome and see why it does not seem to apply to most women.

Rubin (1979) writes,

> Think about the language we unquestioningly use to characterize this period of life: *the empty nest*. Not *the awakening*, not *the emergence*, not words that might suggest that inside that house all those years there lived someone besides a mother; no, we say *the empty nest*. . . . Indeed, the very words *empty nest* conjure up a vision of a lonely, depressed woman clinging pathetically and inappropriately to a lost past—a woman who has lived for and through her children. . . . [p. 14]

At present, more than half of all children leave their parents' house by the age of 19 (Neugarten & Brown-Rezanka, 1978). This means that most women have many years left to their lives in which they are not "active" mothers. Thus, there is a *potential* for the empty-nest syndrome, and some women may experience an empty-nest syndrome that is severe enough to require psychiatric care. Bart (1971) examined middle-aged women in psychiatric hospitals. She concluded that women who could be categorized as "Supermoms" were particularly likely to be depressed when their children left. These women had been overly involved in mothering; for them, an empty nest was often traumatic.

However, many surveys conducted on a door-to-door basis show that women are not depressed when their children leave home, a point we discussed in the chapter on love relationships. In fact, women may be even happier than when their children were living with them. Glenn (1975) examined data from six national surveys conducted in the United States. He concluded that middle-aged women whose children have left home reported greater happiness, enjoyment of life, and marital satisfaction than women of the same age who had at least one child at home.

Furthermore, Radloff (1975, 1980) found that women whose children had left home had somewhat *lower* depression scores than those whose children still lived at home. Of course, we cannot conclude from her study that women are overjoyed when children leave home; they may indeed be somewhat depressed. However, these depressions appear to be rare and brief. Women seem to be relatively happy after their children have left home.

Older women as daughters.   We are accustomed to thinking of adult women as mothers and grandmothers, but adult women are often daughters as well, having responsibilities to their elderly parents. In fact, over 80 percent of middle-aged couples have at least one living parent (Hess & Waring, 1983).

Middle-aged women and men seem to worry considerably about their parents. A survey in Chicago showed that they reported concern about their parents' health and increased need for moral support (Neugarten & Brown-Rezanka, 1978). Furthermore, daughters are somewhat more likely than sons to worry a great deal about parents' illness. A term, the **caught generation** describes many middle-aged people, particularly women, who find themselves torn among several sets of competing obligations. They are responsible to their own children and spouses, and in addition they are anxious about their elderly parents' poor health (Baruch, et al., 1983; Lang & Brody, 1983; Marshall, et al. 1983).

Hess and Waring (1983) are concerned about what will happen if the government reduces support for the elderly. They point out that women in particular have much to lose if government support decreases. Elderly women (who constitute, as we said, the major portion of elderly people) will not be able to remain financially and physically independent of their children. Their children—primarily middle-aged women—will be increasingly obligated to care for their ill or impoverished parents.

There is a common perception that adult children often abandon their elderly parents. However, there seems to be little evidence for this idea. Most children visit their parents regularly (Edinburg, 1982). Other research, summarized by Hess and Waring (1978), shows that elderly parents have frequent contact and help from at least one of their offspring.

Many questions about older women's relationships with their parents remain unanswered. Except for a popularized book on the topic, *My Mother/ My Self* (Friday, 1977), there has not been much written about how middle-aged women interact with their elderly mothers. Also, think about how this topic has been neglected in fiction, in movies, and on television. Aside from "On Golden Pond," have you ever read about or seen any interaction between an adult woman and her mother?

Older women as grandmothers.   Robertson (1977) describes the stereotype of the grandmother:

> Traditionally, grandmothers have been portrayed as jolly, white-thatched bespectacled old ladies who lavish goodies and attention on their grandchildren. Not infrequently, the media alludes to grandmothers as happy-go-lucky, meddlesome intruders in family life who are politely tolerated because they add a unique dimension to family interaction. [p. 165]

About three-fourths of people over the age of 65 in the United States have grandchildren (Troll, 1982). How do the women, in particular, view their role as grandmother? In a study by Robertson (1977), about 80 percent of grandmothers actively enjoyed the role. They were proud, excited, thrilled, and so forth, when they first learned that they were going to be a grandmother. They often reported that they liked grandparenting more than parenting because grandchildren could be enjoyed and then sent home.

Only a small proportion of grandmothers report that the grandparent role had little effect on them (Neugarten & Weinstein, 1964). Robertson (1977) found that women who placed less emphasis on the grandmother role were likely to be younger, married, more educated, and employed, in contrast to the women who were more involved in grandmothering.

What do grandmothers do? In terms of activities, they are most likely to babysit and drop by for visits, playing games and reading books when they visit (Robertson, 1977). According to research discussed by Troll, grandmothers try to influence their grandchildren in a wide range of areas, such as lifestyle, work and education, and interpersonal issues. In contrast, grandfathers mainly confine their advice to work and education. However, a substantial number of grandmothers said that good grandparents should not interfere with their grandchildren's upbringing (Wood & Robertson, 1976). Notice that some grandmothers consciously avoid the meddlesome grandmother image we discussed earlier.

Widowhood

In her review of women in widowhood, Barrett (1977) remarks that the death of a spouse is consistently seen as a major source of stress, one that requires more readjustment than any other life event. The stressfulness of widowhood extends across people of all ages and backgrounds. We know that black and white women respond similarly when they grieve the death of a husband (Hess & Waring, 1983). It is clear that the spouse's death disrupts a strong emotional bond, a companionship that typically lasted more than half a lifetime. Routine kinds of daily behavior are also disrupted and so are relationships with other people.

Women live longer than men, typically marry men older than themselves, and are less likely to remarry. As a result, there are many more widows than widowers in the United States. According to a 1977 Bureau of the Census report, there were about 5.6 widows for every one widower. Furthermore, in the future, women may spend an increasing proportion of their lives as widows, since the difference between male and female life expectancies is continuing to increase (Hess & Waring, 1983).

Let us now examine the stresses of widowhood in more detail. Clearly, the first stress facing a widow is the pain of bereavement. Widows often have the feeling that nothing in life is worthwhile. They are unable to understand the loss, and they feel a sense of injustice about their spouse's death. A common physical symptom is the inability to sleep. Widows frequently experience the illusion that their husbands are still with them (Barrett, 1977, 1981).

Loneliness is a major problem for widows. Lopata (1979), in her book *Women as Widows*, points out that many women have never before been alone in their homes, since they went from the home of their parents directly into the home in which they lived with their husbands. Now the widow is in a home by herself, without the usual conversation and companionship. Many of her activities outside the home were previously centered on her husband's relatives, friends, and work associations. A widow may also find that there are many social situations where an unaccompanied woman feels awkward, or she might not even be invited (Trager, 1984).

According to a study by Lopata (1981), women show a strong tendency to idealize their late husbands. Some women even say that their husbands were free from all irritating habits. They may also idealize the quality of the life they shared with their husbands. This tendency toward "husband sanctification" was more likely in older women than in younger women, and more likely in white women than in black women.

Who suffers most from the loss of a spouse, women or men? Stroebe and Stroebe (1983) reviewed dozens of studies on this question and they concluded that men seem to suffer more. They based their conclusion on evidence from many different areas: psychological depression, psychiatric disorders, physical illness, death rates, and suicide rates. In all cases, men appear to be more mentally and physically disturbed by the death of their wives, in contrast to women's reactions to the death of their husbands.

The reason for this sex difference is still a mystery. However, the authors favor an explanation involving social support. A spouse provides a person with a protective screen—a reassurance that one is worthwhile—as well as a source of material support and help. When the spouse dies, the survivor must find other sources of social support. It is simply more acceptable for women to admit that they are lonely and need companionship. Women are also more likely to have confidants other than their husbands, whereas husbands typically share their feelings only with their wives. Women may find widowhood easier because it is easier for them to find social support from their friends.

Men may have a more difficult experience with widowhood than women do, but the experience is traumatic for women, nonetheless. Can anything help a widow deal with her grief? Barrett (1978) examined several kinds of group treatments, all of which were based on the idea that widowed women can help each other cope with the stresses of widowhood. All of the varieties of group treatment proved to be helpful in terms of raising the women's self-esteem. One of the methods was a consciousness-raising technique, which we discussed in Chapter 12. These groups focused on increasing the widows' awareness of how their experiences as widows related to them as women. Women who had participated in these consciousness-raising groups showed the greatest amount of life change in a follow-up session conducted six months after the original treatment began. As Barrett concludes, this information should be useful for mental-health professionals; appropriate therapy can help widows cope with their grief.

Widowed men are likely to remarry if they are under 70. In contrast, only 5 percent of women who are widowed after age 55 ever remarry (Troll, 1982). One reason for this low remarriage rate in widows is simply that there are not many unmarried men in the socially "appropriate" age range, that is, the same age or older. Another reason, however, is that many women simply have no interest in remarriage (Barrett, 1977). Perhaps the idealization of the dead husband, which Lopata observed, is partly responsible. If he was such a saint, who could hope to live up to that standard?

Remarriage seems to have more health benefits for men than for women. You will recall from our earlier discussion that widowed men are more likely than widowed women to die soon after the death of their spouse. Another study demonstrated that death rates among widowed males who remarried were very much lower than among those who did not remarry. However, there was no difference between the death rates of widowed females who did or who did not remarry (Helsing, Szklo, & Comstock, 1981). Females seem to be more resilient in this area; they are better able to survive the stress of living without a spouse.

Living Arrangements

Women are more likely than men to live alone. In fact, 70 percent of all women aged 55 years and over live by themselves, in contrast to only 36 percent of men in this age group (Szinovacz, 1983). As Troll (1982) noted, older people prefer whenever possible to live in their own homes.

Living with an adult child is the least popular choice for most old people, particularly if it involves moving (Markson & Hess, 1980). Elderly people move in with their children only if they do not have enough money to live alone, if their health is poor, or—less often—if their spouses have died (Troll, 1982). When people over the age of 65 live with their children, they are twice as likely to live with their daughters as with their sons. When three generations live in one household, a relatively rare arrangement today, there are disadvantages for the elderly person in terms of reduced social activity and loss of privacy. However, the benefits include affection, enjoyment, household help, and decreased worry (Troll, 1982).

Many people believe that a majority of the elderly live in nursing homes. However, only about 5 percent of the population 65 and over lives in an institution. Most people in nursing homes are women; according to one estimate, 70 percent of nursing home residents are women. Women are more likely than men to live in nursing homes because of their longer life expectancies, health and financial problems, and absence of caretakers. Wives tend to nurse their sick husbands, but fewer men nurse their wives when their health is poor (Edinburg, 1982; Hess & Waring, 1983).

Many older women live in poverty. According to Hess and Waring (1983), 28 percent of old women with no husband present were living below the poverty level in 1980. Women are likely to find themselves without any income after the death of their husbands, or—if they worked outside the home— their Social Security benefits and pensions may be limited (Troll & Turner, 1979; Turner, 1982). As Jacobs (1979) remarks:

> There is real deprivation and consequent anxiety and danger for many older women. There is also the danger that critics, seeking reinforcement for their prejudices, will continue to believe that older women deserve their troubles.

They claim that such women's unhappiness is a result of personality defects or unrealistic expectations instead of recognizing that many older women are unhappy because their essential human needs are unmet. [p. 14]

Satisfaction with Life

A glance through some of the topics we have discussed in this chapter shows that many older women have every right to be unhappy. Some women may have physical problems, such as breast cancer and menopause. They may be unhappy about retiring. Some older women (though not most) may be depressed about their children's leaving home. Many worry about the health of their parents. Widowhood may be the most important source of grief and readjustment. Many older women are likely to be poor. Furthermore, suppose an older woman has no physical problems and no concerns about retirement, the departure of children, parents' health, widowhood, or poverty. Even this woman faces negative reactions from others for being an old woman in a culture that condemns older females for their wrinkles and other signs of age.

It is puzzling, therefore, that many studies do *not* show older women to be any less satisfied with their lives than other people. Palmore and Kivett (1977) interviewed about 500 men and women between the ages of 46 and 70 who belonged to a health-insurance plan. Women and men reported that they were equally satisfied with their lives. Age did not seem to make a difference; the older women were just as satisfied as the younger women. Liang (1982) reanalyzed the data from four different surveys, involving a total of over 8,000 people. He concluded that there were no systematic sex differences in terms of life satisfaction. Also, Bird (1979) compared present-day surveys with surveys conducted 20 years ago. The comparison showed that middle-aged women today are more satisfied with their lives and are more mentally healthy than middle-aged women were in the 1960s.

Clearly, however, there are individual differences in life satisfaction, and there are important factors related to life satisfaction. Johnson (1983) points out that health, finances, and family relationships are particularly crucial. She argues that if women have good family relationships, they are better able to tolerate health and finance problems. However, if family relationships are disappointing, then health and financial problems are intensified; these women are likely to feel depressed or even devastated.

Bart and Grossman (1978) are more pessimistic about women's satisfaction with their lives. They point out that studies are frequently conducted using people who are well-off financially, and therefore likely to be happier. Their point is justified; notice that the study by Palmore and Kivett involved people who could afford health insurance. Bart and Grossman also believe that women may be particularly hesitant to complain about their families to strangers.

At any rate, we do not have any substantial evidence that older women are overwhelmed by unhappiness. As Markson (1983b) concludes, "... most old women are hardy; even in adversity they are brave. They offer us a model from which we can learn about the financial, emotional, and social supports needed by all of us throughout the life course" (p. 330).

It's important, too, to remember the theme of individual variation that we have stressed throughout this book. In particular, women vary in the ways they achieve happiness. Baruch and her colleagues (1983) found that there is no ready-made blueprint for happiness in women's lives. One woman might find happiness through her husband and children, whereas another might be equally happy with a riskier, less traditional lifestyle.

To some extent, the feminist movement—with its emphasis on greater options for women—may encourage older women to be hopeful. One survey found that women tended to be more optimistic than men regarding the years ahead of them (Borges, et al., 1984). As many women grow older, they find that they have skills and confidence beyond their expectations. For instance, a 40-year-old woman in a computer firm reports,

> The group I have working for me consists of forty people, all skilled. I get a tremendous satisfaction out of solving a problem. I feel very good about myself. If you'd asked me how I felt at twenty-five, I'd have said, "I don't feel so hot." My ability to work is a good part of the way I feel today. I've developed confidence in my technical competence, and social competence as well, and I have been able to get my act together. [Baruch, et al., 1983, p. 103]

Final Words

To conclude this book, I asked a 69-year-old friend of mine to reflect about her life and old age. Anne Hardy is a woman whose name appropriately echoes Markson's point that old women are hardy. When she was 58, she and her husband Duane left their comfortable community in Rochester, New York, to work in the South for several organizations that are concerned with social change. She writes about this period in her life.

> When our children were through college and on their own, our feeling was that it was time to close out the marketplace phase of our lives. We never had the empty-nest feeling. It was, instead, a kind of liberation, a time to move into a new phase. Just as marriage had been a new phase, followed by parenthood, this was another. The caring, the sharing of concerns, the readiness to be of help to each other when necessary, would continue with our children, unchanged by the fact that we were no longer living under one roof, but we were ready to move on, just as they were. We had both done a great deal of volunteer work in our free time for many years, and now we had the opportunity to do it full time. Our needs are modest, so we were able to accept subsistence salaries until we were able to "retire" on Social Security, at which time we continued to work full time but no longer drew salaries.
>
> ... I am very conscious that my life hasn't been "typical," if there is such a thing. I've had many advantages denied to others. We have had fairly low income at times but were never really poor and certainly never hungry; my health has, for the most part, been good; we have loving, caring children; and best of all, I've had, in my husband, a superb companion and best friend. With today's economic stresses and disrupted families, I doubt it's a norm.

After ten years of work in the South, Anne and her husband Duane have moved back North. Anne is still involved in organizations such as Women's International League for Peace and Freedom, the Nuclear Freeze Campaign, and the U.S.-China People's Friendship Association.

"Retirement" has many advantages. It's possible to be involved in many activities, yet not be pressured by them. We set our own schedules. We're free of regimentation. If something interesting to do comes up, we can do that and shift other commitments around. It's a more flexible, less rigid, less scheduled life.

At the age of 69, I still don't feel "old," although chronologically, I'm not "young." I think one ages—given reasonable health—as one has been gradually aging in all the years before, very much depending on the quality of life one has built. My interests haven't changed, except that we have the added joy of six grandchildren in our lives. Elderly people are as diverse as young people. Differences between them remain; previous likes and dislikes remain, for the most part. I am still me, "old" or not, though I feel that I have become more understanding, less judgmental, more open to new experiences, still trying to grow as a person.

Some concessions to age are made, of course, a recent one of ours being the decision that it would be wiser to remain in our pleasant apartment than to buy a house with its accompanying maintenance needs, in spite of the fact that at this moment we are in excellent health, and that we would prefer the privacy of our own home.

We have begun to experience the loss of relatives and friends, and chronic and serious illnesses are beginning to appear among our associates. It's sad, of course, but it has the positive side of drawing us closer to those of our families and friends who are still in our lives, makes us more loving, more willing to overlook small irritants, more giving. There is a heightened sense of the importance of savoring today, since this is the only tomorrow we will ever have.

There are serious concerns and hopes about the future, naturally, both in regard to personal matters such as health and loss of close ones, and in regard to national and international events. What kind of world will our children and grandchildren inherit, if they inherit any world at all? What will the employment picture be for them? What will it be like when our children reach their later years, and when our grandchildren reach their employment years? I have lost much of my sense that we can influence the course of events; I have increasingly stronger conviction that we are in the hands of multinationals and conglomerates, of Eisenhower's "military-industrial complex." That feeling can be an immobilizing one. But to do nothing is to go along with what's happening. I know it's a cliché, but the future is *now*. This is the only world any of us has, and if we don't like it, or if we are worried about the direction it's going, we have to work to change it. "This is the way it is" is something we can't settle for. We have to work toward being able to say, "That is the way it *was*, and we have helped to improve it." I console myself a bit with the recollection that 40 years ago, when we debated whether we should bring children into the world, I had the same concerns—and we're all still here!

A Fundamentalist relative asked me recently what I felt about eternity. I answered that for me eternity is being created daily in what I do, how I live vis-à-vis other human beings, what kinds of values I gave and continue to give our children so that they in turn would have good values to pass on to their world and their children.

□ SECTION SUMMARY ▪ Social Aspects of Later Adulthood

1. According to the double standard of aging, aging presents more problems for women in our society than it does for men.
2. Women tend to think of themselves as younger than men who are the same age, but both men and women assign women to older age categories than men; people think that a relationship is unlikely to succeed if the woman is much older than the man.
3. People also respond differently to women than to men in the areas of sexuality and emotional appeal (though the nature of the responses depends upon whether the judgments are public or private).
4. Older men are judged to be more competent than older woman.
5. There is some evidence that people become less gender-role stereotyped as they grow older, but we cannot draw any clear-cut conclusions.
6. The empty-nest syndrome may occur for some women, but most women seem to be relatively happy after their children have left home.
7. Middle-aged daughters worry about their elderly parents; they are the "caught generation."
8. Women report that they enjoy being grandmothers; they typically try to influence their grandchildren in a wide range of areas.
9. There are many more widows than widowers; major issues for widows include loneliness and idealization of the late husband. Group treatment, such as consciousness raising, is beneficial.
10. Older widows seldom remarry, and remarriage has more health benefits for men than for women.
11. Older women are most likely to live alone, but some live with children or in nursing homes; many live in poverty.
12. Older women seem to be as satisfied with their lives as other groups of people, despite health and personal problems.

Chapter Review Questions

1. Some physicians might be tempted to say to their patients who are older women, "Keep a stiff upper lip—it's no big deal" when discussing health issues. Discuss why this attitude would be inappropriate when dealing with a woman who is experiencing difficulty with menopause or a woman who has recently had a mastectomy.
2. One of the themes in this book is that women tend to be relatively invisible; this tendency is particularly true for older women. Discuss this theme, pointing out how older women have not received enough atten-

tion in the following areas: (a) psychological research, in general; (b) representation in the media; (c) discussion of menopause; and (d) research on retirement.

3. This chapter mentions several times that there is a discrepancy between what people believe about older women and what the older women actually experience. Discuss this discrepancy in the following areas: (a) psychological reactions during menopause; (b) adjustment to retirement; (c) choosing an age category, such as "middle-aged"; and (d) satisfaction with life.

4. Discuss the physical and psychological reactions to menopause, and describe how menopause may be inappropriately blamed for some psychological reactions.

5. From what you know about retirement, describe (a) a woman who is likely to adjust well to retirement, (b) a woman who is likely to adjust poorly to retirement, and (c) a woman who is likely to remain interested in her occupational area following retirement.

6. What is the double standard of aging? Describe how it operates in the following areas: (a) attitudes toward wrinkles and other signs of physical aging; (b) discussing one's age; (c) categorizing people as "middle-aged" or "elderly"; (d) the age difference between a woman and her husband; and (e) judgments of older people's competence.

7. Suppose that you were appointed to a national commission aimed at meeting the needs of elderly women. What kinds of concerns would you identify, and what would you recommend to improve the lives of elderly women?

8. Why does the term the "caught generation" apply to middle-aged women? Why might the responsibilities faced by these women account for some of the psychological symptoms that are typically attributed to menopause?

9. Describe some of the psychological reactions that women experience when they become widows. Discuss sex differences in reactions to widowhood and speculate about why men might benefit more from remarriage than women do.

10. The chapter discussed many legitimate reasons why older women might be dissatisfied with their lives. List as many of these as you can, and offer reasons why older women are reasonably satisfied, to supplement those listed in the chapter.

☐ NEW TERMS

life-span approach
osteoporosis
mastectomy
menopause
climacteric

hot flash
estrogen-replacement therapy
double standard of aging
empty-nest syndrome
caught generation

☐ RECOMMENDED READINGS

Baruch, G., Barnett, R., & Rivers, C. (1983). *Lifeprints: New patterns of love and work for today's women*. New York: McGraw-Hill. ■ Baruch and her coauthors describe a large-scale study aimed at identifying the factors that contribute to a middle-aged woman's sense of well-being; the book stresses the importance of individual differences.

Giele, J. Z. (Ed.) (1982). *Women in the middle years: Current knowledge and directions for research and policy*. New York: Wiley. ■ This book describes adulthood in women, not just the middle years. In addition to chapters that focus on psychology, there are also discussions from medical, sociological, and anthropological perspectives.

Lesnoff-Caravaglia, G. (Ed.) (1984). *The world of the older woman*. New York: Human Sciences. ■ This book focuses on a variety of topics related to women and aging, such as discrimination against older women, institutionalized older women, and widowhood.

Markson, E. W. (Ed.) (1983). *Older women*. Lexington, Mass.: Lexington Books. ■ Markson's book contains 16 chapters dealing with four topics that are important to older women: physical appearance, work, family, and health.

☐ ONE LAST QUESTION

You have now read 14 chapters about the psychology of women, from the months before their birth up until old age. In order to review the entire book as comprehensively as possible, set aside several hours for one final task: On separate pieces of paper, list each of the four themes of this book. Then skim through each of the chapters and note any mention of the themes on the appropriate piece of paper. (You can check whether your lists are complete by looking at the entries "Themes 1, 2, 3, and 4" in the subject index.) After you have completed the task, try to synthesize the material within each of the four themes.

REFERENCES

Abbey, A. (1982). Sex differences in attributions for friendly behavior: Do males misperceive females' friendliness? *Journal of Personality and Social Psychology, 42*, 830–838.

Abel, T., & Joffe, N. F. (1950). Cultural background of female puberty. *American Journal of Psychotherapy, 4*, 90–93.

Abplanalp, J. M. (1983). Premenstrual syndrome: A selective review. In S. Golub (Ed.), *Lifting the curse of menstruation* (pp. 107–123). New York: Haworth.

Abplanalp, J. M., Haskett, R. F., & Rose, R. M. (1980). The premenstrual syndrome. *Psychiatric Clinics of North America, 3*, 327–347.

Abramowitz, C. V., & Dokecki, P. R. (1977). The politics of clinical judgment: Early empirical returns. *Psychological Bulletin, 84*, 460–476.

Abramowitz, S., Weitz, L., Schwartz, J., Amira, S., Gomes, B., & Abramowitz, C. (1975). Comparative counselor inferences toward women with medical school aspirations. *Journal of College Student Personnel, 16*, 128–130.

Abramson, P. R., Goldberg, P. A., Greenberg, J. H., & Abramson, L. M. (1977). The talking platypus phenomenon: Competency ratings as a function of sex and professional status. *Psychology of Women Quarterly, 2*, 114–124.

Action for Children's Television. (1978, Spring), *7*(3).

Adair, J. G. (1973). *The human subject; The social psychology of the psychological experiment.* Boston: Little, Brown.

Adams, M. (1976). *Single blessedness.* New York: Basic.

Adler, N. E. (1981). Sex roles and unwanted pregnancy in adolescent and adult women. *Professional Psychology, 12*, 56–66.

Ainsworth, M. S. (1973). The development of infant-mother attachment. In B. M. Caldwell & H. N. Riccuiti (Eds.), *Review of child developmental research.* Chicago: University of Chicago.

Albee, G. W. (1981). The prevention of sexism. *Professional Psychology, 12*, 20–28.

Albrecht, S. L., Bahr, H. M., & Goodman, K. L. (1983). *Divorce and remarriage.* Westport, Conn.: Greenwood.

Allen, I. L. (1984). Male sex roles and epithets for ethnic women in American slang. *Sex Roles, 11*, 43–50.

Allgeier, A. R. (1983). Sexuality and gender roles in the second half of life. In E. R. Allgeier & N. B. McCormick (Eds.), *Changing boundaries* (pp. 135–157). Palo Alto, Calif.: Mayfield.

Allgeier, E. R. (1983). Reproduction, roles and responsibilities. In E. R. Allgeier & N. B. McCormick (Eds.), *Changing boundaries* (pp. 163–181). Palo Alto, Calif.: Mayfield.

Almquist, E. M. (1977). Women in the labor force. *Signs, 2*, 843–855.

Almquist, E. M., & Wehrle-Einhorn, J. L. (1978). The doubly disadvantaged: Minority women in the labor force. In A. H. Stromberg & S. Harkess (Eds.), *Women working* (pp. 63–88). Palo Alto, Calif.: Mayfield.

Alpaugh, P. K., & Birren, J. E. (1975). Are there sex differences in creativity across the adult life span? *Human Development, 18*, 461–465.

Alper, T. (1974). Achievement motivation in college women: A now-you-see-it-now-you-don't phenomenon. *American Psychologist, 29*, 194–203.

American Academy of Pediatrics. (1983). Report of the Task Force on Opportunities for Women in Pediatrics. *Pediatrics, 71,* supplement.

American Institute of Public Opinion. (1975, April). *Gallup Opinion Index #118.* Princeton, N.J.: Author.

American Medical Association, Council on Scientific Affairs. (1983). Fetal effects of maternal alcohol use. *Journal of the American Medical Association, 249,* 2517–2521.

American Psychiatric Association. (1980). *Diagnostic statistical manual of mental disorders* (Third Edition). Washington, D.C.: American Psychiatric Association.

American Psychological Association. (1975). Report of the Task Force on Sex Bias and Sex-Role Stereotyping in Psychotherapeutic Practice. *American Psychologist, 30,* 1169–1175.

American Psychological Association. (1981). Ethical principles of psychologists. *American Psychologist, 36,* 633–638.

American Psychological Association. (1983). *Publication manual of the American Psychological Association* (Third Edition). Washington, D.C.: Author.

American Psychological Association. Task Force on Sex Bias and Sex Role Stereotyping in Psychotherapeutic Practice (1978). Guidelines for therapy with women. *American Psychologist, 33,* 1122–1123.

Andelin, H. B. (1963). *Fascinating womanhood.* Santa Barbara, Calif.: Pacific Press.

Andersen, B. L. (1981). A comparison of systematic desensitization and directed masturbation in the treatment of primary orgasmic dysfunction in females. *Journal of Consulting and Clinical Psychology, 49,* 568–570.

Andersen, B. L. (1983). Primary orgasmic dysfunction: Diagnostic considerations and review of treatment. *Psychological Bulletin, 93,* 105–136.

Anderson, K. Higgins, C., Newman, E. S., & Sherman, S. R. (1978). Differences in attitudes toward retirement among male and female faculty and other university professionals. *Journal of Minority Aging, 3,* 5–13.

Angrist, S. S. (1969). The study of sex roles. *Journal of Social Issues, 25,* 215–232.

Antill J. K., Cotton, S., & Tindale, S. (1983). Egalitarian or traditional: Correlates of the perception of an ideal marriage. *Australian Journal of Psychology, 35,* 243–255.

Antill, J. K., & Cunningham, J. D. (1979). Self-esteem as a function of masculinity in both sexes. *Journal of Consulting and Clinical Psychology, 47,* 783–785.

Antill, J. K., & Cunningham, J. D. (1982). Sex differences in performance on ability tests as a function of masculinity, femininity, and androgyny. *Journal of Personality and Social Psychology, 42,* 718–728.

Archer, D. (1982). Biochemical findings and medical management of the menopause. In A. M. Voda, M. Dinnerstein, & S. R. O'Donnell (Eds.), *Changing perspectives on menopause* (pp. 39–48). Austin, Tex.: University of Texas Press.

Archer, D., Iritani, B., Kimes, D. D., & Barrios, M. (1983). Face-ism: Five studies of sex differences in facial prominence. *Journal of Personality and Social Psychology, 45,* 725–735.

Arenson, G. (1984). *Binge eating.* New York: Rawson.

Aries, E. J., & Johnson, F. L. (1983). Close friendship in adulthood: Conversational content between same-sex friends. *Sex Roles, 9,* 1183–1196.

Arieti, S., & Bemporad, J. (1978). *Severe and mild depression: The psychotherapeutic approach.* New York: Basic.

Aristotle. (1943). *The generation of animals* (A. L. Peck, Trans.). Cambridge, Mass.: Harvard University Press.

Arvey, R. D. (1979). Unfair discrimination in the employment interview: Legal and psychological aspects. *Psychological Bulletin, 86,* 736–765.

Ashmore, R. D., & Del Boca, F. K. (1979). Sex stereotypes and implicit personality theory: Toward a cognitive-social psychological conceptualization. *Sex Roles, 5,* 219–248.

Ashton, E. (1983). Measures of play behavior: The influence of sex-role stereotyped children's books. *Sex Roles, 9,* 43–47.

Asso, D. (1983). *The real menstrual cycle.* Chichester, England: Wiley.

Association for Women in Psychology Ad Hoc Committee on Sexist Language. (1975, November). Help stamp out sexism: Change the language! *APA Monitor, 16.*

Astin, H. S. (1974). Sex differences in mathematical and scientific precocity. In J. C. Stanley, D. P. Keating, & L. Fox (Eds.), *Mathematical talent: Discovery, description, and development* (pp. 70–86). Baltimore, Md.: Johns Hopkins University Press.

Atchley, R. C. (1976). Selected social and psychological differences between men and women in later life. *Journal of Gerontology, 31,* 204–211.

Atkeson, B. M., Calhoun, K. S., Resick, P. A., & Ellis, E. M. (1982). Victims of rape: Repeated assessment of depressive symptoms. *Journal of Consulting and Clinical Psychology, 50,* 96–102.

Atkinson, A. K., & Rickel, A. U. (1984). Depression in women: The postpartum experience. In A. U. Rickel, M. Gerrard, & I. Iscoe (Eds.), *Social and psychological problems of women: Prevention and crisis intervention.* Washington, D.C.: Hemisphere.

Atkinson, J., & Huston, T. L. (1984). Sex role orientation and division of labor early in marriage. *Journal of Personality and Social Psychology, 46,* 330–345.

Backhouse, C., & Cohen, L. (1978). *The secret oppression: Sexual harassment of working women.* Toronto: Macmillan of Canada.

Backhouse, C., & Cohen, L. (1981). *Sexual harassment on the job.* Englewood Cliffs, N.J.: Prentice-Hall.

Bahr, S. J. (1974). Effects on power and division of labor. In L. Hoffman & F. I. Nye (Eds.), *Working mothers* (pp. 167–185). San Francisco: Jossey-Bass.

Bahrick, H. P., Bahrick, P. O., & Wittlinger, R. P. (1975). Fifty years of memory for names and faces: A cross-sectional approach. *Journal of Experimental Psychology: General, 104,* 54–75.

Bakan, D. (1966). *The duality of human existence.* Chicago: Rand McNally.

Ballou, J. W. (1978). *The psychology of pregnancy.* Lexington, Mass.: Lexington.

Bar-Tal, D., & Saxe, L. (1976). Physical attractiveness and its relationship to sex-role stereotyping. *Sex Roles, 2,* 123–133.

Barbach, L. (1980). *Women discover orgasm: A therapist's guide to a new treatment approach.* New York: Free Press.

Bard, M., & Sangrey, D. (1979). *The crime victim's book.* New York: Basic.

Barness, L. A. (1977). Breast milk for all. *New England Journal of Medicine, 297,* 939–940.

Barnett, R. C. (1981). Parental sex-role attitudes and child-rearing values. *Sex Roles, 7,* 837–846.

Barnett, R. C., & Baruch, G. K. (1978). Women in the middle years: A critique of research and theory. *Psychology of Women Quarterly, 3,* 187–197.

Baron, A. S. (1977). Selection, development and socialization of women into management. *Business Quarterly, 28,* 61–67.

Barrett, C. J. (1977). Women in widowhood. *Signs, 2,* 856–868.

Barrett, C. J. (1978). Effectiveness of widow's groups in facilitating change. *Journal of Consulting and Clinical Psychology, 46,* 20–31.

Barrett, C. J. (1981). Intimacy in widowhood. *Psychology of Women, 5,* 473–487.

Barron, N. (1971). Sex-typed language: The production of grammatical cases. *Acta Sociologica, 14,* 24–72.

Bart, P. B. (1971). Depression in middle-aged women. In V. Gornick & B. K. Moran (Eds.), *Woman in sexist society* (pp. 163–186). New York: Basic.

Bart, P. B., & Grossman, M. (1978). Menopause. In M. T. Notman & C. C. Nadelson (Eds.), *The woman patient: Vol. 1: Sexual and reproductive aspects of women's health care* (pp. 337–354). New York: Plenum.

Bart, P. B., & O'Brien, P. H. (1984). Stopping rape: Effective avoidance strategies. *Signs, 10*, 83–101.

Baruch, G., Barnett, R., & Rivers, C. (1983). *Lifeprints.* New York: McGraw-Hill.

Basow, S. (1986). *Gender stereotypes: Traditions and alternatives.* (Second Edition). Monterey, Calif.: Brooks/Cole.

Baxer, J. C. (1970). Interpersonal spacing in natural settings. *Sociometry, 33*, 444–456.

Beck, A. T., & Greenberg, R. L. (1974). Cognitive therapy with depressed women. In V. Franks & V. Burtle (Eds.), *Women in therapy* (pp. 113–131). New York: Brunner/Mazel.

Beckman, L. J. (1979). The relationship between sex roles, fertility, and family size preferences. *Psychology of Women Quarterly, 4*, 43–60.

Beckman, L. J. (1978). The relative rewards and costs of parenthood and employment for employed women. *Psychology of Women Quarterly, 2*, 215–234.

Beckman, L. J., & Houser, B. B. (1982). The consequences of childlessness on the social-psychological well-being of older women. *Journal of Gerontology, 37*, 243–250.

Bell, A. P., & Weinberg, M. S. (1978). *Homosexualities.* New York: Simon and Schuster.

Bell, I. (1979). The double standard: Age. In J. Freeman (Ed.), *Women: A feminist perspective* (pp. 233–244). Palo Alto, Calif.: Mayfield.

Bellinger, D. C., & Gleason, J. B. (1982). Sex differences in parental directives to young children. *Sex Roles, 8*, 1123–1139.

Belovitch, T. E. (1980). The experience of abortion. In C. L. Heckerman (Ed.), *The evolving female* (pp. 92–106). New York: Human Sciences.

Bem, S. L. (1974). The measurement of psychological androgyny. *Journal of Consulting and Clinical Psychology, 42*, 155–162.

Bem, S. L. (1975). Sex role adaptability: One consequence of psychological androgyny. *Journal of Personality and Social Psychology, 31*, 634–643.

Bem, S. L. (1977). On the utility of alternative procedures for assessing psychological androgyny. *Journal of Consulting and Clinical Psychology, 45*, 196–205.

Bem, S. L. (1981). Gender schema theory: A cognitive account of sex typing. *Psychological Review, 88*, 354–364.

Bem, S. L. (1983). Gender schema theory and its implications for child development: Raising gender-aschematic children in a gender-schematic society. *Signs, 8*, 598–616.

Bem, S. L. (1985). Androgyny and gender schema theory: A conceptual and empirical integration. In T. B. Sonderegger (Ed.), *Nebraska Symposium on Motivation, 1984: Psychology and gender* (pp. 179–226). Lincoln, Nebr.: University of Nebraska Press.

Bem, S. L., & Lenney, E. (1976). Sex-typing and the avoidance of cross-sex behavior. *Journal of Personality and Social Psychology, 33*, 48–54.

Bemis, K. M. (1978). Current approaches to the etiology and treatment of anorexia nervosa. *Psychological Bulletin, 85*, 593–617.

Benbow, C. P., & Stanley, J. C. (1980). Sex differences in mathematical ability: Fact or artifact? *Science, 210*, 1262–1264.

Benbow, C. P., & Stanley, J. C. (1983). Sex differences in mathematical reasoning: More facts. *Science, 222*, 1029–1031.

Benderly, B. L. (1982, October). Rape-free or rape-prone? *Science, 3*, 40–43.

Benedek, E., & Vaughn, R. (1982). Voluntary childlessness. In M. Kirkpatrick (Ed.), *Women's sexual experience* (pp. 205–222). New York: Plenum.

Bequaert, L. H. (1976). *Single women, alone and together.* Boston: Beacon.

Berg, J. H., Stephen, W. G., & Dodson, M. (1981). Attributional modesty in women. *Psychology of Women Quarterly, 5,* 711–727.

Berg-Cross, L., Berg-Cross, G., & McGeehan, D. (1979). Experience and personality differences among breast- and bottle-feeding mothers. *Psychology of Women Quarterly, 3,* 344–356.

Bergmann, B. (1982, February 3). Women's economic condition in the 1980s: Bad and getting worse. In *Hearing before the Joint Economic Committee, Congress of the United States, Ninety-Seventh Congress* (pp. 74–83). Washington, D.C.: U.S. Government Printing Office.

Berkowitz, L. (1986). *A survey of social psychology* (Third Edition). New York: Holt, Rinehart and Winston.

Berman, P. W. (1976). Social context as a determinant of sex differences in adults' attraction to infants. *Developmental Psychology, 12,* 365–366.

Berman, P. W. (1980). Are women more responsive than men to the young? A review of developmental and situational variables. *Psychological Bulletin, 88,* 668–695.

Berman, P. W., O'Nan, B. A., & Floyd, W. (1981). The double standard of aging and the social situation: Judgments of attractiveness of the middle-aged woman. *Sex Roles, 7,* 87–96.

Bernard, J. (1972). *The future of marriage.* New York: World Publishing.

Bernard, J. (1974). *Sex differences: An overview.* New York: MSS Modular Publications.

Bernard, J. (1981). *The female world.* New York: Free Press.

Berry, K. (1982, February). Childbirth—Letting gravity help. *Ms. Magazine,* p. 20.

Bestor, D. K. (1982). *Aside from teaching, what in the world can you do?* Seattle: University of Washington Press.

Beuf, A. (1974). Doctor, lawyer, household drudge. *Journal of Communication, 24,* 142–145.

Bielby, D. (1978). Maternal employment and socioeconomic status as factors in daughters' career salience: Some substantive refinements. *Sex Roles, 4,* 249–266.

Bingham, W., & House, E. (1973, January). Counselors view women and work: Accuracy of information. *The Vocational Guidance Quarterly, 21,* 262–268.

Bird, C. (1979, June). The best years of a woman's life. *Psychology Today, 12,* 20–26.

Bishop, N. (1984). Abortion: The controversial choice. In J. Freeman (Ed.), *Women: A feminist perspective* (Third Edition, pp. 39–53). Palo Alto, Calif.: Mayfield.

Blaubergs, M. S. (1978). Changing the sexist language: The theory behind the practice. *Psychology of Women Quarterly, 2,* 244–261.

Blaubergs, M. S. (1980). An analysis of classic arguments against changing sexist language. *Women's Studies International Quarterly, 3,* 135–147.

Blechman, E. A. (1984). Women's behavior in a man's world: Sex differences in competence. In E. A. Blechman (Ed.), *Behavior modification with women* (pp. 3–33). New York: Guilford Press.

Block, J. H. (1973). Conceptions of sex role: Some cross-cultural and longitudinal perspectives. *American Psychologist, 28,* 512–526.

Block, J. H. (1976). Issues, problems, and pitfalls in assessing sex differences: A critical review of *The psychology of sex differences. Merrill-Palmer Quarterly, 22,* 283–308.

Block, J. H. (1978). Another look at sex differentiation in the socialization behaviors of mothers and fathers. In J. A. Sherman & F. L. Denmark (Eds.), *The psychology of women: Future directions in research* (pp. 30–87). New York: Psychological Dimensions.

Block, J. H. (1983). Differential premises arising from differential socialization of the sexes: Some conjectures. *Child Development, 54*, 1335–1354.

Block, J. H. (1984). *Sex role identity and ego development.* San Francisco: Jossey-Bass.

Blum, B. L. (Ed.) (1980). *Psychological aspects of pregnancy, birthing, and bonding.* New York: Human Sciences.

Blumstein, P. W., & Schwartz, P. (1977). Bisexuality: Some social psychological issues. *Journal of Social Issues, 33*, 30–45.

Blumstein, P., & Schwartz, P. (1983). *American couples.* New York: William Morrow.

Bograd, M. (1982). Battered women, cultural myths and clinical interventions: A feminist analysis. *Women & Therapy, 1*, 69–77.

Bohannan, P. (Ed.). (1970). *Divorce and after.* Garden City, N.Y.: Doubleday.

Bond, G. R., & Lieberman, M. A. (1980). The role and function of women's consciousness raising: Self-help, psychotherapy, or political activation? In C. L. Heckerman (Ed.), *The evolving female* (pp. 268–306). New York: Human Sciences.

Borges, M. A., Levine, J. R., & Dutton, L. J. (1984). Men's and women's ratings of life satisfaction by age of respondent and age interval judged. *Sex Roles, 11*, 345–350.

Borman, K. M., Quarm, D., & Gideonse, S. (Eds.) (1984). *Women in the workplace: Effects on families.* Norwood, N.J.: Ablex.

Boskind-White, M., & White, W. C. (1983). *Bulimarexia: The binge/purge cycle.* New York: Norton.

Bowker, L. H. (1983). *Beating wife-beating.* Lexington, Mass.: Lexington Books.

Brabant, S. (1976). Sex-role stereotyping in the Sunday comics. *Sex Roles, 2*, 331–337.

Braiker, H. B. (1984). Therapeutic issues in the treatment of alcoholic women. In S. C. Wilsnack & L. J. Beckman (Eds.), *Alcoholic problems in women* (pp. 349–368). New York: Guilford.

Braito, R., & Anderson, D. (1983). The ever-single elderly woman. In E. W. Markson (Ed.), *Older women* (pp. 195–225). Lexington, Mass.: Lexington Books.

Braito, R., Dean, D., Powers, E., & Bruton, B. (1981). The inferiority game: Perceptions and behavior. *Sex Roles, 7*, 65–72.

Bram, S. (1984). Voluntarily childless women: Traditional or nontraditional? *Sex Roles, 10*, 195–206.

Brandenburg, J. B. (1982). Sexual harassment in the university: Guidelines for establishing a grievance procedure. *Signs, 8*, 320–336.

Brannon, R. (1978). Measuring attitudes (toward women, and otherwise): A methodological critique. In J. Sherman & F. Denmark (Eds.), *Psychology of women: Future directions in research.* New York: Psychological Dimensions, Inc.

Brant, R. S. T. (1980). The child victim. In S. L. McCombie (Ed.), *The rape crisis intervention handbook* (pp. 185–198). New York: Plenum.

Brazelton, T. B. (1974). *Toddlers and parents.* New York: Delta.

Breines, W., & Gordon, L. (1983). The new scholarship on family violence. *Signs, 8*, 490–531.

Brend, R. M. (1975). Male-female intonation patterns in American English. In B. Thorne & N. Henley (Eds.), *Language and sex: Differences and dominance* (pp. 84–87). Rowley, Mass.: Newbury House.

Brewer, J. I., & de Costa, E. J. (1967). *Textbook of gynecology* (Fourth Edition). Baltimore: Williams & Wilkins.

Brewer, M. B. (1982). Further beyond nine to five: An integration and future directions. *Journal of Social Issues, 38*, 149–157.

Briere, J., & Lanktree, C. (1983). Sex-role related effects of sex bias in language. *Sex Roles*, *9*, 625–632.

Brinson-Pineda, B. (1985). Hispanic women: Toward an agenda for the future. In A. G. Sargent (Ed.), *Beyond sex roles* (Second Edition, pp. 252–257). St. Paul, Minn.: West.

Brodsky, A. M. (1977). Therapeutic aspects of consciousness-raising groups. In E. I. Rawlings & D. K. Carter (Eds.), *Psychotherapy for women* (pp. 300–309). Springfield, Ill.: Charles C. Thomas.

Brodsky, A. M. (1980). A decade of feminist influence on psychotherapy. *Psychology of Women Quarterly*, *4*, 331–344.

Brodsky, A. M., & Hare-Mustin, R. T. (1980). Psychotherapy and women: Priorities for research. In A. M. Brodsky & R. T. Hare-Mustin (Eds.), *Women and psychotherapy* (pp. 385–409). New York: Guilford.

Brooks, J., Ruble, D., & Clarke, A. (1977). College women's attitudes and expectations concerning menstrual-related changes. *Psychosomatic Medicine*, *39*, 288–298.

Brooks, L. (1984). Counseling special groups: Women and ethnic minorities. In D. Brown & L. Brooks (Eds.), *Career choice and development* (pp. 355–368). San Francisco: Jossey-Bass.

Brooks, V. R. (1981). *Minority stress and lesbian women*. Lexington, Mass.: Lexington Books.

Brooks, V. R. (1982). Sex differences in student dominance behavior in female and male professors' classrooms. *Sex Roles*, *8*, 683–690.

Brooks-Gunn, J., & Matthews, W. S. (1979). *He & she: How children develop their sex-role identity*. Englewood Cliffs, N.J.: Spectrum.

Brooks-Gunn, J., & Ruble, D. N. (1983). The experience of menarche from a developmental perspective. In J. Brooks-Gunn & A. C. Petersen (Eds.), *Girls at puberty* (pp. 155–177). New York: Plenum.

Brophy, J. E., & Good, T. L. (1974). *Teacher-student relationships: Causes and consequences*. New York: Holt, Rinehart and Winston.

Broverman, I. K., Broverman, D. M., Clarkson, F. E., Rosenkrantz, P. S., & Vogel, S. R. (1970). Sex-role stereotypes and clinical judgments of mental health. *Journal of Consulting and Clinical Psychology*, *34*, 1–7.

Broverman, I. K., Vogel, S. R., Broverman, D. M., Clarkson, F. E., & Rosenkrantz, P. S. (1972). Sex-role stereotypes: A current appraisal. *Journal of Social Issues*, *28*, 59–78.

Brown, A., Goodwin, B. J., Hall, B. A., & Jackson-Lowman, H. (1985). A review of psychology of women textbooks: Focus on the Afro-American woman. *Psychology of Women Quarterly*, *9*, 29–49.

Brown, P., & Fox, H. (1979). Sex differences in divorce. In E. S. Gomberg & V. Franks (Eds.). *Gender and disordered behavior: Sex differences in psychopathology* (pp. 101–123). New York: Brunner/Mazel.

Brownmiller, S. (1975). *Against our will: Men, women and rape*. New York: Bantam.

Brownmiller, S. (1984). *Femininity*. New York: Simon and Schuster.

Bruch, H. (1978). *The golden cage: The enigma of anorexia nervosa*. Cambridge, Mass.: Harvard University Press.

Brush, L. R. (1980). *Encouraging girls in mathematics: The problem and the solution*. Cambridge: Mass.: Abt Books.

Bry, B. H. (1984). Substance abuse in women. In A. U. Rickel, M. Gerrard, & I. Iscoe (Eds.), *Social and psychological problems of women: Prevention and crisis intervention* (pp. 253–272). Washington, D.C.: Hemisphere.

Bryden, M. P. (1979). Evidence for sex-related differences in cerebral organization. In

M. A. Wittig & A. C. Petersen (Eds.), *Sex-related differences in cognitive functioning* (pp. 121–143). New York: Academic.

Buczek, T. Z. (1981). Sex biases in counseling: Counselor retention of the concerns of a female and male client. *Journal of Counseling Psychology, 28,* 13–21.

Budoff, P. W. (1983). *No more menstrual cramps and other good news.* New York: Putnam.

Bugental, D. E., Love, L. R., & Gianetto, R. M. (1971). Perfidious feminine faces. *Journal of Personality and Social Psychology, 17,* 314–318.

Bureau of Labor Statistics. (1985). *Handbook of labor statistics.* Washington, D.C.: U. S. Government Printing Office.

Burgess, A. W., & Holmstrom, L. L. (1974). Rape trauma syndrome. *American Journal of Psychiatry, 131,* 981–986.

Burgess, A. W., & Holmstrom, L. L. (1979). Rape: Sexual disruption and recovery. *American Journal of Orthopsychiatry, 49,* 648–657.

Burgess, A. W., & Holmstrom, L. L. (1980). Rape typology and the coping behavior of rape victims. In S. L. McCombie (Ed.), *The rape crisis intervention handbook* (pp. 27–40). New York: Plenum.

Burlew, A. K. (1982). The experiences of black females in traditional and nontraditional professions. *Psychology of Women Quarterly, 6,* 312–326.

Burt, M. R. (1980). Cultural myths and supports for rape. *Journal of Personality and Social Psychology, 38,* 217–230.

Burt, M. R., & Estep, R. E. (1981). Apprehension and fear: Learning a sense of sexual vulnerability. *Sex Roles, 7,* 511–522.

Butler, A. (1976). Breast cancer. *Canadian Nurse, 72,* 17–22.

Butler, R. N. (1978). Prospects for middle-aged women. In Select Committee on Aging (Ed.), *Women in midlife—Security and fulfillment* (Part I, pp. 323–333). Washington, D.C.: U.S. Government Printing Office.

Byrne, D. (1979). Determinants of contraceptive values and practices. In M. Cook & G. Wilson (Eds.), *Love and attraction* (pp. 301–307). Oxford, England: Pergamon.

Cahill, S. E. (1983). Reexamining the acquisition of sex roles: A social interactionist approach. *Sex Roles, 9,* 1–13.

Caldwell, M. A., Finn, S., & Marecek, J. (1981). Sex-role identity, sex-role behavior, and satisfaction in heterosexual, lesbian, and gay male couples. *Psychology of Women Quarterly, 5,* 488–494.

Caldwell, M. A., & Peplau, L. A. (1982). Sex differences in same-sex friendship. *Sex Roles, 8,* 721–732.

Caldwell, M. A., & Peplau, L. A. (1984). The balance of power in lesbian relationships. *Sex Roles, 10,* 587–599.

Caldwell, R. A., Bloom, B. L., & Hodges, W. F. (1984). Sex differences in separation and divorce. In A. U. Rickel, M. Gerrard, & I. Iscoe (Eds.), *Social and psychological problems of women: Prevention and crisis intervention* (pp. 103–120). New York: Hemisphere.

Campbell, A. (1975). The American way of mating: Marriage sí, children only maybe. *Psychology Today, 8,* 37–43.

Campbell, A., Converse, P. E., & Rodgers, W. L. (1976). *The quality of American life.* New York: Russell Sage Foundation.

Campbell, F. L., Townes, B. D., & Beach, L. R. (1982). Motivational bases of childbearing decisions. In G. L. Fox (Ed.), *The childbearing decision* (pp. 145–159). Beverly Hills, Calif.: Sage.

Cann, A., & Haight, J. M. (1983). Children's perceptions of relative competence in sex-typed occupations. *Sex Roles, 9,* 767–773.

Carpenter, C. J., & Huston-Stein, A. (1980). The relation of children's activity preference to sex-typed behaviors. *Child Development, 51,* 862–872.

Carroll, J. L., Volk, K. D., & Hyde, J. S. (1985). Differences between males and females in motives for engaging in sexual intercourse. *Archives of Sexual Behavior, 14,* 131–139.

Cash, T. F., Gillen, B., & Burns, D. S. (1977). Sexism and "beautyism" in personnel consultant decision making. *Journal of Applied Psychology, 62,* 301–310.

Cassata, M. (1983). The more things change, the more they are the same: An analysis of soap operas from radio to television. In M. Cassata & T. Skill (Eds.), *Life on daytime television: Tuning-in American serial drama* (pp. 85–100). Norwood, N J.: Ablex.

Celentano, D. D., McQueen, D. V., & Chee, E. (1980). Substance abuse by women: A review of the epidemiologic literature. *Journal of Chronic Diseases, 33,* 383–394.

Chambless, D. L., & Goldstein, A. J. (1980). Anxieties: Agoraphobia and hysteria. In A. M. Brodsky & R. T. Hare-Mustin (Eds.), *Women and psychotherapy* (pp. 113–134). New York: Guilford Press.

Chance, J. E., & Goldstein, A. G. (1971). Internal-external control of reinforcement and embedded-figures performance. *Perception & Psychophysics, 9,* 33–34.

Check, J. V. P., & Malamuth, N. M. (1983). Sex role stereotyping and reactions to depictions of stranger versus acquaintance rape. *Journal of Personality and Social Psychology, 45,* 344–356.

Cherry, F., & Deaux, K. (1978). Fear of success versus fear of gender-inappropriate behavior. *Sex Roles, 4,* 97–102.

Cherry, F., & Eaton, E. L. (1977). Physical and cognitive development in children of low-income mothers working in the child's early years. *Child Development, 48,* 158–166.

Cherry, L. (1975). The preschool teacher-child dyad: Sex differences in verbal interaction. *Child Development, 46,* 532–535.

Cherry, L., & Lewis, M. (1976). Mothers and two-year-olds: A study of sex-differentiated aspects of verbal interaction. *Developmental Psychology, 12,* 278–282.

Chesler, P. (1972). *Women and madness.* New York: Doubleday.

Chesler, P. (1976). *Women, money, and power.* New York: Bantam.

Chiriboga, D. A., & Cutler, L. (1977). Stress responses among divorcing men and women. *Journal of Divorce, 1,* 95–106.

Chow, E. N. (1985). The acculturation experience of Asian American women. In A. G. Sargent (Ed.), *Beyond sex roles* (Second Edition, pp. 238–251). St. Paul, Minn.: West.

Church, M. L. (1982). Effects of teenage motherhood. In M. Kirkpatrick (Ed.), *Women's sexual experience* (pp. 151–166). New York: Plenum.

Clarke, A. E., & Ruble, D. N. (1978). Young adolescents' beliefs concerning menstruation. *Child Development, 49,* 231–234.

Clarke-Stewart, K. A. (1973). Interactions between mothers and their young children: Characteristics and consequences. *Monographs of Society for Research in Child Development, 38* (Serial No. 153).

Clayton, R. R., & Voss, H. L. (1979). Shacking up: Cohabitation in the 1970s. In J. G. Wells (Ed.), *Current issues in marriage and the family* (Second Edition, pp. 77–96). New York: Macmillan.

Cohen, D., & Wilkie, F. (1979). Sex-related differences in cognition among the elderly. In M. A. Wittig & A. C. Petersen (Eds.), *Sex-related differences in cognitive functioning* (pp. 145–159). New York: Academic.

Cohen, S. L., Bunker, K. A., Burton, A. L., & McManus, P. D. (1978). Reactions of male subordinates to the sex-role incongruency of immediate supervision. *Sex Roles, 4*, 297–311.

Coleman, E. (1982). Changing approaches to the treatment of homosexuality: A review. In W. Paul, J. D. Weinrich, J. C. Gonsiorek, & M. E. Hotvedt (Eds.), *Homosexuality: Social, psychological, and biological issues* (pp. 81–88). Beverly Hills, Calif.: Sage.

Collier, H. V. (1982). *Counseling women.* New York: Free Press.

Combs, M. W., & Welch, S. (1982). Blacks, whites, and attitudes toward abortion. *Public Opinion Quarterly, 46*, 510–520.

Condry, J. C., & Condry, S. (1976). Sex differences: A study of the eye of the beholder. *Child Development, 47*, 812–819.

Condry, J. C., & Dyer, S. L. (1976). Fear of success: Attribution of cause to the victim. *Journal of Social Issues, 32*, 63–83.

Connor, J. M., Serbin, L. A., & Ender, R. A. (1978). Responses of boys and girls to aggressive, assertive and passive behaviors of male and female characters. *Journal of Genetic Psychology, 133*, 59–69.

Constantinople, A. (1973). Masculinity-femininity: An exception to a famous dictum? *Psychological Bulletin, 80*, 389–407.

Constantinople, A. (1982). A critique of "In search of token women in academia." *Psychology of Women Quarterly, 7*, 163–169.

Cook, A. S., West, J. S., & Hamner, T. J. (1982). Changes in attitudes toward parenting among college women: 1972 and 1979 samples. *Family Relations, 31*, 109–113.

Cooper, H. M. (1979). Statistically combining independent studies: Meta-analysis of sex differences in conformity research. *Journal of Personality and Social Psychology, 37*, 131–146.

Copeland, E. J. (1982). Oppressed conditions and the mental health needs of low-income black women: Barriers to services, strategies for change. *Women & Therapy, 1*, 13–26.

Courtney, A. E., & Whipple, T. W. (1983). *Sex stereotyping in advertising.* Lexington, Mass.: Lexington Books.

Cowan, G. (1984). The double standard in age discrepant relationships. *Sex Roles, 11*, 17–24.

Cowan, M. L., & Stewart, B. J. (1977). A methodological study of sex stereotypes. *Sex Roles, 3*, 205–216.

Crandall, V. J. (1969). Sex differences in expectancy of intellectual and academic reinforcement. In C. D. Smith (Ed.), *Achievement related motives in children.* New York: Russell Sage Foundation.

Crandall, V. J. (1975). Sex differences in expectancy of intellectual and academic reinforcement. In R. Unger & F. Denmark (Eds.), *Women: Dependent or independent variable?* (pp. 649–685). New York: Psychological Dimensions.

Crawford, M. (1984). Personal communication.

Crawford, M. (1985). Personal communication.

Crawford, M., & English, L. (1984). Generic versus specific inclusion of women in language: Effects on recall. *Journal of Psycholinguistic Research, 13*, 373–381.

Crew, J. C. (1982). An assessment of needs among black business majors. *Psychology, 19*, 18–22.

Crombie, G. (1983). Women's attribution patterns and their relation to achievement: An examination of within-sex differences. *Sex Roles, 9*, 1171–1182.

Crosby, F. J. (1982). *Relative deprivation and working women.* New York: Oxford University Press.

Cross, E. (1985). Reflections: On being black and female. In A. G. Sargent (Ed.), *Beyond sex roles* (Second Edition, pp. 233–237). St. Paul, Minn.: West.

Crowley, J., Levitin, T., & Quinn, R. (1973, March). Seven deadly half-truths about women. *Psychology Today, 6,* 94–96.

Crull, P. (1980). The impact of sexual harassment on the job: A profile of the experiences of 92 women. In D. A. Neugarten & J. M. Shafritz (Eds.), *Sexuality in organizations* (pp. 67–71). Oak Park, Ill.: Moore.

Culp, R. E., Cook, A. S., & Housley, P. C. (1983). A comparison of observed and reported adult-infant interactions: Effects of perceived sex. *Sex Roles, 9,* 475–479.

Cummings, S., & Taebel, D. (1980). Sexual inequality and the reproduction of consciousness: An analysis of sex-role stereotyping among children. *Sex Roles, 6,* 631–644.

Cunningham, S. (1983, April). Courts recognizing 'battered wife syndrome.' *APA Monitor, 14,* 24, 27.

Dalton, K. (1977). *The premenstrual syndrome and progesterone therapy.* London: W. Heinemann Medical Books.

Dalton, K. (1983). *Once a month.* Claremont, Calif.: Hunter House.

Dan, A. J. (1979). The menstrual cycle and sex-related differences in cognitive variability. In M. A. Wittig & A. C. Petersen (Eds.), *Sex-related differences in cognitive functioning* (pp. 241–260). New York: Academic.

Dan, A. J., Graham, E. A., Beecher, C. P., Bart, P. B., Komnenich, P., Krueger, J., Pitel, M., & Ruble, D. (1980). Synthesis and new directions. In A. J. Dan, E. A. Graham, & C. P. Beecher (Eds.), *The menstrual cycle* (Vol. 1, pp. 339–345). New York: Springer-Verlag.

Daniels, P., & Weingarten, K. (1982). *Sooner or later: The timing of parenthood in adult lives.* New York: Norton.

Danza, R. (1983). Menarche: Its effects on mother-daughter and father-daughter interactions. In S. Golub (Ed.), *Menarche* (pp. 99–105). Lexington, Mass.: Lexington Books.

Darley, J. M., & Fazio, R. H. (1980). Expectancy confirmation processes arising in the social interaction sequence. *American Psychologist, 35,* 867–881.

Darrow, W. (1970). *I'm glad I'm a boy; I'm glad I'm a girl.* New York: Windmill Books.

Datan, N., & Rodeheaver, D. (1983). Beyond generativity: Toward a sensuality of later life. In R. B. Weg (Ed.), *Sexuality in the later years* (pp. 279–288). New York: Academic.

David, H. P., & Matejcek, Z. (1981). Children born to women denied abortion: An update. *Family Planning Perspectives, 13,* 32–34.

Davidson, C., & Davidson, V. M. T. (1977). Variations in gender-role equality among classes: A research note. *Sex Roles 3,* 459–467.

Davidson, C. V., & Abramowitz, S. I. (1980). Sex bias in clinical judgment: Later empirical returns. *Psychology of Women Quarterly, 4,* 377–395.

Davidson, L. R. (1981). Pressures and pretense: Living with gender stereotypes. *Sex Roles, 7,* 331–347.

Davis, M., & Weitz, S. (1981). Sex differences in body movements and positions. In C. Mayo & N. M. Henley (Eds.), *Gender and nonverbal behavior* (pp. 81–92). New York: Springer-Verlag.

Davis, S. W., Williams, J. E., & Best, D. L. (1982). Sex-trait stereotypes in the self- and peer descriptions of third grade children. *Sex Roles, 8,* 315–331.

Dayhoff, S. A. (1983). Sexist language and person perceptions: Evaluation of candidates from newspaper articles. *Sex Roles, 9,* 543–555.

Deaux, K. (1976a). Sex: A perspective on the attribution process. In J. H. Harvey, W. J. Ickes, & R. F. Kidd (Eds.), *New directions in attribution research, Vol. 1* (pp. 335–352). Hillsdale, N.J.: Erlbaum.

Deaux, K. (1976b). *The behavior of women and men.* Monterey, Calif.: Brooks/Cole.

Deaux, K. (1979). Self-evaluation of male and female managers. *Sex Roles, 5,* 571–580.

Deaux, K. (1984). From individual differences to social categories: Analysis of a decade's research on gender. *American Psychologist, 39,* 105–116.

Deaux, K. (1985). Sex and gender. *Annual Review of Psychology, 36,* 49–81.

Deaux, K., & Emswiller, T. (1974). Explanations of successful performance on sex-linked tasks: What's skill for the male is luck for the female. *Journal of Personality and Social Psychology, 29,* 80–85.

Deaux, K., & Hanna, R. (1984). Courtship in the personals column: The influence of gender and sexual orientation. *Sex Roles, 11,* 363–375.

Deaux, K., & Lewis, L. L. (1984). Structure of gender stereotypes: Interrelationships among components and gender label. *Journal of Personality and Social Psychology, 46,* 991–1004.

Deaux, K., & Ullman, J. C. (1983). *Women of steel.* New York: Praeger.

Deaux, K., White, L., & Farris, E. (1975). Skill versus luck: Field and laboratory studies of male and female preferences. *Journal of Personality and Social Psychology, 32,* 629–636.

Delaney, J., Lupton, M. J., & Toth, E. (1976). *The curse.* New York: Dutton.

Dellas, M., Gaier, E. L., & Emihovich, C. A. (1979). Maternal employment and selected behaviors and attitudes of preadolescents. *Adolescence, 14,* 579–589.

deMonteflores, C., & Schultz, S. (1978). Coming out: Similarities and differences for lesbians and gay men. *Journal of Social Issues, 34,* 59–72.

Denckla, M. B., & Rudel, R. (1974). Rapid "automatized" naming of pictured objects, colors, letters, and numbers by normal children. *Cortex, 10,* 186–202.

Denmark, F. L. (1977). The psychology of women: An overview of an emerging field. *Personality and Social Psychology Bulletin, 3,* 356–367.

Densen-Gerber, J. (1984). Sexual abuse of children: Emerging issues. *New York Pediatrician, 2,* 3–6.

Depner, C. E., & Veroff, J. (1979). Varieties of achievement motivation. *Journal of Social Psychology, 107,* 283–284.

deWolf, V. A. (1981). High school mathematics preparation and sex differences in quantitative abilities. *Psychology of Women Quarterly, 5,* 555–567.

Diamond, D. L., & Wilsnack, S. C. (1978). Alcohol abuse among lesbians: A descriptive study. *Journal of Homosexuality, 4,* 123–142.

Dill, B. T. (1980). "The means to put my children through": Child-rearing goals and strategies among Black female domestic servants In L. Rodgers-Rose (Ed.), *The Black woman* (pp. 107–123). Beverly Hills, Calif.: Sage.

Dipboye, R., Fromkin, H., & Wiback, R. (1975). Relative importance of applicant sex, attractiveness, and scholastic standing in evaluation of job applicant resumes. *Journal of Applied Psychology, 60,* 39–43.

DiPietro, J. A. (1981). Rough and tumble play: A function of gender. *Developmental Psychology, 17,* 50–58.

Dobash, R. E., & Dobash, R. P. (1978). Wives: The 'appropriate' victims of marital violence. *Victimology, 2,* 426–442.

Doherty, W. J., & Jacobson, N. S. (1982). Marriage and family. In B. B. Wolman (Ed.), *Handbook of developmental psychology* (pp. 667–680). Englewood Cliffs, N.J.: Prentice-Hall.

Donahue, T., & Costar, J. (1977). Counselor discrimination against young women in career selection. *Journal of Counseling Psychology, 24,* 481–486.

Douvan, E., & Adelson, J. (1966). *The adolescent experience.* New York: Wiley.

Downs, A. C. (1981). Sex-role stereotyping on prime-time television. *Journal of Genetic Psychology, 138,* 253–258.

Downs, A. C. (1983). Letters to Santa Claus: Elementary-school-age children's sex-typed toy preferences in a natural setting. *Sex Roles, 9,* 159–163.

Downs, A. C., & Gowan, D. C. (1980). Sex differences in reinforcement and punishment on prime-time television. *Sex Roles, 6,* 683–694.

Dreyer, P. H. (1982). Sexuality during adolescence. In B. B. Wolman (Ed.), *Handbook of developmental psychology* (pp. 559–601). Englewood Cliffs, N.J.: Prentice-Hall.

Droege, R. C. (1967). Sex differences in aptitude maturation during high school. *Journal of Counseling Psychology, 14,* 407–411.

Dunham, G. (1979). Timing and sources of information about and attitudes toward menstruation among college females. *Journal of Genetic Psychology, 117,* 205–207.

Dunnette, M. D., & Motowidlo, S. J. (1982). Estimating benefits and costs of antisexist training programs in organizations. In H. J. Bernardin (Ed.), *Women in the work force* (pp. 156–182). New York: Praeger.

Dwyer, C. A. (1974). Sex differences in reading: An evaluation and a critique of current theories. *Review of Educational Research, 43,* 455–467.

Dwyer, C. A. (1976, May). Test content and sex differences in reading. *Reading Teacher, 29,* 753–757.

Dziech, B. W., & Weiner, L. (1984). *The lecherous professor: Sexual harassment.* Boston: Beacon.

Eagly, A. H. (1978). Sex differences in influenceability. *Psychological Bulletin, 85,* 86–116.

Eagly, A. H., & Carli, L. L. (1981). Sex of researchers and sex-typed communications as determinants of sex differences in influenceability: A meta-analysis of social influence studies. *Psychological Bulletin, 90,* 1–20.

Eagly, A. H., & Wood, W. (1985). Gender and influenceability: Stereotype versus behavior. In V. E. O'Leary, R. K. Unger, & B. S. Wallston (Eds.), *Women, gender, and social psychology* (pp. 225–256). Hillsdale, N.J.: Erlbaum.

Eberts, E. H., & Lepper, M. R. (1975). Individual consistency in the proxemic behavior of preschool children. *Journal of Personality and Social Psychology, 32,* 841–849.

Eccles, J., Adler, T., & Meece, J. L. (1984). Sex differences in achievement: A test of alternate theories. *Journal of Personality and Social Psychology, 46,* 26–43.

Edelsky, C. (1976a). Subjective reactions to sex-linked language. *Journal of Social Psychology, 99,* 97–104.

Edelsky, C. (1976b). The acquisition of communicative competence: Recognition of linguistic correlates of sex roles. *Merrill-Palmer Quarterly, 22,* 47–59.

Edinburg, G. M. (1982). Women and aging. In C. C. Nadelson & M. T. Notman (Eds.), *The woman patient: Vol. 2: Concepts of femininity and the life cycle* (pp. 169–194). New York: Plenum.

Edney, J. J., & Jordan-Edney, N. L. (1974). Territorial spacing on a beach. *Sociometry, 37,* 92–104.

Ehrhardt, A. A., Greenberg, N., & Money, J. (1970). Female gender identity and absence of fetal hormones: Turner's syndrome. *Johns Hopkins Medical Journal, 126,* 237–248.

Eisenberg, N., & Lennon, R. (1983). Sex differences in empathy and related capacities. *Psychological Bulletin, 94,* 100–131.

Ellis, A. (1984). Current psychotherapies. In R. J. Corsini (Ed.), *Encyclopedia of psychology* (Vol. 1, pp. 339–341). New York: Wiley-Interscience.

Emmerich, W., Goldman, K. S., Kirsch, B., & Sharabany, R. (1977). Evidence for a transitional phase in the development of gender constancy. *Child Development, 48,* 930–936.

Entwisle, D. R., & Doering, S. G. (1981). *The first birth.* Baltimore, Md.: Johns Hopkins University Press.

Ephron, N. (1975). *Crazy salad.* New York: Bantam Books.

Epstein, C., & Paludi, M. (1985). *Performance evaluation research: Some conceptual and methodological issues.* Paper presented at the annual meeting of the American Psychological Association, Los Angeles.

Equal Employment Opportunity Commission Guidelines on discrimination because of sex. (1980). *Federal Register, 45,* 74676–74677.

Erikson, E. H. (1968). *Identity: Young and crisis.* New York: Norton.

Ernster, V. L. (1975). American menstrual expressions. *Sex Roles, 1,* 3–13.

Eron, L. D. (1980). Prescription for reduction of aggression. *American Psychologist, 35,* 244–252.

Eskilson, A., & Wiley, M. G. (1976). Sex composition and leadership in small groups. *Sociometry, 39,* 183–194.

Etaugh, C., & Brown, B. (1975). Perceiving the causes of success and failure of male and female performers. *Developmental Psychology, 11,* 103.

Etaugh, C., & Foresman, E. (1983). Evaluations of competence as a function of sex and marital status. *Sex Roles, 9,* 759–765.

Etaugh, C., & Kasley, H. C. (1981). Evaluating competence: Effects of sex, marital status and parental status. *Psychology of Women Quarterly, 6,* 196–203.

Etaugh, C., Levine, D., & Mennella, A. (1984). Development of sex biases in children: 40 years later. *Sex Roles, 10,* 911–922.

Etaugh, C., & Malstrom, J. (1981). The effect of marital status on person perception. *Journal of Marriage and the Family, 43,* 801–805.

Etaugh, C., & Riley, S. (1983). Evaluating competence of women and men: Effects of marital and parental status and occupational sex-typing. *Sex Roles, 9,* 943–952.

Fagot, B. (1978). The influence of sex of child on parental reactions to toddler children. *Child Development, 49,* 462.

Fagot, B., & Littman, I. (1976). Relation of pre-school sex-typing to intellectual performance in elementary school. *Psychological Reports, 39,* 699–704.

Falbo, T. (1977). Relationships between sex, sex role, and social influence. *Psychology of Women Quarterly, 2,* 62–72.

Falbo, T. (1982). PAQ types and power strategies used in intimate relationships. *Psychology of Women Quarterly, 6,* 399–405.

Farley, L. (1978). *Sexual shakedown: The sexual harassment of women on the job.* New York: McGraw-Hill.

Farmer, H. S. (1983). Career and homemaking plans for high school youth. *Journal of Counseling Psychology, 30,* 40–45.

Farmer, H. S., & Backer, T. E. (1977). *New career options for women: A counselor's sourcebook.* New York: Human Sciences.

Faunce, P. S., & Phipps-Yonas, S. (1979). Women's liberation and human sexual relations. In J. H. Williams (Ed.), *Psychology of women: Selected readings* (pp. 228–240). New York: Norton.

Faux, M. (1984). *Childless by choice.* Garden City, N.Y.: Anchor.

Feather, N. T., & Simon, J. G. (1975). Reactions to male and female success and failure in sex-linked occupations: Impressions of personality, causal attributions, and perceived likelihood of different consequences. *Journal of Personality and Social Psychology, 31,* 20–31.

Featherman, D. L., & Hauser, R. M. (1976). Sexual inequalities and socioeconomic achievement in the United States: 1962–1973. *American Sociological Review, 41,* 462–483.

Federbush, M. (1974). The sex problems of school math books. In J. Stacey, S. Bereaud, & J. Daniels (Eds.), *And Jill came tumbling after: Sexism in American education* (pp. 178–184). New York: Dell.

Feild, H. (1978). Attitudes toward rape: A comparative analysis of police, rapists, crisis counselors, and citizens. *Journal of Personality and Social Psychology, 36,* 156–179.

Feild, H., & Caldwell, B. (1979). Sex of supervisor, sex of subordinate and subordinate job satisfaction. *Psychology of Women Quarterly, 3,* 391–399.

Feldman, S. S., Biringen, Z. C., & Nash, S. C. (1981). Fluctuations of sex-related self-attributions as a function of stage of family life cycle. *Developmental Psychology, 17,* 24–35.

Feldman-Summers, S., & Ashworth, C. D. (1981). Factors related to intentions to report a rape. *The Journal of Social Issues, 37,* 53–70.

Feldman-Summers, S., Gordon, P. E., & Meagher, J. R. (1979). The impact of rape on sexual satisfaction. *Journal of Abnormal Psychology, 88,* 101–105.

Feldman-Summers, S., & Kiesler, J. (1974). Those who are number two try harder: The effects of sex on attributions of causality. *Journal of Personality and Social Psychology, 30,* 846–855.

Feldstein, J. H. (1976). Sex differences in social memory among preschool children. *Sex Roles, 2,* 75–79.

Feldstein, J. H., & Feldstein, S. (1982). Sex differences on televised toy commercials. *Sex Roles, 8,* 581–587.

Fengler, A. P. (1975). Attitudinal orientations of wives toward their husbands' retirement. *International Journal of Aging and Human Development, 6,* 139–152.

Fennema, E., & Sherman, J. (1977). Sex-related differences in mathematics achievement, spatial visualization and affective factors. *American Educational Research Journal, 14,* 51–71.

Ferree, M. M. (1980). Working class feminism: A consideration of the consequences of employment. *The Sociological Quarterly, 21,* 173–184.

Feshbach, S., & Malamuth, N. (1978, November). Sex and aggression: Proving the link. *Psychology Today, 12,* (6), 11–117.

Fidell, L. S. (1970). Empirical verification of sex discrimination in hiring practices in psychology. *American Psychologist, 25,* 1094–1098.

Fidell, L. S. (1973, April). *Put her down on drugs: Prescribed drug usage in women.* Paper presented at the Western Psychological Association Meeting, Anaheim, Calif.

Fidell, L. S. (1981). Sex differences in psychotropic drug use. *Professional Psychology, 12,* 156–162.

Fidell, L. S. (1982). Gender and drug use and abuse. In I. Al-Issa (Ed.), *Gender and psychopathology* (pp. 221–236). New York: Academic.

Field, T. M., & Widmayer, S. M. (1982). Motherhood. In B. B. Wolman (Ed.), *Handbook of developmental psychology* (pp. 681–701). Englewood Cliffs, N.J.: Prentice-Hall.

Fields, M. O. (1978). Wife beating: Facts and figures. *Victimology, 2,* 643–647.

Finucci, J. M., & Childs, B. (1981). Are there really more dyslexic boys than girls? In A. Ansara, N. Geschwind, A. Galaburda, M. Albert, & N. Gartrell (Eds.), *Sex differences in dyslexia* (pp. 1–9). Towson, Md.: Orton Dyslexia Society.

Fischer, J. L., & Narus, L. R. (1981). Sex-role development in late adolescence and adulthood. *Sex Roles, 7,* 97–106.

Fisher, W. A. (1983). Gender, gender-role identification, and response to erotica. In E. R. Allgeier & N. B. McCormick (Eds.), *Changing boundaries* (pp. 245–284). Palo Alto, Calif.: Mayfield.

Fisher, W. A., & Byrne, D. (1978). Sex differences in responses to erotica? Love versus lust. *Journal of Personality and Social Psychology, 36,* 117–125.

Fitzpatrick, M. L. (1977). Nursing. *Signs, 2,* 818–834.

Fodor, I. G. (1982). Gender and phobia. In I. Al-Issa (Ed.), *Gender and psychopathology* (pp. 179–197). New York: Academic.

Fodor, I. G., & Thal, J. (1984). Weight disorders: Overweight and anorexia. In E. A. Blechman (Ed.), *Behavior modification with women* (pp. 373–398). New York: Guilford.

Foreit, K. G., Agor, T., Byers, J., Larue, J., Lokey, H., Palazzini, M., Patterson, M., & Smith, L. (1980). Sex bias in the newspaper treatment of male-centered and female-centered news stories. *Sex Roles, 6,* 475–480.

Forisha, B. L. (1978). *Sex roles and personal awareness.* Morristown, N.J.: General Learning Press.

Fox, G. L. (1977). Sex-role attitudes as predictors of contraceptive use among unmarried university students. *Sex Roles, 3,* 265–283.

Fox, G. L. (Ed.) (1982). *The childbearing decision.* Beverly Hills, Calif.: Sage.

Fox, G. L., & Inazu, J. K. (1980). Mother-daughter communication about sex. *Family Relations, 29,* 347–352.

Fox, J. H. (1977). Effects of retirement and former work life on women's adaptation in old age. *Journal of Gerontology, 32,* 196–202.

Fox, L. H. (1980). Conclusions: What do we know and where should we go? In L. H. Fox, L. Brody, & D. Tobin (Eds.), *Women and the mathematical mystique* (pp. 195–208). Baltimore, Md.: Johns Hopkins University Press.

Fox, L. H., Tobin, D., & Brody, L. (1979). Sex-role socialization and achievement in mathematics. In M. A. Wittig & A. C. Petersen (Eds.), *Sex-related differences in cognitive functioning* (pp. 303–332). New York: Academic.

Fraiberg, S. (1977). *Every child's birthright.* New York: Basic Books.

Frances, S. J. (1979). Sex differences in nonverbal behavior. *Sex Roles, 5,* 519–535.

Frank, A. (1972). *The diary of a young girl.* New York: Pocket Books.

Frank, E., Anderson, A., & Rubenstein, D. (1978). Frequency of sexual dysfunction in "normal" couples. *New England Journal of Medicine, 299,* 111–115.

Frank, E., & Stewart, B. D. (1984). Physical aggression: Treating the victims. In E. A. Blechman (Ed.), *Behavior modification with women* (pp. 245–272). New York: Guilford.

Frasher, J. M., Frasher, R. S., Wims, F. B. (1982). Sex-role stereotyping in school superintendents' personnel decisions. *Sex Roles, 8,* 261–268.

Freedman, J. (1978). *Happy people.* New York: Harcourt Brace Jovanovich.

Freud, S. (1965). *New introductory lectures on psychoanalysis.* New York: Norton. (Original work published in 1933)

Friday, N. (1977). *My mother/my self.* New York: Dell.

Friederich, M. A. (1982). Aging, menopause and estrogens: The clinician's dilemma. In A. M. Voda, M. Dinnerstein, & S. R. O'Donnell (Eds.), *Changing perspectives on menopause* (pp. 335–345). Austin, Tex.: University of Texas Press.

Friederich, M. A. (1983). Dysmenorrhea. In S. Golub (Ed.), *Lifting the curse of menstruation* (pp. 91–106). New York: Haworth.

Friedman, E. A. (1978). The physiological aspects of pregnancy. In M. T. Notman & C. C. Nadelson (Eds.), *The woman patient. Vol. I: Sexual and reproductive aspects of women's health care* (pp. 55–71). New York: Plenum.

Friedman, L. J. (1977). *Sex role stereotyping in the mass media: An annotated bibliography.* New York: Garland.

Frieze, I. (1979). Perceptions of battered wives. In I. Frieze, D. Bar-Tal, & J. Carrol (Eds.), *New approaches to social problems* (pp. 79–108). San Francisco: Jossey-Bass.

Frieze, I. (1983). Investigating the causes and consequences of marital rape. *Signs, 8,* 532–553.

Frieze, I., & Ramsey, S. J. (1976). Nonverbal maintenance of sex roles. *Journal of Social Issues, 32,* 133–142.

Frieze, I., Whitley, B. E., Jr., Hanusa, B. H., & McHugh, M. C. (1982). Assessing the theoretical models for sex differences in causal attributions for success and failure. *Sex Roles, 8,* 333–343.

Frodi, A., Macaulay, J., & Thome, P. R. (1977). Are women always less aggressive than men? A review of the experimental literature. *Psychological Bulletin, 84,* 634–660.

Frueh, T., & McGhee, P. E. (1975). Traditional sex role development and amount of time spent watching television. *Developmental Psychology, 11,* 109.

Fuchs, F. (1982). Dysmenorrhea and dyspareunia. In R. C. Friedman (Ed.), *Behavior and the menstrual cycle* (pp. 199–216). New York: Marcel Dekker.

Fyans, L. J., Jr. (Ed.) (1980). *Achievement motivation: Recent trends in theory and research.* New York: Plenum.

Gambrill, E. D., & Richey, C. A. (1980). Assertion training for women. In C. L. Heckerman (Ed.), *The evolving female* (pp. 222–267). New York: Human Sciences.

Game, A., & Pringle, R. (1983). *Gender at work.* North Sydney, Australia: George Allen & Unwin.

Gannon, L. (1982). The role of power in psychotherapy. *Women & Therapy, 1,* 3–11

Gansberg, J. M., & Mostel, A. P. (1984). *The second nine months.* New York: Tribeca.

Ganson, H. C. (1975). *Cohabitation: The antecedents of dissolution of formerly cohabiting individuals.* Unpublished master's thesis, Ohio State University.

Garai, J. E., & Scheinfeld, A. (1968). Sex differences in mental and behavioral traits. *Genetic Psychology Monographs, 77,* 169–199.

Garfinkel, P. E., & Garner, D. M. (1982). *Anorexia nervosa.* New York: Brunner/Mazel.

Garland, H., Hale, K. F., & Burnson, M. (1982). Attributions for the success and failure of female managers: A replication and extension. *Psychology of Women Quarterly, 7,* 155–162.

Geis, B. D., & Gerrard, M. (1984). Predicting male and female contraceptive behavior: A discriminant analysis of groups high, moderate, and low in contraceptive effectiveness. *Journal of Personality and Social Psychology, 46,* 669–680.

Gelles, R. J. (1979). *Family violence.* Beverly Hills, Calif.: Sage.

Gentemann, K. M. (1984). Wife beating: Attitudes of non-clinical population. *Victimology, 9,* 109–120.

Gerdes, E. P., & Garber, D. M. (1983). Sex bias in hiring: Effects of job demands and applicant competence. *Sex Roles, 9,* 307–319.

Gerrard, M., McCann, L., & Geis, B. D. (1984). Antecedents and prevention of unwanted pregnancy. In A. U. Rickel, M. Gerrard, & I. Iscoe (Eds.), *Social and psychological problems of women: Prevention and crisis intervention.* Washington, D.C.: Hemisphere.

Gerson, M. (1980). The lure of motherhood. *Psychology of Women Quarterly, 5,* 207–218.

Gerson, M. (1984). Feminism and the wish for a child. *Sex Roles, 11,* 389–399.

Gerson, M., Alpert, J. L., & Richardson, M. S. (1984). Mothering: The view from psychological research. *Signs, 9,* 434–453.

Gettys, L. D., & Cann, A. (1981). Children's perceptions of occupational sex stereotypes. *Sex Roles, 7,* 301–308.

Giele, J. Z. (1982a). Women in adulthood: Unanswered questions. In J. Z. Giele (Ed.), *Women in the middle years: Current knowledge and directions for research and policy* (pp. 1–35). New York: Wiley.

Giele, J. Z. (Ed.). (1982b). *Women in the middle years: Current knowledge and directions for research and policy.* New York: Wiley.

Giesen, C. B., & Datan, N. (1980). The competent older woman. In N. Datan & N. Lohman (Eds.), *Transitions of aging* (pp. 57–72). New York: Academic.

Gigy, L. L. (1980). Self-concept of single women. *Psychology of Women Quarterly, 5,* 321–340.

Gilbert, L. A. (1980). Feminist therapy. In A. M. Brodsky & R. T. Hare-Mustin (Eds.), *Women and psychotherapy* (pp. 245–265). New York: Guilford.

Gilbert, L. A. (1981). Toward mental health: The benefits of psychological androgyny. *Professional Psychology, 12,* 29–38.

Gilbert, L. A., Deutsch, C. J., & Strahan, R. F. (1978). Feminine and masculine dimensions of the typical, desirable, and ideal woman and man. *Sex Roles, 4,* 767–778.

Giles-Sims, J. (1983). *Wife battering: A systems theory approach.* New York: Guilford Press.

Gilkes, C. T. (1982). Successful rebellious professionals: The black woman's professional identity and community commitment. *Psychology of Women Quarterly, 6,* 289–311.

Gilligan, C. (1982). *In a different voice.* Cambridge, Mass.: Harvard University Press.

Gitelson, I., Petersen, A., & Tobin-Richards, M. (1982). Adolescents' expectancies of success, self-evaluation, and attributions about performance on spatial and verbal tasks. *Sex Roles, 8,* 411–419.

Glazer, N. Y. (1984). Paid and unpaid work: Contradictions in American women's lives today. In K. Borman, D. Quarm, & S. Gideonse (Eds.), *Women in the workplace: Effects on families* (pp. 169–186). Norwood, N.J.: Ablex.

Glenn, N. D. (1975). Psychological well-being in the postparental stage. *Journal of Marriage and the Family, 37,* 105–110.

Glenn, N. D., & McLanahan, S. (1981). The effects of offspring on the psychological well-being of older adults. *Journal of Marriage and the Family, 43,* 409–422.

Glenwick, D. S., Johansson, S. L., & Bondy, J. (1978). A comparison of the self-images of female and male assistant professors. *Sex Roles, 4,* 513–524.

Goffman, E. (1979). *Gender advertisements.* Cambridge, Mass.: Harvard University Press.

Gold, A. R., & Adams, D. B. (1981). Motivational factors affecting fluctuation of female sexual activity at menstruation. *Psychology of Women Quarterly, 5,* 670–680.

Gold, A. R., Brush, L. R., & Sprotzer, E. R. (1980). Developmental changes in self-perceptions of intelligence and self-confidence. *Psychology of Women Quarterly, 5,* 231–239.

Gold, D., & Andres, D. (1978a). Relations between maternal employment and development of nursery school children. *Canadian Journal of Behavioral Science, 10,* 116–129.

Gold, D., & Andres, D. (1978b). Developmental comparisons between adolescent children with employed and nonemployed mothers. *Merrill-Palmer Quarterly, 24,* 243–254.

Goldberg, D. C., Whipple, B., Fishkin, R. E., Waxman, H., Fink, P. J., & Weisberg, M. (1983). The Grafenberg spot and female ejaculation: A review of initial hypotheses. *Journal of Sex and Marital Therapy, 9,* 27–37.

Goldberg, P. A. (1968). Are women prejudiced against women? *Transaction, 5,* 28–30.

Goldberg, S., & Lewis, M. (1969). Play behavior in the year-old infant: Early sex differences. *Child Development, 40,* 21–31.

Goldberg, W. G., & Tomlanovich, M. C. (1984). Domestic violence victims in the emergency department. *Journal of the American Medical Association, 251,* 3259–3264.

Goldstein, A. G., & Chance, J. E. (1965). Effects of practice on sex-related differences in performance on embedded figures. *Psychonomic Science, 3,* 361–362.

Gollin, A. E. (1980). Comments on Johnson's "On the prevalence of rape in the United

States." *Sex Roles, 6*, 346–349.

Golub, S. (1976a). The magnitude of premenstrual anxiety and depression. *Psychosomatic Medicine, 38*, 4–14.

Golub, S. (1976b). The effect of premenstrual anxiety and depression on cognitive function. *Journal of Personality and Social Psychology, 34*, 99–104.

Golub, S. (1983). Menarche: The beginning of menstrual life. In S. Golub (Ed.), *Lifting the curse of menstruation* (pp. 17–36). New York: Haworth.

Golub, S., & Harrington, D. M. (1981). Premenstrual and menstrual mood changes in adolescent women. *Journal of Personality and Social Psychology, 4*, 961–965.

Gomberg, E. S. (1979). Problems with alcohol and other drugs. In E. S. Gomberg & V. Franks (Eds.), *Gender and disordered behavior* (pp. 204–240). New York: Brunner/Mazel.

Gomberg, E. S. (1982). Historical and political perspective: Women and drug use. *Journal of Social Issues, 38*, 9–23.

Gomberg, E. S., & Lisansky, J. M. (1984). Antecedents of alcohol problems in women. In S. C. Wilsnack & L. J. Beckman (Eds.), *Alcohol problems in women* (pp. 233–259). New York: Guilford.

Good, T. L., Sikes, J. N., & Brophy, J. E. (1973). Effects of teacher sex and student sex on classroom interaction. *Journal of Educational Psychology, 65*, 74–87.

Goodman, M. J. (1980). Toward a biology of menopause. *Signs, 5*, 739–753.

Goodman, M. J. (1982). A critique of menopause research. In A. M. Voda, M. Dinnerstein, & S. R. O'Donnell (Eds.), *Changing perspectives on menopause* (pp. 273–288). Austin, Tex.: University of Texas Press.

Gove, W. R. (1979). Sex, marital status, psychiatric treatment: A research note. *Social Forces*, 89–93.

Gove, W. R. (1980). Mental illness and psychiatric treatment among women. *Psychology of Women Quarterly, 4*, 345–362.

Gove, W. R., & Tudor, J. F. (1973). Adult sex roles and mental illness. *American Journal of Sociology, 78*, 812–835.

Grady, K. E. (1981). Sex bias in research design. *Psychology of Women Quarterly, 5*, 628–636.

Gray-Little, B., & Burks, N. (1983). Power and satisfaction in marriage: A review and critique. *Psychological Bulletin, 93*, 513–538.

Green, J. (1982). Recent trends in the treatment of premenstrual syndrome: A critical review. In R. C. Friedman (Ed.), *Behavior and the menstrual cycle* (pp. 367–395). New York: Marcel Dekker.

Green, S. K., Buchanan, D. R., & Heuer, S. K. (1984). Winners, losers, and choosers: A field investigation of dating initiation. *Personality and Social Psychology Bulletin, 10*, 502–511.

Greenglass, E. R., & Devins, R. (1982). Factors related to marriage and career plans in unmarried women. *Sex Roles, 8*, 57–71.

Griffin, S. (1979). *Rape: the power of consciousness.* San Francisco: Harper & Row.

Grimm, J. W. (1978). Women in female-dominated professions. In A. H. Stromberg & S. Harkess (Eds.), *Women working: Theories and facts in perspective* (pp. 293–315). Palo Alto, Calif.: Mayfield.

Gross, A. D. (1978). The relationship between sex differences and reading ability in an Israeli kibbutz system. In D. Feitelson (Ed.), *Cross-cultural perspectives on reading and reading research* (pp. 72–88). Newark, Del.: International Reading Association.

Gross, M. M., & Geffner, R. A. (1980). Are the times changing? An analysis of sex-role prejudice. *Sex Roles, 6,* 713–722.

Grossman, F. K., Eichler, L. S., Winickoff, S. A. (1980). *Pregnancy, birth, and parenthood.* San Francisco: Jossey-Bass.

Groth, A. N., & Birnbaum, H. J. (1979). *Men who rape: The psychology of the offender.* New York: Plenum.

Gubrium, J. F. (1975). Being single in old age. *International Journal of Aging and Human Development, 6,* 29–40.

Gunnar, M. R., & Donahue, M. (1980). Sex differences in social responsiveness between six months and twelve months. *Child Development, 51,* 262–265.

Gutek, B. A., Nakamura, C. Y., Gahart, M., Handschumacher, I., & Russell, D. (1980). Sexuality and the workplace. *Basic and Applied Psychology, 1,* 225–265.

Guttentag, M., & Bray, H. (1976). *Undoing sex stereotypes: Research and resources for educators.* New York: McGraw-Hill.

Guttentag, M., & Bray, H. (1977). Teachers as mediators of sex-role standards. In A. G. Sargent (Ed.), *Beyond sex roles* (pp. 395–411). St. Paul, Minn.: West.

Haas, A. (1979). Male and female spoken language differences: Stereotypes and evidence. *Psychological Bulletin, 86,* 616–626.

Haas, L. (1982). Determinants of role-sharing behavior: A study of egalitarian couples. *Sex Roles, 8,* 747–760.

Haber, S. (1980). Cognitive support for the career choices of college women. *Sex Roles, 6,* 129–138.

Hafter, D. M. (1979). An overview of women's history. In M. Richmond-Abbott (Ed.), *The American woman* (pp. 1–27). New York: Holt, Rinehart and Winston.

Hahn, S. R., & Paige, K. E. (1980). American birth practices: A critical review. In J. E. Parsons (Ed.), *The psychobiology of sex differences and sex roles* (pp. 145–175). Washington, D.C.: Hemisphere.

Hailwood, E. (1984, December). Unspeakable practices, unnatural facts. *Toronto Life,* 54–59.

Hall, J. A. (1978). Gender effects in decoding nonverbal cues. *Psychological Bulletin, 85,* 845–857.

Hall, J. A. (1984). *Nonverbal sex differences: Communication accuracy and expressive style.* Baltimore: Johns Hopkins University Press.

Hall, J. L., & Frederickson, W. A. (1979). Sex-role stereotyping, a function of age and education, as measured by a perceptual-projective device. *Sex Roles, 5,* 77–84.

Hall, S. M., & Havassy, B. (1981). The obese women: Causes, correlates, and treatment. *Professional Psychology, 12,* 163–170.

Hamilton, D. L. (1979). A cognitive-attributional analysis of stereotyping. In L. Berkowitz (Ed.), *Advances in experimental social psychology, Vol. 12* (pp. 53–84). New York: Academic.

Hamilton, D. L. (1981a). Stereotyping and intergroup behavior: Some thoughts on the cognitive approach. In D. L. Hamilton (Ed.), *Cognitive processes in stereotyping and intergroup behavior* (pp. 333–353). Hillsdale, N.J.: Erlbaum.

Hamilton, D. L. (1981b). Illusory correlation as a basis for stereotyping. In D. L. Hamilton (Ed.), *Cognitive processes in stereotyping and intergroup behavior* (pp. 115–144). Hillsdale, N.J.: Erlbaum.

Hammen, C. L. (1982). Gender and depression. In I. Al-Issa (Ed.), *Gender and psychopathology* (pp. 133–152). New York: Academic.

Hammond, J. A., & Mahoney, C. W. (1983). Reward-cost balancing among women coal-miners. *Sex Roles, 9,* 17–29.

Hansen, R. D., & O'Leary, V. E. (1985). Sex-determined attributions. In V. E. O'Leary, R. K. Unger, & B. S. Walston (Eds.), *Women, gender, and social psychology* (pp. 67–99). Hillsdale, N.J.: Erlbaum.

Hare-Mustin, R. T., & Broderick, P. C. (1979). The myth of motherhood: A study of attitudes towards motherhood. *Psychology of Women Quarterly, 4,* 114–128.

Harmon, L., Birk, J., Fitzgerald, L., & Tanney, M. (Eds.). (1978). *Counseling women.* Monterey, Calif.: Brooks/Cole.

Harris, L. J. (1977). Sex differences in the growth and use of language. In E. Donelson & J. Gullahorn (Eds.), *Women: A psychological perspective* (pp. 79–94). New York: Wiley.

Harris, R., Linn, M. W., Good, R., & Hunter, K. (1981). Attitudes and perceptions of perinatal concepts during pregnancy in women from three cultures. *Journal of Clinical Psychology, 37,* 477–483.

Harrison, A. O. (1977). Black women. In V. E. O'Leary, *Toward understanding women* (pp. 131–146). Monterey, Calif.: Brooks/Cole.

Hartman, M. (1976). A descriptive study of the language of men and women born in Maine around 1900 as it reflects the Lakoff hypothesis in "Language and woman's place." In B. L. Dubois & I. Crouch (Eds.), *The sociology of the languages of American women* (pp. 81–90). San Antonio, Tex.: Trinity University Press.

Harway, M. (1980). Sex bias in educational-vocational counseling. *Psychology of Women Quarterly, 4,* 412–423.

Hass, A. (1979). *Teenage sexuality: A survey of teenage sexual behavior.* New York: Macmillan.

Haugh, S. S., Hoffman, C. D., Cowan, G. (1980). The eye of the very young beholder: Sex typing of infants by young children. *Child Development, 51,* 598–600.

Hayler, B. (1979). Abortion. *Signs, 5,* 307–323.

Hedrick, T. E., & Chance, J. E. (1977). Sex differences in assertive achievement patterns. *Sex Roles, 3,* 129–139.

Heide, W. S. (1984). Now, for the feminist menopause that refreshes. In G. Lesnoff-Caravaglia (Ed.), *The world of the older woman* (pp. 162–174). New York: Human Sciences.

Heilman, M. E., & Guzzo, R. A. (1978). The perceived cause of work success as a mediator of sex discrimination in organizations. *Organizational Behavior and Human Performance, 21,* 346–357.

Heiman, J. (1975). The physiology of erotica: Women's sexual arousal. *Psychology Today, 8,* 90–94.

Heiman, J., & Verhulst, J. (1982). Gender and sexual functioning. In I. Al-Issa (Ed.), *Gender and psychopathology* (pp. 305–320). New York: Academic.

Helsing, K. J., Szklo, M., & Comstock, G. W. (1981). Factors associated with mortality after widowhood. *American Journal of Public Health, 71,* 802–809.

Hendel, D. D. (1980). Experiential and affective correlates of math anxiety in adult women. *Psychology of Women Quarterly, 5,* 219–230.

Henley, N. M. (1973). Status and sex: Some touching observations. *Bulletin of the Psychonomic Society, 2,* 92–93.

Henley, N. M. (1977). *Body politics.* Englewood Cliffs: Prentice-Hall.

Henley, N. M. (1985). Psychology and gender. *Signs, 11,* 101–119.

Hennig, M., & Jardim, A. (1977). *The managerial woman.* New York: Pocket Books.

Henretta, J. C., & O'Rand, A. M. (1980). Labor-force participation of older married women. *Social Security Bulletin, 43,* 10–15.

Henshaw, S. K., Binkin, N. J., Blaine, E., & Smith, J. C. (1985). A portrait of American women who obtain abortions. *Family Planning Perspectives, 17*, 90–96.

Henshaw, S. K., & O'Reilly, K. (1983). Characteristics of abortion patients in the United States, 1979 and 1980. *Family Planning Perspectives, 15*, 5–15.

Herman, D. (1984). The rape culture. In J. Freeman (Ed.), *Women: A feminist perspective* (Third Edition, pp. 20–38). Palo Alto, Calif.: Mayfield.

Herman, J. (1981). *Father-daughter incest.* Cambridge, Mass.: Harvard University Press.

Herman, J., & Hirschman, L. (1981). Father-daughter incest. In S. Cox (Ed.), *Female psychology* (pp. 206–221). New York: St. Martin's.

Herman, J. B., & Gyllstrom, K. K. (1977). Working men and women: Inter- and intra-role conflict. *Psychology of Women Quarterly, 1*, 319–333.

Herzog, D. B. (1985). Pharmacotherapy of anorexia nervosa and bulimia. *Pediatric Annals, 13*, 915–923.

Hess, B., & Waring, J. (1978). Parent and child in later life: Rethinking the relationship. In R. M. Lerner & A. B. Spanier (Eds.), *Child influences on marital and family interaction* (pp. 241–268). New York: Academic.

Hess, B., & Waring J. (1983). Family relationships of older women: A women's issue. In E. W. Markson (Ed.), *Older women: Issues and prospects* (pp. 227–251). Lexington, Mass.: Lexington Books.

Hewes, G. (1957). The anthropology of posture. *Scientific American, 196*(2), 123–132.

Hilberman, E. (1978). The impact of rape. In M. T. Notman & C. C. Nadelson (Eds.), *The woman patient, Vol. 1* (pp. 303–322). New York: Plenum.

Hill, C. T., & Stull, D. E. (1981). Sex differences in effects of social and value similarity in same-sex friendship. *Journal of Personality and Social Psychology, 41*, 488–502.

Hill, J. (1982). Smoking, alcohol, and body mass relationships to early menopause: Implications for risk of cardiovascular disease. In A. M. Voda, M. Dinnerstein, & S. R. O'Donnell (Eds.), *Changing perspectives on menopause* (pp. 160–169). Austin, Tex.: University of Texas Press.

Hill, S. Y. (1984). Vulnerability to the biomedical consequences of alcoholism and alcohol-related problems among women. In S. C. Wilsnack & L. J. Beckman (Eds.), *Alcohol problems in women* (pp. 121–154). New York: Guilford.

Hines, M. (1982). Prenatal gonadal hormones and sex differences in human behavior. *Psychological Bulletin, 92*, 56–80.

Hirsch, M. D. (1981). *Women and violence.* New York: Van Nostrand Reinhold.

Hite, S. (1976). *The Hite report.* New York: Dell.

Hobbs, D., Jr., & Wimbash, J. (1977). Transition to parenthood by black couples. *Journal of Marriage and the Family, 39*, 677–689.

Hochschild, A. R. (1975). *Attending to, codifying and managing feelings: Sex differences in love.* Paper presented at the meeting of the American Sociological Association, San Francisco.

Hochschild, A. R. (1979). Emotion work, feeling rules, and social structure. *American Journal of Sociology, 85*, 551–575.

Hoffman, L. W. (1972). Early childhood experience and women's achievement motives. *The Journal of Social Issues, 28*, 129–156.

Hoffman, L. W. (1974a). Psychological factors. In L. W. Hoffman & F. I. Nye (Eds.), *Working mothers* (pp. 32–62). San Francisco: Jossey-Bass.

Hoffman, L. W. (1974b). Effects of maternal employment on the child—A review of the research. *Developmental Psychology, 10*, 204–228.

Hoffman, L. W. (1979). Maternal employment: 1979. *American Psychologist, 34*, 859–865.

Hoffman, L. W., & Manis, J. D. (1978). Influences of children on marital interaction and parental satisfaction and dissatisfaction. In R. M. Lerner & G. B. Spanier (Eds.), *Child influences on marital and family interaction* (pp. 165–213). New York: Academic.

Hoffnung, M. (1984). Motherhood: Contemporary conflict for women. In J. Freeman (Ed.), *Women: A feminist perspective* (Third Edition, pp. 124–138). Palo Alto: Mayfield.

Hogan, H. W. (1978). IQ self-estimates of males and females. *Journal of Social Psychology, 106*, 137–138.

Hogan, R. A., Fox, A. N., & Kirchner, J. H. (1977). Attitudes, opinions, and sexual development of 205 homosexual women. *Journal of Homosexuality, 3*, 123–136.

Holahan, C. K. (1981). Lifetime achievement patterns, retirement and life satisfaction of gifted aged women. *Journal of Gerontology, 36*, 741–749.

Holmes, T. H., & Rahe, R. H. (1967). The social readjustment rating scale. *Journal of Psychosomatic Research, 11*, 213–218.

Holroyd, J. C., & Brodsky, A. M. (1977). Psychologists' attitudes and practices regarding erotic and nonerotic physical contact with patients. *American Psychologist, 32*, 843–849.

Holstrom, L. L. (1972). *The two-career family.* Boston: Schenkman.

Holt, L. H., & Weber, M. (1982). *The American Medical Association book of womancare.* New York: Random House.

Holt, Rinehart and Winston. (1976). *The treatment of sex roles and minorities.* New York: Author.

Hopke, W. E. (1981). *The encyclopedia of careers and vocational guidance* (2 volumes). Chicago: J. G. Ferguson.

Hopkins, E. (1984, June 18). Modern bride. *New York Magazine, 17*, 54–67.

Hopkins, J., Marcus, M., & Campbell, S. B. (1984). Postpartum depression: A critical review. *Psychological Bulletin, 95*, 498–515.

Horgan, D. (1983). The pregnant woman's place and where to find it. *Sex Roles, 9*, 333–339.

Horner, M. S. (1968). *Sex differences in achievement motivation and performance in competitive and non-competitive situations.* Unpublished doctoral dissertation, University of Michigan.

Horner, M. S. (1972). Toward an understanding of achievement-related conflicts in women. *Journal of Social Issues, 28*, 157–175.

Horner, M. S. (1978). The measurement and behavioral implications of fear of success in women. In J. W. Atkinson & J. O. Raynor (Eds.), *Personality, motivation, and achievement* (pp. 41–70). Washington, D.C.: Hemisphere.

Horos, C. V. (1974). *Rape.* New Canaan, Conn.: Tobey.

Horwitz, A. V. (1982). Sex-role expectations, power, and psychological distress. *Sex Roles, 8*, 607–623.

House, W. C. (1974). Actual and perceived differences in male and female expectancies and minimal goal levels as a function of competition. *Journal of Personality, 42*, 493–509.

House, W. C., & Perney, V. (1974). Valence of expected and unexpected outcomes as a function of locus of goal and type of expectancy. *Journal of Personality and Social Psychology, 29*, 454–463.

Houser, B. B., Beckman, S. L., & Beckman, L. J. (1984). The relative rewards and costs of childlessness for older women. *Psychology of Women Quarterly, 8*, 395–398.

Hunter College Women's Studies Collective. (1983). *Women's realities, women's choices.* New York: Oxford University Press.

Hurst, M., & Zambrana, R. E. (1981). *Determinants and consequences of maternal employment: An annotated bibliography 1968–1980.* Washington, D.C.: Business and Professional Women's Foundation.

Huston, A. C. (1983). Sex-typing. In E. M. Hetherington (Ed.), *Carmichael's manual of child psychology* (Fourth Edition). New York: Wiley.

Hutt, C. (1978). Biological bases of psychological sex differences. *American Journal of Diseases of Children, 132*, 170–177.

Hyde, J. S. (1981). How large are cognitive gender differences? A meta-analysis using ω^2 and d. *American Psychologist, 36*, 892–901.

Hyde, J. S. (Ed). (1986). *The psychology of gender: Advances through the meta-analysis.* Baltimore: Johns Hopkins.

Hyde, J. S., & Phillis, D. E. (1970). Androgyny across the lifespan. *Developmental Psychology, 15*, 334–336.

Iglitzin, L. B. (1972). The child's eye view of sex roles. *Today's Education, 61*, 23–25.

Images (1984, December 31). *Time*, pp. 24–47.

Instone, D., Major, B., & Bunker, B. B. (1983). Gender, self confidence, and social influence strategies: An organizational simulation. *Journal of Personality and Social Psychology, 44*, 322–333.

Intons-Peterson, M. J., & Reddel, M. (1984). What do people ask about a neonate? *Developmental Psychology, 20*, 358–359.

Ireson, C. J. (1984). Adolescent pregnancy and sex roles. *Sex Roles, 11*, 189–201.

Jacklin, C. N. (1983). Methodological issues in the study of sex-related differences. In B. L. Richardson & J. Wirtenberg (Eds.), *Sex role research* (pp. 93–100). New York: Praeger.

Jacklin, C. N., DiPietro, J. A., & Maccoby, E. E. (1984). Sex-typing behavior and sex-typing pressure in child/parent interaction. *Archives of Sexual Behavior, 13*, 413–425.

Jacklin, C. N., & Maccoby, E. E. (1983). Issues of gender differentiation. In M. D. Levine, W. B. Carey, A. C. Crocker, & R. T. Gross (Eds.), *Developmental-behavioral pediatrics* (pp. 175–184). Philadelphia: W. B. Saunders.

Jacklin, C. N., Maccoby, E. E., & Dick, A. E. (1973). Barrier behavior and toy preference: Sex differences (and their absence) in the year-old child. *Child Development, 44*, 196–200.

Jacobs, R. H. (1979). *Life after youth.* Boston: Beacon Press.

Jakubowski, P. A. (1977a). Assertive behavior and clinical problems of women. In E. I. Rawlings & D. K. Carter (Eds.), *Psychotherapy for women* (pp. 147–167). Springfield, Ill.: Charles C. Thomas.

Jakubowski, P. A. (1977b). Self-assertion training procedures for women. In E. I. Rawlings & D. K. Carter (Eds.), *Psychotherapy for women* (pp. 168–190). Springfield, Ill.: Charles C. Thomas.

Janoff-Bulman, R. (1979). Characterological versus behavioral self-blame: Inquiries into depression and rape. *Journal of Personality and Social Psychology, 37*, 1798–1809.

Jay, T. B. (1980). Sex roles and dirty word usage: A review of the literature and a reply to Haas. *Psychological Bulletin, 88*, 614–621.

Jeffords, C. R. (1984). The impact of sex-role and religious attitudes upon forced marital intercourse norms. *Sex Roles, 11*, 543–552.

Jelliffe, D. B., & Jelliffe, E. F. P. (1977). Current concepts in nutrition. Breast is best: Modern meanings. *New England Journal of Medicine, 297*, 912–915.

Jennings, J., Geis, L., & Brown, V. (1980). Influence of television commercials on women's self-confidence and independent judgments. *Journal of Personality and Social Psychology, 38*, 203–210.

Jensen, I., & Gutek, B. (1982). Attributions and assignment of responsibility for sexual harassment. *Journal of Social Issues, 38*, 121–136.

Johnson, A. G. (1980). On the prevalence of rape in the United States. *Signs, 6*, 136–146.

Johnson, C. K., & Price-Bonham, S. (1980). Women and retirement: A study and implications. *Family Relations, 29*, 380–385.

Johnson, C. L., & Johnson , F. A. (1977). Attitudes toward parenting in dual-career families. *American Journal of Psychiatry, 134*, 391–395.

Johnson, D. D. (1973–1974). Sex differences in reading across cultures. *Reading Research Quarterly, 9*, 67–86.

Johnson, E. S. (1983). Suburban older women. In E. W. Markson (Ed.), *Older women: Issues and prospects* (pp. 179–193). Lexington, Mass.: Lexington Books.

Johnson, M. (1976). An approach to feminist therapy. *Psychotherapy: Theory, Research and Practice, 13*, 72–76.

Johnson, M. M., Stockard, J., Rothbart, M. K., & Friedman, L. (1981). Sexual preference, feminism, and women's perceptions of their parents. *Sex Roles, 7*, 1–18.

Johnson, P. (1976). Women and power: Toward a theory of effectiveness. *Journal of Social Issues, 32*, 99–110.

Johnson, P. (1982). Sex differences, women's roles and alcohol use: Preliminary national data. *Journal of Social Issues, 38*, 93–116.

Jones, B. E., Gray, B. A., & Parson, E. B. (1981). Manic-depressive illness among poor urban Blacks. *American Journal of Psychiatry, 138*, 654–657.

Jordan, B. (1983). *Birth in four cultures.* Montreal: Eden Press.

Jordan, H., & Glynn, A. (1984, Summer). Sexual harassment in the military. *Militarism Resource Project News, 1*, 3–10.

June, L. N., & Fooks, G. M. (1980). Key influencers on the career directions and choices of black university professionals. *Journal of Non-White Concerns in Personnel & Guidance, 8*, 157–166.

Kahn, S. E., & Richardson, A. (1983). Evaluation of a course in sex roles for secondary school students. *Sex Roles, 9*, 431–440.

Kahn-Hut, R., Daniels, A. K., & Colvard, R. (1982). *Women and work.* New York: Oxford University Press.

Kaltreider, N. B., & Margolis, A. G. (1977). Childless by choice: A clinical study. *American Journal of Psychiatry, 134*, 179–182.

Kanin, E. J., & Parcell, S. (1981). Sexual aggression: A second look at the offended female. In L. H. Bowker (Ed.), *Women and crime in America* (pp. 223–233). New York: Macmillan.

Kannel, W. B., & Brand, F. N. (1983). Cardiovascular risk factors in the elderly woman. In E. W. Markson (Ed.), *Older women* (pp. 315–327). Lexington, Mass.: Lexington.

Kanter, R. M. (1977). *Men and women of the corporation.* New York: Basic Books.

Kanter, R. M., & Stein, B. A. (1980). *A tale of "O": On being different in an organization.* New York: Harper & Row.

Kaplan, A. G., & Yasinski, L. (1980). Psychodynamic perspectives. In A. M. Brodsky & R. T. Hare-Mustin (Eds.), *Women and psychotherapy* (pp. 191–215). New York: Guilford.

Kardener, S. M., Fuller, M., & Mensh, I. N. (1973). A survey of physicians' attitudes and practices regarding erotic and nonerotic contact with patients. *American Journal of Psychiatry, 130*, 1077–1081.

Karkau, K. (1973). *Sexism in the fourth grade.* Pittsburgh, Pa.: Know, Inc.

Katz, J., & Cronin, D. M. (1983). Sexuality and college life. In O. Pocs (Ed.), *Human sexuality 83/84* (pp. 25–30). Guilford, Conn.: Dushkin.

Katz, P. A. (1979). The development of female identity. In C. B. Kopp & M. Kirkpatrick (Eds.), *Becoming female: Perspectives on development* (pp. 3–28). New York: Plenum.

Katz, S., & Mazur, M. A. (1979). *Understanding the rape victim.* New York: Wiley.

Kaufman, D. R. (1978). Associational ties in academe: Some male and female differences. *Sex Roles, 4,* 9–21.

Kaufman, D. R., & Richardson, B. L. (1982). *Achievement and women: Challenging the assumptions.* New York: The Free Press.

Keiffer, M. G., & Cullen, D. M. (1974). Women who discriminate against other women: The process of denial. *International Journal of Group Tensions, 4,* 21–33.

Kelley, H. H., Cunningham, J. D., Grisham, J. A., Lefebvre, L. M., Sink, C. R., & Yablon, G. (1978). Sex differrences in comments made during conflict within close heterosexual pairs. *Sex Roles, 4,* 473–392.

Kelly, J. A., Kern, J. M., Kirkley, B. G., Patterson, J. N., & Keane, T. M. (1980). Reactions to assertive versus unassertive behavior: Differential effects for males and females and implications for assertiveness training. *Behavior Therapy, 11,* 670–682.

Kelly, J. B. (1982). Divorce: The adult perspective. In B. B. Wolman (Ed.), *Handbook of developmental psychology* (pp. 734–750). Englewood Cliffs, N.J.: Prentice-Hall.

Kemper, S. (1984). When to speak like a lady. *Sex Roles, 10,* 435–444.

Kennell, J. H., & Klaus, M. H. (1984). Mother-infant bonding: Weighing the evidence. *Developmental Review, 4,* 275–282.

Kerzner, L. J. (1983). Physical changes after menopause. In E. W. Markson (Ed.), *Older women* (pp. 299–313). Lexington, Mass.: Lexington.

Kesler, M. S., Denney, N. W., & Whitely, S. E. (1976). Factors influencing problem solving in middle-aged and elderly adults. *Human Development, 19,* 310–320.

Key, M. R. (1975). *Male/female language.* Metuchen, N.J.: Scarecrow Press.

Kilmann, P. R., & Mills, K. H. (1983). *All about sex therapy.* New York: Plenum.

Kilpatrick, D. G., Resick, P., & Veronen, L. (1981). Effects of a rape experience: A longitudinal study. *The Journal of Social Issues, 37,* 105–122.

Kimball, M. M. (1981). Women and science: Critique of biological theories. *International Journal of Women's Studies, 4,* 318–338.

Kimball, M. M., & Gray, V. A. (1982). Feedback and performance expectancies in an academic setting. *Sex Roles, 8,* 999–1007.

Kitzinger, S. (1983). *Woman's experience of sex.* New York: Putnam.

Klaus, M. H., Jerauld, R., Kreger, N. C., et al. (1972). Maternal attachment: Importance of the first post-partum days. *New England Journal of Medicine, 286,* 460–463.

Klaus, M. H., & Kennell, J. H. (1982). Labor, birth, and bonding. In M. H. Klaus & J. H. Kennell (Eds.), *Parent-infant bonding.* St. Louis, Mo.: C. V. Mosby.

Klein, F. (1978). *The bisexual option: A concept of one hundred percent intimacy.* New York: Arbor House.

Kleinke, C. L. (1981). *Opening lines.* Paper presented at the meeting of the Western Psychological Association, Los Angeles, Calif.

Knaub, P. K., Eversoll, D. B., & Voss, J. H. (1983). Is parenthood a desirable adult role? An assessment of attitudes held by contemporary women. *Sex Roles, 9,* 355–362.

Koeske, R. (1980). Theoretical perspectives on menstrual cycle research: The relevance of attributional approaches for the perception and explanation of premenstrual emotionality. In A. J. Dan, E. A. Graham, & C. P. Beecher (Eds.), *The menstrual cycle, Vol. 1* (pp. 8–25). New York: Springer.

Koeske, R. (1983). Lifting the curse of menstruation: Toward a feminist perspective on the menstrual cycle. In S. Golub (Ed.), *Lifting the curse of menstruation* (pp. 1–16). New York: Haworth.

Koeske, R., & Koeske, G. F. (1975). An attributional approach to moods and the menstrual cycle. *Journal of Personality and Social Psychology, 31,* 473–478.

Koff, E. (1983). Through the looking glass of menarche: What the adolescent girl sees. In S. Golub (Ed.), *Menarche* (pp. 77–86). Lexington, Mass.: Lexington Books.

Kogan, N. (1974). Creativity and sex differences. *Journal of Creative Behavior, 8,* 1–14.

Kogan, N. (1979). A study of age categorization. *Journal of Gerontology, 34,* 358–367.

Kohlberg, L. (1966). A cognitive-developmental analysis of children's sex-role concepts and attitudes. In E. E. Maccoby (Ed.), *The development of sex differences* (pp. 82–173). Stanford, Calif.: Stanford University Press.

Kohlberg, L., & Ullian, D. Z. (1974). Stages in the development of psychosexual concepts and attitudes. In R. C. Friedman, R. M. Richart, & R. L. Van de Wiele (Eds.), *Sex differences in behavior* (pp. 209–222). New York: Wiley.

Konopka, G. (1976). *Young girls: A portrait of adolescence.* Englewood Cliffs, N.J.: Prentice-Hall.

Korner, A. F. (1969). Neonatal startles, smiles, erection and reflex sucks as related to state, sex, and individuality. *Child Development, 40,* 1039–1053.

Korsch, B. M. (1983). More on parent-infant bonding. *Journal of Pediatrics, 103,* 249–250.

Koss, M. P., & Oros, C. J. (1982). Sexual experiences survey: A research instrument investigating sexual aggression and victimization. *Journal of Consulting and Clinical Psychology, 50,* 455–457.

Kotkin, M. (1983). Sex roles among married and unmarried couples. *Sex Roles, 9,* 975–985.

Krail, K. A., & Leventhal, G. (1976). The sex variable in the intrusion of personal space. *Sociometry, 39,* 170–173.

Kramarae, C. (1981). *Women and men speaking.* Rowley, Mass.: Newbury House.

Krause, N. (1984). Employment outside the home and women's psychological well-being. *Social Psychiatry, 19,* 41–48.

Kravetz, D. (1980). Consciousness-raising and self-help. In A. M. Brodsky & R. T. Hare-Mustin (Eds.), *Women and psychotherapy* (pp. 267–283). New York: Guilford.

Kravetz, D., Marecek, J., & Finn, S. E. (1983). Factors influencing women's participation in consciousness-raising groups. *Psychology of Women Quarterly, 7,* 257–271.

Kriedberg, G., Butcher, A. L., & White, K. (1978). Vocational role choice in second- and sixth-grade children. *Sex Roles, 4,* 175–181.

Kutner, N. G., & Levinson, R. M. (1978). The toy salesperson: A voice for change in sex-role stereotypes? *Sex Roles, 4,* 1–7.

LaFrance, M., & Carmen, B. (1980). The nonverbal display of psychological androgyny. *Journal of Personality and Social Psychology, 38,* 36–49.

LaFrance, M., & Mayo, C. (1978). *Moving bodies: Nonverbal communication in social relationships.* Monterey, Calif.: Brooks/Cole.

Lakoff, R. (1973). Language and woman's place. *Language in Society, 2,* 45–80.

La Leche League International (1981). *The womanly art of breastfeeding.* Franklin Park, Ill.: Author.

Lamb, M. E. (1982). Early contact and maternal-infant bonding: One decade later. *Pediatrics, 70,* 763–768.

Lane, S. I. (1981, Winter). Speak up, speak out, say no. *Southern Exposure,* 114–119.

Laner, M. R. (1978). Media mating II: "Personals" advertisements of lesbian women. *Journal of Homosexuality, 4,* 41–61.

Lang, A. M., & Brody, E. M. (1983). Characteristics of middle-aged daughters and help to their elderly mothers. *Journal of Marriage and the Family, 45,* 193–202.

Langlois, J. H., & Downs, A. C. (1980). Mothers, fathers, and peers as socialization agents of sex-typed play behaviors in young children. *Child Development, 51,* 1217–1247.

Language in the News (1984, Winter). *Women and Language, 8,* 29–32.

Lanier, H. B., & Byrne, J. (1981). How high school students view women: The relationship between perceived attractiveness, occupation, and education. *Sex Roles, 7,* 145–148.

L'Armand, K., & Pepitone, A. (1982). Judgments of rape: A study of victim-rapist relationship and victim sexual history. *Personality and Social Psychology Bulletin, 8,* 134–139.

Larwood, L., & Gutek, B. A. (1984). Women at work in the USA. In M. J. Davidson & C. L. Cooper (Eds.), *Women at work* (pp. 237–267). Chichester, England: Wiley.

Latané, B., & Dabbs, J. M., Jr. (1975). Sex, group size and helping in three cities. *Sociometry, 38,* 180–194.

LaTorre, R. A., & Wendenburg, K. (1983). Psychological characteristics of bisexual, heterosexual and homosexual women. *Journal of Homosexuality, 9,* 87–97.

Lavine, L. O. (1982). Parental power as a potential influence on girls' career choice. *Child Development, 53,* 658–663.

Lawrence, R. A. (1980). *Breast-feeding.* St. Louis, Mo.: Mosby.

Laws, J. L. (1975). The psychology of tokenism: An analysis. *Sex Roles, 1,* 51–67.

Laws, S. (1983). The sexual politics of pre-menstrual tension. *Women's Studies International Forum, 6,* 19–31.

Lee, A. G., & Scheurer, V. L. (1983). Psychological androgyny and aspects of self-image in women and men. *Sex Roles, 9,* 289–306.

Leiblum, S. R., & Pervin, L. A. (Eds.). (1980). *Principles and practice of sex therapy.* New York: Guilford.

Leiblum, S. R., Pervin, L. A., & Campbell, E. H. (1980). The treatment of vaginismus: Success and failure. In S. R. Leiblum & L. A. Pervin (Eds.), *Principles and practice of sex therapy* (pp. 167–192). New York: Guilford.

Leifer, M. (1980). *Psychological effects of motherhood.* New York: Praeger.

Leland, J. (1982). Gender, drinking and alcohol abuse. In I. Al-Issa (Ed.), *Gender and psychopathology* (pp. 201–220). New York: Academic.

Leland, J. (1984). Alcohol use and abuse in ethnic minority women. In S. C. Wilsnack & L. J. Beckman (Eds.), *Alcohol problems in women* (pp. 66–96). New York: Guilford.

Lemkau, J. P. (1979). Personality and background characteristics of women in male-dominated occupations: A review. *Psychology of Women Quarterly, 4,* 221–240.

Lemkau, J. P. (1980). Women and employment: Some emotional hazards. In C. L. Heckerman (Ed.), *The evolving female: Women in psychosocial context.* New York: Human Sciences.

Lennane, K. J., & Lennane, R. J. (1973). Alleged psychogenic disorders in women—a possible manifestation of sexual prejudice. *The New England Journal of Medicine, 288,* 288–292.

Lenney, E. (1977). Women's self-confidence in achievement settings. *Psychological Bulletin, 84,* 1–13.

Lenney, E. (1979). Androgyny: Some audacious assertions toward its coming of age. *Sex Roles, 5,* 703–719.

Lenney, E. (1981). What's fine for the gander isn't always good for the goose: Sex differences in self-confidence as a function of ability area and comparison with others. *Sex Roles, 7,* 905–924.

Leo, J. (1984a, April 9). The revolution is over. *Time, 123,* 74–83.

Leo, J. (1984b, April 23). "Some day, I'll cry my eyes out." *Time, 123,* 72–73.

Lerner, P. M., Orlos, J. B., & Knapp, J. R. (1976). Physical attractiveness, physical effectiveness and self-concept in late adolescents. *Adolescence, 11,* 314–326.

Leserman, J. (1980). Sex differences in the professional orientation of first-year medical students. *Sex Roles, 6,* 645–660.

Lesnoff-Caravaglia, G. (1984). Double stigmata: Female and old. In G. Lesnoff-Caravaglia (Ed.), *The world of the older woman* (pp. 11–20). New York: Human Sciences.

Lessard, S. (1976). Aborting a fetus: The legal right, the personal choice. In A. G. Kaplan & J. P. Bean (Eds.), *Beyond sex-role stereotypes* (pp. 144–152). Boston: Little, Brown.

Levenson, H., Burford, B., Bonno, B., & Davis, L. (1975). Are women still prejudiced against women? A replication and extension of Goldberg's study. *Journal of Psychology, 89,* 67–71.

Lever, J. (1976). Sex differences in the games children play. *Social Problems, 23,* 478–487.

Lever, J., & Brush, M. G. (1981). *Premenstrual tension.* New York: McGraw Hill.

Levin, J., & Arluke, A. (1985). An exploratory analysis of sex differences in gossip. *Sex Roles, 12,* 281–285.

Levine, A., & Crumrine, J. (1975). Women and the fear of success: A problem in replication. *American Journal of Sociology, 80,* 964–974.

Levinson, D. J. (1978). *The seasons of a man's life.* New York: Knopf.

Levinson, R. M. (1981). Images of males and females in children's media during the seventies, or Kidvid and Kiddie Lit revisited. *Studies in Popular Culture, 4,* 82–89.

Levinson, R. M. (1982). Sex discrimination and employment practices: An experiment with unconventional job inquiries. In R. Kahn-Hut, A. K. Daniels, & R. Colvard (Eds.), *Women and work* (pp. 54–64). New York: Oxford University Press.

Levitin, T., & Chananie, J. D. (1972). Responses of female primary school teachers to sex-typed behaviors in male and female children. *Child Development, 43,* 1309–1316.

Levitin, T., Quinn, R. P., & Staines, G. L. (1971). Sex discrimination against the American working woman. *American Behavioral Scientist, 15,* 237–254.

Levy, J. (1972). *Lateral specialization of the human brain: Behavioral manifestations and possible evolutionary basis.* Corvallis: Oregon State University Press.

Levy, S. M. (1980–1981). The adjustment of the older woman: Effects of chronic ill health and attitudes toward retirement. *International Journal of Aging and Human Development, 12,* 93–110.

Levy, S. M. (1981). The aging woman: Developmental issues and mental health needs. *Professional Psychology, 12,* 92–102.

Lewinsohn, P. M., Biglan, A., & Zeiss, A. M. (1976). Behavioral treatment of depression. In P. O. Davidson (Ed.), *The behavioral management of anxiety, depression and pain.* New York: Brunner/Mazel.

Lewis, E. (1983). The group treatment of battered women. *Women & Therapy, 2,* 51–58.

Lewis, H. R., & Lewis, M. E. (1983). All about the clitoris. In O. Pocs (Ed.), *Human sexuality 83/84* (pp. 52–54). Guilford, Conn.: Dushkin.

Lewis, M. (1972). Parents and children: Sex-role development. *School Review, 80,* 229–240.

Liang, J. (1982). Sex differences in life satisfaction among the elderly. *Journal of Gerontology, 37,* 100–108.

Linkie, D. M. (1982). The physiology of the menstrual cycle. In R. C. Friedman (Ed.), *Behavior and the menstrual cycle* (pp. 1–21). New York: Marcel Dekker.

Linn, L. (1971). Physician characteristics and attitudes toward legitimate use of psychotherapeutic drugs. *Journal of Health and Social Behavior, 12,* 132–140.

Lipman-Blumen, J., Handley-Isaksen, A., & Leavitt, H. J. (1983). Achieving styles in men and women: A model, an instrument, and some findings. In J. T. Spence (Ed.), *Achievement and achievement motives* (pp. 151–204). San Francisco: W. H. Freeman.

Lipman-Blumen, J., Leavitt, H. J., Patterson, K. J., Bies, R. J., & Handley-Isaksen, A. (1980). A model of direct and relational achieving styles. In L. J. Fyans, Jr. (Ed.), *Achievement motivation: Recent trends in theory and research* (pp. 135–168). New York: Plenum.

Liss, L. (1975). Why academic women do not revolt: Implications for affirmative action. *Sex Roles, 1*, 209–223.

Liss, M. B. (1981). Patterns of toy play: An analysis of sex differences. *Sex Roles, 7*, 1143–1150.

Liss, M. B. (Ed.). (1983). *Social and cognitive skills: Sex roles and children's play*. New York: Academic.

Liss-Levinson, N., et al. (1981). *Women and psychotherapy: A consumer handbook*. Washington, D.C.: Federation of Organizations for Professional Women.

Little Miss Muffet fights back. (1974). New York: Feminists on Children's Media.

Livingston, J. A. (1982). Responses to sexual harassment on the job: Legal, organizational, and individual actions. *Journal of Social Issues, 38*, 5–22.

Lockheed, M. E., & Hall, K. P. (1976). Conceptualizing sex as a status characteristic and applications to leadership training strategies. *Journal of Social Issues, 32*, 111–124.

Lohr, J. M., & Nix, J. (1982). Relationship of assertiveness and the short form of the Bem Sex-Role Inventory: A replication. *Psychological Reports, 50*, 114.

Loewenstein, S. F., Bloch, N. E., Campion, J., Epstein, J. S., Gale, P., & Salvatore, M. (1981). A study of satisfactions and stresses of single women in midlife. *Sex Roles, 7*, 1127–1141.

Lopata, H. Z. (1971). *Occupation housewife*. New York: Oxford University Press.

Lopata, H. Z. (1979). *Women as widows: Support systems*. New York: Elsevier.

Lopata, H. Z. (1981). Widowhood and husband sanctification. *Journal of Marriage and the Family, 43*, 439–450.

Lopata, H. Z., & Norr, K. F. (1980). Changing commitments of American women to work and family roles. *Social Security Bulletin, 43*, 3–14.

LoPiccolo, L. (1980). Low sexual desire. In S. R. Leiblum & L. A. Pervin (Eds.), *Principles and practice of sex therapy* (pp. 29–64). New York: Guilford.

Lott, B. (1978). Behavioral concordance with sex role ideology related to play areas, creativity and parental sex typing of children. *Journal of Personality and Social Psychology, 36*, 1087–1100.

Lott, B. (1981). A feminist critique of androgyny: Toward the elimination of gender attributions for learned behavior. In C. Mayo & N. M. Henley (Eds.), *Gender and nonverbal behavior* (pp. 171–180). New York: Springer-Verlag.

Lott, B., Reilly, M. E., & Howard, D. R. (1982). Sexual assault and harassment: A campus community case study. *Signs, 8*, 296–319.

Luker, K. (1984). *Abortion and the politics of motherhood*. Berkeley, Calif.: University of California.

Lull, J., Mulac, A., & Rosen, S. L. (1983). Feminism as a predictor of mass media use. *Sex Roles, 9*, 165–177.

Lynn, M., & Shurgot, B. A. (1984). Responses to lonely hearts advertisements: Effects of reported physical attractiveness, physique, and coloration. *Personality and Social Psychology Bulletin, 10*, 349–357.

Macaulay, J. (1985). Adding gender to aggression research: Incremental or revolutionary change? In V. E. O'Leary, R. K. Unger, & B. S. Wallson (Eds.), *Women, gender, and social psychology* (pp. 191–224). Hillsdale, N.J.: Erlbaum.

Maccoby, E. E. (1972). The meaning of being female. *Contemporary Psychology, 17*, 369–372.

Maccoby, E. E., & Jacklin, C. N. (1974). *The psychology of sex differences*. Stanford: Stanford University Press.

Maccoby, E. E., & Jacklin, C. N. (1980). Sex differences in aggression: A rejoinder and reprise. *Child Development, 51,* 964–980.

MacDonald, C. T. (1980). An experiment in mathematics education at the college level. In L. H. Fox, L. Brody, & D. Tobin (Eds.), *Women and the mathematical mystique* (pp. 115–137). Baltimore, Md.: Johns Hopkins University Press.

MacKinnon, C. A. (1979). *Sexual harassment of working women*. New Haven: Yale University Press.

Macklin, E. D. (1978). Review of research on nonmarital cohabitation in the United States. In B. I. Murstein (Ed.), *Exploring intimate life styles* (pp. 197–243). New York: Springer-Verlag.

Maddux, H. C. (1975). *Menstruation.* New Canaan, Conn.: Tobey.

Magnus, E. M. (1980). Sources of maternal stress in the postpartum period: A review of the literature and an alternative view. In J. E. Parsons (Ed.), *The psychobiology of sex differences and sex roles* (pp. 177–208). Washington, D.C.: Hemisphere.

Malamuth, N. M., & Donnerstein, E. (1984). Pornography and sexual aggression. New York: Academic.

Manahan, N. (1982). Homophobia in the classroom. In M. Cruikshank (Ed.), *Lesbian studies* (pp. 66–69). Old Westbury, N.Y.: The Feminist Press.

Mancini, J. A., & Orthner, D. K. (1978). Recreational sexuality preferences among middle-class husbands and wives. *Journal of Sex Research, 14,* 96–106.

Mandelbaum, D. R. (1978). Women in medicine. *Signs, 4,* 136–145.

Mannion, K. (1981). Psychology and the lesbian: A critical review of the research. In S. Cox (Ed.), *Female psychology* (pp. 256–274). New York: St. Martin's.

Manstead, A. S. R., Proffitt, C., & Smart, J. L. (1983). Predicting and understanding mothers' infant-feeding intentions and behavior: Testing the theory of reasoned action. *Journal of Personality and Social Psychology, 44,* 657–671.

Marecek, J. (1978). Psychological disorders in women: Indices of role strain. In I. H. Frieze, J. Parsons, P. Johnson, D. Ruble, & G. Zellman (Eds.), *Women and sex roles: A social psychological perspective* (pp. 255–276). New York: Norton.

Marecek, J., & Johnson, M. (1980). Gender and the process of therapy. In A. M. Brodsky & R. T. Hare-Mustin (Eds.), *Women and psychotherapy* (pp. 67–93). New York: Guilford.

Marecek, J., & Kravetz, D. (1977). Women and mental health: A review of feminist change efforts. *Psychiatry, 40,* 323–329.

Marecek, J., Kravetz, D., & Finn, S. (1979). A comparison of women who enter feminist therapy and women who enter traditional therapy. *Journal of Consulting and Clinical Psychology, 47,* 734–742.

Marini, M. M. (1978). Sex differences in the determination of adolescent aspirations: A review of the research. *Sex Roles, 4,* 723–753.

Markson, E. W. (Ed.). (1983a). *Older women: Issues and prospects.* Lexington, Mass.: Lexington Books.

Markson, E. W. (1983b). Epilogue. In E. W. Markson (Ed.), *Older women: Issues and prospects* (pp. 329–331). Lexington, Mass.: Lexington Books.

Markson, E. W., & Hess, B. B. (1980). Older women in the city. *Signs, 5,* S127–S141.

Markus, H., Crane, M., Bernstein, S., & Siladi, M. (1982). Self-schemas and gender. *Journal of Personality and Social Psychology,* 38–50.

Marrett, C. B., & Gates, H. (1983). Male-female enrollment across mathematics tracks in predominantly black high schools. *Journal for Research in Mathematics Education, 14*, 113–118.

Marsh, J. C. (1982). Public issues and private problems: Women and drug use. *Journal of Social Issues, 38*, 153–165.

Marshall, V. W., Rosenthal, C. J., & Synge, J. (1983). Concerns about parental health. In E. W. Markson (Ed.), *Older women: Issues and prospects* (pp. 253–273). Lexington, Mass.: Lexington Books.

Marten, L. A., & Matlin, M. W. (1976). Does sexism in elementary readers still exist? *The Reading Teacher, 29*, 764–767.

Martin, C. A., Warfield, M. C., & Braen, G. R. (1983). Physician's management of the psychological aspects of rape. *Journal of the American Medical Association, 249*, 501–503.

Martin, D. (1976). *Battered wives.* New York: Pocket Books.

Martinez, G. A., & Dodd, D. A. (1983). 1981 milk feeding patterns in the United States during the first 12 months of life. *Pediatrics, 71*, 166–170.

Martinko, M. J., & Gardner, W. L. (1983). A methodological review of sex-related access discrimination problems. *Sex Roles, 9*, 825–839.

Martyna, W. (1980). Beyond the "He/Man" approach: The case for nonsexist language. *Signs, 5*, 482–493.

Masson, J. M. (1984). *The assault on truth: Freud's suppression of the seduction theory.* New York: Farrar, Straus, & Giroux.

Masters, W. H., & Johnson, V. E. (1966). *Human sexual response.* Boston: Little Brown.

Masters, W. H., & Johnson, V. E. (1970). *Human sexual inadequacy.* Boston: Little, Brown.

Matlin, M. W. (1979). *Human experimental psychology.* Monterey, Calif.: Brooks/Cole.

Matlin, M. W. (1983a). *Cognition.* New York: Holt, Rinehart and Winston.

Matlin, M. W. (1983b). *Perception.* Boston: Allyn and Bacon.

Matlin, M. W. (1983c). *Attitudes toward masculine-generic and gender-neutral language.* Paper presented at the meeting of Eastern Psychological Association, Philadelphia.

Matlin, M. W. (1985). Current issues in psycholinguistics. In T. M. Shlechter & M. P. Toglia (Eds.), *New directions in cognitive science* (pp. 217–241). Norwood, N.J.: Ablex.

Mattison, A. (1979). *Animals.* Cambridge, Mass.: Alice James Books.

May, R. R. (1976). Mood shifts and the menstrual cycle. *Journal of Psychosomatic Research, 20*, 125–130.

McArthur, L. Z., & Eisen, S. V. (1976). Achievements of male and female storybook characters as determinants of achievement behavior by boys and girls. *Journal of Personality and Social Psychology, 33*, 467–473.

McClelland, D. C., Atkinson, J. W., Clark, R. A., & Lowell, F. L. (1953). *The achievement motive.* New York: Appleton-Century-Crofts.

McCombie, S. L. (1980). *The rape crisis intervention handbook.* New York: Plenum.

McConnell-Ginet, S. (1978). Intonation in a woman's world. *Signs, 3*, 541–559.

McConnell-Ginet, S., Borker, R., & Furmer, N. (Eds.). (1980). *Women and language in literature and society.* New York: Praeger.

McCormick, N. B., & Jesser, C. J. (1983). The courtship game: Power in the sexual encounter. In E. R. Allgeier & N. B. McCormick (Eds.), *Changing boundaries* (pp. 64–86). Palo Alto, Calif.: Mayfield.

McCrady, B. S. (1984). Women and alcoholism. In E. A. Blechman (Ed.), *Behavior modification with women* (pp. 428–449). New York: Guilford.

McCray, C. A. (1980). The black woman and family roles. In L. Rodgers-Rose (Ed.), *The black woman* (pp. 67–78). Beverly Hills, Calif.: Sage.

McFalls, J. A. (1983). Where have all the children gone? The future of reproduction in the

United States. In O. Pocs (Ed.), *Human sexuality 83/84* (pp. 86–88). Guilford, Conn.: Dushkin.

McGhee, P. E., & Frueh, T. (1980). Television viewing and the learning of sex-role stereotypes. *Sex Roles, 6,* 179–188.

McHugh, M. C., Koeske, R. D., & Frieze, I. H. (1981). *Guidelines for nonsexist research.* Washington, D.C.: American Psychological Association.

McKenna, W., & Kessler, S. J. (1977). Experimental design as a source of sex bias in social psychology. *Sex Roles, 3,* 117–128.

McMillan, J. R., Clifon, A. K., McGrath, D., & Gale, W. S. (1977). Women's language: Uncertainty or interpersonal sensitivity and emotionality? *Sex Roles, 3,* 545–560.

McNett, I., Taylor, L., & Scott, L. (1985). Minority women: Doubly disadvantaged. In A. G. Sargent (Ed.), *Beyond sex roles* (Second Edition, pp. 226–232). St. Paul, Minn.: West.

McPherson, K. S., & Spetrino, S. K. (1983). Androgyny and sex typing: Differences in beliefs. *Sex Roles, 9,* 441–451.

Mead, M. (1980). A proposal: We need taboos on sex at work. In D. A. Neugarten & J. M. Shafritz (Eds.), *Sexuality in organizations* (pp. 53–56). Oak Park, Ill.: Moore Publishing.

Mednick, M. T. S. (1978). Psychology of women: Research issues and trends. *New York Academy of Sciences Annals, 309,* 77–92.

Meece, J. L., Parsons, J. E., Kaczala, C. M., Goff, S. B., & Futterman, R. (1982). Sex differences in math achievement: Toward a model of academic choice. *Psychological Bulletin, 91,* 324–348.

Mehrabian, A. (1968). Relationship of attitude to seated posture, orientation, and distance. *Journal of Personality and Social Psychology, 10,* 26–30.

Mester, R. (1978). Induced abortion and psychotherapy. *Psychotherapy and Psychosomatics, 30,* 98–104.

Meyer, B. (1980). The development of girls' sex-role attitudes. *Child Development, 51,* 508–514.

Meyer-Bahlburg, H. F. L. (1980). Homosexual orientation in women and men: A hormonal basis? In J. E. Parsons (Ed.), *The psychobiology of sex differences and sex roles* (pp. 105–130). Washington, D.C.: Hemisphere.

Meyerowitz, B. E. (1981). The impact of mastectomy on the lives of women. *Professional Psychology, 12,* 119–127.

Miles, C. (1935). Sex in social psychology. In C. Murchinson (Ed.), *Handbook of social psychology* (pp. 699–704). Worcester, Mass.: Clark University Press.

Miller, J., & Garrison, H. H. (1982). Sex roles: The division of labor at home and in the workplace. *Annual Review of Sociology, 8,* 237–262.

Miller, J. A., Jacobsen, R. B., & Bigner, J. J. (1982). The child's home environment for lesbian versus heterosexual mothers: A neglected area of research. *Journal of Homosexuality, 7,* 49–56.

Milow, V. J. (1983). Menstrual education: Past, present, and future. In S. Golub (Ed.), *Menarche* (pp. 127–132). Lexington, Mass.: Lexington Books.

Mirandé, A., & Enríquez, E. (1979). *La Chicana: The Mexican-American woman.* Chicago: University of Chicago.

Mischel, H. N. (1974). Sex bias in the evaluation of professional achievements. *Journal of Educational Psychology, 66,* 157–166.

Mischel, W. (1966). A social-learning view of sex differences in behavior. In E. Maccoby (Ed.), *The development of sex differences* (pp. 56–81). Stanford, Calif.: Stanford University Press.

Mischel, W. (1968). *Personality and assessment.* New York: Wiley.

Monahan, L., Kuhn, D., & Shaver, P. (1974). Intrapsychic versus cultural explanations of the "fear of success" motive. *Journal of Personality and Social Psychology, 29,* 60–64.

Money, J., & Ehrhardt, A. A. (1972). *Man and woman: Boy and girl.* Baltimore and London: John Hopkins University Press.

Money, J., & Tucker, P. (1975). *Sexual signatures: On being a man or a woman.* Boston and Toronto: Little, Brown.

Moore, D. (1979). *Battered women.* Beverly Hills, Calif.: Sage.

Moore, E. C. (1977). Fertility regulation: Friend or foe of the female? In J. Money & H. Musaph (Eds.), *Handbook of sexology* (Vol. 3). New York: Elsevier.

Moore, K. A., & Sawhill, I. V. (1978). Implications of women's employment for home and family life. In A. H. Stromberg & S. Harkess (Eds.), *Women working: Theories and facts in perspective* (pp. 201–225). Palo Alto, Calif.: Mayfield.

Moore, M. (1978). Discrimination or favoritism? Sex bias in book reviews. *American Psychologist, 33,* 936–938.

Moore, T. W. (1975). Exclusive early mothering and its alternatives. *Scandinavian Journal of Psychology, 16,* 256–272.

Morgan, C. S., & Walker, A. J. (1983). Predicting sex role attitudes. *Social Psychology Quarterly, 46,* 148–151.

Morgan, M. (1973). *The total woman.* Old Tappan, N.J.: Spire Books.

Morgan, W. G. (1974). The relationship between expressed social fears and assertiveness and its treatment implications. *Behavior Research & Therapy, 12,* 255–257.

Morin, S. F. (1977). Heterosexual bias in psychological research on lesbianism and male homosexuality. *American Psychologist, 32,* 629–637.

Mortimer, J. T., & Sorenson, G. (1984). Men, women, work, and family. In K. M. Borman, D. Quarm, & S. Gideonse (Eds.), *Women in the workplace: Effects on families* (pp. 139–167). Norwood, N.J.: Ablex.

Moss, H. A. (1967). Sex, age, and state as determinants of mother-infant interaction. *Merrill-Palmer Quarterly, 13,* 19–36.

Moss, H. A. (1974). Early sex differences and mother-infant interaction. In R. C. Friedman, R. M. Richart, & R. L. Vande Wiele (Eds.), *Sex differences in behavior* (pp. 149–163). New York: Wiley.

Moss, H. A., & Robson, K. S. (1968). Maternal influences in early social visual behavior. *Child Development, 39,* 401–408.

Motowidlo, S. J. (1982). Sex role orientation and behavior in a work setting. *Journal of Personality and Social Psychology, 42,* 935–945.

Moulton, J. (1977). The myth of the neutral "man." In M. Vetterling-Braggin, F. A. Elliston, & J. English (Eds.), *Feminism and philosophy* (pp. 124–137). Totowa, N.J.: Littlefield, Adams.

Moulton, J., Robinson, G. M., & Elias, C. (1978). Sex bias in language use: "Neutral" pronouns that aren't. *American Psychologist, 33,* 1032–1036.

Moyer, K. E. (1976). *The psychobiology of aggression.* New York: Harper & Row.

Moynihan, D. P. (1965). *The Negro family: The case for national action.* Washington, D.C.: U.S. Department of Labor, Office of Policy Planning and Research.

Murray, S. R. (1981). Who is that person? Images and roles of black women. In S. Cox (Ed.), *Female psychology: The emerging self* (pp. 113–123). New York: St. Martin's.

Murray, S. R., & Scott, P. B. (1982). Introduction [to a special issue on black women]. *Psychology of Women Quarterly, 6,* 259.

Murstein, B. I. (Ed.). (1978). *Exploring intimate life styles.* New York: Springer-Verlag.

Myers, B. J. (1984). Mother-infant bonding: The status of this critical period hypothesis. *Developmental Review, 4*, 283–288.

Myers, T., & Gilbert, S. (1983). Wifebeaters' group through a women's center: Why and how. *Victimology, 8*, 238–248.

Nadelson, C. C. (1978a). An overview of problems in sexual functioning. In M. T. Notman & C. C. Nadelson (Eds.), *The woman patient: Vol. 1. Sexual and reproductive aspects of women's health care* (pp. 281–292). New York: Plenum.

Nadelson, C. C. (1978b). "Normal" and "special" aspects of pregnancy: A psychological approach. In M. T. Notman & C. C. Nadelson (Eds.), *The woman patient: Vol. 1. Sexual and reproductive aspects of women's health care* (pp. 73–86). New York: Plenum.

Nadelson, C. C., Polonsky, D. C., & Mathews, M. A. (1982). Marriage and midlife: The impact of social change. In C. C. Nadelson & M. T. Notman (Eds.), *The woman patient: Vol. 2. Concepts of femininity and the life cycle* (pp. 145–158). New York: Plenum.

Nash, S. C. (1975). The relationship among sex-role stereotyping, sex-role preference, and sex differences in spatial visualization. *Sex Roles, 1*, 15–32.

Nash, S. C. (1979). Sex role as a mediator of intellectual functioning. In M. A. Wittig & A. C. Petersen (Eds.), *Sex-related differences in cognitive functioning* (pp. 263–302). New York: Academic.

Nathanson, C. A. (1980). Social roles and health status among women: The significance of employment. *Social Science and Medicine, 14A*, 463–471.

National Center for Education Statistics. (1981). *Digest of education statistics 1981* (DOE Publication No. NCES 81–400). Washington, D.C.: U.S. Government Printing Office.

National Commission on Working Women. (1979). *National Survey on working women.* Washington, D.C.: Author.

Nelson, K. (1973). Structure and strategy in learning to talk. *Monographs of the Society for Research in Child Development, 38* (Serial No. 149).

Neugarten, B. L. (Ed.). (1968). *Middle age and aging.* Chicago: University of Chicago Press.

Neugarten, B. L. (1973). A new look at menopause. In C. Tavris (Ed.), *The female experience.* Del Mar, Calif.: Communications/Research/Machines.

Neugarten, B. L., & Brown-Rezanka, L. (1978). Midlife women in the 1980's. In Select Committee on Aging (Ed.), *Women in midlife—Security and fulfillment* (Part I, pp. 23–38). Washington, D.C.: U.S. Government Printing Office.

Neugarten, B. L., & Gutmann, D. L. (1964). Age-sex roles and personality in middle age: A thematic apperception study. In B. L. Neugarten, et al. (Eds.), *Personality in middle and later life: Empirical studies* (pp. 44–89). New York: Atherton.

Neugarten, B. L., & Weinstein, K. (1964). The changing American grandparent. *Journal of Marriage and the Family, 26*, 197–205.

Newcombe, N., Bandura, M. M., & Taylor, D. G. (1983). Sex differences in spatial ability and spatial activity. *Sex Roles, 9*, 377–386.

Newland, K. (1980). Women, men and the division of labor. *Worldwatch paper 37.* Washington, D.C.: Worldwatch Institute.

Newman, B. M. (1976). The study of interpersonal behavior in adolescence. *Adolescence, 11*, 127–142.

Newson, J., & Newson, E. (1968). *Four years old in an urban community.* Harmondsworth, England: Pelican Books.

NiCarthy, G. (1982). *Getting free: A handbook for women in abusive relationships.* Seattle, Wash.: The Seal Press.

Nicholls, J. G. (1975). Causal attribution and other achievement-related cognitions: Effects of task outcome, attainment value, and sex. *Journal of Personality and Social Psychology, 31*, 379–389.

Nichols, M. (1982). The treatment of inhibited sexual desire (ISD) in lesbian couples. *Women & Therapy, 1*, 49–66.

Nieva, V. F., & Gutek, B. A. (1980). Sex effects on evaluation. *Academy of Management Review, 5*, 267–276.

Nieva, V. F., & Gutek, B. A. (1981). *Women and work: A psychological perspective.* New York: Praeger.

Nilsen, A. P., Bosmajian, H., Gershuny, H. L., & Stanley, J. P. (1977). *Sexism and language.* Urbana, Ill.: National Council of Teachers of English.

"No comment." (1982, June/July). *National NOW Times*, p. 5.

Norman, W. H., Johnson, B. A., & Miller, I. W., III. (1984). Depression: A behavioral-cognitive approach. In E. A. Blechman (Ed.), *Behavior modification with women* (pp. 275–307). New York: Guilford.

Norwood, J. L. (1982). *The female-male earnings gap: A review of employment and earnings issues* (Report 673). U.S. Department of Labor.

Notman, M. T. (1978). A psychological consideration of mastectomy. In M. T. Notman & C. C. Nadelson (Eds.), *The woman patient: Vol. 1. Sexual and reproductive aspects of women's health care* (pp. 247–255). New York: Plenum.

Notman, M. T., & Nadelson, C. (1982). Changing views of the relationship between femininity and reproduction. In C. C. Nadelson & M. T. Notman (Eds.), *The woman patient* (Vol. 2, pp. 31–42). New York: Plenum.

Nyquist, L., Slivken, K., Spence, J. T., & Helmreich, R. L. (1985). Household responsibilities in middle-class couples: The contribution of demographic and personality variables. *Sex Roles, 12*, 15–34.

Oakley, A. (1974). *Woman's work: The housewife, past and present.* New York: Vintage.

O'Barr, W. M., & Atkins, B. K. (1980). "Women's language" or "powerless language"? In S. McConnell-Ginet, R. Borker, & N. Furman (Eds.), *Women and language in literature and society* (pp. 93–110). New York: Praeger.

Oberston, H. K., & Sukoneck, H. (1976). Psychological adjustment and life style of single lesbians and single heterosexual women. *Psychology of Women Quarterly, 1*, 172–188.

O'Bryant, S. L., & Brophy, J. E. (1976). Sex differences in altruistic behavior. *Developmental Psychology, 12*, 554.

O'Connell, A. N., & Russo, N. F. (Eds.). (1980). Eminent women in psychology: Models of achievement [Special issue]. *Psychology of Women Quarterly, 5*(1).

O'Connell, A. N., & Russo, N. F. (1983). *Models of achievement: Reflections of eminent women in psychology.* New York: Columbia University Press.

Offermann, L. R. (1986). Visibility and evaluation of female and male leaders. *Sex Roles, 14*, 533–543.

O'Hare, J., & Taylor, K. (1983). The reality of incest. *Women & Therapy, 2*, 215–229.

O'Keefe, E. S. C., & Hyde, J. S. (1983). The development of occupational sex-role stereotypes: The effects of gender stability and age. *Sex Roles, 9*, 481–492.

O'Leary, V. E., Unger, R. K., & Wallston, B. S. (Eds.). (1985). *Women, gender, and social psychology.* Hillsdale, N.J.: Erlbaum.

Olesen, V. L., & Katsuranis, F. (1978). Urban nomads: Women in temporary clerical services. In A. H. Stromberg & S. Harkess (Eds.), *Women working: Theories and facts in perspective* (pp. 316–338). Palo Alto, Calif.: Mayfield.

Olsen, N. J., & Willemsen, E. (1978). Studying sex prejudice in children. *The Journal of Genetic Psychology, 133,* 203–216.

On campus with women. (1978, March). *Project on the status and education of women.* Washington, D.C.: Association of American Colleges.

Orbach, S. (1978). *Fat is a feminist issue.* New York: Berkeley.

O'Reilly, J. (1983, September 5). Wife beating: The silent crime. *Time,* 23–24, 26.

Orenstein, H., Orenstein, E., & Carr, J. E. (1975). Assertiveness and anxiety: A correlational study. *Journal of Behavior Therapy & Experimental Psychiatry, 6,* 203–207.

Orlofsky, J. L. (1982). Psychological androgyny, sex-typing, and sex-role ideology as predictors of male-female interpersonal attraction. *Sex Roles, 8,* 1057–1073.

Padawer, W. J., & Goldfried, M. R. (1984). In E. A. Blechman (Ed.), *Behavior modification with women* (pp. 341–372). New York: Guilford.

Paige, K. E. (1971). Effects of oral contraceptives on affective fluctuations associated with the menstrual cycle. *Psychosomatic Medicine, 33,* 515–537.

Paige, K. E. (1978). Commentary. In J. A. Sherman & F. L. Denmark (Eds.), *The psychology of women: Future directions in research* (pp. 239–247). New York: Psychological Dimensions.

Paige, K. E., & Paige, J. M. (1981). *The politics of reproductive rituals.* Berkeley, Calif.: University of California Press.

Palmer, P. (1984). Housework and domestic labor: Racial and technological change. In K. B. Sacks & D. Remy (Eds.), *My troubles are going to have trouble with me: Everyday trials and triumphs of women workers* (pp. 80–91). New Brunswick, N.J.: Rutgers University Press.

Palmore, E., & Kivett, V. (1977). Changes in life satisfaction: A longitudinal study of persons aged 46–70. *Journal of Gerontology, 32,* 311–316.

Paludi, M. A. (1984). Psychometric properties and underlying assumptions of four objective measures of fear of success. *Sex Roles, 10,* 765–781.

Paludi, M. A. (1985). Personal communication.

Paludi, M. A., & Bauer, W. D. (1983). Goldberg revisited: What's in an author's name? *Sex Roles, 9,* 387–390.

Paludi, M. A., & Strayer, L. A. (1984). What's in an author's name? Differential evaluations of performance as a function of author's name. *Sex Roles, 12,* 353–361.

Pandey, J., & Griffitt, W. (1974). Attraction and helping. *Bulletin of the Psychonomic Society, 3,* 123–124.

Pape, R. E. (1982). Female sexuality and pregnancy. In M. Kirkpatrick (Ed.), *Women's sexual experience* (pp. 185–197). New York: Plenum.

Parke, R., & O'Leary, S. (1976). Family interactions in the newborn period: Some findings, some observations, and some unresolved issues. In K. Riegel & J. Meacham (Eds.), *The developing individual in a changing world, II* (pp. 653–663). The Hague: Mouton & Co.

Parlee, M. B. (1973). The premenstrual syndrome. *Psychological Bulletin, 80,* 454–465.

Parlee, M. B. (1974). Stereotypic beliefs about menstruation: A methodological note on the Moos Menstrual Distress Questionnaire and some new data. *Psychosomatic Medicine, 36,* 229–240.

Parlee, M. B. (1978). Psychological aspects of menstruation, childbirth, and menopause. In J. A. Sherman & F. L. Denmark (Eds.), *The psychology of women: Future directions in research* (pp. 181–238). New York: Psychological Dimensions.

Parlee, M. B. (1981). Appropriate control groups in feminist research. *Psychology of Women Quarterly, 5,* 637–644.

Parlee, M. B. (1982). Changes in moods and activation levels during the menstrual cycle in experimentally naive subjects. *Psychology of Women Quarterly, 7,* 119–131.

Parlee, M. B. (1983). Menstrual rhythms in sensory processes: A review of fluctuations in vision, olfaction, audition, taste and touch. *Psychological Bulletin, 93,* 539–548.

Parsons, J. E., & Goff, S. B. (1980). Achievement motivation and values: An alternative perspective. In L. J. Fyans, Jr. (Ed.), *Achievement motivation: Recent trends in theory and research* (pp. 349–373). New York: Plenum.

Peplau, L. A. (1983). Roles and gender. In H. H. Kelley, E. Berscheid, A. Christensen, J. Harvey, & D. Peterson (Eds.), *Close relationships* (pp. 220–264). San Francisco: Freeman.

Peplau, L. A. (1985). Personal communication.

Peplau, L. A., & Amaro, H. (1982). Understanding lesbian relationships. In W. Paul, J. D. Weinrich, J. C. Gonsiorek, & M. E. Hotvedt (Eds.), *Homosexuality: Social, psychological, and biological issues* (pp. 233–247). Beverly Hills, Calif.: Sage.

Peplau, L. A., & Gordon, S. L. (1985). Women and men in love: Gender differences in close heterosexual relationships. In V. E. O'Leary, R. K. Unger, & B. S. Wallston (Eds.), *Women, gender, and social psychology* (pp. 257–291). Hillsdale, N J.: Erlbaum.

Peplau, L. A., Padesky, C., & Hamilton, M. (1982). Satisfaction in lesbian relationships. *Journal of Homosexuality, 8,* 23–35.

Peplau, L. A., Rubin, Z., & Hill, C. T. (1977). Sexual intimacy in dating relationships. *Journal of Social Issues, 33,* 86–109.

Perl, H., & Abarbanell, G. (1979). *Guidelines to feminist consciousness raising.* Los Angeles: Authors.

Perlmutter, E., & Bart, P. B. (1982). Changing views of "The change": A critical review and suggestions for an attributional approach. In A. M. Voda, M. Dinnerstein, & S. R. O'Donnell (Eds.), *Changing perspectives on menopause* (pp. 187–199). Austin, Tex.: University of Texas Press.

Perry, J., & Whipple, B. (1983). Can women ejaculate? Yes! In O. Pocs (Ed.), *Human sexuality 83/84* (pp. 64–66). Guilford, Conn.: Dushkin.

Personal Products. (1981). *Growing up and liking it.* Milltown, N.J.: Author.

Petersen, A. C. (1976). Physical androgyny and cognitive functioning. *Developmental Psychology, 12,* 524–533.

Petersen, A. C. (1980). Biopsychosocial processes in the development of sex-related differences. In J. E. Parsons (Ed.), *The psychobiology of sex differences and sex roles* (pp. 31–55). Washington, D.C.: Hemisphere.

Petersen, A. C. (1983). Menarche: Meaning of measures and measuring meaning. In S. Golub (Ed.), *Menarche* (pp. 63–76). Lexington, Mass.: Lexington Books.

Peterson, C. C., & Peterson, J. L. (1973). Preference for sex of offspring as a measure of change in sex attitudes. *Psychology, 10,* 3–5.

Pheterson, G. I., Kiesler, S. B., & Goldberg, P. A. (1971). Evaluation of the performance of women as a function of their sex, achievement, and personal history. *Journal of Personality and Social Psychology, 19,* 114–118.

Phillips, R. D., & Gilroy, F. D. (1985). Sex-role stereotypes and clinical judgments of mental health: The Brovermans' findings reexamined. *Sex Roles, 12,* 179–193.

Phillips, S., King, S., & DuBois, L. (1978). Spontaneous activities of female versus male newborns. *Child Development, 49,* 590–597.

Piliavin, J. A., & Unger, R. K. (1985). The helpful but helpless female: Myth or reality? In V. E. O'Leary, R. K. Unger, & B. S. Wallston (Eds.), *Women, gender and social psychology* (pp. 149–189). Hillsdale, N.J.: Erlbaum.

Pinkston, E. M., Reese, N. M., LeBlanc, J. M., & Baer, D. M. (1979). Independent control of aggression and peer interaction by contingent teacher attention. *Journal of Applied*

Behavior Analysis, 12, 102–106.

Pitcher, E. G., & Schultz, L. H. (1983). *Boys and girls at play: The development of sex roles.* New York: Praeger.

Playboy Magazine. (1983). Sex on campus. In O. Pocs (Ed.), *Human sexuality 83/84* (pp. 177–182). Guilford, Conn.: Dushkin.

Pleck, J. H. (1978). Males' traditional attitudes toward women: Conceptual issues in research. In J. A. Sherman & F. L. Denmark (Eds.), *The psychology of women: Future directions in research* (pp. 619–644). New York: Psychological Dimensions.

Pleck, J. H. (1983). Husbands' paid work and family roles: Current research issues. In H. Z. Lopata & J. H. Pleck (Eds.), *Research in the interweave of social roles: Jobs and families, Vol. 3* (pp. 251–333). Greenwich, Conn.: JAI Press.

Plumb, G. (1983). A holistic approach to postpartum depression. *Women & Therapy, 2*, 5–17.

Pocs, O., Godow, A., Tolone, W. L., & Walsh, R. H. (1983). Is there sex after 40? In O. Pocs (Ed.), *Human sexuality 83/84* (pp. 190–192). Guilford, Conn.: Dushkin.

Pogrebin, L. C. (1983). Nonsexist sexuality. In G. W. Albeem, S. Gordon, & H. Leitenberg (Eds.), *Promoting sexual responsibility and preventing sexual problems* (pp. 66–95). Hanover, N.J.: University Press of New England.

Polivy, J. (1977). Psychological effects of mastectomy on a woman's feminine self-concept. *Journal of Nervous and Mental Disease, 164*, 77–82.

Poloma, M. M., & Garland, T. N. (1971). The married professional woman: A study in the tolerance of domestication. *Journal of Marriage and the Family, 33*, 531–540.

Pope, H. G., & Hudson, J. I. (1984). *New hope for binge eaters: Advances in the understanding and treatment of bulimia.* New York: Harper & Row.

Porter, N. P., & Geis, F. L. (1981). Women and nonverbal leadership cues: When seeing is not believing. In C. Mayo & N. M. Henley (Eds.), *Gender and nonverbal behavior* (pp. 39–61). New York: Springer-Verlag.

Posner, J. (1979). It's all in your head: Feminist and medical models of menopause (strange bedfellows). *Sex Roles, 5*, 179–189.

Potkay, C. E., Potkay, C. R., Boynton, G. J., & Klingbeil, J. A. (1982). Perceptions of male and female comic strip characters using the adjective generation technique (AGT). *Sex Roles, 8*, 185–200.

Prather, J. E., & Fidell, L. S. (1978). Drug use and abuse among women: An overview. *The International Journal for the Addictions, 13*, 863–885.

Prescott, S. (1978). Why researchers don't study women: The responses of 62 researchers. *Sex Roles, 4*, 899–905.

Price-Bonham, S., & Skeen, P. (1982). Black and white fathers' attitudes toward children's sex roles. *Psychological Reports, 50*, 1187–1190.

Pursell, S., Banikiotes, P. G., & Sebastian, R. J. (1981). Androgyny and the perception of marital roles. *Sex Roles, 7*, 201–215.

Rabe, M. B., & Matlin, M. W. (1978). Sex-role stereotypes in speech and language tests. *Language, Speech, and Hearing Services in Schools*, 70–76.

Radloff, L. S. (1975). Sex differences in depression: The effects of occupation and marital status. *Sex Roles, 1*, 249–265.

Radloff, L. S. (1980). Depression and the empty nest. *Sex Roles 6*, 775–781.

Radlove, S. (1983). Sexual response and gender roles. In E. R. Allgeier & N. B. McCormick (Eds.), *Changing boundaries: Gender roles and sexual behavior* (pp. 87–105). Palo Alto, Calif.: Mayfield.

Ragan, J. M. (1982). Gender displays in portrait photographs. *Sex Roles, 8*, 33–43.

Raskin, P. A., & Israel, A. C. (1981). Sex-role imitation in children: Effects of sex of child, sex of model, and sex-role appropriateness of modeled behavior. *Sex Roles, 7*, 1067–1076.

Rathus, S. A. (1983). *Human sexuality.* New York: Holt, Rinehart and Winston.

Rawlings, E. T., & Carter, D. K. (1977). Feminist and nonsexist psychotherapy. In E. I. Rawlings & D. Carter (Eds.), *Psychotherapy for women.* Springfield, Ill.: Charles C. Thomas.

Rebecca, M., Hefner, R., & Oleshansky, B. (1976). A model of sex-role transcendence. In A. G. Kaplan & J. P. Bean (Eds.), *Beyond sex-role stereotypes: Readings toward a psychology of androgyny* (pp. 90–97). Boston: Little, Brown.

Reid, P. T. (1979). Racial stereotyping on television. A comparison of the behavior of both black and white television characters. *Journal of Applied Psychology, 64*, 465–471.

Reinisch, J. M. (1981). Prenatal exposure to synthetic progestins increases potential for aggression in humans. *Science, 211*, 1171–1173.

Reis, H. T., & Wright, S. (1982). Knowledge of sex-role stereotypes in children aged 3 to 5. *Sex Roles, 8*, 1049–1056.

Reitz, R. (1977). *Menopause: A positive approach.* Harmondsworth, England: Penguin Books.

Rekers, G. A., Amaro-Plotkin, H. D., & Low, B. P. (1977). Sex-typed mannerisms in normal boys and girls as a function of sex and age. *Child Development, 48*, 275–278.

Renetzky, A. (Ed.) (1985). *Career employment opportunities directory* (4 volumes). Santa Monica, Calif.: Ready Reference Press.

Resick, P., Calhoun, K. S., Atkeson, B. M., & Ellis, E. M. (1981). Social adjustment of victims of sexual assault. *Journal of Consulting and Clinical Psychology, 49*, 705–712.

Reuben, D. (1969). *Everything you always wanted to know about sex but were afraid to ask.* New York: David McKay.

Rheingold, H. L., & Cook, K. V. (1975). The contents of boys' and girls' rooms as an index of parents' behavior. *Child Development, 46*, 459–463.

Rhyne, D. (1981). Bases of marital satisfaction among men and women. *Journal of Marriage and the Family, 43*, 941–955.

Rich, A. (1976). *Of woman born.* New York: Norton.

Rich, A. (1980). Compulsory heterosexuality and lesbian existence. *Signs, 5*, 631–660.

Rich, A. R., & Schroeder, H. E. (1976). Research issues in assertiveness training. *Psychological Bulletin, 83*, 1081–1096.

Richardson, D., Vinsel, A., & Taylor, S. P. (1980). Female aggression as a function of attitudes toward women. *Sex Roles, 6*, 265–271.

Richter, J. (1983). *Crossing boundaries between work and home.* Paper presented at the Eastern Psychological Association.

Rierdan, J., & Koff, E. (1980). The psychological impact of menarche: Integrative versus descriptive changes. *Journal of Youth and Adolescence, 9*, 49–58.

Riess, B. F., & Safer, J. M. (1979). Homosexuality in females and males. In E. S. Gomberg & V. Franks (Eds.), *Gender and disordered behavior: Sex differences in psychopathology* (pp. 257–286). New York: Brunner/Mazel.

Riger, S., & Galligan, P. (1980). Women in management: An exploration of competing paradigms. *American Psychologist, 35*, 902–910.

Riger, S., & Gordon, M. T. (1981). The fear of rape: A study in social control. *Journal of Social Issues, 37*, 71–92.

Robertson, J. F. (1977). Grandmotherhood: A study of role conceptions. *Journal of Marriage and the Family, 39*, 165–174.

Robinson, J. P., Yerby, J., Fieweger, M., & Somerick, N. (1977). Sex-role differences in time use. *Sex Roles, 3*, 443–458.

Robson, K. S., & Moss, H. A. (1970). Patterns and determinants of maternal attachment. *Journal of Pediatrics, 77,* 976–985.

Rodin, J., Silberstein, L., & Striegel-Moore, R. (1985). Women and weight: A normative discontent. In T. B. Sonderegger (Ed.), *Nebraska Symposium on Motivation, 1984: Psychology and gender* (pp. 267–307). Lincoln, Nebr.: University of Nebraska Press.

Rofé, Y., Lewin, I., & Padeh, B. (1981). Emotion during pregnancy and delivery as a function of repression-sensitization and number of children. *Psychology of Women Quarterly 6,* 163–173.

Rogers, T. B., Kuiper, N. A., & Kirker, W. S. (1977). Self-reference and the encoding of personal information. *Journal of Personality and Social Psychology, 35,* 677–688.

Rohner, R. P. (1976). Sex differences in aggression: Phylogenetic and enculturation perspectives. *Ethos, 4,* 57–72.

Rollin, B. (1976). *First, you cry.* Philadelphia: J. B. Lippincott.

Romer, N. (1981). *Sex-role cycle.* Old Westbury, N.J.: Feminist Press.

Romer, N., & Cherry, D. (1980). Ethnic and social class differences in children's sex-role concepts. *Sex Roles, 6,* 245–263.

Rosen, B., & Jerdee, T. H. (1974a). Effects of applicants' sex and difficulty of job on evaluations of candidates for managerial positions. *Journal of Applied Psychology, 59,* 511–512.

Rosen, B., & Jerdee, T. H. (1974b). Influence of sex role stereotypes on personnel decisior *Journal of Applied Psychology, 59,* 9–14.

Rosen, B., & Jerdee, T. H. (1978). Perceived sex differences in managerially relev characteristics. *Sex Roles, 4,* 837–843.

Rosenbaum, M. (1978). Female sexual dysfunctions: A clinical approach. In M. T. Nc & C. C. Nadelson (Eds.), *The woman patient: Vol. 1. Sexual and reproductive a of women's health care* (pp. 292–302). New York: Plenum.

Rosenberg, F. R., & Simmons, R. G. (1975). Sex differences in the self-concept in cence. *Sex Roles, 1,* 147–159.

Rosenfield, S. (1980). Sex differences in depression: Do women always have high *Journal of Health and Social Behavior, 21,* 33–42.

Rosenkrantz, P. S., Vogel, S. R., Bee, H., Broverman, I. K., & Broverman, D. M. (role stereotypes and self concepts in college students. *Journal of Con Clinical Psychology, 32,* 287–295.

Rosenthal, N. B. (1984). Consciousness raising: From revolution to re-eva *chology of Women Quarterly, 8,* 309–326.

Rosenthal, R. (1976). *Experimenter effects in behavioral research* (enla York: Halsted.

Ross, E. (1980). "The love crisis": Couples advice books of the late 109–122.

Ross, L., Anderson, D. R., & Wisocki, P. A. (1982). Television viewing attitudes. *Sex Roles, 8,* 589–592.

Ross, M. W., Rogers, L. J., & McCulloch, H. (1978). Stigma, sex and at gender differentiation and sexual variation. *Journal of Homos*

Rossi, A. S. (1980). Mood cycles by menstrual month and social we Graham, & C. P. Beecher (Eds.), *The menstrual cycle, Vol. 1 (* Springer-Verlag.

Rossi, A. S., & Rossi, P. E. (1977). Body time and social time: Moc cycle phase and day of week. *Social Science Research, 6, 2*

Rothbart, M. K. (1983). *Longitudinal observation of infant te* manuscript, University of Oregon, Department of Psychol

Rothbart, M. K., & Maccoby, E. E. (1966). Parents' differential reactions to sons and daughters. *Journal of Personality and Social Psychology, 4*, 237–243.

Rothbart, M. K., & Rothbart, M. (1976). Birth order, sex of child, and maternal help-giving. *Sex Roles, 2*, 39–46.

Roy, M. (1982). *The abusive partner.* New York: Van Nostrand.

Rubin, J. Z., Provenzano, F. J., & Luria, Z. (1974). The eye of the beholder: Parents' views on sex of newborns. *American Journal of Orthopsychiatry, 43*, 720–731.

Rubin, L. B. (1979). *Women of a certain age: The midlife search for self.* New York: Harper & Row.

Rubin, R. B. (1981). Ideal traits and terms of address for male and female college professors. *Journal of Personality and Social Psychology, 41*, 966–974.

Rubin, Z., Hill, C. T., Peplau, L. A., & Dunkel-Schetter, C. (1980). Self-disclosure in dating couples: Sex roles and the ethic of openness. *Journal of Marriage and the Family, 42*, 305–318.

Rubin, Z., Peplau, L. A., & Hill, C. T. (1981). Loving and leaving: Sex differences in romantic attachments. *Sex Roles, 7*, 821–835.

Ruble, D. (1977). Premenstrual symptoms: A reinterpretation. *Science 197*, 291–292.

Ruble, D., Balaban, T., & Cooper, J. (1981). Gender constancy and the effects of sex-typed televised toy commercials. *Child Development, 52*, 667–673.

Ruble, D., Boggiano, A. K., & Brooks-Gunn, J. (1982). Men's and women's evaluations of menstrual-related excuses. *Sex Roles, 8*, 625–638.

Ruble, D., & Brooks-Gunn, J. (1982). A developmental analysis of menstrual distress in adolescence. In R. C. Friedman (Ed.), *Behavior and the menstrual cycle* (pp. 177–216). New York: Marcel Dekker.

Ruble, D., & Ruble, T. L. (1982). Sex stereotypes. In A. G. Miller (Ed.), *In the eye of the beholder: Contemporary issues in stereotyping* (pp. 188–252). New York: Praeger.

Ruble, T. L. (1983). Sex stereotypes: Issues of change in the 1970s. *Sex Roles, 9*, 397–402.

Ruble, T. L., Cohen, R., & Ruble, D. N. (1984). Sex stereotypes: Occupational barriers for women. *American Behavioral Scientist, 27*, 339–356.

Russell, D. (1975). *The politics of rape.* New York: Stein and Day.

Russell, D. (1982). *Rape in marriage.* New York: Macmillan.

Russell, D., & Howell, N. (1983). The prevalence of rape in the United States revisited. *Signs, 8*, 688–695.

Russo, N. F. (1978). Beyond adolescence: Some suggested new directions for studying female development in the middle and later years. In J. A. Sherman & F. L. Denmark (Eds.), *The psychology of women: Future directions in research* (pp. 89–134). New York: Psychological Dimensions.

Russo, N. F., & Sobel, S. B. (1981). Sex differences in the utilization of mental health facilities. *Professional Psychology, 12*, 7–19.

Rutter, M. (1982). Social-emotional consequences of day care for pre-school children. In E. F. Zigler & E. W. Gordon (Eds.), *Day care: Scientific and social policy issues* (pp. 3–32). Boston: Auburn House.

Saario, T. N., Jacklin, C. N., & Tittle, C. K. (1973). Sex role stereotyping in the public schools. *Harvard Educational Review, 43*, 386–416.

Sachs, J. (1975). Cues to the identification of sex in children's speech. In B. Thorne & N. Henley (Eds.), *Language and sex: Difference and dominance* (pp. 152–171). Rowley, Mass.: Newbury House.

Sadker, M. P., & Sadker, D. M. (1982). *Sex equity handbook for schools.* New York: Longman.

Sagi, A., & Hoffman, M. L. (1976). Empathetic distress in the newborn. *Developmental Psychology, 12*, 175–176.

St. John-Parsons, D. (1978). Continuous dual-career families: A case study. *Psychology of Women Quarterly, 3*, 30–42.

St. Peter, S. (1979). Jack went up the hill ... but where was Jill? *Psychology of Women Quarterly, 4*, 256–260.

Sanday, P. R. (1981). The socio-cultural context of rape: A cross-cultural study. *Journal of Social Issues, 37*, 5–27.

Sandmaier, M. (1980). *The invisible alcoholics.* New York: McGraw-Hill.

Sang, B. E. (1978). Lesbian research: A critical evaluation. In G. Vida (Ed.), *Our right to love* (pp. 80–87). Englewood Cliffs, N.J.: Prentice-Hall.

Saretsky, L. (1977). Sex related countertransference: Issues of a female therapist. *The Clinical Psychologist, 30*, 11–12.

Sassen, G. (1980). Success anxiety in women: A constructivist interpretation of its source and its significance. *Harvard Educational Review, 50*, 13–24.

Scadron, A., Witte, M. H., Axelrod, M., Greenberg, E. A., Arem, C., & Meitz, J. E. G. (1982). Attitudes toward women physicians in medical academia. *Journal of the American Medical Association, 247*, 2803–2807.

Scarf, M. (1979, November). The more sorrowful sex. *Psychology Today, 12*, 45–52, 89–90.

Schab, F. (1982). Early adolescence in the South: Attitudes regarding the home and religion. *Adolescence, 17*, 605–612.

Schacter, F. F., Shore, E., Hodapp, R., Chalfin, S., & Bundy, C. (1978). Do girls talk earlier? Mean length of utterance in toddlers. *Developmental Psychology, 14*, 388–392.

Schaffer, K. F. (1980). *Sex-role issues in mental health.* Reading, Mass.: Addison-Wesley.

Schau, C. G., Kahn, L., Diepold, J. H., & Cherry, F. (1980). The relationships of parental expectations and preschool children's verbal sex typing to their sex-typed toy play behavior. *Child Development, 51*, 266–270.

Schlesier-Stropp. (1984). Bulimia: A review of the literature. *Psychological Bulletin, 95*, 247–257.

Schmuck, P. A. (1975). Deterrents to women's careers in school management. *Sex Roles, 1*, 339–353.

Schneider, B. E. (1982). Consciousness about sexual harassment among heterosexual and lesbian women workers. *Journal of Social Issues, 38*, 75–97.

Schneider, J. W., & Hacker, S. L. (1973). Sex role imagery and use of the generic "man" in introductory texts: A case in the sociology of sociology. *American Sociologist, 8*, 12–18.

Schover, L. R. (1982). Midlife women: Lessons for sex therapy. In M. Kirkpatrick (Ed.), *Women's sexual experience* (pp. 83–86). New York: Plenum.

Schwartz, P., & Strom, D. (1978). The social psychology of female sexuality. In J. Sherman & F. L. Denmark (Eds.), *Psychology of women: Future directions of research.* New York: Psychological Dimensions.

Scott, W. J., & Morgan, C. S. (1983). An analysis of factors affecting traditional family expectations and perceptions of ideal fertility. *Sex Roles, 9*, 901–914.

Seaman, B., & Seaman, G. (1978, November). Pennyroyal, tansy, and other home cures for "those days." *Ms., 7*, 25–29.

Seavey, C. A., Katz, P. A., & Zalk, S. R. (1975). Baby X: The effect of gender labels on adult responses to infants. *Sex Roles, 1*, 103–110.

Seiden, A. M. (1978). The sense of mastery in the childbirth experience. In M. T. Notman & C. C. Nadelson (Eds.), *The woman patient. Vol. I: Sexual and reproductive aspects of women's health care* (pp. 87–105). New York: Plenum.

Selby, J. W., Calhoun, L. G., & Brock, T. A. Sex differences in the social perception of rape victims. *Personality and Social Psychology Bulletin, 3*, 412–415.

Seligman, M. E. P. (1974). Depression and learned helplessness. In R. J. Friedman & M. M. Katz (Eds.), *The psychology of depression: Contemporary theory and research* (pp. 83–113). Washington, D.C.: Winston-Wiley.

Sells, L. W. (1980). The mathematics filter and the education of women and minorities. In L. H. Fox, L. Brody, & D. Tobin (Eds.), *Women and the mathematical mystique* (pp. 66–75). Baltimore, Md.: Johns Hopkins University Press.

Selnow, G. W. (1985). Sex differences in uses and perceptions of profanity. *Sex Roles, 12*, 303–312.

Semaj, L. T. (1982). Polygamy reconsidered: Causes and consequences of declining sex ratio in African-American Society. *Journal of Black Psychology, 9*, 29–43.

Senneker, P., & Hendrick, C. (1983). Androgyny and helping behavior. *Journal of Personality and Social Psychology, 45*, 916–925.

Serbin, L. A., Connor, J. M., & Iler, I. (1979). Sex-stereotyped and nonstereotyped introductions of new toys in the preschool classroom: An observational study of teacher behavior and its effects. *Psychology of Women Quarterly, 4*, 261–265.

Serbin, L. A., & O'Leary, K. D. (1975, December). How nursery schools teach girls to shut up. *Psychology Today, 9*, 57–58, 102–103.

Serbin, L. A., O'Leary, D. D., Kent, R. N., & Tonick, J. J. (1973). A comparison of teacher response to the preacademic and problem behavior of boys and girls. *Child Development, 44*, 796–804.

Sharp, C., & Post, R. (1980). Evaluation of male and female applications for sex-congruent and sex-incongruent jobs. *Sex Roles, 6*, 391–401.

Shaw, E. (1977). Professional schools and their impact on black women. In *Conference on the educational and occupational needs of black women*, Vol. 2: Research papers. Washington, D.C.: National Institute of Education.

Shepard, W., & Hess, D. T. (1975). Attitudes in four age groups toward sex role division in adult occupations and activities. *Journal of Vocational Behavior, 6*, 27–39.

Shepard, W., & Peterson, J. (1973). Are there sex differences in infancy? *JSAS: Catalog of Selected Documents in Psychology, 3*. (Ms. No. 474).

Shepard-Look, D. L. (1982). Sex differentiation and the development of sex roles. In B. B. Wolman (Ed.), *Handbook of developmental psychology* (pp. 403–433). Englewood Cliffs, N.J.: Prentice-Hall.

Sherif, C. W. (1979). Bias in psychology. In J. A. Sherman & E. T. Beck (Eds.), *The prism of sex* (pp. 93–133). Madison, Wis.: University of Wisconsin.

Sherman, J. A. (1971). *On the psychology of women: A survey of empirical studies.* Springfield, Ill.: Charles C. Thomas.

Sherman, J. A. (1978). *Sex-related cognitive differences.* Springfield, Ill.: Charles C. Thomas.

Sherman, J. A. (1981). Girls' and boys' enrollment in theoretical math courses: A longitudinal study. *Psychology of Women Quarterly, 5*, 681–689.

Sherman, J. A. (1982a). Mathematics and critical filter: A look at some residues. *Psychology of Women Quarterly, 6*, 428–444.

Sherman, J. A. (1982b). Continuing in mathematics: A longitudinal study of the attitudes of high school girls. *Psychology of Women Quarterly, 7*, 132–140.

Sherman, J. A. (1983). Factors predicting girls' and boys' enrollment in college preparatory mathematics. *Psychology of Women Quarterly, 7*, 272–281.

Sherman, J. A., Koufacos, C., & Kenworthy, J. A. (1978). Therapists: Their attitudes and information about women. *Psychology of Women Quarterly, 2*, 299–313.

Shields, S. A. (1975). Functionalism, Darwinism, and the psychology of women: A study in social myth. *American Psychologist, 30*, 739–754.

Shields, S. A. (1982). The variability hypothesis: The history of a biological model of sex differences in intelligence. *Signs, 7*, 769–797.

Shields, S. A., & Cooper, P. E. (1983). Stereotypes of traditional and nontraditional child-bearing roles. *Sex Roles, 9*, 363–376.

Shotland, R. L., & Straw, M. K. (1976). Bystander response to an assault: When a man attacks a woman. *Journal of Personality and Social Psychology, 34*, 990–999.

Shusterman, L. R. (1976). The psychosocial factors of the abortion experience: A critical review. *Psychology of Women Quarterly, 1*, 79–106.

Sidorowicz, L. S., & Lunney, G. S. (1980). Baby X revisited. *Sex Roles, 6*, 67–73.

Siegel, R. J. (1983). Accumulated inequalities: Problems in long-term marriages. *Women & Therapy, 2*, 171–178.

Silbert, M. H., & Pines, A. M. (1984). Pornography and sexual abuse of women. *Sex Roles, 10*, 857–868.

Silvern, L. E., & Ryan, V. L. (1979). Self-rated adjustment and sex-typing on the Bem Sex-Role Inventory: Is masculinity the primary predictor of adjustment? *Sex Roles, 5*, 739–763.

Simmons, R. B., & Rosenberg, F. (1975). Sex, sex roles, and self-image. *Journal of Youth and Adolescence, 4*, 229–258.

Simons, M. A. (1979). Racism and feminism: A schism in the sisterhood. *Feminist Studies, 5*, 384–401.

Sinnott, J. D. (1982). Correlates of sex roles of older adults. *Journal of Gerontology, 37*, 587–594.

Sinnott, J. D. (1984). Older men, older women: Are their perceived sex roles similar? *Sex Roles, 10*, 847–856.

Skrypnek, B. J., & Snyder, M. (1982). On the self-perpetuating nature of stereotypes about women and men. *Journal of Experimental Social Psychology, 18*, 277–291.

Smead, V. S. (1983). Anorexia nervosa, buliminarexia, and bulimia: Labeled pathology and the Western female. *Women & Therapy, 2*, 19–35.

Smith, C., & Lloyd, B. (1978). Maternal behavior and perceived sex of infant: Revisited. *Child Development, 49*, 1263–1265.

Smith, E. J. (1982). The black female adolescent: A review of the educational, career, and psychological literature. *Psychology of Women Quarterly, 6*, 261–288.

Smith, M. L. (1980). Sex bias in counseling and psychotherapy. *Psychological Bulletin, 87*, 392–407.

Smith, M. O. (1985). Examining reading problems as a means to uncovering sex differences in cognition. In T. Schlechter & M. Toglia (Eds.), *New directions in cognitive science* (pp. 147–157). Norwood, N.J.: Ablex.

Smith, P. A., & Midlarsky, E. (1985). Empirically derived conceptions of femaleness and maleness: A current view. *Sex Roles, 12*, 313–328.

Smith, R. W. (1979). A social psychologist looks at scientific research on homosexuality. In V. L. Bullough (Ed.), *The frontiers of sex research* (pp. 64–70). Buffalo, N.Y.: Prometheus Books.

Smye, M. D., & Wine, J. D. (1980). A comparison of female and male adolescents' social behaviors and cognitions: A challenge to the assertiveness literature. *Sex Roles, 6*, 213–230.

Snow, L. F., & Johnson, S. M. (1977). Modern day menstrual folklore. *Journal of the American Medical Association, 237*, 2736–2739.

Sohn, D. (1980). Critique of Cooper's meta-analytic assessment of the findings on sex differences in conformity behavior. *Journal of Personality and Social Psychology, 39*, 1215–1221.

Sohn, D. (1982). Sex differences in achievement self-attributions: An effect-size analysis. *Sex Roles, 8*, 345–357.

Solomon, K., & Levy, N. B. (Eds.). (1982). *Men in transition: Theory and therapy.* New York: Plenum.

Sommer, B. (1982). Cognitive behavior and the menstrual cycle. In R. C. Friedman (Ed.), *Behavior and the menstrual cycle* (pp. 101–127). New York: Marcel Dekker.

Sommer, B. (1983). How does menstruation affect cognitive competence and psychophysiological response? In S. Golub (Ed.), *Lifting the curse of menstruation* (pp. 53–90). New York: Haworth.

Sommer, B. (1984, August). PMS in the courts: Are all women on trial? *Psychology Today, 18*, 36–38.

Sontag, S. (1979). The double standard of aging. In J. H. Williams (Ed.), *Psychology of women: Selected readings* (pp. 462–478). New York: Norton.

Sorrels, B. D. (1983). *The nonsexist communicator.* Englewood Cliffs, N.J.: Prentice-Hall.

Soto, D. H., & Cole, C. (1975). Prejudice against women: A new perspective. *Sex Roles, 1*, 385–394.

Spanier, G. B. (1983). Married and unmarried cohabitation in the United States: 1980. *Journal of Marriage and the Family, 45*, 277–288.

Spence, J. T., Helmreich, R. L., & Stapp, J. (1974). The Personal Attributes Questionnaire: A measure of sex role stereotypes and masculinity-femininity. *JSAS Catalog of Selected Documents in Psychology, 4*, 43. (Ms. No. 617)

Spence, J. T., Helmreich, R. L., & Stapp, J. (1975). Ratings of self and peers on sex role attributes and their relation to self esteem and conceptions of masculinity and femininity. *Journal of Personality and Social Psychology, 32*, 29–39.

Staines, G. L., Pleck, J. H., Shepard, L. J., & O'Connor, P. (1978). Wives' employment status and marital adjustment: Yet another look. *Psychology of Women Quarterly, 3*, 90–120.

Staines, G. L., Tavris, C., & Jayaratne, T. E. (1974). The queen bee syndrome. *Psychology Today, 7*, 55–60.

Stake, J., & Katz, J. F. (1982). Teacher-pupil relationships in the elementary school classroom: Teacher-gender and pupil-gender differences. *American Educational Research Journal, 19*, 465–471.

Star, B. (1978). Comparing battered and non-battered women. *Victimology, 3*, 32–44.

Stein, A. H., Pohly, S. R., & Mueller, E. (1971). The influence of masculine, feminine, and neutral tasks on children's achievement behavior, expectancies of success, and attainment values. *Child Development, 42*, 195–207.

Stein, G. (1982). The maternity blues. In I. F. Brockington & R. Kumar (Eds.), *Motherhood and mental illness* (pp. 119–154). London: Academic.

Steinberg, R., & Shapiro, S. (1982). Sex differences in personality traits of female and male master of business administration students. *Journal of Applied Psychology, 67*, 306–310.

Steinem, G. (1983). *Outrageous acts and everyday rebellions.* New York: Holt, Rinehart and Winston.

Stericker, A., & LeVesconte, S. (1982). Effect of brief training on sex-related differences in visual-spatial skill. *Journal of Personality and Social Psychology, 43*, 1018–1029.

Sternberg, R. J. (1974). *How to prepare for the Miller Analogies Test.* Woodbury, N.Y.: Barron's Educational Series.

Sternglanz, S. H., & Serbin, L. A. (1974). Sex role stereotyping in children's television programs. *Developmental Psychology, 10*, 710–715.

Stewart, A. J., & Chester, N. L. (1982). Sex differences in human social motives: Achievement, affiliation, and power. In A. J. Stewart (Ed.), *Motivation and Society* (pp. 172–218). San Francisco: Jossey-Bass.

Stewart, F., Guest, F., Stewart, G., & Hatcher, R. (1981). *My body, my health.* New York: Bantam.

Stipek, D. J. (1984). Sex differences in children's attributions for success and failure on math and spelling tests. *Sex Roles, 11,* 969–981.

Stockburger, D. W., & Davis, J. O. (1978). Selling the female image as mental patient. *Sex Roles, 4,* 131–134.

Storms, M. D. (1981). A theory of erotic orientation and development, *Psychological Review, 88,* 340–353.

Straus, M. A., Gelles, R. J., & Steinmetz, S. K. (1980). *Behind closed doors: Violence in the American family.* Garden City, N.Y.: Anchor Books.

Stricker, G. (1977). Implications of research for psychotherapeutic treatment of women. *American Psychologist, 32,* 14–22.

Stroebe, M. S., & Stroebe, W. (1983). Who suffers more? Sex differences in health risks of the widowed. *Psychological Bulletin, 93,* 279–301.

Strommen, E. A. (1977). Friendship. In E. Donelson & J. E. Gullahorn (Eds.), *Women: A psychological perspective* (pp. 154–167). New York: John Wiley.

Stuart, R. B., & Jacobson, B. (1979). Sex differences in obesity. In E. S. Gomberg & V. Franks (Eds.), *Gender and disordered behavior* (pp. 241–256). New York: Brunner/Mazel.

Sunday, S., & Lewin, M. (1985). *Integrating nuclear issues into the psychology curriculum.* Paper presented at Eastern Psychological Association.

Sussman, N. M., & Rosenfeld, H. M. (1982). Influence of culture, language, and sex on conversational distance. *Journal of Personality and Social Psychology, 42,* 66–74.

Suter, L., & Miller, H. (1973). Income differences between men and career women. *American Journal of Sociology, 78,* 962–974.

Swacker, M. (1975). The sex of the speaker as a sociolinguistic variable. In B. Thorne & N. Henley (Eds.), *Language and sex: Difference and dominance* (pp. 76–83). Rowley, Mass.: Newbury House.

Szinovacz, M. E. (Ed.). (1982). *Women's retirement: Policy implications of recent research.* Beverly Hills, Calif.: Sage.

Szinovacz, M. E. (1983). Beyond the hearth: Older women and retirement. In E. W. Markson (Ed.), *Older women: Issues and prospects* (pp. 93–120). Lexington, Mass.: Lexington Books.

Tangri, S. S., Burt, M. R., & Johnson, L. B. (1982). Sexual harassment at work: Three explanatory models. *Journal of Social Issues, 38,* 33–54.

Tavris, C., & Offir, C. (1977). *The longest war: Sex differences in perspective.* New York: Harcourt Brace Jovanovich.

Tavris, C., & Wade, C. (1984). *The longest war: Sex differences in perspective* (Second Edition). New York: Harcourt Brace Jovanovich.

Taylor, J. W. (1984). Structured conjoint therapy for spouse abuse cases. *Social Casework, 65,* 11–18.

Taylor, M. C., & Hall, J. A. (1982). Psychological androgyny: Theories, methods, and conclusions. *Psychological Bulletin, 92,* 347–366.

Taylor, S. E. (1981). A categorization approach to stereotyping. In D. L. Hamilton (Ed.), *Cognitive processes in stereotyping and intergroup behavior* (pp. 83–114). Hillsdale, N.J.: Erlbaum.

Taylor, S. E., Fiske, S. T., Etcoff, N. L., & Ruderman, A. J. (1978). Categorical and contextual basis of person memory and stereotyping. *Journal of Personality and Social Psychology, 36*, 778–793.

Taylor, S. E., & Langer, E. J. (1977). Pregnancy: A social stigma? *Sex Roles, 3*, 27–35.

Taynor, J., & Deaux, K. (1973). When women are more deserving than men: Equity, attribution, and perceived sex differences. *Journal of Personality and Social Psychology, 28*, 360–367.

Teglasi, H. (1978). Sex-role orientation, achievement motivation, and causal attributions of college females. *Sex Roles, 4*, 381–397.

Terborg, S., & Ilgen, D. (1975). A theoretical approach to sex discrimination in traditionally masculine occupations. *Organizational Behavior and Human Performance, 13*, 352–376.

Tevlin, H. E., & Leiblum, S. R. (1983). Sex-role stereotypes and female sexual dysfunction. In V. Franks & E. D. Rothblum (Eds.), *The stereotyping of women: Its effects on mental health* (pp. 129–150). New York: Springer-Verlag.

Thomas, A., & Stewart, N. (1971). Counselor response to female clients with deviate and conforming career goals. *Journal of Counseling Psychology, 18*, 352–357.

Thompson, S. K. (1975). Gender labels and early sex-role development. *Child Development, 46*, 339–347.

Thomson, M. E., & Kramer, M. S. (1984). Methodologic standards for controlled clinical trials of early contact and maternal-infant behavior. *Pediatrics, 73*, 294–300.

Thorne, B., & Henley, N. (1975). Difference and dominance: An overview of language, gender. and society. In B. Thorne & N. Henley (Eds.), *Language and sex: Difference and dominance* (pp. 5–42). Rowley, Mass.: Newbury House.

Tiger, L. (1969). *Men in groups.* New York: Random House.

Till, F. J. (1980). *Sexual harassment: A report on the sexual harassment of students.* Washington, D.C.: National Advisory Council on Women's Educational Programs.

Tishler, S. L. (1978). Breast disorders. In M. T. Notman & C. C. Nadelson (Eds.), *The woman patient. Vol. 1: Sexual and reproductive aspects of women's health care* (pp. 233–246). New York: Plenum.

Tobias, S. (1978). *Overcoming math anxiety.* New York: Norton.

Tobias, S., & Weissbrod, C. (1980). Anxiety and mathematics: An update. *Harvard Educational Review, 50*, 63–70.

Tolor, A., Kelly, B. R., & Stebbins, C. A. (1976). Assertiveness, sex-role stereotyping, and self-concept. *Journal of Psychology, 93*, 157–164.

Towson, S. M. J., & Zanna, M. P. (1982). Toward a situational analysis of gender differences in aggression. *Sex Roles, 8*, 903–914.

Treadway, C. R., Kane, F. J., Jr., Jerrahi-Zadeh, A., & Lipton, M. A. (1975). A psychoendocrine study of pregnancy and puerperium. In R. K. Unger & F. L. Denmark (Eds.), *Woman: Dependent or independent variable?* (pp. 591–604). New York: Psychological Dimensions.

Tremaine, L. S., & Schau, C. G. (1979). Sex-role aspects in the development of children's vocational knowledge. *Journal of Vocational Behavior, 14*, 317–328.

Tremaine, L. S., Schau, C. G., & Busch, J. W. (1982). Children's occupational sex-typing. *Sex Roles, 8*, 691–710.

Tresemer, D. (1977). *Fear of success.* New York: Plenum.

Trigg, L. J., & Perlman, D. (1976). Social influences on women's pursuit of a nontraditional career. *Psychology of Women Quarterly, 1*, 138–150.

Troll, L. E. (1982). *Continuations: Adult development and aging.* Monterey, Calif.: Brooks/Cole.

Troll, L. E., & Turner, B. F. (1979). Sex differences in problems of aging. In E. Gomberg & V. Franks (Eds.), *Gender and disordered behavior: Sex differences in psychopathology.* New York: Brunner/Mazel.

Tsai, M., Feldman-Summers, S., & Edgar, M. (1979). Childhood molestation: Variables related to differential impacts on psychological functioning in adult women. *Journal of Abnormal Psychology, 88,* 407–417.

Tuch, R. H. (1975). The relationship between a mother's menstrual status and her response to illness in her child. *Psychosomatic Medicine, 37,* 388–394.

Turner, B. F. (1982). Sex-related differences in aging. In B. B. Wolman & G. Stricker (Eds.), *Handbook of developmental psychology* (pp. 912–936). Englewood Cliffs, N.J.: Prentice-Hall.

Turner, C., & Turner, B. F. (1982). Gender, race, social class, and self-evaluations among college students. *The Sociological Quarterly, 23,* 491–507.

Turrini, P. (1980). Psychological crises in normal pregnancy. In B. L. Blum (Ed.), *Psychological aspects of pregnancy, birthing, and bonding* (pp. 135–150). New York: Human Sciences.

Ungar, S. B. (1982). The sex-typing of adult and child behavior in toy sales. *Sex Roles, 8,* 251–260.

Unger, R. K. (1979). Toward a redefinition of sex and gender. *American Psychologist, 34,* 1085–1094.

Unger, R. K. (1981). Sex as a social reality: Field and laboratory research. *Psychology of Women Quarterly, 5,* 645–653.

Unger, R. K. (1983). Through the looking glass: No wonderland yet! (the reciprocal relationship between methodology and models of reality). *Psychology of Women Quarterly, 8,* 9–32.

Unger, R. K. (1985). Epilogue: Toward a synthesis of women, gender, and social psychology. In V. E. O'Leary, R. K. Unger, & B. S. Wallston (Eds.), *Women, gender, and social psychology* (pp. 349–358). Hillsdale, N.J.: Erlbaum.

Unger, R. K., Brown, V. H., & Larson, M. V. (1983). Physical attractiveness and physical stigma: Menstruation and the common cold. In S. Golub (Ed.), *Menarche* (pp. 107–111). Lexington, Mass.: Lexington Books.

Unger, R. K., & Siiter, R. (1975). Sex-role stereotypes: The weight of a "grain of truth." In R. K. Unger (Ed.), *Sex role stereotypes revisited: Psychological approaches to women's studies.* New York: Harper & Row.

U.S. Bureau of the Census. (1979). *Statistical abstract of the United States: 1979.* Washington, D.C.: U.S. Government Printing Office.

U.S. Bureau of the Census (1985). *Household and family characteristics: March 1984.* Washington, D.C.: U.S. Government Printing Office.

U.S. Commission on Civil Rights. (1980). *Characters in textbooks.* Washington, D.C.: U.S. Government Printing Office.

U.S. Department of Labor. (1980). *Perspectives on working women: A databook.* Washington, D.C.: U.S. Government Printing Office.

U.S. Department of Labor. (1982). Twenty facts on women workers. Washington, D.C.: U.S. Government Printing Office.

Valanis, B. G., & Perlman, C. S. (1982). Home pregnancy testing kits: Prevalence of use, false-negative rates, and compliance with instructions. *American Journal of Public Health, 72,* 1034–1036.

Van Buskirk, S. S. (1977). A two-phase perspective on the treatment of anorexia nervosa. *Psychological Bulletin, 84,* 529–538.

Vance, E. B., & Wagner, N. N. (1977). Written descriptions of orgasm: A study of sex differences. In D. Byrne & L. A. Byrne (Eds.), *Exploring human sexuality* (pp. 201–212). New York: Thomas Y. Crowell.

Vandenberg, S. G., & Kuse, A. R. (1979). Spatial ability: A critical review of the sex-linked major gene hypothesis. In M. A. Wittig & A. C. Petersen (Eds.), *Sex-related differences in cognitive functioning* (pp. 67–95). New York: Academic.

Vanek, J. (1978). Housewives as workers. In A. H. Stromberg & S. Harkess (Eds.), *Women working: Theories and facts in perspective* (pp. 392–414). Palo Alto, Calif.: Mayfield.

Veevers, J. (1979). Voluntary childlessness: A review of issues and evidence. *Marriage and Family Review, 2,* 1–26.

Verbrugge, L. M. (1982). Sex differences in legal drug use. *Journal of Social Issues, 38,* 59–76.

Vida, J. E. (1982). The developmental crisis of pregnancy. In M. Kirkpatrick (Ed.), *Women's sexual experience* (pp. 199–204). New York: Plenum.

Voda, A. M. (1982). Menopausal hot flash. In A. M. Voda, M. Dinnerstein, & S. R. O'Donnell (Eds.), *Changing perspectives on menopause* (pp. 136–159). Austin, Tex.: University of Texas Press.

von Baeyer, C. L., Sherk, D. L., & Zanna, M. P. (1981). Impression management in the job interview: When the female applicant meets the male "chauvinist" interviewer. *Personality and Social Psychology Bulletin, 7,* 45–51.

Waber, D. P. (1979). Cognitive abilities and sex-related variations in the maturation of cerebral cortical functions. In M. A. Wittig & A. C. Petersen (Eds.), *Sex-related differences in cognitive functioning* (pp. 161–186). New York: Academic.

Walker, L. E. (1979). *The battered woman.* New York: Harper & Row.

Walker, L. E. (1980). Battered women. In A. M. Brodsky & R. T. Hare-Mustin (Eds.), *Women and psychotherapy* (pp. 339–363). New York: Guilford.

Walker, L. E. (1981). Battered women: Sex roles and clinical issues. *Professional Psychology, 12,* 81–91.

Walker, L. E. (1984a). *The battered woman syndrome.* New York: Springer-Verlag.

Walker, L. E. (1984b). Battered women, psychology, and public policy. *American Psychologist, 39,* 1178–1182.

Wallston, B. S. (1981). What are the questions in psychology of women? A feminist approach to research. *Psychology of Women Quarterly, 5,* 597–617.

Wallston, B. S., Foster, M., & Berger, M. (1978). I will follow him: Myth, reality, or forced choice? Job seeking experiences of dual career couples. *Psychology of Women Quarterly, 3,* 9–21.

Wallston, B. S., & Grady, K. E. (1985). Integrating the feminist critique and the crisis in social psychology: Another look at research methods. In V. E. O'Leary, R. K. Unger, & B. S. Wallston (Eds.), *Women, gender, and social psychology* (pp. 7–33). Hillsdale, N.J.: Erlbaum.

Wallston, B. S., & O'Leary, V. E. (1981). Sex makes a difference: Differential perceptions of women and men. In L. Wheeler (Ed.), *Review of personality and social psychology, Vol. 2* (pp. 9–41). Beverly Hills, Calif.: Sage.

Walshok, M. L. (1981). *Blue-collar women.* Garden City, N.Y.: Anchor.

Walster, E. H., & Walster, G. W. (1978). *A new look at love.* Reading, Mass.: Addison-Wesley.

Ward, C. (1981). Prejudice against women: Who, when, and why? *Sex Roles, 7,* 163–171.

Ward, R. A. (1977). The impact of subjective age and stigma on older persons. *Journal of Gerontology, 32,* 227–232.

Warr, P., & Parry, G. (1982). Paid employment and women's psychological well-being. *Psychological Bulletin, 91,* 498–516.

Warren, L. W., & McEachren, L. (1983). Psychosocial correlates of depressive symptomatology in adult women. *Journal of Abnormal Psychology, 92,* 151–160.

Warren, M. P. (1983). Physical and biological aspects of puberty. In J. Brooks-Gunn & A. C. Petersen (Eds.), *Girls at puberty* (pp. 3–28). New York: Plenum.

Washington, A. C. (1982). A cultural and historical perspective on pregnancy-related activity among U. S. teenagers. *Journal of Black Psychology, 9,* 1–28.

Webbink, P. (1981). Nonverbal behavior and lesbian/gay orientation. In C. Mayo & N. M. Henley (Eds.), *Gender and nonverbal behavior* (pp. 253–259). New York: Springer-Verlag.

Weg, R. B. (1983). Introduction: Beyond intercourse and orgasm. In R. B. Weg (Ed.), *Sexuality in the later years* (pp. 1–10). New York: Academic.

Weinberg, G. (1983). Homophobia. In O. Pocs (Ed.), *Human sexuality 83/84* (pp. 198–200). Guilford, Conn.: Dushkin.

Weingarten, K. (1978). The employment pattern of professional couples and their distribution of involvement in the family. *Psychology of Women Quarterly, 3,* 43–52.

Weiss, R. S. (1975). *Marital separation.* New York: Basic.

Weissman, M. M. (1980a). Depression. In A. M. Brodsky & R. T. Hare-Mustin (Eds.), *Women and psychotherapy* (pp. 97–112). New York: Guilford.

Weissman, M. M. (1980b). The treatment of depressed women. In C. L. Heckerman (Ed.), *The evolving female* (pp. 307–324). New York: Human Sciences.

Weissman, M. M., & Klerman, G. L. (1979). Sex differences and the epidemiology of depression. In E. S. Gomberg & V. Franks (Eds.), *Gender and disordered behavior* (pp. 381–425). New York: Brunner/Mazel.

Weitz, R. (1982). Feminist consciousness raising, self-concept, and depression. *Sex Roles, 8,* 231–241.

Welch, S., & Booth, A. (1977). Employment and health among married women with children. *Sex Roles, 3,* 385–398.

Wheeler, L., & Nezlek, J. (1977). Sex differences in social participation. *Journal of Personality and Social Psychology, 35,* 742–754.

Whisnant, L., Brett, E., & Zegans, L. (1975). Implicit messages concerning menstruation in commercial education materials prepared for young adolescent girls. *American Journal of Psychiatry, 132,* 815–820.

White, J. W. (1983). Sex and gender issues in aggression research. In R. G. Geen & E. I. Donnerstein (Eds.), *Aggression: Theoretical and empirical reviews, Vol. 2* (pp. 1–26). New York: Academic.

Whiting, B. B., & Edwards, C. P. (1973). A cross-cultural analysis of sex differences in the behavior of children aged three through eleven. *Journal of Social Psychology, 91,* 171–188.

Whiting, B. B., & Edwards, C. P. (1976). A cross-cultural analysis of sex differences in the behavior of children aged three through eleven. In S. Cox (Ed.), *Female psychology: The emerging self* (pp. 50–62). Chicago: Science Research Associates.

Whitley, B. E. (1983). Sex-role orientation and self-esteem: A critical meta-analytic review. *Journal of Personality and Social Psychology, 44,* 765–788.

Whitley, B. E. (1985). Sex-role orientation and psychological well-being: Two meta-analyses. *Sex Roles, 12,* 207–225.

Wideman, M. V., & Singer, J. E. (1984). The role of psychological mechanisms in preparation for childbirth. *American Psychologist, 39,* 1357–1371.

Widom, C. S., & Burke, B. W. (1978). Performance, attitudes, and professional socialization of women in academia. *Sex Roles, 4,* 549–562.

Wiest, W. M. (1977). Semantic differential profiles of orgasm and other experiences among men and women. *Sex Roles, 3,* 399–403.

Will, J. A., Self, P. A., & Datan, N. (1976). Maternal behavior and perceived sex of infant. *American Journal of Orthopsychiatry, 49,* 135–139.

Williams, G. D., & Williams, A. M. (1982). Sexual behavior and the menstrual cycle. In R. C. Friedman (Ed.), *Behavior and the menstrual cycle* (pp. 155–176). New York: Marcel Dekker.

Williams, J. E. (1982). An overview of findings from adult sex stereotype studies in 25 countries. In R. Rath, H. S. Asthana, D. Sinha, & J. B. H. Sinha (Eds.), *Diversity and unity in cross-cultural psychology.* Lisse, Netherlands: Swets and Zeitlinger.

Williams, J. E., & Bennett, S. M. (1975). The definition of sex stereotypes via the adjective check list. *Sex Roles, 1,* 327–337.

Williams, J. E., Bennett, S., & Best, D. (1975). Awareness and expression of sex stereotypes in young children. *Developmental Psychology, 11,* 635–642.

Williams, J. E., & Best, D. L. (1982). *Measuring sex stereotypes.* Beverly Hills, Calif.: Sage.

Williams, L. R. (1983). Beliefs and attitudes of young girls regarding menstruation. In S. Golub (Ed.), *Menarche* (pp. 139–148). Lexington, Mass.: Lexington Books.

Wilsnack, S. C., & Beckman, L. J. (1984). *Alcohol problems in women.* New York: Guilford.

Wilson, R. A. (1966). *Feminine forever.* New York: M. Evans.

Wolfe, L. (1980, September). The sexual profile of that Cosmopolitan girl, *Cosmopolitan,* 254–265.

Wolff, C. (1977). *Bisexuality.* London: Quartet Books.

Women on Words & Images. (1972). *Dick and Jane as victims.* Princeton, N.J.: Author.

Women's Action Alliance. (1981). *The radio and television commercial monitoring project: Summary report.* New York: Author.

Women's work: Undervalued, underpaid. (1983, January). *Women at Work,* p. 3.

Woods, N. F. (1982). Menopausal distress: A model for epidemiologic investigation. In A. M. Voda, M. Dinnerstein, & S. R. O'Donnell (Eds.), *Changing perspectives on menopause* (pp. 160–169). Austin, Tex.: University of Texas Press.

Woods, N. F., & Earp, J. L. (1978). Women with cured breast cancer: A study of mastectomy patients in North Carolina. *Nursing Research, 27,* 279–285.

Wooley, S. C., & Wooley, O. W. (1979). Obesity and women: II. A neglected feminist topic. *Women's Studies International Quarterly, 2,* 81–92.

Wooley, S. C., & Wooley, O. W. (1980). Eating disorders: Obesity and anorexia. In A. M. Brodsky & R. T. Hare-Mustin (Eds.), *Women and psychotherapy* (pp. 135–158). New York: Guilford.

Woolley, H. T. (1910). Psychological literature: A review of the recent literature on the psychology of sex. *Psychological Bulletin, 7,* 335–342.

Wright, P. H. (1982). Men's friendships, women's friendships and the alleged inferiority of the latter. *Sex Roles, 8,* 8–20.

Yalom, M., Estler, S., & Brewster, W. (1982). Changes in female sexuality: A study of mother/daughter communication and generational differences. *Psychology of Women Quarterly, 7,* 141–154.

Yarkin, K. L., Town, J. P., & Wallston, B. S. (1982). Blacks and women must try harder:

Stimulus persons' race and sex attributions of causality. *Personality and Social Psychology Bulletin, 8,* 21–30.

Yogev, S., & Vierra, A. (1983). The state of motherhood among professional women. *Sex Roles, 9,* 391–397.

Young, C. J., MacKenzie, D. L., & Sherif, C. W. (1980). In search of token women in academia. *Psychology of Women Quarterly, 4,* 508–525.

Young, C. J., MacKenzie, D. L., & Sherif, C. W. (1982). "In search of token women in academia": Some definitions and clarifications. *Psychology of Women Quarterly, 7,* 166–169.

Young. D. (1982). *Changing childbirth: Family birth in the hospital.* Rochester, N.Y.: Childbirth Graphics.

Zambrana, R. E., Hurst, M., & Hite, L. (1979). The working mother in contemporary perspective: A review of the literature. *Pediatrics, 64,* 862–870.

Zanna, M. P., & Pack, S. J. (1975). On the self-fulfilling nature of apparent sex differences in behavior. *Journal of Experimental Social Psychology, 11,* 583–591.

Zellman, G. L., & Goodchilds, J. D. (1983). Becoming sexual in adolescence. In E. R. Allgeier & N. B. McCormick (Eds.), *Changing boundaries* (pp. 49–63). Palo Alto, Calif.: Mayfield.

Zigler, E., & Muenchow, S. (1983). Infant day care and infant-care leaves: A policy vacuum. *American Psychologist, 38,* 91–94.

Zilbergeld, B. (1978). *Male sexuality.* Boston: Little, Brown.

Zimmerman, D. H., & West, C. (1975). Sex roles, interruptions and silences in conversation. In B. Thorne & N. Henley (Eds.), *Language and sex: Difference and dominance* (pp. 105–129). Rowley, Mass.: Newbury House.

Zuckerman, D. M. (1980). Self-esteem, personal traits, and college women's life goals. *Journal of Vocational Behavior, 17,* 310–319.

Zuckerman, D. M., & Sayre, D. H. (1982). Cultural sex-role expectations and children's sex-role concepts. *Sex Roles, 8,* 853–862.

Zuckerman, D. M., Singer, D. G., & Singer, J. L. (1980). Children's television viewing, racial and sex-role attitudes. *Journal of Applied Social Psychology, 10,* 281–294.

Zuckerman, M., & Wheeler, L. (1975). To dispel fantasies about the fantasy-based measure of fear of success. *Psychological Bulletin, 82,* 932–946.

NAME INDEX

Bar-Tal, D., 287
Bart, P. B., 104, 438, 468, 469, 480, 485
Baruch, G., 465, 480, 481, 486, 490
Basow, S., 283
Bauer, W. D., 139
Baxer, J. C., 212
Beach, L. R., 379
Beck, A. T., 406
Beckman, L. J., 183, 184, 377, 380, 421
Bee, H., 259
Beecher, C. P., 104
Bell, A. P., 304, 307
Bell, I., 464, 466
Bellinger, D. C., 61
Belovitch, T. E., 351, 352, 354
Bem, S. L., 24, 46, 53, 54, 55, 71, 78, 87, 265, 276, 277, 278, 280
Bemis, K. M., 413, 414
Bemporad, J., 386
Benbow, C. P., 202, 203
Benderly, B. L., 433
Benedek, E., 379
Bennett, S. M., 74, 260, 262, 270
Bequaert, L. H., 316, 320
Berg, J. H., 135
Berg-Cross, G., 375
Berg-Cross, L., 375
Berger, M., 177
Beckman, L. J., 380
Bergmann, B., 159
Berkman, S. L., 380
Berkowitz, L., 265
Berman, P. W., 223, 224, 478, 479
Bernard, J., 195, 297, 301, 317
Bernstein, S., 53
Berry, K., 369
Best, D., 74, 75, 264
Bestor, D. K., 155
Beuf, A., 76
Bielby, D. D., 150, 153
Bies, R. J., 128
Biglan, A., 406

Bigner, J. J., 304
Bingham, W., 154
Binkin, N. J., 353
Bird, C., 485
Biringen, Z. C., 479
Birk, J., 155
Birnbaum, H. J., 433
Birren, J. E., 196
Bishop, N., 351, 352
Blaine, E., 353
Blaubergs, M. S., 254
Blechman, E. A., 398, 421
Bloch, N. E., 318, 320
Block, J. H., 31, 50, 60, 230, 261
Bloom, B. L., 303
Blum, B. L., 383
Blumstein, P., 293, 294, 298, 301, 313, 314, 315, 317, 322, 336, 338, 339
Boggiano, A. K., 105
Bograd, M., 443, 446, 447, 448
Bohannan, P., 302
Bond, G. R., 402
Bondy, J., 167
Bonno, B., 140
Booth, A., 184
Borges, M. A., 486
Borker, R., 240
Borman, K. M., 188
Boskind-White, M., 414
Bosmajian, H., 250
Bowker, L. H., 450
Boynton, G. J., 69
Brabant, S., 69
Braen, G. R., 425
Braiker, H. B., 418
Braito, R., 289, 317, 318, 320, 321
Bram, S., 377
Brand, F. N., 465
Brandenburg, J. B., 452, 458
Brannon, R., 260
Brant, R. S. T., 435
Bray, H., 67
Brazelton, T. B., 180
Breines, W., 446
Brend, R. M., 209

Brett, E., 91
Brewer, J. I., 470
Brewer, M. B., 453
Brewster, W., 341
Briere, J., 253
Brinson-Pineda, B., 257
Brock, T. A., 432
Broderick, P. C., 379
Brodsky, A. M., 386, 396, 402, 421
Brody, E. M., 481
Brody, L., 203
Brooks, J., 114
Brooks, L., 85
Brooks, V. R., 208, 307
Brooks-Gunn, J., 32, 33, 34, 41, 43, 91, 92, 93, 100, 105, 109
Brophy, J. E., 64, 222
Broverman, D. M., 259, 270, 389, 390
Broverman, I. K., 259, 270, 389, 390
Brown, A., 17, 18
Brown, B., 143, 144
Brown, P., 301, 303
Brown, V., 258
Brown, V. H., 116
Brownmiller, S., 412, 427
Brown-Rezanka, L., 480, 481
Bruch, H., 413
Brush, L. R., 131, 132, 206
Bruton, B., 289
Bry, B. H., 415, 416
Bryden, M. P., 199
Buchanan, D. R., 290
Buczek, T. Z., 395, 420
Budoff, P. W., 100, 101, 108, 118
Bugental, D. E., 215
Bundy, C., 196
Bunker, B. B., 167
Bunker, K. A., 168
Bureau of Labor Statistics, 160
Burford, B., 140
Burgess, A. W., 426, 427, 428, 429
Burke, B. W., 167

Gambrill, E. D., 403
Game, A., 152
Gannon, L., 401
Gansberg, J. M., 371, 372, 375, 383
Ganson, H. C., 295
Garai, J. E., 31
Garber, D. M., 157
Gardner, W. L., 153
Garfinkel, P. E., 414
Garland, H., 145
Garland, T. N., 178
Garner, D. M., 414
Garrison, H. H., 178
Gates, H., 203
Geffner, R. A., 141
Geis, B. D., 349, 350, 351
Geis, F. L., 232, 233
Geis, L., 258
Gelles, R. J., 442, 444
Gentemann, K. M., 444, 445
Gerdes, E. P., 157
Gerrard, M., 349, 350, 351
Gershuny, H. L., 250
Gerson, M., 377, 378, 380
Gettys, L. D., 76
Gianetto, R. M., 215
Gideonse, S., 188
Giele, J. Z., 464, 490
Giesen, C. B., 472, 479
Gigy, L. L., 318
Gilbert, L. A., 262, 263, 280, 400
Gilbert, S., 447
Giles-Sims, J., 448, 449
Gilkes, C. T., 166
Gillen, B., 144
Gilligan, C., 220, 270, 351
Gilroy, F. D., 391
Gitelson, I., 134
Glazer, N. Y., 178
Gleason, J. B., 61
Glenn, N. D., 380, 480
Glenwick, D. S., 167
Glynn, A., 452
Godow, A., 340
Goff, S. B., 128, 202, 204, 205
Goffman, E., 213, 256
Gold, A. R., 110, 131, 132

Gold, D., 181
Goldberg, D. C., 333
Goldberg, P. A., 138, 140, 141, 156, 157
Goldberg, S., 32, 41
Goldberg, W. G., 442
Goldfried, M. R., 410, 411
Goldman, K. S., 52
Goldstein, A. G., 200
Goldstein, A. J., 410, 411
Gollin, A. E., 425
Golub, S., 90, 92, 103, 109, 118
Gomberg, E. S., 416, 417, 418
Gomes, B., 155
Good, R., 364
Good, T. L., 64
Goodchilds, J. D., 334, 335, 434
Goodman, K. L., 301
Goodman, M. J., 462, 467
Goodwin, B. J., 17, 18
Gordon, L., 446
Gordon, M. T., 426
Gordon, P. E., 429
Gordon, S. L., 291, 293, 301, 322
Gove, W. R., 387, 388, 389, 391, 392, 408
Gowan, D. C., 70
Grady, K. E., 9, 11, 21
Graham, E. A., 104
Gray, B. A., 407
Gray, M. W., 203
Gray, V. A., 130
Gray-Little, B., 299
Green, J., 107
Green, S. K., 290
Greenberg, E. A., 169
Greenberg, J. H., 141
Greenberg, N., 28
Greenberg, R. L., 406
Greenglass, E. R., 317
Griffin, S., 425
Griffitt, W., 222
Grimm, J. W., 164
Grisham, J. A., 292
Gross, A. D., 198
Gross, M. M., 141

Grossman, F. K., 371
Grossman, M., 485
Groth, A. N., 433
Gubrium, J. F., 320
Guest, F., 348, 353, 461
Gunnar, M. R., 32
Gutek, B. A., 151, 152, 153, 157, 163, 165, 170, 179, 189, 452, 456, 457
Gutmann, D. L., 479
Guttentag, M., 67
Guzzo, R. A., 145
Gyllstrom, K. K., 183

Haas, A., 208, 210, 211, 339
Haas, L., 179
Haber, S., 153
Hacker, S. L., 252
Hafter, D. M., 245, 246
Hahn, S. R., 368, 369
Haight, J. M., 76
Hailwood, E., 431
Hale, K. F., 145
Hall, B. A., 17, 18
Hall, J. A., 208, 212, 213, 214, 215, 216, 217, 218, 236, 240, 280
Hall, J. L., 263
Hall, K. P., 232
Hall, S. M., 412
Hamilton, D. L., 265, 266, 267, 269, 283
Hamilton, M., 313
Hammen, C. L., 406, 408
Hammond, J. A., 165, 171, 172
Hamner, T. J., 377
Handley-Isaksen, A., 128
Handschumacher, I., 452, 456, 457
Hansen, R. D., 144, 145
Hanna, R., 290
Hanusa, B. H., 134
Hardy, A., 486–487
Hare-Mustin, R. T., 379, 386, 421
Harmon, L., 155
Harrington, D. M., 103
Harris, L. J., 196
Harris, R., 364

Mills, K. H., 344, 345, 346, 356
Milow, V. J., 106, 112
Mirande, A., 371
Mischel, H., N., 141
Mischel, W., 49, 279
Monahan, L., 126
Money, J., 25, 26, 28, 29
Moore, D., 442
Moore, E. C., 348
Moore, K. A., 179
Moore, M., 140
Moore, T. W., 181
Morgan, C. S., 263, 377
Morgan, M., 299
Morgan, W. G., 231
Morin, S. F., 305, 306
Mortimer, J. T., 153, 181
Moss, H. A., 31, 40, 376
Mostel, A. P., 371, 372, 375, 383
Motowidlo, S. J., 162, 278
Moulton, J., 251, 252
Moyer, K. E., 227
Moynihan, D. P., 299
Mueller, E., 130
Muenchow, S., 181
Mulac, A., 258
Murray, S. R., 17, 255
Murstein, B. I., 293
Myers, B. J., 377
Myers, T., 447

Nadelson, C. C., 300, 343, 344, 345, 363, 377
Nakamura, C. Y., 452, 456, 457
Narus, L. R., 479
Nash, S. C., 199, 201, 479
Nathanson, C. A., 184
National Center for Education Statistics, 64
National Commission on Working Women, 183
Nelson, K., 196
Neugarten, B. L., 467, 470, 479, 480, 481, 482
Newcombe, N., 201

Newland, K., 178
Newman, B. M., 81
Newman, E. S., 473
Newson, E., 60
Newson, J., 60
Nezlek, J., 225
NiCarthy, G., 449
Nicholas, M., 343
Nicholls, J. G., 130, 134
Nieva, V. F., 151, 152, 153, 157, 170, 179, 189
Nilsen, A. P., 250
Nix, J., 231
"No comment," 444
Norman, W. H., 406, 407, 409
Norr, K. F., 473
Norwood, J. L., 160
Notman, M. T., 377, 466
Nyquist, L., 178

Oakley, A., 175
O'Barr, W. M., 210
Oberston, H. K., 307
O'Brien, P. H., 438
O'Bryant, S. L., 222
O'Connell, A. N., 6, 21
O'Connor, P., 179
Offermann, L. R., 233
Offir, C., 48
O'Hare, J., 435, 436
O'Keefe, E. S. C., 76
O'Leary, K. D., 64
O'Leary, S., 223
O'Leary, V. E., 21, 138, 144, 145, 147, 241
Oleshansky, B., 280
Olsen, N. J., 62
Olesen, V. L., 164
O'Nan, B. A., 478, 479
On Campus with Women, 161
O'Rand, A. M., 473
Orbach, S., 412
O'Reilly, J., 444, 448
O'Reilly, K., 351
Orenstein, E., 231
Orenstein, H., 231
Orlofsky, J. L., 287
Oros, C. J., 425

Orlos, J. B., 80
Orthner, D. K., 337

Pack, S. J., 272, 273
Padawer, W. J., 410, 411
Padeh, B., 367
Padesky, C., 313
Paige, J. M., 92, 112
Paige, K. E., 92, 104, 112, 360, 368, 369
Palazzini, M., 256
Palmer, P., 164
Palmore, E., 485
Paludi, M., 123, 127, 139, 140
Pandey, J., 222
Pape, R. E., 363
Parcell, S., 436
Parke, R., 223
Parlee, M. B., 16, 102, 103, 105, 106, 108, 374
Parry, G., 185, 186
Parson, E. B., 407
Parsons, J. E., 128, 153, 199, 202, 204, 205
Patrick, G. T. W., 5
Patterson, J. N., 403
Patterson, K. J., 128
Patterson, M., 256
Payne, B. D., 75
Pearse, W. H., 369
Pepitone, A., 432
Peplau, L. A., 225, 287, 290–294, 296, 298, 301, 312, 313, 322, 335, 336, 339
Perl, H., 402
Perlman, C. S., 361
Perlman, D., 153
Perlmutter, E., 468, 469
Perloff, R. M., 71
Perney, V., 130
Perry, J., 333
Perri, M., 287
Personal Products, 92
Perun, P. J., 150
Pervin, L. A., 344, 346
Petersen, A. C., 91, 93, 134, 200, 202

Peterson, C. C., 33, 270
Peterson, J., 31
Peterson, J. L., 33, 270
Pheterson, G. I., 140, 157
Phillips, R. D., 391
Phillips, S., 31
Phillis, D. E., 479
Phipps-Yonas, S., 330, 341
Piliavin, J. A., 221, 222
Pines, A. M., 434
Pinkston, E. M., 64
Pitcher, E. G., 73
Pitel, M., 104
Playboy, 336
Pleck, J. H., 178, 179, 262
Plumb, G., 374
Pocs, O., 340
Pogrebin, L. C., 345
Pohly, S. R., 130
Polivy, J., 466
Poloma, M. M., 178
Polonsky, D. C., 300
Pope, H. G., 414
Porter, N. P., 232, 233
Posner, J., 468, 469
Post, R., 157
Potkay, C. E., 69
Potkay, C. R., 69
Powers, E., 289
Prather, J. E., 396
Prescott, S., 9
Price-Bonham, S., 58, 474
Pringle, R., 152
Proffitt, C., 375
Provenzano, F. J., 35
Pursell, S., 299

Quarm, D., 188
Quinn, R. P., 151, 156, 159

Rabe, M. B., 66
Radloff, L. S., 408, 480
Radlove, S., 333
Ragan, J. M., 215
Rahe, R. H., 302
Ramsey, S. J., 214
Raskin, P. A., 50
Rathus, S. A., 90, 328, 341, 357

Rawlings, E. T., 399, 400, 401
Rebecca, M., 280
Reddel, M., 33
Reed, L., 133
Reese, N. M., 64
Reid, P. T., 256
Reilly, M. E., 455, 456
Reinisch, J. M., 229
Reis, H. T., 75, 287
Reitz, R., 469, 471
Rekers, G. A., 214
Renetzky, A., 155
Resick, P., 425, 427, 429, 430
Rest, J., 133
Reuben, D., 469
Rheingold, H. L., 39, 40
Rhyne, D., 300
Rich, A., 310, 363, 372, 403
Richardson, A., 67
Richardson, B. L., 122, 123
Richardson, D., 227
Richardson, M. S., 377, 380
Richey, C. A., 403
Richter, J., 183
Rickel, A. U., 374
Rierdan, J., 93
Riess, B. F., 312
Riger, S., 172–173, 426
Riley, S., 320
Rivers, C., 465, 481
Robertson, J. F., 481, 482
Robinson, G. M., 252
Robinson, J. P., 178
Robson, K. S., 31, 376
Rodeheaver, D., 340
Rodgers, W. L., 380
Rodin, J., 412, 421
Rofe, Y., 367
Rogers, L. J., 305
Rogers, T. B., 18, 19
Rohner, R. P., 230
Rollin, B., 466, 467
Romer, N., 75, 79
Rose, R. M., 101, 103
Rosen, B., 156, 162, 168, 169
Rosen, S. L., 258
Rosenbaum, M., 343, 344
Rosenbaum, R. M., 133

Rosenberg, F. R., 80, 81
Rosenfeld, H. M., 212
Rosenfield, S., 301, 408
Rosenkrantz, P. S., 259, 270, 389, 390
Rosenthal, C. J., 481
Rosenthal, N. B., 402
Rosenthal, R., 10
Ross, E., 326
Ross, L., 258
Ross, M. W., 305
Rossi, A. S., 106, 107
Rossi, P. E., 107
Rothbart, M. K., 31, 32, 59, 61, 306
Roy, M., 444
Rubenstein, D., 343
Rubin, J. Z., 35
Rubin, L. B., 465, 480
Rubin, R. B., 249
Rubin, Z., 290, 291, 294, 296, 335, 336
Ruble, D., 70, 91–93, 100, 103, 104, 105, 114, 153, 157, 248, 260
Ruble, T. L., 153, 157, 248, 260
Rudel, R., 197
Ruderman, A. J., 267, 268, 269
Russell, D., 425, 430, 437, 438, 442, 452, 456, 457
Russo, N. F., 6, 21, 386, 464
Rutter, M., 181
Ryan, V. L., 279

Saario, T. N., 66
Sachs, J., 208
Sadker, D. M., 67, 87
Sadker, M. P., 67, 87
Safer, J. M., 312
Sagi, A., 32
St. John-Parsons, D., 174, 185
St. Peter, S., 68
Salvatore, M., 318, 320
Sanday, P. R., 433
Sandmaier, M., 415

Strommen, E. A., 286
Stuart, R. B., 411
Stull, D. E., 225
Sukoneck, H., 307
Sunday, S., 379
Sussman, N. M., 212
Suter, L., 160
Sutherland, E., 147
Swacker, M., 208
Synge, J., 481
Szinovacz, M. E., 472, 473, 484
Szklo, M., 484

Taebel, D., 76
Tangri, S. S., 456
Tanney, M., 155
Tavris, C., 48, 170, 332, 333, 335
Taylor, D. G., 201
Taylor, J. W., 448
Taylor, K., 435, 436
Taylor, L., 157, 301, 354
Taylor, M. C., 280
Taylor, S. E., 267, 268, 269, 364, 382
Taylor, S. P., 227
Taynor, J., 143
Teglasi, H., 135
Terborg, S., 156
Tevlin, H. E., 343, 345
Thal, J., 411, 412, 413
Thomas, A., 155
Thome, P. R., 226
Thompson, S. K., 52
Thomson, M. E., 377
Thorne, B., 210
Tiger, L., 224
Till, F. J., 454
Tindale, S., 278, 299
Tishler, S. L., 466
Tittle, C. K., 66
Tobias, S., 205
Tobin, D., 203
Tobin-Richards, M., 134
Tolone, W. L., 340
Tolor, A., 231
Tomlanovich, M. C., 442
Tonick, J. J., 64
Toth, E., 92, 112, 114

Town, J. P., 143
Townes, B. D., 379
Towson, S. M. M., 227, 229, 230
Treadway, C. R., 363
Tremaine, L. S., 76, 77
Tresemer, D., 127
Trigg, L. J., 153
Troll, L. E., 481, 483, 484
Tsai, M., 436
Tuch, R. H., 104
Tucker, P., 29
Tudor, J. F., 387, 391
Turner, B. F., 84, 479, 484
Turner, C., 84
Turrini, P., 363, 366

Ullian, D. Z., 51
Ullman, J. C., 171, 172, 188
Ungar, S. B., 72
Unger, R. K., 3, 6, 12, 16, 17, 21, 116, 123, 220–222, 241, 261
U. S. Bureau of the Census, 297, 477
U. S. Commission on Civil Rights, 66
U. S. Department of Labor, 151, 152, 160, 163, 165, 176, 180

Valanis, B. G., 361
Van Buskirk, S. S., 414
Vance, E. B., 331, 332
Vandenberg, S. G., 202
Vanek, J., 175
Vaughn, R., 379
Veevers, J., 380
Verbrugge, L. M., 416
Verhulst, J., 343, 345, 346
Veroff, J., 128, 147
Veronen, L., 425, 427
Vida, J. E., 365
Vierra, A., 377
Vinsel, A., 227
Voda, A. M., 468
Vogel, S. R., 259, 270, 389, 390
Volk, K. D., 337

von Baeyer, C. L., 271
Voss, H. L., 293
Voss, J. H., 379

Waber, D. P., 199, 202
Wade, C., 332, 333, 335
Wagner, N. N., 331, 332
Walker, A. J., 263
Walker, L. E., 441, 442, 443, 444, 446, 447, 448, 449, 461
Wallston, B. S., 6, 9, 11, 21, 138, 143, 147, 177, 241
Walsh, R. H., 340
Walshok, M. L., 171, 172
Walster, E. H., 290
Walster, G. W., 290
Ward, C., 140
Ward, R. A., 476
Warfield, M. C., 425
Waring, J., 465, 480, 481, 482
Warr, P., 185, 186
Warren, L. W., 407, 408
Warren, M. P., 90
Washington, A. C., 353, 354
Waxman, H., 333
Webbink, P., 305
Weber, M., 361
Weg, R. B., 340
Weinberg, G., 307, 309
Weinberg, M. S., 304, 307, 312
Weiner, B., 133
Weiner, L., 451, 452, 453, 454, 455, 456, 457, 458, 461
Weingarten, K., 182, 379
Weinstein, K., 482
Weisberg, M., 333
Weiss, R. S., 303
Weissbrod, C., 205
Weissman, M. M., 406, 407, 409
Weist, W. M., 331
Weitz, L., 155
Weitz, R., 402
Weitz, S., 213
Welch, S., 184, 353
Wendenburg, K., 314

SUBJECT INDEX

Attractiveness, 80, 287, 346, 411–415
Attributions
  and depression, 409
  for own success and failure, 132–137
  in premenstrual women, 104
  for violence against women, 424, 428,
    430–432, 433–434, 437, 443, 446,
    454–455
  for women's and men's performance,
    138–145
Autosomes, 25

Battered women, 441–450
  attitudes toward, 444–445
  the batterer, 443–444
  the battering cycle, 442
  characteristics of, 443
  in dating relationships, 442
  and divorce, 302
  leaving a battering relationship, 448
  and marital rape, 438–440
  myths about, 446
  shelters, 448
  therapy, 447
Bedrooms, decoration of, 39–40
Behavioral-cognitive approach, 398, 409
Behaviorism, 398, 410–411, 414
  See also Social-learning theory
Bem Sex-Role Inventory (BSRI), 276–280,
  299
Bereavement, 482–484
Bias against women (*see* Theme 2)
Biases in research (*see* Research problems)
Bible, 247–248
Binge-purge syndrome, 414–415
Bipolar scales, 276
Birth centers, 369
Birth control, 347–351
Birth order, 152–153
Bisexual women, 314–315
Black females
  abortion, 353
  achievement motivation, 124
  adolescents, 83–85
  and alcoholism, 415
  attributions for success of, 143–144
  beliefs about stereotypes, 75
  "black matriarchy," 85, 299
  decision to have children, 377

  and depression, 407
  divorce, 297, 301
  domestic workers, 164
  employment and, 151, 152, 157–158,
    164, 166
  fear of success, 127
  invisibility of, 17, 255
  and language, 249
  math courses, 203
  in the media, 255, 256–257
  motherhood, 371
  pregnancy, 364
  and psychotherapy, 394
  rape, 425, 428
  salary, 160
  sex-typing in, 58
  single black women, 317
  and stereotypes, 75, 263–264
  variability of, 18
  in widowhood, 483
Black matriarchy, 85, 299
Blame-the-victim approach, 424, 428,
    430–432, 433–434, 437, 438, 443, 446,
    454–455
Blue-collar jobs, 171–172
Body image, 79–80
Body language (*see* Nonverbal communication)
Body posture, 213–214
Books, sexism in, 65–66, 68–69
Brain, lateralization in, 199–202
Breaking up
  divorce, 301–303, 431
  love relationships, 294–296
Breast cancer, 466–467
Breast development, 79–80, 90
Breast feeding, 374–376
Bulimia, 414–415

Cancer, 466–467
Career choice, 154–155
  in adolescence, 82–83
  in black females, 84–85
Career counselors, 85, 154–155
Careers (*see* Work)
Castration complex, 47
Caught generation, 481
Cervix, 367
Cesarean births, 369
Chicana women, 152, 249, 371

See also Hispanic women
Childbirth
    biology of, 366–367
    emotional reactions to, 367–368
    family-centered approach, 368–369
    and menstrual pain, 100
    prepared childbirth, 368
Child-care tasks, 182–183
Child-free women, 377–380
Childhood, 46–85
    adolescence, 79–84
    children's behavior and beliefs, 72–79
    factors that shape sex-typing, 56–72
    theories about sex-typing, 46–56
Children
    battering of, 444
    decision to have, 377–380
    and maternal employment, 152,
        179–183
    and sexual abuse, 435–436
Chinese religion, 248
Christianity, 245
Chromosomes (see Genetics)
Clerical work, 164
Climacteric, 467–471
    See also Menopause
Clitoral hood, 326–327, 332
"Clitoral orgasm," 330–331
Clitoris, 26, 326–333, 397
Clothing, 214
Coalminers, 171
Cognitive abilities
    during menstrual cycle, 108–109
    sex differences in, 194–207
Cognitive-developmental theory, 50–53,
    60, 67
Cohabitation, 293–294, 295–296
Coitus, 110, 112
    See also Rape
Comic strips, 69
Communication patterns in dating,
    291–292
Communication styles, 207–219
Communion, in stereotypes, 261
Commuting marriages, 177–178
Competition, 232
Concept formation, 196
Condoms, 348
Confidence rape, 426–427
Conflict, reactions to, 292

Consciousness-raising (CR) groups,
    401–402, 409, 436, 467, 483
Conservation (Piagetian), 50–52
Contingency training, 82
Contraceptives
    in birth control, 347–351
    and menstrual pain, 101
    and mood changes, 104
    and premenstrual syndrome, 107–108
Conversations, 207–211
Corpus luteum, 98–99
Creativity, 196
Crime, in premenstrual syndrome,
    105–106
Crying, in infancy, 31–32, 372
Counselors, career, 85, 154–155
Cross-cultural studies
    aggression, 230
    body position, 214
    depression, 407
    in evaluation of others, 141
    household tasks, 178
    menstruation, 90–91, 92, 112
    pregnancy, 364
    on rape, 433
    reading, 198
    religion, 247
    stereotypes, 75, 264
Cuban women, 364
    See also Hispanic women

Date rape, 436–437
Dating, 286–293
Day-care centers, 181
Decoding ability, 216
Dependency, 32, 40–41, 60–61, 65, 479
Depression, 302–303, 406–409
    empty-nest syndrome, 480
    following rape, 429, 438–439
    postpartum depression, 374
Devaluation of women (see Theme 2)
Dieting, 411–415
Direct achieving style, 128
Discrimination (see Stereotypes; Theme
    2)
Disorders (see Psychological disorders)
Division of the Psychology of Women, 5
Divorce, 301–303, 431
Doctors, 166, 167
Domestic violence (see Battered women)

Double standard of aging, 476–479
Double standard of mental health, 389–391, 393–396
Drugs, 387, 395–396
Dual-career families, 176–179, 182–183
Dysfunction, sexual, 342–346
Dysmenorrhea, 92, 100–101
Dyspareunia, 345

Eating disorders, 411–415
Education
    of black females, 84–85
    and sexual harassment, 453–459
    about sexuality, 335, 349
    See also Schools
Education level
    and breast feeding, 375
    and decision to have children, 377
    and employment, 151
    and psychological disorders, 406–407
    of single women, 317–318
    and stereotypes, 263
Egalitarian marriage, 299
Ejaculation, 333
Elderly women (see Later adulthood)
Embedded figures test, 200–201
Embryo, 25–26
Emotion management, 291, 296
Emotions, decoding, 81
Empathy, 223–224
Employed women
    definition of, 150
    and love relationships, 294
    and marriage, 299, 301
    and psychological disorders, 406–407
    single employed women, 318, 320
    and stereotypes, 264, 271
    in textbooks, 65
    therapists' questions about, 395
    See also Work
Empty-nest syndrome, 480
Endometrium, 95–99
Equal Rights Amendment, 228–229
Erogenous zones, 327–328
Estrogen, 95–99, 361, 367, 374, 467, 468
Estrogen-replacement therapy, 468
Ethnic group
    and children's stereotypes, 75
    and employment, 152
    and slang, 249

See also Asian women; Black women; Chicana women; Cross-cultural studies; Cuban women; Hispanic women; Jewish women; Native American women; Puerto-Rican women
Euphemisms, 113–114
Evaluations of women's and men's performance, 138–145
Excitement phase, 327–329
Executives, 156, 166, 173–174, 458
Expectations and social cognition, 266–267
Experimenter expectancy, 10
Experimenter, sex of, 10, 236–237

Favoritism (see Theme 2)
Fear of success, 6, 125–127, 173, 278
Feminist, definition of, 4
Feminist therapy, 400–401, 403–404
Fetus, 26
Filled pauses, 208
Follicle-stimulating hormone (FSH), 95–99
Follicles, 95–99
Foreplay, 338
Frequency distributions, 192–193
Freudian approach, 8, 47–48, 305, 330–331, 397–398, 435
Friendship, 81–83, 224–225

G-spot, 328, 333
Gays, 57, 304–315, 339–340, 343
Gaze, 215–216
Gender constancy, 51
Gender, definition of, 3–4
Gender identity, 51–52
Gender-role transcendence, 280–281
Gender roles (see Stereotypes)
Gender schema theory, 53–55, 62, 67
Gender segregation, 62–63, 164
Gender stereotypes, definition of, 244
    See also Stereotypes
Generic masculine, 250–254
Genetics, 24–25, 28–30, 202, 204, 229
Genital development, prenatal, 25–29
Genital herpes, 341
Genital stage, 48
Goddesses, 247–248
Gonads, development of, 25–30
Gonorrhea, 341

Gossip, 211
Grandmothers, 481–482
Greeting cards, 36–37

Happiness (*see* Satisfaction)
Harassment (*see* Sexual harassment)
Health
    and employed women, 184
    See also Childbirth; Later adulthood;
        Menstruation; Pregnancy; Psychologi-
        cal disorders
Heart problems, 465–466
Helping
    parents' responses to children's re-
        quests, 60–61
    sex differences in helping, 220–226
    as shown in media, 70
Hemispheres, of brain, 199, 202
Hindu religion, 248
Hispanic women, 152, 249, 364, 371, 377,
    394–395, 415, 428
History of psychology of women, 4–7
Homemakers, 174–175
Homophobia, 57, 308–312
Homosexuality, 57, 304–315, 339, 343
Hormones
    in childbirth, 367
    and lesbianism, 305
    in menopause, 467, 468
    in menstruation, 95–99
    and postpartum depression, 374
    in pregnancy, 361
    prenatal hormones, 25–30
    and spatial ability, 202
    See also Androgen; Estrogen; Follicle-
        stimulating hormone; Luteinizing
        hormone; Progesterone
Hot flash, 468
Housewives, 174–175
Housework, 174–179, 256, 300
Humanism, 398–399
Husbands
    alcoholism and, 417
    battering by, 441–450
    childcare tasks and, 182–183
    household responsibilities, 176–179
    marriage, 298–301
    rape by, 437–438
    retirement of, 474
    widowhood, 482–484

Hypothalamus, 95–99
Hypothesis formulation, 8–9

Illusion of sex differences, 17
    See also Theme 2
Imitation, 48–50
Incest, 435–436
Independence, 32, 40–41, 60–61, 65
Individual differences among women (*see*
    Theme 4)
Infancy, 23–43
    prenatal development, 24–33
    responses to infant girls and boys,
        33–42
    sex differences in infancy, 30–33
Infantilization, 249–250, 365
Influenceability, 235–237
Inhibited sexual desire, 343
Intelligence quotient (IQ), 195
Intercourse, 110, 112
    See also Rape
Interpersonal relations in adolescence,
    81–82
Interruptions, in communications, 208
Intonation, 209
Intrauterine devices, 348, 350
Invisibility of women (*see* Theme 3)

Jewish religion, 247
Jewish women, 75
Jobs (*see* Employed women; Work)
Judgments about females and males (*see*
    Theme 2)

Kissing, 339

Labia, 26–27, 326–327
Labia majora, 326–327
Labia minora, 326–327
Labor (childbirth) 366–368
Lamaze preparation, 368
Language
    in adulthood, 196–200
    in infancy, 32, 40, 196
    representation of women, 248–254
Latency stage, 48
Later adulthood
    attitudes toward other women, 475–479
    child-free women, 380
    family relationships, 479–482

Minority females
  abortion, 353
  achievement motivation, 124
  adolescents, 83–85
  and alcoholism, 415
  American Indian women, 152
  Asian women, 249, 257, 428
  attributions for success of, 143–144
  beliefs about stereotypes, 75
  "black matriarchy," 85, 299
  Chicana women, 152, 249, 371
  Cuban women, 364
  decision to have children, 377
  and depression, 407
  divorce, 297, 301
  domestic workers, 164
  employment and, 151, 152, 157–158,
      164, 166
  fear of success, 127
  Hispanic women, 152, 249, 364, 371,
      377, 394–395, 415, 428
  invisibility of, 17, 255
  Jewish women, 247
  and language, 249
  math courses, 203
  in the media, 255, 256–257
  motherhood, 371
  Native American women, 152
  pregnancy, 364
  and psychotherapy, 394
  Puerto-Rican women, 394
  rape, 425, 428
  salary, 160
  sex-typing in, 58
  single black women, 317
  and stereotypes, 75, 263–264
  variability of, 18
  in widowhood, 483
  See also Cross-cultural studies
Mittelschmerz, 98
Modeling, 48–50
Modern marriage, 299
Mons pubis, 326–327
Mood changes
  in menopause, 469–470
  in menstrual cycle, 102–108
Mortality rates, 465
Motherhood
  breast feeding, 374–376
  decision to have children, 377–380

postpartum disturbances, 373–374
  reality of motherhood, 371–373
  stereotypes about, 371
  See also Parental behavior
Mothers
  and daughters' career choices, 153
  and discussion of sexuality, 335
  and information about menstruation,
      91, 93–94
  in middle age, 480
  representation of, 248
  satisfaction with retirement, 474
Mullerian ducts, 26
Mullerian inhibiting substance, 26
Multiple orgasms, 332–333
Murder, in rape cases, 435
Mythology, 247–248

Narcissism, 397
Native American women, 152
"Natural childbirth," 368
Nature-nurture argument, 30, 34
Networks, 162–163
"Never married" women, 316–321
Nonemployed women, definition of, 150
Nonsexist therapy, 399–401
Nontraditional employment, 54, 77, 82–83,
      128, 152–153, 155, 157
  attitude toward women in, 167–168
  blue-collar jobs, 171–172
  characteristics of women in, 165–167
Nonverbal communication, 211, 218, 256
  and rape, 437, 456
Nurses, 152, 163–164
Nursing (breast feeding), 374–376
Nursing homes, 484
Nurturance, 222–223

Observational learning, 48–50
Occupations (see Employed women;
      Work)
Old age (see Late adulthood)
Operational definitions, 9, 220
Oral contraceptives, 247–249
Oral stage, 47
Orgasm, theories of, 330
Orgasmic dysfunction, 344
Orgasmic phase, 330
Orgasmic platform, 329–330
Oriental women, 249, 257, 428
Osteoporosis, 466

Ova, 95–99
Ovaries, 25–26, 95–99
Overweight women, 411–413
Ovulation, 97–99

Painful intercourse, 345
Parental behavior, 39, 56–61, 84
   See also Fathers; Motherhood; Mothers
Participants in research, 9–10
Passive behavior, 63, 230–231
Peers, 61–63
Penis, 25–27, 28–29, 47–48, 330–331, 425
Penis envy, 47–48
Perceptual abilities
   and the menstrual cycle, 108–109
   sex similarities in infancy, 31
Persistence of attachment, 303
Personal space, 212–213
Personality characteristics, children's be-
   liefs about, 73–75
Personality disorders, 386–387
Person-centered explanations, 6, 123,
   172–173, 280, 403
"Personals" advertisements, 289–290, 312
Persuasion, 234–235
Phallic stage, 47–48
Phobic disorders, 410–411, 436
Physical abilities and the menstrual cycle,
   108–109
Pitch, 209
Pituitary glands, 95–99
Placenta, 361, 367
Plateau phase, 328–330
Play, 37–39, 57–58, 65, 72–73
"Playing dumb," 289
Politeness, 210
Pornography, 306, 434–435, 440
Postpartum depression, 374
Postpartum period, 373–374
Posture, 213–214
Poverty, 484–485
Power
   in feminist therapy, 400–401
   in lesbian relationships, 313
   in marriage, 298–299, 301
   in nonverbal communication, 217
   and psychological disorders, 392
   in rape, 431–432
   in schools, 63–64
   in sexual harassment, 453

in violence, 424
Practical significance, 11, 203
Predicting sex of unborn child, 32
Preference for same sex, 51, 52, 62–63,269
Pregnancy, 360–366
   abortion, 351–354
   attitudes toward pregnant women,
      364–366
   biology of, 361
   emotional reactions to, 362–364
   physiological reactions to, 362–364
Prejudice
   access discrimination, 156–158
   evaluation of accomplishments,
      138–141
   against other sex, 51, 52, 62–63, 269
   in stereotypes, 269–271
   treatment discrimination, 159–163
   See also Theme 2
Premenstrual syndrome (PMS), 92,
   100–108
Premenstrual tension, 101–108
Prenatal development, 24–30
   abnormal prenatal development, 28–29
   genetics, 24–25
   normal prenatal development, 25–27
Prepared childbirth, 368
Problem-solving ability, 196
Process-oriented behavior, 281
Professors, 162, 167, 377, 451–460, 473
Progesterone, 95–99, 107–108, 361, 367,
   374, 467
Promotions (in employment), 162, 166
Property, view of women as, 430–431
Prostaglandins, 100
Psychiatric problems (see Psychological
   disorders)
Psychoactive drugs, 395–396, 409, 411,
   414, 415–418
Psychoanalytic theory, 47–48, 305,
   330–331, 397–398, 435
Psychological disorders
   eating disorders, 411–415
   female role and, 391–392
   phobias, 409–411
   postpartum disorders, 373–374
   psychotherapy and sexism, 393–396
   psychotherapy approaches, 397–404
   sex ratios in disorders, 386–392
   substance abuse, 415–418

See also Mental health
Psychotherapy, 393–405, 447–448
Puberty, 79, 90
Pubic hair, 79, 90
Puerto-Rican women, 394
See also Hispanic women
Punishment, 48–50, 57–61, 64–65

Queen Bee, 170–171

Race (see Minority women)
Rape, 425–441
   attitudes toward, 430
   child sexual abuse, 435–436
   date rape, 436–437
   fear of, 425–426
   marital rape, 437–438
   myths about, 433–436
   rape attack, 426–427
   rape prevention, 438–439
   victim's reaction to, 427–430
Rape-trauma syndrome, 428–430
Reading ability, 198–199
Reasoning ability, 196
Reciprocity, 292–293
Refractory period, 333
Reinforcement, 48–50, 57–61, 64–65
Relational achieving style, 128
Relative deprivation, 160
Religion, 247–248
Remarriage, 483–484
Reproductive system, prenatal development of, 25–30
Research problems
   communicating the findings, 12–13, 192
   designing the study, 9–10
   formulating the hypotheses, 8–9
   interpreting the data, 11–12
   in love relationships, 306–307
   in menstrual research, 102–104
   with older women, 464
   performing the study, 10–11
   in personality and social behavior, 219–220, 236–237
Researcher expectancy, 10
Resolution phase, 330
Retirement
   adjustment to, 473–474
   of husbands, 474
   planning for, 472–473
Rivalry between women, 286–287

Role strain, 183–184
Romanticism, 290–291, 312
Rooming-in, 376–377
"Rough and tumble" play, 73, 230
Salaries, 154–155, 159–160
   and marital power, 298
Same-sex preference, 51–52, 62–63
Satisfaction
   and employment status, 184–186
   in later adulthood, 485–486
   lesbian relationships, 313
   in marriage, 300–301
   about retirement, 472–475
   single women, 318
   See also Mental health
Scholastic Aptitude Test (SAT), 198, 202–208
Schools
   and mathematics, 203–206
   programs on menstruation, 91
   sex education, 90–92
   sex segregation in employment, 164
   and sex-typing, 63–68
   sexual harassment in, 453–459
   treatment discrimination in, 162
"Second sex," 248
   See also Theme 2
Secondary sex characteristics, 79
Secretaries, 152
Segregation according to sex, 62–63, 164
Selective recall, 267, 395
Self-attribution, 133–137
Self-blame, 132–137, 428, 437, 443
Self-concepts
   in adolescence, 79–81
   black females and, 83–85
   after menarche, 93–94
Self-confidence, 129–132, 136, 166–167, 442, 486
Self-consciousness, 80–81
Self-disclosure, 225, 292
Self-fulfilling prophecy, 10, 100, 271–274
Self-report method, 9, 11, 223, 224
Self-selection, 186
Sensate focus, 346
Sex, definition of, 3–4
Sex as a stimulus variable, 16–17, 138, 212–213, 216
Sex as a subject variable, 16, 138, 212–213, 216

Sex-biased language, 248–254
Sex chromosomes, 25
Sex differences
    attitudes toward rape, 431–432
    attitudes toward sexual harassment,
        456
    biased judgments, 36
    in children's play, 73
    cognitive abilities, 194–206
    communication styles, 207–219
    dating, 287–292, 294–296
    divorce, 301–303
    early studies of, 5
    educational aspirations, 85
    frequency distributions, 192–193
    infancy, 30–32
    marital satisfaction, 300–301
    occupational stereotypes, 76–77
    personality and social behavior,
        219–237
    self-attribution, 135–136
    self-confidence, 129–132, 167
    sexual response cycle, 331–333
    sexual role playing, 336–337
    stability of self-image, 80
    widowhood, 483–484
    See also Sex similarities
Sex education, 90–92, 334–335
Sex reassignment, 28–29
Sex segregation, 62–63, 164
Sex similarities
    achievement motivation, 124
    cognitive abilities, 194–206
    communication styles, 207–219,
        291–292
    employed men and women, 165–167
    fear of success, 124, 127
    gender stereotypes, 17, 262
    infancy, 30–32
    overlapping frequency distributions,
        192–193
    personality and social behavior,
        219–237
    response to erotica, 338–339
    self-attributions, 134–135
    self-confidence, 129–132
    self-esteem, 80
    sexual behavior, 335
    sexual response cycle, 331–332

Theme 1 (defined), 16
    See also Sex differences; Theme 1
Sex-typing, 41
    definition of, 24, 41
    and play, 72–73
    theories of, 46–56
Sexism, 4, 55, 269–271
    and psychological disorders, 389–391,
        393–394
    reducing sexism, 67–68
    See also Theme 2
Sexual abuse, 435–436
Sexual dysfunction, 342–347
Sexual harassment, 163, 172, 396–397,
    424, 451–460
    attitudes toward, 455–456
    responses to, 456–459
    victims' reactions to, 453–455
Sexual preference, 304–315, 339–340,
    343
Sexual revolution, 341–342
Sexual unresponsiveness, 343–344
Sexuality
    abortion, 351–354
    in adolescence, 81
    birth control, 347–351
    early sexuality, 335–336
    interest in, 337
    among lesbians, 339–340
    and the menstrual cycle, 110
    older women, 340, 478
    after rape, 429, 431
    role playing, 336–337
    sex differences and similarities,
        331–333
    sex education, 334–335
    sexual activities, 338–339
    sexual anatomy, 326–327
    sexual dysfunction, 342–346
    sexual response cycle, 327–330
    theories of orgasm, 330–331
    therapy for dysfunction, 346
Shelters for battered women, 448, 450
Siblings and sex-typing, 56–57
Simple phobias, 410–411
Single women
    advantages and disadvantages, 320–321
    attitudes toward, 319–320
    characteristics of, 317–318

Situation-centered explanations, 6, 123, 172–174, 280, 403
Sleep patterns, 31
Smiling, 32, 40, 215–216
Social behavior
  adolescence, 81–82
  adulthood, 219–239
  infancy, 32
Social class, 75, 262, 365–366, 406–407, 444
  See also Minority women
Social cognition, 264–271
  See also Attributions; Cognitive-developmental theory; Gender-schema theory
Socialization (*see* Childhood; Infancy)
Social-learning theory, 48–53, 59–60, 67, 69, 306, 411
Social phobias, 410–411
Spatial abilities, 200–202, 204
Sperm, 25, 361
Spermicidal foams, 348
Statistical approach to reviewing research, 235–236
Statistical significance, 11, 203
Steelworkers, 172
Stereotypes
  about achievement, 126–127
  in adolescence, 82–83
  beliefs about men and women, 259–275
  about child-free women, 378–379
  in children, 73–78
  and employed mothers, 179–182
  and employment, 157–158, 168–169
  in history, 245
  and language, 248–253
  in later adulthood, 479
  in the media, 55, 68–71, 250, 254–258
  about motherhood, 371
  philosophers and stereotypes, 245–247
  about psychological disorders, 389–391, 393–396
  psychological disorders, promoted by stereotypes, 418
  religion and mythology, 247–248
  and sexual dysfunction, 345–346
  sexual role playing, 336–337
  about sexuality in the elderly, 340
  social cognition approach to, 264–274

and violence against women, 424
  See also Theme 2
Subjects in research, 9–10
Substance abuse, 307, 387, 415–418
Success, fear of, 6, 125–127, 173, 278
Suicide, 106, 374
Surprise attack, 426
Swearing, 210
Symbolic models, 48

Tactile sensitivity, 31
Teachers, 63–68, 163–164, 166
Television, sexism in, 65, 70–71, 254–258
Temperament, infant, 31–32
Tenure decisions, 162
Testes, 25–26
Tests, sexism in, 65–66
Textbooks, sexism in, 65–66
Thematic Apperception Test, 123–124
Theme 1 (sex similarities), 16–17, 30–32, 80, 122, 124, 127, 129–132, 134–137, 165–167, 192–237, 262, 291–292, 331–333, 335, 338–339
Theme 2 (differential treatment), 16–17, 33–34, 63, 65–66, 70, 73–78, 82–83, 93, 113, 122, 126–127, 138, 154–158, 165–167, 168–169, 171, 212, 216, 242–283, 340, 345–346, 365, 389–391, 408, 418, 424–461, 476–479
Theme 3 (invisibility), 3, 17, 64–65, 66–67, 70, 83, 93, 113, 245, 250–254, 255, 345–346, 360, 440, 464–465, 469, 471
Theme 4 (variability), 17, 83–84, 100–102, 109, 122, 216–217, 307, 318, 326, 327–328, 362–364, 367–368, 374, 430, 468, 486–487
Theories of sex typing, 46–56
Therapist bias, 389–391
Therapy, 309–310, 393–405, 447–448
Thinking, 108–109, 194–207
Thinness, 411–415
Title IX, 67–68
Token women, 169–171, 268–269
Touch, 214–215
Toys, 37–40, 50, 65, 72–73, 200–201
Traditional employment, 163–165
Traditional marriage, 298–299
Tranquilizers, 395–396, 415
Treatment discrimination, 159–163

Trimester, 361
Tubal ligation, 348
Turner's syndrome, 28–29

Undifferentiated people, 277
Urethral opening, 327
Uterus, 95–99

Vagina, 99, 327, 397, 468
"Vaginal orgasm," 330–331
Vaginismus, 344–345
Variability among women (*see* Theme 4)
Vasectomy, 348
Vasocongestion, 328–329, 343
Verbal ability, 32, 40, 196–200
Verbal analogies, 197
Verbal communication styles, 207–211
Verbal fluency, 197
Victimization of women (*see* Battered
    women, Rape, Sexual harassment)
Violence against women, 423–461
    battering, 441–450
    rape, 425–441
    sexual harassment, 163, 172, 396–397,
        424, 451–460

Voice quality, 208–209
Voiceovers, 255

Weight, body, 411–415
Widowhood, 482–484
Withdrawal (birth control), 348
Wives, 176–179, 297–303, 387, 391–392,
    437–438, 441–450
Wolffian ducts, 26
Word usage, 209–210
Words for women, 249–250
Work
    applying for work, 155–158
    attribution patterns and, 144–145
    children and, 179–182
    children's beliefs about, 76–78
    marriage and, 176–179
    nontraditional employment, 165–173
    personal adjustment and, 183–186
    predictors of employment, 150–152
    retirement from, 472–475
    traditional employment, 163–165
    vocational choice, 152–153
    See also Employed women
Working women, definition of, 150